人 谢正则 飞光 三
来

Bing Elliot Xie

12 - 14 - 200/

Opium Regimes

Opium Regimes

China, Britain, and Japan, 1839–1952

EDITED BY

Timothy Brook
and
Bob Tadashi Wakabayashi

UNIVERSITY OF CALIFORNIA PRESS
Berkeley   Los Angeles   London

University of California Press
Berkeley and Los Angeles, California

University of California Press, Ltd.
London, England

Library of Congress Cataloging-in-Publication Data

Opium regimes : China, Britain, and Japan, 1839–1952 / edited by Timothy Brook
and Bob Tadashi Wakabayashi.
    p.   cm.
Includes bibliographical references and index.
    ISBN 0-520-22009-9 (alk. paper).—ISBN 0-520-22236-9 (alk.
paper)
    1. Opium trade—China—History.   2. Drug traffic—China—
History.   3. Narcotics, Control of—China—History.   4. China—Relations—
Great Britian.   5. Great Britain—Relations—China.   6. China—Relations—
Japan.   7. Japan—Relations—China.   I. Brook, Timothy, 1951- .   II.
Wakabayashi, Bob Tadashi, 1950- .
HV5840.C6065   2000
363.45'0951—dc21   99-35149
                                                                                  CIP

Manufactured in the United States of America

09   08   07   06   05   04   03   02   01   00
        10   9   8   7   6   5   4   3   2   1

The paper used in this publication meets the minimum requirements of ANSI/
NISO Z39.48-1992 (R 1997) (*Permanence of Paper*).

In honor of
Eguchi Keiichi,
whose pursuit of a tabooed topic
inspired us to produce this book

CONTENTS

ILLUSTRATIONS AND TABLES

ACKNOWLEDGMENTS

The research in this volume was first presented at a conference on the history of opium in East Asia held in Toronto in May 1997. We organized the conference when we discovered that opium was more than a common interest of ours in our research on Japan's wartime occupation of China but had become a major topic of scholarly investigation among the generation of scholars then emerging from writing their doctoral dissertations. The number of participants grew so large that we were not able to include in this volume all of the papers. References to those presented on that occasion by Alvyn Austin, Thomas Burkman, Catherine Carstairs, Rich Connors, Paul Howard, John Jennings, Man-houng Lin, Bernard Luk, Daniel Malleck, Kathryn Meyer, Richard Newman, and Douglas Sechter, as well as one of us, may be found in the bibliography.

The conference was the fourth in a series of annual symposia organized by the Joint Centre for Asia Pacific Studies of the University of Toronto and York University, and was co-sponsored by the Department of History of York University. In addition to the support of our two universities, we received major funding from the Social Sciences and Humanities Research Council of Canada and the Connaught Foundation of the University of Toronto. Critical to the success of the project were Carol Irving, who handled the conference business, and Lynne Russell, who ran the errands that made the conference a success, provided editorial assistance, and injected much-needed good humor into the long process of getting from conference to book. We thank both of them for their willing support for the academic work of the Centre.

Through the daunting task of working a set of conference papers into a coherent volume, we benefited from the advice and ideas of many of our contributors. We wish to thank, in particular, Alan Baumler, Gregory Blue, and Bin Wong. Among those outside the conference who read the manuscript, we are grateful to Kenneth Pomeranz and Joshua Fogel for the written comments they provided. In addition, Tim would like to acknowledge the members of his spring 1998 colloquium on modern Chinese history at Stanford University who gave him helpful feedback on several of the chapters while the manuscript was still in process. At the University of California Press, Sheila Levine, Rachel Berchten, and [name] contributed greatly to getting the manuscript into the book that it has become, and we owe them our thanks as well.

Finally, and most of all, we want to express our personal appreciation to Fay Sims and Yumiko Wakabayashi for their tolerance in what proved to be a bigger project than either of their spouses ever cared to admit.

Timothy Brook
Bob Tadashi Wakabayashi

ABBREVIATIONS

ANC	Anti-Narcotics Commission
BFO	British Foreign Office Archives, Public Record Office, London
CCP	Chinese Communist Party
DGQL	Junji chu, lufu dang diguozhuyi qinlüe dalei, diyi yapian zhanzheng (Grand Council copy archive, imperialist aggression category, First Opium War), Number One Historical Archives, Beijing
EDG	Zhongguo di'er lishi dang'anguan (China Number Two Historical Archives), Nanjing
EIC	East India Company
GHQ	General Headquarters (of the American occupation of Japan)
GMD	Guomindang (Nationalist Party)
IAOA	International Anti-Opium Association
IMTFE	International Military Tribunal for the Far East, Tokyo
IPS	International Prosecuting Section
JJY	Junji chu lufu dang, falü dalei, jinyan (Grand Council copy archive, legal category, opium prohibition), Number One Historical Archives, Beijing
JY	Gongzhong dang, falü dalei, jinyan (Palace Memorial Archive, legal category, opium prohibition), Ming-Qing Archives, Beijing

MAE	Archives of the Ministère des Affaires Étrangères, Paris
MAE / Nantes	Archives of the Ministère des Affaires Étrangères, Nantes
MPS	Ministry of Public Security Archive, Beijing
MZSW	Junji chu lufu dang, minzushiwu dalei, Weiwuer (Grand Council copy archive, minority affairs category, Uighurs), Number One Historical Archives, Beijing
NAOA	National Anti-Opium Association
NCC	National Christian Council of China
NLM	New Life Movement
NOPC	National Opium Prohibition Committee
OSB	Opium Suppression Bureau
OTRJ	Organization of Tianjin Resident Japanese
OWP	*Opium, A World Problem*
PRC	People's Republic of China
SMP	Shanghai Municipal Police Files, Washington
SSD	Special Service Department
USDS	United States Department of State archives, National Archives and Records Administration, Washington
USNA	U.S. National Archives
WCMN	*West China Missionary News*
YMCA	Young Men's Christian Association
YWCA	Young Women's Christian Association
YPZZ	*Yapian zhanzheng dang'an shiliao* (Archival documents on the Opium War)

INTRODUCTION

Opium's History in China

Timothy Brook and Bob Tadashi Wakabayashi

Without opium, Chinese history in the nineteenth and twentieth centuries would have been far different. Opium thrust the states of East Asia, and the imperial Qing state most of all, into the "modern" world of unequal treaties and gunboat diplomacy. It gave foreign powers the financial wherewithal to make colonial empire-building feasible. It presented Chinese states from the Qing empire to the People's Republic with unparalleled opportunities to intervene in the lives of Chinese people, and indeed demanded that they do so. On those lives opium had an impact greater than that of any other internationally traded commodity. As smokers, Chinese consumed this addictive substance in volumes that beggar comparison with any other item in their history with the exception of tea—though that comparison belittles opium's potency. As dealers, they set up commercial organizations and networks to handle the trade so as fully to realize its profit-making potential. As peasant farmers, they produced poppy harvests large enough to keep opium in circulation and in consumption long after foreign imports had stopped. As anti-imperialist revolutionaries, they struggled to rid their country of this stain of backwardness and sign of subjugation to foreign commercial and political interests. And as politicians, they devised elaborate regulations to remove the drug from social use and to limit or monopolize distribution so as to keep the huge revenues that opium could yield out of private hands (and sometimes in their own).

Opium's addictiveness has proven irresistible to buyers, profitable to producers and dealers, alluring to states—and endlessly fascinating to those of us who know it only indirectly through history. With so much power vested in one simple substance, with so much evidently to be won and lost, it is not surprising that opium has inspired more in the way of strong reactions than dispassionate research. The sensationalism that seems naturally to attach itself to opium is hardly new. As the great early scholar of China's international trade, H. B. Morse, wrote in 1907 in the introduction to his own examination of this commodity,

> Opium presents a thorny subject to handle for any writer. If he is a partisan of the opium trade, his tendency is strong to leave the ground with which he is familiar, that of commercial dealings and statistics, and try to demonstrate the innocuousness of the drug as smoked by the Chinese—to compare it to the relatively harmless ante-prandial glass of sherry. If his mission is to denounce the opium traffic, he invariably seems impelled, by an irresistible inclination, to leave the high moral ground on which he is unassailable, and descend into the arena of facts and figures, with which he is not likely to be so familiar, and among which his predisposition will lead him to pass by or to misinterpret those which make against his case. The writer who tries to investigate the facts with no predisposition to either side, is likely to find himself branded as a trimmer by the one party and a Laodicean on the other, with no opportunity to defend himself.[1]

These contrary accusations of indifference—whether to the actual "facts" of trade and consumption on one side, or to the moral responsibility of the traders on the other—continue to color the ways in which opium gets represented in the history of China, and more especially in the history of China's relations with foreign states. But it is moral failure that prevails in most accounts. A popular historiography targets foreigners as morally culpable for having used opium to intoxicate, impoverish, and demoralize the Chinese people—deploying what Chinese in the twentieth century have dubbed "policies to empoison" *(duhua zhengce)*. The charge originated at the time of the Opium Wars, when Western critics of the trade invoked the principles of fair diplomacy and temperance to condemn British conduct. Karl Marx as a journalist decried the "flagrant self-contradiction of the Christianity-canting and civilization-mongering British Government" for its energetic pursuit of what he called its "free trade in poison."[2] Charles King, an American merchant in Guangzhou and a Christian temperance advocate, published a blast against British policy in the spring of 1839—even before the outbreak of armed hostilities—charging that government with duplicity in this "deadly traffic" for allowing the East India Company to be "employed in growing the drug in one place, and disowning it in another." Noting from published British documents that the number of consumers in China had increased sixfold between 1820 and 1835, King declared that any continuation of the opium trade in the face of official opposition from China could only lead to "the impoverishment of the empire, and the disruption of every tie of morality and order."[3] The strong views of King and Marx, although not universal, were increasingly voiced through the nineteenth century. They were not heard as widely as some would have liked, as one anti-opium activist observed forty years later:

> Although to many persons something is known of the traffic in opium which is being carried on between India and China by the British Government, I am sure that the country generally cannot be aware of the true character of that traffic; of the dreadful wrongs it inflicts upon the Chinese people; of the total disregard it indicates of our high responsibilities in those regions; or of the retribution which must await this country, unless we repent and speedily put away the iniquity from us.[4]

This man hopefully assumed that the trade would not withstand scrutiny in public opinion, were it to be scrutinized. However, it would take several decades before public opinion swung far enough his way to pressure the British government to give up the opium regime on which its empire had once relied.

Those who profited from the trade were dubious about the value of sacrificing economic benefits in favor of moral considerations. They felt that opium was being fetishized to the exclusion of other interests. Some academic scholarship has also questioned the moral superiority of the anti-opium argument. Historians of this stripe insist that the first Opium War was a conflict between an expansive West and a tradition-bound China. The "problem" of opium was secondary to this struggle between states over issues of commercial access and extraterritoriality. It was even suggested that war might just as easily have broken out over molasses, rice, or cotton.[5] Most Chinese opinion, not surprisingly, has resisted this "collision of cultures" view by arguing that foreigners wantonly, even consciously, used opium to victimize the Chinese people.[6] A more recent variation on this theme portrays opium as the symbol of China's sad inability to reform itself so as to resist foreign aggression. This interpretation dovetails nicely with the political claim of the People's Republic of China that it has succeeded on both points whereas all previous regimes failed, that it has vanquished the foreign threat of opium and strengthened China in the process. Either way, a history based on moral reproach sits well with an aggrieved sense of nationalism among most Chinese, and resonates with many of the Western and Japanese observers who accept guilt for the opium trade.

Although we do not approach the question of opium in nationalistic terms in this book, we do not deny the salience of this critique. Opium was *not* a harmless commodity like molasses. It was an addictive substance with noxious and sometimes tragic effects for users, their families, and the social networks in which they lived. Abuse of opium eroded self-esteem and shamed both the nation and the colonized individual. Trafficking in opium tilted the balance of global trade to benefit the West, robbing the Qing empire of the silver that had been flowing in for several centuries. It also cast a decided pall on the reputation of Chinese living in the diaspora outside China; opium was viewed as further evidence that this was a pernicious and untrustworthy ethnic group.[7]

Our focus here is less on the debilitating effects of opium on users or the insult to national pride—although these must be the backdrop to any study. Rather, we focus on the opium trade's political and economic effects. The artificially high price at which opium traded enabled a rate of capital accumulation that could not but capture the attention of state elites and create political pressures to confuse moral judgments on trafficking. Opium was certainly too attractive for Britain or its colonial client states to resist, so long as its consumption was restricted to Chinese and did not cross to whites (every colonial state in the region except the Philippines operated an opium monopoly). The Qing state in its turn was drawn into complex relations with the individuals, businesses, and states involved with opium, pursuing endless negotiations with foreigners around the legality and volume of the trade. Within its own borders, it had to engage in the multiple tasks of policing, taxing, and educating its people, thus formulating its own opium regime to manage the flow of opium into and around China.

We use the term *regime* to signify a system in which an authority declares its right to control certain practices, and develops policies and mechanisms to exercise that right within its presumed domain. The system can be a formal organization, such as the League of Nations, that seeks to direct, modify, or suppress the practices of governments. Or, like the National Anti-Opium Association, which strove to play a visible public role in China between 1924 and 1937, a regime can be a network of individuals who pursue published political goals to achieve a positive social outcome. We can consider the East India Company in similar terms: a corporate group operating within a well-organized network of authority to obtain a particular end—in this case, profitable exchange—through the regulation of public conduct. The East India Company's aims happened to be explicitly economic. Yet the company was nothing if not active in politics, as it had to be to ensure that Parliament continued to support its monopolies. The term *regime* usually signifies a state's established government. The association is apt in this instance because the state was interested in opium. However, it usually delegated its management to a specialized administrative system that supervised distribution and revenue (the French in their colonies used the term *régie*). What characterizes a regime more generally is its ability to impose conformity to policies that are profitable to it in the public realm.[8]

Employing this concept allows us to highlight the systematic and comprehensive character of drug-control structures and to stress their capacity

for operating in the political realm—and their awareness that it was necessity to do so. The status of opium as a monopoly/contraband commodity makes this kind of political engagement inevitable. Supervision must be
exercised at all stages from poppy planting to final sale. Wholesalers, carriers, distributors, retailers, and consumers must be licensed and checked.
Supply must be gatekept and traffic policed to cut out competitors at each
stage in the lucrative trade. Grouping the many different types of organization under this one rubric allows us to cross standard conceptual boundaries and to recognize the thoroughly political character of contraband
trade, whether the entity that manages it is an established state or not.

The opium regimes we consider in this volume include formal state
governments, both Chinese and foreign, state agencies, and businesses and
civic organizations that acted in the public sphere to induce political outcomes. As the individual chapters show, the complex interweaving of commodity trading, addiction, and state intervention that took place because
of opium prompted the formation of regimes to pursue political, economic, and even cultural arrangements that otherwise would not have been
possible. The face of East Asia was refigured in the process. To track these
changes, we start our coverage in the middle decades of the nineteenth
century, by which time opium had become established as a major commodity linking Asian trade with British imperial power, notably through
Singapore and Hong Kong. We take the story forward from the emerging
patterns of distribution and consumption in the latter part of the nineteenth century, to the multistranded attempts to bring the drug under the
supervision of state entities, civic associations, and international bodies during the first three decades of the twentieth. We complete the arc of opium's
history in East Asia by focusing on the crisis in drug control precipitated
by Japan's military adventurism in the 1930s and 1940s, which contributed
greatly to the energetic and effective suppression of the opium trade by
the Communist government of the People's Republic of China in the
1950s.

OPIUM TO CHINA

The origins of the opium trade in East Asia can be traced from well before
the nineteenth century. Opium was not native to China. Textual evidence
of opium in a Chinese pharmacopoeic manual of the eighth century suggests that Muslim traders were already carrying opium from West to East
Asia. This long genealogy anchors the history of a medicine that was prescribed for diarrhea up into the twentieth century and for that frequent
complaint in traditional medical lore, male impotence. The history of
opium as an object of recreational consumption begins much later, not
until the seventeenth century, when Dutch and English traders were

extending their ever-growing networks in Southeast Asia into China. They made the drug available by lacing tobacco, a drug substance coming around the globe from the other direction, with opium. This substance, *madak,* was more potent and pleasurable for smokers to consume than raw opium. The earliest Chinese to consume it, as the court discovered early in the 1720s, were "worthless young men" from Taiwan, as first memorialized to the throne. This text portrays opium as a commodity that "cunning barbarians" used "to trick Chinese out of their money"—a complaint that would be repeated up to the present. When other reports from officials on the south coast followed, the Yongzheng emperor (r. 1723–1735) banned the sale and distribution of opium. His edict of 1729 identified dealers rather than smokers as legally culpable, reserving the damning epithet *hanjian* (Chinese traitor) for those retailing the opium, not those consuming it.[9]

Subsequent edicts repeated the restrictions and imposed more specific penalties. It is impossible to say whether such legislation had any effect on the trade, which in any case continued to grow, albeit slowly. About two hundred chests (one chest weighs about 63.5 kilograms) of opium entered China in 1729. Sixty years later that amount had only doubled. Most of that increase probably occurred after 1773, when the East India Company began to ship opium to China through subcontracting agents known as "country traders." The floodgates opened a little wider in the early decades of the nineteenth century, especially after the East India Company lost its monopoly on the opium trade in India in 1813. In response, the annual average for 1817–1820 rose to more than four thousand chests. The imperial government's response was harsh when it perceived that consumption was spreading from commoners to the elite, and from southerners to residents of the capital and denizens of the court. But new legislation proved powerless against the deadly combination of expanding Chinese demand and skyrocketing British supply. When the activist official Lin Zexu was appointed imperial maritime commissioner in 1838 to stop the opium trade, the annual flow of the drug into China had risen to well over thirty thousand chests.

The British empire could not survive were it deprived of its most important source of capital, the substance that could turn any other commodity into silver. Thus followed the "Opium War" (1839–1842) in response to Lin's tough measures against foreign opium suppliers. As we have already noted, British opinion was not unified behind this assault on what many perceived as China's legitimate right to ban imports of opium. "A ghastly bloody farce" is what the satirical magazine *Punch* called it in 1842.[10] The war resulted famously in military defeat and the granting of more concessions to foreign traders, notably the opening of five "treaty ports" along the southeast coast and the abolition of the trade monopoly that the Qing government had imposed on foreign merchants trading into Guangzhou (Canton). These concessions further frustrated official attempts to reduce imports. However, the focus at the time was less on the addictive consequences of opium than on the hemorrhaging of the Chinese economy through the rapid outflow of silver to pay for the opium imports.

The British felt frustrated as well, for bilateral trade did not grow as handsomely as some had hoped. By 1854, when China became third after the United States and France among suppliers of imports to an over-extended Great Britain, the value of goods (principally tea and silk) from China totaled more than nine times the value of British exports to China. The gap could be filled only by Indian opium, and in ever-increasing amounts. Without it, Britain could not hope to reverse its dreadfully skewed balance of payments with China into the black—short of asking the British to give up drinking tea (or to grow tea in India, which they eventually did do). Nor could Britain dream of maintaining its ever more expensive presence in India, or paying for its imperial stepping-stones in Singapore and Hong Kong. Nor, as J. Y. Wong has argued, could Britain afford to buy raw cotton from the United States in the huge quantities it needed to keep the mills of Manchester running.[11] The entire imperial system on which Britain's trade was delicately balanced depended on the funds it could extract from other commodity trades through opium, either in tax or profit. And as the scale of the empire grew, so too did that dependence. Given Britain's desperate need to maintain its world trade position, a minor incident in 1856 involving a Chinese vessel under expired British registration known as the *Arrow* was sufficient to launch hostilities a second time in what is called the "Second Opium War" (1856–1860). With the signing of the Treaty of Tianjin at the end of the first phase of this war in 1858, opium was conditionally legalized as an import. The Qing ban on opium may have been only a minor barrier among the forces determining the scale of the trade. Still, without it, blocking the flow of opium into China became even more difficult.

OPIUM IN CHINA

Opium's place in China expanded, deepened, and changed over the course of the next hundred years, which is why the subject demands a historical perspective. As opium went from medicine to mass drug food, patterns of consumption altered, demand increased, and the understanding of opium use changed. Both Chinese and Europeans could be found who took a benign view of opium, insisting that its moderate consumption was less of a social evil than alcohol abuse in the West. We might be tempted to dismiss this observation as cynical hypocrisy and point to the ban on opium importation into Britain in 1856 as evidence of a double standard. The moderation implicit in Morse's "ante-prandial glass of sherry" could be found among some opium smokers. On the other hand, the glass-of-sherry argument falls far short of adequately describing the actual experience of rum consumption among the European poor or the indigenous peoples in European colonies, many of whom spent their adult lives inebriated. To be fair to the comparison, since English courts did not regard rum sots as criminals, neither should opium sots be placed beyond the law. This analogy is implicit in Thomas Allom's picture of Chinese in an opium den, drawn on his visit to Guangzhou at the time of the First Opium War. In it he shows people in poses of intoxication that viewers would recognize from pictures of the drunken lower classes in England (fig. 1). But middle-class mores in the nineteenth century were disinclined to countenance either type of intoxication. Accordingly, the anti-opium lobby found its supporters in the temperance movement.

The defense of opium as innocuous when consumed in moderation may be sound from a biological, and even a cultural, point of view.[12] But if a historical point of view problematizes the exculpatory judgments one sometimes finds in nineteenth-century writings, it must do so by recognizing that the concept of "opium" was altering more quickly than these observers could guess. Changing notions among Europeans regarding intoxication, pharmaceuticals, and the role of the state in regulating dangerous substances, combined with the burgeoning scale of use in China, was changing the social meaning of opium. At the start of the nineteenth century, opium had been a foreign import consumed mostly by men in the southern coastal region. The very wealthy enjoyed it as an object of recreational consumption, the very poor as a palliative to help manage physical exhaustion and hunger. In the second half of the nineteenth century, conditions changed. Opium was more often locally grown than imported (a successful instance of private import substitution), and it was consumed among all strata of society, including the middle, usually as a homosocial recreation. A pair or small group of men, poorly or well attired, sprawled on an opium couch, became the recognizable image of "Chinese opium smokers"—or more broadly, of "Chinese" *tout court*—that Westerners liked to photograph. Figures 2 and 3 show smokers at different locations on the social spectrum. Its consumption in turn became more extensively commercialized, retailed not just in elegant halls in the big coastal cities (see fig. 10, pp. 172–173) but in little "smoke shops" *(yanshi)* throughout the countryside. Opium was also becoming an item of female consumption. Women appear to have smoked less than men, and with lower rates of addiction. But smoke they did, at home alone (see fig. 4) or in the company of other women.

Evidence of all these changes appears in the diary of Takezoe Shin'ichirō, secretary of the Japanese legation in Beijing. When Takezoe traveled from the capital into the western interior in May 1876, he crossed through the province of Shanxi and found it quite overgrown with poppies

Figure 1. An opium den in Guangzhou as depicted by Thomas Allom in his *China, in a Series of Views* (1843), vol. 3, preceding p. 54. The histrionic poses of intoxication that the smokers strike are more suggestive of rum than of opium consumption.

and steeped in opium. He estimated with deep dismay—and gross exaggeration—that 70 percent of the people in Shanxi, men and women alike, smoked opium. Takezoe's prediction of long-term effects ironically anticipates the rhetoric that Chinese would later use to worry about opium and challenge the right of Japanese to peddle the drug in their country:

> It is in the nature of opium to consume the energies of the smoker and shorten his life. This poison is worse than venom. I fear that in another one hundred years' time the four hundred millions of China will be utterly enervated and the race will approach extinction. The Father-and-Mother of the people [Emperor Guangxu] should take measures as soon as possible.[13]

The individual consequences of drug abuse could be alarming, as Takezoe notes. But the integration of opium into China's culture and economy was having other effects, as new research is now showing. Poppy production in the poorer interior regions created a golden opportunity for peasant farmers subsisting in otherwise marginal economies. The production and distribution of native opium did many things in the process: facilitate Chinese capital accumulation, expand the money supply, knit internal trade networks, and redistribute wealth away from the coast.[14] In time it would

Figure 2. Lower-class opium smokers in Sichuan, as reproduced in Omar Kilborn, *Heal the Sick* (1916), facing p. 110.

also redistribute political power away from the coastal provinces that had initially benefited owing to foreign trade and the rise of a new compradore class and Republican elites.[15]

The spread of poppies across fields, and of opium across society, was not something to which the Qing state was indifferent. Li Hongzhang, who directed China's foreign relations during the first two decades of Guangxu's reign (1876–1907), was not persuaded that imported opium had a place in China. Constrained by China's international treaty obligations to allow opium into the country, he could only keep the moral argument alive and hope to shame Britain with it. As he put it in a letter of 24 May 1881 to the secretary of the British Society for the Suppression of Opium, "China views the whole question from a moral standpoint; England from a fiscal." These were state postures, however. "China" included peasants, transport coolies, merchants, and even officials such as Li Hongzhang who found the trade too lucrative—and smokers who found it too pleasurable—to abandon in favor of moral goods. Nor does Li's opposition of moral to fiscal interests fully characterize the relationship that the Chinese state then had, and more particularly would later have, with opium. Li's appeal to the

Figure 3. Upper-class opium smokers surrounded by elegant accessories, photographed by Mr. Mencarini and reproduced in Mrs. Archibald Little, *The Land of the Blue Gown* (1902), p. 39.

foreigners was phrased as morality, but his chief concern was to stop the drain of silver—to which his solution, realized in 1891, was import substitution.[16] As many of the contributors to this volume demonstrate, fiscal concerns could not but influence decisions about whether and how to suppress the traffic. In any case the Qing state was not able to take effective action against the importing of opium, although by the 1890s the amount of opium coming into China began to lessen. Still, it accounted for half of the value of Britain's exports to China.[17] The decline in this higher-quality imported opium was more than offset by the lower-grade domestic product, however, which was flooding the market without any involvement of foreigners.

A turning point came in 1906. Fired by reformist zeal in the wake of the disastrous Boxer Rebellion (1900), the Qing government launched a major campaign of eradication when assured of the international cooperation needed to make such a campaign viable. The Guangxu emperor issued a series of edicts that autumn calling for phased abolition based on a gradual reduction of native production, just as Takezoe had hoped three decades

Figure 4. A wealthy Manchu woman smoking opium at home; the girl to the right is an attendant. Published by S. Kojima in his *View and Custom of North China* (1910).

before. This program was the first coordinated national campaign in Chinese history to bring drugs under control. Despite lapses during the first decade and a half of Republican rule when central policy proved precariously difficult to impose, the 1906 campaign did cut back opium production and put suppression on the agendas of all subsequent Chinese states. Opium did not suddenly disappear, but the ideal was now firmly established that it should. Only with the advent of an aggressively centralizing regime in 1949 was a Chinese government able take the matter fully in hand.

A notable component of the 1906 suppression campaign was Britain's willingness to comply, on condition that the Chinese government suppress native production. In 1907 the British and Chinese governments negotiated a schedule of import reductions, starting with a three-year trial period, designed to end imports by 1917. By that time, Britain could afford to bow to public pressure and allow its drug trade in China to lapse. As all colonial players in the international opium trade had come to recognize, opium eroded the productive capacity of colonial subjects, fed a stratum of tax farmers who were difficult to control, and generated an unstable revenue.

It was now also a blemish on a regime's reputation and good grounds for local political opposition. These pressures were making themselves felt by 1906, when imported Indian opium accounted for less than a tenth of all the opium consumed in China, according to official figures.[18] The burden of suppression had thus already shifted from the British Other to the Chinese Self. However, the intransigence of addiction at home would prove as difficult to break in the twentieth century as the intransigence of foreign encroachment had been in the nineteenth.

ILLEGALIZATION AND ITS ILLS

With a suppression campaign underway in the country of greatest use, international negotiations soon followed to bring the opium trade to a close. The United States took the lead by setting up an International Opium Commission in Shanghai in 1909 to explore ways and means of suppressing drugs, particularly opium's inexpensive and potent derivative, morphine. The United States pressed for a second opium conference at The Hague in the winter of 1912, with a follow-up meeting in 1913. The Hague Convention urged members to restrict opium and its derivatives to medical uses, but allowed those states already involved in producing opium to phase it out gradually through a system of export licensing. The agreement made each contracting power responsible for developing its own legislation, which the United States did in 1914 with the Harrison Act, and Great Britain did in 1920 with the Dangerous Drugs Act. After the First World War, the League of Nations assumed the task of coordinating drug control through its Opium Advisory Committee. The committee's two conventions at Geneva in the winter of 1924–1925 produced a new agreement to regulate the international drug trade, but one that allowed domestic monopolies to keep running for another fifteen years.[19] A prolonged timetable for suppression encouraged producer states to close their doors to outside scrutiny. But in China's case the challenge of bringing dangerous drugs under control was vexed by the precariousness of every Chinese regime's hold over the country, particularly the poppy-growing interior.[20]

The imposition of international controls stimulated another complicating development. By increasing the cost of doing business, it encouraged dealers to process opium into the more potent, less detectable, and far more toxic forms of morphine and heroin through industrial production. As smokable opium was edged aside by refined narcotics, drug use became a more powerfully addictive activity. Trafficking then took on an entirely new immoral hue. Since the consumption of refined narcotics could no longer be moderate, the much higher profits from refined narcotics made the urge to expand the trade irresistible, regardless of the human cost. The opium trade also lost its association—at least among Chinese who regarded moderate opium smoking as socially acceptable—with the innocent peasant poppy-grower, whose livelihood depended on the drug trade's continuance.[21]

The legal consequence of government monopoly was the criminalization of opium traded outside the monopoly. Criminalization did not necessarily translate into effective control, especially because most of those who sold outside the monopoly also worked within it and were engaged simply in selling over quota. Instead, by increasing the profitability of handling a now scarce commodity, illegalization encouraged criminal organizations to get into the trade, thereby paradoxically tightening opium's grip on society. Thus, as the new international regulations came into force, states and gangs found themselves in intense competition over the trade. They also found themselves doing business with each other to create mutually satisfying arrangements, with states using gangsters for political purposes and gangsters gaining political influence. As Brian Martin has noted in the context of 1920s Shanghai, "Prohibition encouraged the growth of a vast, illicit traffic that provided the economic basis for the development of organized crime in the major cities and helped define the ways in which criminal organization interacted with the world of politics."[22] The consumption of contraband drugs not only created the financial basis for the spectacular growth of organized crime in the 1920s and 1930s. It also provided the newly emergent and unstable Guomindang state with revenue. Moreover, this also gave the Guomindang state the intelligence and strong-arm capacities of organized crime that it felt it needed to silence its political enemies.

The tide of international illegalization and domestic criminalization occurred at the same time that public associations and spokesmen were mounting anti-opium propaganda campaigns to persuade consumers to give up the drug and to pressure the government when they felt it was not sufficiently vigilant on the issue. Their rhetoric, which highlighted national, moral, and personal consequences for the smoker, was largely identical to the government's. The mildest appeal was to the health of the nation, which opium was construed as undermining (see fig. 13, p. 255). A more powerful appeal to delegitimize opium consumption associated it discursively with other vices, most particularly prostitution (see fig. 5). During the Republican era, this way of gendering the opium vice was not difficult to effect, given the proliferation, at least in Shanghai, of "flower-smoke rooms" *(huayan shi),* unlicensed brothels where opium was also retailed.[23] The most dramatic appeal in the anti-opium propaganda of the time was not the shame of moral or even national debilitation, but the threat of personal ruin and execution (fig. 6). In actual fact, however, execution was for opium addicts a rare and exemplary penalty, being reserved rather for those who dealt in refined narcotics.

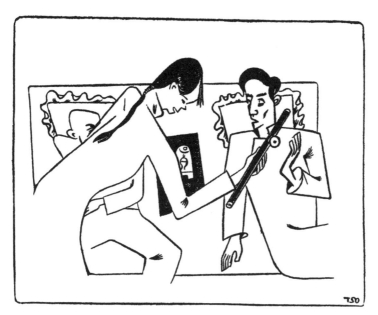

Figure 5. An anti-opium cartoon associating opium addiction with prostitution, which appeared in the inaugural issue of the magazine *Judu zhuankan* 1, no. 1 (December 1935): 19. It illustrates a story revealing how one puff taken at the behest of a prostitute was enough to addict a man for life.

JAPAN AND OPIUM

As imperial Britain extricated itself from the nineteenth-century opium regime it had operated in China, imperial Japan began to assemble its own. Japan's first colonial experience with an opium regime was in Taiwan, where it began a successful program to control addiction after occupying the island in 1895.[24] With their expansion to the Asian mainland, first to Korea and then to Manchuria, Japanese discovered the irresistible power of opium to accumulate capital. Imperial Japanese subjects were smuggling opium into China as early as the 1890s, but the nature and scale of their activities began to change decisively during the interwar period, when first the great *zaibatsu* corporations and then the imperial government itself smuggled not just opium but refined drugs (first morphine, then heroin). Japan ratified the four international treaties between 1912 and 1931 that banned the sale and export of narcotic drugs for nonmedicinal purposes. But Japan soon found itself under censure in the League of Nations, where former trafficking nations criticized it for violating those treaties.

The importance of opium in Japan's calculations increased exponen-

Figure 6. The descent of the opium smoker through addiction, rehabilitation, poverty, and execution, as depicted by a poster produced by the municipal Public Health Bureau of Beijing (1936). Panels, right to left, top to bottom: *a.* "Before ever smoking opium, he is healthy in body and content in spirit." *b.* "After starting to smoke opium, he bankrupts his family, loses his job, confuses his mind, and reduces his body to kindling." *c.* "Because he smokes opium, he is arrested and forced to undergo detoxification in an addiction treatment clinic." *d.* "After being rehabilitated in the clinic, his health is restored and he is approved for discharge." *e.* "After being rehabilitated, he goes back to smoking opium." *f.* "Nabbed again by the police." *g.* "The only thing to do now is take him out and execute him!" Reproduced with permission of the Hoover Institution, Stanford California.

tially during its Asia-Pacific War (1931–1945), particularly in the early phases.[25] Japanese opium operations in China sprang from three motives. First, opium funded undercover operations that facilitated aggression against Chinese territory outside of Japan's control. Second, opium profits went to right-wing societies in Japan, and there is even some evidence linking laundered wartime opium monies with postwar conservative parties.[26] Finally, and above all, the Japanese imperial government needed to finance a series of increasingly expensive client states in occupied China; opium seemed the only expeditious way to do this. According to the last Qing emperor, Pu Yi, whom the Japanese installed as head of state in Manchukuo, that puppet regime received 300 million yuan, or about one-sixth of its total revenues, from opium.[27] The Nationalist Party (Guomindang) averred that Japan used drugs to poison China into submission, and some Japanese war criminals detained on the mainland, such as Furumi Tadayuki, testified to that effect in the 1950s.[28] But as Timothy Brook and Kobayashi Motohiro argue in their chapters, the Japanese used opium mainly because it raised sorely needed revenue—just as it did for Chinese warlords, criminals, the Guomindang, and even the Chinese Communist Party (CCP).[29] Imperial Japan lacked the wherewithal to be a colonial power by conventional means. Its leaders therefore latched on to opium as a poor empire's fiscal panacea.

Japanese opium operations in China developed in three overlapping stages.[30] Stage one lasted from the 1890s through the Manchurian Incident (1931), which ended with the Tanggu Truce in May 1933. During this stage, imperial subjects smuggled drugs into Chinese treaty ports under the cloak of extraterritoriality. These riff-raff carpetbaggers or "continental adventurers" *(tairiku rōnin)*, as they were known, enjoyed at least tacit support from consular authorities in treaty port concessions and from imperial armed forces in colonial areas such as the Guandong (Kwantung) Leased Territories. The volume of morphine that Japanese were bringing into China by the 1910s was considerable. Of the close to fifty thousand kilograms of morphine that Japanese dealers bought from Great Britain in 1915, for example, most was going to China under extraterritorial privilege.[31] Japanese treaty port officials did little to staunch the flow, and were discouraged from doing so when they tried. Yoshida Shigeru, a postwar prime minister of Japan who at the time was serving as consul in Tianjin, described the situation in that city in December 1922:

> Of the 5,000 Japanese residents in Tianjin, 70 percent deal in morphine or other illegal substances. Almost all businesses traffic in these goods, even eateries and general stores, not just medicinal firms. . . . Police crackdowns here are not as strict as in Dalian, and the consulate's policy is to arraign only the most flagrant violators. We prosecute only those caught by [Chinese] customs authorities or those uncovered in other crimes. We don't arrest criminals or investigate crimes on our own. If we did so thoroughly, no Japanese would be left in Tianjin.[32]

Even when a Japanese subject came before consular officials for drug dealing, penalties were light. In his memoirs, Ishii Itarō recalled the trial of a Korean over which he presided as judge in 1918. After he handed down a six-month jail term, the consular police chief pulled him aside and said, "Look, we'd blow our budget if we had to feed that guy for six months.

Consul Yoshida [Shigeru] would have said two months at the most." Ishii commented: "After all, I was still a rank amateur, so my first experience was a real knee-slapper. After three or four tries, I got better."[33]

Stage two in the history of Japanese opium operations began in June 1933 with the creation of a demilitarized zone (DMZ) in East Hebei as stipulated by the Tanggu Accords, and ended with the establishment of the Kōain (Asia Development Board) in December 1938. Trafficking by carpetbaggers continued during this stage, with connivance from consular officials, but it expanded south of the Great Wall into East Hebei. Only Chinese units were actually forced to leave this DMZ, whereas Japanese forces and their campfollowers could enter at will. The zone was placed under Yin Rugeng's Regime for East Hebei Autonomy and the Containment of Communism, set up in November 1935. There, imperial subjects could sell opium with impunity. Furthermore, *zaibatsu* such as Mitsubishi shōji and Mitsui bussan liberally interpreted provisions in the Tanggu Accords to extend the DMZ out to sea and smuggle Iranian opium into north China under formal Foreign Ministry direction.[34] Trafficking was no longer confined to individuals in Guandong or the treaty ports; the *zaibatsu* now operated in China proper with imperial government backing.

Stage three came with the creation in December 1938 of the Kōain, headed by the premier plus his army, navy, foreign, and finance ministers—a body that later became the Japanese government's Greater East Asia Ministry. The Kōain ran opium operations through its Kalgan branch office, working hand in glove with the Mengjiang regime in Mongolia, which was also headquartered there after its creation in 1939. Eguchi Keiichi, the historian who spearheaded academic research on what he terms "Japan's opium war," shows that Japanese officials controlling this puppet regime encouraged local consumption of the drug and taxed profits from it. They set up monopolies, got farmers to grow poppies on a large scale, bought up the harvests, processed the sap into raw opium, refined that opium into heroin and morphine, and exported these narcotics to other parts of China and to Southeast Asia. Thus, in stage one individuals trafficked in treaty port concessions and colonies under the protection of extraterritoriality. In stage two the *zaibatsu* extended smuggling south of the Great Wall by exploiting provisions of the Tanggu Truce under Foreign Ministry direction. Finally in stage three the Japanese imperial government itself manufactured and exported narcotics from Mengjiang into other regions of China.

Japan tried to parry foreign criticism of its opium operations in China.[35] But its trafficking was condemned by the League of Nations in the 1930s and continued to be exposed by non-Japanese observers in the 1940s.[36] The Tokyo War Crimes Tribunal took up the issue from 30 August to 6 September 1946, and behind-the-scenes questioning of principals such as

Tanaka Ryūkichi yielded still more information to Allied prosecutors.[37] In their own postwar settling of accounts, the Guomindang government executed 149 imperial Japanese subjects on drug-related charges as B- and C-class war criminals, and the People's Republic detained war criminals involved with drugs until 1956. Yet despite the prominence that Japan enjoyed as a narcotics regime during the war, its record as a narcotic imperialist is much less well known than Britain's.[38]

THE ARC OF OPIUM'S HISTORY

This collection of new research on the opium trade in East Asia covers the period from roughly 1839 to 1952. Our point of departure, 1839, was the year in which the Qing emperor sought to impose a new regime for opium on two fronts: he dispatched Commissioner Lin Zexu to Canton, and he ordered an investigation of opium coming into China over the northwest border. Our terminus, 1952, marks the final suppression of opium in China, at least for this stage of its history. Our purpose in bringing this wide-ranging work together is to introduce fresh perspectives on a topic that, until recently, most historians assumed was adequately understood and therefore of little interest. In the last few years the scholarly community has started to see opium as a more complex phenomenon with a multi-stranded history. This is not to say that our contributors dismiss the moral judgments long since passed on the opium trade. But we seek to move beyond these conventions. Our chapters investigate the complex global and local processes that channeled the drug to and from certain places, created particular markets, and extracted enormous volumes of wealth. All of these actions entailed costs, and some yielded benefits. Costs and benefits affected victims and victimizers differently. Our intention is less to repeat the narrative of British, or even Japanese, victimization of China than to explore more fully how costs and benefits arose and played out in political contexts.

The book is organized in four parts. Part 1, "The International Context," introduces the nineteenth-century foundations of the opium trade. Gregory Blue tracks the economic and political considerations involved in creating the British opium regime in Asia. He locates opium in what he terms a "cohesive trade structure" that Britons, Indians, and Chinese created through the energetic pursuit of profitable trade. Britain dominated, and gained greatest advantage from, this structure. A "bifurcated framework of formal colonialism and the 'imperialism of free trade'" characterized the British presence in Asia in the nineteenth century. Through it, Britain was able to impose the legalization of opium in China after 1858, and thereby secure an important financial pillar of its far-flung political empire. Bob Tadashi Wakabayashi then turns our gaze to nineteenth-century Japan. The Tokugawa and Meiji regimes, both before and after 1868, enjoyed almost total success at controlling opium within Japan's borders, and both used this control to enhance state consolidation and centralize power. Just as British politicians and merchants had established an opium regime in China earlier in the nineteenth century, Meiji Japanese moved to establish their own. Japan would eventually go beyond Britain by selling not just opium but also refined narcotics, doing so in the face of ever-mounting Chinese resistance and international censure. Wakabayashi examines the historical origins of the Japanese involvement in this opium trade by analyzing changing Japanese views of opium use in Qing China. He shows how the mechanisms of *sakoku* (national isolation) furthered political consolidation in Tokugawa Japan, and he argues that Meiji Japan used opium to move away from being a co-victim of Western imperialism, to become a co-predator in China.

In Part 2, "Distribution and Consumption," we consider how opium was being distributed and consumed in China and by whom. Here, to a considerable extent, we move away from the conventional focus on imperialists operating from the outside and shift attention to the pivotal roles that Chinese played in enjoying opium and developing the trade in it. All five chapters in this part focus on locations at the interstices of China's relations with the outside world. Carl Trocki shows how much the development of Singapore, the most important opium entrepôt between India and China, hinged on Chinese economic networks. Opium in Singapore, as in other colonial possessions, was handled through privately held monopolies granted by the colonial state, known as "opium farms." These were owned and operated by Chinese *kongsi* or shareholding partnerships (*gongsi* in Mandarin, now the standard term for a limited liability company). The *kongsi* discovered that exploiting the Malay hinterland could only be profitable if they were able to recoup labor costs through opium sales. This arrangement is what in turn made British colonialism affordable in Singapore. As Trocki has noted elsewhere, "Opium was the trap in which the *kongsi* economies were captured by colonial capitalism. Having trapped the local economies, British merchants were able, perhaps even forced, to leave the details of the opium trade to others, but they relied on its presence."[39] Without this well-oiled link in the chain of opium shipments and receipts, the British empire could not have bridged the distance between its colony in India and its market in China. However, when the British attempted to replicate their Singapore success in Hong Kong, they found it impossible to trap the local economy there, thus exposing any notion of establishing a genuine colonial foothold in China as impossible. As Christopher Munn shows in the next chapter, the British quickly abandoned the one flawed attempt by Scotsmen to run an opium farm in Hong Kong and shrewdly gave it to Chinese merchants who could turn a profit. Marx may have criticized the British monopolistic position as "incompatible with the development of legitimate commerce."[40] But in fact the local integuments of commercial activity throughout East Asia derived form and vigor from the power of opium to concentrate capital.

David Bello's chapter moves us away from the coastal periphery and the agents of colonialism operating there, which past studies of the opium trade have made familiar. He chooses instead to look at the networks by which Muslim traders brought opium into China across the northwest border. His work demonstrates that before 1839 the Qing drug problem was not solely or even mainly a coastal issue involving the British. He also indicates, as Munn does, that without energetic Chinese mercantile involvement, the opium trade could never have penetrated the Chinese economy to the extent that it did. Motohiro Kobayashi then takes us to another periphery, this time the northeast coast. He tracks the activities of another group of outsiders, Japanese and Korean, who plied the drug trade later in the nineteenth century in the port city of Tianjin. The profitability of this trade, which spread rapidly and produced revenues quickly, would lure Japanese imperial government organs to take it over in the twentieth century.

In the final chapter of part 2, Alexander Des Forges moves from distribution to consumption to examine the opulent world of high-class recreational consumption in coastal Shanghai. At one level opium may have been tainted as a noxious foreign substance, yet it enjoyed a conspicuous place in the new urban culture of leisure that the hybridizing environment of Sino-foreign contact was creating. The culture of consumption and enjoyment that took shape in Shanghai would never have emerged without the opium that was streaming in from India, through Hong Kong and the treaty ports as well as over the northwest border. And yet opium would not have continued to circulate within China without the effective demand that made this appropriation of opium into the culture of consumption possible.

Part 3, "Control and Resistance," turns to the ways in which national and regional efforts to control or suppress opium served to promote the integration and penetration of the modern Chinese state. In these chapters, *state* is used to signify political regimes with different orders of magnitude. All imply greater consolidation and centralized control vis-à-vis centrifugal forces such as local elites, though at different levels. Examples would be the Qing empire as a whole, provincial or warlord or collaborator regimes, and the Guomindang. This term *state* connotes the conditions that those regimes aspired to attain as often as it indicates a political entity powerful enough to assert effective control over administration and revenue throughout its realm. Contrary to what one might expect, these chapters show that opium contributed to, rather than detracted from, strengthening state power by co-opting local elites, and even peasants, into new state structures. This effect occurred whether the state's aim was to suppress the drug outright, or to control it gradually and thereby milk the trade for revenue, at least temporarily. Whether controls worked depended on many factors, not all of which functioned as the state might wish. These included state power (which in China before 1949 was variable and weak), the profitability of the revenue, the cooperation of local elites, the ability of poppy-growing peasants to survive by disguising their poppies or cultivating other crops, and the degree of domestic and international pressure brought to bear on the opium trade.

The Chinese state faced considerable challenges in establishing opium regimes. Getting a grip on opium meant penetrating local society to an extent that went beyond normal Qing imperial practices. Bin Wong begins this section with a chapter on Chinese state-making and the impact of opium control on that process. He looks back to earlier efforts by the Qing state to control society in order to appreciate its impressive campaign of 1906 as an attempt "to resecure a neo-Confucian social order." The difficulties that modern China faced in its state-making enterprise would have been simplified had the British not imported opium into China, he argues. In that sense China "bore the burden of opium." But the great challenge of framing new state institutions and state-society relations would have been on the agenda in any case. In the next two chapters, Judith Wyman and Joyce Madancy look at two provinces to assess the Qing suppression campaign. Wyman stresses how successful representatives of the central government were in enforcing the 1906 campaign in Sichuan. By contrast, Madancy focuses on the local side of the equation in Fujian. She describes how provincial officials worked to win the cooperation of elites and co-opt them into their power structure, using opium policy to orchestrate new relations between the state and local elites.

Moving further into the Republican period, Edward Slack studies how those relations played out in the National Anti-Opium Association, set up by activists within and beyond the Chinese Christian community to press the state to rid China of opium. The movement struck a sympathetic chord among some sectors of the emerging urban elite. However, the Guomindang state was not keen to have a competitor regime in spheres crucial for state-building and revenue. Hence it used both co-optation and coercion to force the association to disband in 1937, just nine days before Japan's invasion. The Guomindang felt pressured not just to take up the cause of opium control, but to take it over. Thus arose the second "successful" opium campaign in China, which Jiang Jieshi (Chiang Kai-shek) mounted in 1935. In his study of it, Alan Baumler describes how Jiang was able to gain the upper hand in the trade over his warlord counterparts by getting almost complete control over supply and distribution. Jiang worked on the fine line between control and suppression. Whether the ambitious six-year plan would have achieved its declared goal of total elimination cannot be known, for the plan was thrown into chaos when Japan invaded two years later. Opium suppression lost its priority at the beginning of the war, but the Guomindang government rapidly re-emphasized it as a key component of the war effort and kept the original plan going in west China.

Lucien Bianco rounds out part 3 from the other side of opium suppression by shifting our attention down to the cultivators whose livelihoods, and even survival, were directly affected by the state's opium regimes. Growing opium could be a life-saving option for cultivators in bad times and a great boon in good. Suppression and control led to a nightmare of oppressive demands by tax agents (when revenue demands were uppermost) or crop destruction by opium-control officials (when suppression was on the agenda), or sometimes both in the same season! The unevenness with which the state policed the rural sector in the Republican era added to the instability of the relations between them and the high degree of suspicion with which they viewed each other. Guomindang campaigns made progress in the 1930s. But the project to rid China of opium—like the larger project that loomed behind it, the consolidation of the central state—remained far from complete when Japan invaded in 1937.

Japan's occupation of north China and its invasion of central China in the summer of 1937 forced all these projects into abeyance. The fourth and final part of this volume, "Crisis and Resolution," examines the tremendous impact of Japan's onslaught. Japan threw existing opium regimes into disarray, but then quickly reconstituted them in ways designed to increase revenues to itself and the client states it set up to run its occupation. Timothy Brook reconstructs the formation of the agencies of collaboration in central China in 1938 under the aegis of a state entity called the Reformed Government, through which Japan sought, among other goals, to manage the opium/narcotics trade. He concludes that the revenue opium generated was essential for keeping both the regime and its military patrons financially solvent. But solvency came at a cost of legitimacy, which even collaborators needed to claim. Motohiro Kobayashi in the next chapter carries the story forward into the Wang Jingwei regime, which replaced the Reformed Government in Nanjing in 1940 and survived to the end of war. Wang strove for a higher degree of autonomy from Japan than did the leaders of the Reformed Government, but he was placed in a tug-of-war over opium revenues because of Japan's need to purchase war matériel from other collaborator regimes in China. Without opium, Kobayashi concludes, Japan could not have waged "total war." It was beyond Wang Jingwei's capacity to resist that necessity. A dramatic public incident in that tug-of-war was the anti-opium movement that broke out in the streets of Nanjing in December 1943, which Mark Eykholt reconstructs in the following chapter. University students took to the streets to smash opium dens and to demand that the Wang regime take a more active role in stamping out opium consumption—and by so doing, loosen Japan's control. The Chinese in occupied areas were not as quiescent as resistance propaganda liked to suggest.

The powerfully negative wartime image of opium as a drug of conquest—however melodramatized by Guomindang propaganda—may have helped to inspire the political resolve and popular support that allowed the Communist Party to mount suppression campaigns in 1950 and 1952. This would bring the trade forcibly to an end within just a few years of the party's assumption of state power. That process is the subject of the final chapter in the volume. Zhou Yongming is the first scholar to do research on the Chinese Communist campaigns to suppress opium. The scarcity of materials on these campaigns he attributes to the pressured international environment in which they were carried out, at a time when the Chinese government did not wish its difficulties with opium to be made known to a hostile United States, with which it was unofficially at war in Korea. The success of the suppression campaign in the early 1950s was relatively complete, although it has been eroded since the 1980s with the decline of state socialism.

CONCLUSIONS

The study of opium in East Asian history is an ongoing project, and whatever conclusions can be drawn at this stage are provisional. If there are two we would offer, they are these: First, despite the common assumption that opium is a single, unitary thing, it was historically many things and was capable of undergoing transformation from one to another. As a physical substance, it was the sap exuding from the head of ripe poppies that Indian and Chinese peasants collected and sold, the tarry paste that merchants boiled up into marketable form, the commodity that businessmen used to capitalize commercial and industrial ventures elsewhere, the raw material that wholesalers refined to produce more intense narcotics, and the toxins running in smokers' veins. As a substance observed, it was a palliative medicine, an item of recreational consumption, an addictive drug food, a form in which capital could be stored, a sign of national and ethnic degradation, and a mechanism for transferring wealth and power between regions and nations. The variability of opium's identity is confirmed and further complicated by David Courtwright's sensible reminder that "what we think about addiction very much depends on who is addicted."[41] For opium to be the drug of choice for the wealthy is very different, in culture and consequence, than when it is the drug of sole resort for the poor. And when opium is the drug of Chinese, rather than of Britons or Japanese, it reinforces assumptions about which race or ethnic group is mastering history and which is mastered by it.

Our second conclusion follows from the first. Given the polymorphous character of a substance that changed in meaning according to its context, opium generated a wide range of problems for those who opposed its consumption. These problems were never amenable to straightforward solutions, although many were tried, from modest control to violent suppression. Because opium could be many things to many people, it usually eluded whatever controls that regimes, legislators, and moralists placed on it. The narcotic, economic, political, and even cultural pulls of opium went so strongly in favor of its continued use—despite the increasingly popular perception that opium was a bad thing. Almost every proposal for its limitation foundered as soon as it was launched.

We hope that this volume will map out a new state of the field. Our contribution fits together the numerous new studies now appearing into a coherent temporal arc: from British imperialism in the nineteenth century, to Chinese capital-formation and state-making earlier in the twentieth century, to Japanese imperialism through the 1930s and 1940s, and finally to the resolution of that long phase of China's "opium problem" in the 1950s. Each of the chapters furnishes a piece in this long arc. With this structure in place, it now may be possible to appreciate more fully the complex history of the buying, selling, and banning of opium over the past two centuries. It was a history of exploitation favoring few at the expense of many. But what kept it going were vast complicities that are best understood by probing the economics, politics, and cultural practices at work below the surface—not by repeating the moral claims that glossed the surface. This phase of opium's history in East Asia is over, but our understanding of it will continue to grow as scholars delve more thoroughly into the historical records of the trade and as we reflect more deeply on the narcotics-based regimes that flourish in our own time.

NOTES

1. Morse, *Trade and Administration of the Chinese Empire,* p. 323.

2. Karl Marx, "The Opium Trade" (3 September 1858), in Marx and Engels, *On Colonialism,* pp. 219–20. Marx's journalism on the *Arrow* incident is discussed in J. Y. Wong, *Deadly Dreams,* pp. 165–67, although not perhaps with a sufficiently full sensitivity to his rhetoric.

3. King, *Opium Crisis,* pp. 5, 6, 30, 69.

4. Mander, *Our Opium Trade with China,* p. 1.

5. For examples see Chang, *Commissioner Lin and the Opium War,* p. 15; Morse, *International Relations of the Chinese Empire,* 1:539; Fairbank, Reischauer, and Craig, *East Asia,* p. 136.

6. Communist historiography before and after 1949 was more moderate,

emphasizing only the economic aspect. For example, Fan Wenlan in his authoritative *Zhongguo jindai shi* stresses the role of opium as the "decisive commodity in Sino-British trade" (p. 5). Equally reticent to voice moral arguments was Hu Sheng, whose study of imperialism was in the 1950s the most widely read account of China's nineteenth-century foreign relations. Hu declined to pursue the notion that the British were deliberately poisoning or enslaving the Chinese people, and instead saw opium more simply as a device in Britain's larger imperialist strategy to impose a colonial relationship on China; see his *Imperialism and Chinese Politics*, pp. 12–17. This disinclination to emphasize opium may be related to the political context of opium suppression in the 1950s that Yongming Zhou explores in the last chapter of this volume.

7. On the racialization of drug use in Canada, see Carstairs, "'Deport the Drug Traffickers.'" Filipinos, conditioned to regard the Chinese in their midst with suspicion, blamed them for introducing the vice of opium to the Philippines; Alip, *Chinese in Manila*, p. 21.

8. We are indebted to Alan Baumler for his suggestions regarding the concept of "regime."

9. Howard, "Opium Suppression in Late-Qing China," pp. 4–8. On the use of the term *hanjian* during the first Opium War, see Waley, *Opium War through Chinese Eyes*, pp. 222–23. Spence, "Opium Smoking in Ch'ing China," provides a broad account of opium consumption in nineteenth-century China

10. *Punch* 3 (1842): 126, quoted in Munn, "Anglo-China," chapter 1, p. 7.

11. J. Y. Wong, *Deadly Dreams*, pp. 409–10.

12. This argument is presented in Newman, "Opium Smoking in Late Imperial China." Lodwick, *Crusaders against Opium*, pp. 76–85, argues that those who represented opium as relatively harmless were not disinterested in their advocacy, as H. B. Morse suspected (see note 1).

13. This excerpt from the diary of Takezoe Shin'ichirō (1842–1917) is quoted in Keene, *Modern Japanese Diaries*, p. 141. Oka Senjin (1832–1913), in his travelogue of China in 1884–1885, registers the same shock and dismay that caused many Japanese to abandon the sinophilia with which they were culturally prepared to regard China; see Fogel, *Literature of Travel in the Japanese Rediscovery of China*, pp. 75–77.

14. Hao, *Commercial Revolution in Nineteenth-Century China*, pp. 68–69. Lin Man-houng, "National Opium Market within China."

15. Baumler, "Playing with Fire: The Nationalist Government and Opium in China, 1927–1941."

16. Wang Jinxiang, *Zhongguo jindu jianshi*, pp. 52–54. Li's letter is quoted in Lodwick, *Crusaders against Opium*, p. 24. The Qing gave permission to plant poppies in 1891; see Madancy, "Ambitious Interlude," p. 122.

17. Harcourt, "Black Gold," p. 14, table 3.

18. Liang-lin Hsiao, *Foreign Trade Statistics*, p. 52.

19. The history of international controls is sketched in Walker, *Opium and Foreign Policy*, pp. 14–19, 35–40; Lodwick, *Crusaders against Opium*, pp. 137–44; and Meyer and Parssinen, *Webs of Smoke*, pp. 21–33. As the hosts of the Hague conferences, the Dutch were in the awkward position of having to go along with the implementation of international controls while at the same time wanting to protect the commercial

interests that their opium monopoly in Java served, in regard to which see Rush, *Opium to Java*, pp. 232–33.

20. Burkman, "Opium in China and the League of Nations."

21. Baumler, "Playing with Fire: The Nationalist Government and Popular Anti-opium Agitation in 1927–28."

22. Martin, *Shanghai Green Gang*, p. 45. For the nexus between drugs and politics in the 1930s, see Wakeman, *Policing Shanghai*, pp. 120–31, 260–75.

23. Hershatter, *Dangerous Pleasures*, pp. 49–50.

24. See Jennings, *Opium Empire*, pp. 19–28.

25. Aspects of Japanese drug trafficking in China are sketched in Meyer and Parssinen, *Webs of Smoke*, pp. 89–100, 185–229.

26. *Asahi shinbun*, 8 July 1993.

27. In *From Emperor to Citizen*, p. 384, Aisin-Gioro Pu Yi quotes the figure from Furumi Tadayuki; he gives no dates for the period covered.

28. *Asahi shinbun*, 5 April 1998; *Sekai* 649 (June 1998): 170–71.

29. Yung-fa Chen, "The Blooming Poppy under the Red Sun."

30. Much of the information that follows, but not the periodization, is from Eguchi, *Nit-Chū ahen sensō*.

31. Walker, *Opium and Foreign Policy*, p. 30.

32. Okada et al., *Zoku Gendai shi shiryō*, 12:190–91.

33. Ishii, *Gaikōkan no isshō*, pp. 38–40. This passage is cited in Liu Mingxiu [Itō Kiyoshi], *Taiwan tōchi to ahen mondai*, pp. 134–36, and Eguchi, *Shiryō*, p. 27n. 31, though both, for complicated postwar political reasons, decline to identify the defendant as Korean.

34. Okada et al., *Zoku Gendaishi shiryō*, 12:98–101.

35. Postwar confession by Lieutenant-General Sassa Shinnosuke in *Sekai* 648 (May 1998): 133–34; Ikeda, *Rikugun sōgi iinchō*, pp. 43–44. Drug dealing was depicted in novels of the time. Kuroshima Denji's 1930 fictional retelling of the Jinan Incident of 1928 in his *Busō seru shigai* portrayed the incident as having been set off in part by Japanese opium traffickers (in *Kuroshima Denji zenshū*, vol. 3). Lin Yutang's 1939 novel, *Moment in Peking*, shows imperial subjects peddling narcotic-laced candy to Chinese schoolchildren in treaty port concessions. Partial translations of Lin's novel appeared in Japan, but with those scenes expurgated.

36. E.g., the Institute of Pacific Relations published Frederick Merrill's *Japan and the Opium Menace* in 1942.

37. Awaya, Adachi, and Kobayashi, *Tōkyō saiban shiryō*, pp. 41–61.

38. The reason for this is explored in Wakabayashi, "Japanese Wartime Operations and Postwar Political Correctness."

39. Trocki, *Opium and Empire*, p. 52.

40. Marx, "The Opium Trade" (31 August 1858), in Marx and Engels, *On Colonialism*, p. 214.

41. Courtwright, *Dark Paradise*, p. 3.

PART ONE

The International Context

ONE

Opium for China
The British Connection

Gregory Blue

Opium in Chinese history is a large subject, as Jonathan Spence has observed.[1] This chapter is restricted to discussing its international aspects during the "long nineteenth century," a period usually defined as running from 1789 to 1914 but which I will frame more generously as extending from the late-eighteenth-century "Atlantic revolutions" to the 1920s or, to use other terms of reference, from the British conquest of Bengal to the upsurge of Asian nationalism between the two world wars and the displacement of Britain by the United States as the world's leading creditor nation. Using these non-Chinese processes to demarcate the subject may serve as a reminder that China's complex involvement with opium during this period was considerably more than a domestic affair. Organized into a multifaceted series of stages running from production to consumption, the nineteenth-century opium "industry" was a vivid example of transnational enterprise, an instance perhaps of the cultural hybridity that Bruno Latour sees as typical of the modern era.[2] To capture the industry's international character as well as to set the stage for later chapters exploring its specifically Chinese dimensions, my discussion must extend geographically beyond East Asia to include Britain, South Asia, and North America.

From the 1780s to the eve of the First World War, the opium trade was instrumental in integrating China into the world market and in harnessing that country to the institutions of European, and especially British, colonialism. During this period the economies of China, India, and Britain were structurally linked to one another in a trade triangle that until the 1860s was one of the most important components of the world economy, and thereafter continued for several decades to play a significant role in world trade. By the first half of the nineteenth century the flow of trade among the three countries involved the export of British manufactures to South

Asia, the export from India of opium and cottons for sale in China, and the purchase by British merchants of Chinese teas, silks, and bullion either for consumption in Britain or for re-export. The sale of Indian opium to China thus constituted a significant part of this triangular structure throughout the nineteenth century; for much of the period it was an essential part.

THE OPIUM TRADE PRIOR TO 1860

The Western trade in opium to China developed through several distinct phases. The earliest began in the seventeenth century and lasted until the 1760s; during this time the drug was mainly shipped either from Portuguese Goa in Portuguese and British vessels, or from Bengal by the Dutch, who held the monopoly on the export opium trade there. In either case it entered China—whether directly or via Macao—through Canton (Guangzhou), which from 1757 was designated by the imperial government as the only port open to European traffic. That opium was already considered a problem by the Qing in this period is evident from the Yongzheng emperor's 1729 edict banning its sale. The ban was vigorously enforced for a time, but became more sporadic in application as the Qianlong period (1736–1795) progressed. The second phase of the trade, lasting from the 1760s until the end of the century, followed British victories at Plassey in 1757 and Buxar in 1764 through which the East India Company (EIC) gained de facto sovereignty over Bengal, Bihar, and Orissa, and thereby acquired effective control over some of India's major opium-producing regions. The company resurrected the old Mogul monopoly on opium, and between 1764 and 1781 devised several systems for contracting out rights in the drug. At first company officials and other British merchants were allowed to use the trade to enhance their private fortunes, but after passage of the 1773 India Act a new system geared to increasing EIC revenues was introduced with the aim of using the China trade to bolster the company's then precarious accounts. In 1781, as part of Warren Hastings's program of putting the British administration in India on a stable financial footing during the American revolutionary war, the company took over the purchase of all opium produced in its territories. The Bengal administration itself briefly tried selling the bulk of its opium at Canton without the use of intermediaries, as a means for covering purchases of tea intended for the British and American markets. Carrying opium in EIC ships was soon criticized by company directors in London, however, both for incurring losses and for jeopardizing legal forms of Sino-British trade, since opium was contraband in China.[3] Having grown rapidly over the previous century, the remunerative tea trade burgeoned after Parliament in 1784 passed the Commutation Act, by which the British duty on tea was reduced from 125 percent to 12.5 percent to counter the new threat of American competition. Thereafter most of the opium trade from Calcutta to China was left in the hands of private merchants working under EIC license; the opium thus traded, however, remained essential to the company not only as its major commodity saleable at Canton for offsetting the increasingly massive purchases of tea but also as its key means for acquiring the bills of exchange that allowed company officials to remit the wealth they accumulated in India back to Britain.[4]

In 1793, when leading the British delegation to Beijing, Lord Macartney, the former governor of Madras, revealed himself to be quite precisely informed about the quantity and value of what he called the "the contraband trade" in opium.[5] Four years later, with Britain facing the continued pressures of war with France, the company initiated a new phase of the opium trade when it extended its monopoly over the production as well as sale of the drug in those parts of India under direct British rule.[6] By restricting and regulating production, the company was able to keep opium prices on the Chinese market high while reversing the tendency under the contract system to debasement of the product. According to the new arrangement, the company sold "export opium"[7] at auction in Calcutta to private merchants known as the "country traders,"[8] who engaged in taking it to China. This they did under company license until the EIC monopoly on the China trade was abolished in 1833. The 1797 introduction of the monopoly on production coincided closely with important legal changes in China. Edicts issued by the Jiaqing emperor again outlawed the smoking of opium in 1796 and its importation in 1800. Though the ban on imports formally changed the status of the drug, opium by this time was too crucial to British finances in India and too much in demand in China for the trade to be abandoned. To protect its legal forms of trade, the company devised the subterfuge of issuing ships' orders that on paper forbade the licensed private traders from smuggling opium to China, while at the same time the company administration at Calcutta secretly required those traders to carry Indian opium precisely to that market. In addition, the late eighteenth and early nineteenth centuries saw growth in exports of opium to China from states in western India under native rule as well as from Persia and Turkey, with American merchants as the main vendors of Turkish opium in 1800–1830. Competition from these sources led the British East India Company to lower prices and increase exports from territories under its control as one strategy of winning a greater market share. At the same time it succeeded in gaining increasing control over the hitherto competing supply of "Malwa" (western Indian) and Persian opium, a feat it managed partly by introducing a system of transit passes for opium moved through its territories and partly by extending the territory under its direct rule.[9] Indeed, one of the advantages of the trade for the company was that it provided revenues necessary for the military campaigns by which British rule in India was further extended at this time.

Conditions for trading in opium at Canton meanwhile went through an evolution of their own. Between 1800 and 1821 Western traders continued to carry opium to their factories at Whampoa, just south of Canton, for transfer to Chinese buyers. Morse observes that to ensure the acquiescence of local officials in the contraband trade after the Jiaqing imperial prohibition of 1796, the traders paid bribes instead of the former custom duties.[10] A contemporary British source noted that, of the Bengal presidency's total exports for 1818–1819, China received one-fifth, an amount made up primarily of opium.[11] In 1821 a renewed crackdown by the Qing government on opium and the corruption that attended it resulted in the trade being driven out of the Pearl River to a new base on Lintin Island where armed British ships received consignments of the drug from India and passed it on to Chinese fast boats, which carried it off for distribution on the coast. This remained the situation throughout the so-called Lintin era (1821–1839), which lasted until the outbreak of hostilities between China and Britain in 1839. A crucial step in the worsening of relations between the two countries came in 1833–1834 when, along with expanding the electoral roll and abolishing slavery in the British empire, the new reform-minded Whig government in London ended the company's monopoly on direct trade between China and Britain, a privilege that had been left in place when its monopoly on direct trade between Britain and India was abolished in 1813.[12] From 1834 to 1838 the opium trade from British India to China underwent another dramatic spurt of growth. While noting that this trade continued to be essential to the finances of the British administration in India in the 1830s, Michael Greenberg underlines its global significance with the comment that "opium was no hole-in-the-corner petty smuggling trade, but *probably the largest commerce of the time in any single commodity.*"[13] This commodity was crucial to the establishment of what were becoming the great Western trading firms in Asia. Led by William Jardine, the scion of one of those houses, these dealers in Indian opium pushed successive British governments to use force to compel the Qing to change the trading system in ways favorable to British interests.[14] They finally got their way with Palmerston and the Whigs in 1839.

The story of the Opium War and the events leading up to it has been told often and does not need repeating here.[15] It is useful to recall, however, that the causes of the war have long been the subject of debate. The Indian historian Tan Chung has identified three commonly encountered positions in the historiography regarding this issue.[16] The view that the British initiated the war to force opium on China is commonly associated with Chinese nationalist analyses, including those of a Marxist cast,[17] but Tan documents that it is well attested in the Western literature, for instance in the works of the influential American missionary Samuel Wells Williams.[18] A second position, which Tan sees represented in the post–Second World War literature by Greenberg and Chang Hsin-pao, is that the war was essentially about balancing trade and gaining access to the Chinese market. On this reading, opium was the item that just happened to be in demand, but the war could have been over molasses if the Chinese government had been impeding access to a market for that.[19] Finally, there is John Fairbank's position that the war resulted from a clash of cultures in which a traditional Chinese sense of superiority and xenophobia had to be broken down.[20] Interestingly, essentially similar positions were already found in the nineteenth-century debates about the opium trade and the 1839–1842 war. It was accepted among much of the political class in Britain at the time of the war, and not only among the war's critics, that the opium trade was the casus belli. Not only was this asserted by the Earl of Stanhope in his motion against the war in the House of Lords in April 1840, after Gladstone had already made the same argument in a speech against the war in the Commons, but it was also clearly accepted by Lord Melbourne, the prime minister, whose government entered into the state of war.[21] The "trade war" thesis may be seen as implicit in the instruction of Palmerston, who as foreign secretary oversaw British military activities, to Captain Elliot, the British representative in Canton when the crisis broke.[22] It was up to the Duke of Wellington, Tory leader of the opposition in the House of Lords, who during the debate rallied his party against censuring the Whig government for the hostilities, to make the patriotic "cultural" argument that the cause of war was not opium, but the right of British subjects not to be subjected to Chinese law.[23]

The British victory in the Opium War resulted, as is well known, in China's being forced to make significant concessions: indemnification for the confiscated opium; the opening of the first five "treaty ports" to Western trade; abolition of the mercantilist Cohong structure and other impediments to trade; and the surrender of Hong Kong.[24] What the British victory did not bring was the legalization of opium, as its importation into China remained technically illegal. Continued opposition from the court in Beijing and the strength of anti-opium opinion in Britain can both be plausibly cited as factors explaining why British negotiators did not insist that the Qing government legalize the trade. However, as John Fairbank has pointed out, the main reason for British acquiescence in continued Chinese prohibition was that the negotiators actually did agree on an arrangement that in effect accommodated British desires regarding the trade.[25] Originally proposed as a compromise by the chief Manchu negotiator, Qiying, this arrangement was written into the 1842 Treaty of Nanjing and then institutionalized in the system of so-called bilateral regulation of trade.[26] The British side of the trade was accordingly placed under the authority of British consular agents in the treaty ports, and the Qing authorities refrained from interfering with it. Although the government of the United States, pushed by public opinion, condemned the opium trade in principle, that condemnation was negated in practice by the American administration's granting of consular status to the main U.S. opium trader, Russell & Co., and by inclusion in the Treaty of Wangxia of the principle of extraterritoriality, which prevented Chinese authorities from prosecuting American opium traders.[27] Under the system of bilateral regulation the imports of opium from British India to China fluctuated around 30,000 chests per annum between 1841 and 1847, then increased to around 40,000 in the late 1840s, and eventually rose to around 60,000 in the late 1850s.[28]

OPIUM AFTER THE SECOND ANGLO–CHINESE WAR

Opium was again an issue in the outbreak of the Arrow War in 1856, when the British initiated hostilities over the Qing authorities' seizure of a Chinese opium-running boat after the craft's British registration had expired. The *Arrow* had been operating in a typical manner to exploit the bilateral regulation system. Britain's military victory was diplomatically codified first in the 1858 Treaty of Tianjin and then again, following further hostilities, in the 1860 Convention of Beijing, which was imposed once the British had managed to re-establish their control in India after the so-called Sepoy Mutiny.[29] Under trade articles added to the 1858 treaty, the Qing agreed to legalize the importation of opium to China, although how the legalization clause originated remains something of a puzzle. Various accounts depict it as resulting from a proposal by the American representative, W. B. Reed, which contradicted his government's explicit instructions regarding opium, and from the reluctant acceptance of Reed's proposal by the British plenipotentiary Lord Elgin, who had to overcome a professed personal distaste for the opium trade.[30] It is not clear whether Elgin's inner struggle continued when he was appointed the first viceroy of India shortly thereafter. In any event, two consequences followed from the new arrangement. First, the amount of opium coming from India continued to rise both in numbers of chests and in its proportion of China's total imports; opium constituted 33 percent of those imports in 1868, and 39 percent in 1880, when the number of chests per annum peaked at 80,000.[31] Thereafter the number of chests fell to about 50,000 per annum, a level at which it remained until 1905.

This decline in imports was partly the result of a second consequence of legalizing the inflow of Indian opium, namely the rapid growth of domestic opium cultivation. Although remaining illegal for three decades after 1860, Chinese domestic cultivation expanded greatly in those years, until domestically produced opium was eventually made legal—and tax-able—in 1890.[32] Expanded domestic cultivation can be seen as a sponta-neous form of import substitution undertaken by Chinese peasants, land-lords, and merchants. By 1870 it was recognized in Britain as a threat to Indian revenues similar to that posed by Malwa opium forty years earlier.[33] Partly in response to this threat the British forcefully negotiated for Chinese import duties and internal transit *(likin)* taxes to be consolidated in the hands of the inspectorate general of customs.[34] Despite British hopes of guaranteeing opium imports by promoting a greater Qing stake in them, the possibility of exploiting this arrangement to increase Chinese imperial revenues was resisted. Although the Qing negotiators were compelled to accept the fiscal consolidation in the Chefoo Convention,[35] the regime's continuing disapproval of the opium trade was shown in the 1880 treaty revision with the U.S. government, by which American merchants were forbidden to deal in opium. Domestic Chinese opium nevertheless pro-vided British supporters of the trade with a useful argument for countering Western criticisms of the Indian opium industry and for dismissing Chinese complaints about the opium trade as self-interested, on the grounds that Chinese growers were simply trying to find ways to monopolize the market. When the British ambassador Rutherford Alcock and the Qing chief ne-gotiator Wenxiang proposed an end to the opium trade in 1869, at the time of the renegotiation of the Treaty of Tianjin, the British Parliament rejected that proposal along with the revised Treaty Convention.[36] Two arguments frequently advanced in favor of the trade can be called the eco-nomic and the cultural. According to the former, prohibition was bound to fail because it contravened the law of supply and demand. Economic rationality required regulation by means of taxes, an approach that was deemed perfectly compatible with free trade in the drug. The cultural ar-gument, on the other hand, held that opium was to the East what alcohol was to the West, a parallel expressed clearly by George Campbell, secretary of state for India from 1868 to 1874, who suggested that Parliament might treat the issue "simply as a matter of race": "as the Aryan races prefer alcohol, so the Turanian consume opium."[37]

BRITISH OPPOSITION TO THE OPIUM TRADE

Despite such justifications, criticism of the opium trade continued to be voiced and, indeed, to grow in both China and the West through the last decades of the nineteenth century.[38] If before 1895 the international bal-ance of power allowed British authorities at home and in Asia to turn a deaf ear to protests in China, successive governments in London were stead-ily subjected to denunciations by the vocal anti-opium movements in Brit-ain and the United States.[39] These movements, now comprehensively documented by Kathleen Lodwick, drew support from several constituencies. From among British manufacturers, for example, concern was repeatedly expressed that opium was soaking up Chinese demand.[40] However, the most consistent and ultimately the most influential source of opposition, starting in the 1830s, was missionary objections to the opium trade and to the British government's role in it. The missionaries' objections arose both from their personal observation of addicts and from the fact that attempts at conversion were frustrated by the Chinese perception that the British opium trade demonstrated the immorality of Christians.[41] Among physicians, opinion about whether opium was harmful remained divided into the last decades of the century, partly because of the strength of pro-opium views in the Indian medical service.[42] As more and more medical missionaries reported back from China with evidence of the harms of addiction, however, the missionary case against opium gained increasing credibility in Western public opinion.[43] A characteristic feature of the anti-opium literature was its regular incorporation of elite and popular Chinese opinion that was critical of addiction and the opium trade. This feature runs counter to Edward Said's conclusion that the nineteenth-century Western mentality was uniformly one in which "the Orient is all absence."[44]

Throughout the middle decades of the century the British anti-opium movement had spokesmen in both the main parties in Parliament. Its representatives, including such distinguished advocates as Shaftesbury and Wilfrid Lawson, regularly drew attention to the legal, political, economic, and moral objections to the trade and forced successive governments to justify their involvement with it.[45] In 1874 the Society for the Suppression of the Opium Trade was founded by Edward Pease, member of one of the great Quaker industrialist families of England.[46] With Shaftesbury as its first president and with the Liberal MP Joseph Pease as its early champion in Parliament,[47] this society acted as an umbrella for promoting the increasingly effective opposition to the India-China opium trade. Through its journal, *The Friend of China*, it publicized the growing anti-opium sentiment in clerical and popular opinion in Britain and the hostility to the trade that predominated in missionary communities in China and India.[48] Clear crossbench opposition to the trade was demonstrated in 1875, when the Commons debated Conservative MP Mark Stewart's motion on behalf of the Society urging the government to consider withdrawing from the trade. Pease as seconder described the Indian treasury as dependent on opium.[49] In 1891, with opinion in Britain increasingly aware of the problems of opium addiction, Pease shrewdly introduced a Commons resolution condemning the Indian opium revenue as "morally indefensible." In the ensuing debate the undersecretary of state for foreign affairs was led to declare that if the Chinese government chose to raise a prohibitive duty on opium or even exclude it altogether, Britain would not use force to impose

the drug on China.[50] Although this may have accorded with a strict interpretation of the treaty situation in 1890, the statement was nevertheless
greeted by the anti-opium movement as a significant concession.[51] Though
a formal vote on Pease's resolution was adjourned sine die, the Tory government was embarrassed by the clear majority against dismissing this anti-
opium motion.[52]

Because of its importance for Government of India revenues, criticisms
of the lucrative opium trade were bound to elicit further attempts at re-
buttal. In 1892 the Royal Society for the Arts organized a debate dominated
by speakers who favored the trade.[53] Then in 1893–1894, under pressure
of the 1891 Commons motion and the threat of a potentially divisive new
debate on opium, Gladstone's government established the Royal Commission on Opium in India.[54] Although much of the anti-opium group in Parliament eventually voted against the Royal Commission because its brief
was formulated to exclude any investigation into conditions in China, two
of the group's members, Arthur Pease and Henry Wilson, nevertheless
joined the nine-man body. The final report shows that the opponents of
the opium trade were right in perceiving the commission as an instrument
intended to rebut criticism of the Indian opium industry and to justify the
opium policies of the governments of the United Kingdom, India, and
other British colonial holdings in Asia. Among the arguments set forth were
the old standards that opium was to Asia what alcohol was to the West, that
opium used in moderation was not harmful to Asians, and that the Chinese
complaints about the opium trade, which Western critics cited, were simply
motivated by anti-Western commercial ambitions.[55]

A minority report condemning the trade was filed by Henry Wilson,
drawing on evidence supplied by his assistant, Joseph G. Alexander, who
in 1893 had gone to China at the anti-opium lobby's expense. From his
discussions with various authorities there, including Zhang Zhidong and
Li Hongzhang, emerged the proposal that China and Britain together undertake measures to suppress the opium trade.[56] Though this idea was bur-
ied by the Royal Commission, it would return in the following decade as a
basis for negotiation and eventual implementation. In the meantime, the
Royal Commission's conclusion that the opium trade was legitimate failed
to carry public opinion even in Britain. Instead it elicited a series of strong
counterblasts. Arnold Foster's study refuting the Royal Commission's conclusions on the basis of his critical re-examination of its own evidence was
endorsed by the archbishop of Canterbury, William Temple, and more
than one hundred other prominent persons. Similarly, the memorial condemning the Indian opium industry that Joshua Rowntree, head of the
Representative Board of Anti-Opium Organizations, sent to all MPs in 1900
was signed by the archbishop of Canterbury and other Church of England
leaders as well as by the heads of the Wesleyan, United Methodist, and Free

Evangelical churches. A still more imposing line-up of leading churchmen supported the memorial forwarded by the archbishop of Canterbury to the prime minister in 1902.[57]

BRITAIN'S OPIUM TRADE TO CHINA: THE SUPPRESSION PHASE

In China, the promulgation of a new imperial edict banning opium in September 1906 was succeeded in 1907–1911 by the dramatic reduction in Chinese production and consumption of the drug, aspects of which are treated in part 2 of this volume. Following the movement against foot-binding, the anti-opium campaign promoted by the Qing government reflected the intensification in China over the previous decade of aversion to the drug. That aversion was part of the rise in nationalist sentiment at the turn of the century, stimulated by such factors as the 1895 defeat at the hands of Japan, the subsequent new imperialist incursions by other powers, and the humiliation delivered by the anti-Boxer expeditionary forces in 1900.[58]

The timing of the 1906 edict suggests, however, that it was not only feelings within China that affected the success of the Chinese anti-opium campaign at this time. Leaving aside both the British concerns about political challenges in East Asia and the political impact of Russia's 1905 defeat and subsequent revolution, two developments in the foreign powers' attitude specifically to the opium trade had a bearing on the Chinese movement. The first, of an ideological nature, emerged indirectly from the Philippines Opium Committee. This committee held hearings on behalf of the American government in 1903–1905 and was charged with examining problems of addiction in the newly acquired territory. It eventually recommended a system of opium prohibition there. In weighing the issues involved, however, the committee also examined the prevalence of opium addiction in China, and while roundly condemning the Indian opium trade, it interpreted the apparent weakness of Chinese official efforts to control opium as a sign that the Chinese "race" was bereft of proper national character. This was a view widely discussed in China, where it piqued national pride and intensified the desire to be rid of the drug.[59]

The second development, which had more precise diplomatic implications, involved a change in the attitude of the United Kingdom. In December 1905 the Liberals were returned to power after ten years in opposition, a period during which leading members of the party, including Edward Grey and John Morley, respectively foreign secretary and secretary of state for India in the new cabinet, had associated themselves with the anti-opium associations in criticizing the trade as morally reprehensible.[60] In April 1906, a private member's motion put by Liberal MP Theodore Taylor again condemned the opium trade as "morally indefensible" and called on the new government to take measures to bring it to a speedy end.[61] Despite opposition from Morley, who now had responsibility for Indian revenues and who argued that the share of opium in the Indian budget had already been declining over the previous decade,[62] the motion was carried. These new developments were significant for two reasons. First, in the course of the parliamentary debate Morley had publicly reiterated the pledge previously given in 1891 that if the Chinese government should undertake to suppress the opium traffic, the British government would not resort to force to maintain it.[63] Second, after the motion passed, Morley indicated that the Qing should be encouraged to restrict opium imports and that new negotiations should be undertaken with them regarding the trade.[64] The result was the 1907 Sino-British agreement in which the British government promised to reduce the export of Indian opium to China by 5,100 chests per annum (10 percent of the 1907 total) provided that native Chinese production be stopped first. Successful adherence to the schedule, which was to be considered for renewal after three years, would have brought an end to the trade after ten years.

Ending the trade was not a simple process, however.[65] Exports to China still made up three-quarters of the Indian government's opium revenue and were not to be sacrificed lightly, especially as the finances of the Government of India were in a difficult state.[66] The authorities in India and other British colonies in Asia anticipated that the Chinese would prove unable to achieve domestic suppression and that failure on their part would allow the Government of India, against its critics, to justify maintaining its part in the trade. The success of the Chinese suppression campaign in 1907–1910 came as a surprise, but was hard to dispute once confirmation came in 1910 from Alexander Hosie, when he finished his inspection of China's opium-producing provinces on behalf of the British government.[67] In January 1911 the government of India began issuing certificates on the restricted consignments of opium intended for China, and in May a new Sino-British treaty was signed confirming the two sides' commitment to the 1907 ten-year timetable.[68] This included reiteration of the British undertaking to end all opium shipments from India to China in 1917, a stipulation pushed through despite strong agitation in both Britain and China for ending the trade even sooner.[69]

In addition, American enthusiasm for the 1909 Opium Conference held in Shanghai and for the 1912 International Opium Tribunal held in The Hague made Whitehall increasingly sensitive to the trade's international reputation, although Delhi tended to be more thick-skinned.[70] Sir John Pratt's confidential Foreign Office memorandum of 1929 indicates that from 1908 a rift over opium policy was opening between the Foreign Office on one side and the India Office, the Government of India, and the Colonial Office on the other. Eventually, in May 1913, the Indian government actually did stop the export of opium for the China market ahead of the negotiated schedule, following a dramatic statement by E. S. Montagu, the undersecretary of state for India, that "for the first time in [the] modern history of India, . . . we are selling not an ounce of poppy for China," and that Britain was prepared never again to sell opium for shipment to China.[71] It is clear, however, that this step was taken then not because of diplomatic considerations or a sense that the trade was immoral, but rather because of pleas from the opium traders themselves to stop the supply. These firms had accumulated extra stocks in the treaty ports on the assumption that either the suppression campaign would fail or prohibition would drive up the price of the drug. Despite an upturn in demand in 1912–1913, they found themselves with a glut when Chinese provincial authorities began excluding opium from entering their jurisdictions.[72] In order to maintain their hold on the market, the merchants were obliged to continue buying the certified export opium as long as this was put on the market at Calcutta, and this meant in turn that they had to hold the opium in their own warehouses. These considerations led them to demand a stoppage of the Indian supply. In this regard Pratt's 1929 memorandum confirms the analyses of Owen and Lodwick that the opium traders' interests were crucial in shifting the British government's attitude to ending exports.[73]

WORLD WAR I AND THE INTERWAR PERIOD

The 1913 stoppage of the direct traffic proved to be only a temporary hindrance to Indian opium entering China, where the breakdown of central government control after the revolution of 1911–1912 introduced a new set of circumstances. In May 1913 the foreign and Chinese opium merchants in Shanghai and Hong Kong formed an opium combine and collectively took over the accumulated stocks in the expectation that the stoppage would drive prices up. Chinese banks backed the venture with 1.5 million taels, and the British-owned Hong Kong and Shanghai Bank provided 2.5 million taels. With the glut clearing, prices soon soared. In 1915, confronted by Japan's Twenty-one Demands and an acute need for funds, the Chinese government entered into a revenue-generating accommodation with the opium merchants whereby it would buy their remaining stocks and market them on its own account. Faced with a public outcry in China as well as with American and British protests, however, the government actually dared sell only a portion of the stocks. The rest it burned publicly at the end of 1918, exactly eighty years after Lin Zexu had carried out a similar operation at Canton. This time the British representative, Sir John Jordan, who for a decade had been arguing against the trade within the Foreign Office, reported with approval: "The foreign trade in opium, which began in the eighteenth century, has thus come to a dramatic end in the burning of the surplus Indian stocks, and it only remains for foreign governments to keep a strict watch on exports."[74]

The Government of India, however, proceeded to export increased amounts of "non-certified" opium to the Straits Settlements and Hong Kong (where the monopolies on opium sales were responsible for about half of all government revenues) as well as to Macao, French Indochina, the Dutch East Indies, and Japan.[75] From all of these locations opium continued to gravitate in considerable quantities to China. In effect a profitable transit trade had developed, with at least the connivance of the respective colonial governments and with the implicit support of British authorities in India. In 1918 a particular scandal arose over revelations that Japan had been transshipping regular consignments of opium into China through its concession in Tianjin. Over the urgings of Jordan and the Foreign Office that India stop export completely, Delhi continued to hold to the old line, arguing that "they were under no obligation to take drastic measures, at the sacrifice of Indian revenues, to prevent any of their opium from being smuggled by third parties into China, especially at a time when China was not enforcing her policy of suppression."[76]

For such thinking the governments of Britain, India, and the Straits Settlements were subjected to criticism throughout the 1920s. Article 23 of the League of Nations Covenant stipulated general supervision of previous international undertakings on opium and narcotics as falling within the League's mandate. The League consequently organized two conferences on opium and narcotics; these were held in 1924–1925, with the United States agreeing to participate. The ostensible task of the conferences was to examine how things stood with regard to agreements reached at the 1912 Hague Convention.[77] Within this framework, strong objections to the opium policies of Britain and the other colonial powers were pressed not only by China, but also by the United States; and both countries eventually withdrew from the conferences, the U.S. over Government of India resistance to limiting opium production to amounts necessary for medical and scientific uses.[78] When they eventually ran their course, the League conferences had two formal outcomes: on the one hand, the Geneva Conventions of 1925,[79] by which the signatories committed themselves to regulate their participation in the international commerce in opium and industrial narcotics; and, on the other, the establishment of the League's controversial Opium Advisory Committee. Comprised of representatives of the main colonial powers and officially responsible for monitoring the production, manufacture, and trade in opium products, the Opium Committee, however, had a major credibility problem. Lacking American and Chinese support, it was soon dubbed "the Smugglers' Reunion" by American journalists at Geneva, who charged the states represented on it with collusion in the trade.[80]

Meanwhile, having promoted an opium restriction campaign in Assam as part of the 1919–1921 Non-Cooperation Movement, the Indian National Congress in 1924 established its own Assam Opium Enquiry Committee, with a mandate to present evidence to the Geneva conference. Backing up its arguments with a hitherto confidential Government of India assessment, the Enquiry's report charged the Indian government's representative in Geneva with having misled the international conference about the extent to which opium smoking constituted a problem in India. Marshalling an impressive roster of Indian witnesses—including former addicts—who favored total prohibition, the Assam Enquiry Committee proposed a new anti-opium mass campaign to be led by Gandhi.[81] "We believe that if opium, as a poison, is regarded as a dangerous drug in the West, it should equally be regarded as a dangerous drug in the East," wrote Gandhi's confidant, C. F. Andrews, on behalf of the committee. "We do not think that human nature in the East is different from human nature in the West."[82] The statement exemplified the nationalist reaction across Asia to imperial definitions of "separate identity."[83]

Throughout the 1920s informed observers of world drug trends saw that the production and consumption of opium was again on the rise in China. Colonial governments and European communities in Asia accordingly reacted to criticisms of their involvement in the opium trade with charges that a congenital Chinese need for opium, as well as the difficulty of controlling opium smuggling, made all plans for prohibiting smoking or stopping the trade to neighboring territories unfeasible.[84] In contrast, confidential Foreign Office reports at the time indicated that the use of opium was more widely condemned by Chinese in the Straits than by the foreigners, who stubbornly argued that their Chinese work force, and hence the economy of the territories, simply could not do without it.[85] The allegations about Chinese character and behavior made by the Colonial Office and by most colonial governments—British and otherwise—typically went together with claims that government monopolies on opium were the sole effective means for regulating consumption, and with denials that such monopolies played any important role in generating colonial revenues. The Foreign Office response formulated by Pratt was that these denials were "believed by no one."[86]

Under siege on so many fronts, the Government of India in 1926 finally adopted a policy of gradually reducing opium exports for other than scientific and medical purposes until the export ceased altogether.[87] American anti-drug campaigner Ellen La Motte nevertheless revealed that rather than curtailing the cultivation of opium in its territories the Government of India was actually proposing to increase production, for despite previous denials it had been found that Indian opium made high-quality heroin.[88] By 1930 the Indian export of opium for other than medical and scientific purposes had officially shriveled to a negligible amount.[89] As pointed out at the time, however, the colonial power's perpetration of the view that opium use was an exotic Chinese vice served to obscure the fact that the world's main drug-related danger was now the new "industrial" narcotics—morphine, heroin, and cocaine—produced in the capital-intensive pharmaceutical laboratories of the "civilized" West and Japan.[90]

CONCLUSION

The history of opium testifies to the possibility that the logic of social change can run counter to purely formal expectations. One would think that of the two main approaches to drug control developed over the last three centuries—prohibition and criminalization on the one hand, and legalization and licensing on the other—the latter would be a more subtle and flexible form of regulation that ought to rely less on legal and physical coercion. It is perhaps a historical irony that in nineteenth-century Asia legalization was instead associated with the military impositions of the world's hegemonic state and was cemented by force into the bifurcated framework of formal colonialism and the "imperialism of free trade." Born with Britain's Asian empire and lasting to within two decades of Indian independence, the long nineteenth-century opium trade can be seen as a multinational, collaborative institution that bound Indian peasants, British and Indian governments, a vast mass of Chinese consumers, and an array of Western, Parsee, Sephardic, and most of all Chinese merchants together in an immense revenue-generating system. It was also a system that gave rise to a genuinely cross-cultural opposition, for from the outset it elicited a broad front of international resistance that included otherwise ideologically disparate groups around the shared view that legalization in the service of colonial power was politically, economically, physically, and especially morally unacceptable. By the beginning of the twentieth century this alliance linking rising nationalist movements in China and India with religious anti-imperialist and temperance forces in Britain and the United States put increasing pressures on British and British Indian governments. Whether these forces would by themselves have been sufficient to undermine such a long-standing pillar of the colonial order is difficult to say. In the event, however, they were reinforced by several other factors, namely, the growing need for British governments to respond to domestic and international criticism; the official American promotion of prohibition both domestically and internationally; the emergence of the United States as a global financial and diplomatic power after World War I; the proliferation of opium production within China; and, finally, the growth of demand for new industrial drugs. All of these factors played a role in turning the historical page on the trade in processed Indian opium.

At the outset of this chapter I suggested that the opium industry of the "long nineteenth century" might be considered a cultural hybrid of the sort that Bruno Latour sees as typical of "modernity." In his view, "modernity" is a phenomenon constituted by two linked but contrary processes, namely, the proliferation of culturally constructed hybrids and the simultaneous quest to identify isolatable "essences," with the latter quest tending to obscure the process of hybridization. Leaving aside the question of how much light this model sheds on "the modern constitution" as such, one can argue that Latour's analysis does at least evoke the structure of imperial power during the late colonial era. Within the "formal" colonial order, his paired processes of hybridization and essentialization can be seen as institutionalized in the structural bifurcation between the institutions of Western law governing citizens under direct colonial rule and the officially sanctioned institutions of "customary law" applicable to subjects organized under various forms of indirect rule.[91] In this system, which the British elaborated in India and then applied, with desired modifications, to Africa, the symbiosis of the two sets of institutions was typically obscured by the process of conceiving each subsystem as the expression of distinct cultural or racial essences. Beyond the "formal" empires of the European powers, China, Persia, and the Ottoman empire were also subjected to Western economic and political hegemony as spheres of Europe's nineteenth-century "informal empire," and within this framework they too were transformed through interactions with Western imperial power.[92] Many of the new institutions—economic, political, social, and cultural—that emerged from such interactions can be considered hybrids in the sense that they sprang from such common (if unequal) relationships, and while fusing features of previously distinct societies, they constituted phenomena of new and unique character.

At the economic level, the history of the opium trade between British India and China illustrates the degree to which markets are socially constructed. While the opium industry served as an all too obviously constructed institutional nexus binding China, Britain, and India together for a century and a half, there always existed throughout the period—in accord with the Latour model—persistent attempts to deny the collaborative nature of the opium network by portraying it as essentially the result either of Chinese depravity and corruption or of the overweening greed of British governments and merchants—in either case, as deriving from some trait characteristic of one participant only, which the other was only accommodating or submitting to. The Chinese case in this regard was perhaps stronger before 1870, the British after 1913; but over the long nineteenth century each side contributed to, and was shaped by, the cohesive trade structure that linked them. Explaining that cohesive system adequately calls for the study of each country's changing involvement with opium across time, the specification of evolving international power relations, and the analysis of the long interplay between the push of British Indian supply and the pull of Chinese demand for the drug.

One further feature of the international opium trade that has been obscured by the focus on national interests and antagonisms is the prominent degree of collaboration involved in the opium system. However, collaboration did not only involve those tied into the chain of production and distribution of the drug, and those who profited from it in various ways; it was also a strategy cultivated by those opposed to the trade. In other words, collaboration was important not only for initiating and maintaining the trade, but also for bringing about its demise, as Kathleen Lodwick points out when she observes that "opium suppression became a reality only when public opinion in Britain and China favored it."[93] By contributing to the mobilization of broad political movements that converged in their opposition to the trade, the coordination of anti-opium agitation across cultures played a key political role in bringing about the demise of the trade in Indian opium to China, though mercantile and diplomatic conditions no doubt shaped the timing of the 1913 British stoppage. The fact that from the 1830s on Western anti-opium agitators regularly confronted their audiences with Chinese objections to the drug and exposed British interests behind the trade shows that, as in the anti-slavery and women's rights movements,[94] and despite clear ideological differences, cross-cultural communication could be effective among those fighting against the opium trade in their respective societies.

NOTES

1. Spence, "Opium Smoking in Ch'ing China," p. 228.

2. Latour, *We Have Never Been Modern,* pp. 10–12.

3. These criticisms figured in the impeachment of Warren Hastings; cf. Lambert, ed., *House of Commons Sessional Papers,* vol. 140, 9th Report, pp. 55ff.

4. Fearful of fluctuation in the company's liquid funds, company headquarters at Leadenhall Street in London placed strict restrictions on direct remittances from India to Britain.

5. For 1792, 2,500 chests worth £250,000 (Cranmer-Byng, *Embassy,* p. 260).

6. Dodwell, *Indian Empire,* p. 86.

7. "Provision opium" was the corresponding phrase designating opium for sale within India. Among Chinese users, opium was typically smoked; in India, it was usually eaten, except in Assam, where it was also smoked.

8. Country traders engaged in the intra-Asian trade, as opposed to the trade between England and India, or England and China, over which the company

exercised its monopoly directly until Parliament opened those routes to private competition in 1813 and 1833 respectively.

9. Between 1780 and 1830 the EIC tried various mechanisms to control the export of opium from the native states. These included a system of attempting to buy all the opium they produced and another of regulating their trade through treaty. The device finally adopted involved facilitating shipment of native states' opium through Bombay in exchange for a transit fee not to exceed the cost of sending the opium further afield for export; cf. Beveridge, *Comprehensive History*, 3: 197–99. The 1843 British conquest of Sind enabled the company to control all opium exports from the subcontinent by this means; Inglis, *Opium War*, pp. 188ff.

10. Morse, *Trade and Administration of the Chinese Empire*, pp. 340–41.

11. Prinsep, "Remarks on the External Commerce and Exchanges of Bengal," p. 84.

12. The 1834 legislation deprived the company not only of its monopoly on the China trade but of any international trading role (Davis, *The Chinese*, 1:102), though it governed India until 1858. The 1813 termination of the monopoly on direct trade to India was a victory for British textile manufacturers intent on exporting to the subcontinent; Lloyd, *British Empire*, p. 133.

13. Greenberg, *British Trade and the Opening of China*, p. 104 (his italics); similarly, Wakeman, "Canton Trade and the Opium War," p. 172. Morse, *International Relations of the Chinese Empire*, 1:556, shows the average number of chests of opium imported annually into China growing from about 4,000 in 1800–1810 to about 8,000 in 1821–1828, and to 30,000 in 1835–1839.

14. Discussing the Lintin era, Paul Johnson claims that no British merchant then felt there was anything wrong with selling opium to China (*Birth of the Modern*, p. 682). If true before the 1830s, this was only because merchants dismissed the well-known views of Chinese officials, Protestant missionaries, and D. W. C. Olyphant, the American merchant who financed the anti-opium missionary journal *The Chinese Repository*. For the decades after 1830, Johnson's claim is untenable. Qualms were emerging even within the core houses. Hugh Matheson refused to join Jardine, Matheson & Co. in 1834 because of his moral objection to opium. Donald Matheson left the firm in 1849 when he too repudiated the trade; he went on to join the executive committee of the Society for the Suppression of the Opium Trade, for which he testified before the 1893–1894 Royal Commission on Opium. Cf. Lodwick, *Crusaders against Opium*, pp. 95, 193; Latourette, *History of Christian Missions in China*, p. 231.

15. Standard accounts include Fairbank, *Trade and Diplomacy on the China Coast;* Chang, *Commissioner Lin and the Opium War;* Inglis, *Opium War;* Wakeman, "Canton Trade"; Fay, *Opium War;* Tan, *China and the Brave New World;* and Rodzinski, *History*, vol. 1, chapter 27. The much-debated phrase "opium war" was coined by *The Times* on 25 April 1840.

16. Tan, *China and the Brave New World*, chapters 1 and 2.

17. E.g., Hu Sheng, *Imperialism and Chinese Politics*.

18. S. Wells Williams, *Middle Kingdom*, 2:564.

19. Tan, *China and the Brave New World*, p. 10; Chang, *Commissioner Lin.*, p. 15.

20. Tan, *China and the Brave New World*, pp. 6, 13. Although Tan's typology is useful analytically, these positions did not always exclude one another, even in the

writings of the authors just mentioned. Tan himself notes (p. 12) that Chang gives evidence supportive of the "opium" thesis. Fairbank's description of the role of British opium traders in the outbreak of war and his view of the opium trade as "the most long-continued and systematic international crime of modern times" ("Creation of the Treaty System," p. 213) might also lend weight to that thesis.

21. *Hansard,* 1840, vol. 4: for Stanhope, cols. 1–26; for Melbourne, cols. 27–34, esp. 31. That Stanhope was president of the Royal Medical-Botanical Society and a fellow of the Royal Society indicates that within the medical profession there was already at this time strong condemnation of the opium trade based on recognition of the drug's deleterious effects.

22. Secret instruction, 18 Oct 1839 (F.O. 17/37), cited in Costin, *Great Britain and China,* p. 60: "H.M. govt by no means disputes the right of the Government of China to prohibit the importation of opium. . . . But these fiscal prohibitions ought to be impartially and steadily enforced." However, it is quite conceivable that what Palmerston thought opportune to dispute in negotiations was not the same as his motive for entering hostilities.

23. For Wellington, *Hansard,* 1840, vol. 4, col. 34–43, esp. 38. He also stressed the importance of opium to British Indian finances.

24. A consequence in British India was the expansion of tea cultivation, in which a large role was played by Robert Fortune's massive 1851 importation of plants from China; cf. Brockway, *Science and Colonial Expansion,* p. 27.

25. See Fairbank, *Trade and Diplomacy on the China Coast,* chapter 9 and pp. 222–23.

26. Immediately before signing the treaty, British plenipotentiary Sir Henry Pottinger suggested that opium be legalized, and in the following years he and John Davis as the first two governors of Hong Kong regularly repeated the idea. Morse, *International Relations of the Chinese Empire,* 1:546ff.

27. Fairbank, *Trade and Diplomacy on the China Coast,* p. 208.

28. Morse, *International Relations of the Chinese Empire,* 1:556.

29. On the British need to re-establish control in India first, see Costin, *Great Britain and China,* p. 275.

30. Morse, *International Relations of the Chinese Empire,* 1:553–56. A more plausible scenario comes from W. A. P. Martin, one of Reed's translators in China. According to him, it was Elgin who convinced Reed to omit the article forbidding the opium trade from the U.S. draft treaty; cf. Foster, *American Diplomacy,* p. 299. Reed's other translator, S. W. Williams, condemned the legalization of opium and especially criticized the British for imposing a tariff rate "lower than that paid on tea and silk entering England" (*Middle Kingdom,* 2:657).

31. Hyde, *Far Eastern Trade,* p. 217. Rothermund, *Economic History,* p. 39, indicates that in 1871 opium constituted 20 percent of India's exports. That the lion's share of these opium exports continued to be for the China market is shown by the Government of India's judgment in 1872 that its income from the monopoly on the sale of opium to China had averaged about one-sixth of total government revenue in recent years (Moulton, *Northbrook's Administration,* p. 23). Feuerwerker, "Economic Trends," indicates that opium remained China's single largest import until 1890, when it was overtaken by cotton goods (pp. 9, 48–49). The long

symbiosis of the opium and tea trades makes it worth noting that 1890 was the year India and Ceylon overtook China in providing most of the world's tea; Lloyd, *British Empire*, p. 227.

32. Feuerwerker judges it impossible to calculate the increase in land given to domestic production ("Economic Trends," p. 9). However, Rev. Arthur Moule, a forceful critic of the British opium trade, did estimate that in 1882 imported opium was equivalent to a third of the native crop (*New China and Old*, p. 93).

33. *Hansard*, 1870, vol. 3, col. 495; Owen, *British Opium Policy*, pp. 248ff.

34. The consolidation proposal was negotiated by Sir Thomas Wade following a suggestion by I.G. director Sir Robert Hart; see Owen, *British Opium Policy*, pp. 251ff; Morse, *International Relations of the Chinese Empire*, 2: 294–304.

35. The Chinese put the negotiated stipulations into effect from 1877, but British ratification of the opium clause was delayed until 1885 because of the feeling among opium traders and their supporters that better terms should be won; see Owen, *British Opium Policy*, pp. 272ff; Morse, *Trade and Administration of the Chinese Empire*, p. 350.

36. Turner's *British Opium Policy* included translations of Wenxiang's speech and memorial (pp. 123–27); see also Owen, *British Opium Policy*, chapter 9; Morse, *International Relations of the Chinese Empire*, 2:217ff.

37. *Hansard*, 1875, vol. 4, col. 600.

38. Owen, *British Opium Policy*, pp. 262ff.

39. Among the many critiques of the opium trade two pre-1890 works that deserve special mention are: *China and the Chinese . . . The Evils Arizing from the Opium Trade* (1849) by the London barrister Henry Sirr, and *British Opium Policy* (1876) by F. S. Turner, secretary of the Anglo-Oriental Society for the Suppression of the Opium Trade.

40. At the time of the First Opium War two hundred thirty-five British manufacturers and merchants protested against the trade on the grounds that opium was supplanting Chinese demand for British manufactures. Cf. S. W. Williams, *Middle Kingdom*, 2:562–63. Over later decades anti-opium advocates in Parliament and elsewhere regularly reiterated this point. Karl Marx similarly noted in 1858 that Chinese imports of British manufactures since 1840 had remained stationary while opium imports had grown (*Marx on China*, pp. 62–64).

41. See, for example, Medhurst's influential discussion in *China*, p. 371.

42. The 1895 Royal Commission found that medical opinion within the Indian Service was itself divided (Owen, *British Opium Policy*, p. 318). Note that in reviewing the late-nineteenth-century medical literature, Terry and Pellens found in 1928 that lax prescribing by physicians was cited as one of the major causes of opium and morphine addiction in the West (*Opium Problem*, pp. 98–101, 122–23).

43. See Lodwick, *Crusaders against Opium*, p. 65. Arthur Moule's 1902 book, *New China and Old*, p. 98, cites among others the missionary scholar Joseph Edkins on the medical damage wrought by opium in China. Edkins's own 1899 historical study of opium cited extensively from Chinese botanical and official literature as well as from Western works in coming to the conclusion that opium was "a universal poison" in the China of his day (*Opium*, p. 53).

44. Said, *Orientalism*, p. 208. Suffice it to say that Chinese views about opium and the opium trade were cited favorably in the parliamentary speeches (referred

to elsewhere in this chapter) by Stanhope in 1840, Ashley in 1843, Lawson in 1870, Stewart in 1875 and 1891, Pease in 1875 and 1891, and Taylor in 1906.

45. A Tory Evangelical and promoter of both foreign and domestic missions, the seventh Earl of Shaftesbury (1801–1885) was Victorian England's most effective social reformer, the driving force behind the Factory Acts, the Collieries Regulation Acts, the Lodging House Act, the Ten Hours Act, etc. His detailed indictment of the opium trade (*Hansard*, 1843, vol. 3, cols. 361–405) after the First Opium War (when he was still styled Lord Ashley) was often cited by later advocates of suppression. In 1857 he maneuvered unsuccessfully to have the trade declared illegal by the Law Lords (*Hansard*, 1857, vol. 1, pp. 2027ff.); on his controversial attitude to Palmerston during the Arrow War, see Finlayson, *Shaftesbury*, pp. 446–47. The Liberal radical Wilfred Lawson led the charge for the anti-opium societies in a powerful 1870 speech that recalled Shaftesbury's objections (*Hansard*, 1870, vol. 3, cols. 480–90), and that thereafter was itself frequently cited as a landmark in the cause of the Society for the Suppression of the Opium Trade (e.g., *Hansard*, 1875, vol. 4, cols. 617–18).

46. The Pease family had been active for generations in movements for social and political reform. Joseph Pease (1772–1846), a founder of the Peace Society, was also one of the more egalitarian members of the Anti-Slavery Society; in the 1830s he also campaigned for "the protection of the natives of India" and against the emerging "coolie trade." His daughter Elisabeth was a prominent feminist who involved herself deeply in campaigns against slavery in India and the United States as well as against the Indian opium industry; cf. Ware, *Beyond the Pale*, pp. 90–96.

47. Joseph Whitwell Pease (1828–1903), Liberal MP from 1865 until 1903— not to be confused with his father, also named Joseph (1799–1872), the first Quaker Member of Parliament—was a great-nephew of the Joseph Pease discussed in the previous note.

48. Paul Johnson's *Birth of the Modern* ironically singles out a few early-nineteenth-century Quakers for selling medicinal opium in Britain (p. 768), but neglects to mention that Quakers played a central role in agitating against the opium trade later on.

49. *Hansard*, 1875, vol. 4, cols. 571ff; col. 587 on Treasury dependence. Stewart's motion was followed up the next year in a passionate speech by the MP for Methyr, who approvingly cited Prince Gong's lengthy criticism of the opium trade (1876, vol. 4, cols. 550–52).

50. Ibid., cols. 316–17.

51. On treaties: Fergusson in *Hansard*, 1890–1891, vol. 4, col. 315. On anti-opium satisfaction: Pease, ibid., col. 901; Lodwick, *Crusaders against Opium*, p. 57; Owen, *British Opium Policy*, pp. 312–13.

52. *Hansard*, 1890–1891, vol. 4, cols. 285–344, 383–84. Government and anti-opium spokesmen alike noted the rise of public concern about opium (cols. 308–9, 315). The anti-opium motion stood partly because pro-opium MPs demanding a Royal Commission on Opium tactically refused to support the government (cols. 340, 382).

53. Lodwick, *Crusaders against Opium*, p. 76. Despite his youthful eloquence against the opium trade, Gladstone condoned it in 1860 after joining Palmerston's cabinet the previous year. According to Owen (*British Opium Policy*, pp. 314–15),

Gladstone's firm support for the trade in 1893 may have been motivated by a political desire not to alienate powerful cabinet ministers at a time when party unity was imperative for his Irish Home Rule Bill. Although this might have been the case, M. J. Gilbert shows that a similar calculation to solidify Liberal support for the Irish bill led Gladstone and the party whips to concede anti-opium MPs a free vote on the initial motion for a Royal Commission on Opium (Gilbert, "Lord Lansdowne in India").

54. Owen, *British Opium Policy*, chapter 11; Lodwick, *Crusaders against Opium*, pp. 85ff.

55. Lodwick, *Crusaders against Opium*, pp. 85–97.

56. Ibid., pp. 58–59. While noting that the origins of the proposal are unclear, Lodwick observes that Moule suggested it at the 1877 London missionary conference and Zhang spoke of it in 1883 (p. 193n. 80). Li insisted that Britain end Indian exports before China suppressed domestic production; Owen, *British Opium Policy*, p. 326.

57. Lodwick, *Crusaders against Opium*, pp. 52, 63, 101. Papal condemnation of opium use and the trade came only in 1892, but the head of Britain's Roman Catholics, Cardinal Manning, had already joined Shaftesbury and the archbishop of Canterbury in condemning the trade in 1881, and Roman Catholic bishops in the U.K. published memorials against the trade in the following decade; Owen, *British Opium Policy*, pp. 263, 312.

58. Hevia, "Making China 'Perfectly Equal,'" documents the Western powers' intention to humiliate the Qing.

59. Taylor, *American Diplomacy*, pp. 22, 40–46; Lodwick, *Crusaders against Opium*, pp. 112–15. It is hard to imagine that Chinese reactions to the Opium Committee were unrelated to the extension of the Chinese Exclusion Act, which barred Chinese immigration to the United States and animated the mass boycott of U.S. goods in China in 1905.

60. Milner's program of bringing indentured Chinese laborers to work in Britain's newly acquired South African gold districts was a heated issue in the January 1906 election campaign. British public opinion was indignant at conditions approximating slavery there, and among the British working class there was resentment that the exploitation of degraded Chinese workers was displacing white Britons from employment. The Liberals stopped the influx of coolies after taking power, but whether opinion about the opium trade affected the election's outcome is unclear. Opium was an important part of the image of Chinese degradation at the time; cf. Lloyd, *British Empire*, p. 262.

61. *Hansard*, 1906, vol. 7, col. 505.

62. Ibid., col. 507.

63. Ibid., cols. 513–14; Newman, "India and the Anglo-China Opium Agreements," p. 534.

64. Wolpert, *Morley*, pp. 219–20.

65. Richard Newman's "India and the Anglo-China Opium Agreements" considers the issues and developments from 1907 until 1914 in detail. See also Morse, *International Relations of the Chinese Empire*, 3:436–38.

66. Dodwell, *Indian Empire*, p. 326; Wolpert, *Morley*, pp. 218–19. Pratt, *Memorandum*, p. 24, specifies the Indian export for 1906 as 67,000 chests, of which 51,000

were intended for sale in China, and 16,000 for non-China markets. The Straits Settlements took a large proportion of the latter. Opium was still the Qing government's largest source of customs duty and the Government of India's third largest source of revenue (Newman, "India and the Anglo-China Opium Agreements," p. 525).

67. Owen, *British Opium Policy*, pp. 341–42; Newman, "India and the Anglo-China Opium Agreements," p. 548.

68. Newman, "India and the Anglo-Chinese Opium Agreements," pp. 550–51.

69. Chan, "Government, Merchants and Industry," pp. 410–11, recognizes the role of popular pressure in Britain and China. One work that no doubt contributed to aversion to the opium trade was *The Yangtze Valley and Beyond* (1899) by the widely read Isabella Bird Bishop. Her chapter on the problems of opium reinforced themes well established in the missionary literature, such as the association of drug addiction with ill health, impoverishment, and the selling of wives and children. Depicting Chinese opinion on the subject, Bird wrote: "The Chinese condemn all but the most moderate smoking and gambling as twin vices, and not a voice is raised in defense of either of them, even by the smokers themselves. The opium habit is regarded as a disease" (2:283–84).

70. The Shanghai conference was chaired by the Anglican bishop of the Philippines, Charles Brent, one of the three members on the Philippines Opium Committee, whose record of moral opposition to opium is discussed by Taylor, *American Diplomacy*, pp. 37–38 and passim. He later represented the American government at the 1912 and 1924–1925 international opium conferences. In 1910 he was one of the moving forces in the ecumenical movement at the Edinburgh World Missionary Conference.

71. *Hansard*, fifth series, 1913, vol. 52, col. 2190; Owen, *British Opium Policy*, p. 348.

72. Dodwell, *Indian Empire*, p. 326; Newman, "India and the Anglo-Chinese Opium Agreements," pp. 553ff; Pratt, *Memorandum*, pp. 20, 35, the latter regarding the temporary upturn in demand.

73. Owen, *British Opium Policy*, pp. 347–48; Lodwick, *Crusaders against Opium*, pp. 175–76. There are two curious parallels here. One is with the British 1807 abolition of the slave trade, which served as an inspiration for the later anti-opium movement. After decades of anti-slavery agitation, the slave trade was finally outlawed when sugar markets became glutted and a variety of British commercial interests including West Indian planters stood to suffer from further importation of slaves to the Caribbean (E. Williams, *Capitalism*, pp. 149–50). A second parallel is with 1839, when an opium glut in Calcutta threatened to bring down the Indian economy (Owen, *British Opium Policy*, p. 144; Inglis, *Opium War*, pp. 123–24).

74. Pratt, *Memorandum*, pp. 23–24.

75. Ibid., pp. 30–31.

76. Ibid., pp. 19–20, and p. 36 for India's similar attitude in 1907.

77. Buell, *Conferences*, pp. 80, 103–5. Article 23 of the League Covenant had stipulated general supervision of previous international undertakings on opium and narcotics, particularly those agreed at the 1912 Hague Convention. The two League conferences ran more or less concurrently from November 1924 to February 1925. The first was devoted to the suppression of opium smoking, the second to limiting

opium production and the manufacture of related drugs. Conventions on both were signed in February 1925, but without agreement on limiting production.

78. Ibid., pp. 99, 111. On the rekindling of British-American animosities over opium and colonialism in Asia, see Taylor, *American Diplomacy*, pp. 216–17.

79. Reproduced in Buell, *Conferences*, pp. 176–90.

80. Inglis, *Forbidden Game*, pp. 165ff.

81. *Assam Opium Enquiry Report:* for recommendations, see pp. 51–52. The charge of misleading the Geneva Conference was made (pp. 38–39) against John Campbell, the first representative of the Government of India, who had been replaced after clashing sharply with the Americans; see Buell, *Conferences*, pp. 104–6; Taylor, *American Diplomacy*, pp. 187–89.

82. Introduction, *Assam Opium Enquiry Report*, p. 4. Andrews's comparison referred to Great Britain's Dangerous Drugs Act of 1920.

83. See Mamdani, *Citizen and Subject*, for similar reactions to constructed identities in late colonial Africa.

84. See Buell, *Conferences*, pp. 94–95, for the British motion criticizing China at the 1924 conference. Pratt, *Memorandum*, p. 35, observed that the Chinese might well think the "duty to cooperate in preventing smuggling" a remarkable new discovery on the part of the Western powers, since even during World War I, when Yuan Shikai's government had made serious attempts to suppress the domestic cultivation and use of opium, the smuggling had clearly been into China, not out.

85. Pratt, *Memorandum*, pp. 32, 41.

86. Ibid., p. 41.

87. Taylor, *American Diplomacy*, p. 302.

88. Inglis, *Forbidden Game*, p. 164.

89. Rothermund, *Economic History*, p. 81. Even in 1944, the British still resisted American pressure to stop exports of "quasi-medical" opium; Taylor, *American Diplomacy*, pp. 325–26.

90. Gavit, *Opium*.

91. Mamdani, *Citizen and Subject*.

92. Kesaba, "Treaties and Friendships."

93. Lodwick, *Crusaders against Opium*, p. 66.

94. Ware, *Beyond the Pale*, chapters 2–3.

TWO

From Peril to Profit

Opium in Late-Edo to Meiji Eyes

Bob Tadashi Wakabayashi

Neither China nor Japan worried much about opium in 1800. Things were far different by 1900. China proved unable to reverse a narcotics plague that vitiated all efforts to halt chaos within and invasion from abroad; indeed, many late-Qing reformers saw opium as the root cause of that dual malaise. By contrast, the almost total absence of drug abuse in Japan greatly aided reform efforts, first under the old Tokugawa (or Edo) order and later under a new Meiji regime. This chapter poses three overarching issues for East Asia as an integral unit of historical research. First, although a trend toward academic specialization has split China and Japan apart, the two societies can profitably be studied in tandem during the nineteenth century when they faced a common Western threat—if to varying degrees. Second, some elements in a loosely shared "great tradition," such as *sakoku* and the Canton system, helped Japan yet thwarted China in state-building and self-strengthening. Third, the Edo to Meiji perception of Japan's "success" as opposed to China's "failure" at narcotics control had less than salutary consequences. Tokugawa-era Japanese had shared with Qing Chinese a sense of danger from the West. But after overcoming this first opium peril, Japanese in Meiji times discerned a new one—this time emanating from China. It spawned malice and contempt toward the Chinese people, plus a desire to profit from their addiction to drugs.

SAKOKU AND STATE CONSOLIDATION

Early in the nineteenth century, most Japanese felt secure and satisfied in their "closed country" or *sakoku*, a term translated from the Dutch in 1801. Although the term itself had been recently coined, the policies forming it were of long standing: a proscription of Christianity, Tokugawa government controls over foreign trade at specific locations, bans on Japanese travel abroad, and the stipulation of which alien nationals could enter and reside in Japan for what purposes. After Edo quashed the 1637–1638 Shimabara Rebellion, Christianity eked out an underground existence in remote parts of Kyushu. Inbound Japanese trade, like the Qing trade at Canton, came under strict control at Nagasaki, where resident aliens lived in segregated areas—the Dutch on Dejima and the Chinese in a "Chinese compound." Outbound Japanese trade took place at Ezō (present-day Hokkaidō) through Matsumae domain, and at one trading post in Korea run by Tsushima domain officials.[1] Aside from them, Japanese were forbidden to travel overseas. The Chinese, Koreans, Dutch, and Ryukyuans were the only aliens allowed to enter or live in Japan—and only for specific purposes of trade or diplomacy. But unlike Qing vassal states such as Korea or Annam, which also were "closed countries," Tokugawa Japan adopted *sakoku* autonomously, so it was free to choose policies of *kaikoku* to "open the country" given different needs in another day. Edo stipulated which peoples, goods, and ideas could enter and leave the country. In that sense *sakoku* contained prototypical mechanisms to determine citizenship, restrict immigration and emigration, control customs, and establish censorship. After 1868 the Meiji imperial regime would take over, refine, and utilize these state control mechanisms to suppress opium.

Few people in the Edo period begrudged the constraints imposed by *sakoku*, for most presumed that Japan enjoyed riches aplenty as long as each person accepted his allotted share as determined by social status. Socioeconomic ills derived from improper distribution, not an absolute deficiency. When non-Dutch Westerners—the Russians, British, and Americans—began to ask for trading rights after 1800, most Japanese saw them as being lured by Japan's natural abundance. Common sense held that Japan had no need of wealth from abroad. Foreigners came to take away native wealth, so a powerful state was needed to fend them off; Edo's 1825 edict to "expel barbarians" *(jōi)* enjoyed universal support. Yet almost no Japanese thought of taking the next logical step—that of pursuing foreigners overseas to gain plunder. Imperialism and colonialism were thus impossible for Tokugawa Japan. But by Meiji times common sense told the Japanese that their land was too poor to sustain an adequate standard of living. They now presumed a need to exploit foreign sources of wealth, so a powerful state was needed to pursue trade and conquest abroad. This sea change in attitude—from passivity in plenitude at home to aggressive acquisitiveness abroad—was central to the emergence of modern Japan. But after "opening" their land, Japanese leaders insisted on the same degree of autonomy as when it was "closed," and their views of opium played a key role in those efforts. Some far-sighted Tokugawa thinkers had seen foreign relations in a menacing light even before 1840, and news of the

Opium War and Taiping Rebellion buttressed that view up to the 1860s. Japanese in Edo times saw the West victimizing the Qing empire by means of opium, Christianity, and aggressive warfare. They feared similar threats to Japan and strove to overcome these in the 1850s and 1860s by enacting and enforcing treaty provisions that banned opium imports. After opening their land, Meiji leaders perceived a menace from Chinese opium imports and would overcome this peril only through war. Finally, after venturing overseas to win concessions in Qing treaty ports, many Japanese began to traffic in opium there under the protection of extraterritoriality.

LIPS AND TEETH: PRE-1840

Tokugawa adulation for the Confucian Way and other aspects of Chinese moral culture gave way to a Japan-centered world view long before 1800. Students of Western learning first used the value-neutral term *Shina*, adapted from various European renditions of the word *China*, to denote the Qing empire.[2] Other thinkers adopted the honorific term *Zhongguo* or "Middle Kingdom" for Japan, which they might also call "the Divine Realm" or "the Imperial Realm." Knowledge of the larger world derived largely from second- or third-hand Chinese and Western sources of uneven quality, and Edo leaders were often less than zealous about gathering information on recent events. Thus they all but ignored 1809 reports that the Thirteen Colonies had revolted against Britain and formed a new nation.[3] By and large it was thinkers outside of the central government before 1840 who studied world affairs, and they did so with grave concern. Men such as Honda Toshiaki, Hayashi Shihei, Satō Nobuhiro, Aizawa Seishisai, Watanabe Kazan, and Takano Chōei wrote of an imminent life-and-death struggle between the world's major powers. Honda, Hayashi, and Satō presumed that the Qing empire was the world's foremost power. In 1806 Satō feared that "a crafty Manchu emperor" might decide to invade Japan; then "the resulting disasters would be far worse than attacks by Russia."[4] By the 1820s and 1830s Satō's fear of Qing prowess receded; his *Kondō hisaku* of 1823 blithely asserted that a radically reorganized Japanese state could gain a foothold in "Manshū" whence "conquering Tungusland, all of China *[Shina]*, and Korea would be easy."[5] Aizawa, Watanabe, and Takano, who viewed current affairs in the framework of ancient Chinese history, were more realistic. Aizawa likened the world scene in 1825 to the Warring States era of 403 to 221 B.C., when seven great kingdoms vied for supremacy. He posited the Qing empire, Russia, Ottoman Turkey, Britain, Spain, the Mogul empire, and Japan as the corresponding seven powers of his own day. Japan was at best comparable to the weak state of Yan or, more properly, to the impotent yet venerable Zhou, which depended on the mercy of stronger states for survival. Aizawa saw the Russian, Qing, and Ottoman empires as the world's greatest powers, and he expressly likened Czarist Russia to Qin, the ruthless Legalist state that unified China in 221 B.C. He believed that Russia would conquer the Qing before taking on Ottoman Turkey, but first would take over Japan and recruit Wakō-type raiders to ravage the eastern China seaboard as they had five centuries before. Watanabe Kazan and Takano Chōei, both writing on the eve of the Opium War in 1839, dropped the Mogul and Ottoman empires from this scenario. They believed that Russia, the Qing, and Britain were the greatest powers of their day, and claimed that Russia and Britain were bent on world conquest. Above all, they warned that the British were ready to pounce on Japan before tackling the Qing, so Edo must not give Britain any pretext to justify an attack. Also in 1839 Tokugawa Nariaki—the daimyo of Mito and Aizawa's overlord—contended that Russia would conquer and make Japan into a base of operations from which to assault the far mightier Qing.[6]

These men were exceptional even for having studied foreign affairs before 1840. If their assumptions, information, and inferences were faulty, their strategic thinking reveals three key points. First, they depicted a hostile world of lurking predators. As Watanabe put it, Japan was little more than "a slab of meat on the road before Westerners."[7] Second, giving the lie to their puffed-up "Divine Realm" rhetoric, they held that Japan was at most a pawn to help Russia or Britain capture the great Qing empire. Third, few Japanese before 1840 felt threatened by their Manchu neighbor, whose power had slipped somewhat after 1800. Instead, they believed that Japan and the Qing faced a common peril from the West. The classical metaphor they used to describe Edo-Beijing relations was that of mutual, yet clearly unequal, dependence: "If the lips [Japan] fall away, the teeth [the Qing] will lie naked and exposed."[8]

MIRROR FOR YIN: 1840S AND 1850S

News of the First Opium War (1840–1842) shocked Japanese worldwatchers. Up to then they had feared a British or Russian attack on Japan designed to secure forces needed for subduing the far mightier Qing empire. This conflict now showed that Britain could get by without Japan's help. As reports filtered in, Tokugawa observers metaphorically deemed the war "an overturned cart with tracks for all to see" or "a mirror for Yin," that is, a lesson in what to avoid. But the only available sources of information about the war—Dutch and Chinese reports—were perforce unverifiable because *sakoku* precluded overseas travel until the 1860s. As a result, Japanese leaders and thinkers came away with highly differing and even contradictory "lessons" about the Opium War and, by extension, about the larger menace that Westerners posed in East Asia.

Historian Katō Yūzō has analyzed the five Dutch and seven Chinese re-

ports extant from 1839 to 1842 and examined the original sources from
which the twelve reports were compiled.[9]

1. Dutch 1, received in August 1839, describes events up to the
   summer of 1839.
2. Dutch 2, received in July 1840, describes conditions up to
   the start of 1840.
3. Chinese 1, received in August 1840, describes events to the
   end of 1839.
4. Dutch 3, received in August 1840, tells of conditions up to the
   start of 1840.
5/6. Chinese 2 and 3, received in December 1840, describes events
   to the fall of 1840.
7. Chinese 4, received in April 1841, discusses the situation to the
   fall of 1840.
8. Chinese 5, received in July 1841, describes events to the spring
   of 1841.
9. Chinese 6, received in January 1842, tells of events to the end of 1841.
10. Chinese 7, received in February 1842, depicts conditions to
   the end of 1841.
11/12. Dutch 4 and 5, received in August 1842, cover between 1840
   and 1842.

The Dutch reports derived from two types of English periodicals published
in the Qing empire. Those like the *Canton Press* and *Canton Register* usually
sided with British commercial interests to support the opium trade, whereas
missionary-run journals like *The Chinese Repository* tended to criticize that
trade on ethical grounds.[10] Such English periodicals came from Shanghai
and Canton via British Singapore to Dutch-held Batavia, where articles were
translated and excerpted in Dutch. The translated redactions then went to
Dejima, where Dutch officials compiled and send gists to Tokugawa officials, who in turn prepared loose Japanese renditions. Thus the Dutch reports took a very roundabout linguistic route: (1) original Chinese oral
accounts → (2) English periodical articles → (3) Dutch summaries → (4)
Japanese translations. Omissions and distortions might creep in along the
way, but the Dutch accounts were fairly accurate. They were comprehensive
in nature, but lacked an on-the-spot feel for events given the redacted nature of the original sources. Thus the Dutch reports conveyed a state-level
macro view of events in dry digest form. They tended to treat opium as a
trade item while downplaying or ignoring its malevolent effects on Qing
state and society. And they were often silent or pro-British as to how the
war broke out and which side was in the right. Finally, the Dutch reports
tended to depict Britain as having won a quick, overwhelming victory owing
to superior cannon and warships.

By contrast, the Chinese reports were compiled from Qing court documents and nonofficial accounts of local fighting. Although less factually accurate, these were more vivid than the Dutch reports, and their greater frequency conveyed a sense of events unfolding over time. Moreover, they were intelligible in their original language; only one was translated into Japanese. The Chinese reports stressed that opium had been a blight in terms of state revenues and human suffering for several decades, that the Daoguang emperor was wise to outlaw further imports, that Lin Zexu was right to seize opium stocks from British smugglers and Chinese collaborators, and that the war had ended in a split decision that, if anything, favored the Qing. True, high court officials had misled the emperor, ousted Lin, and adopted a policy of surrender by which they paid six million dollars to ransom Canton. But local bands of Chinese "braves" then inflicted major defeats on Britain such as at Sanyuanli near Canton. Modern historians later exposed such accounts as having been fabricated.[11] But many Japanese in the late Tokugawa era believed this myth of Chinese militia victories nonetheless. Finally, the first Chinese report of August 1840, which set the tone for those that followed, held that British authorities knew full well the evils of addiction, banned opium sales and shot violators at home, and yet still insisted on importing the drug to the Qing empire. In fact, Britain did not prohibit the using, importing, or manufacturing of opium in 1840.[12] So this Chinese report, too, was false. But it seemed credible at the time, and it reinforced images of British duplicity, depravity, and rapacity in Japanese minds.[13]

Thus the Japanese got mixed signals about the Opium War. Students of Western tactics and gunnery such as Takashima Shūhan and Egawa Tarōzaemon perceived a Western military and technological threat that had to be met as such. They held that Edo should strengthen coastal defenses by developing Western-style cannon, warships, and infantry tactics.[14] The logical extension of their ideas entailed policies of *kaikoku,* or opening Japan to the West, in order to buy advanced weapons and learn to build these firsthand. This view seemed to prevail in 1842, when Edo went back on its 1825 expulsion edict and ordered that provisions be supplied to Western ships on request. Although soon rescinded by Edo government conservatives such as Torii Yōzō, this 1842 edict in effect sanctioned trade and diplomacy with the West. It was a first step toward *kaikoku* that Perry would exploit in 1853.[15] Yet it is wrong to conclude that "accurate" Dutch reports of the Opium War produced "progressive" policies of *kaikoku.* Chinese reports of the war—plus studies of the West by Wei Yuan and Xu Jiyu as well as other Chinese works in the 1840s and 1850s—seemed to present a case for *sakoku* and *jōi.*[16] As noted above, some of the early Chinese reports implied that the Qing had come off better than Britain and that military hardware was not a factor in any case. Instead, a Qing victory proved elusive because court officials stabbed their emperor and the Canton braves in the back. Also, the Qing empire had long been vulnerable to attack from abroad because it suffered from grave ills within—the poverty, crime, disorder, and moral dissolution resulting from opium use at all levels of society, but especially among officials and in the military. And, of course, opium could never have entered the empire if Beijing had enforced the same strict controls over foreign trade at Canton that Edo did in Nagasaki. Also, the British could sell opium precisely because the Chinese used it without thinking of the consequences for state and society. Thus, it might be concluded, the West posed a menace to Japan only if the Japanese people made themselves vulnerable to it. If this were the case, the best countermeasure would be to keep the nation closed to foreign trade beyond that already allowed, and to expel forcibly any Westerners who dared to smuggle in contraband items. After unity and patriotism were forged at home, Tokugawa Japan might risk a limited military engagement to test superior Western power. The idea of total war fought to an unconditional surrender was still unknown, and as the Canton braves had reputedly shown, the armed expulsion of barbarians seemed well within the realm of possibility.

Later Tokugawa treatments of the Opium War, some serious and some fictional, seemed to reflect and support the case for seclusion and armed expulsion, and these works popularized that argument among the reading public.[17] Such treatments include Saitō Chikudō's *Ahen shimatsu* (1843), Shionoya Tōin's *Ahen ibun* (1847), Satō Nobuhiro's *Suiriku senpō roku* and *Sonka zateki ron* (both 1849), and Mineta Fūkō's *Kaigai shinwa* (1849). To different degrees, these authors all contended that the British were evil for dealing in opium and the Qing were foolish to cling to their egocentric, outdated Middle Kingdom world view. In his two 1849 works Satō retracted his earlier ideas about Japan's ability to conquer Asia; he now portrayed Japan as relying on the Qing empire to fend off Westerners. Mineta's illustrated *Kaigai shinwa* was especially influential. He vividly stressed the terrible effects that opium had on Qing society and state finances, and he confirmed the justness of Lin Zexu's crusade against the drug and its peddlers—both foreign and domestic. Mineta sympathetically portrayed helpless Chinese victims of British rapacity. In describing the invaders' orgies of rape and pillage, he wrote: "each night five to six hundred maidens, their lives ruined, would end their miserable lives." He lauded the patriotic "braves" who expelled the British barbarians from Canton (see fig. 7). Mineta pilloried the Qing officials Yilibu and Qishan for bribing enemy forces with six million dollars while quashing the patriotic militia who strove to fight on as the Daoguang emperor ordered.[18] In the 1850s sequels such as *Kaigai shinwa shūi* and *Kaigai yowa*—together with Shionoya Tōin's *Kakka ron* and Iwagaki Gesshū's *Seisei kaishin hen*—circulated in print or manuscript. Iwagaki's 1858 work stretched popular imaginations to the limit by describing how Tokugawa Nariaki might lead 8,000 elite troops in a four-teen-ship task force to save the Qing empire from British aggression. The Japanese would boldly attack London, take Queen Victoria captive, and then partition the United Kingdom among Russia, Spain, France, the Netherlands, Prussia, and Portugal. On Nariaki's triumphant return, the Xian-feng emperor would bestow words of praise and gratitude for those distinguished services.[19]

In the meantime, Commodore Matthew Perry had forced Edo to sign a Treaty of Amity in 1854, which in effect formally sanctioned the earlier 1842 edict that had permitted Western ships to obtain provisions at Japanese ports. Perry's treaty did not call for regular trade as such, but it did open five ports besides Nagasaki and called for stationing a U.S. consul in Japan. This consul, Townsend Harris, arrived in 1856. According to his half-veiled threats, Japan could stop the British from importing opium only by signing a U.S. treaty.[20] Thus Harris used news of the 1858 Treaty of Tianjin, which ended the Second Opium War, to extract a formal trade pact plus more stipulations on ports and foreign residence from Ii Naosuke and Hotta Masayoshi. News of this treaty—signed by Edo in violation of the Kōmei emperor's will—soon spread throughout Japan. Indignant thinker-activists such as Sakuma Shōzan and Yoshida Shōin likened Ii and Hotta to Yilibu and Qishan—the Qing officials who sold out Canton and suppressed local braves striving to obey the Daoguang emperor's orders for expelling barbarians.[21] Sakuma railed that Harris had extorted this treaty through deceit. Harris had claimed that if Japan signed a U.S. treaty explicitly prohibiting opium imports, this precedent would force Britain to follow suit, and Japan would avoid the tragic fate that had befallen Qing China. Sakuma claimed that this was a lie: "Even the great power Qing failed to stop British marauders from violating bans on opium; how can a weak power like Japan stop Britain with a mere treaty? . . . The British break treaty provisions and commoners suffer as a result. Reason dictates that we must not victimize our own people to help foreign nations gain profits."[22] Sakuma did not oppose formal trade and diplomatic relations per se, but he insisted that Edo should abrogate this particular treaty and send delegates to America with orders to negotiate a new one based firmly on the principles of truth and equality.[23] Yoshida Shōin also saw through Harris's arguments. Yoshida argued that such feigned goodwill would do nothing to stop Americans from smuggling opium into Japan—as in fact they were doing in the Qing empire. Yoshida was xenophobic but not benighted. Later he would try to violate *sakoku* by stowing away on one of Perry's ships and by extending Japan's outbound trade, then restricted to Korea and Ezo, to U.S. shores. Yet he insisted on doing this from a position of strength and on Japanese terms: "If we are strong enough to control foreigners, there is nothing wrong with staying home to trade, and venturing abroad

Figure 7. Cantonese "braves" attacking foreign soldiers at Sanyuanli, published by Mineta Fūkō in his *Kaigai shinwa* (Edo: n.p., 1849).

to do so would even be better. But if we agree to trade because we fear barbarian power, even venturing abroad to trade would be bad, and staying at home would even be worse."[24]

In the 1850s men such as Sakuma and Yoshida no longer clung to the specific policies making up *sakoku;* instead they sought to uphold the principle of national sovereignty behind it. That is, they refused to surrender Japan's right to enact any laws it deemed fit and to enforce these against infringement by foreigners. Whether the Edo regime or the imperial court exercised that right was of secondary concern. We should also note that these men made opium-smuggling their prime test case in upholding these principles of sovereignty and autonomy—even though anti-opium legislation did not yet exist in Tokugawa Japan. Furthermore, their advocacy of armed force to keep the country closed was by no means irrational. Sir Ernest Satow, a British diplomat in Japan in the 1860s, noted the Japanese reaction to the Western threat during the 1850s:

Nor can it be wondered that Japan . . . which had seen the humiliation of China consequent upon a dispute with a Western Power arising out of trade questions at the very moment when she was being torn by a civil war which owed its origins to the introduction of new religious beliefs from the West, should have believed that the best means of maintain peace at home and avoiding an unequal contest with Europe, was to adhere strictly to traditions of the past two centuries *[sakoku/jōi]*.[25]

Japanese in the 1850s might argue to expel Westerners and keep their country closed, or they might seek large-scale trade and cultural borrowing by opening their country to the West. Either way, the point was for Japan to uphold its freedom of choice by acting on its own initiative.

Two measures were imperative whatever that choice might be: signing equal treaties that forced foreigners to obey Japanese domestic laws, including any against opium that might be enacted, and fostering the armed strength to enforce those laws against would-be violators. Indeed, Nakaoka Shintarō ascribed universal moral validity to *sakoku* and *jōi* in 1866 by likening those concepts explicitly to what the American colonists did to British colonial rulers beginning in 1776.[26] Furthermore, *sakoku* and *jōi* also dovetailed with the idea of deportation—with drug-related offenses included among the grounds for that punishment. Moreover, contrary to what many historians believe, Harris was not the first foreigner to sign a treaty with Japan that included an anti-opium clause. Edo had already concluded supplemental commercial pacts with the Netherlands and Czarist Russia that expressly banned opium imports. The treaty with Russia is worth noting for its stress on equality: "The Japanese government strictly forbids opium imports. Knowing about the evils that stem from opium, the Russian government also strictly bans it. Since this prohibition is the same in each nation, both shall be scrupulous in obeying it." Upon prompting from the daimyo of Kagoshima, Tokushima, and Morioka, as well as from its own officials, the Tokugawa regime also concluded similar treaties with Britain and France after it signed the one with Harris.[27]

CHINESE OPIUM: 1860s TO 1895

By the early 1860s Tokugawa bans on overseas travel were a dead letter and ports other than Nagasaki were open to non-Dutch Western trade and residence. So the specific policies in *sakoku* no longer obtained except for the ban on Christianity—which was discreetly rescinded in 1873. Yet both the Edo and Meiji regimes insisted on outlawing foreign opium in diplomatic treaties. Such efforts bore fruit vis-à-vis Western states but failed with the Qing empire, which had never posed a threat in Edo times, yet refused to sign a treaty with the Meiji state prohibiting opium imports. Meanwhile, a momentous change took place in Japanese attitudes toward the Qing regime and Chinese people. Gone was the "lips-and-teeth" metaphor that presumed common victimization at Western hands; now China was seen as the main potential source of opium poisoning in Japan. Nor did Meiji

Japanese take the "mirror for Yin" to heart. Earlier, they had overcome the opium peril while empathizing with their neighbor afflicted by it; now they evinced open contempt for the Manchu state and Chinese people who sank ever deeper into addiction. This attitude justified overseas aggression—an idea barely conceivable in Edo times. After victory in the 1894–1895 Qing-Meiji War[28] gave Japan a toehold on the continent, unscrupulous carpetbaggers or *tairiku rōnin* as well as ordinary Japanese residents in Qing treaty ports began to traffic in drugs. In short, Japan eagerly joined Western imperialist states in exploiting for profit the Chinese people's vulnerability to opium.

Japanese disdain for China began to emerge in the 1860s after the Edo regime itself repudiated *sakoku* by sending missions abroad. Three future leaders—Takasugi Shinsaku, Hibino Teruhiro, and Nōtomi Kaijirō—joined such a mission to Shanghai from 2 June to 31 July 1862, just as Taiping, Anglo-French, and foreigner-led Ever-Victorious Army forces were launching attacks nearby. These three men were among the first Japanese to view actual conditions in the land that they had always idealized as home to Confucius and the sages. These sojourners were shocked to see the Chinese *(Shinajin)* living in squalid hovels and cringing like slaves before haughty Westerners. As Takasugi noted, "Shanghai is part of China *[Shina]*, but it may as well belong to the British or French as far as I can tell." Thus "Shina" was acquiring negative associations: filth, poverty, weakness, backwardness, and servility toward foreigners. The trio also saw that the ruling Qing gentry and scholar-officials failed to perceive, or chose to ignore, the danger to state sovereignty that came with relying on Western military aid to suppress a rebellion. Hibino and Nōtomi took pains to note that some 200,000 catties of opium worth 1.2 million dollars flowed into Shanghai each year, and that circuit intendants regulating the trade in this drug were themselves addicted to it. Finally, the trio argued that "[in 1851] the 'Long Hairs' first avowed loyalty to the Ming, but now worship Christianity and use it to deceive stupid commoners and raise destructive havoc." Or, "the 'Long Haired' rebels don't really justify their uprising by appealing to Ming loyalty; they delude stupid commoners with their vile creed, and have spread poison over ten provinces."[29] ("Long Hair" refers to the Taiping style of allowing hair to grow long on the entire head—as under the native Ming dynasty—rather than shaving the head except for a queue, as dictated by Manchu rulers.)

Based on other accounts in the 1860s, Japanese speculated as to what the outcome of this massive rebellion would be for Japan. For example, a returned castaway named Monta held that the rebels might overcome foreign intervention, topple the dynasty, and go on resisting Western incursion; then these new Han Chinese rulers might protect Japan from an invasion.[30] In contrast, Kusaka Genzui, a student of Yoshida Shōin, said:

"Britain and France cannot launch an attack on our Divine Realm as well because the Long Hairs are so strong. If the Long Hairs ever succumb to Britain and France, we would surely face an onslaught."[31] Historian Inoue Kiyoshi contends that Britain did indeed give up territorial designs on Japan for fear of meeting similarly ferocious resistance from the Japanese people.[32] This charge cannot be proven. But it is clear that in the last years of Tokugawa rule some Japanese observers detected that the Manchu dynasty sought help from drug-peddling foreigners to suppress native Chinese rebels. These Japanese also observed that Christianized Taiping rebels—and by extension, the native Chinese masses as a whole—were a powerful force that might possibly protect, but more likely would menace, Japan.[33]

The Qing and their foreign allies quashed the Taiping Rebellion by 1864. Yet the specter of a Chinese peril remained and became associated with opium rather than Christianity. As early as the 1830s, Matsuura Seigan, retired daimyo of Hizen, adjacent to Nagasaki, had written that Chinese sailors habitually smoked opium and suffered illness or death from large doses. Later on, news of the Opium War reinforced this image of widespread daily Chinese opium use—much as Japanese routinely drank *sake*. *Sakoku* permitted idealization of China through the reading of books by Confucian scholars; *kaikoku* entailed large-scale cheek-by-jowl contact by commoners. Under *sakoku*, Chinese resident aliens were confined to the Nagasaki "Chinese compound." With *kaikoku*, Chinese were allowed to register as domestic servants of Western nationals and began to live in the foreign concessions of all newly opened ports. Disputes based on sociocultural differences often arose. In early-Meiji times, Chinese were the largest foreign community in Japan. In 1867 more than 300 Chinese lived in Kōbe, 660 lived in Yokohama, and they outnumbered Westerners in both cities. In 1868 some 743 Chinese lived in Nagasaki, 288 of whom resided in the foreign concession, as opposed to 195 Westerners. And by 1875 the Chinese accounted for 1,300 out of 2,496 foreign nationals living in the Yokohama foreign concessions. This sudden increase in the number of resident Chinese and their greater day-to-day contact with Japanese in society spread fears of a looming opium epidemic—whether justified or not.

Although opium was present in Edo times, its nonmedicinal use was virtually nil. Ten thousand farmers grew poppies as a cash crop by the 1860s, mainly around Osaka. But the first domestic prohibition on opium use came in Meiji times, in 1868. Under Meiji law, growers had to submit their poppies to state officials, who processed these into opium for medical purposes. Anyone who sold opium to smokers or who tempted others to smoke was subject to execution. Meiji law restricted opium use to medical purposes. Doctors and druggists who dispensed opium-based medicines had to file reports on each occasion. Moreover, Japanese poppies were poor in quality and expensive to process compared with varieties obtained from India or Persia through Western importers. This influx of cheap opium imports after the end of *sakoku* destroyed a once-profitable domestic cash crop until World War I, but the Meiji regime took pains to contain the influx. In 1876 it began to set up what evolved into a state monopoly under which foreign firms—but not individuals—sold opium to the Meiji government, and not directly to Japanese subjects. Foreign nationals might bring in 1,800 grams for personal use as medicine but could not dispose of it otherwise while in Japan.[34] Moreover, this state monopoly did not at first seek to raise revenue; it was a means to control the supply and distribution of imported opium under existing treaties. But after Meiji leaders discovered just how cheap and plentiful foreign opium was, they realized the fiscal benefits that might accrue from such a monopoly given a large population of addicts.[35] That condition was intolerable in Japan, but it already existed in Taiwan, where the Chinese opium habit had taken root.

Japan's lack of self-sufficiency in opium for medicinal use exacerbated fears of foreigners smuggling it in for more sinister purposes—a fear that seemed borne out by sporadic reports of drug-related crimes. An 1868 newspaper article stated that Chinese were selling large amounts of opium and that five Nagasaki courtesans who tried the drug had died. Such reports prompted local authorities in 1868 and the Tokyo government in 1870 to threaten with fines or deportation any Chinese who used or supplied opium to Japanese. Yet the sense of peril intensified. Records in Kanagawa Prefecture (where Yokohama was located) show that four Westerners and no Japanese were arrested on drug charges between 1872 and 1876, whereas twenty-six Chinese were arrested between April 1873 and December 1876.[36] Although this number was small, Japanese authorities argued that opium use took place secretly in Chinese homes, so the number of violators actually caught and prosecuted constituted the tip of an iceberg. Moreover, some Chinese carried in plain sight pipes and utensils that could only be used for smoking opium. Hence Japanese constables insisted that they had to search Chinese homes in order to enforce domestic opium laws.[37]

This Japanese sense of vulnerability stemmed partly from faulty treaty protection against Chinese opium imports; ironically enough, the Meiji regime felt safer with Westerners. Meiji Japan inherited the "unequal" treaties that Edo had signed with Western states, but these still affirmed in principle Japan's right to enforce domestic laws banning opium as a narcotic in spite of provisions for extraterritoriality. Under extraterritoriality, sovereign state A insists that its nationals be subject to its own laws for offenses allegedly committed in non-sovereign state B, and suspects are tried in foreign consular courts rather than by the judiciary in state B. Although Westerners were tried in consular courts, they did not enjoy extraterritoriality in Japan as regards opium. This was true in the celebrated case of John Hartley, a British subject arrested for opium-smuggling in 1877 and 1878. Britain and the other Western powers had signed treaties that respected in principle Japan's right to control narcotic substances. So the British government did not permit Hartley to claim immunity from Japanese drug laws on the grounds that buying and using opium were legal acts in Britain. His sole defense was to argue that he brought opium to Japan for personal use as medicine, in which case he was limited to 1,800 grams. However, he lied about the amount and his intended purpose, and British consular officials found him guilty at his 1878 retrial. Thus the main difference between Western and Chinese residents in early-Meiji Japan was that Westerners did not use opium for social purposes, and therefore did not insist on the right to do so in opposition to Japanese law.[38] Westerners brought opium to Japan, as they did to China, but did not use it widely as a narcotic in either country; and the Meiji state stopped its own subjects from trying to use the drug. By contrast, the Meiji state signed an "equal" treaty with the Qing in 1871, but it worked to Japan's detriment; and, as Mōri Toshihiko and Xu Yueting show, the Qing had a separate agenda in designing it. Its architects, Li Hongzhang and Zeng Guofan, knew that past Qing treaties with the West—*tiaoyue* or *jōyaku*, literally "itemized agreements"—were perforce unequal because each was signed after the Qing lost a war. So these two Qing leaders set about crafting a new type of agreement with Japan—*tiaogui* or *jōki*, literally "itemized stipulations"—to be signed voluntarily on an equal footing in peacetime, not under duress in wartime; and they schemed to apply this new deal as leverage in negotiating treaty revision with the West. Li and Zeng knew that under conventional bilateral trade pacts, each party gained the right to station diplomatic officials who regulated its citizens' business in the other country. But they purposely omitted the stipulation of this right in their final draft with Japan because they feared that Western states would exploit it under most-favored-nation arrangements. And in stark contrast with past Qing diplomatic practices, Li all but forced this carefully prepared draft upon the Japanese delegates and badgered them to sign it.[39]

But Mōri and Xu fail to examine the implications of their thesis for the issue of opium. This 1871 Qing-Meiji *tiaogui* was "equal" in that Article III enjoined each side to honor the other's right of extraterritoriality.[40] This made for a queer situation. Japanese subjects on Qing soil could not use or import opium because Meiji law prohibited those acts on pain of death. On the other hand, Qing subjects could use and import opium in Japan— and claim immunity from Japanese law—because their government had legalized opium imports in 1858–1860—though under duress. While negotiating this 1871 *tiaogui*, Li Hongzhang dismissed Japanese requests to insert a clause that expressly banned opium—as found in *tiaoyue* signed between Japan and Western states—because such a clause would reveal that

Japan could outlaw opium imports whereas the Qing could not. Such a disclosure of Qing weakness would further damage the dynasty's international stature and obstruct treaty revision with the West. The Meiji regime chose not to force this issue because of Japanese weakness relative to the Qing, so in 1873 the treaty was ratified as drafted in 1871. Li also refused Japanese requests to revise Article III for these same reasons.[41]

Given the history of egregious Japanese aggression that followed, we tend to think of Japan as the swaggering bully and China as a meek victim from the start of modern times. That image, although accurate from the 1880s onward, distorts reality in the 1860s and 1870s. Japanese opposition parties and journalists were loudly jingoistic, but the Meiji government itself desperately struggled to overcome acute foreign and domestic threats to order. By contrast, the Tongzhi Restoration was achieving great success in restoring domestic stability and fiscal strength, so the Qing empire was far richer and stronger than Japan, and Meiji leaders trimmed their sails accordingly. Thus, prior to the 1874 Taiwan Expedition, Japanese diplomats performed a modified form of the kowtow and sought Qing recognition that Taiwanese "barbarians" lay "outside of Middle Kingdom civilization." In other words, Japan sought official recognition that Taiwan was not Qing territory and therefore could be attacked.[42] The Qing refused. But the point is that Meiji leaders admitted Japan's weakness and tried to settle disputes over opium by diplomatic means. When this failed because of Qing intransigence, Japan cautiously took sterner measures. In 1876 the Meiji regime declared that Chinese resident aliens must obey Japanese anti-drug laws and that violators would first be detained and only then turned over to Qing authorities for trial. In 1878 Japanese officials became stricter. They declared that police would enter Chinese homes to make arrests, confiscate smoking pipes, and deport in perpetuity any Chinese convicted of drug-related offenses. Such forcible searches of residences provoked hostile protests from the resident Chinese, who petitioned consular officials for support. Those protests rested on certain culture-bound assumptions—that opium use was an accepted part of social gatherings, took place in private homes, and did not threaten public safety. Therefore, the Chinese held, opium use should not constitute a criminal offense.[43] Unlike the arguments expounded by resident Englishmen in late-nineteenth-century China, there was little hypocrisy in these protests by resident Chinese in Meiji Japan. They brought opium to Japan, but did so for their own use. What they objected to was zealous Japanese attempts to block their habit from spreading to the surrounding society.

Conflicts over importing, possessing, and using opium led to violent clashes between resident Chinese and Japanese authorities, the worst of which took place in 1883 and 1886. In September 1883 a Nagasaki constable tried to detain Chinese opium suspects without prior permission from Qing consular officials. An unruly crowd of Chinese residents soon assaulted him, and he ended up killing one person and wounding several in the melee. After a Qing consul protested, Nagasaki police were ordered not to draw swords and ethnic tensions rose. Yellow journalists incited anti-Chinese sentiment throughout Japan, setting the stage for more violence when Li Hongzhang's Beiyang warship, the *Tingyuan*, called at Nagasaki in August 1886. After police tried to arrest drunken Chinese sailors rioting on shore, more sailors landed and Chinese residents joined the fray until police, rioters, and Nagasaki citizens involved in the violence came to number in the hundreds. Within a few years, jingoistic military tunes boasted lyrics like "Peace talks have broken off; settle scores with the runty Chinks," or "Haven't we sunk the *Tingyuan* yet?"[44] Actual fighting in the Qing-Meiji War ended in February 1895 after Beiyang fleet commander Ding Richang committed suicide through an opium overdose rather than face a mutiny.[45] In April 1895 the Qing empire agreed to submit its subjects to Japanese anti-drug laws—but only after having lost this war. By contrast, Britain had agreed to end all unequal treaties with Japan in July 1894—as a result of diplomatic negotiations before that war had begun.[46]

IMPLICATIONS

The Edo and Meiji regimes were keenly aware of the opium peril and intent on overcoming it. In stark contrast, Qing efforts in this regard failed, and China proved unable to suppress opium until after World War II. And, on the other hand, Britain and other Western states did not pass anti-opium laws like those that Japan enacted in 1868 until the twentieth century. A number of points stand out in Japan's early and nimble response. (1) Laws banning opium were unknown in the Edo era. But *sakoku* effectively blocked drug abuse in Japan and gave the Meiji state ready-made mechanisms for that purpose. Thus Meiji anti-opium crusades did not need to uproot addiction—just prevent it. (2) A knowledge of Qing affairs impressed Edo-era Japanese with the acute need to control opium as a narcotic substance. Seeing that lax Qing prohibitions on opium use at home precluded an ability to stop imports from abroad, the Edo regime insisted on banning opium in foreign treaties signed in the 1850s. (3) Later, the Meiji state enacted strict domestic laws against opium in 1868, the first year of its life, and diplomats extended those treaties and laws not only to Westerners, but also to Qing subjects who up to then had been immune from these. (4) Japan's state-run opium monopoly was meant to control the supply and distribution of imported opium—not to raise revenue. Only later did Meiji leaders find that such a monopoly could be lucrative. (5) The Meiji state and its subjects pursued opium profits abroad because they agreed that drug addiction was intolerable at home. (6) The state began by setting up a colonial opium monopoly in Taiwan that garnered huge revenues—though it did uproot addiction eventually.[47] (7) Seeing that the Chinese could not purge themselves of addiction, Japanese individuals began to exploit that vulnerability by trafficking in Qing treaty ports under protection of extraterritoriality—a colonial privilege extracted through war. Thereafter, Japanese might scorn the Chinese for being weak and irresolute, but sympathy was out of the question.

Opium was mainly an issue of power and profit in modern Sino-Japanese relations, but it also stemmed from sociocultural differences. People in all Qing socioeconomic strata tolerated opium use, whereas *sakoku* precluded that for Tokugawa Japan. By Meiji times, the Japanese state and people alike came to view opium as an evil because its abuse led not only to personal degeneracy and destitution, but to national debility as well. The Japanese linked this private vice to state fortunes, and so made it a patriotic issue that overrode individual freedom of choice. Any foreigner who brought opium to Japan was a subversive, and any Japanese who used or sold it at home was a traitor; neither could be tolerated in respectable society. Not until after the May Fourth Movement would grassroots anti-drug movements attain such rhetorical heights on a nationwide scale in China.[48] That the Japanese resolutely overcame the opium peril "proved" their superiority to peoples who feebly succumbed to it. And in the heyday of Social Darwinism, the feebleness of inferior peoples warranted no respect.

Nothing flaunts this attitude better than a 1884 woodblock print titled "The Beijing Pillow of Dreams" (fig. 8), conceived by Fukuzawa Yukichi and produced by his nephew Imaizumi Hidetarō. Western statesmen heap coarse insults on a Chinese giant—caricatured with pig-tail and long fingernails—as he puffs on an opium pipe, oblivious to the Lilliputian French invaders who bind him with telegraph wires and apply a moxa that fails to rouse him from his comatose stupor.[49] In 1849 Mineta Fūkō lauded the braves at Canton who died trying to rid their land of British opium, and he expressed remorse for Chinese maidens raped by foreign armies. In 1884 Fukuzawa exuded sheer contempt for the Chinese people partly because their opium habit invited foreign subjugation. Such derision fostered aggressive Japanese policies in league with the Western imperial powers. In 1884 Fukuzawa also published in his newspaper, the *Jiji shinpō*, reputedly leaked European plans for a partition of China, which he likened to the three partitions of Poland in 1773, 1793, and 1795. He even included a map of the soon-to-be-sliced-up Qing melon (fig. 9).[50] It shows the dynastic house relegated to its Manchu homeland; pretender Chinese regimes claiming Gansu, Sichuan, and Guizhou; Germany controlling Shandong and Henan; Russia holding Korea, Shanxi, and Shaanxi; Britain owning Jiangsu, Anhui, Zhejiang, Hebei, and Jiangxi; France taking Annam, Yunnan, Hunan, Guangxi, Guangdong, and western Fujian; and Japan left

Figure 8. "The Beijing Pillow of Dreams," a woodblock print conceived by Fukuzawa Yukichi and produced by his nephew Imaizumi Hidetarō, 1884. Reprinted
from Keiō gijuku, *Fukuzawa Yukichi zenshū*, 20: 284; by permission of the Fukuzawa Yukichi kenkyū sentā, Tokyo.

with Taiwan and eastern Fujian. Fukuzawa justified this partition scheme
through a Western-inspired rationale: The comity of nations might censure
a lone aggressor, but if several aggressors ganged up on the victim, all would
share the onus and the moral stigma on each thus became negligible.[51] In
his eyes, Japan had no choice but to "leave Asia behind and join the West"
(datsu-A, nyū-Ō). This entailed ravaging the Chinese people, who seemed
to lack even the will to defend themselves.

But moral opposition to opium was quickly building in Western societies
during the final third of the nineteenth century. By the 1870s and 1880s
British reformers were declaring that the opium trade was more reprehensible than the slave trade had ever been. Englishmen should now look
beyond profit; they should abolish drug trafficking in the name of a higher
good—just as they had abolished trafficking in humans earlier on.[52] By the
twentieth century, conscientious Westerners admitted moral duplicity in
selling opium as a narcotic—while not using it as such themselves—to addicted Chinese masses. The Japanese, by contrast, embraced that moral

Figure 9. A cartoon map of China carved up like a melon, published by Fukuzawa Yukichi in his newspaper, *Jiji shinpō*, 1884. Reprinted from Keiō gijuku, *Fukuzawa Yukichi zenshū*, 10: 77; by permission of the Fukuzawa Yukichi kenkyū
sentā, Tokyo.

duplicity just as Westerners were rejecting it through international treaties
and the League of Nations. As dope smuggler Uchikawa Mikitarō argues
in *Busō seru shigai*, a fictionalized account of the 1928 Jinan Incident: "It's
okay for us to sell heroin here [in China]; but don't ever consume it like
the Chinks do."[53] Modern Japan, it would seem, was doomed to remain at
least one step behind in its quest to "join" the West.

NOTES

1. Toby, *State and Diplomacy in Early Modern Japan;* Tashiro, *Kinsei Nit-Chō tsūkō
bōeki shi kenkyū;* Uchida Ginzō, *Kinsei no Nihon*, pp.154–202; also Iwao, *Nihon no
rekishi.*

2. Watanabe, *Higashi Ajia no ōken to shisō*, pp.170, 180–81; Fogel, "On Japanese Expressions for 'China,'" pp. 5–16.

3. Numata, Matsumura, and Satō, *Nihon shisō taikei*, vol. 64, *Yōgaku jō*, p. 560.

4. Satō Kenji, *Satō Nobuhiro bugakushū jō*, p. 322.

5. Bitō and Shimazaki, *Nihon shisō taikei*, vol. 45, *Andō Shōeki, Satō Nobuhiro*, pp. 435–36.

6. *Mitohan shiryō bekki jō*, p. 98.

7. Satō, Uete, and Yamaguchi, *Nihon shisō taikei*, vol. 55, *Watanabe Kazan, Takano Chōei, Sakuma Shōzan, Yokoi Shōnan, Hashimoto Sanai*, p. 66.

8. Wakabayashi, *Anti-Foreignism and Western Learning in Early-Modern Japan;* also Wakabayashi, "Rival States on a Loose Rein," pp. 17–22.

9. Katō, *Kurofune zengo no sekai*, pp. 261–84.

10. By contrast, Mori Mutsuhiko holds that the Dutch reports derive from the *Singapore Free Press;* see Mori, "Ahen senso jōhō toshite no Tōfōsetusho."

11. See Wakeman, *Strangers at the Gate*, pp. 11–58; Polachek, *Inner Opium War;* Natsui, "Kanton kō-Ei tōsō."

12. See Niimura, "Eikokujin kara mita Chūgoku no ahen kyūin," and Sechter, "The Legal, Medical, and Social Status of Opium."

13. Katō, *Kurofune zengo no sekai*, pp. 266–67, 174. This largely corroborates Satō Shōsuke, *Yōgakushi kenkyū josetu*, pp. 301–23.

14. Etō, *Katsu Kaishū zenshū*, vol. 11, *Rikugun rekishi I*, pp. 9–12, 22–32, and 106–40.

15. Katō, *Kurofune zengo no sekai*, p. 285.

16. See Ōba, *Edo jidai no Nit-Chō hiwa*, pp. 242–48; Ōba, *Edo jidai ni okeru Tōsen mochiwatarisho no kenkyū*, pp. 187–99.

17. Masuda, *Seigaku tōzen to Chūgoku jijō*, pp. 86–87. Joshua Fogel has translated this segment of Masuda's book in *Sino-Japanese Studies* 4, no. 1 (October 1991): 44–63.

18. I summarize Mineta's work and discuss its implications in "Opium, Expulsion, Sovereignty."

19. For this summary of the plot, see Takeuchi, *Nihonjin ni totte no Chūgoku zū*, p. 387.

20. For the text of Harris's five-hour harangue to Hotta Masayoshi, see Etō, *Katsu Kaishū zenshū*, vol. 16, *Kaikoku kigen II*, pp. 128–44; and Gaimushō, *Nihon gaikō nenpyō narabini shuyōbunsho, jō: 1840–1945*, pp. 10–16.

21. Wakabayashi, "Opium, Expulsion, Sovereignty," pp. 17–21.

22. Shinano kyōiku kai, *Fukkoku Shōzan zenshū*, 5:143.

23. Ibid., p. 144.

24. Yamaguchi ken kyōiku kai, *Yoshida Shōin zenshū*, 5:292.

25. Satow, *A Diplomat in Japan*, p. 44.

26. Kunaishō ed., *Shōho Junnanroku kō, kōhen*, p. 427.

27. Satō Saburō, *Kindai Nit-Chū kōshō shi no kenkyū*, pp. 188–89.

28. I do not use the term *Sino-Japanese War of 1894–1895* because it anachronistically imparts a sense of widespread Han Chinese national consciousness that did not exist in the late nineteenth century.

29. Nohara, "Kyokutō o meguru kokusai kankei," pp. 86–89.

30. Ibid.

31. Fukumoto, *Kusaka Genzui zenshū*, pp. 430–31.

32. Inoue, *Nihon gendaishi I: Meiji ishin*, pp. 204–5.

33. Haga, "Ahen sensō."

34. The above follows Satō Saburō, *Kindai Nit-Chō kōshō shi no kenkyū*, pp. 185–90, 201–5; also Jennings, *Opium Empire*, pp. 8–11.

35. Yamada, *Ōrudo Shanhai ahen jijō*, pp. 17–21.

36. Ibid., p. 11.

37. Satō Saburō, *Kindai Nit-Chū kōshō shi no kenkyū*, pp. 190–200.

38. Ibid.

39. Mōri, *Taiwan shuppei*, pp. 189–96.

40. Gaimushō, *Nihon gaikō nenpyō narabini shuyō bunsho, jō: 1840–1945*, p. 45.

41. Satō Saburō, *Kindai Nit-Chū kōshō shi no kenkyū*, pp. 192–93.

42. Mōri, *Taiwan shuppei*, pp. 25–64.

43. Satō Saburō, *Kindai Nit-Chū kōshō shi no kenkyū*, pp. 190–200.

44. Yamada, *Ōrudo Shanhai ahen jijō*, pp. 20–21.

45. Rawlinson, *China's Struggle for Naval Development*, p. 190.

46. Satō Saburō, *Kindai Nit-Chū kōshō shi no kenkyū*, pp. 214–16.

47. Liu Ming-hsiu [Itō Kiyoshi], *Taiwan tōchi to ahen mondai*.

48. See Kasahara, "Chūka kokumin kyodokukai ni tsuite no ichi kōsatsu," pp. 2–16.

49. Keiō gijuku, *Fukuzawa Yukichi zenshū*, 20:284.

50. Ibid., 10:77.

51. Ibid., 10:72–80.

52. Niimura, "Igirisujin no ahen bōekikan," p. 29.

53. Kuroshima, *Busō seru shigai*, p. 5.

PART TWO

Distribution and Consumption

THREE

Drugs, Taxes, and Chinese Capitalism in Southeast Asia

Carl A. Trocki

The history of opium in Southeast Asia is probably as old as it is in China. Opium passed through Southeast Asia on its way to China and was certainly a major item of trade for the Dutch East India Company since the seventeenth century. It is possible that the practice of smoking opium, an innovation that went a long way toward making the drug a true mass consumption commodity, may have been developed by Southeast Asians. Englebert Kaempfer's observations about opium use among Javanese in the 1690s is perhaps the earliest evidence of opium smoking.[1]

The Dutch also sold opium in Sumatra and they probably found markets for the drug throughout the archipelago. There is little evidence, however, that the Dutch shipped opium to China before the nineteenth century. Rather it seems that Chinese junk traders probably purchased opium in Java and took it to China themselves. In the eighteenth century, after the British East India Company came to dominate the opium-producing regions of Bengal and Varanasi, British country traders took control of the opium trade and brought the drug to Aceh, the Malay Peninsula, Riau, Sulu, and numerous other places. They traded it for Straits produce such as tin, pepper, spices, and other commodities that had a market in China.

As the China market grew, however, the Southeast Asian market tended to decrease in significance. China's vast population and enormous wealth made it the most lucrative market of the age. It did not take long, moreover, for the Southeast Asian market to become saturated. Aside from the Southeast Asian elites and the few other Southeast Asians who had disposable cash incomes, the market represented by the indigenous populations of the region was limited. Nonetheless, throughout the nineteenth century, while exports of Indian opium to China grew persistently until the 1880s, Southeast Asia accounted for a steady 20 percent share of Indian opium

output. Although some was simply bought by European traders on speculation and ultimately intended for transshipment to China, much of the
opium delivered to Southeast Asian ports seems to have stayed in the region. This means that the market in Southeast Asia was expanding at about
the same rate as that in China.

The major reason for this expansion was the growth in the number of
Chinese immigrants to Southeast Asia. It was the establishment of significant settlements of Chinese laborers in the Nanyang that created the nexus
between opium and capitalism. These Chinese, most of whom were wage-
earners engaged in the production of exportable commodities, constituted
an important and ever-expanding market for opium. They, and all others
who wished to buy opium, purchased their opium from agencies known as
"opium farms," which were privately held monopolies for the processing
and retail sale of opium.

This chapter examines the opium revenue farming systems in Southeast
Asia during the nineteenth century as well as the links between these institutions and the growth of capitalist enterprises in the region. First, it will
look at the question of how and why opium taxes were farmed, and then
why it was primarily Chinese who were both the farmers and the consumers.
Next, it will look at the relationship between capitalism, the colonial state,
and the opium farms. Finally, it will attempt to explain the demise of the
farming system. The major argument offered here is that capital accumulation was intimately linked to the sale of opium to "captive" consumers.
During this period, there was a close connection between the production
of marketable commodities and the creation of consumer markets among
the labor forces that produced the commodities. In most instances, opium
was the first, and for a long time the major, item of mass consumption. It
was also the chief item of taxation. In both of these functions opium served
as one of the chief building blocks for capitalist enterprise as well as for
the colonial state in Southeast Asia. Although this link is primarily visible
in regard to Chinese capital, it can also be seen to have had a flow-on effect
for European capital.

OPIUM FARMS IN SOUTHEAST ASIA

The opium trade in Southeast Asia involved all European colonial regimes.
Britain enjoyed primacy in carriage and distribution of opium, but other
European colonial powers needed opium to finance their colonial governments, and all relied on the British to provide it. In regard to the opium
trade, they were of one mind with the British. Despite strategic and economic competition among the colonial powers, all agreed that the opium
trade should continue and that, within their dominions, they should control it and profit from it. Every single Southeast Asian colony, and Siam as

well, relied on some sort of opium farm or state monopoly for an important share of its revenue during the nineteenth and early twentieth centuries. These revenue-collecting institutions were at the heart of European colonialism in Southeast Asia.[2]

What was an opium farm? And how did it work? The operations of the opium farms were remarkably similar in most parts of Southeast Asia, particularly by the late nineteenth century. On a periodic basis, usually every three years, the government would advertise for tenders for the farm. Normally a number of individuals would submit bids promising to pay the government a fixed rent, usually on a monthly basis during the coming three years. Often, but not always, the farm would be awarded to the highest bidder. The winning farmer would then have the exclusive right to process raw opium into *chandu* (smokable opium) and retail it to consumers, or to provide it at fixed prices to licensed opium shops, divans, or other approved retailers. The farm was always limited territorially. In Singapore and Penang, it was usually for only the actual territory controlled by the British government. In Java, the Netherlands East Indies government parceled out the island in districts, usually regencies. Sumatra too was divided into residencies. Siam was divided into provinces, and Burma and the Philippines, among other places, were likewise divided into some sort of farming territories wherever there was a sufficiently affluent population.[3] There were also opium farms in British India and in most of the princely states of the subcontinent, where they produced what was known as the "abkaree" revenue. The opium revenue, as well as the revenue from liquor sales, coconut toddy, cannabis preparations (usually called *baang*), gambling, markets, pawnbroking, pork sales, and prostitution, as well as a number of other concessions, were all farmed out at various places and times in Southeast Asia during this period. This income was usually labeled "excise revenue" in colonial budgets. Similar systems existed in Hong Kong, in the Chinese treaty ports, and in Taiwan under Japanese rule. Among all of the different types of farms, the opium farms were almost always the most lucrative.[4]

The Straits Settlements was an extreme case. Trade was free and therefore could not be a source of taxation. With few permanent inhabitants, little or no agriculture, and no other products of the land, there was very little to tax. The situation stimulated commerce, but offered no solution to the problem of paying administrative expenses. Even though the traders agreed that someone should suppress piracy and maintain lighthouses on some of the more dangerous reefs, they were unwilling to accept a tax on trade to pay for these services.[5] The solution for most fiscal needs was the farming system. The Dutch had established farms in Melaka and Java by the eighteenth century, and the British followed their example, continuing the practice in Melaka and creating them in Penang. Major William Farquar, the second-in-command under Thomas Stamford Raffles, established Singapore's first revenue farms shortly after the colony's founding in 1819. The farms were placed on a more solid footing by John Crawfurd when he was resident from 1824 to 1828. For the next eighty years the entire colony was largely dependent upon the revenue from farms.[6]

The opium farm was the mainstay of the revenue. For more than a century the income gained from selling opium to the inhabitants of these settlements regularly provided between 40 and 60 percent of the locally collected revenue.[7] Other colonial settlements did not forgo the taxing of trade; moreover, they were sometimes able to tax land, agricultural production, or other exports, or to collect a capitation tax. Even with these resources, they still had budget deficits, which metropolitan governments were reluctant to cover. For all these other territories, the opium farm offered an important supplementary revenue. Between 1886 and 1895, for example, the Netherlands Indies opium farm supplied about 35 percent of the tax revenue.[8] In the French colony of Cochinchina the opium farm contributed about 30 percent of the colonial revenues between 1861 and 1882. It was also the largest single item of the budget.[9] In 1901–1902 the Siamese opium farm generated five million baht out of a total government revenue of 36 million baht, and by 1905–1906 opium farm revenue had risen to ten million baht out of a total of 52 million, or about 20 percent of the government's total revenues.[10] Although opium farms provided smaller proportions of the revenue in British Burma and the Philippines, they were, nonetheless, significant revenue generators.[11]

THE FARMS AND THE CHINESE

The opium farmers were invariably Chinese. In addition to skill in financial management, the successful farmer needed several kinds of resources. For processing the drug he needed some sort of building, equipment, and trained personnel. He was also required either to own or to control a network of retail outlets. These were opium shops, where small quantities (anywhere from a "pot" of one or two tahils, to "tubes" of several hoons) of *chandu* were sold on a take-away basis; or divans or opium dens, where the drug was smoked on the premises. The shop licenses were purchased from the government or sometimes from the farmer himself. Generally, the farmer preferred it if the shopkeepers were "his" men. Whatever the case, they had to buy their supplies from the farmer.

Beyond these facilities, it was also necessary for the farmer to control a fairly large body of private security personnel. Part of the contract was that the farmer was responsible for the integrity of his monopoly. The state passed laws to protect the revenue farming system, but it was the farmer's business to police it. The whole object of the institution was to spare the government the expense of building and maintaining an infrastructure. It was a form of outsourcing. The farmer thus controlled a private police force as well as a network of informers. In Singapore the police were called *chintengs* or revenue peons, and in the 1880s about eighty men were employed in this function. Very often these individuals were part of the local Chinese secret society or triad organization. In Java, the informers were called *matamata* or "eyes," and were often Javanese. The major job of these police and informers was to prevent the smuggling of contraband opium into the farmer's territory. In order to carry out these functions, these groups had considerable powers of search and seizure, which were occasionally abused.

These facilities were all part of the farmer's overhead. In addition, he had to purchase his stocks of raw opium on the open market and, of course, pay the government its monthly rent. What remained was his profit. It is clear that the profits could be immense, and normally the opium farmers were the wealthiest and most powerful Chinese in all of Southeast Asia. The evidence for this is quite compelling. Song Ong Siang's *One Hundred Years of Chinese History in Singapore* and more recent studies on Chinese economic leadership in colonial Southeast Asia make it clear that opium farmers ranked among the wealthiest, most powerful, and most respected Chinese in Siam and in all of the European colonies of Southeast Asia. In fact, it was necessary to already have wealth, power, and respect in order to become an opium farmer; thus it was a profession that attracted those who already had gained money and influence. It also helped them to keep it.[12]

The sources usually speak of the farmer as an individual, but by the middle of the nineteenth century, most opium farms were held by corporate bodies of investors, usually called a *kongsi* after the Chinese term for "company" *(gongsi)*. These *kongsi*, or syndicates, were generally run by cliques of the wealthiest merchants in the area. Some members undertook the actual management of the farm while others simply invested money and held shares. There were many types of *kongsi* in nineteenth-century Southeast Asia, ranging from a small group of laborers and perhaps a petty shopkeeper who invested in a small mine or a plantation, to large triad organizations, to family businesses and clan societies. The opium farming *kongsis*, however, were probably the largest locally based forms of economic organization in colonial Southeast Asia before the twentieth century. At the time, the farms were responsible for the largest cash flows in the region. Literally hundreds of thousands, sometimes millions, of dollars flowed through their coffers every month.

By the late nineteenth century many of the farms for densely populated territories, such as Singapore, Hong Kong, Saigon, and even Shanghai, demanded such large investments that funds were drawn from all over the region, and in some cases wealthy Chinese residents in one colony would buy up or invest in the farms of another colony or territory. As early as 1880, the Singapore farms came under the control of a group of Penang merchants. At the same time, a one-time farmer from Singapore had interests in the Hong Kong opium farm. Even early in the nineteenth century, merchants in Penang and Singapore frequently held farms or interests in farms in the Dutch territories of Riau and Sumatra. Later they also held interests in Javanese farms. In 1886 Lee Keng-yam, a Melaka Chinese, headed a syndicate that held both the Singapore farms and the Hong Kong farms, as well as "some Dutch farms." As time passed, the farms for adjacent territories were frequently merged by the holders. This happened even when they spanned different political boundaries. For instance, from 1870 onward the farms for the British territories of Singapore and Melaka were held by the same *kongsi* that held the farms for the Malay state of Johor and the Dutch territory of Riau.[13]

The opium farms were large, complex enterprises that involved enormous amounts of capital. As a type of economic organization they were found throughout Southeast Asia and the southern Chinese littoral. In fact, when we step back and look at it in its entirety, we see that by the late nineteenth century the opium farming syndicates constituted a large, segmented network of interconnected *kongsis* stretching from Burma to Shanghai and extending as far south as Australia. In most cases the wealthiest local Chinese clique exercised a level of control or at least participated in the farms in their area, but almost all of them depended on outside connections that usually reached beyond the borders of their particular territory. The farms thus constituted a more or less separate economic system that was dominated exclusively by Chinese. It was, moreover, a network that integrated the opium economies of Southeast Asia and connected them with those of the southern Chinese territories controlled by foreigners (i.e., Hong Kong, Macao, Taiwan, and the foreign concessions in Shanghai and in other treaty ports).

All of these farming systems depended on the Chinese. Chinese merchants were always the farmers, and very often Chinese laborers were also the major consumers. John Cameron, the Singapore newspaper editor, maintained that "by greatly enhancing the cost to the consumer the consumption is kept within narrow bounds. To the laboring classes it is all but banned and forbidden fare, and even to the rich its indulgence to excess would be a serious item of expenditure."[14] In fact, most of the other evidence available indicates that the most reliable consumers were the poorest class of laborers, the Chinese coolies. Indeed, it is hard to see how the opium farm could have paid half of Singapore's revenue if it did not sell opium to the greater portion of its population. In 1848, in one of the first substantial critiques of the opium farming system, Dr. R. Little, a Singapore surgeon, noted: "Now certain trades are greater consumers of opium than others. Amongst the principal are carpenters, box makers, blacksmiths, barbers, hunters, coolies, boatmen, and gambier planters including gardeners. These trades seem almost entirely to be devoted to the drug. I should say fully 85 percent are opium smokers."[15] When one considers that in the mid nineteenth century gambier planters alone made up more than 50 percent of Singapore's population, it is hard to see how opium could have been forbidden to anyone who could claim some kind of cash income. It is this relationship between cash and opium that is the focus of this chapter.

CHINESE FARMERS AND CHINESE SMOKERS

Initially, the development of the opium trade in Southeast Asia was limited because of the low population density and the relative lack of affluence. By the middle of the nineteenth century, however, the weight of the Chinese migration to Southeast Asia had significantly changed this equation. Chinese laborers had been migrating to Southeast Asia as laborers since the early eighteenth century, and although at the time they constituted one of several markets for imported opium, their numbers were relatively small. The growing opportunities offered by European settlements in Southeast Asia, together with the increasing population pressures in South China, the disruption resulting from the Taiping Rebellion, and other factors, caused a major explosion of Chinese migration to the region in the years after 1850. This migration began to burgeon at the same time that European merchants in Southeast Asian ports, such as Singapore, began to realize that they would not get rich by speculating in the opium trade to China, or in any branch of the China trade for that matter. The advent of clipper ships and then of steam power ended the necessity for secondary opium markets in places like Singapore. The security that Chinese capitalists found in European settlements gave them the opportunity to dominate the trade in Southeast Asian commodities to China. The China trade offered relatively few opportunities for European merchants in Southeast Asia.

The "salvation" for European merchants in the region was the trade in local products for shipment back to Europe and North America. If clipper ships and steamers took the China trade out of these merchants' hands, they also offered an expeditious means of shipping Southeast Asian commodities to the West. Furthermore, the activities of Chinese merchants, laborers, craftsmen, and retailers made this commodity trade viable. They delivered the goods. Success went to those European capitalists and local rulers who could exploit the services, the production, and the consumption of the Chinese. Perhaps John Crawfurd said it most bluntly: "I entertain so high an opinion of the industry, skill and *capacity of consumption* of the Chinese, that I consider one Chinaman equal in value to the state to *two* natives of the Coromandel coast and to four Malays at least" (italics in the original).[16] They were not only productive, they consumed, and above all they consumed opium. The opium farms were the means by which both the state and the emerging Chinese capitalists could profit.

Although there were opium farms in virtually every European colony and in Siam, there was a fairly high degree of local variation in the organization and scope of these farms. For the purposes of this discussion, it is useful to recognize several different types of farms: the Malayan pattern, the Javanese pattern, and the urban pattern. The primary differences between the first two systems relate to the ethnicity of the consumers and to the nature of the local economy. In the Malayan pattern most of the consumers were Chinese, whereas in the Javanese pattern they tended to be Southeast Asians. Another distinction was that in the Malayan pattern the farmers and the coolies who consumed the opium were usually involved in one specific type of commodity production. In the Javanese pattern the economic interests of the farmers and the general economy were far more diverse but tended to focus on the rice economy, and most of the consumers were peasant agriculturists. The third type of farm could be found in all large Asian cities and served users of a variety of ethnic backgrounds. Its special features arose from its consuming base in the urban working classes.

The Malayan system was found throughout the Malay world: that is, from the provinces of southern Siam and along both coasts of the Malay Peninsula including Singapore. It was also found in parts of Sumatra during the nineteenth century and throughout the entire island of Borneo. Some variations of it seem to have existed in certain parts of the Philippines as well, prior to 1899. The purest examples of the Javanese pattern were to be found on the island of Java and in the central plain of Siam, and to some extent this pattern also characterized the French systems in Cochinchina and Tongkin.

The differences in the two systems stemmed from key ecological factors: the Malayan system was found in the underpopulated regions of the wet tropics, where the major life form was the rainforest. The consuming population was thus largely composed of Chinese immigrants. The "Javanese" areas were places where fairly dense populations of Southeast Asian peasants had been able to establish themselves. These were more fertile areas, characterized by alluvial or volcanic soils that had given rise to more intensive forms of rice agriculture.

In the Malay states such as Perak and Johor, by the mid nineteenth century the picture was fairly simple. Virtually all of the opium consumers were Chinese coolies who worked in the tin-mining settlements, as in Perak, or on pepper and gambier plantations, as in Johor. Generally these were financed by Chinese merchants in the Straits Settlements. For much of the nineteenth century the Malayan farms could be subdivided by region and by type of industry. The merchants of Penang who invested in tin mining controlled the farms of the Malay and Siamese states that were the centers of tin mining. The Singapore merchants, on the other hand, generally drew their income from the pepper and gambier agriculture, which was based on Singapore Island, Johor, and the Riau Archipelago. For much of the nineteenth century the two economies were more or less separate systems.

The management of Chinese labor, however, was common to both areas. Almost all the laborers were very recent migrants and were housed in "*kongsi* lines" or long attap sheds located near their work sites. The coolies had either migrated voluntarily at their own expense or had been imported from China as "piglets" under something like the credit-ticket scheme, or some other type of indenture, in which the coolie broker who recruited them paid for their transportation from China. Other laborers, who came without debts, usually had a bit more latitude in choosing their employers, but they often ended up in the same sort of situation. The coolie might begin his career in the mines or plantations of the Malayan jungle with a debt of about fifteen to twenty dollars, or about a year's wages, and the cards were already stacked against him. Although his expenses were fairly low, his life was hard and lacking in virtually all amenities. Very often the only available form of diversion was the local opium shop. This was usually owned, wholly or in part, by the same capitalists who held the coolie's debt. The food shop, butcher shop, pawnshop, gambling concession, and all of the other goods and services offered to the coolies were managed under similar "company store" arrangements. It was thus very easy for the coolie to slide deeper and deeper into debt and, in the process, become addicted to opium. Such arrangements were central to the labor control system in these parts of Southeast Asia.

Opium was a key element in the creation of debt because it served so many purposes. Not only was it useful for the capitalist, but it was also highly attractive to the coolie in the jungle. The pipe in the evening served as his "rainy-day woman," and was probably as close to sexual pleasure as he was likely to get, unless he found it among his fellows. Swallowing a bit of opium in the middle of the day eased the pain in his muscles and made it possible for him to go on working through the heat. It also dulled the pain of standing for hours at a time knee-deep in bone-chilling jungle streams and mining sluices shoveling mud to separate out the ore. In contrast to the contemporary anti-opium propaganda, much evidence suggests that opium did not immediately turn its users into soporific vegetables or sunken-chested hulks. Some commentators report that coolies could work half the day, sit down for a rest, take a few puffs from an opium pipe, and then get up "refreshed" and work for several more hours. This view was expressed by John Anderson, a Singapore merchant who was interviewed by the Royal Commission on Opium, which was to investigate the trade in 1894. He spoke of seeing thousands of "Chinese miners working in swarms at tin mines, displaying physical energy and endurance that the white man, under similar conditions, could not have and apply, and at the same time keep his full health. . . . I have seen these Chinamen after working all but naked for hours together in water up to their knees, go back to their quarters, and either before or after their meal, or both, smoke a pipe or pipes of opium apparently without prejudicial effect."[17]

It can be argued, and indeed it was by many defenders of the system, that opium was a necessary "work drug" for the Chinese laborers. In addition to killing the pain of daily labor, opium was also the coolie's prophylactic against diarrhea caused by dysentery and the range of intestinal parasites that plagued one in the jungle. It also reduced fever for those attacked by malaria, blackwater fever, dengue, typhoid, and other ailments. In a world with virtually no form of medical care and in conditions that might be considered among the unhealthiest in the world, opium appeared to solve many problems. Lenore Manderson's description of health conditions on late-nineteenth-century Malayan estates, which is typical of the age, focuses mainly on bad drainage as the key to health conditions on the mines and estates.[18]

In his doctoral dissertation on the farms of Indochina Jacques Dumarest noted that despite its baneful intoxicating effects, opium was a useful medication for the numerous illnesses that are found in the Far East: "Opium constitutes a precious medication for the numerous maladies that one finds in the Far East. It is, in its turn and according to the time, both a stimulant and a relaxant, an analgesic and a bringer of sleep." It was also used against cholera, dysentery, and malaria as well as beri-beri and neurasthenia. It was a common element in many native and European remedies. Local Europeans in Indochina "smoked a little to immunize themselves against 'la cochinchinette,'" described as persistent intestinal "intoxications" thought to be caused by "salts of lead and other impurities found in the drinking water of Saigon."[19] Of course, opium only appeared to cure these afflictions; it did not actually cure anything, but simply masked the symptoms and made it possible for an individual to ignore the messages of his body and to go on working for yet another day. In all probability, opium made it possible for the coolie to wear out his body even more quickly but in a relatively painless fashion.

Other observers had a far more critical view of the impact of opium on its users. As early as 1809 a witness before the Penang Grand Jury claimed that opium so debilitated the mind and body that "those who use it are in a short time so debased as to become incapable of any exertion, and their bodies . . . rendered totally unfit and unable to perform or undergo any corporal labour or fatigue." As a result, "they are under the necessity of resorting to robbery, plunder and depredation to enable them to procure . . . this pernicious drug."[20] Those who follow the drug debates in the

United States in the late twentieth century will realize that people have been saying some of the same things about drugs for centuries. There is no need to discount this report any more than John Anderson's, but we do not have much clear evidence about how long it took for an individual to be transformed from the coolies that Anderson saw to those described by the Penang witness. There is also no reliable information on how long an individual could smoke opium before he became addicted, nor do we know how long a habit could be maintained at a given level.

The amounts that the average smoker used were matters of speculation and incidental reports. J. D. Kerr said that in China the heaviest opium smokers consumed between 16.2 and 90 grams per day. Laurent said that a heavy smoker consumed 20 to 40 grams a day; a Singapore doctor had a patient who used 243 grams daily. The price of opium in Singapore stayed below one dollar per tahil (37.6 grams) until 1862. By 1864 it had risen to two dollars; at the same time, rice was two dollars per picul (about 60 kilograms). Descours-Gatin argues that in eighteen days an ordinary smoker spent as much on opium as he would to feed himself for two months, but if we take the above figures, a worker who made five dollars per month could easily spend his entire wage in just a few days on opium.[21] If the worker were willing to smoke dross (the remains left from a previous smoker), he could economize. These cheaper preparations are probably what most of the poorer smokers used. That the system was designed to get coolies into debt seems obvious. Even more so is the proposition that the system depended on most of them never getting out of debt, and on a significant proportion of them being permanently trapped by opium in the cycle of labor, indebtedness, addiction, and ultimately death.

Given the prospects of survival in the jungles, however, one might suspect that the coolies probably took the easiest way out. Manderson's statistics for the late nineteenth and early twentieth centuries in Malaya show that death rates on the plantations generally varied between about 50 and 250 per 1,000 workers annually, but in other cases 50 percent of new arrivals could die within the first year.[22] Warrington Smyth, an English mining engineer who worked for the Siamese government, estimated that the death rate for mining coolies in southern Siam was about 60 percent overall, and for new arrivals it was even higher. The main causes of death were fever and dysentery. Smyth's greatest concern was that word of an epidemic would cause a panic among the laborers and they all would flee. He indicated that a mine owner could lose 70 percent of his work force through desertion. This was the other great incentive to provide the coolies with a regular supply of opium. Without opium, coolies would desert. With it, at least they could forget their problems for a while.[23]

One could argue that regardless of the level of suffering and the dismal existence of the Chinese coolie in the jungle, his life would possibly have been even shorter and more brutish had he been condemned to stay in China. There he faced unemployment, landlessness, overcrowding, disease, warfare, and banditry as well as grinding poverty. Moreover, he probably would have been so poor that he would not have been able to afford opium. In the jungles of Malaya, Sumatra, Borneo, or the islands, at least there seemed to be a chance that a coolie (if he could resist the temptation of opium) could save his money, guard his health, and perhaps rise out of the muck. He could become, if not a wealthy *taukeh* (boss or merchant) himself, at least possessed of enough money to come home with a small share of capital, find a wife, and have a better life than he might have had otherwise. Even if he was unsuccessful, he might have passed his short life with the comfort of opium. Dr. Little saw another possible future for these workers. In 1848 he wondered how different life would be for the Chinese coolies he saw in Singapore if, instead of buying opium, they spent their hard-earned money on better food, clothing, and houses. They could then afford to marry, settle down, and develop a taste for the finer things.[24] His was an idealistic vision, which would have had little short-term benefit for the Singapore capitalists or for the Singapore treasury.

Opium was not peripheral to the system as Dr. Little seems to have assumed; it was central. Were it not for opium, there would have been little profit for the capitalist. His tin, pepper, gambier, and even gold would have been barely competitive on the world market. If the cost of employing labor were not recaptured by the capitalist and recycled, as it were, there would have been no profit. This was certainly the case for the pepper and gambier economy that characterized all of the Chinese laboring settlements of Singapore, Johor, Riau, and later Negri Sembilan.[25] Since the sale of gambier and pepper in the Singapore market could pay for little more than the cost of the labor, there would have been no profit unless the investor could recoup the labor costs. This was done through the mechanism of the opium farm. Smyth makes the point that mining capitalists also depended on the opium revenue: "The Chinese 'tauke' is in a position to work mines which no one else could possibly make pay. Very often he does not look to the actual mining for a profit but to the gambling, opium, and spirit shops attached to the kongsi, and to the food and stores with which he supplies his coolies."[26]

All of the Chinese settlements in the jungle produced exportable commodities. The investors who hired the labor and financed the production also held shares in the opium farms. They could easily afford to "pay" their coolies three or four dollars per month, partly because this was usually only a bookkeeping transaction. Emily Sadka pointed out that the administrators of British Malaya not only understood the connection between opium farming and commodity production, but acted to facilitate it. Generally, they made sure that the largest investors in a district also received the farms.[27]

Opium thus served a number of purposes among the Chinese in the Malay world. In the first instance, it met what may seem the misguided but very real physical and psychic needs of the users. This is why there was a demand. Because they earned a cash income, they could afford to buy opium. They paid the long-term costs of satisfying those needs both in terms of contracting a chemical dependency as well as in whatever damage was done to them physically by the difficulty of their labors. Opium also left them in debt and deprived them of their wages. Opium thus served the colonial state and provided an easily collected revenue from those who were least able and least likely to protest the exaction. It served the Chinese entrepreneurs by giving them a large cash flow together with the means of continually compounding their profits through the relationship between opium farming and commodity production. By providing the workers with opium, they were often able to recoup a very large proportion of their labor costs. It was thus possible to bring important commodities to market at very low prices. This factor served the needs of European capitalists and, by extension, European industry, which was thus able to procure strategic commodities at rock-bottom prices. It seemed the perfect system for the rulers of Southeast Asian colonies.

The problem for the governments, however, lay in the fact that the different mining and planting zones were not coterminous with political or administrative territories. For instance, the pepper and gambier area around Singapore included the Dutch territories in Riau, the Malay state of Johor, and the other British territory of Melaka. Goods, labor, and capital moved freely within this early "growth triangle." On the other hand, all of the farms were leased separately by the different governments. This circumstance required that if they wished to protect the integrity of their monopolies, the various administrations had to cooperate in leasing the farms, often letting them as a package or at least agreeing to give them to the same holder. If they did not, then the holder of the most valuable farm, such as that of Singapore, often needed to buy all of the other farms in surrounding territories in order to prevent smuggling. Otherwise, competing syndicates would buy farms in adjoining territories and work to undercut him. The rulers of these other territories were often tempted to demand premium prices for their farms simply on the basis of their nuisance value. There was, thus, every incentive for farming syndicates to transgress political boundaries and to become truly "international."

This circumstance placed the Chinese opium farmers in an anomalous but vital position. On the one hand, they became the customs officers for the newly created colonial territories. The opium farming districts were among the first "borders" in colonial Southeast Asia that were actively enforced. On the other hand, both capital needs and the practical necessity of combating smugglers meant that these "foreign Asians" also transgressed colonial administrative and political boundaries. Their syndicates regularly combined the farms of adjacent polities under a single administrative center and just as often sought capital from outside sources. It may seem ironic, but the recognition and reassertion of these boundaries by Chinese opium farmers gave a reality to the territories that would ultimately become the new nations of Southeast Asia.

Because of the potential for smuggling, the opium farms were almost always connected to the secret societies that flourished in Chinese communities throughout Southeast Asia. The historical development of the societies was largely affected by their relationship to the farms. Initially, perhaps in the early nineteenth century, the societies seem to have been simply ritual brotherhoods that underlaid the partnership agreements that bound the mining and planting *kongsis* together. These appear at first to have been partnerships among laborers, planters, and capitalists. The societies also provided self-defense forces for settlements in the jungle that were far away from colonial protection. As time passed, the societies became the muscle for the planters, mine owners, and *taukehs*. They came to be made up of toughs who intimidated the coolies and protected the economic interests of the merchants. In particular they were necessary to protect the opium farms, or conversely to attack the farms of rival syndicates. This was certainly their role in places like Singapore, Penang, and the tin-mining states of western Malaya during the mid nineteenth century.

In the years when competing opium syndicates fought for control of the various farming territories, the secret societies flourished because they had direct access to the major economic institutions of the region. By the late 1860s, however, their influence began to wane. One cause for this seems to have been the efforts by the moneyed interests of the Straits Settlements to reach compromises in controlling the opium farms. In 1870, the "Great Opium Syndicate" was formed in Singapore.[28] This syndicate represented the combined capital of Hokkien, Teochew, and Johor interests in the settlement, and also united the opium farms of Singapore, Johor, Riau, and Melaka. This development was a serious blow to the triad societies because it meant that the merchants could dispense with a large number of their enforcers. The result was that after 1870 more and more "illegal" societies began to appear, representing, it seems, those who no longer shared in the largesse of the opium farmers. There was thus a natural tendency toward industrywide monopoly combinations. Unfortunately, such combinations also worked against the fiscal interests of the colonial states, which hoped that competition would increase their revenues. In Malaya and other places with similar farming systems, by 1870 it probably began to seem that the farming syndicates had become an indispensable branch of government, and one upon which the colonial governments were largely dependent. Their very success now began to work against them.

PEASANTS AND *TAUKEHS*

Although the Javanese type of opium farm was found in areas where there were fairly dense populations of Southeast Asian peasants, there were still many Chinese consumers. As in the other areas, however, the farmers were almost always Chinese. In Java the smoking of opium had been practiced since the seventeenth century. By the nineteenth, the economies of the business had become more closely regulated. Every regency had its own opium farm and the business was highly competitive. One account described the opium farm auction as the "battle of kings," in which the wealthiest, most powerful Chinese in Java gathered to outdo one another in their fight for the concession.[29]

Colonial governments in these places had to be a little more circumspect about the opium farming system. Particularly towards the end of the nineteenth century, when colonial governments felt the need to justify their existence by claiming that they were working for the welfare of the natives, it was difficult to explain the opium farms to the metropolitan public. In Malaya, Burma, and the Philippines, on the other hand, the farms could be justified on the ground that they merely served the "sojourning" Chinese, who would not remain if they did not get their opium—and thus the work would not get done. The French and Dutch often tried to claim that opium smoking was primarily a Chinese vice. In Cochinchina, they pointed out that the average Chinese smoker consumed 1.4 kilograms annually, compared to only 200 grams for the average Vietnamese smoker. Moreover, while nearly 40 percent of the Chinese population used opium, only 2 percent of the Vietnamese used it. Of course, the Chinese population was overwhelmingly young, male, and gainfully employed. They were, moreover, far outnumbered by the Vietnamese, who had a much more balanced age and sex distribution and who did not usually participate in the cash economy. Among the Vietnamese, the French claimed that only the very rich or the very poor smoked opium—those who had long hours of nothing to do, *les personnes oisives* (the idle rich) or *l'oisiveté* (the unemployed).[30] These arguments, too, tended to downplay the impact of opium on the native population. In Siam, after several decades of unsuccessfully attempting to ban opium in the kingdom, a farming system was finally permitted and opium sales were legalized. This took place on the eve of the Bowring Treaty, which opened Siam to European commerce. Here too, the claim was made that the farm was primarily to serve the Chinese consumer.[31]

Despite the rather tortured arguments about only providing opium for Chinese users and forbidding it to the "natives," it seems clear that in both Java and Indochina, natives formed an important group of users. This was probably also the case in central Siam. Cochinchina represented the largest opium-consuming area in the colony, and Tongkin in the north was the second largest consuming area. It is difficult to ascertain the precise number of users in either place, and even more difficult to distinguish Vietnamese from Chinese users. In Java, the natives were the major users of the drug. In both places, farmers prepared several cheaper grades of opium intended for the less affluent native smokers.[32] These varied in quality. Such products often represented even greater profits for the opium dealer, since these preparations were little more than recycled opium that had already been sold to someone else at full price.[33]

The other major difference between these (Javanese-type) farms and those in British Malaya was that the farmers, if they were to succeed, found it necessary to form patronage relationships with existing Southeast Asian elites. This was especially important in Siam, where patronage was at the heart of the entire political economy, but it was also true in Java.[34] Because the native participants in the alliances in Siam were members of the government, the farming system was more deeply entrenched in the Thai state than elsewhere. There were very close links between the Chinese revenue farmers and the Thai elite. Not only did influential Chinese gain Siamese titles, but many of them intermarried with the Thai elite, both in the court and among the provincial elite families. By contrast, the appearance of these alliances was far less welcome in the Netherlands Indies, where the Dutch rulers were suspicious of such informal linkages. Nevertheless, Chinese farmers there regularly cultivated patronage links with Javanese officials.

Something similar happened in French Indochina. Very soon after establishing themselves in Cochinchina, the French attempted to do away with the opium farms that had existed under the Nguyen regime, and tried to place them under a government monopoly, or at least give the farms to European investors. Neither alternative was successful, and by 1864 the colonial government gave the farms to a Cantonese syndicate in Saigon. Later the Hokkien merchants saw the profits that the Cantonese syndicate gained, and formed the Banhap *kongsi* to bid for the farms themselves.[35] This group held the farms until 1881, but there were continual squabbles with the government over the terms of the contract.[36]

The Banhap clique was known for its methodical organization of the farms. In each district it set up a central trading post for opium. It also named a European agent in each district who had charge of relations with the French colonial authorities. These agents, called the first *douaniers Cochinchinois* or Cochinchinese customs agents, had extensive powers to pursue smugglers, powers they quickly misused to enrich themselves and gain commercial advantages.[37] Abuses such as these made it obvious that the farmers had gained an excessive amount of power within the colony. This was also the case in British and Dutch colonies, though other factors made such activity more tolerable in those places.

At the heart of the problem was the increasing unease on the part of all colonial governments about the commercialization of the Southeast Asian peasantry. If peasants smoked opium, they needed a cash income or at least a source of cash. Often this meant going into debt, either to the opium farmer himself or to one of the opium shopkeepers, in order to pay for opium. In most cases, a person's land or future rice crop could be pledged against such obligations. As a result, colonial administrators and local elites found that Chinese were developing networks of debtors throughout the countryside and acquiring control of both land and produce.

These developments helped lead the French to a speedy elimination of the farms and to the creation of government monopolies. In Indochina the "native welfare argument" was an important part of the government's campaign to take over the farms and organize a government monopoly or *régie*. Use of opium by the Vietnamese population was portrayed as the work of "greedy" Chinese opium farmers. Some have seen the French policy as one of divide and rule. Vietnamese representatives on the Colonial Council pressured the French to control the Chinese, who they claimed were abusing, exploiting, and mistreating the Vietnamese. It was said that the Chinese had gained a monopoly over trade in Cochinchina. The French were thus able to exploit ethnic tensions and push the Chinese out of the farming business.[38]

THE URBAN FARMS

In the long run, wherever they were located, the farms got progressively larger and more valuable with the passage of time. There was a direct relationship between the growth of the economy and the increase in opium smoking. Not only did revenues grow, but so too did the number of users and the amount of opium consumed. Again, it is difficult to draw conclusions about cause and effect. On the one hand, we might conclude that as people got more money, they tended to spend it on opium. On the other hand, perhaps the need to satisfy a habit gave people an incentive to work for a cash income. Whatever the case, opium and commercialization went together. Wherever there was cash, there was opium to soak it up, and people who used opium needed cash to pay for it.

Farms that included large urban areas grew the fastest, and ultimately these became the most important opium farming territories. As this happened, new complications in the farming system began to appear. The connection between the farming system and one particular productive industry tended to become less and less important. The "islands" of commodity production that had characterized the Southeast Asian economic landscape in the mid nineteenth century (the gambier and pepper plantations, the tin mines, the gold mines, etc.) now became less prominent as urban economies expanded and became the focus of more permanent population clusters. In the middle of the nineteenth century probably a majority of Singapore's opium users, for instance, actually resided in the rural parts of the island and made their living as pepper and gambier planters. By the 1880s, however, many of the planters had moved on to Johor and Riau and the urban area had grown both in physical size and in influence. The Singapore farm thus became a truly urban farm, serving a variegated population of coolies, craftsmen, dock laborers, rickshaw pullers, and the entire range of city-based occupations. In Singapore, for instance, at the turn of the century, there were twenty thousand rickshaw pullers in the city. These enormous populations of young men, mostly single and engaged in hard physical labor, were ideal consumers for opium.

This level of occupational as well as ethnic variety meant that a link to the gambier industry was much less necessary for success in revenue farming ventures. It now became necessary to control only urban neighborhoods, and as colonial police forces became better trained and more numerous there was less need to rely on secret societies and other bodies of violent individuals. Similar trends occurred in other large Southeast Asian cities such as Batavia, Penang, Saigon, Bangkok, and possibly Manila. The same was true in Hong Kong. These developments began to bring the farms within the grasp of colonial administrations.

Because of their sheer size, the urban farms now required large amounts of capital to finance them. Often these sums could not be raised from within a single urban center, and even less often would there be more than one group of capitalists capable of raising such sums in one center. It was not only possible but also necessary for the colonial government to seek bidders from outside a given colony. Anyone would do, so long as he had the money and the will. All of these factors tended to enhance the power of the government vis-à-vis the farmers and the partnership between revenue farmers and colonial states began to be seen as less and less necessary.[39] In fact, in many places it now became possible to believe that the farms themselves were no longer necessary.

THE END OF THE FARMING SYSTEM

The French and the Dutch in their colonies in Indochina and the Netherlands Indies were less willing to tolerate excessive power in the hands of the Chinese than were the British. After 1881 the French again attempted to organize a government monopoly. They abolished the farming system in 1883 and created a government monopoly (*régie directe*) but it was still under the control of the same Chinese who had previously run the opium farm. It was actually run in very much the same fashion as before, but the degree of government control and profit was increased.[40] By the 1890s even the Dutch began to worry about their "partnership" with the Chinese and, when the French *régie* in Indochina appeared to prove successful, the Dutch were quick to emulate it in Java, where they established their own government monopoly.[41]

In Java the move toward eliminating the farm was spurred by its increasing value and the increasing level of competition that now appeared in the bidding process. Although colonial governments generally welcomed competition, they found that Chinese were often willing to bid far more than the farms were worth. Once having gained the contract, the farmers would petition for relief and attempt to renegotiate the contract on more favorable terms. The government was often at a disadvantage in such situations because it was difficult to re-auction the farms if the farmer went bankrupt. The chance of receiving equivalent bids, particularly after one farmer had gone broke, was unlikely. The value of the farm would have been diminished in everyone's eyes. Often the government found it best to accept a deal with the farmer, but such compromises were costly, both in pride and in anticipated revenue.

The other eventuality, after furious bidding wars, was that the disappointed competitor would resort to smuggling. An individual could simply bid to control the farms of an adjoining regency and would then have a base from which to undercut his rival. There was a fairly well established pattern of such cross-border smuggling. Growing dissatisfaction with the farming system in Java came to a head in the mid 1890s, following a wave of bankruptcies and spectacular failures among some of the more prominent farming syndicates.[42]

Even within the British colonies there had always been a certain level of debate regarding the morality, usefulness, and appropriateness of the farms. Most Europeans supported the institution, however, and few Asian voices were raised in objection to it. The British in both the Straits Settlements and Malaya maintained the farming system for the longest period of time, only abolishing it in 1909. Here too, however, the appearance of significant financial troubles led to the abolition of the farms. In the years between 1907 and 1909, Southeast Asia was hit by one of its periodic economic crashes. Commodity prices in the Singapore market fell precipitously in mid 1907, shortly after a syndicate of Penang Chinese led by Khaw Joo Choe, a member of the powerful Khaw clan, had just offered an enormously large increase in the annual opium farm rent. Shortly before that, the same syndicate had also acquired the farms for Penang, parts of

Sumatra, parts of southern Siam, and for Bangkok itself. The collapse of this syndicate was taken as a major wake-up call by the British and Siamese governments. This financial crisis, together with a new wave of pressures against the opium trade generated by events in the Philippines and in China, now led the British government in Malaya to abandon the farming system completely. The Siamese government, whose farms were closely integrated into the financial systems of the Straits Settlements, also abolished their farms at that time.[43]

In the Philippines the farming system ended slightly earlier than those in British Malaya and Siam, but no opium monopoly replaced it. Rather, the Philippines were the first Asian possession in which opium was forbidden altogether. Following the annexation of the islands by the United States in 1899, the U.S. Congress, under pressure from missionary interests and others, sent a commission of inquiry to the new colony. The result of this mission was a complete prohibition against opium smoking in the Philippines. The United States was the first major Western power to move decisively to ban opium in any part of Asia. This was the first step in the process of banning the opium trade on an international level.[44]

The American policy in the Philippines came with the British and Chinese agreement to end the trade in China. These events ended opposition to the abolition of the opium farms in British Malaya and Siam, but did little more. Both the Siamese and the British now followed the French and the Dutch and replaced their farming systems with government-run monopolies. This turned out to be good business. The new monopolies proved far more profitable than the old opium farms.[45] Profits continued to rise until 1920, when Britain and other European powers were finally forced to effectively restrict opium use in their colonies. In that year net profits from opium sales reached the all-time high of more than twenty million dollars for the three Straits Settlements. Even after a decade of restrictive measures, net profits for the Straits opium monopoly were still in excess of $8 million in 1929. Opium profits and actual usage only declined in a serious way with the global depression and the slump in trade during the 1930s.

THE RESULTS OF THE OPIUM EMPIRE

The opium farming system not only paid for free trade in the Straits Settlements and made a few Chinese businessmen very wealthy, it also had some important structural results. The establishment of commodity-producing settlements also created Southeast Asia's first class of wage-earners. Opium turned them into wage-spenders, or what we now call consumers. These coolies now produced for a market, sold to the market, calculated the value of their labor in the market, and bought from the market. They probably constituted the first mass market in Southeast Asia. Even though opium was only one among the products that these laborers purchased, for indeed all of their necessities came from the same stores controlled by the same *taukehs*, it can be argued that opium gave their consumption a different character. On the one hand, opium was not a necessity, but on the other, it was an item for which the demand was potentially unlimited. The need for food, clothing, and tools could be satisfied, but the need for opium by an addict was sure to grow. Opium needs to be understood as a very different sort of commodity; as a drug, its impact on the market should be compared with that of other mass consumer drug products such as tobacco, alcohol, tea, coffee, and sugar. Mass consumption of essential non-necessities is one of the first hallmarks of the modern, industrial-age market.

For Chinese coolies of nineteenth-century Southeast Asia the opiate of the masses was the real thing, whereas the twentieth-century consumer often has only Coca-Cola. The opium farming system had a similar impact on the peasant economies of Java, Siam, and Vietnam. It brought peasants into the cash economy as modern consumers. It also made them into debtors, very often stripping them of control over their lands and labor and replacing earlier forms of debt bondage with the new, improved commercialized system of dependence.

The opium farming system also was the primary vehicle of capital accumulation for Chinese during a large part of the nineteenth century. The revenue farms were their cash cows, providing capital that could be freely redirected into an array of investments. Although we do not know the average interest that could be earned from a share in an opium farming *kongsi*, it was not inconsiderable; moreover, in a largely unregulated economy, the opium farms were relatively secure.[46] The farmers were men of substance who had the confidence of the government. Shares in the revenue farms were something like shares of stock. They were negotiable and could be bought and sold.[47] In addition to providing liquid capital for investment, the opium farms also served as a vehicle for attracting and accumulating savings from within the community. It is no accident that the first Asian banks in the region were organized by revenue farmers. Although they were still a subservient bourgeoisie, the revenue farmers had played a major role in creating Southeast Asia's first local capitalist class.

Jennifer Cushman's account of the rise and fall of the Khaw / Na Ranong dynasty shows how opium farming could serve as a springboard from traditional Chinese business to complex corporate endeavors.[48] At the beginning of the twentieth century Khaw Sim Bee, along with his brothers, cousins, in-laws, and other affiliates, controlled vast holdings of tin mines both in British Malaya and in southern Siam. Sim Bee was also the Siamese governor of Ranong province in southern Siam and held a number of revenue-farming concessions, government positions, and other honors from the Thai government. The family controlled tin smelting works and steam dredges, owned the Eastern Shipping Company, and had its own insurance company. At the core of this empire was the extensive, interlocked amalgamation of revenue farms controlled by Khaw Joo Choe. In 1907 this included Singapore, Melaka, Penang, a number of farms in southern Siam and in Sumatra, and an important share of the Bangkok opium farm. These holdings were expected to play a vital role in providing a source of ready cash for the other enterprises in the empire. When the farming syndicate collapsed in the economic downturn of 1907, the entire corporate construct began to disintegrate.

Although European merchants and speculators found much to criticize in the opium farming system, it was actually of great benefit to them. Because it was so closely tied to commodity production by the Asian masses (whether Chinese coolie or Javanese or Vietnamese peasant made no difference), opium farming had the effect of bringing products to market far more cheaply than would have been possible otherwise. This effect enhanced the marketability of Southeast Asian products in the West; it also saved the Europeans from taxation.

Perhaps the colonial governments reaped the greatest benefit from the opium farming system. The farms supplied hard currency for the day-to-day operations of colonial administrations. The statistics show that the opium farm was, for most of the nineteenth century, one of the major props of every colonial state. This was even more the case in Siam, where tax revenues from traditional sources (such as the land tax and others that came through the *krom* or government divisions) were highly irregular. The revenue farming income was a dependable and never-failing source of revenue for the state during the period during which Chulalongkorn undertook the modernization of Siamese governmental structures.[49]

Opium and the opium farming system supplied the necessary framework within which the new state structures of Southeast Asia were erected. The farms served similar functions in British Malaya, in the Netherlands East Indies, and in French Indochina. The revenue farms, and in particular the opium farms, were analogous to the bamboo scaffolding one sees on the construction sites of the modern skyscrapers of Hong Kong, Southeast Asia, and China. It looks messy, incredibly low-tech, and very much out of place in a modern urban setting. And yet it does the job cheaply and effectively where almost nothing else could substitute.

The opium farms marked the boundaries of the new political-administrative structures. The licensing of farms to cover specific territories was very often the first move by a colonial government to give reality to its claim of sovereignty within the domain it claimed. Prior to the nineteenth century, there were no real land boundaries in Southeast Asia, and very often colonial administrative lines did not coincide with pre-existing political or cultural divisions. The redrawing of boundaries was one of the main legacies of the European empire in Asia. All modern Southeast Asian states are the product of colonial mapping. The opium farms were the first regular institutions that effectively marked and affirmed the administrative boundaries of the new political units. In most cases, the opium farmer's *chintengs, mata-mata,* or revenue peons were the first customs agents of the colonial states. The smuggling struggles between farming syndicates in the nineteenth century were, in effect, one of the arenas where these lines were asserted. The act of policing the borders defined them and made them real. Even though Chinese revenue farmers held farms in a number of different territories, the very fact that they recognized the sovereignty and legitimacy of the new colonial regimes that laid claim to the areas was an important step in the revolution of meaning that was taking place in the region. When it was no longer necessary to hold up the edifice, the farms were pulled down and discarded and replaced with government monopolies. The new states, however, remained. So did the classes of Chinese capitalists, coolies, and consumers: the new political economy had been created.

Opium and the opium farming system need to be seen as having played a key role in the fiscal, economic, political, and administrative development of Southeast Asia. They supported the state financially in an era when few other resources were available to colonial administrations. They were important in the creation of markets, consumers, commodities, and capitalists. Opium farms structured the key relationship between the colonial state and indigenous capital that was fundamental to the colonial political economy. When the farms were eliminated, that relationship underwent an important change. Finally, the opium farms, as expressions of colonial territoriality, helped to enforce the new map that Europeans had drawn in the region.

NOTES

1. Engelbert Kaempher, a German physician working for the Dutch East India Company, recorded that the Javanese "mix with it, tobacco diluted with water so that when kindled the head spins more violently. In Java, I saw flimsy sheds [made of] reeds in which this kind of tobacco was set out [for sale] to passers-by. No commodity throughout the Indies is retailed with greater return by the Batavians than opium, which [its] users cannot do without, nor can they come by it except it be brought by ships of the Batavians from Bengal and Coromandel" (Kaempfero, *Amoenitatum exoticarum,* p. 650).
2. Butcher, "Demise of the Revenue Farm System."
3. Brown, "Ministry of Finance"; John Cameron, "The Opium Farm," *The*

Straits Times, 11 April 1863; Cameron, *Our Tropical Possessions in Malayan India;* Crawfurd, *History of the Indian Archipelago;* Rush, *Opium to Java;* Trocki, "Rise of Singapore's Great Opium Syndicate"; Wickberg, *Chinese in Philippine Life,* p. 115; Butcher, "Demise of the Revenue Farm System."

4. Singapore had a gambling farm briefly during the 1820s and early 1830s; for three or four years it earned more than the opium farm, but the Indian government, under pressure from Parliament, decided that it was immoral and therefore abolished it. Johor maintained a gambling farm, as did many other Malay rulers, the Dutch, and the Siamese, but none earned more revenue than opium.

5. Turnbull, *History of Singapore.*

6. Trocki, *Opium and Empire;* Lin Ken Wong, "Revenue Farms of Prince of Wales Island."

7. Trocki, *Opium and Empire.*

8. Diehl, "Revenue Farming and Colonial Finances," p. 208.

9. Descours-Gatin, *Quand l'opium finançait la colonisation en Indochine,* pp. 100–1; Nankoe, Gerlus, and Murray, "Origins of the Opium Trade," p. 189.

10. Brown, "End of the Opium Farm in Siam," p. 233.

11. Brown, "Imperialism, Trade and Investment," pp. 80–88; Le Failler, "Le mouvement international anti-opium et l'Indochine"; Butcher, "Demise of the Revenue Farm System"; Rush, *Opium to Java.*

12. Song, *One Hundred Years' History of the Chinese in Singapore.*

13. Cushman, *Family and State;* Cushman and Godley, "Khaw Concern," pp. 267–71; Godley, *Mandarin Capitalists from Nanyang,* and "Thio Thiau Siat's Network," pp. 262–66; Brown, "End of the Opium Farm in Siam"; Butcher, "Demise of the Revenue Farm System"; Le Failler, "Le mouvement international anti-opium"; Rush, *Opium to Java;* Song, *One Hundred Years' History;* Trocki, "Demise of Singapore's Great Opium Syndicate"; Wickberg, *Chinese in Philippine Life.*

14. Cameron, *Our Tropical Possessions in Malayan India,* p. 217.

15. R. E. Little, "On the Habitual Use of Opium in Singapore," pp. 20–21.

16. Crawfurd, Untitled note, p. 410.

17. Royal Commission on Opium, *First Report,* 5:175.

18. Manderson, *Sickness and the State,* pp. 132–33.

19. Dumarest, "Les monopoles de l'opium et du sel en Indochine," pp. 32–33.

20. Quoted in H. R. C. Wright, *East-Indian Economic Problems of the Age of Cornwallis and Raffles,* pp. 167–68.

21. Descours-Gatin, *Quand l'opium financait la colonisation en Indochine,* pp. 213–14.

22. Manderson, *Sickness and the State,* pp. 128–35.

23. Smyth, *Five Years in Siam,* 2:20–21.

24. R. E. Little, "On the Habitual Use of Opium," pp. 73–74.

25. Trocki, *Prince of Pirates.*

26. Smyth, *Five Years in Siam,* 1:328.

27. Sadka, *Protected Malay States,* pp. 333–34: "Capitalists who already had a large stake in the country were in a strong position when it came to tendering for the farms, for a number of reasons; they were in a position to expand their enterprises if their applications were successful, and restrict production and immigration in an

attempt to break the farm if they were not; and since their prosperity was of some importance to the state, there was an incentive to support them financially by giving them the farms."

28. Trocki, "Demise of Singapore's Great Opium Syndicate."

29. Rush, *Opium to Java,* p. 41.

30. Descours-Gatin, *Quand l'opium financait la colonisation en Indochine,* p. 213–14.

31. Viraphol, *Tribute and Profit,* p. 234.

32. The first grade was *chandu,* which was made from good-quality Bengal opium. In Java, the second-quality opium was *cacak,* intended for the "mass market," which was made with cheaper Turkish opium and adulterated with burnt sugar, lemon juice, and *jijing* or opium dross (the burnt remains of good opium). *Jijing* was also sold as yet a cheaper grade to poorer smokers. Finally, there was *tiké,* made from *cakak,* chopped leaves, and other adulterants. Similar cheap grades existed in other places. These were sold to the less affluent natives and the poorer Chinese. Rush, *Opium to Java,* pp. 53–55.

33. Ibid.

34. Ibid.; Wilson, "Revenue Farming, Economic Development and Government Policy."

35. Dumarest, "Les monopoles de l'opium," pp. 44–45.

36. Nankoe, Gerlus, and Murray, "Origins of the Opium Trade," pp. 184–86.

37. Dumarest, "Les monopoles de l'opium," p. 45.

38. Nankoe, Gerlus, and Murray, "Origins of the Opium Trade," pp. 190–91.

39. Trocki, *Opium and Empire.*

40. Nankoe, Gerlus, and Murray, "Origins of the Opium Trade," p. 191.

41. Rush, *Opium to Java.*

42. Ibid.

43. Brown, "End of the Opium Farm in Siam."

44. Owen, *British Opium Policy in China and India,* pp. 327–28.

45. For the British in Singapore, this shift led to a decade of enormous profits from opium. In 1909, the year before the opium farms were abolished in the Straits Settlements, the Singapore farm brought the government slightly more than $2.5 million, which was $400,000 short of the contracted amount. In 1910 the government shifted to a state monopoly, and although profits for that first year fell back to only $1.8 million, the situation quickly improved. In 1911 the government netted $3 million, and by 1914 net profits from opium sales were in excess of $5 million annually. In the Netherlands Indies there was a similar trend. In 1895 the opium farm delivered f17.7 million, and in 1925 the government-controlled *régie* delivered f41.9 million. Trocki, *Opium and Empire,* pp. 203–4; Diehl, "Revenue Farming and Colonial Finance," p. 208.

46. Trocki, *Opium and Empire,* and "Demise of Singapore's Great Opium Syndicate."

47. Trocki, *Prince of Pirates.*

48. Cushman, "The Khaw Group," pp. 58–79; Cushman, *Family and State.*

49. Wilson, "Revenue Farming, Economic Development and Government Policy": "The administrative reorganization of the 1880s and 1890s was a major act of statecraft, one that created a viable modern state, recognised as such by all outside

observers and other nations. The role of the tax farms in all of this was to provide a basic level of revenue stability that made it possible for the restructuring of the administrative system to take place. At some point—it is not clear when—the payments of *suai* [traditional taxes] must have dropped to very little. The imposition of a capitation tax must have taken some time to implement and enforce.''

FOUR

The Hong Kong Opium Revenue, 1845–1885

Christopher Munn

For nearly a century, between 1845 and 1941, the Hong Kong government drew a large revenue from opium.[1] During the nineteenth century this revenue was usually derived from a tax on the retail sale and processing of opium within the colony, and was raised through a monopoly, or farm, leased periodically to the highest bidder. The Hong Kong monopoly was a variant of the many colonial opium monopolies in the region. In particular, it closely resembled the Singapore monopoly, which successive governors of Hong Kong held up as a successful model worth imitating. Like its Singapore counterpart, the Hong Kong opium monopoly linked imperial processes with local trading systems and played an important role in creating Chinese capital and strengthening Chinese elites. The Hong Kong monopoly also had its own special problems and characteristics. Much more than the Singapore monopoly, it came to rely heavily on its export market in the Chinese communities of North America and Australia. This long-range trade complemented the profitable traffic in labor between Hong Kong and the New World, but it also produced instability in the opium revenue through competition from rival colonial farms. Because Hong Kong was also the central depot for the wholesale export of opium to China, the Hong Kong government found it necessary to differentiate this larger, vital imperial trade from the local retail trade covered by the monopoly: it was concerned both to prevent the larger trade from submerging the retail monopoly and to prevent the monopoly from driving the larger trade away from its base in Hong Kong. Later in the century, it also sought to protect China's revenue from being undermined by the smuggling fostered by the colony's opium industry. The government's difficulties in balancing these interests and its attempts to obtain a larger revenue led to periodic crises, some of which threatened to destroy the delicate relationship between government and Chinese capitalists that formed the basis of the monopoly.

The Hong Kong government's greatest preoccupation was with the outstanding success of the Singapore monopoly. Hong Kong officials could never understand why their own opium monopoly produced only a fraction of the revenue brought in by the Singapore monopoly when Hong Kong had a larger Chinese population, access to millions of smokers on the mainland, and a flourishing export market. Successive governors tried various methods to stimulate the revenue, by stirring up competition for the farm, for example, or by changing the terms on which the monopoly was let. Nearly all of these strategies resulted in immediate gain and long-term loss, as competitors came to terms among themselves or took their business elsewhere. In 1885 the Hong Kong companies that had run the monopoly during its early decades were finally ousted by big Chinese capitalists from Singapore.

The struggle between government and monopolists for a larger cut of the opium revenue fostered a fiscal instability that mirrored, and contributed to, a wider political instability, in which the Hong Kong government experienced special difficulties in coming to terms with its local collaborators. The British established their colony at Hong Kong during a prolonged period of war and confusion. They found no indigenous elites or expatriated *kongsi* to help them manage a rapidly growing, largely unassimilated, and partly transient Chinese population. They neither sought nor received much assistance from the neighboring Chinese authorities, who, when not actively undermining the colony, were resolutely uncooperative, even after their defeat in the Second Opium War. Despite the huge influx of Chinese capital into the colony in the mid 1850s and beyond, the co-option of elites was a slow and clumsy process, troubled by conflict and mutual distrust. The colonial authorities governed the early colony through a mixture of coercion and selective, unstable collaboration, which gradually gave way in the 1870s to a more systematic, though still problematic, cooperation between government and Chinese bourgeoisie.[2] The development of the early opium monopoly epitomizes these problems and, because it gave rise to so much controversy and ink-spilling, provides a rare opportunity for studying the relations between government and collaborators at close hand. This chapter traces that development by outlining the troubled history of the monopoly between the years 1845 and 1885, when it was largely in the hands of Hong Kong monopolists. The first part examines attitudes toward opium in early colonial Hong Kong and notes that, whatever controversies the monopoly may have provoked, the moral question of founding a revenue on the sale of a narcotic drug was not a political issue. The second part places the opium monopoly in its fiscal and political context, summarizes its development, and explores some of the crises that plagued it.

EARLY COLONIAL HONG KONG AND THE OPIUM TRADE

The British colony at Hong Kong was a by-product of the Opium War of 1839–1842. Hong Kong's viability as a colony was also closely linked to the opium trade. Early Hong Kong served as "the central warehouse" for "British Indian produce" and had little other trade to sustain it. By the late 1840s, it was estimated, three-quarters of the entire Indian opium crop passed through Hong Kong.[3] Hong Kong broadened its economic base in the 1850s, when it became a center for the coolie trade between China and the New World and began to develop the banking, shipping, and entrepôt functions that have sustained it to this day. For much of the remainder of the century, however, the transshipment of opium to China continued to be a vital part of the colony's trade.[4] Indeed, the opium trade and Hong Kong are so obviously intertwined that it is hardly possible to consider the early history of the colony without some reference to the drug: the colony was founded because of opium; it survived its difficult early years because of opium; its principal merchants grew rich on opium; and its government subsisted on the high land rent and other revenue made possible by the opium trade. Early Chinese traders came to the colony to deal in opium; the drug became standard currency for remittances from Chinese living in Hong Kong to their native places on the mainland; pirated or disputed consignments of opium dominated many judicial proceedings; and opium balls cluttered the colony's numerous pawnbrokers' shops.[5]

British policy had not initially intended that the new colony should be so closely connected with the opium trade, which was technically illegal in China until 1858. Ministers in London directed that the export of opium from the island should be prohibited or discouraged through the imposition of duties, at least until a legal trade in the drug had been agreed upon with the Qing government.[6] This policy reflected a claim, prevalent among promoters both of the Opium War and of the new colony, that, with the opening of a more general commerce with China, British merchants would quickly see their dependence on opium replaced by a more healthy trade in British manufactures.

In fact, the continued growth of the opium trade in the 1840s held back the development of a regular trade between England and China. Legal trade could anyway be carried out more conveniently at the five new treaty ports along the China coast. As the many critics of the new colony pointed out, except as an opium depot or as a military base for the widely predicted second China war, Hong Kong had little to offer. Had it not been for its role as a safe warehouse to the illicit opium stations scattered along the coast, and for parliamentary subsidies, the colony would have been bankrupt and probably abandoned before the end of the 1840s. The "poppy lords," who had invested heavily in land and buildings on the island on the assumption that Hong Kong would be dedicated to the opium trade, were not prepared to allow this to happen.

The colonial government evaded ministerial instructions (which were already hedged by many qualifications) by pointing out that, whatever might be the formal Chinese policy, the opium trade had been de facto legalized all along the coast, "the only interference on the part of the officers of government being to ensure to themselves a large part of the profit." Under these "altered circumstances," concluded the second governor, Sir John Davis, "any scruples on our part, within our own colony, appear to me to be more than superfluous."[7] Hong Kong became the depot for the unrestricted and untaxed transshipment of opium to the opium stations along the China Coast, with all the irregularity and violence that this entailed. Long after the drug was legalized in China as a dutiable commodity, Hong Kong maintained its reputation among Chinese officials, officers of the Imperial Maritime Customs, and British diplomats "as a nest of pirates and smugglers, and as a 'thorn in their side.'"[8]

None of the scruples about the larger opium trade applied to consumption of opium *within* the colony. In his instructions about restricting the export of opium from the island, the secretary of state, Lord Stanley, acknowledged that in view of the large numbers of Chinese migrating to the colony, it would "not appear to be politic to attempt, even if it were practicable to effect, the total exclusion of opium for purposes of consumption." On the contrary, he urged Governor Davis, the aim should be "not to prohibit or impede consumption on the island," but "to raise as large an amount of local revenue as you can realize" by taxing the retail trade in the drug.[9]

Although the new Hong Kong government sought to harmonize many of its policies with those of the neighboring Qing government, it never seriously countenanced a prohibition on the sale or consumption of opium for moral, health, or social reasons. Opium was freely available in Great Britain and its other colonial possessions. Taxing its consumption had precedents in other British possessions in the region, most notably in Singapore, where since 1820 the opium monopoly had contributed between a third and a half of total government revenue.[10] The policy of raising a revenue out of opium consumption had a few prominent opponents in Hong Kong, including one chief justice,[11] but it was not to be expected that a community dominated by opium merchants would tolerate criticism of the substance for very long. The local press, which was contentious on many other subjects, survived mainly on merchant subscriptions.[12] Those most prone to criticize, the missionaries, were compromised by the prominence of opium merchants among the sponsors of local missionary enterprises: these enterprises ranged from prestige projects, such as the construction of Hong Kong's Anglican cathedral and James Legge's translation of the Confucian classics, to village schools and the practical fieldwork conducted by the Medical Missionary Society. The cultivation of goodwill by the local opium lobby could turn into hostile pressure if the morality of what it was doing was ever brought into question. When in 1860 a Hong Kong missionary, Dr. Happer, circulated a pamphlet in England attacking the opium trade, the Morrison Education Society, which was dominated by the great opium merchants, refused to continue its annual grant of $250 to the schools under his care until he agreed to "clarify" his "misstatements."[13]

The rare colonial defenses of the drug appeared when the larger opium trade was under attack: in the early 1840s, for example, when war aroused opposition to the trade, or in the mid 1870s, with the rise of the anti-opium movement in London. European defenders of opium consumption in Hong Kong drew mainly on the arguments deployed to justify the larger international trade in the substance, throwing much of the moral responsibility for the problems of opium on the Chinese people and their government. They could also draw on their own "expertise" accumulated through direct observation of the effects of opium on Chinese consumers. Some tried opium smoking themselves and found it to have no effect at all.[14]

Defenses of opium consumption not only assumed that responsibility for the effects of the drug rested with the individual Chinese consumer, they also turned the question of responsibility on its head by praising the Chinese opium smoker for making a wise choice of recreational drug. The most common arguments drew on comparisons between opium and alcohol consumption, regarding the "Chinese Opium sot" as preferable to the "Foreign Drunkard."[15] In contrast to Indian and Malay opium eaters, and even in comparison with their Hokkien compatriots in Singapore, Hong Kong's opium smokers were said to be moderate and restrained.[16] Opium was acknowledged to be dangerous if taken to excess, but, the defenders argued, it was as misleading to set down the helpless, skeletal addict as representative of the average opium smoker as it was to assume that "the entire population of England were dram-drinkers because the Canadian backwoodsman was addicted to the immoderate use of spirits."[17]

A table prepared by the colonial surgeon, Dr. Phineas Ayres, on more than a hundred opium smokers admitted to the colony's jail in 1886 showed a daily consumption ranging from about eight grains a day to more than a hundred, with most smokers taking around twenty or thirty grains a day. In his replies to the questionnaire from the Royal Commission on

Opium in 1893, Ayres relied on his studies of opium addiction among prisoners to support his claim that the proportion of opium smokers among Hong Kong's population, even among its "criminal population," was no higher than two per thousand. Yet his colleague, J. M. Atkinson, the superintendent of the Civil Hospital, produced a widely differing estimate in his replies to the same questionnaire: "at least 60 per cent of the whole community are consumers," he claimed. Ayres and Atkinson agreed on the race-specific nature of consumption. There was "in the Chinese an hereditary toleration, if not a craving, for opium," Atkinson suggested. In contrast, Europeans, Ayres remarked, found the trouble of preparing and smoking a pipe of opium "excessive," when a cigar, pipe, or cigarette allowed the smoker the freedom to "ride, walk, read, and write, and talk and pursue his ordinary avocations." Addiction was also gender specific. The only women, and the only Europeans, observed to have contracted a serious habit of opium smoking were two or three of the tiny community of European prostitutes.[18]

Government estimates of consumption patterns from opium production in the colony were no more helpful than the contradictory claims by medical experts. The manufacturers and purveyors of prepared opium resisted official inquiries. In 1883, when Hong Kong had a (mostly Chinese, preponderantly male) population of about 160,000, the government finally obtained the production figure of two chests per day prepared for local consumption (reduced through boiling into about 2,000 taels of prepared smokable opium): by Ayres's calculations, this would supply between forty and sixty thousand addicts. By the 1870s and 1880s, the more important market for the colony's prepared opium was not the local population but the overseas Chinese communities in California, Australia, and elsewhere. In 1882 more than 70 percent of opium prepared in Hong Kong (or five out of seven chests processed every day) went to these destinations.[19] Managed by Hong Kong–based Chinese companies, which made use of European and American steamships and banks, the export of prepared opium from Hong Kong to the Chinese communities in the New World intersected neatly with the two great trades that sustained Hong Kong's early economy: the import of opium into China, and the export of labor out of China. The involvement of coolie brokerages (most notably the Wo Hang firm) in the refining and export of opium from Hong Kong echoes the connection between the control of labor and the trade in the drug that Carl Trocki describes elsewhere in Southeast Asia (see chapter 3 in this volume), just as the trans-Pacific links and the growing connections and rivalries in the region reflect the increasing internationalization of Chinese capital.

Such progress pleased Hong Kong's rulers. In 1879 Governor Hennessy derived great satisfaction from the way in which the flourishing opium industry illustrated "the growing confidence and prosperity of the Chinese

Subjects of the Queen in this Colony, and the extension of the commercial relations between Hong Kong and the Chinese communities in Australia and the United States.''[20] The government did its best to nurture this early industrial export. Envious of the large opium revenue raised from the smaller Chinese population in Singapore, it also sought to maximize its own cut from this lucrative and expanding industry.

THE HONG KONG OPIUM MONOPOLY

Revenue was a serious concern for the Hong Kong government throughout the nineteenth century. Between the two Opium Wars the colony depended for much of its income on grudging parliamentary grants. Land, the government's main source of revenue, was an unstable asset: lucrative premiums on land leases were a limited resource easily squandered by money-hungry governors, and land rents, which were controversially high, depended on the staying power of merchants and speculators. Land rents and property rates directly or indirectly affected all of the colony's inhabitants, but the bulk of *indirect* taxation, consistent with a policy of regressive taxation, fell on smaller Chinese tradesmen and on the poorer majority of the colony's Chinese population. Most indirect taxation was raised through farms or franchises, which the government periodically auctioned off or sold privately to the highest or most favored bidder. The farms included monopolies on salt-weighing, stone-quarrying, and (briefly) gaming houses, as well as franchises for building and operating markets, running slaughterhouses, managing public privies, collecting night-soil, and maintaining rural rope-walks. With minor exceptions, the farms were held by Chinese merchants or contractors based within the colony. Collectively, they accounted for between 10 and 25 percent of annual colonial revenue in the first four decades of the colony. By far the largest and most enduring farm was the opium monopoly, which alone accounted for between 4 and 22 percent of annual revenue in this period.

According to the architect of Hong Kong's taxation system, Governor Davis, the revenue farm was best adapted to a Chinese population: "as the farmers themselves are Chinese, their perfect knowledge of their own countrymen joined to the personal interest which they have in the collection, renders them incomparably the best tax-gatherers in a case of this kind."[21] By auctioning off revenue collection rights to middlemen, the government was able to secure an income with minimal trouble and liability: it was relieved of much of the bother and friction of collecting tax direct from the people; it was assured of an income, since the rental was payable monthly in advance and the farmers were heavily bonded; and it could distance itself from the farms if things went wrong. The farms also had political value. By ousting pre-existing Chinese forms of revenue collection or private protection rackets, they helped to confirm British sovereignty over the new colony. They encouraged and empowered local elites over whom the government believed it could exercise some degree of control. For the farmers themselves, the farms offered them the possibility of becoming extremely rich, of building up positions of power and influence in society, and of channeling resources into indigenous forms of charity and political influence, such as the Tung Wah Hospital.[22] Their importance to the colonial revenue offered them some limited but direct influence over the shaping of government policy: the development of the opium farm, in particular, owed much to the advice and demands put forward by monopolists and their competitors.

The revenue farms were also the source of considerable problems. The damage to society—in the suppression of trade, the inflation of prices, the diversion of general wealth into the hands of a few, and the abuse of policing rights granted with the farms—is impossible to quantify.[23] For the farmers themselves, bidding for the monopolies could be something of a gamble. The earnings they could expect from the farms were easily eroded by invasions of their monopoly, by poorly framed legislation, and by the frequent unwillingness of the courts to uphold their powers. Attempts by the government to foster competition for the opium monopoly also tended to disrupt the market and undermine the quiet and profitable stability that opium merchants sought for themselves. For the government, the revenue farms never seemed to deliver the income it had expected from them. In farming out the collection of opium revenue to Chinese monopolists, officials constantly feared that they were grossly underselling one of the colony's greatest yet most undeveloped assets.

The Hong Kong opium monopoly changed in form over the years and was finally absorbed by the government in 1914. It was governed by a succession of ordinances and regulations and periodically interrupted by attempts by the government to raise opium revenue through the granting of licenses at fixed prices. Introduced in 1844 as a tax on the retail sale of opium, raw or prepared, in quantities of less than a chest, it was held as a single farm sold by public auction to the highest bidder for a period of a year. The monopoly was first leased in March 1845 to two Europeans, George Duddell and Alexander Mathieson, who were able to hold on to it for only three months.[24] Their failure to make the monopoly work illustrates why so few of the opium monopolies in colonial Asia were held by European outsiders. A sustained attack by Chinese interests, supported by official corruption, nullified the monopoly and helped transfer it into the hands of the government's most prominent collaborator, Lo Aqui, who had served as one of the main suppliers to the British expedition during the Opium War. The British had rewarded Lo's services with extensive grants of land in the new colony of Hong Kong, where he settled hundreds of his followers as tenants and employees. His gambling, prostitution, and alleged piratical enterprises were widely understood to be under the protection of senior British officials, to whom he lent money and paid bribes.[25] During a prosecution for invasion of the Duddell-Mathieson monopoly in April 1845, Chief Magistrate William Caine (allegedly one of the principal beneficiaries of Lo's bribes) ruled that the monopoly did not extend to opium purchased for the purpose of export, however small the quantity purchased might be.[26] With this loophole legally confirmed, the monopoly instantly collapsed. A new ordinance, passed in July, plugged the loophole by making the sale of opium in quantities of less than a chest *for any purpose* subject to the monopoly. During the same month the monopoly was put up for re-auction and leased by Lo Aqui and his partner Fung Attai at a monthly rental of $1,710, more than twice the rental ($710) paid by Duddell and Mathieson.[27]

Even with friends in the government and the backing of stronger legislation, Lo Aqui and his partners ran into similar difficulties with invasions of their monopoly. Their attempts to enforce the monopoly through an intrusive revenue police aroused opposition from both European and Chinese traders. Complaints began to emerge that the faltering monopoly had become a front for piracy and an extension of Lo's sleazy gangster empire.[28] European merchants claimed that the fortified warehouses they had erected to store the opium they had expected to be able to sell locally now lay empty because of Lo's oppressive monopoly on the retail trade: the shadow colony that they, accompanied by the Chinese opium refiners, had been forced to establish on the nearby island of Cumsingmoon in order to escape the oppressive monopoly was, they protested, expensive and insecure.[29] The Chinese shopkeepers of Hong Kong submitted a petition against the monopoly:

> Your people whether engaged in a small or large trade, have from their arrival in this Colony, all principally derived their profits from the sale of Opium. Last year however this commodity was made a monopoly, and every one who dealt in it was exposed to very heavy fines. As soon as the Merchants of the different places heard of this, they were loath to come hither, and hence we have found it difficult to dispose of our goods, and the trade has been much reduced and is decaying, so that we fear, that all the shops in future will be shut and none be opened, and thus the commerce of Your Honorable Colony on that account to be destroyed.[30]

The opium farm played a prominent part in the hearings conducted by the House of Commons Select Committee in 1847 into the poor performance of the China trade and the depression into which Hong Kong had sunk. The experience of Lo's *imperium in imperio* confirmed in the colonial mind the dangers of delegating power to an "unprincipled native," a theme that was to re-emerge in future crises involving the monopoly. In July 1847, its returns having already declined, the monopoly was discontinued and replaced by a less lucrative system of individual annual licenses issued at fixed fees in unlimited numbers to businesses retailing raw opium in quantities of less than a chest, refining and selling prepared opium, or simply running opium divans. This system was tightened in 1853, with a prohibition on the import of raw opium in quantities of less than a chest by unlicensed dealers.

The new scheme produced a declining opium revenue, which by the early 1850s was barely a third of what it had been at its peak in 1846. To remedy this, the government set up an entirely new regime in 1858, coinciding with the decriminalization of opium imports into China during the Second Opium War. The new monopoly, which was sold through a process of sealed tenders and not necessarily to the highest bidder, freed up the larger trade in raw opium and reserved to the monopolist only the boiling of opium and the sale of prepared opium. The new monopoly went to Chan Tai-kwong, a protégé of the Bishop of Hong Kong, whose attractive tender of £7,075 for a twelve-month period was almost three times the annual opium revenue in 1857 and more than 12 percent of the government revenue for that year.[31] As one of the most respectable Chinese in the colony, the anglicized, Anglicanized Chan was everything that Lo Aqui was not.[32] Chan appears to have functioned as a respectable front for the rising Wo Hang company, heavily involved in the coolie trade and the general entrepôt trade of the colony.[33] Despite his advantages, Chan found it impossible to preserve his monopoly against European and other invaders; nor, during a series of well-publicized disputes, did the colonial courts help him in his struggle.[34] In May 1858 Chan became embroiled in an official investigation into whether the colonial secretary, W. T. Bridges, had accepted bribes from Chan in return for the monopoly. This, in turn, fed into a generalized inquiry into abuses of power in the senior ranks of the civil service. Later that summer, following the collapse of the monopoly, Chan fled the colony along with twenty-five thousand other Chinese residents in response to proclamations by the Qing government, which was still at war with Britain. The Hong Kong government was left with little choice but to negotiate a stop-gap lease of the monopoly with the rivals of the Wo Hang company, the Yan Wo, who took it for six months at less than half the monthly rental offered by Chan Tai-kwong. The Yan Wo obtained the monopoly again in 1859 at a rent (£6,812 10s per annum) close to that agreed with Chan a year earlier. From then on, income from the monopoly showed a long-term increasing trend.[35]

Despite the early instability and controversy surrounding the revived monopoly, the legislation of 1858 became the basis of the monopoly until 1889. Under this system the government leased the farm for periods of between six months and three years to a small number of closely connected local firms. In its efforts to maximize revenue, from the late 1870s onwards the government sought to bring in outside competition, tighten enforcement, and prevent dumping by outgoing monopolists. The opium farmers were empowered to grant sublicenses under their monopoly and to protect the monopoly with a revenue police backed up with fines of up to five hundred dollars (increased to one thousand dollars in 1879) and imprisonment for up to six months, either of which could be imposed by the magistrates on those caught attempting to invade the monopoly. From the late 1870s, with the increasing value of the opium revenue and the growing bureaucratization of government, the monopoly was heavily policed by officially regulated excise officers funded by the monopolist. Prosecutions were common and sentences were stiff.

After the false starts in the 1840s and 1850s, the monopolists became ever more elaborate in their management of the monopoly and increasingly skilled at holding it at the lowest possible price. They managed this through the working of a flexible, three-tier operation, which kept the control of the monopoly in a few hands, minimized local competition, baffled government attempts to inquire into profits, and, for a while, resisted or absorbed the outside competition brought in by the government. At the lowest tier were a number of opium firms, most of them situated on Bonham Strand or Jervois Street and owned by merchants who had migrated to the colony in the 1850s. For purposes of bidding for the monopoly these firms grouped together into a second tier of companies (usually no more than two, the Yan Wo and the Wo Hang), which allowed one of the company's firms to put forward one genuine tender backed up with several much lower dummy tenders. This helped them to obtain and maintain the monopoly at a low price through negotiation and accommodation among themselves rather than through hostile competition or through negotiation with an often unpredictable colonial government. It also enabled them to pool resources, police and consolidate the monopoly, and deter less powerful opposition. One of the two companies, the Yan Wo, was able to hold the monopoly in this way for all but one year during the 1860s. The third and highest tier came with the deal struck between the Yan Wo and the Wo Hang in 1874, which effectively brought all opium retailers and processors in the colony under one umbrella organization. A direct response to the government's attempts to stimulate the revenue, this amalgamation served to nullify the government's efforts to nurture competition for the monopoly.

Despite the steady increase in the opium revenue, the government was not satisfied. It was aware of the much higher opium farm rent in Singapore (which was consistently double or even triple that in Hong Kong during these years) and of the increasing amounts of prepared opium leaving the colony on European steamers bound for California and Australia. It concluded that the Yan Wo company, which was gradually shutting out rival firms by refusing to grant them sublicenses, was holding back large amounts of revenue because it was the only company capable of bidding successfully for the farm. The competition that the government had hoped to cultivate in its annual tendering exercise had been snuffed out and, in the words of the governor Sir Arthur Kennedy, "practically the government was in the hands of the monopolists."[36]

In 1872 Kennedy appointed a commission to investigate the problem. The commission failed to determine how much revenue the government was losing, or even to come up with an estimate of the colony's opium production.[37] It recommended that the government should take the monopoly into its own hands or, failing that, lease it for longer terms to encourage substantial competitors to come forward.[38] The government chose the latter and invited tenders for the lease of the monopoly for a period of one to three years. This measure broke the Yan Wo's hold on the monopoly, and in January 1873 the lease went to Li Tak-cheong of the rival Wo Hang company, who had put in a high bid for a three-year period. Unlike the Yan Wo, Li was willing both to build up the value of the farm and to tolerate rivals by granting sublicenses: this would, Kennedy predicted, "result in a greater number of tenders being offered for the privilege" and would "break down the [Yan Wo's] combination, which will ultimately make the farm more remunerative for the colony."[39]

The Wo Hang's policy had the very opposite effect. In March 1874, just over a year into its tenure of the farm, the Wo Hang entered into an agreement with the Yan Wo to form a combination known as the Sun Yee company. This pooling of resources and management of competing interests resembled other business associations in Hong Kong at this time:[40] it was intended partly to make the best of the growing export market for opium prepared in Hong Kong but mainly to keep the rental for the Hong Kong opium farm as low as possible. Under the terms of the combination, a council composed of representatives of the various shareholding companies worked the monopoly by putting forward one genuine tender at each sale of the farm together with a number of fictitious, lesser tenders made "with a view to blinding the government."[41] Shareholders bound themselves for a period of fifty years, under a penalty of half a million dollars, never to oppose the council's bid. The result was that, when the opium farm was put up for sale toward the end of the Wo Hang's three-year lease in late 1875, the highest of the tenders submitted was $68,400 less than the total amount paid for the 1873–1875 lease, representing a decline in annual revenue between 1875 and 1876 of $20,000 (or nearly 15 percent). Seeing part of the way through the smokescreen put up to blind it, the government refused to accept any of the bids and called for fresh tenders.

A higher tender of $132,000 per annum, put forward by Li Tak-cheong, was finally accepted, with the result that the revenue for the three-year period was about the same as that for the preceding three-year period, although the sudden dip in revenue in 1876 made it seem like a decline.[42]

Kennedy's successor, John Pope Hennessy, resolved to extract much more from the Hong Kong farm. Hennessy, a controversial governor, granted some respect to Chinese opinion and attempted a more deliberate cultivation of the Chinese bourgeoisie. His determination to increase the opium revenue was the only policy advanced by him to receive approval from a European colonial community increasingly alarmed by his "native race craze" and by his desire to instill some element of humanity into the colony's brutal penal system. The problem with the opium monopoly, he suggested, was simply the government's imperfect knowledge "of the Chinese, of their business habits, and of the mode in which they would endeavor to get this farm." The solution, he proposed, was for the government to obtain advice and assistance from leading Chinese merchants on the best means of securing both a "fair share" for the government and a "handsome profit" for the farmer. As governor of Labuan, he pointed out, he had tripled the opium revenue of that colony by acting on the advice of Chinese merchants in Singapore.[43]

Hennessy's strategy in Hong Kong included both seeking help from his merchant friends in Singapore and threatening to take the monopoly into government hands. Notifications in August 1878 inviting tenders for a one- to three-year farm lease appeared in the newspapers of various European colonies in the region and carried the warning that if the highest tender should be less than the "fair price" for the farm the government would use its powers to grant individual licenses "and take such further steps as may be necessary to raise a fair price."[44] The incumbent monopolist, Li Tak-cheong, tendered a bid for $156,000 per annum on behalf of the Sun Yee combine. On the surface, this bid, which was nearly 20 percent higher than the current rent for the farm, showed a gracious willingness on the part of the Sun Yee to play Hennessy's game. Hennessy, however, decided, on the confidential advice of "some of my Chinese friends in Hong Kong," that this was not enough, and reopened the tendering. After several months of tense negotiation, Li progressively amended his offer until it reached $201,000 for one year, proof to many of the inordinate profits the farmers had been making from the monopoly. Hennessy rejected this, and accepted instead the offer of $205,000 per annum for three years from Li's competitor and a complete outsider, the Singaporean Tan King-sing, representing a Mr. Ban Hap (alias Ngan Chan Wai), a Hokkien Chinese based in Saigon, who had a stake in the opium farms at Singapore, Saigon, and Annam. Ban Hap's bid represented an increase in the annual opium revenue of 55 percent.

One theme stood out in the congratulations that followed this coup: Hennessy's success in resisting "the sea of intrigue, falsehood, over-reaching, and finesse" and in defeating "all the powers of cunning and chicanery of which the celestial nature is capable."[45] By bringing in a "better class" of anglicized Chinese from outside the Chinese subcontinent, the progressive, pro-Chinese Hennessy had, uniquely, found common ground with the conservative, anti-Chinese colonial community while promoting his policy of cultivating the Chinese elite within Hong Kong. The dense, impenetrable Chinese combination "laboriously built up, and held together for a long series of years, with so much tenacity and closeness," the *Daily Press* observed, had finally been replaced by a man with whom the colonial government believed it could do business.[46] Even the outgoing monopolist, Li Tak-cheong, reportedly admitted that "nothing could have been more just and fair than the mode in which the farm was disposed of by the Government."[47] The chief justice, Sir John Smale, though a critic of the opium trade, also publicly endorsed Hennessy's choice of Tan King-sing: "I came up with this gentleman from Singapore and a more intelligent man I have seldom met with—a man whose general observations and conversation at the table were most sensible, and therefore I judge him to be an exceedingly able, and intelligent man."[48]

The introduction of Ban Hap had certainly succeeded in breaking the Sun Yee combine, but the Yan Wo half of the combine quickly came to terms with Ban Hap to produce another combination. The surge in prosecutions for invading the opium monopoly and the increase in the maximum penalty in December 1879 give some sense of the difficulties experienced by Ban Hap in enforcing the monopoly within Hong Kong.[49] The new monopoly faced smuggling and evasion, and its unpopular sublicensing system was challenged in court.[50] "A most determined opposition was got up with the intent of ruining" the outsiders.[51] Deprived of the Hong Kong farm, the two companies that made up the Sun Yee combine moved their production to other colonies in the region, first to the usual refuge of Macao, where they picked up the opium boiling monopoly, and later to Penang, where Li Tak-cheong obtained a license to boil large quantities of opium under the Penang monopolist. From Macao the Sun Yee sent large quantities of cheap prepared opium into Hong Kong. Still in possession of much of the American and Australian markets, they continued to make use of Hong Kong's connections by arranging with steamship lines to load their product on board outside Hong Kong waters.[52]

Ban Hap's secret negotiations with the Yan Wo in 1880 were an attempt to resolve these problems and ward off bankruptcy. The Yan Wo had never been completely happy with the articles drawn up for the Sun Yee combine at a time when, having lost the Hong Kong monopoly to the Wo Hang, it was at a disadvantage. In early 1880 the Yan Wo abandoned the Sun Yee and went into partnership with Ban Hap in a new combination known as the Man Wo Sang.[53] This combination enabled Ban Hap to see through his three-year monopoly , but it provoked extensive and expensive litigation, which brought the workings of the monopolists into the open and confirmed suspicions that, far from breaking the old cartel, the bringing in of competition from outside had merely resulted in another cartel. Worse than that, it had driven the larger part of Hong Kong's lucrative prepared opium industry to other colonies.

For two years, in 1883 and 1884, the government suspended the farm, again issued individual licenses, and supervised the preparation of opium in what looked suspiciously like a state enterprise. An "Opium Department" issued licenses to boilers, managed a centralized boiling factory, and persuaded the Wo Hang and Yan Wo to return to Hong Kong from their inconvenient exile in Penang and Macao to take part in this great enterprise. The final yield of the opium revenue for 1883 was $246,450, the highest ever.[54] In 1884, however, the revenue suddenly dropped by more than half to its lowest level in over a decade. The Wo Hang, Yan Wo, and other licensees now furiously boiling opium under the harmonious government scheme had hurried back to Hong Kong in 1883 not so much to admit defeat as to make the most of the last few months of business before the U.S. government doubled the duty on prepared opium on 1 July 1883.[55] Added to increasingly restrictive U.S. immigration policies and to fears that boiling establishments would soon open in San Francisco, this measure raised serious doubts about the future of the Hong Kong opium revenue, nearly three-quarters of which was now dependent on exports.[56] The Hong Kong government managed the monopoly for a further year, despite qualms about possible objections from the anti-opium lobby in England.[57] An ill-advised policy of initially denying new boiling licenses to the Yan Wo and Wo Hang in 1884 because they refused to give up their boiling establishments in Macao and Penang further depressed the revenue for that year. The aim, Governor Bowen explained, was to encourage the small boiling firms in the colony and "to prevent the two large firms from obtaining, at nominal cost, the great advantage of figuring in foreign markets as mercantile houses of Hong Kong." This policy, and the U.S. restrictions, nearly obliterated the colony's opium export industry. After a few months the government gave up, halved its duty on prepared opium for export, and lured the two large firms back to the colony.[58]

In 1885, keen to distance itself from the monopoly, the government leased the farm to the Yan Wo, the only credible bidders, for $159,000. The highly unstable experiments of the late 1870s and early 1880s, though they had brought substantial short-term gains, had, the colonial treasurer admitted in December 1884, seriously disrupted the local industry, "whilst the Government has come perilously near to losing its revenue on exported opium altogether."[59] The 1885 farm was the Yan Wo's swan song, after more than twenty-five years of involvement in the monopoly. Late in 1885, a Singapore syndicate led by Lee Keng-yam offered $182,400 a year for a three-year monopoly, thus effectively breaking up "the little clique of firms at Hong Kong, which, during some years past, have been endeavoring to impose their own terms on the Government of this Colony."[60]

Later in the 1880s tougher measures to reduce the smuggling of opium into China came to the Hong Kong government's rescue. An amendment made to the Chefoo Convention in 1885 standardized the taxes charged on opium by the Chinese government and required measures to be taken to plug the main artery for smuggling opium into China, the free port of Hong Kong.[61] Legislation of 1887 prohibited the importation of opium into Hong Kong in quantities of less than a chest, except under license, and required strict reporting on the movements of opium into and out of the colony.[62] By the 1890s prosecutions for breaches of the opium regulations exceeded prosecutions for any other single criminal offense. In helping the Chinese government to protect its revenue, the Hong Kong government helped its own opium revenue enormously. In exempting the farmer from most of these restrictions, while enforcing them strictly against everyone else, the government effectively added to this official monopoly the monopoly on smuggling opium into China. The successful bid for the 1889–1891 monopoly from the same Singapore syndicate nearly tripled the rental, and the monopoly maintained high yields until it was taken over by the government in 1914.

This fruitful cooperation between government and farmer—between watertight, strictly enforced legislation and bureaucratic efficiency on the one hand and international Chinese capital and entrepreneurial flair on the other—was something that earlier administrations had merely dreamed of. Both sides had at last achieved the returns they were looking for. Even more satisfactorily, the government could now argue that the farm, and the controls and checks connected with it, was a positive aid in the growing campaign to reduce opium smoking. When in 1891 the Colonial Office asked the Hong Kong government to consider whether the opium monopoly might once more be placed directly under the government in order "to diminish the evil resulting from it without seriously crippling the revenue," the governor, Sir William Robinson, replied that the current system was more likely "to diminish the evils attendant upon an undue consumption of opium than any other that can be devised."[63]

CONCLUSION

The history of the early Hong Kong opium monopoly is the story of a prolonged battle between an avaricious colonial government, which wanted the benefits of both a stable monopoly and genuine competition, and a resourceful, flexible, constantly mutating local Chinese opium cartel, which ousted or absorbed rivals until it was itself finally defeated by outside competition in the mid 1880s. Feeding this struggle was the nagging suspicion that monopolists were abusing the privileges granted to them by the government and corrupting the institutions of colonial government. Although blown out of proportion by European commentators, abuse of power (or rather the undermining of colonial power), corruption, and collusion were clear features of the early opium monopoly and were perhaps an inevitable part of the system of narrow collaboration on which the early colonial government depended.

Each of these features has a practical explanation. Abuses under the first monopoly (1845–1847) were linked both to the instability of early colonial rule and to the monopolists' declining ability to make the farm pay its way. Bribes or "retainers" secured access and assistance at senior levels of government. "Collusion" turned potentially destructive, all-or-nothing competition into productive cooperation, which spread the fruits of the monopoly, minimized the tax paid and money spent on policing, and replicated the self-regulation that served Chinese businesses well in their relations with the Qing government.[64]

Sustained by the free trade ideal then opening China to the freer importation of opium and the freer exportation of labor, colonial opinion did not view the problem in these terms. To colonists jealous of their own privileges and suspicious of any measures that conferred trust and power on Chinese, and particularly to a government striving to enlarge its revenue, the experience of the opium monopoly confirmed what they saw as some of the worst and most incurable features of "the Chinese": the tendency to convert any amount of power into private gain; the corrupting of European methods of government by their readiness to purchase power and influence; and the secretive, exclusive, "clannish" manner in which they managed their affairs. In its attempts to address these difficulties, and especially in its efforts to maximize revenue from the opium farm, the government more often than not merely deepened the problems it faced and added to the political instability of the early colony. These problems are illustrated in the successive struggles, controversies, and disappointments that characterized the early Hong Kong opium monopoly: the out-of-control *imperium in imperio* operated by the government's earliest collaborator, Lo Aqui, which outraged nearly every section of the community; the scandal attached to the short-lived monopoly of the new-style, Christianized middleman Chan Tai-kwong in 1858; the grand alliance of established opium firms following the government's ill-judged attempts to stir competition in the early 1870s; the turmoil that followed Governor Hennessy's promising but doomed efforts to bring in a substantial, experienced, and highly respectable monopolist, Ban Hap, to break the entrenched Hong Kong combination in the late 1870s; and the rapid rise and fall of the government's own opium monopoly in 1883–1884. The government learned from the failures of its monopoly that it could not operate successfully without the help of Chinese capitalists.

By the 1880s, forces largely external to the colony removed the difficulties that had troubled the Hong Kong opium revenue since its beginnings in 1845. Restrictions on the movement of all forms of opium into and out of the colony reduced the widespread smuggling that had eroded the revenue from the farm. The transformation from a largely overseas market to a largely domestic market removed many of the uncertainties caused by competition from other farms. The replacement of the local combination of opium firms with substantial and durable capital from outside at last produced partners with whom the colonial government was happy to do business. By 1910, when Hong Kong's last opium farmer signed his three-year contract, the government was receiving an annual rent of $1,183,200, or the equivalent of 17 percent of its annual revenue.[65]

A final external force, the anti-opium movement, introduced the last stage in the Hong Kong opium monopoly: the take-over of the monopoly by the government in 1914 as part of general imperial policy, with the aim of eventually suppressing opium use. Under this system, the opium revenue soared to still higher levels, peaking at more than eight and a half million dollars in 1918 and benefiting greatly from the effects on supply and price of opium suppression policies elsewhere and of civil war in China. By then, the concern of the Hong Kong government was not how to squeeze an acceptable opium revenue from a recalcitrant and uncooperative farmer, but what to do about the "awful spectre" of the inevitable loss, one day, of the millions of dollars that the opium revenue was now annually bringing in.[66] That day did not come until 25 December 1941, when the colonial government in Hong Kong handed over power to the invading Japanese army.

NOTES

I acknowledge with much pleasure and gratitude the considerable help given to me in preparing this paper by Carl T. Smith of the Hong Kong Branch of the Royal Asiatic Society. I also thank Timothy Brook and Lynne Russell for their valuable comments on earlier drafts.

1. The fullest account of Hong Kong's nineteenth-century opium monopoly is Cheung, "Opium Monopoly in Hong Kong." For the twentieth-century government monopoly see Miners, "Hong Kong Government Opium Monopoly," pp. 275–99. Traver, "Colonial Relations and Opium Control Policy in Hong Kong," provides a brief but helpful introduction to the monopoly.

2. These developments are discussed in Sinn, *Power and Charity,* and in Jung-fang Tsai, *Hong Kong in Chinese History.*

3. Memorandum by W. H. Mitchell "Upon the Present Condition, Trade and Prospects of the Colony of Hong Kong," 1 November 1850, Great Britain, Public Record Office, CO 129/34, pp. 327–28.

4. *Friend of China,* 19 July 1845, p. 856. See, for example, the report on Hong Kong's opium trade in 1892 by Sir James Russell (the colony's chief justice and former treasurer, and an expert on the trade), which estimated that, up to 1887, practically all opium from India, Persia, and Turkey destined for China was trans-shipped through Hong Kong: "Correspondence on the Subject of the Consumption of Opium in Hong Kong and the Straits Settlements," August 1896, CO 882/5, p. 44.

5. For a discussion of remittances through the medium of opium, see Memorandum by Mitchell, p. 330; for opium as a feature of court proceedings see almost any court page from the colony's early newspapers.

6. Stanley to Davis, 8 February 1844, CO 129/6, pp. 18–27. See also Aberdeen to Pottinger, 4 January 1843, CO 129/3, pp. 73–76.

7. Davis to Stanley, 28 December 1844, CO 129/7, p. 340.

8. Memorandum by Sir Julian Pauncefote on Hart's proposal to establish a Chinese customs station in Hong Kong, CO 129/172, p. 478.

9. Stanley to Davis, 8 February 1844, CO 129/6, pp. 19–20.

10. Trocki, *Opium and Empire,* p. 96.

11. Sir John Smale, chief justice of Hong Kong between 1866 and 1881, described the "three evils" of Hong Kong as the opium trade, the licensing of brothels, and female slavery. Smale was widely regarded in the colony as a crank. Norton-Kyshe, *History of the Laws and Courts of Hong Kong,* 2:347.

12. The *Hongkong Register,* one of the colony's three early newspapers, was financed by Jardine, Matheson & Co.; it and the others at any given time relied heavily on government printing contracts. *Friend of China* (which was no enemy to the opium trade) complained on 12 June 1844 (p. 396) that "the opium millionaires of East Point" (Jardine Matheson & Co.) had withdrawn their annual subscription to the newspaper because the *Friend* had merely dared "to introduce the great firm into our columns."

13. Happer declined to "clarify," and the funds for his school were raised by private subscription; *Hongkong Register,* 2 and 5 January 1861.

14. The reaction by the diarist John Wright, a minor civil servant in the colony, is typical: "Sunday 15 August 1852. Smoke a pipe of opium to try effect, it had none, so I suppose I did not do it properly." The colonial surgeon Phineas Ayres (discussed below) had smoked the drug "hundreds of times" and "never felt any effect at all." John Wright, Diary, 15 August 1852; replies by Dr. Phineas Ayres to questions from the Royal Commission on Opium, 19 December 1893, Colonial Surgeon's Report for 1893, *Hong Kong Sessional Papers,* 28/94.

15. Foreshadowing arguments by the Hong Kong government in the early twentieth century that the criminalization of opium in Hong Kong would merely drive opium smokers to more dangerous substances such as morphine or cocaine, the *Friend of China* commented in 1848, "It is impossible for the Emperor to alter the taste of the people, and however earnest he may be in the laudable desire, he can

never effect a change, and if he did, they would only be driven to another vice—drinking samshoo." The symmetry is extended by the fact that, in exchange for the opium exported from India to China, the main British import from China—tea—was promoted on the ground that it would offer the working classes a healthy substitute for spirits: this was a prominent theme in the evidence given to the House of Commons Select Committee of 1847. "Opium," remarked *The Times*'s Hong Kong correspondent in that year, "has become to the Chinese what tea is to the English; it must be had, at whatever cost." *Friend of China*, 14 May 1848, p. 194; *The Times*, 1 January 1847, p. 6a.

16. Cunynghame, *Opium War*, pp. 237–38; memorandum by Russell, 14 March 1883, CO 129/207, 555; Colonial Surgeon's reports for 1876, 1877, and 1878, *Hongkong Government Gazette*, 14 April 1877, p. 208, 6 July 1878, p. 324, and 9 July 1879, p. 405.

17. Cunynghame, *Opium War*, p. 238.

18. *Hong Kong Sessional Papers*, 28/94.

19. Opium retained for preparation in the colony represented about 2.5 percent of all the raw opium passing through Hong Kong at this time. The estimated total export of prepared opium from Hong Kong to California and Australia in 1882 was about 1.7 million taels; in 1870 the figure was estimated to be as high as 2.5 million taels, valued at nearly two million dollars. Memorandum by Russell, 14 March 1883, CO 129/207, pp. 548–50.

20. Hennessy to Hicks Beach, January 1879, CO 129/184, p. 34.

21. Davis to Stanley, 29 June 1844, CO 129/6, p. 304.

22. Cheung, "Opium Monopoly in Hong Kong," pp. 85–91.

23. To illustrate the speculation under these schemes, one market, operated by the former opium monopolist George Duddell in the mid 1850s, was leased to him by the government at £637 10s per annum and then immediately sublet by him to someone else at £1,625 per annum. Bowring to Russell, 4 September 1855, CO 129/51, pp. 226–27.

24. Duddell and Mathieson were two minor entrepreneurs in early colonial Hong Kong. Mathieson (who had no connection with the great opium dynasty of Matheson) died shortly after the collapse of his monopoly. Duddell involved himself in land speculation and other government franchises (such as markets and seamen's boarding houses), and by the time of his departure from Hong Kong in 1858 he had amassed a considerable fortune. Vernon, *George Duddell*.

25. *Hongkong Register*, 27 May 1845, pp. 84–85, and 27 July 1847, p. 120; Tarrant, *Hongkong*, pp. 69, 92. For an account of Lo Aqui's career see Carl T. Smith, *Chinese Christians*, pp. 108–10.

26. *China Mail*, 1 May 1845, p. 42; Magistracy case no. 327, 22 April 1845, CO 129/27, pp. 335–36.

27. Opium Monopoly Contracts, Public Records Office, Hong Kong, HKRS 149; Davis to Stanley, 7 August 1845, CO 129/13, pp. 3–4.

28. *Friend of China*, 6 May, 11 July, and 12 and 19 December 1846, pp. 1184, 1260, 1432, 1440; George Smith, *Narrative of an Exploratory Visit*, p. 513; Jamieson How & Co. to Caine, 6 May 1846, CO 129/27, p. 335; petition of Chuen Shunyih, 11 September 1845, BFO 233/186, pp. 14–15; *China Mail*, 28 May 1846, p. 59; *Hongkong Register*, 30 June 1846, p. 103.

29. *Hongkong Register*, 22 July, 5 August, and 18 November 1845, pp. 119, 127, 194; Davis to Aberdeen, 22 August 1845, BFO 17/100, pp. 323–24; Boustead & Co. to Frederick Bruce, 20 May 1846, CO 129/16, pp. 389–96; William Scott to Benjamin Hawes, 25 July 1846, CO 129/18, p. 592.

30. Petition from the Shopkeepers of Hong Kong, December 1846, CO 129/20, pp. 176–77 (official translation): original in BFO 233/186, no. 12.

31. Bowring to Labouchere, 23 March 1858, CO 129/67, pp. 303–6.

32. For an account of Chan's career see Carl T. Smith, *Chinese Christians*, pp.7–8, 136–37.

33. Chan's bid was financed mainly by Leong-attoy, Li Tuk-cheong, and Li Chun, the last two being members of the Li family's Wo Hang firm, which was to play an important part in financing future bids for the opium monopoly and in the gambling monopoly of 1868.

34. *Hongkong Register*, 20 April 1858, p. 70, and 11 May 1858, p. 84.

35. The temporary mass exodus of Chinese from the colony was partly responsible for this low rental and for the shortage of bidders. Bowring to Lytton, 29 March 1859, CO 129/73, p. 307.

36. Kennedy to Kimberly, 10 March 1873, CO 129/162, p. 406.

37. Witnesses produced estimates of the gross annual receipts of the opium farmers ranging between $577,124 (suggested by European merchants involved in the trade) and $159,684 (from Ho Leong, the manager of the Yan Wo).

38. Report of the Commission on the Opium Monopoly, *Hongkong Government Gazette*, 23 November 1872, pp. 495–500.

39. Kennedy to Kimberly, 28 January 1873 and 10 March 1873, CO 129/162, pp. 123–24 and 403–8.

40. See Hayes, "Nam Pak Hong Commercial Association"; Sinn, *Power and Charity*, pp. 28–29; Jung-fang Tsai, *Hong Kong in Chinese History*, pp. 62–64; Yu and Liu, *Shijiu shiji de Xianggang*, pp. 370–71.

41. Articles of agreement of the Sun Yee Company, March 1874; *China Mail*, 9 February 1880.

42. Kennedy to Carnarvon, 23 February 1876, CO 129/173, pp.134–40.

43. "Votes and Proceedings of the Legislative Council of Hongkong," 12 November 1877, p. 523.

44. *Hongkong Government Gazette*, 24 August 1878, p. 407; *China Mail*, 21 August 1878.

45. *China Mail*, 17 January 1879.

46. *Hongkong Daily Press*, 18 January 1879.

47. Memorandum by Tonnochy, 9 September 1881, CO 129/194, p. 362.

48. Legislative Council proceedings, *Hongkong Daily Press*, 20 January 1879.

49. The number of people prosecuted for breaches of the opium regulations rose from four in 1878 to 117 in 1879 and 195 in 1880. Sentences tended to be stiff, with fines of fifty or even two hundred dollars and the full three-month prison term specified in default of payment.

50. *China Mail*, 1 October 1879, p. 3.

51. Memorandum by Russell, 14 March 1883, CO 129/207, pp. 542–43.

52. Ibid., pp. 543–44.

53. Ibid., pp. 44–45; *China Mail,* 9 February 1880; articles of agreement of the Man Wo Sang Company, 9 March 1880, CO 129/207, pp. 576–85.

54. From this, $8,375 in government expenses connected with the monopoly has to be subtracted. Bowen to Derby, 22 March 1884, "Correspondence on the Subject of the Consumption of Opium," p. 11.

55. March to Derby, 11 August 1883, ibid., pp. 9–10.

56. Bowen to Derby, 19 July 1884, ibid., pp. 12–14; memorandum by Lister, 22 December 1884, ibid., pp.17–18.

57. The single tender for the monopoly had offered an amount for the whole year equal to less than what the government-run monopoly had produced in five months in 1883. Bowen to Derby, 28 August 1883, p. 8; Marsh to Derby, 22 October 1883, p. 10.

58. Bowen to Derby, 19 July 1884, pp. 13–14.

59. Memorandum by Lister, 22 December 1884, pp. 17–18.

60. Bowen to Derby, 6 November 1885, CO 129/223, pp. 12–13.

61. Report by Sir James Russell, 6 January 1892, "Correspondence on the Subject of the Consumption of Opium," p. 44.

62. Ordinance no. 22 of 1887.

63. Robinson to Knutsford, 22 January 1892, p. 43.

64. For a discussion of this theme see Rowe, *Hankow,* especially vol. 1, chapter 8.

65. Miners, "Hong Kong Government Opium Monopoly," p. 276.

66. Ibid., pp. 285, 295.

FIVE

Opium in Xinjiang and Beyond

David Bello

The Opium War of 1839–1842 occurred as the consequence of a creeping narcotic collaboration between the subjects of the Qing empire, its Eurasian neighbors, and its Western mercantile supplicants. The structure of human relations produced by this collaboration was decades in the making and extended throughout and beyond China to wherever opium was produced, transported, consumed, or profited from. These relations, being not simply concrete objects but practices and interdependencies, could not be confined to a discrete space and controlled, as the imperial bureaucracy sought to do in the southeastern coastal zone of Guangdong in 1839. Rather, by the time the government of the Daoguang emperor, the sixth ruler of China's last dynasty, was forced to confront the opium problem, that problem was not restricted to a single city or province or region of the empire, but was localized and differentiated too intensively for the dynasty's centralized bureaucracy to control.

The direction that this confrontation would take was charted between 1836 and 1839 as the court thrashed out an activist policy embodied in a set of thirty-nine regulations and in the person of Imperial Commissioner Lin Zexu. The policy was intended to reassert central authority over the vast imperial dominions, which the government believed were being drained of silver by the opium traffic. During this period information was compiled clearly showing that opium had taken root in many localities of the interior where it was being produced by imperial subjects and brought in by Inner Asians, none of whom were directly connected to the British

Dates used in the text are given for each document according to the Chinese lunar calendar in the order of year / month / day.

coastal traders. Moreover, opium produced by these sources was circulating overland via mountain passes and along interprovincial and Inner Asian trade routes rather than by sea.

Information collected from the provinces showed that during the 1830s, and in some cases clearly earlier, opium was being traded, cultivated, and consumed all over China's interior, particularly on the frontiers of its western territories in Yunnan, Guizhou, Sichuan, Gansu, Shaanxi, and Xinjiang. In each of these locations the opium problem manifested itself somewhat differently even as it linked them together in a network of production, transportation, and consumption. Xinjiang was a particularly important part of this network because it possessed unique regional characteristics that created unusual problems for Qing control of opium. It was the only place in the empire that imported opium from foreign territories in Inner Asia and the northern Indian subcontinent while producing its own opium and sending both types eastward into China proper. It was also unique in that it was the only locality in China at the time that was involved in the opium trade with a non-Western state, the Khanate of Kokand.

This latter fact alone makes an examination of the opium problem in Xinjiang particularly valuable for any study of the problem between the British and Qing empires, which has been treated as virtually synonymous with the nineteenth-century opium problem in China. In the wider context provided by Qing Xinjiang's relations with its neighbors, patterns emerge that suggest that a culture clash between Chinese and Western notions of law, diplomacy, economics, and the like was not the main source of difficulty between Britain and China in the 1830s and 1840s. They indicate instead that the main source of difficulty between China and all foreigners,Western and otherwise, was power in the form of commodified and addictive opium.

Before going into the specifics of the dynamics of opium in Xinjiang and their significance for the rest of the Qing empire, I would like to examine the legal and political context of the opium problem itself in more detail in order to provide an adequate frame of reference for understanding the main issues of opium prohibition that arose in Xinjiang.

As early as 1729, the Qing dynasty's official perspective relegated opium to the coast and its riverine areas.[1] Dynastic statutes threatened to punish boatmen and various port officials for collusion with opium traffickers, thus enshrining the coastal nature of the opium trade in law. The distribution of opium use, however, did not remain so neatly restricted and by 1813 eunuch traffickers and addicts of the Forbidden City were being banished as slaves to Heilongjiang.[2] This destination was changed to Xinjiang under the next set of extensive regulations issued in 1820. According to a memorial by the famous official and chief of the Grand Council Mu-zhang-a written in 1840, a censor from the Board of Punishments suggested that exiling criminals to the same region as that of the auxiliary capital, known as Shengjing (Mukden), the pre-Qing capital of the Manchus, was inappropriate and so Xinjiang was duly pressed into service. Xinjiang's role as the empire's sole destination for virtually all exiled opium offenders became an important issue in subsequent deliberations over opium control in the province.[3] In a sense, as military governor of Xinjiang, Yi-shan implied early in 1840, the coastal opium problem was being exported to Xinjiang in the form of traffickers and addicts who had had their capital sentences commuted to banishment. In Xinjiang, these people had already generated fifty-four legal cases involving opium, mostly by turning themselves in.[4]

Officials in the Jiaqing reign (1796–1820) were even more conscious of not only the geographical extent of opium smoking but also its cultivation. It was also in 1813 that the first official sanctions against "the villainous people of the interior who plant poppy and gather its juice to make opium" appeared. Although the statute does not specify precisely where in the interior poppies were planted and scraped for their juice, opium was plainly no longer only being imported through coastal ports from abroad. Early in the nineteenth century, opium was not a major issue in Sino-British foreign relations, but it was already a domestic problem with its own dynamics that would ultimately test the limits of the Qing state to enforce its will in places far from the empire's coastal zone.[5]

One of the farthest of those places, in terms of both distance and culture, was Xinjiang, for which there is unofficial evidence of local cultivation of poppies in a poem by Ji Yun, a famous literatus who spent a year in exile there in 1770. Although it is far from clear to what use the poppies were put, the fact that they were being cultivated is suggestive, as is the date, which is well before the 1819 boom in the drug trade on the coast.[6]

Despite the presence of opium in the interior, the government's legislative focus continued to be directed toward the coastal trade, which was the main source of opium in China and which was believed to be draining China of silver. However, local cultivation in Zhejiang was the central theme of a series of memorials originating from Censor Shao Zhenghu that resulted in two imperial decrees in 1830 and 1831 that established new, more stringent regulations.[7] Local cultivation was also referred to in 1831 by the famous Qing general Yang Yuchun, who reported that there was opium being sold, but not cultivated, in Gansu.[8] Opium had reached far into the Chinese interior by the early 1830s.

By 1836 the highest levels of the central government were still unaware that any opium problem existed in Xinjiang, much less one involving both local production and cross-border traffic. The empire's senior bureaucrats, however, were all too cognizant that the opium problem was no longer confined to the coasts and that none of the existing regulations were effective enough to change this situation. This prompted legalization proposals, which represented the views of a clique of Guangdong officials under the leadership of the famous scholar-bureaucrat Ruan Yuan. The legalization faction, however, was soon discredited by revelations of corruption among the cohong merchants in Guangzhou with whom this clique had financial ties.[9]

The elimination of the legalizers cleared the way for the formulation of the strictest set of opium prohibition laws yet adopted by the dynasty. The driving force behind these laws was a group of metropolitan censors who constituted the forefront of hard-liners on opium among the bureaucracy. These men felt that if addicts stopped smoking, the traffic would automatically disappear. The solution was capital punishment for addicts, to either deter or eliminate them. The thirty-nine regulations on opium prohibition, often called the "New Regulations," that resulted were inspired by these censors, who believed that addict demand stimulated foreign traffic in coastal urban centers. To gain control over these locales would be to gain control over the opium problem.[10]

These assumptions were debatable in terms of the Han interior and its multi-ethnic borders; for, while it was certainly true that the bulk of opium in China could be found in the empire's coastal zone, the interior was no longer completely dependent on the coast to supply its opium needs. Moreover, the New Regulations caused great controversy among the officials of the provinces, many of whom argued that strict compliance with them would mean mass executions of addicts.[11] Although technically this was true, in practice there were many loopholes in the New Regulations, such as amnesties for voluntary handover of opium and for first offenses, that many local officials were quick to slip through.

One of the most eloquent voices echoing the concerns of the local officialdom of the rural Han interior was that of Shanxi Circuit Investigating Censor Guo Baiyin, who early in 1839 expressed doubt about the coastal, urban assumptions of the New Regulations even before they were formally promulgated. Guo's position was succinctly formulated in his assertion that "provinces like Guangxi, Sichuan, Yunnan, and Guizhou are places where barbarian ships cannot reach and foreign opium cannot penetrate. All these places come by opium from the locals' poppy-planting and paste-making."[12]

Guo's argument was that the effect of opium was different in western China, where it was locally cultivated, than in the eastern urban coastal regions, where it was sold by foreigners. Whereas foreign opium drained silver and wasted the wealth of the populace, the effect of locally cultivated opium, known as "little dirt" *(xiaotu)*, was more insidious. It exhausted the soil and deprived the state of taxes because its production remained secret. These qualities made little dirt a serious problem in its own right.

Guo also called for greater awareness of the important role played by little dirt in the agricultural economy of the west. With a farmer's sensitivity to seasons, he observed that the New Regulations could not be put into effect in many rural regions until the spring of 1839. By then opium would already have sprouted and peasants would be more likely to actively resist search and seizure operations because of their irrevocably heavy investments in the crop. Although the opium crop would be eradicated, it would be too late for these peasants to plant a new crop of grain. Thus taxes would continue to be lost.[13]

It is difficult to be sure what effect Guo's memorial had, beyond immediately generating an imperial decree for search and seizure operations to be launched in Guizhou and Yunnan.[14] This action in itself is instructive because it is clearly contrary to Guo's view that opium cannot be hastily eradicated from the countryside, which depended on it for income.

An opium problem was discovered in Xinjiang during this period of increasing severity by the central government. Actually, Beijing's attention was drawn to Xinjiang only after Vice Minister of the Court of Judicial Review Hui Feng complained in September 1839 that he had heard of no reports on opium cases from the territory.[15] The imperial decree issued in the fifth month, twenty-seventh day of 1839 ordering an investigation of the opium problem in Xinjiang was attentive to that region's particular characteristics and acknowledged that because the towns of western, southern, and northern Xinjiang are located in border zones over a wide expanse of territory, there are many points that border on foreign territories and it is therefore difficult to guarantee that there are no incidents of foreigners smuggling opium through the checkpoints for purposes of sale and resale.

Nevertheless, despite these obstacles, smuggling was to be strictly prohibited. Still, the court realized that conditions in Xinjiang were fundamentally different from those of the provinces of China proper and that these differences might hinder the implementation of the New Regulations. Consequently, senior military and civil officials in Xinjiang were to make concerted personal inquiries, deliberate, and then offer their suggestions to the throne for the adaptation of the New Regulations.[16] The court, however, assumed that the opium problem in Xinjiang was one of smuggling by foreigners. This was to prove only partly true.

The military governor of Ili and the highest Qing official in Xinjiang, Yi-shan, submitted a long memorial in response to the central government's decree on adapting the New Regulations to Xinjiang. It is important to note at the outset that Yi-shan's comments were predicated on the principle, commonly held by many officials at the time, that "the scourge of opium originated overseas and only gradually entered China."[17] Thus, to effectively prohibit opium on the coast was to stop up its flow into China proper.

Yi-shan compared traffic on the coast with that in Xinjiang, and found the latter negligible mainly because the foreign ships of the coast could carry much more opium than the foreign camels of the Inner Asian interior. Moreover, although he acknowledged the possibility of its existence, he had heard of no local cultivation. From this he concluded that foreign smuggling in Xinjiang was comparatively difficult and negligible in quantity, and therefore felt that strict enforcement of tough opium laws in such a sensitive border zone would be unnecessarily and dangerously disruptive. His solution was leniency for foreign first offenders trafficking in small amounts. Traffickers in large amounts and others guilty of "knowingly committing" opium crimes would continue to be harshly dealt with.[18]

Subsequent events, among them the discovery of cultivation and of extensive traffic throughout the territory, were to disprove Yi-shan's statements regarding the paucity of opium in Xinjiang. Within months two "barbarian criminals," a forty-three-year-old Kokandi trader named Ai-lin-bai and a fifty-eight-year-old Muslim from Tashkent named Nasir, were caught smuggling around 425 kilos of opium into Tarbagatai, Xinjiang's northernmost major town. The Daoguang emperor himself, while observing that this amount was hardly negligible, nevertheless decreed that as first offenders ignorant of the law, they were to avoid the beheadings and strangulations demanded by the Board of Punishments.[19]

This was a standard formulation used in incidents involving foreign smugglers in Xinjiang, all of whom, as far as I can determine, avoided any punishment beyond confiscation of their opium or a brief stint in the cangue followed by expulsion. The general excuse for such toleration was that foreign merchants were ignorant of Chinese law and were too widely scattered to be efficiently informed about it. Such ignorance would have been impossible if standing orders to inform traders at checkpoints and in town markets, in their own languages, were being carried out. The real reason was probably related to Yi-shan's concern about avoiding incidents in Xinjiang, which was in a constant state of simmering revolt and had already proven prohibitively expensive to defend against the neighboring Khanate of Kokand, whose merchants were intimately involved in the drug traffic.[20]

The authors of the New Regulations were convinced that previous prohibition laws had failed because they had not been vigorously implemented by officials, many of whom looked upon them as a dead letter and executed them in a perfunctory way.[21] Certainly a major reason for the impotence of state police powers both on the coast and in the interior was indeed the laxity and / or corruption of local officialdom.[22] However, this situation was exacerbated in Xinjiang by the peculiarities of its administrative structure, which were intimately connected to the fact that Han, Mongols, and Manchus resident there were a tiny minority in comparison with the indigenous population of Uighurs and other Inner Asian peoples.[23]

The Qing dynasty had finally taken the whole region from the Zhungar

Mongols in 1759, dubbed it the "New[ly Opened] Frontier" *(Xinjiang)* and divided the immense expanse into three "Marches" *(lu),* known as the Eastern March, the Northern March, and the Southern March. This division roughly corresponded to the geographical and social conditions that obtained at the time of the Qing conquest. The Tian Mountains, Xinjiang's basic geographic dividing line, bisected Xinjiang into northern and southern halves. The Eastern March, northeast of the Tian Mountains, was composed of a few city-states that had been under Han influence since Ming times and by the nineteenth century had partly fallen under the civilian administration of the Shaan(xi)-Gan(su) governor general.[24] The Northern March, also to the north of the Tian Mountains, was steppe that was sparsely populated by Mongol and Kazakh nomads and was almost immediately exposed to Han and Muslim agricultural colonization. The Southern March, south of the Tian Mountains, was composed of oasis towns populated by East Turkestani Muslims, mostly Uighurs and other Central Asians.[25]

The towns of the Southern March were administered by superintendents *(banshi dachen),* who were supervised by a councillor *(canzan dachen)* stationed, at this time, in Yarkand. The councillor was the highest Qing authority in the Southern March and subordinated only to the military governor at Ili in the Northern March, which also had a councillor in the northern town of Tarbagatai. The tasks of all these officials were largely military, and officials of the more urbanized Southern March had to rely upon indigenous structures for the bulk of the civil administration their existence necessitated.[26]

The complex society of the oasis towns of the Southern March proved particularly resistant to incorporation into the Qing empire via the traditional bureaucratic structure invented by the Han and modified by the Manchus, both of whom were largely unfamiliar with Inner Asian Islamic language and culture.[27] In practice, this meant that there could be no low-level officialdom composed of Han district magistrates and their runners to act as intermediaries between the general populace and the higher levels of the bureaucracy, as was the norm in China proper.

Instead there was a layer of local East Turkestani officialdom, generically known as "begs" *(boke),* who acted as intermediaries between the local Muslims and Qing civil and military officers in the Southern March, which was also known as Altishahr (Turki for "Six Cities"), Kashgaria, and Eastern Turkestan. These begs, who were of varying status and responsibility, constituted, among many other things, the Qing's frontline police investigators in the Southern March.[28]

Reliance on begs was unavoidable because the dynasty simply lacked the official manpower to adequately police this area. Actually, had it had the personnel, the begs would still have been necessary, as an early 1840 memorial from Xinjiang makes clear. The memorialist, the councillor of Yarkand, En-te-heng-e, was responding to the decree requesting evaluations of the New Regulations. En-te-heng-e submitted a long list of modifications intended for exclusive application in the cities of the Southern March, titled "Regulations for the Investigation and Prohibition of Opium in the Cities of the Southern March" (hereafter "Regulations: Southern March"). One section of these regulations specifically prohibited Han troops, who manned the various checkpoints scattered throughout Xinjiang, from inspecting incoming foreign trade goods for opium. The councillor proposed to use begs for this purpose instead, in order to prevent "incidents" between Han and Muslim traders.[29]

Xinjiang, both because of its frontier character and because of its East Turkestani population, also lacked structures of social control usually associated with Han gentry society, which would otherwise have helped to relieve the official administrative burden. In essence, one of the social effects of the geography of Xinjiang was to preclude the development of gentry social structures. By 1842 in Hami, for example, there was a total of only thirty successful candidates for the official exams, all of whom held either the lowest or no official position. Hami, which had had the longest exposure to Han political and cultural influence of any place in Xinjiang, had still not produced a gentry that could mediate between officialdom and the local masses for purposes of tax collection, security, and the like. This is precisely why begs were required in the Southern March.[30]

Some of the complications caused by dependency on the beg system, and by conditions in the Southern March in general, are revealed by the first case of local cultivation discovered in Xinjiang, which occurred in the vicinity of Kürla in the Kara-shahr region of the Southern March.[31]

The case provides a detailed description of how cultivators operated in Xinjiang and demonstrates that high market prices for opium stimulated cultivation by local Han merchants, who intended to transport their crop eastward into China proper. Gu Mengxun, a native of Shaanxi province, ran a shop in Kürla in partnership with Zhao Deshou. During April 1839 business was bad, and Gu told Zhao that since the price of opium was currently high, they should find a location to plant poppies and then decoct the paste to make into opium. Zhao agreed and the two went prospecting for a likely spot in the wilds east of Kürla.

Gu, however, was not the only Han merchant looking for an opium plot that day. While out looking around, Gu and Zhao ran into two acquaintances, Xie Zhi and Zhong Yun, who were engaged in a similar search. The four decided to form a partnership and find a plot together. Approximately fifty kilometers east of Kürla the four stumbled on a fifth agricultural entrepreneur, Ren Ju, as he was sowing his plot, and the partnership acquired a fifth shareholder.

A month later, the partnership had cleared an acre or so of wilderness, planted their poppy, built some sheds, and were living on their new fields with Guo Fengde, hired at five hundred strings of cash per month to cook for them while they tended their crop. The poppies were ready to be scraped for their juice within three months, but this had not yet been done when Zhao, on a supply run back to Kürla, was arrested by the Hakim Beg of Kara-shahr Tuo-hu-ta and his patrol, who were out searching for poppy cultivators. Zhao then led the authorities to the wilderness hideout of his partners, who were all arrested along with the cook Guo and taken back to Kürla, where they would be held until remanded to the regional administrative center of Kara-shahr. As the five men arrived under guard in Kürla and were passing through crowds of onlookers in the Muslim section of town, they were approached by two associates, Li Yun and Old Man Liu, who got word to the prisoners of a plan to free them.

Li and Liu got nine of their associates together and successfully ambushed the escort party on its way to Kara-shahr. The men rushed the transport carts, shouting and brandishing clubs and scattering the Muslim escorts, freeing Gu and his five compatriots. Gu and Zhao were recaptured by the beg and Guo turned himself in; in addition, Li Yun and his men were soon caught by the sergeant in command of the Kürla outpost, Zhao Zhongming, but the rest escaped.

At the trial in Kara-shahr, Gu, as chief conspirator, was sentenced to military life exile to "an insalubrious region of the furthest frontier," while Zhao, as an accomplice, received the lighter, but still quite serious, punishment of regular life exile at a distance of fifteen hundred kilometers from his native place. These punishments, however, were not the only ones meted out. Although Hakim Beg Tuo-hu-ta was ultimately not punished, Sergeant Zhao Zhongming was held responsible for failing both to send troops to escort the prisoners back to Kara-shahr and to detect the cultivators' operation in the first place.

The Daoguang emperor's personal comments on this case asserted that problems with opium prohibition in Xinjiang were a direct result of the "invariably perfunctory manner of the generals and senior officials of the various towns, all of whom are unwilling to make conscientious investigations." The authors of the decree were convinced that official laxity and a vast, isolated terrain were the two conditions that made Xinjiang an ideal place for the cultivation and smuggling of opium; indeed, Xinjiang's physical expanse was precisely what was held to encourage official apathy, which itself was enhanced by an excessive reliance on begs. Thus it was considered even more imperative for local officials to be as vigorous as possible in their pursuit of these crimes. The decree's expressions of anger and astonishment at the existence of both opium smuggling and cultivation in such a distant corner of the empire demonstrate that the court had reached a new and unwelcome level of awareness of the extent of the opium problem. They also reveal an acute understanding of the relationship between physical space and bureaucratic laxity.[32]

The court was quite correct in believing that Xinjiang's geography, in addition to its complex and problematic administrative structure, encouraged the clandestine production and sale of opium. The natural conditions for opium cultivation in vast, isolated areas in Xinjiang were outstanding, allowing for the sowing of three crops per year, one each in spring, early fall, and late fall. By contrast, most places in the interior could produce only one crop per year in the spring. Moreover, opium sown during late fall was especially difficult to detect because of its resemblance to sprouts of winter wheat.[33]

The steppe of the Northern March was particularly favorable to local cultivation. A report on search and seizure operations in the region's northernmost major town, Tarbagatai, by its councillor, Tuanduobu, reveals the kind of distances, terrain, and climate encountered on such operations. Mongol horsemen were sent out by the local government to sweep the alpine winter fields of the region in search of cultivators in conjunction with their usual duties of patrolling the region's checkpoints.[34] The Mongols caught nine planters altogether. One of them, Ji Shenglai, stated that the main perpetrators were four grain traders who worked in the area around the towns of Kur-Kara-Usu and Jing He, which were both approximately two hundred miles to the south of Tarbagatai in the region of Kur-Kara-Usu.[35] All the planters involved appear to have been Han.

Enforcement of the opium prohibitions in the Northern March primarily meant mounted operations in the mountains throughout the year. The lot of poppy planters was hardly easier, as the relatively safe alpine fields were far from market towns where their produce could be sold. Since one of Xinjiang's three growing seasons for opium was late fall, it was necessary for both the authorities and the traffickers to operate under some of the most forbidding climactic conditions of the northern steppe. This situation made enforcing the prohibitions in Xinjiang much harder than in an urban environment on the coast or even in a rural one in the more moderate climates of China proper. These conditions also necessitated the use of Inner Asian horsemen such as the Mongols, who possessed the skills and stamina for such conditions that Han troops did not. Military and police operations in Xinjiang were dependent on multi-ethnic cooperation between Han, Manchu, Mongol, Tungan (Chinese Muslim), and East Turkestani. Herein lay another complicating factor that distinguished the prohibition of opium in Xinjiang from that in other parts of the empire.

A further obstacle to the efficient implementation of the New Regulations in Xinjiang was the diversity of geographical, social, and political conditions within the territory itself, as opposed to those that distinguished it

from China proper. The opium problem of the northern steppes was one
of both local cultivation by Han colonists and smuggling by inhabitants of
what was becoming Russian Central Asia. The problem in the southern
oasis towns was mainly smuggling by Kashmiri, Badakshani, and Kokandi
Muslim traders, although there was unquestionably also a good deal of local
cultivation by Han and Muslim farmers. These complexities were recognized by officials such as En-te-heng-e, who emphasized that the Northern
and Southern Marches required separate deliberations for the management of the opium problem.[36]

   The social and ethnographic geography of Xinjiang was also instrumental in the spread of opium cultivation techniques to the region's inhabitants. Some Qing officials believed that opium cultivation had originated
in the Southern March, which contained, in addition to indigenous East
Turkestani Muslims, Afghans from Badakshan, Kashmiris from the northern Indian subcontinent, and Andijans from Kokand. Hui Feng, whose
memorial had initiated investigations in Xinjiang, asserted in the same document that "poppies come from the western regions, where I have heard
that there are large numbers of people in every city who grow them."[37] By
the late 1830s, as officials began to seriously investigate the opium problem
in Xinjiang, cases of both Chinese and Muslim cultivation were appearing.
This is apparent in the "Regulations: Southern March" submitted by En-
te-heng-e in January 1840:

> Both Karashahr and Kucha have had cases of Chinese and Muslim clandestine
> cultivation of opium, which have been reported and processed. Civilians in
> Kashgar's and Barchuk's agricultural colonies, military personnel in Aksu's
> and Ush Turfan's agricultural colonies . . . and various desolate places around
> cities and farms all have Muslims planting opium.[38]

En-te-heng-e provides some indirect evidence for the transmission of
opium cultivation techniques between Muslims and Chinese colonists in
the Southern and Eastern Marches via the agri-colony system. This system
was a series of strategically placed farms whose output was intended to
supply the military garrisons that worked them in peacetime or to enable
Han civilians to settle non-Han areas. All these colonies were potential
nexuses for the circulation of cultivation techniques among Muslim and
Han farmers.[39]

   Officials concerned with the opium problem in Xinjiang not only located the origins of the problem among the local Muslims, but also blamed
trade relations between Qing subjects and some Muslim khanates, as well
as various nomadic Central Asian tribes. Hui Feng's report contains a fairly
detailed account of this complex network and is hence worth closer examination.

   Hui attributed the dearth of opium cases in Xinjiang not to a lack of opium, but to lack of personnel to supervise so vast an area. As we have seen, the Daoguang emperor often expressed extreme skepticism about such excuses and preferred to attribute problems of administrative control to the corruption and laziness of officialdom. Neither corruption nor lack of officials, however, was entirely responsible for the cross-border opium trade in Xinjiang. As Hui himself observed, the trade had sprung up between "foreigners," whose lands bordered on imperial territory, and "officials, Muslims and Mongols" of the oasis towns.

He considered this situation far more serious than in the Han interior because the opium trade was producing large numbers of undependable, potentially disruptive addicts in a strategically sensitive border area.[40] Hui had articulated an important difference between the effect of opium on the coast and at the Inner Asian borders, where the dynasty believed the greater threat to its stability lay. Hui also unconsciously touched upon a contradiction common among officials, namely that official corruption was clearly part of the opium problem, but only an increase in officials could stop the traffic.

In addition to his general warnings about foreign barbarians, Hui Feng also identified nomad tribes (Kara-Khirghiz and Kazakhs) from Russia and merchants from the city of Andijan in Kokand as major opium smugglers. The latter were particularly active and had been selling opium just over the border in the Southern March, from where it was then resold in Gansu. Hui Feng states that he heard about this particular route while acting as surveillance commissioner *(ancha shi)* in Gansu, a position he held from 1829 to 1832.[41] This information is quite valuable not only because it specifically identifies several sources of opium from beyond Xinjiang's western frontier, but also because it provides evidence for a cross-border opium network stretching from Andijan in Kokand to Gansu no later than 1832. There is further evidence for a wider scope of Muslim opium smuggling operations beyond Kokand. The "Regulations: Southern March" asserts that "Kashmir and Badakshan are the worst" smugglers of opium through the border checkpoints.[42] Subcontinental opium was thus flowing into China from both east and west.

Most of the opium that officials in Xinjiang seized was turned in voluntarily by merchants from Kashmir, Badakshan, Andijan / Kokand, and "India," and by East Turkestanis of the Southern March in one of the largest such operations in the interior. In one group of cases more than 2,499 kilos, or thirty-nine chests, were turned over.[43] This voluntary compliance had occurred as a result of a New Regulations' provision guaranteeing that possessors of opium and / or paraphernalia, particularly if they were first offenders, would not be punished if they turned everything over within the year-and-a-half grace period established by the new laws. If local officials' accounts from Xinjiang are to be believed, the Inner Asian traffickers enthusiastically participated in this program.[44]

The fragmentary information on opium seizures suggests that in the Southern March, Muslims from Kashmir, "India," Kokand/Andijan, and Badakshan were the main traffickers, at least those who came forward to take advantage of the grace period. The vast majority of the opium traffic entering the Southern March seems to have come from "India," with the Kashmiris running a close second. Kokand brought in much less opium than Kashmir but far more than Badakshan. However, these totals represent only opium that was voluntarily handed over by traders and inhabitants of the Southern March during the grace period, which began in August 1839.[45] It is quite possible that those handing over the least opium could have been the biggest traffickers.[46]

Regardless of the sincerity of some of the traffickers, to say nothing of the local officials, in Xinjiang the illegal drug trade continued among the populace of the region. Despite the impression that the overwhelming majority of opium in Xinjiang was being either produced or cultivated by Muslims for Han consumption, both groups were identified as cultivators. Moreover, Muslims were only one segment of the opium distribution network in western China, which, after all, could never have penetrated the Han interior without the collusion of Chinese on a large scale.[47] A May 1840 memorial by censor Zhang Bingde provides a rough map of this network's eastern penetration:

> I have heard of a kind of opium from Xinjiang called *qiangtu,* smaller in size than that which comes from Guangdong. Its use in paste-making and smoking is no different from that of [Guangdong's] opium. I, a native of Shanxi, have also heard that when people from Xinzhou in Shanxi go to Xinjiang to trade, each smuggles back *qiangtu.* By way of various passes, such as Jiayu and Hami, it secretly enters the interior and is sold in Shaanxi, Henan, etc. It is, however, especially plentiful in Shanxi.[48]

According to Zhang, Xinjiang was not only producing its own special brand of opium, but was exporting it to other provinces much farther east. This eastward transmission of opium was unquestionably stimulated by the drug's commodification on the east coast by the British, but *qiangtu* was not an import from British India. Local cultivation in the early 1830s already indicated that opium was not a purely Sino-British problem. By 1839, to further complicate matters for the dynasty, it was not even a purely Sino-Western one.

The Kokandi city of Andijan was cited by a number of Qing officials as the primary opium depot for distribution across the frontier into Xinjiang and points east. Although this chapter has so far been largely concerned with opium's effect within the empire's borders, the political geography of Xinjiang necessitates an examination of Qing foreign policy toward Kokand, which was essentially a fragment of a fragment of a fragment of what had been Jenghiz Khan's empire.[49] Kokand was an expansionist Muslim state whose ambitions by the early nineteenth century were largely directed at the Southern March. This resulted in a number of clashes between the khanate and the Qing empire.

In 1839 En-te-heng-e stated that "all foreign merchants" began bringing opium into the Southern March after border inspections were suspended in 1832.[50] The geographical, political, and historical elements that brought opium to the Southern March tell much about Qing border policy in the far west and show why the Qing was as unable to stop the flow of the drug from west to east as it was from east to west.

The history of relations between Kokand and the Qing is complex. It is sufficient for the purposes of this chapter to focus on the origin of the 1830 invasion and some of its aftereffects.[51] From the Qing conquest of Xinjiang in 1759 until approximately 1820, relations between Kokand and the Qing empire were couched in the traditional language of nominal Chinese suzerain and nominal foreign vassal. From the beginning of the nineteenth century, however, cracks began to appear in the relationship that foreshadowed Kokand's rise to regional domination and its transition to a new status as a de facto co-equal of the Qing state. A fundamental change in relations between the two states had occurred, and the 1830 Kokandi incursion into Xinjiang showed that this change could not be reversed. One result of this change was the cross-border opium trade.

Throughout the period of their relations with the Qing, the Kokandis were busily taking advantage of their cultural affinities with the local Muslims of the Southern March even as they sent ostensibly submissive missions to Beijing. They were able to do this because as Turkic Muslims they had racial and religious affinities with the East Turkestanis. Both the Kokandis and the East Turkestanis shared an antipathy toward the Qing rulers, whom they considered pagans as well as invaders. This antipathy manifested itself in an unending series of plots between the Kokandis and the Khojas, Naqshbandi Sufi holy men who had been the former rulers of the Southern March, to expel the Qing.[52] Thus, behind a facade of harmonious relations the Kokandis were making preparations to replace Qing regional hegemony with their own. To this end, the Kokandis worked to exploit weaknesses that afflicted the Qing presence in the Southern March. One serious weakness was the prevalence of a subculture of smuggling, which made a mockery of Qing efforts at local control and smoothed the way for Kokandi military operations.

The infrastructure of smuggling that ran throughout the Southern March was a multicultural construct composed of various Central Asian and

Han traders, many of whom had become permanent residents through marriage with local Uighur women.[53] Such a nexus enmeshed officialdom into an indirect collusion with Kokand. Qing documents reveal official fears that Chinese merchants were assisting their Kokandi counterparts in evading Chinese government trade regulations and that frontier guards were allowing Andijan merchants to bribe them into "inspecting only a part of their merchandise."[54]

This type of commercial penetration was the immediate issue over which Kokandi and Qing interests clashed. As Kokand's economic power grew, its commercial and territorial demands became bolder. These ranged from minor incidents, such as the use of inappropriately familiar language in official communications, to a large-scale (twenty-five- to thirty-thousand-man) invasion of the Southern March in 1830. Two themes that were played continuously throughout this period were Kokandi demands for duty-free passage of goods from their territories into the Southern March and for the right to replace the imperially appointed commissioner of foreign commerce at Kashgar with one of their own begs, who would oversee Kokandi trade affairs. Both these demands were crucial to the maintenance of Kokand's development as a regional power.[55]

The invaders of 1830 were repelled within a few months, yet by 1832 the Kokandis had had all their demands met in exchange for a token resubmission to the Qing throne and a promise to neither instigate nor abet further incidents on the border. In this way the Qing empire attempted to buy peace on its western frontier, which, despite the empire's military victories, it was too weak to secure independently. In general, Qing foreign policy west of the border was to maintain a peaceful status quo in an area Qing leaders had only recently and tenuously incorporated.[56]

By 1840 some officials began to assert that this passive policy was directly responsible for the flow of opium into the Southern March from Kokand and beyond. En-te-heng-e, for example, observed that the original regulations called for inspections of the barbarian traders' goods to be made when they were paying duties at the border checkpoints. After 1832 duties were abolished. Consequently, smuggling could no longer be checked and, as a result, every barbarian was openly selling opium within the borders.[57] Although it seems that any "barbarians" could have avoided inspection and brought opium into Qing territory, it was the Kokandis who were directly responsible for the abolition of these duties and it was they who benefited most, positioned as they were to dominate the western trade routes into the Southern March.[58]

In effect, Kokand was controlling the entry of much of the opium grown in Central Asia and in the northern subcontinent for export eastward to China. The Qing response was constrained by distance, expense, and culture to the point that officials of the Daoguang emperor were reduced to pretending that the Kokandis were completely ignorant of Qing law.[59] Aside from motives of profit, Kokand may have continued to export opium to China possibly in order to destabilize dynastic control of the Southern March, making it ripe for conquest.

The Qing chose to deal with the opium problem in Xinjiang, and in other frontier areas of the empire, by using the bureaucratic structures that served as intermediaries between the dynasty and the various peoples engaged in opium smuggling and cultivation. In southwest China, an area exhibiting many of the socioeconomic dynamics found in the northwest, Ruan Yuan as early as 1831 proposed using the system of "native officials" *(tusi)* to stop indigenous minority cultivation of opium by employing native chiefs to notify their people of the law, personally investigate violations, and confiscate fields used to grow opium.[60] In the northwest, begs were to fulfill a similar role. The existence of such administrative structures and of the non-Han populations they were intended to control made opium suppression in western China far more complex than it was on the coast, where Han gentry structures of control were in place.[61]

Begs and native officials failed to control opium partly because their role had not been to serve as instruments of close control and surveillance. The Qing strategy was to leave these traditional structures of dominance in place in order to remit taxes and solve disputes in the smoothest manner possible. As a result, dynastic officials were reluctant to interfere with most of the cultural practices of the non-Han peoples of western China that did not directly threaten local control for fear of "incidents." Opium disturbed this equilibrium in an unprecedented fashion, in part because opium use had previously been, or was in the process of becoming, part of the culture of many non-Han peoples within and on the borders of western China. Moreover, the opium trade was an important part of their incomes.[62] Both Muslims in the northwest and non-Han peoples in the southwest seem to have been familiar with the cultivation of opium and unwilling to give it up.

Military force was an excessive and prohibitively expensive response for the dynasty, if for no other reason than that the scattered subjects of the empire growing opium deep in the mountains and valleys of western China presented poor targets for large-scale military operations. Moreover, the presence of other states willing to provide military assistance broke the monopoly on armed force that the Qing maintained in its dominions. As was more decisively demonstrated on the coast, state military power outside that of the empire was a crucial factor in sustaining transgressive behavior. The case of Kokand demonstrates that technological superiority, even victory, was unnecessary for the maintenance of resistance. Geographic position and cultural affinity were of greater significance in the power relations of Xinjiang, where there is no evidence of a culture clash between essentialized entities of East and West.

Unfortunately for the dynasty, officialdom's capacity for geographical conceptualization beyond the confines of the empire was quite limited. This is nowhere better demonstrated than in a brief exchange of communications between En-te-heng-e and the imperial authorities in Beijing beginning in August 1840. In reaction to a rumor heard by censor Jiao Yulin, the government ordered En-te-heng-e to discover whether or not the British had an overland route to Xinjiang that they were using for opium smuggling and for the illicit purchase of saltpeter from the local populace.[63] En-te-heng-e replied that the reports of begs and of various superintendents all affirmed that there were no such routes and that no Englishmen had ever reached Xinjiang and tried to purchase saltpeter or anything else. En-te-heng-e also made it clear that the only foreigners moving about in the vast area on the western edge of the Southern March were Kashmiris, Badakshanis, assorted Mongols, and "Indians." A decree issued several months later expressed satisfaction with this report.[64]

Ironically, both Jiao Yulin and En-te-heng-e touched upon a profound spatial truth without fully understanding it, much like the blind men of Indian fable who sought to describe an elephant after each touching only a single part. Technically there was no overland connection between Britain and Xinjiang. Yet various "Indians" were using precisely such routes to bring opium to Xinjiang from the British colony of India, in some sense an appendage of Britain itself, however unenthusiastic. Nevertheless, these barbarians were not Englishmen, as both the rulers of the British empire and their merchant charges in Guangzhou would have been among the first to confirm. Whatever the objective truth of the matter, a fascinating glimpse of the subjective condition of the Qing empire's rulers, by this time already in a vicarious shooting war with those of the British empire, is afforded by this exchange between Beijing and Yarkand. For a few months, the emperor and his senior officials feared themselves literally surrounded by the British barbarians. The epistemological shift engendered by the British attack began, in part, with a wrenching expansion of Qing officialdom's geographic perception.

A shift to regional perspective on the opium problem reveals many affinities between the two Qing imperial poles of Guangdong and Xinjiang.[65] Both encompassed entrepôts for foreign trade and, consequently, each developed an elaborate system of rules for controlling this activity. There were foreign trade representatives and problems of jurisdiction, which occasionally led to violence, in both localities.

Opium was one of the most important factors linking Guangdong, Xinjiang, and the rest of the empire in the late 1830s, and it proved too much for any contemporary system to handle. Whether it came from Andijan, "India," Russia, or the Southern March, opium both exposed weaknesses in structures of local control and exacerbated them. This property was related directly to its commodification by the British on the coast, for opium had long been present in several regions of China, including Xinjiang, without significantly affecting the local socioeconomic order. Commodified opium became a form of power that could not be suppressed via the limited military or police apparatuses of the Qing that did not extend low enough into local society, and indeed were far too dependent upon that society, to function effectively. The opium problem, like so many other problems of the late-Qing and Republican periods, required more comprehensive forms of control that reached down to the local social bedrock and would only come fully into place after 1949.

NOTES

I would like to thank Professors John E. Wills, Jr., and Charlotte Furth for their insightful comments on an earlier draft of this paper.

1. This perspective was certainly based on hard evidence. For example, the *Chongxiu Taiwan fuzhi* (1747), 9:38a–b, citing "the old gazetteer," states that the "red hairs" (the Dutch) produced opium in Java, whose resident Chinese both consumed the drug and smuggled it into Fujian and, ultimately, into Taiwan, where, despite prohibitions, it was ineradicable. There are also several coastal cases extant from the Yongzheng period; *Yongzheng chao hanwen zhupi zouzhe huibian*, 14:23, 15: 901–2. Wang Hongbin, however, provides evidence from Ming dynasty sources that opium came from both "overseas and the western regions," the latter term being a general reference to Xinjiang; *Jindu shijian*, p. 12.

2. *Qing huidian shili*, 828:1a–2b.

3. The exile destination changed again, but only for eunuchs, in the sixth year of the Daoguang emperor (1826) when Na Yancheng requested they be distributed as slaves among the military units of the provinces; see Yu Ende, *Zhongguo jinyan faling bianqian shi*, p. 27. There is some confusion as to dates. Mu-zhang-a writes that after the seventeenth year of the Jiaqing emperor (1812), the location of exile was changed to Xinjiang. The regulation as quoted in the *Qing huidian shili* notes that this change occurred after Jiaqing's twenty-fifth year (1820); *Qing huidian shili*, 828: 2b. Yu Ende cites a third date, the eighteenth year, seventh month of the Jiaqing emperor; Yu Ende, *Zhongguo jinyan*, p. 26. For the memorial by Mu-zhang-a, see *YPZZ*, Daoguang 20/5/1, 2:118. On the Xinjiang exile system, see Waley-Cohen, *Exile in Mid-Qing China*.

4. *YPZZ*, Daoguang 20/1/16, 2:5–6. Yi-shan's main concern over this issue was the implications of the New Regulations promulgated in an effort more strictly to enforce opium prohibition across the empire. Although I will deal with them in more detail below, it is important here to note that their most controversial aspect was capital punishment for addicts, who were given a year and a half from the date of promulgation to reform themselves. After only a few months it was clear to Yi-

shan and to other local officials that these addicts could never reform themselves in so short a time, if ever, and that the execution of the letter of the New Regulations would result in mass executions and fail to solve the opium problem. There were also problems with those whose capital sentences had already been commuted once, but were eligible for a normally irregular second commutation. Yi-shan's memorial deals with a variety of legal issues raised by the New Regulations and it is impossible here to deal with each in detail. However, it should be noted that Mu-zhang-a, responding to Yi-shan's suggestions as chief of the Grand Council, approved most of them except those he and his colleagues found excessively severe or impractical.

5. *Qing huidian shili*, 828:2b.

6. The lines from the poem are quoted in Qi Qingshun, " 'Xinjiang nanlu jinyan zhangcheng' qiantan," n. 99. Qi writes that this poem is evidence "from the early Jiaqing period" (1796–1820) for local cultivation of opium. However, Ji was in exile in Xinjiang between 1770 and 1771, during the Qianlong reign (1736–1795). Qi gives no explanation for this contention. Poppies were also noticed by Hong Liangji, the famous poet, scholar, and official, while he was serving the shortest term of exile in Xinjiang meted out during the Qing. Hong composed a number of essays and poems from his experiences, and in two of these he briefly mentions fields of "poppies as big as bowls." See Hong, *Tianshan kehua*, and Hong, *Yili jishi shi*, pp. 9b and 21a–b, respectively.

7. Zhu Jinpu, "Yapian zhanzheng qian Daoguang chao yanguan de jinyan lun," pp. 59–60; Gongzhong dang (Palace Museum Archives, Taipei): Shang yu (imperial edicts): Daoguang 10/6/24. *Qing huidian shili* cites grand councillor Lu Yinpu's memorial rather than Shao's; *Qing huidian shili*, 828:5a–6a. All memorials concerned quote a report from the governor general of Fujian and Zhejiang, Sun Er-zhun, on local cultivation in that region as the basis for their own recommendations for stricter laws.

8. *Qing huidian shili*, 828:6a–6b, provides the date of Yang's first of five nearly identical reports issued annually between 1831 and 1835. This reference, however, is only an excerpt of Yang's memorial, in which he states that opium had never been cultivated in Gansu because of its cold climate; Gongzhong dang (Number One Archives, Beijing): Falü dalei (legal category): Jinyan (opium prohibition): Daoguang 13/11/29. There are other accounts, mostly local gazetteers from various places in western China, that show that opium was indigenous to many areas there, including Gansu. In fact, the earliest reference to opium in Qing China is from a local Gansu gazetteer in 1657; another from Gansu contains an 1819 reference; Lin Man-houng, "Qingmo shehui liuxing xishi yapian yanjiu," pp. 180–81. There is also a reference to poppies (*ying su*) as indigenous to Gansu in a local gazetteer published in 1778; *Ganzhou fuzhi*, p. 229. In light of this evidence, Yang's investigation of the matter does not seem to have been sufficiently thorough.

9. Polachek, *Inner Opium War*, pp. 119–24, provides the most up-to-date account in English. For a contrasting view of events, see Zhu Jinpu, "Yapian zhanzheng qian Daoguang chao yanguan," pp. 61–66, and Li Yongqing, "Youguan jinyan yundong de jidian, pp. 79–86." Polachek asserts that court factionalism, rather than practical statecraft, resulted in the formation of irrational opium policies; pp. 102, 284–87. Evidence presented by these two Chinese scholars, however, shows that factionalism, along with other "irrational" factors, played less of a role in opium policy-

making than practical, if possibly misguided, concerns arising in response to the silver drain.

10. Zhu Jinpu, "Yapian zhanzheng qian Daoguang chao yanguan," p. 63; *Yapian zhanzheng wenxian huibian,* Daoguang 19/4/23, 1:557–58. The New Regulations, despite their focus on addicts, were equally harsh toward traffickers. In essence, the law equated the two crimes, hence the decision to use capital punishment for addicts, as it was already being used for traffickers. Some Chinese scholars have argued that the initial anti-user focus of the New Regulations had shifted to one of anti-import (i.e., anti–foreign trafficker) by the time Lin Zexu was sent to Guangzhou; Wang Licheng, "Yapian zhanzheng qianxi de jinyan juece pingxi," pp. 9–11.

11. Polachek, *Inner Opium War,* p. 130, notes that nineteen out of twenty-six high-ranking provincial officials expressed disapproval of the ideal of executing addicts. For an example of official reaction in Xinjiang, see the memorial by Yi-shan, military governor of the province, in *YPZZ,* Daoguang 20/1/16, 2:5. This situation is one of several indications of disagreements between local officials and the central government in Beijing.

12. Waiji dang (Outer court records, Taipei), Daoguang 18/12/23, pp. 11–12. A biography of Guo can be found in *Qingshi liezhuan,* 55:21b–24a.

13. Ibid.

14. *YPZZ,* Daoguang 18/12/2, 1:446. Interestingly, the decree left out Guo's assertion about the inability of foreign opium to flow so far from the coast.

15. Ibid., Daoguang 19/7/27, 1:676.

16. Ibid., 1:678.

17. Ibid., Daoguang 21/1/16, 2:3–4.

18. Ibid., 2:4–5.

19. MZSW, frame nos. 1030–1034, Daoguang 20/8/24; WCT Daoguang 20/12/5, pp. 54–55.

20. For a concise account of the revolts in the Southern Marches between 1759 and 1879, see Zhang Zhecheng, "Hezhou, Haohan yu Chashegeer huibian," pp. 32–34. For Qing sensitivity to the local power of Kokand, see Fletcher, "Heyday of the Ch'ing Order in Mongolia, Sinkiang and Tibet," p. 371.

21. *Yapian zhanzheng wenxian huibian,* 1:557. The memorials of General Yang Yuchun, discussed above, are exemplary in this regard.

22. For two brief examples in Xinjiang from Yarkand, see *YPZZ,* Daoguang 20/3/25, 2:64. There are many other cases from sources from all over the empire, including Beijing.

23. The vast majority of the Qing presence in Xinjiang was military and the main forces, usually around 20,000 troops, were stationed in the Northern March at Ili, which was considered the key strategic zone for controlling the whole of Xinjiang. These were garrison troops more than half of which were elite, mounted banner units. By contrast, there were generally around 6,000 Qing troops of all types, only about eight hundred of whom were bannermen, stationed in the Southern March. In the wake of the Kokandi invasion of 1830, troop strength in the Southern March was increased to 15,000 men, 3,000 of whom were transferred from Ili. See Lin Enxian, "Qingdai Xinjiang huanfang bingzhi zhi yanjiu," pp. 168–69; Fletcher, "Heyday of the Ch'ing Order," p. 374. It has been estimated that by 1831 Xinjiang's Uighur population alone was approximately 650,000 people. In other words, the

Southern March's entire garrison, even at its increased strength, was less than 2 percent of the Uighur population, and Xinjiang's entire military establishment was around 5 percent of it; Miao, "Qingdai Weiwuer zu renkou kaoshu," p. 74.

24. Millward, "Beyond the Pass," p. 12; Lin Enxian, "Qingdai Xinjiang huanfang," p. 168. The Eastern March's military affairs were the responsibility of a banner commander in chief *(dutong)*, stationed at Urumchi and subordinate to the military governor at Ili.

25. Fletcher, "Ch'ing Inner Asia," pp. 58–60; Millward, "Beyond the Pass," pp. 12–13; Lin Enxian, *Qingchao zai Xinjiang de Han-Hui geli zhengce*, pp. 3–12.

26. Millward, "Beyond the Pass," pp. 12–13. Lin Enxian, "Qingdai Xinjiang huanfang," pp. 168–69.

27. One example comes from a Tarbagatai dispatch in which a mullah named Ibrahim was cited for his crucial work as a translator. This involved making inquiries, purchasing information, and leading raiding parties. A reward was requested for him; Waiji dang, Daoguang 20 / 12 / 5, p. 54.

28. Lin Enxian, *Qingchao zai Xinjiang*, pp. 68–109. Ranks among begs were numerous. The Hakim begs, who are the ones most frequently encountered in documents relating to opium suppression, were the Muslim equivalent of the Southern March's Qing superintendents. They were the general supervisors of all affairs great and small in a particular town and the environs under its jurisdiction.

29. *YPZZ*, Daoguang 19 / 12 / 22, 1:786. Most of En's proposals were accepted by Mu-zhang-a but a few were rejected on the grounds that they were in fundamental conflict with the New Regulations, especially on the subject of determining the severity of punishment. The Daoguang emperor ordered En to investigate these matters further and respond. En, however, left his post to become Shaan(xi)-Gan(su) governor general early in 1841, and matters were left to his successor, Tu-ming-a, to resolve. In mid 1841 Tu-ming-a memorialized in favor of En's position but the final outcome remains unclear. *YPZZ*, Daoguang 20 / 3 / 27, 2:93; JY, Daoguang 21 / 6 / 17.

30. *Hami zhi*, 46:1a–2a. In 1698, sixty-one years before the Qing conquest of Xinjiang, the Mongolian socioeconomic and military *jasak* system, roughly analogous to the beg system of the south, was implemented in the Eastern March. See Huang Jianhua, "Qing zhi Minguo shiqi Xinjiang Weiwuer zu zhasake zhi yanjiu," p. 149; Lin Enxian, *Qingchao zai Xinjiang*, pp. 57–67. This is yet another complexity of the administrative structure within Xinjiang, where Uighur practices generally obtained in the south and Mongolian in the north.

31. JJY, frame nos. 2952–57, Daoguang 19 / 8 / 24. The following account of the case, unless otherwise noted, is based entirely on this memorial.

32. *YPZZ*, Daoguang 19 / 9 / 22, 1:715. Climate and isolated terrain also helped to create and exacerbate the opium problem in Yunnan, the southern frontier of which possessed conditions quite conducive to opium cultivation. There were also, as in Xinjiang, many isolated and mountainous places where cultivation would be difficult to detect.

33. Zeng, *Zhongguo jingguan xiyu shi*, p. 607.

34. *YPZZ*, Daoguang 20 / 8 / 24, 2:388.

35. Ibid.

36. Ibid., Daoguang 19 / 12 / 22, 1:785.

37. Ibid., Daoguang 19 / 7 / 27, 1:676.

38. Ibid., Daoguang 19 / 12 / 22, 1:787.

39. Fang, *Xinjiang tunken shi,* 2:563–79, provides a detailed overview of the distribution and administrative structure of the three main types of agri-colonies established in Xinjiang between 1716 and 1840. These types were termed military *(juntian* or *tuntian),* civilian *(mintun* or *yingtian),* and Muslim *(Huitian).* It is unclear to what extent Han and Uighurs could intermix in Xinjiang. Millward argues strongly for extensive contact between the two populations; "Beyond the Pass," pp. 154–55, 275–79. However, Lin's book on the subject, *Qingchao zai Xinjiang de Han-Hui geli zhengce,* makes it clear that a "segregation policy" between Han and Muslims was actively pursued by the Qing in Xinjiang. Nevertheless, this system, though certainly pervasive, was hardly absolute, as regulations providing for the enslavement of Han opium criminals to East Turkestani begs, among many other examples, demonstrate. There is clearly a difference between the central government's policies, which themselves are often contradictory, and the problematic realization of those policies by local officials.

40. *YPZZ,* Daoguang 19 / 7 / 27, 1:675–76.

41. Ibid., p. 676; *Qingdai zhiguan nianbiao,* 3:2134–37.

42. *YPZZ,* Daoguang 19 / 12 / 22, 1:786.

43. MZSW, frame nos. 1391–93, Daoguang 19 / 12 / 22. This amount represents confiscations from twenty-one traffickers in Yarkand. Joseph Fletcher's brief account of opium confiscation in Xinjiang asserts incorrectly that "over 97,900 ounces" of opium were confiscated from a single individual; "Heyday of the Ch'ing Order," p. 382. This amount was actually amassed from a series of confiscations from more than twenty and possibly more than thirty-five individuals in late 1839 and early 1840; MZSW, frame nos. 1391–93, Daoguang 19 / 12 / 22; MZSW, unnumbered, Daoguang 19 / 11 / 18; Qi Qingshun, "Xinjiang nanlu," p. 98; *YPZZ,* Daoguang 20 / 1 / 29, 2:23. Even at this reduced per capita figure, these voluntary handovers were among the largest in the interior. Shanxi officials, for example, confiscated a mere 779 kilos (twelve chests) from thirty-one traffickers and thirty-three hundred addicts; *YPZZ,* Daoguang 19 / 2 / 5, 1:502. In Yunnan, a major center of opium cultivation for both local use and extraprovincial sale, the largest confiscation that I have come across amounts to 6,200 kilos (97.5 chests) garnered over a year (mid 1839–mid 1840) from an indeterminate number of offenders; JY, Daoguang 20 / 4 / 19. It should be noted that these amounts were amassed from seizures rather than handovers. A chest weighed about 63.5 kilos.

44. The amounts turned over in Xinjiang, although considerable, were a fraction of those eventually forced out of the Western, mostly British, coastal opium traders, who initially handed over what everyone involved considered a token amount of a thousand-odd chests. After being assured of compensation by the British government, the coastal traffickers ended up joyfully surrendering more than twenty thousand chests, which they had not been able to sell as a result of the effective enforcement of the New Regulations by Commissioner Lin; Wakeman, "Canton Trade," pp. 187–88. The total amount of all opium confiscated in Xinjiang, in contrast, was only 5,546.5 kilos, or about eighty-seven chests; MZSW, frame nos. 1391–93, Daoguang 19 / 12 / 22; JY, Daoguang 20 / 2 / 19; JJY, frame nos. 3109–12, Daoguang 19 / 11 / 24; *YPZZ,* Daoguang 19 / 12 / 12, 1:780–81; *YPZZ,*

Daoguang 20/1/16, 2:3–7; MZSW, frame nos. 1030–34, Daoguang 20/8/24; MZSW, frame nos. 1394–95, Daoguang 20/4/20.

45. MZSW, Daoguang 19/12/22; Qi Qingshun, "'Xinjiang nanlu jingyan zhangcheng,'" pp. 96–97; YPZZ, Daoguang 19/12/13, 1:773. It is possible that the "Indian" traders were actually from the Punjab, which produced opium on its northeastern border with the Raj of Kulu, itself a producer and exporter of opium southward to India proper. Furthermore, even if there were traders from British India itself, it is not clear whether they brought their opium with them or purchased it in either the Punjab or Kulu, where it was being openly sold in the 1820s. William Moorcroft and George Trebeck, British travelers in the Himalayan regions of the subcontinent during the 1820s, in addition to providing information about the Punjab and Kulu, briefly describe opium use in the Sikh empire: "There is considerable demand both for opium and the poppy in the Panjab, as the Sikhs, whose religious creed forbids the use of tobacco, supply its place by opium and an infusion of poppy heads, to both of which they are much addicted, the former being used by the more wealthy, the latter by the poorer people"; Moorcroft and Trebeck, *Travels in the Himalayan Provinces,* 1:141, 171.

46. There is at least one case on record of a merchant who took advantage of the handover program to cover his extensive smuggling operations. He Tianzhong turned over a half kilo of opium during handover operations in Khotan, but was later found to have been part of a large-scale smuggling ring centered in Yarkand but reaching all the way to the Eastern March; YPZZ, 1:772–74; JY, Daoguang 20/2/19.

47. Muslims have often been connected with opium in Chinese history. Arab traders are thought to have introduced it to China during the Tang dynasty, and one scholar has asserted that Muslims were probably responsible for its introduction into Yunnan, via Burma, in 1736; see Edkins, *Opium,* pp. 38–39. Whatever the truth of this assertion, reports from Yunnan, Sichuan, and especially Xinjiang all affirm that Muslims were an important link in both the cross-border and domestic opium trade in both northwest and southwest China. Baoxing, an imperial clansman and governor general of Sichuan, confirmed the extent of Muslim involvement in the opium network in western China when he reported in 1839 that "many of those who sell opium [in Yunnan] are Muslims," who he believed also had networks in Guizhou and Sichuan; DGQL, Daoguang 19/12/18. Yet another memorialist, Jiangnan circuit investigating censor Lu Yinggu, corroborates the presence of Muslims connected with the drug trade in Sichuan, memorializing that in Sichuan "evil Muslim youths repeatedly gather and fight over opium, causing cases of large-scale mayhem and murder"; YPZZ, Daoguang 19/12/17, 1:774. These accounts all hint at widespread opium distribution networks running throughout western China, operated by Muslims and completely independent of those existing on the east coast.

48. YPZZ, Daoguang 20/4/10, 2:96.

49. The khanate of Kokand (1710–1876) had been a part of the Uzbek-dominated Shaybanid khanate (1500–1599), which was originally part of the Chagatai khanate, the portion of Jenghiz Khan's empire that devolved onto his second son, Chagatai. For a concise, if dated, narrative of the permutations that resulted in the khanate of Kokand, see Grousset, *Empire of the Steppes,* chapters 8 and 13.

Grousset's account of the Chagatai khanate's breakup has been revised; see Liu Yingsheng, "Chahetai hanguo de fenlie," pp. 99–105.

50. YPZZ, Daoguang 19/12/22, 1:786.

51. The account of Qing-Kokandi relations that follows is mainly based on Pan Zhiping, Zhongya haohanguo yu Qingdai Xinjiang; Saguchi, "Eastern Trade of the Khoqand Khanate"; and Fletcher, "Heyday of the Ch'ing Order," pp. 361–85.

52. Saguchi, "Eastern Trade," pp. 50, 58; Fletcher, "China and Central Asia," p. 219.

53. Saguchi, "Eastern Trade," pp. 81–86.

54. Ibid., pp. 53, 81. Andijan is a city of Kokand near the border of Xinjiang. In Chinese documents it is generally synonymous with Kokand.

55. For an account of the Kokandi Khan Alim's (1799–1811) futile attempt to address the Jiaqing emperor as "friend" in an official communication, see Pan Zhiping, Zhongya haohanguo, pp. 81–82. An account of the 1830 invasion and the events leading up to it can be found in Fletcher, "Heyday of the Ch'ing Order," pp. 361–75.

56. Pan Zhiping, Zhongya haohanguo, pp. 139–43; Fletcher, "Heyday of the Ch'ing Order," pp. 371–75. Fletcher characterized the subsequent 1835 settlement between China and Kokand as the latter's "first unequal treaty," and also made important comparisons between Qing-Kokandi and Qing-British foreign relations. This agreement granted Kokandi consular jurisdiction over foreign merchants of the Southern March as well as the authority to levy taxes of them. In effect, yet another administrative layer had been added to the region; ibid., pp. 375–85.

57. YPZZ, Daoguang 19/12/22, 1:786.

58. Kokand also tried to act as an emissary to the Qing court for the regions of Kashmir and Badakshan, both of which were major sources of opium smuggling, according to many of the memorials devoted to opium in Xinjiang. Pan Zhiping, Zhongya haohanguo, pp. 147–48. It remains unclear exactly where Kokandi merchants were getting their opium. Fletcher notes that "small amounts of opium" were coming into northern Xinjiang in the 1830s, and this, along with other accounts from Chinese scholars in the early twentieth century, has sustained the impression that opium in Xinjiang came mainly from Russia. See Fletcher, "Sino-Russian Relations," pp. 328–29; Zeng, Zhongguo jingguan xiyu shi, pp. 605, 607, 608–9. Although it is undoubtedly true that Kokand was a central transit point for Chinese and Russian goods, it was also one for goods coming up from India and Afghanistan. Moreover, it was itself a major regional center of agriculture. More research is required before the source of Kokandi opium can be decisively determined, though it is clear that Russian opium was coming into the Northern March and that there were other sources of opium, both domestic and foreign, throughout Xinjiang. A group of foreign merchants questioned by En-te-heng-e in late 1839 said that they had obtained their opium from "Yi-bo-te," whose location remains obscure, but might correspond to the town of Ura-tübe in the Bukhara Khanate on Kokland's western border; JJY frame nos. 3104–8, Daoguang 19/11/18. Cultivation of opium north of the Punjab would at least make it convenient for most of these traders to purchase their opium from this area, through which they had to pass on their way to Yarkand. This and the additional fact that the Kulu region of southwestern Ladakh was exporting opium south into India proper make it unlikely

that opium was being brought to Xinjiang from places south of the Punjab, such as Bengal, which was a main source of Chinese coastal opium.

59. MZSW, frame nos. 1396–1402, Daoguang 21/10/29. It is important to note that the khan, who was writing in part to protest the confiscation of his merchants' opium, is herein addressed as beg, implying that he is part of the Qing administrative structure of the Southern March. His protest was dismissed and I have found no further records of the incident.

60. *YPZZ*, Daoguang 11/5/9, 1:78. This memorial contains a detailed description of Yunnan's indigenous opium culture. Ruan, then governor general of Yunnan and Guizhou, attributed the opium problem in Yunnan to the province's shared frontier with Vietnam as well as to its proximity to Guangdong. Consequently, "barbarian" cultivation, production, and consumption of opium had all found their way into Yunnan. Ruan recommended enforcement procedures that the administrations of two previous governors general had developed, and some do seem to have been adopted by the central government for use in the New Regulations; ibid., 1: 77–78. Space precludes a detailed treatment of the opium network in the western and southwestern provinces of Sichuan, Yunnan, and Guizhou. Nevertheless, it should be noted that a great deal of material exists on the opium problem in all these locations and that some of it relates that opium use had long been endemic among the indigenous peoples along the southern frontier of Yunnan and among those on the Yunnan-Sichuan border. Bandit gangs were also involved with opium in the latter area; Bello, "Opium and the Limits of Empire."

61. Despite obvious problems with using gentry social structures as an unofficial police apparatus to suppress opium, it should be noted that Lin Zexu, bypassing the corrupt official local administration, primarily relied on local gentry in his successful, if short-lived, opium suppression campaign in Guangdong; see Chang, *Commissioner Lin and the Opium War*, p. 29. For a critique of Lin's methods, see Wakeman, "Canton Trade," pp. 186–87. Officials operating in the Southern Marches did not even have this option. An absence of, or weakness in, coastal gentry structures themselves has been noted in Wills, "Maritime China from Wang Chih to Shih Lang," pp. 209–10, 234.

62. Censor Lu Yinggu made several interesting points in this regard. He notes that cultivators in certain border areas of Yunnan had abandoned bean and wheat cultivation for opium, and that local officials were benefiting immensely from the change because the steady and comparatively large incomes opium produced ensured the timely and full collection of taxes. Lu Yinggu considered the wealth that opium could produce to be the major disincentive for both local inhabitants and their official minders to stop opium cultivation, production, and trade; DGQL, Daoguang 19/4/13.

63. *YPZZ*, Daoguang 20/8/4, 2:306–7.

64. For En-te-heng-e's memorial, see Waiji dang, Daoguang 20/12/5, pp. 57–58. Ismail was, presumably, the Hakim beg for Yarkand. For the imperial decree, see *YPZZ*, Daoguang 20/12/5, 2:662. The view that "Hindustan" possessed a common border with the "maritime barbarians" was also held by Xinjiang's military governor, Hui-ji; Li Xingyuan, *Li Xingyuan riji*, 1:96.

65. Many of these affinities were noted by Joseph Fletcher, "Heyday of the Ch'ing Order in Mongolia, Xinjiang and Tibet," p. 384.

SIX

Drug Operations by Resident Japanese in Tianjin

Motohiro Kobayashi

Translated by Bob Tadashi Wakabayashi

OPIUM AND WAR CRIMES

After World War Two ended, the General Headquarters (GHQ) of the occupation of Japan issued a memorandum to the Japanese government dated 12 October 1945 titled "Control of Narcotic Products and Records in Japan." It outlawed the cultivation, manufacture, importing, and exporting of narcotics; and the Ministry of Health and Welfare issued directives to that effect in November 1945 and March 1946. Equally important, the GHQ memorandum also ordered that all existing records related to opium and narcotics be held intact. In this way GHQ repudiated the administration of narcotics by Japan and took control itself.[1] At the same time, the Allied Powers were preparing to prosecute the Japanese for a policy of drug trafficking in China. L. H. Barnard of the International Prosecuting Section (IPS) of the International Military Tribunal for the Far East (IMTFE), or Tokyo War Crimes Trials, used sources left by several American consulates in China and a U.S. treasury department official in Shanghai. On 27 December 1945 he compiled a report on wartime opium and narcotics activities that listed the names of sixty Japanese, thirteen Chinese, and nine Taiwanese.[2] The list included not only military officers and government bureaucrats, but also numerous civilian businessmen who were active in and around Tianjin. One of them, Izumo Yasuke, was a representative of the Kyokutō *gongsi* and had been a respected member of the Tianjin Japanese business community since 1910.[3] If this report is true the implications are immense, for it indicates that even seemingly legitimate Japanese businessmen engaged in drug dealing on the sly. And that, in turn, suggests just how widespread Japanese drug trafficking was in north China.

The Tokyo War Crimes Trials lasted from May 1946 to November 1948. These declared that Japan's wartime opium operations violated international anti-opium treaties and placed Japanese leaders on trial for A-class war crimes. Despite the GHQ memorandum ordering the preservation of records, almost no Japanese primary sources were tendered at the Tokyo War Crimes proceedings; instead, documentary evidence was obtained from Chinese sources or foreigners in China. In addition to the Tokyo trials, B- and C-class war crimes trials were held at various locations in China at which Japanese military personnel and advisors to collaborator regimes were prosecuted. But little is known about the proceedings, the reliability of the evidence, or the types of sources used.[4] It is not even known whether Japanese civilians were tried.

Japanese, especially those who lived in prewar and wartime China, knew about Japan's role in the drug trade, but pangs of guilt purged it from their memories. Moreover, this issue is further complicated by the participation of Koreans in that drug trade—a tragic product of Japan's imperialism that will be treated later in this chapter. For such reasons, Japanese early in the postwar era distanced themselves from this issue and avoided historical analyses of it. Then in the late 1960s the Tokyo War Crimes Trial proceedings were published. Noting their value as source materials, Kuroha Kiyotaka took up the study of this topic and it again became known.[5] In 1982 Eguchi Keiichi chanced to discover a priceless cache of primary sources related to the Mengjiang (J., Mōkyō) Federal Regime for Mongol Autonomy, which he published in 1985. This proved to be an epoch-making find because these documents substantiated to a high degree the Japanese government's wartime involvement in the China drug trade.[6] As Eguchi's later studies convincingly show, imperial Japan pursued a state policy of opium and narcotics trafficking in China from the start of the Sino-Japanese War in 1937.[7]

But when considered in the context of modern Japanese opium and narcotics policy as a whole, this wartime period of direct intervention by the imperial army and government is treated as exceptional rather than the norm. Hence, my goal in this chapter is to examine the larger historical background. I will look at the prewar period, when trafficking was done by private individuals in China rather than by the imperial state itself. We have had a vague knowledge that there was trafficking by resident Japanese in China, but up to now we have lacked concrete evidence in the form of primary sources because of the clandestine nature of these criminal activities. Thus, although the general topic of opium came to light again thanks to Kuroha and a few others, not nearly enough scholarly research has been done on the drug trade run by private individuals in China, except for a recent study by Yamada Gōichi on opium and narcotics trafficking by resident Japanese in Shanghai and Dalian (J., Dairen).[8] Using consular police records in the Japanese Foreign Ministry Archives in Tokyo plus other primary sources, I try to show the nature and extent of these illicit activities by Japanese private individuals in prewar Tianjin, which was a nerve center for the north Chinese economy. Equally important, I hope to show that the Japanese consular police did make a fairly earnest attempt—under extremely difficult circumstances—to bring these traffickers under control in the 1920s and 1930s. Those efforts were doomed to failure, however, owing to the exigencies of Japanese imperialism. My focus on the consular police will also help to delineate the historical shift in perpetrators of Japanese opium operations in China—from private individuals to the imperial state itself.

A TWO-FACED POLICY

From its very inception the Meiji state recognized the evils of opium in the Qing empire and therefore strictly controlled narcotic substances at home so as to prevent their importation from the West. But after the 1894-1895 First Sino-Japanese War, Japan took over Taiwan and for the first time came face to face with the problem of opium—while also discovering that it was extremely lucrative. Thereafter imperial Japan pursued a two-faced policy: banning opium at home while raising revenue through monopolies in overseas colonies and leased territories such as Kwantung (Guandong). (In Korea, which was annexed in 1910, Japan adopted a policy of gradual prohibition of opium use, but stopped short of a monopoly; Japan did not set up monopolies in its Shanghai settlement and Tianjin concession.) Imperial Japan gained an unsavory reputation for this two-faced policy—and for good reason. The city of Dalian in Kwantung was an opium smuggling center, and opium from the Taiwan monopoly flowed into Shanghai and elsewhere. Moreover, the average annual consumption of morphine per one million population in Kwantung was some twenty-seven to forty-four kilograms in 1932-1933—the highest figure in the world—as was the average annual consumption of cocaine in Kwantung.[9] So one must ask: What made imperial Japan adopt this hands-off policy vis-à-vis opium outside the home islands?

After seizing colonies and treaty port concessions, a rapidly modernizing Japan extended its spheres of influence abroad, and Japanese nationals traveled overseas to work in two groups. One group went as fishermen or contract agricultural laborers to the western hemisphere—Hawaii, the continental United States, and Canada, and later to South America, after the United States and Canada passed Japanese exclusion laws. The second group went to various parts of Asia somewhat later in the Meiji and Taishō periods. As Eguchi argues, modern Japan was an imperialist power with feet of clay. Japan boasted colonial holdings plus a world-class army and navy, yet was economically subordinate to the West. Despite achieving independence and seeming autonomy from Western imperial powers, imperial Japan was in fact dependent on them for the wherewithal to uphold great-power status.[10] Hence, aside from a few persons who worked for government or business concerns, the vast majority of these Meiji and Taishō sojourners in Asia came from the lower echelons of Japanese society. These resident Japanese in Asia were the run-off from an economic system that lacked the industrial resources or capacity to support them at home. They had not ventured abroad with dreams of enhancing Japanese prestige and hardly warranted the label "colonizers" or even "immigrants." Instead, they were *kimin*—"good riddance" elements who forsook Japan and were forsaken by it. Lacking capital to engage in commercial ventures, these carpetbaggers or *tairiku rōnin* (continental masterless samurai) viewed drug trafficking as a way to make quick, easy, and huge profits. They were victims of modern Japan's imperial order and in turn its worst victimizers; and they presented China with a new drug menace just as it was striving to rid itself of British opium. China appealed to the Japanese government in the League of Nations and at international anti-opium conferences for help in bringing these lawless carpetbaggers under control. But the clay-footed Japanese imperial system that produced them could hardly be expected to rein them in.

TIANJIN OPIUM

Imperial Japan opened a consulate in Tianjin in 1875 (upgraded to a consulate general in 1902), and won concessions in that treaty port city under the Japan-Qing Trade and Navigation Pact in 1898.[11] This marked Japan's late start in its north China colonial rivalry with Britain and France. The site of Japan's concession was a swamp, however, so there was little influx of settlers until after the 1900 Boxer Incident. Being the closest power to the scene, Japan sent the largest contingent of foreign troops to quell that rebellion and won the right to station a garrison along the Beijing-Tianjin corridor in 1901. The Japanese detachment, which later assumed the name "China Garrison Army," came to number 1,771 men. Hoping to cater to the needs of those troops, residents from Japan flocked to Tianjin, where they rose in number from fifty to about six thousand by the 1920s. This made Tianjin the third largest resident community—behind Shanghai and Qingdao—in China outside of Manchuria. Tianjin served as a convenient way station to Manchuria during the Russo-Japanese War, and to Shandong during World War I, so these carpetbaggers increased after every war or disturbance. In the 1920s resident Japanese in Tianjin ran bars and restaurants, small pharmacies, and general stores; but trading concerns were most numerous, and accounted for about 25 percent of their occupations.[12] A

Tianjin Greater Japan Concessions Bureau was set up as an administrative organ in 1902, and it became the Organization of Tianjin Resident Japanese (OTRJ) in 1907. The OTRJ exercised rights of self-government under the direction of the consul general and bore responsibility for general administrative affairs in the territory.

The Japanese community in Tianjin comprised three general socioeconomic strata: large commercial concerns, smaller locally based firms plus a few professional classes, and small businesses such as eateries, general stores, medicinal outlets, bars, and brothels. Opium and narcotics dealers were to be found among nearly all these strata. The memoirs of Ishii Itarō are revealing on this point. Coming to Tianjin as acting consul in 1917, his main duties centered on deliberating consular court cases. Soon after his arrival he was asked to judge a Korean on charges of smuggling morphine. The consular police chief had told him to be firm in these cases, so Ishii handed down a sentence of six months. The police chief pulled Ishii aside and said that the sentence was too harsh, that Ishii's predecessor, Acting Consul Yoshida, would have handed down a two-month sentence. So Ishii changed the term to two months. Word of Ishii's original sentence had leaked out, however, and he acquired a reputation as a "tough guy who rode roughshod in court."[13] This anecdote shows the slap-on-the-wrist attitude that consular authorities took toward drug smugglers at the time.

In the 1830s British opium merchants first brought their cargoes to Tianjin which later became a British commercial port in 1857. Tianjin is conveniently located on the Baihe river, which flows from the inland to Tanggu on the coast, and is close to Beijing, which had a large population of opium users among the Qing nobility and officialdom. For such geopolitical reasons, Tianjin soon became "the opium market of north China." Long before Meiji Japan acquired concessions there, the British and French were catering to Chinese opium users in their own concessions, so it was only a matter of time before Japan joined in. According to a report by the Tianjin Japanese consulate general in June 1925, Tianjin did not produce its own opium, so it was smuggled in from Siberia, Heilongjiang, Rehe, and Suiyuan by rail, whereas narcotics such as morphine, cocaine, and heroin were brought to Tianjin by the Japanese, British, Americans, Frenchmen, Russians, and Italians by land and sea. More than half of the Chinese high officials, military officers, legislators, and great merchants in Tianjin habitually used opium and exchanged it as gifts, as did journalists such as Meng Zhenhou of the *Minyi bao*. While publishing exposés on Japanese morphine merchants, Meng himself frequented dens in the Japanese concessions and had been arrested there by the consular police. In the mid 1920s strict Japanese enforcement was the rule—at least on the surface— so the price of opium shot up and middle-class users turned to morphine. Chinese high officials and the rich smoked at home, whereas middle- and lower-class smokers frequented dens.[14] Thus Japanese and other foreign traffickers could prosper only because of widespread demand for opium among all strata of Tianjin's Chinese society. At the risk of being misunderstood, I would stress that there was a cozy symbiosis between Chinese users and foreign smugglers.

Unfortunately, though hardly unexpectedly, few documents exist to tell us precisely what proportion of the Tianjin Japanese community dealt in drugs, but a report by Fujiwara Tetsutarō, a Kwantung government-general official, discloses that in the early 1920s there were many, many opium dens and retail outlets in the Japanese and French concessions. For example, there were about seventy opium dens and one hundred retail outlets in the Japanese concession. Fujiwara estimated that roughly 70 percent of the five thousand Japanese living there dealt in morphine or other narcotics. Indeed, it was rare to find a Japanese bar, restaurant, pharmacy, or general store that did *not* deal in these illicit commodities. Tianjin witnessed the greatest volume of such business among all of the Japanese treaty port concessions in China—so much so that residents asserted that "the prosperity of the Japanese community derives from morphine." Even the consulate general took part. It would arrest only those smugglers caught by Chinese customs officials, while turning a blind eye to all others. "If we were to enforce the law strictly and thoroughly," Fujiwara's report claimed, "there would be no Japanese left." That situation obtained not only in Tianjin, but also in other areas of north China such as in Shanhaiguan, Qinhuangdao, Lanzhou, Tanggu, and Jinan.[15] Fujiwara based his report on information supplied by Tianjin consul general Yoshida Shigeru, so it is a highly reliable document showing that seemingly above-board Japanese businesses conducted illicit operations.

Jiang Jieshi and his Guomindang (GMD) began the long process of Chinese national unification by completing the Northern Expedition and setting up a new national government in Nanjing on 10 October 1928. Thereafter the imperial government was forced to adopt a putative policy of controlling Japanese traffickers. On 1 October, the eve of the GMD regime's establishment, the foreign ministry under Tanaka Giichi assumed that pose by issuing a "Directive to Control Opium and Narcotics in China [*Shina*]" that comprised twenty-two articles. These prohibited resident Japanese from: (1) cultivating and processing poppies into raw opium; (2) selling, transferring, possessing, or importing poppies, raw opium, morphine, or cocaine; and (3) importing opium paste or pipes. Furthermore, this October 1928 foreign ministry directive contained regulations that specified which physicians, dentists, pharmacists, and medicinal outlets were permitted to deal in narcotic substances, and it outlined punishments for violators ranging from fines of less than ¥100 to imprisonment for up to three months.[16] The consulate general at Tianjin did, in fact, follow this foreign ministry directive. It punished 357 persons involved in 138 cases in 1929, and 316 persons involved in 124 cases in 1930.[17] But depressed conditions in Japan in the second half of the 1920s, together with the Great Depression and its impact on Tianjin, ultimately made effective compliance with the foreign ministry directive impossible. The Japanese consular police in Tianjin made sweeping arrests of wholesalers, retailers, and opium den operators on 1 October 1929, but later they limited their enforcement efforts to rich wholesalers and adopted a "rather lenient policy" toward small retailers suffering from the Depression. This "lenience" made a dead letter of the foreign ministry directive.[18] And it worsened the situation by bringing to Tianjin waves of destitute Koreans—largely lower-class farmers—who were victims of the Depression in their colonized homeland.

RESIDENT KOREANS AND FISCAL ILLS

Korean participation is a major, if unstudied, dimension of modern Japanese opium operations in China. Japan annexed Korea in 1910 and conducted cadastral surveys between 1912 and 1918. These were designed to abolish the vague, complex land-owning patterns inherited from the past and to establish ownership along modern principles. But in effect what this measure did was to deprive many tillers of their land and thus create a class of landless poor who made their way to Korean cities and to Japan or northeast China.[19] The Korean whom Ishii Itarō sentenced on morphine smuggling charges no doubt was one of them. In the second half of the 1920s the world depression hit Korea as well, and lower-class farmers suffered in particular. Unemployed and destitute, many Koreans left for China, and those already living in Kalgan and Hebei descended on Tianjin as well, so that its Korean population doubled to 639, or about 10 percent of the Japanese community there from 1929 to 1930. Aside from students and those who worked in retail shops or customs houses, about 90 percent of these Koreans were penniless and engaged in illicit occupations such as smuggling various types of goods. Koreans and Japanese opened more than 120 opium dens inside the Tianjin Japanese concessions, and roughly 20 percent of the Koreans themselves became drug addicts. The consular police might send three or four smuggler-addicts a month back to Korea or Japan, but such efforts were just "a drop in the bucket."[20]

In November 1928 the Organization of Tianjin Resident Japanese (OTRJ) tried to cope with depressed business conditions by petitioning the imperial government for low-interest loans using real estate holdings as collateral. But the imperial government rejected this petition. So the OTRJ had to settle for ¥300,000 in loans from private finance companies. Tianjin consul general Okamoto Takezō called on the resident Japanese to take advantage of these admittedly small loans to wash their hands of drugs and take up reputable lines of work.[21] Even though the foreign ministry did lobby on behalf of the OTRJ, OTRJ members were enraged by the imperial government's refusal to help and felt that a paltry ¥300,000 injection into the economy would never produce a recovery. Political and institutional roadblocks stymied efforts to bring reform in the Japanese community as well. At that time, a sixty-member elected body known as the Association of Resident Japanese served as the legislative council for Japan's concessions in Tianjin. But drug traffickers had already made inroads into this association through out-and-out vote-buying. Given the tainted nature of this legislative council, effective law enforcement in Tianjin was nearly impossible.[22] Hence, it is not surprising that a system for licensing Chinese opium dens should arise there, as discussed below.

After the Manchurian Incident began, the Kwantung Army escorted the "last emperor," Aisin-Gioro Pu Yi, from Tianjin, where fighting broke out between Japan's China Garrison Army and peace preservation units under the command of Zhang Xueliang. Tianjin became a battle zone, and many Chinese residents fled from the Japanese concessions. Their flight sharply reduced the OTRJ's income, since those who fled no longer paid taxes; as a result, the OTRJ found itself in a fiscal crisis.[23] In order to gain a new source of revenue, in April 1934 the OTRJ levied a tax on fifteen Chinese-owned and-operated "special hostels" in the Japanese concessions. These establishments were in fact opium dens whose management involved some degree of Japanese control. Actually, Chinese opium wholesalers thought up the idea for these "hostels" to serve as fronts that would store opium stocks used in the manufacture of illegal narcotics. In return for the taxes gained from these "hostels," the Japanese gave tacit approval for their Chinese owners to run illegal opium dens inside. The OTRJ thus garnered annual revenues of sixty to seventy thousand dollars, which went to fund security forces in the concessions.[24] In other words, the OTRJ maintained itself with monies provided by Chinese drug traffickers. So here we have another strange form of Sino-Japanese criminal symbiosis centered on opium. But viewed from the Chinese side, both the consulate general, which was supposed to keep resident Japanese in line, and the imperial government as a whole seemed to be officially sanctioning opium and narcotics operations in Tianjin. Naturally enough, this system of "special hostels" was rife with problems, and spawned many evils in connection with the Green Gang, the Japanese consular police, and carpetbaggers. Finally, when the imperial army began operations to detach north China and place it under Japanese control in the mid 1930s, Japanese and Korean criminal elements again surged into Tianjin, so that from 1935 to 1936 the Japanese population there rose from 6,446 to 8,982, and the Korean from 1,332 to 2,125.[25]

On 1 July 1936, Foreign Minister Arita Hachirō abolished the 1928

"Directive to Control Opium and Narcotics in China *[Shina]*" and replaced it with two separate measures: a "Directive to Control Opium in the Republic of China *[Chūka]*," and another to "Control Narcotics in the Republic of China *[Chūka]*." No reason is given for this move, and we cannot tell if it was made as a result of the "Treaty against Illegal Transactions in Dangerous Drugs" signed in Geneva on 26 June. Presumably the foreign ministry's measure was taken to deal with the new situation in north China. These two directives strengthened administrative controls and stipulated fines for those who "suborn or help non-imperial subjects to perform illegal acts." However, the punishments—up to ¥100 in fines or less than three months imprisonment—remained unchanged from 1928.²⁶ Still, these directives made it illegal for Japanese to employ Chinese for purposes of dealing in opium or narcotics. Because the "special hostel" system sprang up soon after these foreign ministry directives were issued, their immediate effectiveness is doubtful. However, on 10 June 1937, a month or so before the Marco Polo Bridge Incident, Consul General Horinouchi Kanjō directed the Tianjin consular police to launch a roundup of narcotics manufacturers and dealers in the Tianjin-Beijing region. Those raids led to the arrest of twenty-eight persons, including three Japanese in Tianjin and four Japanese in Beijing.²⁷ Before launching these sting operations, the consular police endeavored to dismiss, return to Japan, or transfer to other parts of China internal personnel deemed likely to obstruct or derail these crackdowns.²⁸ Nevertheless, the sting operations uncovered police collaborators in addition to criminal elements. Twelve consular police personnel in Tianjin and other north Chinese cities—including former police inspectors—were served with judicial penalties; and more than forty persons in all were punished in what has been termed "the worst disgrace in the history of the consular police."²⁹ Such was the situation within the Japanese consular police, whose job it was to enforce the law. From this we can surmise just how ubiquitous drug trafficking was among resident Japanese in north China.

WAR AND KOREAN REHABILITATION

The outbreak of the Sino-Japanese War in July 1937 ushered in a series of new developments. On 27 September 1937 the League of Nations general assembly convened in Geneva and its fifth Advisory Committee on Opium and Other Dangerous Drugs discussed the situation in Asia. Britain's delegate urged the governments of China and Japan to note that conditions in the Far East were deteriorating in spite of China's huge efforts to control the opium problem, and that this was a matter for deep regret. The Chinese delegate, Hu Shize (also known as Victor Hu and Hoo Chi Tsai), responded by pointedly criticizing Japan's actions in its occupied areas and treaty port concessions in China. He asserted that although China was doing its utmost to control domestically produced opium, "this situation is made impossible because some regions exist beyond the reach of Chinese law." And, Hu Shize went on, "it is evident that Japan plots to thwart the awakening of China by addicting its masses to drugs. Until Japan abandons this policy of poisoning the world, the League's noble efforts will remain futile. Japan is an enemy of civilization."[30] Based on reports filed at this committee meeting, the *Times* and *Chronicle* began to attack Japanese policies in Manchuria and north China.[31] Indeed, although at a slightly later date, the Japanese consular police themselves noted:

> Resident Japanese in China behave in such a way as to make even their own countrymen assume a hate-Japan stance. They exploit the fact that they are Japanese in order to bully the Chinese into submission left and right. Lamentably, we see every day how resident Japanese deprive the Chinese of even the smallest of privileges, making them homeless and destitute. It is as if we ourselves are sowing the seeds of bitter anti-Japanese sentiment.[32]

Cognizant of these growing anti-Japanese feelings, the foreign ministry could not stand idly by. Imperial Japan was now under world scrutiny for its "China Incident"—in truth an invasion—undertaken on the pretext of "chastising an unruly China," as declared by the Konoe Fumimaro cabinet on 15 August 1937. Japan was waging a "crusade" against the GMD regime for obstinately clinging to a policy of appeasing communism. By 16 January 1938, imperial Japan "refused to deal with" a GMD government that rejected Japanese peace terms, which were: (1) the recognition of an independent Manchu Empire, (2) the conclusion of a Sino-Japanese Anti-Comintern Pact, and (3) the payment of indemnities. To convince the world community of the righteousness of its claims, Japan struck a pose of conducting "virtuous administration" in its occupied areas with help from collaborator regimes under the banner of a "New Order in East Asia."

Against this background, the imperial government redoubled efforts to control drug dealing in Tianjin. On 1 April 1938 it ordered the OTRJ immediately to end the storing and illicit selling of morphine in opium dens, and to abolish the "special hostels" after a six-month grace period. The reasons for this were threefold: the system of hostels spawned consular police corruption, it was difficult maintain in the face of opposition from the League at Geneva, and it reflected badly on Japan in the current wartime situation.[33] For its part, the OTRJ had leeway to comply because it no longer felt strapped for cash. The outbreak of war in 1937 brought a new influx of Japanese and Korean residents whose taxes replenished OTRJ coffers. That, as well as newly enacted entertainment taxes plus an infusion of funds from the foreign ministry, allowed the OTRJ to abandon these "hostels" without undue fiscal pain.[34] But a huge problem remained.

Approximately two hundred Korean-run opium dens were nestled in the Tianjin Japanese concessions. These dens could be abolished, but that meant nothing if their former proprietors began plying their trade on the street. Hence the Tianjin consular police stepped up efforts to enforce laws aimed at Korean traffickers and also strove to rehabilitate them in "model farm villages." These were built at Lutai, fifty-five kilometers outside of Tianjin, and at Qingdao on Jiaozhou Bay.[35] Here I will describe the Lutai experiment.

As noted above, thousands of destitute Koreans immigrated to Tianjin and other points in northeast China beginning in the late 1920s. Their numbers increased after the Manchurian Incident in 1931 and the establishment of the Regime for East Hebei Autonomy in 1935. Many if not most of them dealt in narcotics in league with Chinese criminal elements. After the Sino-Japanese War began in July 1937, Koreans and their Japanese carpetbagger counterparts advanced into all parts of north China close behind imperial army lines, and they earned an extreme degree of Chinese hatred because of their stepped-up drug trafficking. "Model farm villages" were the means by which Japanese authorities interned and hoped to rehabilitate such Koreans. After the war broke out, the North China Area Army, the foreign ministry, and the Korea government-general jointly decided to build these model farming villages for the express purpose of "morally reforming persons now engaged in illicit businesses and returning them to reputable lines of work." One of these enterprises would be located on 3,500 hectares of uncultivated land in Lutai, Mihe prefecture, Hebei province.[36] The village was to accommodate five thousand Koreans in one thousand households, housed on one-hundred-hectare lots with two thousand hectares of paddy land and four hundred hectares of dry fields. The state-backed Tōyō Colonial Company was engaged to do the actual planning and design.[37] Due to major delays caused by floods and rising costs, the construction that began in September 1938 would not be finished until 1942, and the final price tag rose to some ¥2.15 million. Korean settlers began to enter the Lutai facility in 1939 and came to number three thousand by spring 1942. So more than half of the projected enrollment was reached.

Among the criteria for choosing settlers were: "only those healthy and capable of work are qualified; drug addicts and those deemed physically unfit for labor will not be accepted." Such criteria shut the door to those most in need of "rehabilitation"—opium and narcotics dealers, most of whom were also addicts. Hence, we can only wonder just how earnest the authorities really were. In September 1939 the first group of sixty-six Korean settlers in twenty-nine households arrived at Lutai—the resident Koreans in north China who were supposed to be reformed and rehabilitated. Around November 1939, 856 Koreans in 149 households were brought from the Korean peninsula to serve as their instructors. But by 1940 sixteen of the original twenty-nine resident Korean settler households had absconded. Even so, agricultural output from the model farm village measured 50,000 *koku* (1 *koku* is about 5 bushels) of unhulled rice from 1,800 hectares in 1942. This figure surpassed the hope-for target of 40,000 *koku* from 2,000 hectares. From the standpoint of farming productivity, then, this "model village" was a marked success. But given the prevailing circumstances—the outbreak of the Asia-Pacific War in 1941—we can only conclude that the original purpose behind the system had given way to that of boosting agricultural output in order to meet wartime needs for food. In sum, the Lutai "model farm village" did nothing to solve the problem rehabilitating resident Korean drug traffickers in China.

CONCLUSIONS

No matter how seriously the Japanese consular police might have tried to bring opium operations under control, those attempts were stymied by the military, which increasingly took the lead in those operations after 1937. For example, in Nankou, north of Beijing, the Japanese military police exploited China's lack of laws to regulate pharmacists by granting licenses to resident Japanese who had no relevant degrees or qualifications whatsoever.[38] Since pharmaceutical outlets had deep ties with opium dealers, we can be almost certain that the military police granted those licenses to Japanese opium traffickers in return for kickbacks. On another occasion, the military police arrested a Japanese morphine dealer and handed him over to the consular police for trial and sentencing. But the military police officers in question preferred to "dispose of" that morphine themselves rather than turn it over as evidence. The consular police dealt with this situation by making the military police officers provide written verification that they in fact had "disposed of" that morphine, but we will never know how or if that actually happened.[39]

   In north China, a Provisional Government of the Chinese Republic was formed in December 1937. In central China, a Reformed Government of the Chinese Republic was set up in March 1938, then replaced by the Wang Jingwei regime in March 1940. But even after the latter came into being, a parallel North China Political Affairs Committee functioned as a separate collaborator regime in the north. It took some time for the Provisional Government's opium policies and system to get on track, but by July 1939 it had ordered that opium produced within its jurisdiction be sold only to licensed merchants. Later, the Political Affairs Committee established an Opium Suppression Bureau responsible for overseeing and approving the registration of addicts, the importing and exporting of opium, the cultivating of poppies, and the manufacturing of opium paste and smoking implements. This entity also set up a north China opium cartel comprising government-approved merchants responsible for buying and distributing opium.[40] But under all of these collaborator regimes, opium merchants merely needed to obtain official approval and backing to operate. For their part, the regimes gave such approval and backing in return for guaranteed revenues. The opium merchants were Chinese, but in some cases—such as at Taiyuan in Shanxi province—resident Japanese pooled resources or even supplied all of the capital to Chinese who owned the businesses in name only.[41] In other words, some resident Japanese opium dealers skirted consular police crackdowns by moving their operations under the cover of Chinese front men, who in turn functioned openly as part of the collaborator regime's "opium suppression" system. However earnestly the consular police might try to arraign the underground Japanese traffickers, those efforts ran counter to official state policy, which was to raise revenue for collaborator regimes and for the Japanese military from opium. Thus the consular police ended up bringing to justice only those resident Japanese dealers who cut into the profits destined for collaborator governments and the imperial army. Nakajima Chūzaburō, who served as a consul in the Tianjin Japanese consulate general from February 1938 to May 1942, put it this way:

> Many times the Special Service agencies attached to the imperial army would seek some extra cash for entertainment expenses, or whatever. I have heard that some of them raised that money through opium dealings when there was nothing in the budget for those socializing activities. In such cases, it was extremely difficult to enforce laws rigorously when Japanese were involved.[42]

The imperial government made a final attempt to tackle the wartime opium problem in China by issuing its "Regulations to Implement the Directive to Control Narcotics in the Republic of China *[Chūka]*" as an imperial ordinance on 12 August 1941, and a "Directive to Control Narcotics in the Republic of China *[Chūka]*" as a foreign ministry directive on 18 August 1941. These were amendments to directives of the same name issued back in 1936, except that the one intended to "control narcotics" was raised to the level of an imperial ordinance and called for harsher penalties. Whereas previously violators were subject to fines of up to ¥100 and three months in prison, now they were sentenced to "under a year's imprisonment or fined up to ¥200."[43] Aside from the harsher punishments, these changes show that the government would now focus its control efforts on hard drugs. Conversely, the new directives stipulated that the Japanese government would limit its enforcement of opium laws to raw opium. In effect, this brought the letter of the law into line with the reality of the collaborator regimes' control programs. It meant that opium trafficking by resident Japanese—except for that in raw opium—was now all but legal.

In essence, the central government now sanctioned normally illegal drug operations by traffickers—just as it earlier had sanctioned normally illegal military operations by renegade officers—in China. The historical significance of this measure should not be overlooked. Indeed, since the imperial army now took the lead in fostering the drug trade, civilian traffickers in Japanese-occupied areas naturally lined their nests by placing themselves under army protection. Thus, when seen in the overall context of modern Japanese opium and narcotics operations, the Sino-Japanese War that began in 1937 marked a significant change in perpetrators. Private persons, as represented by the civilian traffickers, had been the protagonists before 1937, but now the government itself, as represented by the army and an imperial ordinance, assumed that role. In other words, resident Japanese individuals gave way to the imperial Japanese state. Nevertheless, civilian traffickers continued to operate and prosper. They won tacit recognition and furtive backing in China from the Japanese government until its defeat in August 1945.

NOTES

The views expressed in this chapter are solely those of the author and do not reflect the opinion or position of the Foreign Ministry of Japan.

1. Document AG441,1, dated 12 October 1945, microfilmed in Gaikō shiryōkan (Diplomatic Record Office), Tokyo; see also Kuma, *Mayaku monogatari*, p. 197.

2. Awaya and Yoshida, *Kokusai kensatsu kyoku (IPS) jinmon chōsho*, 38:218–28.

3. Tenshin kōshinjo, *Kita Shina zairyū hōjin kanshō roku*, p. 16.

4. Eguchi, *Nit-Chū ahen sensō*, pp. 200–1.

5. Kuroha, "Mō hitotsu no ahen sensō"; Kurahashi, *Nihon no ahen senryaku;* Liu Mingxiu [Ming-hsiu], *Taiwan tōchi to ahen mondai.*

6. Eguchi, *Shiryō: Nit-Chū sensōki ahen seisaku.* Another document volume is Okada et al., *Zoku Gendai shi shiryō*, vol. 12, *Ahen mondai.*

7. Eguchi, *Nit-Chū ahen sensō*, p. 56. Also, Eguchi, "Nit-Chū sensōki no ahen seisaku"; Eguchi, *Shōgen: Nit-Chū ahen sensō;* and Eguchi, "Nit-Chū sensōki Kainantō no ahen seisan."

8. Yamada, *Ōrudo Shanhai ahen jijō*, pp. 3–57.

9. Eguchi, *Nit-Chū ahen sensō*, pp. 32, 38, 41.

10. Eguchi, *Jūgonen sensō shōshi: Shinpan*, p. 22.

11. Kobayashi, "Tenshin no naka no Nihon shakai," pp. 187–88.

12. Ibid., pp. 189–91.

13. Ishii, *Gaikōkan no isshō*, pp. 39–40.

14. Gaimushō tsūshō kyoku, *Shina ni okeru ahen oyobi mayakuhin* (1925), pp. 228–32.

15. Fujiwara Tetsutarō, "Ahen seido chōsa hōkoku," in Okada et al., *Zoku Gendai shi shiryō*, 12:190–91.

16. However, this did not apply to areas under South Manchurian Railway jurisdiction; *Gaimushōhō* 165 (15 October 1928), in Gaikō shiryōkan.

17. "Shōwa 5-nen zai-Tenshin sōryōjikan keisatsu jimu jōkyō," in Gaikō shiryōkan, *Gaimushō keisatsu shi, Shina no bu, zai-Tenshin sōryōjikan,* vol. 1.

18. Ibid.

19. Miyajima, *Chōsen tochi chōsa jigyō shi no kenkyū.*

20. "Shōwa 5-nen zai-Tenshin sōryōjikan keisatsu jimu jōkyō."

21. Minutes, 15 October 1929. "Tenshin kyoryūmindan, Dai 24-ji kyoryūminkai rinjikai gijiroku." See K.3.2.2.1–3 *Zaigai teikoku kyoryūmindan oyobi minkai kankei zassan: Tenshin no bu,* vol. 2, in Gaikō shiryōkan.

22. Telegram from Tianjin Deputy Consul General Tajiri Akiyoshi to Foreign Minister Shidehara Kijūrō dated 14 August 1930. See K.3.2.2.3–4 *Zaigai kyoryūmindanhō narabini dō sekō kisoku kankei ikken: Tenshin no bu,* in Gaikō shiryōkan.

23. Kobayashi, "Tenshin jiken saikō: Tenshin sōryōjikan, Shina chūton gun, Nihonjin kyoryūmin," pp. 14–15.

24. "Tenshin sokainai enkan seido haishi ni kansuru ken" (28 April 1938), in Gaikō shiryōkan, *Gaimushō keisatsu shi, Shina no bu, zai-Tenshin sōryōjikan keisatsubu.*

25. Tenshin kyoryūmindan, *Tenshin kyoryūmindan sanjūshūnen kinen shi,* p. 484.

26. *Gaimushōhō* 350 (1 July 1936), in Gaikō shiryōkan.

27. "Kinseihin mitsuzō hanbai jiken no kenkyo" (10 June 1937), in Gaikō shiryōkan, *Gaimushō keisatsu shi, Shina no bu, zai-Tenshin sōryōjikan keisatsubu.*

28. Admonition by Ōe chief consular police at the head meeting, dated 22 March 1938, in ibid.

29. "Keisatsukan no shukusei jiken" (31 December 1937), in ibid.

30. Telegram 213 from Acting Bureau Chief Usami Uzuhiko in Geneva to Foreign Minister Hirota Kōki, dated 28 September 1937 (B. 9.9.0.1), in *Kokusai renmei ahen kankei ikken,* vol. 5, in Gaikō shiryōkan.

31. Telegram 800 from Ambassador Yoshida Shigeru in London to Foreign Minister Hirota Kōki, dated 19 October 1937, in ibid.

32. Zai-Chūka minkoku (Pekin) Nihon teikoku taishikan keisatsubu, ed., *Hoku-Shi ryōjikan keisatsushochō kaigiroku* (1940), in Gaikō shiryōkan.

33. "Tenshin sokainai enkan seido haishi ni kansuru ken."

34. Ibid.

35. Ibid.

36. On the Lutai "model farm villages," see Zai-Chūka minkoku (Pekin) Nihon teikoku taishikan keisatsubu, *Hoku-Shi ryōjikan keisatsushochō kaigiroku.*

37. See Inomata, *Watashi no Tōtaku kaikoroku;* Ōkōchi, *Maboroshi no kokusaku gaisha Tōyō takushoku;* Ōkōchi, *Kokusaku gaisha Tōyō takushoku no shūen.*

38. Zai-Chūka minkoku (Pekin) Nihon teikoku taishikan keisatsubu, *Hoku-Shi ryōjikan keisatsushochō kaigiroku.*

39. Ibid.

40. Eguchi, *Nit-Chū ahen sensō,* pp. 82–87, 131–33.

41. See Zai-Chūka minkoku (Pekin) Nihon teikoku taishikan keisatsubu, *Hoku-Shi ryōjikan keisatsushochō kaigiroku.*

42. Nakajima, *Aru ryōjikan no kaisōroku,* p. 185; also pp. 181–86, 198–216.

43. *Gaimushōhō* 473 (15 August 1941) and 474 (1 September 1941), in Gaikō shiryōkan.

SEVEN

Opium / Leisure / Shanghai

Urban Economies of Consumption

Alexander Des Forges

A late-nineteenth-century Shanghai guidebook comments on the double face that opium consumption presents to the visitor:

> Shanghai's opium halls are the best under heaven: the furnishings are elegant and clean, and the teacups and opium bowls are all finely crafted. . . .
>
> The poison of opium has circulated in China for a long time; from the literati to the porters, there is almost no one left untouched.[1]

These two apparently contradictory statements can be found within pages of each other. How and why could opium smoking be represented both as an elegant leisure pursuit and as the dangerous ingestion of a lethal substance? How did this complex constructed image of opium consumption relate to changing understandings of leisure time in Chinese port cities? Shanghai and opium were frequently linked in nineteenth- and early-twentieth-century Western writings on China; the same link often appears in Chinese texts from this period. This chapter focuses on Shanghai guidebooks, miscellaneous accounts, collections of local verse, Shanghai newspapers, novels set in Shanghai, and a discussion of the pleasures and dangers of opium published in Shanghai, all of which demonstrate the centrality of "opium" in the textual construction of late nineteenth-century Shanghai. I place quotation marks around the word *opium* here to emphasize that my interest is not primarily in the substance itself, but rather in the way it was understood and referred to as the center around which sets of practices were organized.

The other chapters in this book detail the institutional, cultural, economic, and ideological characteristics of attempts to control or prohibit opium smoking. In this chapter, I hope to add a dimension to our understanding of the place of opium in Chinese society by looking instead at representations of the consumption of opium, particularly those in which opium smoking is seen neither as an unprecedented scourge nor as a potential source of revenue for the state, but rather as a normal leisure activity; as a practice that could be more or less dangerous depending on one's wealth and self-control, but that was not necessarily a more pressing social problem than gambling or prostitution. Although many of the texts I cite do at times condemn opium consumption, my interest is primarily in the way in which this condemnation is woven together with appreciation of its positive effects, and the extent to which both condemnation and appreciation function within a larger discourse on urban leisure practices and their social effects.

Three closely related themes characterized Shanghai in the late Qing: it was seen as a great business center, a fascinating leisure center, and a place of multifarious dangers. Opium figured significantly in each case, whether as currency, source of relaxation, or cause of harmful addiction. The extent to which the Shanghai economy was based on opium not only as commodity but also as currency was probably unrivaled in other major Chinese cities. Linda Cooke Johnson writes that although bad for the economy as a whole,

> opium sales actually stimulated the indigenous economy and played a significant role in the development of the banking business at Shanghai. Local banks charging high rates of interest on short-term loans to opium merchants in turn issued bank notes drawn on opium loans that served in lieu of hard money in times of silver shortages and contributed to the circulation of currency at the port, without which trade and the economy of the entire area would indeed have come to a standstill.[2]

Whereas opium had been used on occasion since the eighteenth century as a means of payment over long distances (it was lighter than copper cash and more secure than silver),[3] it was not until the second half of the nineteenth century that an entire urban economy emerged that was "addicted" to opium and could not function without it.

This chapter, however, concerns itself primarily with the latter two themes, examining the role of opium in the construction of Shanghai as a place of both recreation and danger, and investigating the double discursive production of opium as integral to both leisure practices *(xiao* [消] *xian)* and self-destructive behavior. The complicated relationship between these discursive strands is hinted at by the multivalent significance of the homophone *xiao** (銷), which denotes both productive and destructive "melting." Opium also constituted an important element in narrative representations of Shanghai in turn of the century novels, where a developing addiction could give the plot both direction and temporal structure.

SHANGHAI / LEISURE / OPIUM

The rapid economic change in nineteenth-century Shanghai—resulting from burgeoning trade, both domestic (with other parts of China) and foreign (with South Asia, Japan, Europe, and the United States)—brought with it new uses and understandings of leisure time, particularly to non-elite urban residents. Wealthy officials and merchants in Shanghai could afford to spend much of their leisure time in private gardens and houses of prostitution, where they ordered in meals, hosted drinking parties, and watched private performances of plays. These relatively private pleasures maintained a continuity with previous elite practices; differences between late-Qing courtesans and their predecessors of even several centuries earlier, though not insignificant, did not affect the structural relationship between the literati or educated merchant and the courtesan. Prior to the middle of the nineteenth century, however, opportunities for non-elite leisure activity in Shanghai were subject to specific spatial and temporal constraints. On ordinary days, temple grounds were the primary space of public recreation; during seasonal festivals there were street processions, operas performed for the spirits, and other public activities.[4] As an early-nineteenth-century author put it in his description of Yangzhou, people go to the temple on Guanyin's birthday "half to burn incense, and half to enjoy themselves."[5] In *Yingruan zazhi* (Random notes from the edge of the sea), an early account of Shanghai city life, Wang Tao voiced his indignation about this "use of space that is intended for expressing reverence for the spirits as a place for illicit meetings."[6] Guild halls provided space for recreation for members of the guild (whether native-place or common-trade association), but here, too, performances were reserved for special occasions.[7] Beginning in the Xianfeng (1851–1861) and Tongzhi (1862–1874) eras, however, space dedicated to leisure-time pursuits independent of temples and guild halls appeared, primarily in the International Settlement and the French concession. The rise of independent theaters, large numbers of teahouses, storytelling halls,[8] opium dens and halls, and public parks literally made space for recreation as such, separate from expressions of religious reverence or native-place solidarity. New leisure practices were among the main topics discussed by new Shanghai guidebooks, leisure papers *(xiaobao)*, travel accounts, and novels.

The purest manifestation of commodified leisure time can be seen in the opium den. Though other Chinese cities had establishments specifically designed for opium smoking as early as the 1830s, according to several authors they were places that were "dirty and hid filth," whereas in Shanghai certain establishments were well kept and beautifully appointed, with *hongmu* furniture and calligraphy done by famous scholars adorning the walls.[9] Indeed, the luxurious surroundings were as much of a draw to some as the opium itself. Alluding to an account written by the Song dynasty prose master Ouyang Xiu,[10] Chi Zhicheng concludes that the real point of smoking opium is not the opium itself; he goes on to describe in detail the intricately carved woodwork, the high-quality accessories, and the electric lights and large mirrors in Shanghai opium establishments, concluding that it is "a world of glass, a cosmos of pearls and jade, that dazzles the eye and sets the heart racing."[11] The most famous establishment in the first two decades of the Guangxu era was Nanchengxin, located in the French concession; illustrations of the main room show a giant hall filled with elegantly appointed couches, ornate decorations, polished stone, and calligraphy (fig. 10). At the center of the room, serving as a focal point, stands a giant clock, reminding the customer (and the viewer of the illustration) that the purpose of the establishment is to enable one to spend time comfortably.[12] Cheap establishments with less attractive decor catered to rickshaw pullers and porters; in 1872 *Shen bao* reported that there were more than 1,700 opium dens in Shanghai, and a decade later one author estimated the number of opium dens in the concession and settlement in the thousands.[13] Writing in 1897, Li Boyuan claimed that there were more stores selling opium in Shanghai than there were stores selling rice, and more opium halls than restaurants.[14]

But the opium den was merely the most specialized venue for the consumption of the drug: opium was readily available at teahouses, storytelling halls and theaters, parks such as Zhang's Garden and Yu Garden, and houses of prostitution.[15] Though the "flower-smoke houses" *(huayan jian)* were often stigmatized as the kind of low-class whorehouses that provided opium on the side, it is clear from literature of the period that houses of prostitution at all status levels supplied opium to their clients. Most institutions dedicated to leisure activities of whatever sort made opium available, rendering opium smoking an integral part of almost any kind of Shanghai relaxation.

We may provisionally note two themes in texts representing Shanghai that correspond neatly with contemporary representations of the practice and experience of opium smoking. First, Shanghai is frequently referred to as "the city that never sleeps" *(buye cheng);* similarly, opium smokers are understood to function on a different circadian rhythm, staying up most of the night and sleeping most of the day, preoccupied while in an opium haze with the marvelous visions that appear before them.[16] Second, guidebooks and reminiscences of Shanghai from this period frequently resort to a rhetoric of a dream and subsequent awakening to give their accounts an appropriate ontological status. Novels from the late nineteenth century set in Shanghai also make extensive use of dreams as narrative devices and to establish narrative frames. Oneiric rhetoric had been central to many earlier travel accounts and novels, but the intensity with which it appeared in this period, coupled with the introduction of opium as one more type of delusional attachment to be overcome in order to escape this world of suffering, represents a significant new development.

DISCOURSES OF LEISURE: PRODUCTIVITY

Money adores movement and abhors lying inert. Heaven created money not to be hoarded in dark corners, but to be used by men.

XIMEN QING IN *JIN PING MEI*[17]

The recreational activities of those to whom Thorstein Veblen would refer as "the leisure class"—wealthy scholars and merchants with aspirations to seem cultured—had been an important factor in the Chinese economy from at least the Song dynasty forward, but this significance was masked in part by the persistent rhetoric of disengagement from the world that characterized literati understandings of gardens and the aesthetic of reclusion.[18] In late-nineteenth-century Shanghai, however, the leisure activities practiced by those who were not members of the leisure class took on unprecedented significance. Leisure time and recreation could no longer be seen as isolated from the urban market, and a new discourse of urban leisure began to appear in guidebooks, travel accounts, and newspapers.

This discourse of leisure consisted of two primary strands differentiated by their understandings of the other expenditures incurred in spending leisure time. These two opposed strands constitute a single discourse, however, because it is rare to find a text that does not present both, and both are grounded on the assumption that one's *jingshen* (spirit, nerves, or psychosomatic well-being) must be treasured and nourished. One of the best examples of this dual discourse on leisure is Zhang Chang's *Yanhua* (On opium, 1878); others include *Huyou zaji* (Random notes on travels to Shanghai, 1876), *Songnan mengying lu* (A record of shadows of dreams south of song, 1883), and *Huyou mengying* (Shadows of dreams of travels to Shanghai, 1893).[19] These four works differ significantly in format, ranging from a collection of aphoristic remarks on opium (*Yanhua*), to a Shanghai guidebook including lists of restaurants and steamship schedules (*Huyou zaji*), to more impressionistic accounts of Shanghai life (*Songnan* and *Huyou mengying*), but they all manifest an attitude towards opium as insistent as it is apparently self-contradictory.

I begin my analysis with the discursive strand that presents leisure as a tonic both to individuals and to society. When the editor of *Xiaoxian bao* (Leisure Times), a Shanghai leisure paper that began to appear in 1897, wrote that "leisure is the opposite *[dui]* of labor," the opposition defined was also an intimate *partnership*. The role of leisure in this urban setting

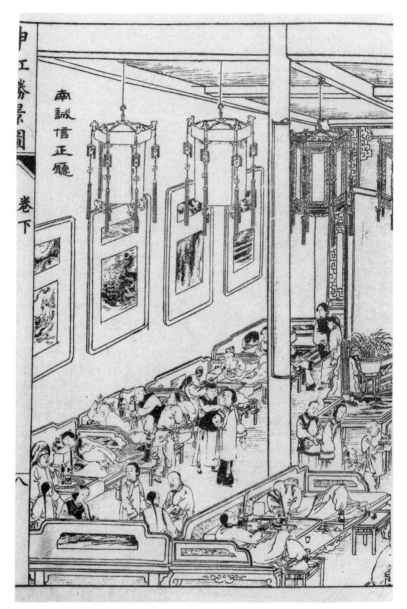

Figure 10. Nanchengxin, a high-class opium den in Shanghai, as depicted in the illustrated collection *Shenjiang shengjing tu,* 1884. Reproduced with permission of the Princeton University Libraries.

was twofold: to refresh those who work, whatever their place in society; and to maintain an economy of consumption that in turn provided a livelihood for other non-elite urban residents. Central to this double function of recreation was a new conception of free time as something that could no longer merely be enjoyed, but had to be actively spent *(xiao)* through the purchase and consumption of commodities. "Since there is this [time for] rest, there is leisure; since there is leisure time, one must have a means of spending it." The leisure paper, for example, could "aid in getting rid of boredom and avoiding depression," and was even likened to a good friend or maidservant.[20] Purchase of leisure-time recreation on the one hand entailed the expenditure of wealth accumulated during hours of labor (leisure as the antithesis of labor), but on the other provided a means of livelihood for a whole class of Shanghai residents (leisure as the opportunity for others to earn money, the foundation that makes labor possible).

We find this rhetoric of leisure articulated coherently as early as 1874, when the editors of *Shen bao* wrote in favor of night theater as "a place of leisure," and encouraged night shows so that "peasants, artisans, and merchants" and others who worked through the day would have amusements during the "long and boring night." The editors also understood that this concept of leisure time served as the foundation of an economy in which not only theater owners, actors, and tea and snack vendors, but even carriage drivers and rickshaw pullers, could earn a living. A similar article several months later claimed that 10,000 households earned their livelihood from the rickshaw trade alone.[21] In the early 1880s it was estimated that in one day the settlement and concession entertainment establishments would go through forty stone of sunflower seeds, five to six hundred *jin* of candles, and twenty to thirty barrels of oil for lamps (exclusive of gas and electric lighting).[22] This logic, which reminds us of Gu Gongxie's eighteenth-century defense of gambling, prostitution, visits to temples, and other leisure activities of the rich in Suzhou as the main source of livelihood for the poor, justifies expenditures by individuals as contributions to the good order of the region and even of the realm as a whole.

> When there is excessive luxury on the part of 10 million people, there is also a way of making a living for 10 million people. If one should try to change these millions' luxury to simplicity, it will certainly cause millions to lose their livelihood. . . . There is a proverb that in saving the frog one starves the snake. In this case, I fear that the attempt to save the frog will not be successful, and the snake will starve anyway.[23]

The practice of "leisure time" leads to the productive circulation of cash envisioned by Ximen Qing, a beneficial flow of cash and commodities referred to in texts as early as *Shiji* (Han dynasty).[24] Shanghai soon acquired the epithet of *xiao*jin zhi guo* (a pot in which to melt gold), originally coined to refer to Hangzhou under the southern Song.[25] (Note the ety-mological connection between the "expenditure" of time in *xiaoxian* and the "melting" of one's resources in *xiao*jin*). This "melting" represented, on the one hand, the depletion of an individual's resources through leisure activity and, on the other, the way in which this now "liquid" asset had been set free to circulate through the milieu and benefit others.

Spending leisure time benefited not only the body politic, but also the individual laboring body, which needed time to rest and recuperate.

> As for the ruler's affairs and the ministers' work . . . if there were no rest-times to regulate them, it would seem to go against the doctrine of taking care of one's spirit *[jingshen]*. Therefore the ancients had the "one day of rest out of every ten" theory. Today's Westerners, for their schedule of rest, take one day out of every seven, and have fixed times for rest in morning and after-noon.[26]

The identification of leisure and labor as opposites enables us to discern the understanding of labor on which the whole discourse of leisure rests: labor is a process involving the expenditure of effort/spirit (*jingshen*) in order to acquire money. This drain on the spirit must be balanced by periods of rest and leisure activity, during which money is spent and the spirit is replenished. The figure of the reclining opium smoker, perhaps chatting with friends, flirting with attendants, or drinking good tea out of high-quality vessels, was one of the central representations of a man at his leisure.[27] It should not come as a surprise, then, that the designation *xiao*jin zhi guo* (pot to melt gold) was also used as early as the 1840s to refer to the bowl of the opium pipe.[28]

Yanhua claims that the opium smoker, without leaving the confines of his or her couch, could experience the delights of a Daoist paradise, expressing no interest in the outside world whatsoever. Relaxing under the influence of opium is likened to Tao Hongjing's and Dong Zhongshu's meditative reclusions, and to the time Bodhidharma spent facing the wall.[29] "It is indeed a good method for dispelling depression." In this view, abuse is dangerous, but so is total abstinence, which almost invariably leads to later abuse. "Everyone has their likes in order to pass the months and years: some like women or sink into alcohol. . . . In excess these can all cause one to . . . lose one's morality of conduct and harm one's body; not criticizing these and only criticizing opium is narrow-minded."[30] As Chi Zhicheng puts it: "On a windy and rainy day, lying on the couch and conversing with a friend, spending only a hundred or so cash *[qingfu]*, one can spend half a day. This is one of the pleasures of life, how could it be the case that one has to be addicted to opium to enjoy it?"[31] The appropriate approach is not to swear off the substance entirely, but to enjoy it in moderation. Other substances in the Chinese materia medica widely acknowledged as beneficial but known to have harmful effects in excess are frequently cited to support this claim by analogy.[32]

Even though opium was often referred to as an addictive substance that could give rise to obsessive behavior on the part of those who consumed it, such an obsession was not necessarily incompatible with high social position; indeed, in some circles, as had been true in the late Ming, a cultured individual could not be said to be refined unless he had some such obsession.[33] Articles printed in *Youxi bao* in 1897 and 1898 made extensive use of the rhetoric of connoisseurship, describing a "stylish" opium smoker whose private couch was "finely worked and superbly beautiful," with a refined inscription and couplet hanging over it. Opium was available in different grades of quality and purity, and it was suggested that only the cognescenti were capable of discriminating the highest grade from the others; it was also considered necessary to pay close attention to the age of the pipe (older being better), the cleanliness of the bowl, and the attentiveness of the service.[34] In some wealthy families in the nineteenth and early twentieth centuries, sons were deliberately introduced to opium at an early age with the aim of rendering them docile and preventing them from squandering the family's wealth on other pursuits. Hong Jingjiang notes that matchmakers frequently asked how much opium the prospective groom could smoke, with the idea that this correlated directly with the family's wealth.[35] Clearly, opium and its accessories and associated practices constituted a sort of language in which statements about an individual or a family's wealth and social status could be made.

DISCOURSES OF LEISURE: DANGER

Yet there was always the danger that the productive circulation of wealth through the relation of expenditure and earning could spiral out of control and lead to waste or even harm.[36] The reasonable expenditure of time and money undertaken by a productive member of society to renew his or her capacity for useful labor could be hard to differentiate from the excessive expenditure practiced by those for whom money had ceased to be of any value. For these excessive spenders, gold was as dirt, to be cast away without a second thought.[37] ("Dirt" *[tu]* was also a slang term for opium.) Time, valuable because it could be spent in other, more productive pursuits, was also spent without regret, hour by hour and day by day.[38] In extreme cases, the body itself could lose its value: vital essences *(jingshen)* would then be expended, and in the end the unfortunate pleasure-seeker literally wastes *(xiao*)* away.[39] The money and essences spent in order to enjoy oneself do not enter into productive and contained circulation (as argued in the previous section), but instead are dissipated or lost to the outside without gain. The fluidity implied in the word *xiao** is no longer beneficial; it has instead become dangerous. The "pot to melt gold" (*xiao*jin zhi guo*) that is Shanghai (or, alternatively, the bowl of the opium pipe) is seen as a threat to both wealth and health.[40] At this point the ideal of monetary frugality merges with alchemical conceptions of the (male) body that can be traced back to some of the earliest Daoist texts. While in earlier vernacular fiction lack of containment (leading to loss of wealth and vital essences) was usually represented by excessive sexuality,[41] by the end of the nineteenth century opium had joined and to some extent replaced sex as the commodity that consumes as it is consumed:

> All those who smoke opium are invariably thin and their blood is congealed; why is it then that their tongues [still] drip saliva? Because there is a limit to how much *jingshen* one person has; if one nourishes it, it stays hidden, but if one raises it, it comes forth. . . . Can *jingshen* be raised again and again? Be careful and swear off [opium].[42]

Working within the medical paradigm in which manifestation, outward display, or emission of spirit or energy is directly opposed to its hidden accumulation and maintenance to nurture the body, the texts present opium smoking as a practice that can draw forth what ought to be carefully kept within, resulting in a body drained of its vital essences. The opium addict's face is represented as bloodless or sallow, with the appearance of withered wood.[43]

Unlike gluttony and licentiousness, two abuses to which it was frequently compared, opium smoking is represented as a learned habit. Whereas desire for food and sex were located squarely within human nature and thought to be instinctive, the craving for opium was understood to be acquired only gradually.[44] *Yanhua* details the stages through which the typical addict would proceed: first, interest in courtesans (or actors)—opium as a means to flirt with objects of sexual attraction; second, interest in refined surroundings and quality accouterments—opium as status object; and so on, down to the time when the individual is so desperate for the opium itself that he or she is willing to contract any debt in order to obtain it, and is no longer interested in sex or status.[45]

Opium addiction came to be seen as a particularly dangerous leisure activity because it was understood to maintain its hold over the addict even when he or she had lost everything else. Unlike other pastimes, which required cash in order to enjoy them properly, the opium smoker could continue until his or her last copper was spent and still feel no regret.[46] Just as one *Shen bao* editor grounded his defense of leisure activities on the livelihood of the poor urban laborer, another editor based his critique of opium selling and prostitution on the general welfare of that same urban worker. For Huang Shiquan, the true danger of dissipated behavior in Shanghai consists in its accessibility to poorer residents and women:

> For houses of prostitution, one must have at least one dollar *[yang fu yitou]* in order to make arrangements. If one's clothes are worn and wrinkled, one cannot even get through the door. Therefore only fashionable youths in light green clothing who throw their gold away like dirt can have wild hearts and misguided intentions. But when an opium den opens, bearers and porters become completely entangled there. It costs only one hundred cash or less to smoke a container of opium.[47]

He further writes of seeing coolies who spend nearly all of their day's earnings each night on opium smoking. Given a choice between eating and satisfying one's cravings for opium, it was thought that an addict would choose to smoke rather than to eat. No matter how poor, old, or sick the individual might become, no redemptive awakening could be expected.[48]

Given the long tradition of butterfly and flower imagery in Chinese poetry about young men in search of pleasure, what better symbol of the dangers of opium for the unwary pleasure-seeker could there be than the Venus flytrap? Huang Shiquan wrote of a foreign plant that could consume insects:

> There was a poet who wrote that "Bees treasure fragrance and return to it" and that "Butterflies search out flowers and enter the realm of intoxication." Dissolute butterflies and wild bees always take flowers to be their livelihood; I had never heard of a flower that can turn and eat butterflies and bees. But then I saw the *Alundakenkeqinsi*[49] flower at the Public Garden: it is different. It comes from the West and can eat moving things.[50]

This veiled allusion to opium's Western origin is made more explicit in later Shanghai texts. In his turn of the century collection of Shanghai verse, Qin Rongguang includes lines reading:

> The opium pipe is a gun that kills bloodlessly; the tiny fire in the bowl can scorch an ocean dry. It melts away one's capital and sucks up the spirit, weakening the people, impoverishing the nation, and speeding China's demise.

Qin's own gloss to this verse notes: "The English use opium to speed China's demise; Chinese do not understand and vie to smoke it; this can be called great stupidity."[51]

In the discursive strand discussed previously, the laborer and society are presented in a synechdochic relationship: money spent by the rich on luxury items eventually benefits society as a whole through the livelihood that it affords the poorest. Here, on the other hand, the poor laborer serves as a *metaphor* for the nation as a whole, susceptible to uncontrollable losses of currency and spirit. The metaphoric link between the individual body and the realm appears frequently in writings that attempt to explain opium's effect on the individual body;[52] over time, authors began to work in the opposite direction and use the figure of the opium addict to think about definitions of "China" as a nation in the imperialist world order.

At this point one might well wonder: How is it that individual texts can on the one hand condemn opium as a poisonous substance and maintain that it should not be tried even once, and on the other praise the refined luxury of opium halls and list smoking there as one of the highest pleasures? How is it that leisure pursuits in general can be presented simultaneously as practices that generate personal and social well-being and as practices that destroy it? I maintain that this apparently conflicted discourse of leisure, particularly that portion dedicated to the discussion of opium, grows out of a specific type of class anxiety. It has been noted above that nineteenth-century Shanghai saw the appearance of new forms of non-elite public leisure practices, and forms of recreation that at one time had been possible only for the elite often in a matter of a few years became much more generally available. Horse-drawn carriages, for example, once the preserve of foreign merchants and the richest Chinese residents, began to be rented out at much lower prices in the 1890s.[53] Opium smoking, as a leisure activity available to and participated in by people from all classes and occupations, no matter how poor, may well have seemed the epitome of this new leisure; one author even refers to opium smokers in the early stages of addiction as "disciples of Mozi" because of their lack of attention to class distinctions: "they enjoy being together even with strangers and those of low social position."[54]

Guidebooks to Shanghai and Shanghai newspapers, which serve as the primary source of this discourse, profit from these anxieties to position themselves as essential arbiters of behavior, without which one ventures into Shanghai at one's peril. At the same time, we find these texts engaged in active attempts to reconstruct a boundary between elite and non-elite by reserving their harshest condemnation of leisure practices for the ones that cost the least. The apparently contradictory statements on the pleasures and dangers of smoking opium can be understood as partial movements to establish a polarity between those who should smoke (the rich and educated, who can afford and appreciate it) and those who should not (the poor, who can ill afford it, as well as those who might be able to afford it in the short run but do not have the strength of will or the self-knowledge to smoke it in the right way, and therefore run the risk of becoming addicted). It would then be all too easy for readers to identify themselves as the former and those abusing opium as the latter.

ADDICTION AND NARRATIVE STRUCTURE

Opium smoking also attracted the attention of authors writing long vernacular fiction set in Shanghai. In *Haishang hua liezhuan* (Lives of Shanghai flowers), one of the earliest novels set in Shanghai (published 1892–1894), we find a relatively "neutral" representation of opium consumption: many of the characters smoke it, and although some experience cravings when they are denied it, opium smoking is seen as no more harmful than indulging in the other leisure activities the Shanghai concession areas have to offer. By the turn of the century, however, the narrative potential implicit in the discourse on opium found in guidebooks, newspapers, and travel accounts could no longer be ignored. Discarding one half of the discourse elaborated above—the understanding of leisure and relaxation as regenerative—novelists began to focus entirely on the power of opium to erode one's standing in a social hierarchy in which wealth is a determining factor, and put this power to work to structure segments of their narratives. In the nineteenth-century French novel, ambition is a "dominant dynamic of plot: a force that drives the protagonist forward, assuring that no incident or action is final or closed in itself until such a moment as the ends of ambition have been clarified, whether through success or else renunciation."[55] In Chinese vernacular fiction beginning as early as *Jin ping mei* and continuing through *Qilu deng* and numerous works published in the nineteenth century, desire plays a role that is just as crucial, though it points the narrative in a different direction. Desire in the Chinese novel serves to structure a downward movement through society, as the protagonist becomes more and more obsessed with the object of desire and less able to detach himself from it, leading to his eventual demise or, in some cases, timely awakening to its ultimately illusory nature. Sex and gambling provided the arenas for desire to play itself out in late-Ming and early- to mid-Qing vernacular fiction, but by the end of the nineteenth century opium takes the stage as well.

It is in *Haishang fanhua meng* (Dreams of Shanghai splendor, published beginning in 1898) that opium first appears as an independent factor in the decline of the addicted individual.[56] Opium smoking causes Wu Chuyun's mother to sell her into prostitution (chapter 13), almost leads another mother to be late to a court hearing that will decide the fate of her daughter (chapter 96), and brings a young man from the countryside to confide in a "maid," only to lose the fortune built up by his father through years of toil (chapter 85). Most striking is the trajectory of Tu Shaoxia, a rich young man who begins to smoke opium early on, loses his fortune through smoking and other pursuits, and is left to pull a rickshaw for a living—and then midway through the novel, with encouragement from his friends, he gives up opium and starts to climb back up into acceptable society. In this case, ridding himself of the addiction is clearly stated as a prerequisite for any upward mobility.[57]

With the publication of Wu Jianren's *Hen hai* (The sea of regret, 1906), featuring an opium addict who is unable to reform himself, opium addiction comes into its own as a desire strong enough to bring an entire narrative to miserable end. Chen Bohe is separated from his fiancée and her family in the chaos of the Boxer Rebellion, and they are able to trace him only months later in Shanghai, where he has used looted wealth to gamble, socialize with courtesans, and begin to smoke opium. By the time Bohe is found, he has gone through all of his ill-gotten gains and spends his time in opium dens in the Hongkou district. His fiancée's father takes Bohe in on the condition that he give up opium, but Bohe is unwilling or unable to do so, and he runs off several times before falling ill and dying in a hospital. In this case, his fiancée and her family were willing to forgive his past transgressions and bring him back into "respectable" society; the sole impediment to his redemption is ultimately his addiction to opium. Unlike guidebooks and reminiscences, which derived their authority in large part from the suggestion that there was a right way and a wrong way to enjoy Shanghai leisure activities, vernacular fiction built its narrative for the most part on the presumption that all such leisure activities (and eventually, opium smoking in particular) would inevitably lead to one's downfall unless one could learn to shun them completely and return to the moral path.

CONCLUSION

In concluding, I would like to call attention to the extent to which the discussion of "opium" in late-nineteenth-century texts becomes an occasion for quasi-metaphorical reflection on issues such as class distinctions and the nature of the "nation." Opium was a uniquely fertile point from which one could begin to think about how relations between classes in a rapidly changing society might develop; focus on the abuse of opium also provided the occasion to conceptualize a social and territorial space that, instead of forming an integral part of a larger system *(tianxia)* in which circulation (of currency, commodities, and information) was beneficial to all concerned, was rather a clearly individuated entity for which balanced circulation with others frequently degenerated (or threatened to degenerate) into uncontrollable outflow. Late-nineteenth-century writers looking back in time to the eighteenth century might have seen Qing society at its height figuratively as a wealthy opium smoker, with leisure time to spend and plenty of wealth to spend it pleasantly, and few negative effects from the habit; such expenditure could even have been understood as a necessary balance to the exertions that supported prosperity. Looking forward to the near future in the Guangxu era, however, "China" perhaps seemed instead to be dangerously close to the figure of the poor opium smoker, unable to afford the necessities of life as he watches his money slip through his fingers and enrich his exploiters.

Opium was not only an important currency and commodity in late-nineteenth-century Shanghai; it also functioned as an important element in contemporary representations of the city. Guidebooks and travel accounts invariably make reference to opium smoking, and opium dens appear in illustrated collections of Shanghai scenes. Why was this the case? Though Suzhou almost certainly had more opium dens in the Tongzhi and early Guangxu eras, Shanghai's establishments are said to be the most luxurious and numerous in China; and even though opium at this point was available in almost any Chinese city or town, fictional characters frequently became addicted to it only after arriving in Shanghai.[58] Shanghai, which was understood as part "Chinese" and part "foreign," as the space in which trade with other nations took place and the point at which a significant amount of opium entered China in the nineteenth century, could only be more closely identified with opium use and abuse as authors began to see "healthy" trade and exchange degenerate into "dangerous" outflow of wealth and the destruction of "national spirit." Shanghai was understood precisely as the zone in which this exchange and/or outflow took place. Clearly it was no coincidence that the same term, *xiao*jin zhi guo*, was used to refer both to Shanghai and to the bowl of the pipe in which opium was smoked.

Yet we must also remember that opium was always represented under the constraints of the specific generic form to which the texts it appears in belong. As other scholars have pointed out, perceptions of opium use differed according to the method by which it was consumed.[59] Similarly, as I show in this chapter, even the more narrowly defined practice of opium smoking appeared in different guises depending on its function within a given text. The discourse of opium presented in guidebooks and newspapers is more than a little reminiscent of discourses on intimacy with courtesans or other obsessions in late-Ming and early-Qing accounts. In vernacular fiction, opium addiction can be thematized to intensify the effect of a bitter critique of the status quo or to serve as an explanation for individual characters' decline in social standing and even self-destruction. In sum, though this chapter focuses narrowly on the images of opium consumption and does not begin to address the issues of control or suppression, multiple distinct understandings of "opium" are evident, often within the same text. For this reason, we are on firmer ground treating opium not as a unitary substance with fixed properties, but rather as an object of several competing discourses. Representations of opium use and abuse should be read not as transparent windows onto a nineteenth-century reality, but rather as cultural products that in turn engender new ways of thinking and writing.

NOTES

1. Ge, *Huyou zaji*, pp. 31, 15.
2. Linda Cooke Johnson, *Shanghai: From Market Town to Treaty Port*, p. 15.

3. Spence, "Opium Smoking in Ch'ing China," pp. 167–68.

4. Huang Shiquan, *Songnan mengying lu*, p. 139.

5. Hanshang mengren, *Fengyue meng*, p. 163.

6. Wang Tao, *Yingruan zazhi*, p. 37.

7. Linda Cooke Johnson, "Shanghai: An Emerging Jiangnan Port."

8. Though the performers in storytelling halls (all female in Shanghai, unlike many other places in Jiangnan) originally performed *tanci*, mostly in Wu dialect, by the middle of the Guangxu era (1880s) it was much more common for them to sing Peking Opera arias instead.

9. Ge, *Huyou zazhi*, p. 30; Huang Shiquan, *Songnan mengying lu*, p. 110; Chi Zhicheng, *Huyou mengying*, pp. 159–60.

10. "Zuiweng ting ji."

11. Chi Zhicheng, *Huyou mengying*, p. 160; see also *Youxi bao*, 14 August 1897, p. 1. *Youxi bao* was the earliest of a variety of daily "leisure papers" published in Shanghai in the decade beginning in 1897. Edited and published by Li Boyuan, *Youxi bao* carried essays on Shanghai city life, anecdotes collected by the editor, his friends, and correspondents, and a significant amount of advertising. Beginning in August 1897, *Youxi bao* was available to readers in Beijing, Tianjin, Hankou, Hangzhou, Suzhou, Nanjing, and Ningbo; the list continued to grow over the years. In the fall of 1897 the publishers of *Zilin Hubao* brought out their answer, a daily titled *Xiaoxian bao*.

12. *Shenjiang mingsheng tushuo* (Famous sites along the Shen River illustrated and described), pp. 64a–b; *Shenjiang shengjing tu* (Illustrated scenes along the Shen River), pp. 15b–16a. *Shenjiang mingsheng tushuo* is a collection of woodblock prints of Shanghai scenes, printed in black and crimson ink. *Shenjiang shengjing tu* is a collection of lithographic prints on similar topics, prints that were frequently reprinted without acknowledgment in later books about Shanghai.

13. Huang Shiquan, *Songnan mengying lu*, pp. 102, 110.

14. *Youxi bao*, 14 August 1897, p. 1.

15. Huang Shiquan, *Songnan mengying lu*, p. 109; Chi Zhicheng, *Huyou mengying*, p. 160; Ping Jinya, "Jiu Shanghai de yandu," p. 12.

16. Ge, *Huyou zaji*, p. 48; Zhang Chang, *Yanhua*, pp. 5b–6a.

17. Cited in Linda Cooke Johnson, *Cities of Jiangnan*, p. 83.

18. On the cultural and economic significance of gardens in the Ming and early Qing, see Clunas, *Fruitful Sites*.

19. *Huyou zaji* was written by Ge Yuanxu, a native of Hangzhou who took refuge from conflict between the Taiping and Qing armies in Shanghai in the early 1860s and remained there. It was reprinted in Chinese- and Japanese-language editions in Japan in 1878, and a revised edition was published in Shanghai in 1887. *Songnan mengying lu* was written by Huang Shiquan, originally from Nanhui county, one of the early editors of *Shen bao*. *Huyou mengying* was written by Chi Zhicheng (1854–1937), who arrived in Shanghai in 1891 but soon moved on to Taiwan to help compile a gazetteer. *Huyou mengying* apparently was written while Chi was in Taiwan; the 1989 reprint edition is based on a manuscript copy done in 1931 and now held by the Wenzhou Museum.

20. A Ying, *Wan Qing wenyi baokan shulüe*, pp. 66–67.

21. Ōno, "Shanhai ni okeru gien no keisei to hatten," pp. 56–57; see also Mack-

erras, *Rise of the Peking Opera,* p. 211, and Mackerras, *Chinese Theatre in Modern Times,* p. 88.

22. Huang Shiquan, *Songnan mengying lu,* p. 117.

23. Gu Gongxie, *Xiao xiaxian ji zhaichao,* excerpted in Xie, *Mingdai shehui jingji shiliao xuanbian,* 2:84–85. Gu, who lived in Qianlong-period Jiangnan, assembled a collection of miscellaneous notes titled *Xiao xiaxian ji,* which appeared in 1818 under the title *Danwu biji* and was excerpted in 1917 and published by Shangwu yinshu guan as *Xiao xiaxian ji zhaichao.*

24. See Sima, *Shiji,* juan 129, pp. 3253–83.

25. Huang Shiquan, *Songnan mengying lu,* p. 127; Qin, *Shanghai xian zhuzhici,* p. 150; *Youxi bao,* 7 September 1897, p. 2. Specific areas within Shanghai were also sometimes referred to in this way: Ge Yuanxu's *Huyou zaji* includes a verse that uses a variant of this phrase, describing the Baoshan jie area in the English Settlement (now Guangdong lu) as *xiao*jin zhi ku* (p. 53).

26. *Xiaoxian bao,* no. 2, excerpted in A Ying, *Wan Qing wenyi baokan shulüe,* pp. 66–67.

27. Ge, *Huyou zaji,* pp. 30, 62, 64; Zhang Chang, *Yanhua,* passim.

28. This usage appears in Wei Yuan's "Jiangnan yin," a ten-verse collection of laments on the difficulties of village life, including floods and taxes as well as opium addiction; Wei Yuan, *Wei Yuan ji,* p. 673. Opinions on the date of composition range from 1831 to Li Hu's contention that the verses were not written until 1849; Yang and Huang, *Wei Yuan sixiang yanjiu,* pp. 421–26.

29. In a relatively ambitious attempt to characterize the opium stupor positively, Zhang refers to these famous religious Daoist, Confucian, and Chinese Buddhist meditative thinkers of the Six Dynasties, Western Han, and Tang, respectively.

30. Zhang Chang, *Yanhua,* pp. 4a–b.

31. Chi Zhicheng, *Huyou mengying,* p. 160.

32. Zhang Chang, *Yanhua,* pp. 3a, 5a.

33. As Judith Zeitlin notes, by the sixteenth century "obsession had become a sine qua non, something the gentleman could not afford to do without" (Zeitlin, *Historian of the Strange,* p. 69).

34. *Youxi bao,* 27 August 1897, p. 2; 2 October 1898, pp. 1–2; 14 August 1897, p. 1. Interestingly, *Youxi bao,* 15 August 1899, pp. 1–2, defends a medicine that is meant to break opium addiction but that does not work on some people by claiming that those people were used to smoking inferior opium that was mixed together with other substances, making it harder to quit. Even when it came to trying to quit opium, a hierarchy of quality was seen to have its effects.

35. Shanghai wenshi yanjiu guan, *Jiu Shanghai de yan, du, chang,* p. 36; see also Spence, "Opium Smoking in Ch'ing China," p. 145.

36. Ge, *Huyou zaji,* p. 56.

37. *Youxi bao,* 30 August 1897, p. 2.

38. Ge, *Huyou zaji,* p. 48; Zhang Chang, *Yanhua,* p. 8a.

39. Huang Shiquan, *Songnan mengying lu,* p. 127.

40. Wei Yuan, *Wei Yuan ji,* p. 673.

41. E.g., Ximen Qing in *Jin ping mei,* Jia Rui in *Honglou meng;* see also McMahon, *Misers, Shrews, and Polygamists.*

42. Zhang Chang, *Yanhua,* p. 9a.

43. Ge, *Huyou zaji*, pp. 48, 67.

44. Zhang Chang, *Yanhua*, pp. 6b, 10a; Han, *Haishang hua liezhuan;* Sun Yusheng, *Haishang fanhua meng.*

45. Zhang Chang, *Yanhua*, pp. 1a–b; Huang Shiquan, *Songnan mengying lu*, p. 114.

46. *Youxi bao*, 6 August 1899, pp. 1–2; Zhang Chang, *Yanhua*, p. 3b.

47. Huang Shiquan, *Songnan mengying lu*, p. 102.

48. Zhang Chang, *Yanhua*, p. 11b.

49. The original (Latin?) term on which this transcription is based has proven impossible to identify.

50. Huang Shiquan, *Songnan mengying lu*, p. 133.

51. Qin, *Shanghai xian zhuzhici*, p. 55.

52. Zhang Chang, *Yanhua*, pp. 9a–10b.

53. Huang Shiquan, *Songnan mengying lu*, p. 113; Chi Zhicheng, *Huyou mengying*, p. 160; *Youxi bao*, 10 May 1899, p. 1.

54. Zhang Chang, *Yanhua*, p. 4b.

55. Brooks, *Reading for the Plot: Design and Intention in Narrative*, p. 39.

56. In the mid-nineteenth-century novel *Fengyue meng* (set in Yangzhou, first published in 1883), there is an opium addict who ends badly in part as a consequence of his addiction. In this work, a bitter exposé of social oppression, opium addiction is not ruinous in isolation, however. It is only that the craving for opium puts the addict at a disadvantage in his struggle to survive in a hostile world.

57. See especially chapters 29, 87, and 88.

58. Suzhou in 1869 had 3,700 opium dens and shops (Spence, "Opium Smoking in Ch'ing China," p. 166); several years later there were fewer than two thousand in Shanghai. It is worth noting that in the case of Wu Zhen, the addicted Yangzhou resident in *Fengyue meng*, the accessories that he uses to smoke come from Shanghai and are far more elaborate than anything made in Yangzhou—this already in the 1840s (see note 56).

59. E.g., Newman, "Opium Licensing System in India"; Sechter, "Legal, Medical, and Social Status of Opium in Britain"; Howard, "Opium Suppression in Late-Qing China." See also Jonathan Spence's discussion of the difficulties faced by the Qing administration when attempting to distinguish between opium for medicinal use and opium for illicit recreational use, in "Opium Smoking in Ch'ing China," pp. 156ff.

PART THREE

Control and Resistance

EIGHT

Opium and Modern Chinese State-Making

R. Bin Wong

China's encounter with opium in the nineteenth and twentieth centuries presented the government with a difficult combination of challenges. First, monitoring and reducing the consumption of opium posed issues of agrarian social control similar to those faced in earlier centuries; in addition, new issues of urban public order with respect to opium consumption surfaced in the twentieth century to complement older concerns for rural social order. Second, controlling the import of this narcotic brought Chinese officials into new forms of negotiations with foreign powers, as the spread of opium consumption through China shaped native and foreign perceptions of China's national character in the late nineteenth and early twentieth centuries. Third, the late-Qing and post-imperial states had an opportunity to raise new revenue from opium production and distribution, but doing so in a manner considered reasonable and acceptable was neither obvious nor easy. In this chapter I will consider these three clusters of challenges to China's government as a lens through which to examine China's modern state-making experience more generally. The first section reviews the social control problems created by spreading opium consumption in light of the eighteenth-century state's vision, strategies, and policies for creating social order. The second section moves on to consider changes in central government challenges, in particular the new types of diplomacy that opium importing made necessary. The third section addresses the political economy of opium within China, in particular the role of opium as a source of government revenue. Together these sections offer a sketch of the arc of modern Chinese state-making seen from the vantage point of opium.

SOCIAL ORDER AND THE PROBLEM OF OPIUM

A basic component of Chinese government success in reproducing itself over the several centuries preceding the nineteenth-century problems with opium were its strategies for creating local social order. The state envisioned empirewide social order to be the cumulative result of maintaining stability across myriad local agrarian communities. Combining moral, material, and coercive measures to promote agrarian social order, officials pursued a variety of goals. They defined religious orthodoxy with their efforts to authorize the pantheon of deities people were expected to worship; they implemented a lecture system *(xiangyue)* with sermonlike speeches to trumpet Confucian virtues. Material measures included efforts to promote agricultural production, store grain for stabilizing food supplies, and reduce taxes in years of poor harvest. Coercive measures centered on household registration in groups expected to engage in mutual surveillance *(baojia)*. To implement many of these strategies, officials relied on the active involvement and even leadership of local elites, many of whom were degree-holding gentry and all of whom shared at least in part the officials' agenda for promoting local order that was crystallized by Zhu Xi (1130–1200). Elite participation in the project of creating a Confucian social order was essential to state success because the bureaucracy lacked the manpower, resources, and local knowledge necessary to penetrate deeply into rural society. Official roles in financing and managing institutions such as local schools and granaries varied inversely with those of elites. Where elites were able and willing to create the institutions of local social order, officials played a reduced role. Official presence was greater in peripheral areas within provinces and across the empire. The eighteenth-century central government—the emperor and officials in the capital— aimed to monitor and regulate social and economic conditions across the empire. The state expected to promote social orthodoxy and economic stability through a vertically integrated bureaucracy that channeled flows of information and resources to facilitate decisions on how to manage different situations.[1]

The Chinese state lacked the capacities for routine surveillance and massive intervention of the sorts we see among contemporary states, but the eighteenth-century bureaucracy certainly took seriously its mission of promoting education and managing subsistence. At times officials made a special effort to develop institutions of local order.[2] These massive efforts required the mobilization of bureaucratic energy, local elite participation, and additional resources. They were in effect campaigns, extraordinary efforts to mount a greater presence in local societies than was routinely maintained. The goal was to institutionalize these new efforts, but as the history of granaries and schools suggests, the reproduction of these instruments of local order was difficult to sustain for more than a few decades and always at a level of intensity well below that required to carry through the campaign itself. Government campaigns to influence local social order represent an important way in which the eighteenth-century state made its presence felt.[3]

The state's presence in society varied in intensity. In principle, officials aimed to promote material security and mold people's behavior in morally correct ways. In practice, these projects were intermittently pursued, on average less intensely in the nineteenth century than in the eighteenth century. Coercive penetration increased, however; militarization and increased taxation meant that the state's benevolent features were eclipsed by its forceful efforts to improve social order through social control. Within this context, the state did little to hold back the nineteenth-century growth of opium production and consumption. The reasons are not yet completely clear, but several possibilities can be mentioned. First, as the early twentieth-century efforts to control production and distribution would show, an extraordinarily great mobilization of energy and determination was required, not the kind of campaign we should necessarily anticipate when the state faced pressing challenges from both foreigners and rebels. Second, the government does not appear to have had good information on the growth of opium use for much of the nineteenth century. Third, there may well have been some ambivalence in assessing how serious a problem opium really was; if it was confined to a leisure-time luxury of the affluent, then its social harm was not obvious to everyone. Despite occasional concerns about effects among soldiers and other lower-class individuals, before the late nineteenth century there was not a general perception of growing popular consumption associated with the dangers of addiction. Lacking was the kind of massive and coordinated campaign push to affect conditions across several provinces at once.

When the government finally mounted a systematic campaign to attack the opium problem in 1906, it drew, at least tacitly, upon a repertoire of techniques already developed in the eighteenth century. Foreign pressures (to be addressed in the next section) helped to motivate these Chinese government efforts. Officials were ordered to reduce production and to control distribution and consumption. No new land was allowed to be planted in opium; if unauthorized lands were planted with opium poppy, the landowners were threatened with losing not only their crop but their title to the land as well. Opium smokers were required to register and would be allowed to buy a decreasing amount over time as they weaned themselves from the habit. The number of shops selling opium was also to decline over several years as the amount of production and the number of consumers were also supposed to be reduced.

Production was difficult to disguise or hide. Peasants who grew opium poppy illegally were therefore easy to spot. But in some areas officials tolerated continued production. In others, however, officials sent out troops to uproot the offending crops. The border between Shanxi and Shaanxi, for instance, was clearly marked by the presence of opium on the Shaanxi side and not on the Shanxi side, where officials pushed hard after 1908 to halt production; in a journey of four hundred miles a British observer did not see a single poppy field in Shanxi, but crossing the border into Shaanxi he immediately saw many.[4] In some cases peasants opposed government attempts to destroy their poppy fields. A British missionary reported a case from Gansu north and east of Liangzhou where "the farmers, in spite of strongly worded proclamations and occasional demonstrations of horse soldiers, refuse to destroy it. Bands of their wives have gone to the magistrate's yamen, saying, 'You may kill us, but we will grow opium.'"[5] Also in Gansu another missionary reported that the district magistrate went to a marketplace on the border of two counties to order the uprooting of the opium poppy, but the people opposed him, saying that "they would willingly uproot their growing plants if the people in the next district would do the same. The cause of this growing on the borders of districts is that the yamen underlings, having been bribed, deceive the magistrate, and, should he appear in person to examine, declare the land in question to be in the neighboring district."[6] Halting opium production was thus not simply a moral issue but an economic one as well. Peasants denied the opportunity to grow the opium poppy were looking at a substantial reduction in income. In different Sichuan counties estimates were made of the relative value of the opium crop compared to the next most profitable use of the land; opium was two to six times as valuable as alternative crops such as wheat, millet, corn, mulberry, and tea. The acting British consul in Chongqing was understandably uncertain about the prospects for reducing opium production in Sichuan, which grew more opium than any other province in the early twentieth century.[7] Other reports from the province by Chinese officials and missionaries suggest that there were reductions in some counties but not in others in response to the government campaign against opium.[8] In some places officials were resolute in their efforts to destroy the crop while in others officials were far more lax. Without a display of force or the threat of its potential use, peasants would not willingly give up a profitable crop. In the western part of Sichuan, where most of the province's opium was grown, efforts to suppress opium cultivation were seen as an attack on the commercial economy. As S. A. M. Adshead remarks:

> Freedom to plant opium was one of the things Szechwan expected from the revolution. In 1912, the Customs reported that "the people, believing that the establishment of a Republic meant license to all to do as they pleased, recommenced planting the poppy in out of the way districts."[9]

Halting opium consumption also entailed economic hardships on those engaged in selling the product. Reform era policies therefore gave opium shops a transition period in which they could shift their capital to other lines of business. Some received more time than others, as the numbers of shops was to be reduced annually. As with production, the regulation of consumption sites varied with the energy and commitment of the officials implementing the policies. In general officials were most successful, not surprisingly, in administrative centers. Opium shops and dens could be closed in the cities and towns while sales in other areas continued. Officials had limited ability to monitor all sites of consumption.[10]

Another way to implement the war against opium was through registering all smokers and regulating the amounts of opium they could purchase. Each opium user was expected to register, giving his name, age, address, and amount of daily consumption. Opium users who were traveling could receive one-month licenses permitting them to buy opium while away from home.[11] The scale of the registration problem can be gauged from estimates of the numbers of people smoking opium in the early twentieth century. The Chinese memorandum to the 1909 International Opium Commission held in Shanghai gave consumption estimates for different provinces generated by Chinese and foreign officials and by missionaries (see table 1).

The dramatically different estimates of opium consumption were accompanied by great variation in the estimated reductions of opium consumption achieved by different provincial leaders during the opium suppression campaign. In some provinces, major efforts were launched, with repeated provincial regulations followed by county-level proclamations. In Fujian, for example, the governor general, the governor, the provincial judge, the head of the police, and various magistrates issued proclamations on implementing the different dimensions of the opium suppression campaign: closing opium dens, limiting the number of retail shops, establishing clinics for treating opium addiction, prosecuting owners of opium dens, outlawing smoking in temples and on boats, and registering smokers. The success of these efforts was corroborated by missionary reports of reduced production, distribution and consumption.[12] In Fujian, a new institution comes into play as the police are enlisted to enforce the opium regulations. But the presence of a new reform-era institution simply adds to a government logic for rule that continues in many ways a logic familiar to the eighteenth-century state. The responsiveness of lower-level officials to higher-level officials' exhortations varied in the opium suppression movement, much as lower-level official response to higher-level officials varied in earlier decades of Qing rule. The logic of sustaining order throughout the empire depended on the capacity and commitment of provincial and lower-level officials to elaborate and implement general directives sent out by the

TABLE 1   Estimated Percentages of Opium Users in China, 1909

Place	Percentage of adult males	Percentage of total population
Manchuria	10	2
Zhili	20–30	
Chefoo, Shandong	33	
Shanghai area	20	
Nanjing	20 before the edict prohibiting opium; 5 by 1909	
Zhejiang		5
Wenzhou		
urban areas	20	
rural areas	10	
Amoy, Fujian		25
Canton area	33–10	
Hunan		
Chinese estimate	20	
missionary estimate		40
Hubei		20
Jiangxi	40 before the edict, 28 by 1909	
Anhui		50 (all adults)
Henan		
urban		15
market towns		5
villages		2
Yunnan		50 (males) and 10 (females) before the edict; by 1909, 45% had stopped, 15% had cut back their consumption, and 40% continued their use of the drug

SOURCE: International Opium Commission, *Report of the International Opium Commission* (1909), 2: 62–66.

central government. As in the eighteenth century, when it depended upon a small group of zealous officials to set an example, the central government could point to Zhang Zhidong, who began his efforts in Shanxi in the 1880s, and Xiliang, who labored to reduce opium production and consumption in Yunnan after 1906. Xiliang appears to have reduced opium cultivation, trade, and consumption by roughly 80 percent.[13] The logic of mounting a successful campaign and the importance of such efforts to creating an effective state were constants from early in the Qing through the flurry of early-twentieth-century reform efforts. Opium suppression was a new campaign in terms of the scale and intensity of effort brought to bear on the problem, but the state-making logic supporting the campaign rested upon an earlier late-imperial formulation. In contrast, the larger contexts for the opium suppression movement were new.

Official efforts at reducing opium consumption were part of a broader movement to oppose what reformers believed to be a pernicious practice. Opposing opium consumption was envisioned by students as an element of a larger struggle to assert Chinese national strength. Inspired by Japanese resistance to opium imports, students mounted resistance to opium smoking in China. Public opinion against opium also expressed itself in less dramatic but perhaps even more significant ways. In cities this shift could be observed in the press, what one observer in Nanjing referred to as "the moral influence exercised by well-thinking newspapers and pamphlets." Opium smoking was no longer fashionable among the urban educated and well to do, as it once had been. Observers in different parts of the empire noted this common trend. In Jiangsu, Alexander Hosie reports, "The progress of the movement in large cities in Soochow is slower than at Shanghae, where there is now a stigma on opium smoking, and where young men shun the opium houses which have in the past been their fashionable after-dinner resorts. There can be no doubt that in Shanghae Chinese public opinion is as strongly as ever in favour of the campaign and the good effect of the movement is unquestionable."[14] In Jiaxing, Zhejiang, "it is reported that before 1906 it was the custom among all classes to discuss business in opium divans; this is now not done. It is also said in that city that it is now considered 'bad form' to offer opium to guests." In Fuzhou, "Opium smoking is no longer a fashionable pastime—a rakish habit which youth felt urged to acquire. It is now regarded as 'bad form', and is distinctly out of favour with young men."[15] Rising public opposition to opium was also noted far from the fashionable eastern provinces in the producing areas of the interior such as Shaanxi, where a missionary of the English Baptist Society wrote to Hosie, "Such a vast change [reduction of opium production] is only possible when supported by popular sentiment. No other change appeals as this has done to the conscience of the people."[16] Max Müller, a British councillor in Sichuan, summarizing changes in public opinion more broadly, notes, "In old days it was considered good form for a young man to smoke opium; now the reverse is the case, and he no longer feels himself bound to indulge in his opium after dinner."[17]

Popular opposition to opium was part of a broader set of social changes involving new groups creating public opinion. Opium's increased consumption in urban areas among adult males had been tied to fashion; opposition to it was equally a statement about changed tastes. These consumption choices fit within a broader social and political perspective that considered the eradication of opium part of a larger project to build a strong and competitive nation. Yet it would be crucially incomplete to view the emergence of popular opposition to opium as based upon thoroughly new sensibilities and logics. The state's strategy for suppressing opium depended fundamentally on mobilizing gentry elites to share in this project of recreating a social order morally reinvigorated by the eradication of the opium blight. In pursuit of this end, the government promoted the founding of anti-opium societies to be headed by gentry leaders. As gentry elites had been entrusted with the neo-Confucian agenda for local order in earlier centuries, now they were called upon to combat a threat to social order as great as any peacetime danger the empire had ever experienced. By the late nineteenth century, gentry elites had come to play more formal roles in politics and social life. The formation of assemblies and various new societies marked the greater participation of elites in politics and a contest between elites and the state over the definition of elite roles in governing. The government wanted to mobilize elite support for promoting social order without sanctioning a more formal political role with enhanced and specified powers.[18] Thus a set of government regulations on opium suppression with regard to anti-opium societies states, "Such society shall be purely for the anti-opium smoking, and the society shall not discuss any other matters, such as political questions bearing on topical affairs or local administration, or any similar matter."[19] Another set of regulations called on all local officials to "instruct reputable gentry and merchants in their jurisdictions to organize Anti-Opium Associations and to publish pamphlets and magazines in simple language to exhort people to break off opium smoking. These publications should not interfere with politics or subjects outside of their province."[20] From the government's point of view, these anti-opium associations were an extension of government capacity and commitments to eradicate opium use. Indeed, a 1906 edict granted anti-opium societies "full authority to enter any place for examination and placing at their disposal officers to enforce their demands for admittance or to make arrests where ordered by such committees." In some provinces these committees were very active. In Fujian "these committees have been busy every night and have accomplished much in enforcing the above decrees. At times they have been attacked and some of them severely beaten, but nothing has deterred them from their purpose. They are still warring nightly."[21] But in other places, such as Sichuan, reports from different counties suggested that no societies were formed.[22] (This contrast is developed in the two following chapters by Wyman and Madancy.) Differences in official-elite relations affected the prospects for anti-opium societies just as they had affected other efforts to create local institutions of social order in earlier centuries.

The larger logic of suppression also included the idea of village elders dissuading others from opium smoking and, if they failed in these efforts, reporting the offenders. Moreover, merely tolerating opium smoking could lead to punishment equal to that of the smoker or owner of an opium den, as an order in Fuzhou made clear: "If such practices are again detected, we will first seal and confiscate the house, and then punish without mercy the Tipaos [constables] and house owners who fail to report such cases as if they were smokers and the proprietors of such opium dens."[23] The late-Qing effort to eradicate opium rested upon an alliance between officials and elites employing a range of instruments to suppress opium; new techniques such as magazines could be called upon, but many of the strategies as well as the underlying social logic of opium suppression engaged officials and elites together in an effort to resecure a neo-Confucian social order. Without elite efforts to complement official initiatives, the suppression movement would not have penetrated as widely or deeply as it did. Elite engagement depended upon the optimism that at least some elites felt about the prospect of eradicating China's opium problem. Elites need not have agreed with officials about all issues facing state and society in the late Qing to have participated in opium suppression according to a political logic that their ancestors would have largely understood. The moral energy fueling the opium suppression movement depended upon faith in the capacity and commitment of the Chinese state and the continued viability of its relations with gentry and other elites to fashion a social and political order that could enter the twentieth-century world. Although some may have felt that they had to act because the state was unable to shoulder the responsibility alone, more elites probably conceived their efforts as a way to complement official actions in a manner resonating with a Chinese tradition of official-elite and state-society relations. From the vantage point of the movement to combat opium, the 1911 Revolution did not come as liberation with the promise of better future possibilities. For opium suppression, the 1911 Revolution meant the end of an opportunity to make a neo-Confucian social order in which opium could be eradicated. In certain local areas, new governments continued to combat the opium trade aggressively in the face of opposition from merchants whose profits were being challenged. But while a local government like that in Canton continued to restrict opium business in 1912, other areas, like those in Sichuan already mentioned, experienced the revolution as an opportunity to plant opium poppy more freely.[24]

In the immediate post-imperial years there was even less possibility of the Chinese state mounting a systematic strategy to approach the opium problem, as the very structures of government were being reconstructed and redefined. Gone was the vertically integrated bureaucracy that formed the skeletal structure for political unification. As local, provincial, and central levels of government expanded in different but overlapping directions, their ranges of operations, as well as the challenges and strategies of ruling urban China, became increasingly distant from the late-imperial agenda for promoting domestic social order. Late-imperial Chinese strategies of local rule had been concerned with both rural and urban social order, but because the vast majority of China's population lived in the countryside and Chinese ideas about social stability were rooted in the soil, the policies for urban social control developed alongside a primary concern for agrarian social order. County seats were of course urban centers. Officials administered the realm from towns and cities. But their administrations were not principally geared to urban social order. As certain cities and towns grew in the nineteenth century, new institutions developed to provide public services and promote social order. Elites played a major role in creating the institutions of public order. For much of the nineteenth century the largely complementary relationship between elites and officials that marked agrarian social order applied to urban settings as well. But the late-nineteenth-century creation of more institutions through which elite interests and concerns were voiced created a contest for power and authority between elites and officials.

Managing the opium problem as an issue of domestic social order reveals important changes in Chinese state-making during the nineteenth and twentieth centuries. The late-Qing state demonstrated a considerable capacity and commitment to attack the opium problem. With noteworthy variations across the empire, the state proved quite successful in stemming the expansion of the opium problem after 1906. These successes and their limitations were firmly grounded in strategies and sensibilities of rule that grew out of a neo-Confucian agenda for local order first elaborated in the Song dynasty and developed in later centuries. The post-imperial period ushered in an era in which a neo-Confucian agenda for rural order no longer made sense. The emergence of new elites, including military and merchant elites, combined with the crystallization of counter-elites in the form of secret societies and bandit groups, made the previous logic of social order difficult to articulate, let alone implement. The Nationalist government's ideological campaign in the 1930s to promote a New Life Movement as a means to reinspire Chinese public order lacked the social substance and political logic that characterized late-imperial initiatives at constructing domestic order. Governing urban China required the development of new institutions, the capacities of which were severely challenged by foreign power and authority in many of the large urban centers. The difficulties of ruling rural China and urban China formed distinctive clusters of issues. To span the two created an even larger challenge. The largest challenge, however, embraced the issues of urban public order, rural social order, and the links between them. This was the challenge of the nation: how to integrate the many local and provincial situations into a politically coherent whole. A systematic solution to the opium problem would be one challenge faced by any successful state-maker in post-imperial China. This solution would entail a changed engagement with foreigners as well as a new domestic order.

THE CHINESE STATE, FOREIGN RELATIONS, AND OPIUM

The late-Qing state's efforts to cope with the problems of opium production and consumption committed it to strategies for promoting local social order and for creating large-scale campaigns. Quite separate from these efforts were discussions entered into by Chinese officials with representatives of foreign governments concerning the reduction of opium imports, a topic with which the Chinese state had grappled in various ways since the fateful efforts of Lin Zexu in the late 1830s to halt what was then a much smaller flow of opium into China. The British responded to a Chinese decision to work toward eliminating opium production and consumption taken in 1906 by signing an agreement in 1907 to reduce annual imports of Indian opium to China by 10 percent each year, provided that domestic production was also reduced by 10 percent each year; if upon review in three years it was found that the Chinese were doing their part, the British would reduce Indian imports to 16,000 chests annually. The International Commission convened at American behest in Shanghai during 1909 was the first of several meetings to discuss what was coming to be seen as the international problem of opium. In practical terms, China at this time was the major site for opium production and consumption, and relations between China and Great Britain formed the principal axis along which most international concerns about opium revolved. The minutes from the proceedings show Chinese skills at engaging in international deliberations. These discussions also revealed how modest the commission's authority was: some delegates were careful not to commit their governments to any new policies as a result of the commission's deliberations. The British neatly avoided any resolutions that could have been construed as affecting their position respecting the import of Indian opium to China. For their part, the Chinese pressed foreign powers who had concessions and settlements in China to enforce the same laws against opium in these areas as they applied in their home countries. They proposed a resolution approved by the commission after arguing that "since each civilized country has its own laws and statutes against the sale of poisons and all medicines containing poisons, we do not think we are asking too much if we request each civilized power to make its laws effective in its respective Concessions and Settlements in China, that is to say, to transfer the operation of its laws as existing in its own country over to China, where the Powers enjoy extra-territorial rights for their subjects."[25] The Chinese pressed especially strongly against the French, who had not seen fit to close opium dens in their concession, despite their strict limitation on opium dens in their Southeast Asian territories. The French noted that they were not allowing any new opium dens in China and were raising the tax on those already open. Their defense was a wish "to be assured that China herself was in earnest" in closing opium dens. The Chinese also criticized the Japanese for their role as the leading supplier of morphia drugs, an addictive alternative to opium peddled throughout the country as a medicinal; the Japanese response was a sympathetic statement of their ignorance of this problem. Thus, the Chinese were able to raise issues about foreign efforts regarding opium in a forum that exposed issues more openly than conventional bilateral discussions. The commission concluded with resolutions condemning opium production, distribution, and consumption and exhorting governments to take measures to resolve these problems. The Chinese could raise issues awkward to foreign delegates, but they were also the object of criticism regarding their efforts at opium suppression. At the sixth session, Sir Alexander Hosie challenged the veracity of Chinese production figures, suggesting that many of the numbers were fabricated; in particular, backward projections of production created fictive numbers assuming a certain percentage decline to the later estimated numbers; this meant that Chinese claims of reducing opium production were necessarily "true" without data to support the assertion. Hosie also noted a wide variety of consumption estimates. The difficulty was not, however, uniquely Chinese. Foreign estimates of production and consumption also varied because it was difficult to gather adequate data on either, a fact Hosie well understood. Hosie's more detailed reports as well as those of Max Müller, a councillor to the British legation, adduce evidence of reduced opium production and consumption.

In 1911 Great Britain agreed to end all Indian opium imports within seven years; moreover, any province establishing clear evidence that both cultivation and domestic sales had been suppressed would not receive Indian imports, except Shanghai and Canton, which were the ports into which Indian opium came. There ensued a series of international conferences to discuss opium problems culminating with a 31 December 1917 declaration that the cultivation and importing of opium into China were both illegal.[26] In the 1920s the League of Nations took up the international concern for opium, establishing an advisory committee for traffic in opium and other dangerous drugs. In 1924–1925 this advisory committee reviewed various policies to suppress opium smoking, including government monopoly, registration of addicts, rationing to addicts, and smuggling. By the mid 1920s international concerns about opium were no longer confined to China. Opium consumption in Southeast Asia and Taiwan engaged the attention of British, Dutch, French, and Japanese colonial governments. These governments believed that China had become the source of opium smuggled into their colonies, undermining their efforts to limit the use of the drug.

The reality of China's growing position in the international drug market was preceded by foreign fears of Chinese and their opium smoking habits, which created domestic political support for policies treating the Chinese as less than equal in international relations, including favoring their exclusion in late-nineteenth-century Australia and United States. Western fears of Chinese opium began with the information that missionaries sent home. Treating opium addicts became one of the principal activities of missionaries. Thus, a Mrs. Piggott of the China Inland Mission reports on her two and a half years in Taiyuan that "the work we had there was chiefly medical work, and the curing of opium-smokers." She goes on to explain how the process of weaning opium addicts offered missionaries an opportunity to proselytize: "We have found that time hangs rather heavily on the hands of these opium smokers while in the Opium Refuge, because they are obliged to stay for three weeks, or sometimes a month, before we feel satisfied to let them go, and as they have nothing to do they are very glad to listen to conversation about the Gospel, and to read books if they are able to read."[27] Although missionaries enjoyed some triumphs, their impact on opium addiction appears to have been very limited.[28] The prevalence of opium addiction among the Chinese gave missionaries a pressing social reason to be in the country, the irony of which some missionaries noted. A China Inland Mission representative in Henan wrote, "We find that such [opium] work helps to clear away the suspicion with which the natives naturally regard us; although I have heard it sarcastically remarked that, 'It was strange that the country which sends the poison should also send the antidote.' "[29]

Because so much of the Christian missionaries' effort was absorbed in combating the evils of opium, it is no wonder that their letters home made frequent mention of opium's dangers. Nor is it surprising that the popular press in the West should begin to create opium-filled images of China. Popular support for exclusion was related to American and Australian images of Chinese as opium addicts. The opium pipe became a symbol of Chinese culture; magazines created the impression that all of China's millions of adults were addicted to the drug. Fears of the spread of opium smoking to the United States from Chinese bringing the habit with them became one ground for supporting Chinese exclusion from the United States. The social logic is captured in an 1882 book titled *Opium Smoking in America and China* by Dr. H. H. Kane, who quotes a letter he received from a Dr. Harris of Virginia City, Nevada:

Opium smoking had been entirely confined to the Chinese up to and before the autumn of 1876, when the practice was introduced by a sporting character who had lived in China, where he had contracted the habit. He spread the practice among his class, and his mistress, "a woman of the town," introduced it among her demimonde acquaintances, and it was not long before it had widely spread among the people mentioned, and then amongst the younger class of boys and girls, many of the latter of the more respected class of families. The habit grew very rapidly, until it reached young women of a more mature age, when the necessity for stringent measures became apparent, and was met by the passing of a city ordinance.

For his own part, Kane describes an insidious process of dark and dangerous mystery that begins in San Francisco's Chinatown in "back rooms and laundries in the low pestilential dens of Chinatown, reeking with filth and overrun with vermin in the cellars of dirty saloons and in houses of prostitution." Opium smoking, Kane warns us, will spread from the edges of Chinatown and infect the rest of American society:

> It is thus seen how fascinating a habit that opium smoking is, and with what rapidity it is spreading all over the country, ensnaring individuals in all classes of society, leading to the downfall of innocent girls and the debasement of married women, and spreading its roots and growing in spite of the most stringent measures looking to its eradication.[30]

Opium was seen as the vice of a weak and depraved people, and such people could not be allowed into the United States. Clear distinctions were drawn between Chinese on the one hand and European immigrants on the other—European immigrants who were considered inferior to earlier European immigrants. As James Gordon Bennett Jr., a New York newspaper editor, opined, "Compared with these base Chinese, the vilest dregs that come into New York from the vilest holes in Europe are refined and attractive people."[31] The Chinese were not fit to participate in American democracy. Linked to this assessment was the judgment that they were unable to create democracy in their own country and thus, having inferior political and social institutions, they could be subjected to foreign control.

For their part, Chinese elites at the turn of the century expected to be able to suppress opium as part of a larger enterprise of building a strong and secure nation. Chinese protested the inclusion of opium paraphernalia in an exhibit on China at the 1903 Louisiana Purchase Exhibition. They wished to project an image of a strong and cultured country. The Chinese delegate to the 1909 International Commission on Opium expressed the hopes of both Chinese officials and elites when he highlighted the common ground between Confucian and Christian moralities:

> With all of the shortcomings of China's old educational system, it had this to commend it, that it insisted upon a thorough study of the ethics of Confucius and Mencius, and the result is a large fund of moral sentiment. This is our

greatest force in entering into this contest, and outside of China also one is conscious of that mighty force, greater than the world's combined navies and armies, greater than the power of all the world's gold and silver—the Christian conscience. With these forces behind us we may enter with confidence into what might be rightly called one of the greatest moral crusades of the twentieth century, for whatever laws the nations of the world may decide to adopt towards each other, we may not forget that there is a law higher than all human laws, a law greater than all economic laws, a law that transcends even the law of nature and that is the eternal law of Heaven, which, through Confucius, says, "do not unto others what thou wouldst not have others do unto you," and which, through Jesus Christ, says "Thou shalt love they neighbor as thyself."[32]

Alas, these fervent hopes proved premature. The Chinese state's inability to eradicate opium use became even greater after 1911. Beyond China, what had been exaggerated nineteenth-century fears of opium smoking spreading through the United States and Australia became the 1920s reality of opium smoking increasing in Southeast Asia. Within China, opium production and consumption were cast as a moral problem. The duty of the state to address the problem, a concern carried forward from late-imperial government assumptions and aspirations, was heightened by foreign perceptions of Chinese weaknesses and depravity associated with opium. But the imperative to eradicate opium was tempered by the much-needed revenue that taxing or controlling opium production and consumption provided to political authorities.

THE POLITICAL ECONOMY OF OPIUM

However morally distasteful opium production and consumption were considered by some, they were also major economic activities. In the eighteenth century grain had been the most important commodity in domestic trade in terms of both value and volume, followed by cotton textiles; these items of daily use bulked large in China's commercial economy. Wu Chengming estimates that grain accounted for nearly 40 percent of interregional trade by value, with cotton cloth a bit less than 30 percent and salt at about 15 percent.[33] During the nineteenth century opium transactions grew to the extent that one scholar has estimated the 1900 value of opium trade to be 130 million taels, compared to 100 million taels for grain and 100 million taels for salt.[34] The economic importance of opium posed not only a major social problem but provided an important political opportunity to raise new revenues. Chronically short of funds, the Qing state in the second half of the nineteenth century constantly searched for new methods to raise additional revenues. Its ability to raise new revenues, largely through the imposition of transit taxes *(likin),* mark it as a successful state meeting one of the basic challenges of state-making—securing resources to pay for expanded government activities.

The Treaty of Nanking (1842) at the conclusion of the Opium War did not actually legalize or regulate opium imports. Imports rose from 20,619 chests in 1838 to about 50,000 chests in 1850 and 85,000 chests in 1860.[35] The 1858 Sino-British Tientsin Treaty formally legalized opium imports with a duty of thirty taels per picul. The 1876 Chefoo Convention added a *likin* tax of eighty taels, to make a total of 110 taels per picul. In 1911 the British government agreed to a tax increase to 350 taels per picul. These opium taxes contributed to a larger increase in government revenues. In 1849 the government raised some 42.5 million taels of revenue, with 77 percent of this coming from agriculture and the balance from commerce; thirty-six years later revenues had climbed to more than 77 million taels, the increase largely due to a quadrupling of the commercial revenues. The development of Chinese central government control over customs revenues is a clear indication of the state's ability to create new infrastructural capacities, with much of the increased revenue raised through the maritime customs collections. But these Chinese increases were nothing compared to the nearly 302 million taels of revenue gathered in 1911, the final year of the dynasty: agricultural taxes had grown from roughly 30 to roughly 50 million taels, with another 45 from miscellaneous sources; more than 207 million came from commercial taxes. Whatever the late-Qing state's weaknesses, raising money was not among them.[36]

When opium revenues were first collected, Robert Hart of the Imperial Maritime Customs Administration proposed using his administration to collect the opium taxes. The central government, however, elected to have provincial officials take charge of these collections, a decision that Hart thought too ambitious. Hart's own preference for dealing with the opium issue was then to support the proposal of one Joseph Samuel, who argued that the British should establish a monopoly with himself in charge of opium production and sales, contracting with the Chinese government to import a set amount each year. An alternative proposed by Gustav Detring was for China to establish its own company to purchase opium and thus control imports. This option was politically unacceptable to Beijing, which could not reconcile its moral opposition to opium with an agreement from which it would profit directly. Hart wrote his London agent, Campbell, "Opium—China's real difficulty is in the existence of so many Treaty Powers each having the 'most favored nation' clause, and the form in which that difficulty shows itself is in the necessity it imposes on China of consulting all before it can enforce on any a rule agreed to by one." Hart's major concern was with regularizing opium revenues for the Chinese government: "the simplest thing would be for India to collect our revenue for us—the next best after that would be Samuel's scheme—and the next best after that will be 'no opium at all.' "[37] Hart's priorities clearly favored the collection of revenue over the reduction of opium consumption. These opium revenues were used for a variety of purposes. Li Hongzhang in the capital province of Zhili used these revenues for provincial defense, Beijing police, patrol boats, coal for cruiser ships, and payment of interest on foreign loans.[38] Initially seen as emergency fiscal measures, opium revenues became regularized in several provinces. As part of its efforts to recentralize control over new taxes initially collected at the provincial levels, the central government took over levies on opium in 1891. Opium revenues from domestic and foreign levies were effectively controlled by the central government as part of the late-Qing state's efforts to create wealth and power. The Qing state failed to survive much beyond the first decade of the twentieth century, but the governments to follow in the next several decades were in many ways even weaker.

Government activities, especially coercive control and extractive activities, did increase in the post-imperial period. But the expansion of government at different levels was not effectively integrated into a common state-building process. Different levels of government each moved to establish claims over revenue sources. Taxing opium production and distribution became increasingly important as different levels of the bureaucracy moved to control different sources of revenue. The Beijing regime retained control over the maritime customs revenues and developed new commercial taxes. Provincial governments asserted control over land taxes after the 1911 Revolution, no longer routinely forwarding a portion of the collection to the central government; moreover, the central government no longer decided how the taxes left at the provincial level would be disbursed. New taxes were levied by local governments seeking to fund new schools and police forces. Higher levels of government in the Republican era continued the late-Qing practice of expecting locales to raise funds to implement political initiatives according to whatever methods they found effective.

Jiang Jieshi (Chiang Kai-shek) retraced the steps taken by the Qing government of legalizing opium sales and registering addicts. But he cut his own path to establish a government opium monopoly. The late-Qing government reforms had included licensing and taxing opium shops as well as setting up officially regulated sales from peasants. But this process of government regulation over what remained a private-sector phenomenon of multiple producers, merchants, and retail shops differed substantially from the conditions of the late 1920s and early 1930s when the Nationalist government created a monopoly. This monopoly basically became a tax farming arrangement with control turned over to drug lord Du Yuesheng, who agreed to give the government a set amount of money in return for monopoly rights over opium sales.[39]

The logic of government control over distribution of opium gained force between the 1860s and the 1930s. Controlling opium distribution reflected fundamental features of Nationalist state-building efforts. First, the challenge of creating social order demanded a large-scale and systematic effort at reducing opium consumption. Without a renewed and even expanded capacity to shape local social order, it became increasingly unclear what kind of society any Chinese government would want to rule. Second, controlling opium revenues became very much an issue of defining power and authority relations between the central and regional or provincial governments; concentration of fiscal authority in central government hands was systematically achieved in the eighteenth century and, after an initial devolution of control over new revenues raised in response to midcentury rebellions, the late-nineteenth-century state labored to regain central government control. Jiang's move on opium revenues represented another such initiative. The expansion of opium production within China made opium revenues ever more possible and thus important. Third, the decision to create an opium monopoly was easier to contemplate in the 1930s than it had been in the 1870s because control over trade had become concentrated in fewer private hands by the latter period. In addition, foreign business involvement had declined. The logic of establishing an opium monopoly was a precursor in logic to efforts in the following decade to establish government monopolies over production and distribution, including tobacco, matches, and sweets, though later efforts would involve more bureaucratic participation and less selling off of government tax authority.[40] Fourth, creating an opium monopoly made sense in international terms as foreign colonial powers had established government monopolies over opium in their Asian territories. Attendees at the League of Nations' International Conferences on Opium and Dangerous Drugs held in the winter of 1924–1925 "unanimously agreed that the establishment of a complete government monopoly has by experience been proved to be the only effective way towards the control of consumption."[41] Not that China's government monopoly quite met the criteria intended by most foreign analyses. A fifth characteristic of Chinese state-making in this period that is displayed in the government's opium monopoly was its willingness to recognize Du's opium empire. This reflects the segmented nature of Nationalist bureaucracy at this time, a bureaucracy in which the two most efficient fiscal branches, maritime customs and the salt administration, were both bureaucracies with heavy foreign presence and considerable autonomy from other units within the government bureaucracy. As long as they delivered the taxes, they were left alone by Jiang and other leaders.[42] The opium monopoly also had its own bureaucracy, which was independent even if considerably less attractive than the bureaucracies created by joint Chinese-foreign efforts. The segmented nature of the bureaucracy and the range of political arrangements to expand the government's revenue base create a broader frame of reference for considering Prasenjit Duara's "state involution," a process of expanded paragovernmental extraction from which the local and provincial governments sponsoring these activities received only a percentage.[43] The Nationalist government's opium monopoly resonates with Duara's concept of "state involution" while also fitting within a continuum of bureaucratic operations to raise revenues. Even at the central government level, there was no coherent and integrated bureaucratic state. Finally, the political allies of the Nationalist government tell us much about the social base of this government and the difficulties of creating a moral vision of statecraft when deals are struck with underworld drug leaders. The government could have continued to tax opium as part of a putative suppression effort and reached an uneasy and less obvious accommodation with Du Yuesheng. The Nationalist government might have been able to avoid the policy decision to form an explicit partnership with criminals, but it would have been hard to avoid turning to opium as a source of revenue.

The importance of opium revenues to the Republican-era political economy derives from the difficulties that governments faced in developing new sources of revenue under conditions of political uncertainty. Opium revenues were especially important in the areas lacking an industrial or commercial base for taxation, though the turn to opium as a revenue source was a more general phenomenon. Reliance on opium for revenues competed with the goal of suppressing opium production and consumption, however much officials stressed their complementarity. The greater the government's success in thwarting consumption, the more difficult it became to maintain the same level of opium revenues. Thus, the twin goals of creating local order and satisfying state needs for revenues became antithetical from the late Qing through the first half of the twentieth century.

OPIUM AND THE ARC OF MODERN CHINESE STATE-MAKING

Opium is related to three different aspects of modern Chinese state-making. First, there is the theme of the decline of the late-imperial state and the subsequent construction of a replacement. The nineteenth-century state failed to reproduce an integrated political order predicated upon domestic social stability rooted in local public order. This capacity to monitor and promote local public order had been a basic component of imperial state success from Southern Song times on. It is easy to miss the importance of these features because they do not fit within conventional categories of state activities defined by European experiences; nor do the features seem all that impressive from a contemporary point of view. Yet the creation and reproduction of a political order spanning an agrarian empire, not surprisingly, required capacities and commitments quite different from those developed within Western traditions. The modesty of the abilities of the late-imperial state by contemporary standards means that these abilities are a poor gauge for measuring what mattered in Chinese politics in earlier centuries. Indeed, the kinds of efforts that the reform-era Qing government took to combat opium include measures difficult to imagine in a twentieth-century Western democracy. No concept of individual liberties or property rights blocked the opium suppression campaign from registering opium smokers and threatening peasants planting opium poppy with confiscation of their land. Although the process of opium suppression by the Communists has not yet been well researched, we can hypothesize that its success was predicated upon the Communist government's willingness to mount a massive campaign that combined the promise of clearing up the decay of the old society with threats against those who resisted. Surveillance no doubt enlisted the participation of people outside the Party who shared with the new government a desire to rid society of opium's destructive presence. In at least some ways, we can plausibly expect the Communist campaign against opium to replicate key features of late-Qing efforts. However, unlike the late-Qing campaign, which was swiftly followed by governmental collapse and the end—temporary, as it turned out—of a vertically integrated bureaucratic system of rule linked to a broader base of elite support, the Communists succeeded in consolidating their control and asserting a new bureaucratic and ideological order across China. Within that order, the repeated launching of campaigns was a practice conventionally seen as a Communist innovation but in fact the practice has precedents among earlier strategies of Chinese state rule. These campaigns augmented what became a bureaucracy with far greater capacities to control society than was imaginable in late-imperial times.

The second aspect of modern Chinese state-making highlighted by opium problems is the relationship of China to foreign countries. The Chinese ability to learn the proper conventions within which to engage foreign diplomats at international meetings on opium affirms the development of new state capacities. Government officials' expertise in diplomatic practices no doubt helped them to secure a reduction in British opium imports. But beyond formal governmental structures and practices, opium contributed to the negative images of Chinese as weak and yet dangerous people; these images in turn fit within racial stereotypes that contributed to notions of China's inferiority, affecting both Chinese and foreign views. Where foreigners could find in opium a reason to believe the Chinese were a lower form of human life, educated Chinese saw opium as a social evil that could be destroyed in the process of creating a vigorous and forward-looking society. Chinese proved unable in the 1920s and 1930s to rid their society of opium, in part because the state continued to lack the power and authority to rid the country of foreign settlements and concessions where the opium trade was centered. The Communist success of 1949 meant the end of foreign concessions and settlements. But the state did not achieve true equality of diplomatic status in the world community until the 1970s. Ostracized from the world order emerging out of the post–World War II era, Chinese isolation allowed an ignorant West to invent racial stereotypes of Chinese yellow hordes becoming Communist blue ants.

The third and final connection between China's state-making and opium concerns political economy. Since increased revenue extraction is a basic feature of state-making experiences, first in Europe and then in other parts of the world, we should not be surprised to see this also taking place in China in the second half of the nineteenth century and into the twentieth century. China expanded its tax base by tapping various commercial revenues, again in a way reminiscent of earlier European state-making. Like other Asian countries from India to southeast Asia, China found that opium could be a valuable source of revenue. What would China's modern state-making dynamics have been like without opium as a significant source of revenue? With a smaller revenue base one might think the Chinese state would have been weaker. But because much of the opium taxes funded competition among warlords and then between the Nationalists and the Communists, we might imagine that the absence of opium might have led to a less fractious competition among powerholders and thus a less violent process of political change. As a response to a smaller revenue base, some powerholders might have turned more actively to foreign governments and banks for loans. With less ability to extract resources domestically, China's state-making arc might have moved more toward an enclave model of new political institutions to deal with foreign powers and fewer institutions to rule domestic society, creating an even greater gap between the Chinese state and the society that earlier Chinese governments had labored to regulate and rule. Ironically, opium kept the Chinese state connected to the countryside even as this linkage was unraveling. The previous multistranded connections were being reduced to a simple revenue tie during the first half of the twentieth century.

The challenges of state-making in modern China would have been considerably simplified had large-scale imports of opium not been introduced by the British. Whatever alternative scenarios we may imagine, the historical connections between opium and Chinese state-making remain empirically important. The dynamics of modern Chinese state-making bore the burden of opium, an issue that Chinese officials and elites perceived as a moral problem with social, economic, and political dimensions unlike those any other country in the world has faced.

NOTES

1. I analyze Chinese government strategies to create local order and compare them with European strategies in *China Transformed,* chapter 5.

2. For example, the Zhili governor general, Nasutu, and the provincial treasurer, Fang Guancheng, ordered local officials to establish a new set of charity granaries in 1747. According to plans outlined by Fang, who became Zhili governor general in 1749, a total of 1,005 granaries were to be established to serve 39,687 villages. The emperor subsequently ordered the governors of Shandong, Henan, Shanxi, Shaanxi, and Gansu provinces to consider emulating this effort in their jurisdictions (Will and Wong, *Nourish the People,* pp. 70–72).

3. These campaigns are a type of extraordinary action somewhat different from that documented so effectively by Philip Kuhn in *Soulstealers.* In the case Kuhn examines, the bureaucracy is set a problem by the emperor whose crisis-level anxiety requires a great expenditure of energy to resolve. In this case the state's basic capacity to rule society does not change, whereas in the granary case a campaign to expand reserves does augment the official capacity to affect food supply.

4. Brenan, "Cultivation and Consumption of Opium in Shansi," p. 33.

5. Hosie, *Despatches from Sir A. Hosie Forwarding Reports Respecting the Opium Question in China,* p. 16.

6. Ibid., p. 17.

7. Sly, "Report on Opium Eradication by Acting Consul Sly," pp. 47–49.

8. Muller, "General Report by Max Muller Respecting the Opium Question in China," pp. 18–21.

9. Adshead, "Opium Trade in Szechwan," pp. 98–99.

10. Evidence of these variations can be found in Hosie, *Despatch from His Majesty's Minister;* Hosie, *Despatches from Sir A. Hosie;* and International Opium Commission, *Report of the International Opium Commission,* 2:62–66, 73–78.

11. International Opium Commission, *Report of the International Opium Commission,* 2:88–90.

12. Ibid., pp. 94–104.

13. Des Forges, *Hsi-liang and the Chinese National Revolution,* p. 101.

14. Hosie, *Despatch from His Majesty's Minister,* p. 10.

15. International Opium Commission, *Report,* 2:75.

16. Hosie, *Despatches from Sir A. Hosie,* p. 11.

17. We do not know how long such a view of fashion persisted. The continued production, marketing, and consumption of opium in the first half of the twentieth century suggest that fashion may well have favored opium again; Muller, "General Report by Max Muller," p. 29.

18. How to interpret the growing formalization of political and social roles for elites in late-Qing China has been the subject of some debate. Some scholars see a process of political and social change parallel to the European development of a "public sphere." I have argued for crucial differences between the Chinese and European cases in my article "Great Expectations: The 'Public Sphere' and the Search for Modern Times in Chinese History." The nature of official and elite efforts to suppress opium conform to those distinctions between European cases in

which an effort is made to demarcate rights and claims as elites battle to limit state penetration, and a Chinese situation in which elites and officials share a common agenda for social order despite conflict and competition over defining their specific roles.

19. International Opium Commission, *Report*, 2:81.

20. Ibid.

21. Ibid., p. 115.

22. Sly, "Report on Opium Eradication."

23. International Opium Commission, *Report*, 2:98.

24. Friedman, "Revolution or Just Another Bloody Cycle?" pp. 302–3; Adshead, "Opium Trade in Szechwan," p. 99.

25. International Opium Commission, *Report*, 1:77.

26. Willoughby, *Foreign Rights and Interests in China*, 1:471–79.

27. Hudson Taylor, *China's Millions*, pp. 87–88.

28. The numbers given in Taylor, *China's Millions*, are small. For example, a missionary commenting on the resumption of "opium work" in Pingyang notes that the refuge cannot accommodate many people. Still, fourteen men and one woman had already been helped to give up opium (p. 51).

29. Hudson Taylor, *China's Millions*, p. 67.

30. Kane, *Opium Smoking in America and China*, pp. 2, 3, 14.

31. Miller, *Unwelcome Immigrant*, pp. 182–83.

32. International Opium Commission, *Report*, 1:70.

33. Wu Chengming, *Zhongguo zibenzhuyi yu guonei shichang*, p. 253.

34. Adshead, *Modernization of the Chinese Salt Administration*, p. 13.

35. Willoughby, *Foreign Rights and Interests in China*, p. 466.

36. Wei Guangqi, "Qingdai houqi zhongyang jiquan caizheng tizhi de wajie," p. 227.

37. Fairbank, Bruner, and Matheson, *I.G. in Peking*, 1:455–56, 465.

38. Spence, "Opium Smoking in Ch'ing China," p. 170.

39. Wakeman, *Policing Shanghai*, pp. 128–29, 262–63.

40. For documents on the Nationalist monopolies see He, *Kangzhan shiqi zhuanmai shiliao*.

41. League of Nations, *Report on the International Conferences on Opium and Dangerous Drugs*, p. 14.

42. Strauss, *Strong Institutions in Weak Polities*.

43. Duara, "State-Involution."

NINE

Opium and the State
in Late-Qing Sichuan

Judith Wyman

Sichuan province was by far the largest producer and consumer of domestic opium in China by the turn of the twentieth century. In 1906 Sichuan produced 40 percent of China's opium. The southwestern region of China, comprising Sichuan, Yunnan, and Guizhou provinces, accounted for 62 percent of total poppy cultivation in the country.[1] Yet by 1910 poppy cultivation in Sichuan had been eradicated and opium consumption and distribution restricted by the state. This successful prohibition lasted until the early years of the Republic. There was every reason to expect that prohibition efforts would fail in Sichuan, a province where opium provided such a critical part of the local and regional economies. One foreign observer raised such doubts when he wrote, "To put the matter tersely, opium prohibition involves Szechuan in a commercial and fiscal revolution. . . . Personally I do not consider that total prohibition is possible."[2] By August 1910, however, foreigners described the campaign in Sichuan as "nothing short of phenomenal."[3] A former British consul of Chongqing, Alexander Hosie, after a thorough investigation of opium prohibition in China, found Sichuan to be the only province with "complete success" in the opium prohibition campaigns.[4] Such enthusiastic reports of the success of the campaign are corroborated by other Western observers as well, including missionaries, travelers, and journalists.[5]

How does one account for such a rapid and effective campaign in a province where the vast majority of the people had a strong vested interest in keeping the drug in circulation? Opium touched virtually all sectors of society in Sichuan. By the time of the imperial edict of 1906, poppy had become the winter crop of choice for many peasant households, bringing high, although risky, profits to farmers, landholders, and merchants. Even the provincial government profited from the lucrative drug, depending on the opium tax to replenish its coffers. Consumption of the drug touched an even wider cross-section of society than did its cultivation. Addiction crossed gender lines and ranged from the poor to the rich, the unskilled to the skilled, and the young to the old. Opium smoking was so socially acceptable that it was commonplace for visitors at rich households to be offered the opium pipe upon arrival. Many people stood to suffer, at least in the short term, from opium prohibition.

Although much research remains to be done on this subject,[6] the astonishing success of the anti-opium campaign in Sichuan appears to have resulted from the assertive leadership of the provincial government, in particular that of Governor General Zhao Erxun during his tenure from June 1908 to February 1911. The importance of a strong state parallels the findings of Joyce Madancy in her examination of the anti-opium movement in Fujian province.[7] Yet in other respects the movements in Sichuan and Fujian were very different. Whereas there was some nonofficial elite participation in the anti-opium campaigns in Sichuan, it was much less significant than nonofficial elite involvement in Fujian. Such a limited role on the part of the nonofficial elite in Sichuan during the late Qing is surprising, given notable trends of nonofficial elite strengthening in other parts of China. As Madancy has shown in Fujian, and as Bryna Goodman, William Rowe, and Mary Rankin have shown in separate studies of Shanghai, Hankou, and Zhejiang, the late Qing was generally a period of nonofficial elite fortification, not decline. If anything, we would expect to see the state in decline at this time.

In fact, the nonofficial elite in Sichuan did assert themselves against the state during the early twentieth century, but not in the area of opium prohibition.[8] Two main factors may have dissuaded them from active participation in the movement, as encouraged by the state in the original opium prohibition edict of 1906.[9] First, many nonofficial elite, either through landholdings or merchant activities, had strong economic investments in the opium economy.[10] With much of the province given over to poppy cultivation as the winter crop, this enterprise probably affected nonofficial elite landholders in Sichuan more than in other provinces. The second factor pertains to the connection between nationalism and the opium prohibition campaign. Whereas in Fujian the importation of foreign opium bore directly on questions of national sovereignty, in Sichuan, where opium was a domestic commodity, it did not. The anti-opium campaign could be construed as a nationalist one only indirectly—opium addiction made China weak as a nation and less able to fight against imperialist foes. The railroad protection movement, not the anti-opium campaign, attracted nationalist fervor, and the nonofficial elite seem to have focused their energies there instead.[11] From the beginning of the twentieth century, this elite had been actively involved in preventing foreign involvement in

Sichuan's railroad project, even persuading the provincial government to relinquish its involvement in the railroad company and allow it to become privately managed. In Sichuan the imperialist threat was manifested, then, not in opium sales but in foreign efforts to control and own Sichuan's railroads.

This oblique relationship between nationalism and opium also explains the relatively limited missionary involvement in the anti-opium campaign in Sichuan. With opium perceived as a domestic commodity, there was less of a need for missionaries, by joining the political fight against opium, to distance themselves from imperialist ties to the drug.

OPIUM AND THE ECONOMY

Opium had been an essential part of Sichuan's economy for at least a decade by the time of the imperial edict of 1906. Production of the drug for nonmedicinal purposes had started in the late 1850s,[12] and later in the nineteenth century a combination of sharp increases in the price of imported Indian opium along with improvement in the quality of Sichuanese opium led to a dramatic expansion of poppy cultivation in the province.[13] By the 1890s export of domestic opium to other provinces had increased to such an extent that it corrected the imbalance in trade caused by the import of cotton, yarn, and Western cloth.[14] By 1900 opium accounted for nearly half of Sichuan's total exports, between twelve million and sixteen million taels, making this province the largest producer of the drug in the country (see table 2).[15] In 1904 Sichuan's opium production was four times greater than the amount of opium imported from India to other regions in China.[16]

Despite the important role played by opium in the province's export trade, however, most of the drug remained in the province for local consumption. In 1904, according to the British opium inspector Alexander Hosie, only 10 percent of the opium produced in Sichuan was exported.[17] Estimates of consumption and addiction, although not reliable, can be used as crude indicators of the extent to which opium was consumed throughout the province. A 1904 report by Hosie claimed that 2.8 million people consumed opium in a province of approximately forty-five million people, that is, 7 percent of the total population, and 17 percent of all adults. Of these consumers, Hosie figured that in the cities 50 percent of adult men and 20 percent of adult women were addicted, with the rates in the countryside somewhat lower, at 15 percent of men and 5 percent of women.[18] Some other foreign observers found Hosie's figures too low.[19]

Opium also provided an important tax base for the provincial government and a desirable crop for many peasant households. In 1906 opium taxes brought 2,552,000 taels a year to the provincial government, 15 per-

TABLE 2   Opium Production in China
in piculs *(dan)*, 1904

Sichuan	200,000
Yunnan	30,000
Guizhou, Manchuria	15,000
Shaanxi, Zhili, Shangdong	10,000
Gansu, Shanxi, Jiangsu, Zhejiang, Henan	5,000
Hubei	4,000
Anhui, Hunan, Guangxi	3,000
Fujian	2,000
Jiangxi, Guangdong	500
Total	269,500

SOURCE: Adshead, *Province and Politics*, p. 51.

cent of Sichuan's total revenue base.[20] Governor General Zhao Erxun was
hard pressed to find substitutes for this source of funding when he accel-
erated the anti-opium campaign in the latter part of the decade. In memorials to the throne in 1909 and 1910, he requested permission to increase taxes on salt, meat, land, and houses as a way to ameliorate the
situation.[21] Poppy cultivation was also an important part of the local peasant
economy (see fig. 11). Planted as a winter crop and harvested in May,
poppy formed part of many farmers' annual rotation of wheat, maize, rice,
and cotton, in some cases substituting for wheat altogether. The profits
were attractive. As early as 1879, British trade representative E. C. Baber
estimated that, per hundred Chinese square feet of field, poppy earned 8.5
taels compared with 4.2 taels for wheat. By 1908 so many farmers had
turned to poppy cultivation as their winter crop that the province was no
longer in a position to export wheat.[22]

The high profits of poppy cultivation, however, sometimes worked to the
disadvantage of tenants, who were charged higher rents for land and subsequently locked into poppy cultivation. In Fuzhou county, a main opium
producing center, for example, rents doubled in 1879.[23] And by the time
of the imperial edict of 1906, some peasant households, presumably small
landowning households, were turning away from poppy cultivation and
back to food production. Although farmers still earned less money per
square foot planting foodstuffs, in the long run it was possible to come out
ahead or at least to break even. By growing their own food they no longer
needed to borrow money to purchase food, money that was often lent to
them at interest rates as high as 20 to 30 percent. In addition, poppy cultivation was extremely labor-intensive. The cultivation of grains and other
produce freed up some of the household labor to earn money by other

Figure 11. A poppy field on the hills opposite Chongqing through which ran the path that foreign missionaries' children took on their way to school. Reproduced from Robert Davidson and Isaac Mason, *Life in West China* (1905).

means. The poppy crop was also fragile; extreme rains could ruin an entire crop.[24]

THE EARLY PHASE: RELUCTANT REFORMERS

Although Sichuan was ultimately acclaimed nationally for its opium prohibition campaign, the province was slow to put the imperial edict into effect. In fact, significant measures were not taken until the summer of 1909 when Governor General Zhao Erxun issued his August proclamation forbidding poppy cultivation. Before then, anti-opium measures were notable primarily for their symbolic value. Xiliang, the governor general when the imperial edict was issued in 1906,[25] did not enforce collection of the new, higher tax, proposed in May 1906, until January 1907.[26] Xiliang also neglected to make any effort to stop cultivation of the poppy during the 1906–1907 period, as mandated by the imperial edict. Xiliang action's were limited to rhetoric, appealing, for example, to the people's sense of nationalism by tying opium addiction to China's weakness as a nation. In a proclamation issued in 1907, he exhorted: "For several decades the grow-ing weakness of the country and the aggravation of foreign pressure has its origin in the indolent and passive spirit of the people which has been caused by opium. . . . It will thus be seen that the eradication of the opium habit constitutes a foundation on which China may hope to derive strength and prosperity."[27]

During this early period of the opium reform movement, Western mis-sionaries in Sichuan also began to consider political solutions to the opium problem, having focused until this point primarily on the medical and so-cial repercussions of opium addiction. Prior to the emperor's edit of 1906, at a May 1905 meeting of the West China Advisory Board representing seven missionary and three Bible societies, a resolution was passed to "send a strong appeal to all who are working for China's emancipation" and "express our conviction that the time has come for taking prompt and efficient measures to regulate the production and traffic in opium—the deadly enemy of all national prosperity, the insidious potent foe of Mis-sionary success."[28] Further political efforts are visible in December 1906, three months after the first imperial edict was issued, when missionary John Parker called for the creation of an anti-opium league in West China, urg-ing students and scholars to start a native branch. "We should," he de-clared, "use all means to create in the Chinese themselves a public opinion on the question. See the great mass meetings held in Canton and Foochow. Why not such things in the cities of West China?"[29]

In response to Parker's call, an anti-opium committee was convened within the month at the Friends Mission Hall in Chongqing. Participants included Parker, missionaries from four local churches, Chinese Christians, some prominent and wealthy Chinese merchants, and representatives from the Baxian magistrate's and daotai's yamen. Eight Chinese Christians were elected to work with four foreigners to create a Chinese anti-opium soci-ety.[30] An anti-opium ballad was written to the tune of the Glory Song.[31] At the meeting the emperor's edict, which urged the people to quit smoking opium, was printed and circulated to the crowd. Officials subsequently posted the edict throughout the city.[32] A second meeting was held in Chongqing on 10 January 1907 in the Zhejiang Guild Hall. Missionaries and Chinese spoke to the 1,500 people attending the meeting.[33] Chong-qing was then divided into six districts, and it was decided that monthly meetings would take place.[34] The numerous opium addicts in attendance at the meeting prompted discussion of the need for the anti-opium society to take an active role in opening opium refuges.[35]

In Chengdu, movement toward establishing a local anti-opium society occurred slightly later, in February 1907, with the arrival of Mr. Alexander of the British Anti-Opium Society. On 25 February 1907, Alexander held a meeting in the Fujian Guild hall that drew two to three thousand people, including Protestant missionaries and important Chinese officials.[36] Speeches were made by Alexander, a police deputy, and the chief director of the provincial university, who, according to an account by a French diplomat, "is very popular in the area and appealed to the crowd's patriotic spirit."[37] An anti-opium committee was created, combining the work of foreign missionaries, Chinese officials, and literati, and it was hoped that an anti-opium society would follow.[38] By January 1908 the missionaries were full of praise for the work of the provincial authorities, conveying at a regional conference their "high appreciation" and "assuring them of [our] hearty co-operation where desired."[39]

Xiliang's successor, Zhao Erfeng, was only slightly more proactive in his efforts to carry out the opium prohibition campaign when he took over as acting governor general in the spring of 1907. In an effort to regulate opium distribution and consumption, Zhao shifted the production and sale of opium to government offices. In Chengdu on 8 August 1907, all opium dens were closed and then reopened as government-owned "Branch Offices,"[40] a change that led to a threefold increase in the price of opium.[41] In this phase of the campaign, the number of dens in Chengdu was reduced to three hundred from eleven to twelve hundred,[42] and in Chongqing to eighty-one from 860,[43] and there was talk of trying to eliminate all dens within five years instead of the allotted ten. The government also took charge of opium production, opening a large building in Chengdu with eighty brick stoves and a capacity to boil 15,000 to 20,000 ounces of opium a day.[44] Efforts were made to bring opium regulation further under the aegis of the government by requiring all smokers to register at police offices, free of charge, during specified days of each month.[45]

Attempts to curtail consumption and distribution were made in other regions as well, but with limited success.[46] In Renshou county in August 1907 local officials posted a four-sheet proclamation detailing opium regulations and the establishment of official opium dens. A local missionary wondered whether the plan would have any impact, however, given that there were no provisions for decreasing cultivation.[47] In November 1907 a missionary reported that private opium dens in Renshou had been closed, but that it was easy to obtain licenses.[48] In Suifu the situation looked promising in September 1907, when opium dens were closed with little resistance.[49] Yet by October missionary reports were less optimistic: "Although the officials have worked hard to close up the opium dens, I am sorry to say that they have not succeeded altogether, although there are not as many now open as there were before the agitation."[50] By September 1908, although the number of licensed opium dens in Suifu was one-third of its former level, there were many private dens.[51] A February 1908 report from the French consulate in Chengdu described Chinese officials as showing weakness in their suppression efforts and as smoking opium in plain public view.[52]

Zhao Erfeng made some attempts to decrease poppy cultivation, but in this area, too, little was accomplished.[53] In early 1908 he issued an edict ordering that land previously planted with poppy must be reduced by half, and that land not previously planted with poppy could not be sown with the seed. Some areas complied. In Yingshan county in August 1908, a missionary reported "much less opium grown in this district this year."[54] In many other areas, however, the prohibition against poppy cultivation was openly defied during the 1908–1909 season. There was no decrease in Liangshan county, an increase in cultivation in Dongxiang and Kaixian, a 50 percent increase in Wanxian, a twofold increase in Baxian, and a sixfold increase in Fuzhou and Nanchuan.[55]

Zhao's greatest challenge was in the area of collecting the *tongshui* opium tax. Under orders issued by the central government in May 1906, the tax on opium was augmented to 115 taels per dan.[56] As the previous tax had been only 10.56 taels for opium consumed within the province and 22 taels for opium that was exported, the new rate represented a sharp increase. Anticipating resistance, Xiliang had postponed collection of this new tax for as long as possible. Finally, under pressure from the central government, Xiliang implemented the tax in January 1907. In late spring, under Zhao Erfeng's watch, violence erupted in the major opium-producing areas of Kaixian and Wanxian, starting with attacks on four opium tax offices and spreading to government schools and mission property.[57] Zhao's appeals to the central government to lower the tax were met with approval and a new rate was set at 32.56 taels per dan for opium sold for local consumption, 22 of which went to the central government, 5.28 to the province as *likin* and 5.28 to the province for the railroad company. The rate of 115 taels for exported opium was still enforced, but was levied outside of the province in the treaty port of Yichang.[58]

ARDENT REFORMER: ZHAO ERXUN

Zhao Erfeng's brother, Zhao Erxun, was more rigorous in his efforts to comply with the anti-opium campaign, writing to the emperor in January 1909 that he had "taken the prohibition of opium to be a matter of the greatest urgency." Zhao supported his assertion with a detailed account of his strategy: obtaining high-yield seeds from the United States to substitute grain for poppy, ordering his edicts to be translated into colloquial Chinese and posted throughout the province, organizing branch officials to collect and sell raw opium, and establishing a strict system of rewards and punishments as incentive for continued enforcement of his instructions.[59]

Like his brother, Zhao Erxun started by focusing on the reduction of opium distribution and consumption. Also like his brother, he enjoyed only limited success in this area. In Chengdu, although official sales of opium decreased from 50,000 ounces to 20,000 per month in 1908, and fell to 10,000 by early 1909, a thriving black market was still operating in non-official opium dens.[60] British reports show a proliferation of private dens in cities and towns in the eastern and western regions of the province as well.[61] Efforts to decrease addiction were equally mixed. On the one hand, there were many success stories. In early 1910 according to French diplomatic reports, the proportion of smokers in the general population had fallen from 35 percent in the cities to 10 percent, and from 20 to 6 percent in the countryside.[62] The class of people smoking opium had narrowed to include the leisure classes and the poor—sedan carriers, boat workers, and artisans. Young people no longer smoked and police and soldiers also abstained. On the other hand, although foreign reports claimed that it was rare to find officials who smoked, reports from Chinese officials detail many officials who proved unable to kick the habit.[63] Moreover, reports from foreign diplomats and missionaries described many people still smoking openly in the villages and towns.[64]

Zhao's primary achievement was in the field of poppy eradication. His proclamation issued during the summer of 1909 forbidding the sowing of poppy seed was taken more seriously than previous orders. During the spring of 1910, when the poppy flower would be visible to all, there was no evidence of the plant in most parts of the province. In Baoning county in May 1910, a local missionary reported, "We are most thankful in this district for the drastic way in which opium growing has been dealt with. . . . In this and other hsiens [counties], very little, if any at all, is being grown this year. . . . Whatever schemes of reform in China may be unsatisfactory in their practical working, this one is certainly being thoroughly carried out."[65] A May 1910 report described "no poppy under cultivation in the Chongqing district."[66] Traveling through the western part of the province, missionaries found the area free of poppy cultivation.[67]

During the summer of 1910 Zhao Erxun implemented even more severe suppression policies. He divided the province into five districts, sending four officials with the rank of daotai and forty-eight lesser officials throughout the province to enforce the prohibition.[68] The success of this phase of the campaign is illustrated in the correspondence of foreigners living in the area. According to a report filed by the American consul in Chongqing in November 1910, the entire province was "cleared of the plant,"[69] with the subsequent increased production of wheat, barley, hemp, maize, tobacco, indigo, beans, and peas prompting a lowering of food prices.[70] The next year showed similar results. By the beginning of 1911 very little poppy was grown in the province. Some foreign reports claimed that opium smoking among the working poor had been effectively stopped and that the only remaining opium smokers were in the leisure classes.[71] On 13 June 1911 the Customs House prohibited the exportation of opium. Opium eradication was by this time a resounding success, according to Customs Commissioner E. von Strauch.[72]

Although Zhao Erxun was the main force behind the opium prohibition movement, he depended upon the willingness and competence of local officials, many of whom came through for him. They posted the proclamations in colloquial Chinese and were diligent in their policing duties.[73] One local official summoned the local elite to tell them that he feared nothing and "was ready to die rather than to allow even one poppy seed to be planted."[74] A variety of methods were used to encourage compliance, from moral persuasion to heavy fines to corporal punishment. The magistrate of Chongqing "administered a 'bambooing' on the spot" if den keepers were found without licenses and delinquent in their tax payments.[75] There were exceptions to this compliance, however. In other places, neither the emperor's edict nor Zhao's proclamation was posted. In the main opium-producing region of Fuzhou, peasants waited to gauge the attitude of the local official before deciding what to do about poppy cultivation. When it was clear that the anti-opium measures would not be enforced, peasants openly disobeyed the proclamation and continued to grow eighty percent as much poppy as before the proclamation. When the daotai of Chongqing traveled to the area to investigate the matter, he was duped by the local poppy farmers, who hid their plants under cover of earth. Upon his departure, the plants were uncovered and more seeds planted. A new prefect ordered the plants cut down, but only within a period of sixty days—long enough to allow the plants to mature and be harvested.[76]

The local elite were much more divided in their views of the anti-opium movement. In some cases efforts were made to promote the campaign. Anti-opium societies were established, moral exhortations were presented, and essays urging people to stop smoking were published in local newspapers. In Wanxian county, the founding of an anti-opium society in March 1907 was attended by some one thousand people.[77] Guild halls and temples in Wanxian were turned into opium prohibition offices, and every month local elite were dispatched to organize rallies focusing on the evils of the drug.[78] Some elite took advantage of the convening of scholars for the *youba* exam to urge them to set up anti-opium societies when they returned to their villages. Local elite in Nanbu county described opium as the "people's hardship and the country's ruin."[79] In an essay published in a Chongqing newspaper in July 1910, the responsibility for opium prohibition was placed on rich official addicts. If they stopped smoking, the writer argued, the profitability of the drug would disappear and peasants would stop planting poppy of their own accord.[80]

Yet elite involvement in the opium prohibition campaign in Sichuan was significantly more circumscribed than it was in Fujian, both by choice and because of external factors. In many regions, the elite was either indifferent or hostile to the campaign, according to a British report written in 1910 on elite responses to the campaign in twenty districts of eastern and western Sichuan. Elite apathy may have been helped along or influenced by provincial attitudes toward elite involvement. In a British report written in late 1907, provincial authorities were described as "giv[ing] little encouragement to such [Anti-Opium] Societies, order[ing] them only to discuss opium and not current politics or questions of local government."[81] This was in contrast to other provinces, according to the author, where "Anti-Opium Societies have been established in many of the capitals, some being under official auspices, others of a private nature."[82]

Some foreigners saw public opinion becoming increasingly positive over the course of the decade. A 1908 British report on the opium prohibition campaign in Sichuan explained that "the movement against opium is really gaining ground among the people."[83] In a 1911 report the French consul in Chengdu attributed much of the success of the prohibition to public opinion openly in favor of the reforms. A letter from a Protestant missionary in Nanchang claimed that "the majority of the population sincerely desires the abolition of the usage of opium."[84] In conversations with the local people, French consul deMargerie found the elite, merchants, farmers, and even opium smokers all in agreement that China needed to rid itself of the opium vice.[85]

A perceived connection between opium addiction and China's weakness as a nation may have played a role in galvanizing the support of some of the people. Already in the late 1890s, according to British traveler Isabella Bird, China's opium problem was given as a reason for the country's defeat at the hands of the Japanese in 1894–1895: "The Chinese said several times to me that the reason that the Japanese beat them was that they were more vigorous men, owing to the rigid exclusion of opium from Japan."[86] In March 1911 a Chinese Christian made an impassioned plea along similar lines. In "The Fight against Opium: A Chinese Statesman on Opium and China," Tong Kaison linked opium eradication with China's prosperity as a nation. "For more than seventy years . . . opium has weakened our productive energies . . . and stagnated the growth of our national prosperity; it is still one of the most potent causes in preventing our country from taking its proper place in the comity of nations," Tong explained. He ended his letter by pleading, "Therefore, for the sake of your national righteousness, for the sake of your national fame, . . . we invoke your continued cooperation until the . . . opium evil has disappeared.''[87] In these exhortations, foreigners and the imperialist powers are noticeably absent as the agents of the opium problem. In some cases, the West is even offered as a model to be followed. Some announcements posted by local officials alluded to the moral and humanitarian efforts made on the part of the foreign powers to stop the importation of opium, and urged the people to be at least as conscientious in their own actions.[88]

The peasants, for their part, appear to have been reluctantly resigned to the anti-opium campaign.[89] In a province that witnessed its own version of the Boxer Movement in the early years of the twentieth century and had the highest rate of violent attacks on foreigners and Chinese Christians in all of China during the late nineteenth century, the anti-opium campaign in Sichuan was notable for its lack of outcry from the poppy cultivators. There were no more than a handful of violent outbreaks in protest of the campaign and one of the most serious of these, the incident in Kaixian in 1907, was as much a protest against foreigners and the New Policies as it was against opium reforms.[90] Peasants were vocal mainly in their demands for lower rents.[91] Nonetheless, given the short duration of the campaign, at most two harvests, it is difficult to determine whether peasants were truly in compliance or simply holding out with the hope that the political winds would soon change. Indeed, as French consul Hauchecorne reported in 1911, many farmers were still holding seed in storage, ready to plant at the first opportunity (an opportunity that arrived during the chaos of the revolutionary activities in the fall of 1911).[92]

CONCLUSION

Sichuan, the largest producer and consumer of domestic opium in China, excelled in its efforts to eradicate opium during the prohibition campaign of the late Qing. This feat was achieved despite the primary role that opium had come to play in Sichuan's economy, polity, and society. Moreover, this accomplishment was the result of the effective leadership and cooperation of central, provincial, and local officials during a period when the Qing state was supposedly in decline. Furthermore, the nonofficial elite, although actively pursuing more important and powerful roles for themselves in most political, economic, and social spheres, were relatively uninvolved in the anti-opium campaign in Sichuan. In part this was the consequence of a strong vested interest in the profits of the opium economy. But more important in Sichuan, where opium was perceived as a domestic commodity, the anti-opium campaign lacked the necessary nationalist flavor. The important patriotic rallying cries were not inspired, as they were in the major cities of Fujian, by images of Commissioner Lin,[93] but by pictures of foreign powers preying on Sichuan's railroads.

NOTES

1. Wen, "Yapian yu jindai xi'nan shehui," p. 4.
2. British Parliamentary Papers, China no. 3 (1909), pp. 47–48, as cited in Adshead, *Province and Politics in Late Imperial China,* p. 90.
3. USDS, American consul at Amoy Julean Arnold, 30 August 1910, p. 13, microfilm series M329 893.114, reel no. 13, pp. 12–13.
4. *Shanghai Times,* 5 July 1911, in USNA, microfilm series M329 893.114, reel 113.
5. See, for example, "Bishop Bashord's Report on Opium in West China," *Chinese Recorder,* April 1910, p. 307.
6. At the present there are no studies in English and very few in Chinese on the subject of opium in Sichuan.
7. Madancy, "Fuzhou Anti-Opium Society."
8. See Hedtke, "Reluctant Revolutionaries."
9. Madancy, "Fuzhou Anti-Opium Society," p. 6.
10. *The Opium Trade, 1910–1941,* part 2, vol. 1, report from British acting consul Smith, Chongqing, 28 February 1910, p. 38. Hedtke, "Reluctant Revolutionaries," p. 16.
11. Adshead reached a similar conclusion in his "Opium Trade in Szechwan," p. 98.
12. BFO 228, Chungking, vol. 627, 1879 annual report, p. 158.
13. Hedtke, "Reluctant Revolutionaries," p. 15.
14. Adshead, *Province and Politics,* p. 51; Adshead, "Opium Trade," p. 96
15. Adshead, *Province and Politics,* p. 51.
16. MAE, NS, Opium, vol. 590, 30 June 1911, p. 258b.
17. 20,000 of 200,000 piculs; *Correspondence Respecting the Opium Question in China,* China no. 1 (1908), p. 39.
18. Ibid.
19. USDS, American consul at Amoy Julean Arnold, 30 August 1910, p. 13; microfilm series M329 893.114, reel no. 13, p. 13.
20. Adshead, *Province and Politics,* p. 92.
21. *Zhengzhi guanbao,* 24:36; 35:183. Thanks to Joyce Madancy for pointing these memorials out to me and for sharing her English translation.
22. *Correspondence Respecting the Opium Question in China,* China no. 1 (1908), p. 39.
23. BFO 228, vol. 627, 1879, p. 160.
24. MAE, NS, Opium, vol. 590, Hauchecorne to Paris, 20 March 1911, p. 112–14.
25. The edict of September 1906 called for suppression of opium production, distribution, and consumption within ten years; Adshead, *Province and Politics,* pp. 71–72.

26. The increase was sharp, from 10.56 taels a picul for domestic opium and 22 taels a picul for exported opium to 115 taels for both; ibid., p. 70.

27. English translation in the *South-China Daily Journal*, 13 May 1907, in MAE, NS, Opium, vol. 585, p. 197.

28. *Chinese Recorder*, September 1905, p. 438; *West China Missionary News* (*WCMN*), July 1905, p. 134.

29. *WCMN*, December 1906, p. 280.

30. *WCMN*, March 1907, p. 4.

31. *WCMN*, December 1907, p. 9.

32. *WCMN*, January 1907, p. 17.

33. *WCMN*, February 1907, p. 11.

34. *WCMN*, March 1907, p. 6.

35. Ibid, p. 5.

36. These important officials included Daotai Chen and Daotai Lin, the directors of the anti-opium bureau; Nian, the director of the Bureau of Mines; Zhou [Tcheou], the chief of police; and the "most important official," the Hanlin graduate Hu Jun [Houkiun]. MAE, NS, Opium, vol. 585, French consul in Chengdu Doire to Bapst in Peking, 2 March 1907, p. 86.

37. Ibid.

38. *WCMN*, March 1907, p. 20.

39. *Chinese Recorder*, April 1908, p. 190.

40. *WCMN*, August 1907, p. 17. MAE, NS, Opium, vol. 586, 16 August 1907, French consul in Chengdu Pierre Bons d'Anty to Boissonnas in Peking. This government monopoly of opium was unique to Sichuan. Cameron claims that the British government did not protest a monopoly of this sort because Sichuan did not buy Indian opium. Meridith Cameron, *The Reform Movement in China, 1898–1912*, p. 150, as cited in Stapleton, "Police Reform in a Late-Imperial Chinese City," p. 260.

41. The price of opium rose from between 100 and 200 cash an ounce to between 370 and 390 an ounce; *WCMN*, October 1907, p. 19.

42. MAE, NS, Opium, vol. 586, 16 August 1907, French consul in Chengdu Pierre Bons d'Anty to Boissonnas in Peking.

43. Adshead, *Province and Politics*, p. 80.

44. *WCMN*, August 1907, p. 17.

45. Ibid. According to Kristin Stapleton's study of the Chengdu police during the late Qing, the prohibition efforts in Chengdu first fell under the supervision of the Opium Suppression Bureau (Jieyan zongju) and later, after the position was created, under the control of the provincial police superintendent; Stapleton, "Police Reform in a Late-Imperial Chinese City," p. 261.

46. *Despatch from His Majesty's Minister in China Forwarding a General Report by Mr. Leech Respecting the Opium Question in China*, China no. 2 (1908), p. 10.

47. *WCMN*, August 1907, p. 15.

48. *WCMN*, November 1907, p. 15.

49. *WCMN*, September 1907, p. 16.

50. *WCMN*, October 1907, p. 18.

51. *WCMN*, September 1908, p. 14.

52. MAE, NS, Opium, vol. 587, 3 February 1907, no. 2, Pierre Bons d'Anty, Chengdu, to French Minister Bapst, Beijing, p. 7.

53. Adshead, *Province and Politics*, p. 79.

54. *WCMN*, December 1908, p. 19.

55. Adshead, *Province and Politics*, p. 90.

56. The *tongshui* tax was an effort to consolidate the various opium taxes into a single tax, a large percentage of which would be remitted to the central government; Adshead, *Province and Politics*, p. 70.

57. BFO 228, vol. 1659, Consul Bristow to Fox, 7 June 1907. *Xinhai geming qian shinianjian minbian dang'an shiliao*, vol. 2, Zhao Erfeng, doc. 440, 1 July 1907, p. 769, and no. 442, 18 July 1907, pp. 770–71.

58. Adshead, *Province and Politics*, pp. 72, 79.

59. *Zhengzhi guanbao*, 15:592.

60. Adshead, *Province and Politics*, p. 90.

61. *The Opium Trade, 1910–1941*, part 2, vol. 1, letters from Smith in Chongqing (February and June 1910), pp. 37–38, and from Wilkinson in Chengdu (March 1910), pp. 45–46.

62. MAE, NS, Opium, vol. 589, Bodard to Paris, no. 3, 18 January 1910, p. 2.

63. Ibid.; *Zhengzhi guanbao*, 12:286–88 (6 October 1908); 24:101–3 (15 September 1909); 34:139–40 (8 July 1910); 35:113 (6 August 1910).

64. *The Opium Trade, 1910–1941*, part 2, vol. 1, letters from Smith in Chongqing (February and June 1910), p. 38, and from Wilkinson in Chengdu (March 1910), p. 47.

65. *WCMN*, May 1910, p. 24.

66. Ibid, p. 11.

67. USDS, American consul at Amoy Julean Arnold, 30 August 1910, p. 11, microfilm series M329 893.114, reel no. 13.

68. Zhou and Liu, *Jindai Chongqing jingji yu shehui fazhan*, p. 323. This book is a Chinese translation of the decennial reports from Chongqing.

69. USDS, American consul at Chongqing Albert W. Pontius, 21 November 1910, p. 1; microfilm series M329 893.114, reel 13.

70. Ibid.

71. MAE, NS, Opium, vol. 590, Hauchecorne to Paris, 20 March 1911, p. 112.

72. Zhou and Liu, *Jindai Chongqing*, p. 331.

73. Wen, "Yapian yu jindai," p. 17.

74. MAE, NS, Opium, vol. 589, no. 40, note 1, 1 November 1910, p. 160.

75. *WCMN*, October 1907, p. 14.

76. USDS, American consul at Amoy Julean Arnold, 30 August 1910, p. 12, microfilm series M329 893.114, reel no. 13.

77. *WCMN*, May 1907, p. 22.

78. Wen, "Yapian yu jindai," p. 17.

79. *Guangyi congbao* 218 (22 November 1909).

80. *Guangyi congbao* 239 (26 July 1910).

81. *Correspondence Regarding the Opium Question in China*, China no. 1 (1908), p. 43.

82. Ibid.

83. *Despatch from His Majesty's Minister in China Forwarding a General Report by Mr. Leech Respecting the Opium Question in China*, China no. 2 (1908), p. 10.

84. MAE, NS, Opium, deMargerie in Chengdu to Peking, no. 48, 10 June 1911, p. 218.

85. Ibid, p. 217.

86. Bird, *Yangtze Valley and Beyond,* p. 498.

87. *WCMN,* March 1911, p. 26.

88. Ibid.

89. *The Opium Trade, 1910–1941,* part 1, 1:38, 47.

90. See Wyman, "Social Change, Anti-Foreignism and Revolution in China," pp. 226–31.

91. *The Opium Trade, 1910–1941,* part 2, vol. 1, British acting consul Smith to Sir J. Jordan, 28 February 1910, p. 39.

92. MAE, NS, Opium, vol. 590, Hauchecorne to Paris, 20 March 1911, p. 112.

93. Madancy, "Poppies, Patriotism and the Public Sphere," p. 4.

TEN

Poppies, Patriotism, and the Public Sphere

Nationalism and State Leadership in the Anti-Opium Crusade in Fujian, 1906–1916

Joyce A. Madancy

Although an important part of the process of forming conceptions of a modern Chinese nation in the early twentieth century rested on the activities and sentiments of patriotic elites outside the official bureaucracy, this chapter addresses the role of the Chinese state in shaping and restricting the manner in which reformist elites pursued nationalistic goals, and the extent to which those goals could be attained. More specifically, I analyze the late-Qing/early-Republican anti-opium campaign as it played out in Fuzhou, the capital city of Fujian province. And within Fuzhou, this analysis focuses particularly on the dynamics of the relationship between the multilayered official bureaucracy created by the Qing state to oversee and conduct the campaign, and one particular nonbureaucratic elite reform group that also plunged into the crusade.

One of the first five treaty ports opened to Western traders by the Treaty of Nanjing in 1842, Fuzhou was a city shaped in large part by China's attempts to restrict the opium trade. As a bustling port and the administrative headquarters both of Fujian's provincial bureaucracy and of the governor general of Fujian and Zhejiang provinces *(Min-Zhe zongdu)*, the population boasted a strong contingent of educated, cosmopolitan elites inclined toward forming progressive organizations supportive of the New Policy *(xinzheng)* reforms of the early twentieth century. The Fujian Anti-Opium Society *(Fujian qudu she)* was one such voluntary elite association that used state authority to legitimize its existence and expand its power well beyond traditional elite public service roles. The society employed the memory of Lin Zexu, a Fuzhou native and China's most revered anti-opium crusader, as a potent nationalistic symbol to reinforce the link between its activities and the goals of the state. However, the late-Qing/early-Republican state was itself severely constrained by international pressures and domestic instability, and ultimately the members of the society discovered that operating under the state policy umbrella brought unforeseen liabilities.

Any discussion of the interaction between the state and extrabureaucratic reform groups inevitably involves addressing the debate concerning the nature and existence of a public sphere in early twentieth-century China. Recent scholarly attempts to delineate China's public sphere have sketched out a rather amorphous space with fluid boundaries between state and society.[1] This chapter attempts to illustrate the pitfalls implicit in such a permeable public sphere, and to trace the changing contours of that space from the very late Qing through the early Republic. The Fujian Anti-Opium Society did indeed come to occupy a public space of sorts in which it was able to pursue its reformist agenda even when the provincial administration lagged behind. But it was a space carved out more by the force of the central state's moral and legal authority than by a nationalistic movement promoted and led by influential elites.

By carrying the story of the opium suppression campaign from its inception in 1906 across the standard historical divide of the 1911 Revolution and into the early-Republican period, this chapter serves as a chronological and conceptual bridge in the literature concerning the evolution of China's public sphere that leaves off either in 1895 with William Rowe's studies of Hankou or in 1911 with Mary Rankin's work on Zhejiang province, and begins again with David Strand's depiction of Beijing politics in the 1920s.[2] Understanding the expansion and contraction of the public sphere from 1906 to 1916—or perhaps it is better conceived of as the softening and hardening of the permeable boundaries between government and this public space—reveals, in this particular case, that the process described by Rankin and Rowe whereby extrabureaucratic elites competed with and distanced themselves from the state was temporarily resolved in the aftermath of the 1911 Revolution. I also hope to help fill a long-standing historiographical gap regarding China's relationship with opium between the work of Lin Man-houng on the construction of China's opium economy in the nineteenth and early twentieth centuries,[3] and studies that document the free-wheeling, highly criminalized opium market of the 1920s and 1930s.[4]

In order to understand the dynamics of state involvement, it is necessary to dissect the anti-opium campaign in Fuzhou from its inception in 1906 until the onset of warlordism sometime after 1915, and to study each of its bureaucratic components. Progressing chronologically, the discussion begins with the "extrabureaucratic bureaucracy"—the Anti-Opium Society mentioned above—formed by progressive local elites prior to the launching of the official campaign. Moving on to the legal and chronological framework within which opium suppression was conducted, the chapter lays out the role of the national opium administration in Beijing and the corresponding civil and military bureaucracies in the province of Fujian, and analyzes the influence of international agreements on the pace and direction of Qing anti-opium policy. Finally, I discuss the impact of the 1911 Revolution and the policies of the new Republican state.

THE FUJIAN ANTI-OPIUM SOCIETY BEFORE 1911

On 20 September 1906 the Qing government announced its intention to eliminate opium in China within ten years, and reformist elites in Fuzhou seized the opportunity afforded by this confluence of their interests with those of the state. The Fujian Anti-Opium Society was formed by ten prestigious local literati on 22 June 1906, three months *before* the issuance of the 1906 imperial edict, and the society served as the vanguard of the province's extrabureaucratic reform efforts throughout the official campaign.[5] Western missionaries noted with approval (and surprise) that the Fuzhou prefect was among those who spoke at the society's inaugural meeting. Several prominent members of the society were Chinese Christians, and foreign missionaries strongly supported the group's activities.[6]

In selecting its leader, the society proved itself a savvy manipulator of nationalistic symbolism, cognizant of the need not only to appeal to provincial loyalties, but also to cement the approval and co-opt the symbolic authority of the central state. It would be difficult to imagine a more suitable chair for the society than Lin Bingzhang, one of its original founders. Lin was a Hanlin scholar who had occupied a number of official positions and was serving as president of the Fuzhou Provincial College when the campaign began.[7] Lin and his father-in-law, Chen Baochen, also brought the prestige and clout of their powerful clans to the campaign.[8] But much more to the point, Lin Bingzhang was the great-grandson of none other than Lin Zexu—the man whose image personified the nationalistic goals and spirit of China's historical battle against opium and imperialist oppression—and the younger Lin's presence suffused Fuzhou's suppression campaign with the aura of a religious crusade.

The members of the society were keenly aware of the power implicit in their geographical and genealogical links to the legendary Commissioner Lin, and over the next decade they presided over his virtual apotheosis. Opium inspection and treatment centers offered Lin Zexu's suggested remedies to those seeking treatment for addiction, and celebratory parades and mass meetings often featured his image.[9] The society's headquarters were located in a shrine dedicated to Lin's memory.[10] Lin Bingzhang's leadership brought a sense of inherited mission, and his active participation served as both model and inspiration for the province's reformist elites and officials. It also reinforced the linkage between the goals and policies of elites and those of the province and the central state.

Perhaps that link was too explicit for the central authorities, because just as Fujian's anti-opium movement gathered momentum, Lin Bingzhang was rewarded for his efforts with an appointment in Beijing. It may well be that this position was a sincere reward for Lin's symbolic and actual leadership in the province's campaign, but it is also possible that Beijing wished either to exploit his symbolic power itself or perhaps to ensure that that power did not get out of hand in Fujian. But even after departing his native province, Lin remained active in the nonofficial side of the movement as a prominent member of a national anti-opium association. After the 1911 Revolution, however, his duties were confined to officialdom. He returned to Fuzhou, where he served as salt controller and held other important provincial posts.[11]

In Fuzhou and in the rest of the province of Fujian, the official launching of the opium reform campaign was briefly delayed by a vacancy in the important post of governor general of Fujian and Zhejiang.[12] According to foreign customs officials, when the imperial edict was issued in 1906, it was the Fujian Anti-Opium Society that seized upon the inaction of the acting governor general. The society allegedly printed copies of the edict and distributed them throughout the greater Fuzhou City area to publicize the campaign.[13]

Although the September edict did little more than simply express the throne's outrage, it was followed by a series of edicts detailing the specific structural and chronological contours of the campaign. In November 1906 the first of those edicts spelled out the court's opium suppression strategy. Among the most important measures was the establishment of a ten-year timetable for the gradual elimination of poppy cultivation throughout China and for the implementation of a comprehensive suppression plan that included closing opium dens, issuing temporary licenses to opium smokers, and manufacturing and disseminating opium remedies. Although provincial and local officials were charged with leading the movement, central authorities explicitly encouraged the voluntary organization of gentry-led anti-opium societies.[14]

According to the regulations promulgated by Beijing, the gradual elimination of poppy cultivation was to take first priority, but it was to proceed alongside the curtailing of consumption. However, in Fujian province, where the local poppy crop was relatively small, anti-consumption measures, such as the closing down of opium dens, were implemented prior to the more long-term restrictions on cultivation. Because the most concentrated consumption occurred in urban centers, elite reform groups were well situated to take a leading role during the early years of the campaign.

There were few restrictions on the activities that these nonofficial groups could undertake—except the discussion of openly political topics—and the Fujian Anti-Opium Society took full advantage of the powers available to it. It became involved in everything from the investigation of illegal smokers and opium dens to participation in the official census of smokers and the allocation of opium smoking licenses. Society members also ran addiction treatment centers, and were even known to have physically uprooted poppy plants in areas around Fuzhou.[15] In addition, the society promoted its cause in a periodical titled *The Fujian Anti-Opium Society Quarterly (Fujian qudu zongshe jibao)*. By 1911 the society had a network of 112 branches scattered throughout the province, including six in Fuzhou itself.[16]

The society's regulations clearly spelled out its intention to work closely with the new provincial police force.[17] And since the head of Fuzhou's police department, Lu Chenghan, also served as president of the official Opium Suppression Office *(jinyan gongsuo)*, the line between state and society was especially porous. Each of Fuzhou's police wards was to be patrolled by teams of police and society inspectors, searching for violations of opium restrictions.[18] The inspectors claimed the right to enter any premises in the city, whether business, private residence, religious establishment, or administrative office.[19] This apparent state sanction of the coercive enforcement of state policy by urban elites was extraordinary in its implication that extensive extrabureaucratic involvement would complement, not impede, the official arm of the campaign.

THE OFFICIAL ANTI-OPIUM BUREAUCRACY IN BEIJING AND FUJIAN

The edicts issued from 1906 through 1908 not only served as the catalyst for nonbureaucratic involvement in opium reform, they also resulted in the construction of an official anti-opium bureaucracy in Beijing and in each province to take charge of the campaign. The nationwide campaign was overseen by the Opium Suppression Bureau-General *(jinyan zongju)*, which was set up in accordance with another edict dated 7 April 1908. Prior to and even after the establishment of this agency, many other important aspects of opium reform, such as the punishment and dismissal of opium-smoking officials as well as the collection of opium taxes, were also handled by the Ministry of Personnel *(Mingzheng bu)* and the Ministry of Finance *(Duzhi bu)*.[20] The bureau-general was headed up by four opium suppression commissioners *(jinyan dachen)*—two Chinese and two Manchus. Later, the four commissioners were joined by three or four proctors *(tidiao)*. The funds for the commission were taken from the taxes collected on domestic opium; it was envisioned that the tapering off of opium tax revenues would be accompanied by reductions in imports and in the amount of land devoted to domestic poppy cultivation, and eventually the entire bureaucracy would naturally become obsolete and wither away.

The commissioners were to focus their energies on three main tasks— inspection, treatment, and enforcement—and their first duty was to draw up regulations and delegate responsibility to the appropriate officials in the provinces. To that end, opium suppression offices *(jinyan gongsuo)* were to be set up in each provincial capital, and led by superintendents *(duban* or *zongli)*. The superintendents were usually influential, high-ranking local officials, and provincial governors or governors general were charged with appointing a bureau chief *(zongban)* to oversee each provincial bureau. In other cities and towns, opium suppression bureaus *(jieyan ju)* were to be initiated by local authorities.[21]

The regulations reflected the throne's desire and ability to establish the pace, priorities, and broad structure of the anti-opium campaign, but they also demonstrated the central government's recognition that methods of suppression had to reflect local conditions. All officials were to put the highest priority on eliminating cultivation of the opium poppy, but provincial officials were given tremendous leeway in setting deadlines for localities under their jurisdiction and were also expected to work to reduce and eventually eliminate opium smoking as well. Although the many edicts handed down from the Qing court served as a template for reform in the provinces, provincial authorities frequently petitioned and were permitted to implement tougher restrictions and impose shorter deadlines within their jurisdictions.[22] The pace of reform, however, was constrained by agreements with the British; ultimately the inability of the central government to respond to provincial requests to accelerate reforms contributed to the growth of anti-Qing sentiment among many reformist officials and elites in 1911.

The central government explicitly dictated that the official anti-opium bureaucracy encourage and embrace nonbureaucratic opium reform groups *(jieyan huishe)*.[23] The purpose of these organizations was not only to provide a relatively regulated avenue for popular anti-opium sentiment, but also to serve as state-sanctioned watchdogs charged with reporting opium violations among local officials. Paradoxically, then, by allowing nonbureaucratic groups a high degree of flexibility in pursuing their reformist objectives, the central government was able to extend its control over local authorities. As the reform effort gained momentum, however, the attempts of the central government to slow the pace of reform to ensure compliance with the terms of the 1908 agreement with the British were perceived by elite and official reformers as evidence that the Manchu dynasty was siding with Western imperialists against the Chinese people.

The throne's blueprint for eliminating the opium problem was a clear manifestation of the Qing government's Confucian approach to the issue.

Military and civil officials were expected to act as exemplars by eliminating opium smoking in their ranks. Officials were subject to strict deadlines for ending their habits, and those who failed to comply were removed from office. Teachers and military officers who smoked opium were given three months to quit or lose their positions. And although local elites were encouraged to form anti-opium organizations and to cooperate with officials, the central authorities urged local bureaucrats to take the lead in the anti-opium campaign.

As in other provinces, the official opium suppression campaign in Fujian was conducted through two parallel but distinct administrative hierarchies—the civilian and military bureaucracies. Although provincial authorities were granted a great deal of leeway in structuring the contours of reform within their borders, they did so under the watchful eye of a central state that determined the pace and content of the suppression campaign, and approved any significant provincial alterations in the national scheme. In Fujian, leading provincial officials—specifically the governor general of Fujian and Zhejiang and the Manchu general of Fuzhou—corresponded regularly with the central government not only to report their general progress, but to seek approval for decisions as critical as major changes in the timelines and policies for suppression and as mundane as seeking permission to fire opium-smoking officials.

In Fujian the implementation of the official opium reform campaign was postponed until the selection of a new governor general of Fujian and Zhejiang, but when that situation was remedied in the spring of 1907 the province began to attack its opium problem in accordance with the regulations issued by the central government. Song Shou, the experienced Manchu official who served as governor general from mid 1907 to November 1911, was charged with overseeing the implementation of the suppression campaign within the civilian bureaucracy and among the general population of Fujian.[24] Song Shou had been serving as the Manchu general of Fuzhou until his promotion, and after his departure Pu Shou became the city's head military man.

Parallel to but autonomous from the opium reform campaign in the provincial civil administration (to be discussed below) was a similar effort within the city's military, spearheaded by Pu Shou, the newly appointed Manchu general of the provincial garrison at Fuzhou.[25] Extrabureaucratic elite reform groups did not seem to be involved in opium suppression among the ranks of the Manchu military, and Pu Shou appeared to be solely responsible for the conduct of the campaign among his men and their dependents in the Manchu quarter of the city. However, even though opium reform within the military remained distinct from the suppression campaign conducted by the civil bureaucracy and nonbureaucratic elites, Pu Shou's actions were still regulated by Beijing.

The final years of the Qing dynasty saw an acceleration in the already precipitous decline of both efficiency and morale among the Manchu bannermen; a serious problem with opium smoking was but one manifestation of that decline.[26] Pu Shou was painfully cognizant of the extent of opium abuse among his officers and soldiers, as well as their families. He claimed that 60 to 70 percent of the soldiers smoked opium, and noted in a memorial to the throne that more than a dozen high-level or expectant officers were "infected" by the habit.[27] Although Manchu troops and their dependents lived in a segregated quarter of Fuzhou, Pu Shou blamed this high rate of addiction on the fact that these men consorted with the general population of Fujian, among whom opium smoking was a long-standing habit. In addition, the continued presence of licensed opium shops and military wives who were themselves opium smokers were unavoidable temptations.[28]

Because poppy cultivation was evidently not a problem among Fuzhou's banner troops, Pu Shou was able to concentrate his energies on reducing addiction, and his first priority was the standardization of enforcement procedures and the designing of investigation and treatment facilities.[29] Pu Shou greatly impressed foreign observers with his efficiency and sincerity in enforcing the restrictions on opium smoking. An American missionary reported that by May 1907, about three months after assuming office, Pu Shou

has made quite a stir in the city by his modern methods of investigation. He goes out on the street or to the soldiers' barracks or out to the forts on the river in citizen's clothes and often they don't know who he is until he has seen all that he cares to. His prosecution of those in his office, and those under his care is no less drastic. This past week he [had] all his petty officials locked up, and he is going to keep them under guard for three months so as to find out for sure who of them smoke, and make them get cured.[30]

Pu Shou established an anti-opium office specifically for bannermen and the units of the Green Standard Army under his jurisdiction.[31] The office, which was located to the west of his yamen in Fuzhou, served as part police station and part clinic, and was separated into two sections, one for officers and the other for soldiers. Pu Shou claimed that he himself went daily to the officers' building to check on his subordinates' progress. He reported to the throne that by the spring of 1909, 392 men (thirteen of whom were high-ranking officers) had successfully undergone examinations and treatment.[32]

When the campaign met with obstacles, however, Pu Shou turned to the central state for permission to bend the rules. In the fall of 1908 Pu Shou was compelled to beg the throne for permission to delay the dismissal and punishment of a number of officers and soldiers, particularly those who had quit smoking but would still be on medication past the government-set deadlines, as well as those in whom he still saw the potential for reform. The central government, however, viewed such a request as simply an excuse for not having completed the assigned task on time, and refused to grant his request.[33] In other cases, when the officers in question were elderly, ill, or had otherwise distinguished service records, the throne was more sympathetic.[34]

Pu Shou was also concerned about the social unrest that might result when unreformed addicts were dismissed and their families could no longer depend on the grain and money allowances allotted to bannermen. "If one person's stipend of money and grain is eliminated, the entire family's cold and hunger can be seen immediately. Hunger and cold [are conditions that produce] urgency. What won't they do [to obtain relief]?" queried Pu Shou. When his request for leniency was refused, he devised a plan to construct handicrafts workshops (gongyisuo) to employ the talents of those who would otherwise have been abandoned. His plan was endorsed by the central government, but whether or not it was actually implemented is not known.[35]

Pu Shou also recognized that certain loopholes in the opium restrictions could hamper his efforts. He found it difficult, for example, to enforce the ban on smoking when processed, smokable foreign opium was readily available in licensed shops. But the rules concerning opium shops came directly from Beijing, which was bound to allow the sale of British opium under the agreement; in their memorials, Pu Shou and Song Shou could only emphasize to the throne the difficulties posed by the ten-year plan for gradual prohibition.[36]

On the civilian side, as directed by the imperial edicts, Fujian's governor general, Song Shou, instructed top provincial officials to establish opium suppression offices (jieyan suo) for the purpose of examining and treating all of Fujian's civil and military officials for evidence of opium use. Officials were first required to sign a pledge stating either that they had never smoked opium or that they had conquered the habit. Several verifying signatures were to be attached, and these claims were double-checked by means of a week-long isolation regimen designed to smoke out any clandestine opium users. Bureaucrats and expectant officials were required to take their meals and to sleep at the opium prohibition bureau during that time under the supervision of a special examining official. All of the examinees changed into clothing provided by the bureau for the duration of their stay, and were forbidden to consume anything from outside. Song Shou reported several violators, who were discovered either through their attempts to smuggle the drug into the bureau or through their inability to forgo the drug for an entire week. Any bureaucrat who attempted to hide his opium habit was to be relieved of his position.[37] Officials who openly admitted to smoking opium, however, apparently were allowed to seek treatment immediately at the bureau.

Other measures addressed opium consumption among all social strata. Song Shou ordered the establishment of six opium hospitals to cure smokers. The poor were responsible for their own food, but were charged no other fees. In early 1909, statistics from two-thirds of the hospitals indicate that more than 3,200 smokers had been cured and released.[38] Smokers among the lower echelons of society were to be allowed to purchase smoking licenses. These licenses provided a minimal, daily opium ration that would gradually diminish over time. Each time a smoker purchased opium, the opium shop would affix its stamp on the license so that the addict was unable to purchase more that day.[39]

Unlike the members of the Fujian Anti-Opium Society, whose efforts were primarily concentrated on the control of opium consumption in the city, Song Shou was also responsible for the elimination of poppy cultivation in and around Fuzhou, a task that he and the central state believed would cut off the supply of opium and thus reduce smoking. The difficulties entailed in simultaneously curtailing domestic cultivation and controlling domestic and foreign imports, however, convinced many provincial authorities, including Song Shou, that the gradual approach suggested by the central government was the wrong strategy regarding the supply side of the opium equation. Song Shou and others realized the hostility with which Chinese opium farmers would view a gradual, piecemeal approach to the suppression of cultivation. Those who were first compelled to change crops or uproot their poppies would undoubtedly resent not only their counterparts who were given extended deadlines, but also the officials who had conceived and enforced the regulation. The central government quickly came to realize that the perceptions of provincial leaders were correct, and approved the blanket prohibition of domestic poppy cultivation.[40] Song Shou was permitted to order all farmers in Fujian province to cease planting the poppy in the fall of 1908, and by May 1910 he reported to the central government that Fujian no longer cultivated the opium poppy.[41]

The authorities in Beijing were not so easily convinced, however, and on 19 April 1910 the Grand Council called on the Ministry of Finance to investigate the claims of provincial officials in Fujian and elsewhere. Beijing's skepticism was justified. Inspectors who clandestinely traveled to Fujian discovered that Song Shou's assertions were false.[42] The Ministry of Finance also refused to approve Song Shou's unilateral prohibition on the importation of opium from neighboring provinces. The prohibition would have contravened the ministry's capacity to levy and collect excise taxes on opium transported between provinces.[43] The Ministry of Finance was apparently only willing to forgo that revenue if Fujian had completely eliminated poppy cultivation (and, presumably, the tax revenue it generated for Fujian) within its borders. Justification for refusing Song Shou's request was muted by the ministry's praise for the work of elites and officials in Fujian, and its assurance that once the Fujianese had eliminated opium smoking, the demand for the imported drug would evaporate on its own.[44] This correspondence clearly demonstrates the hands-on, supervisory role played by the central Chinese state.

The division of labor between the elite-led voluntary associations and the official anti-opium bureaucracy in Fuzhou was often unclear, although as stated earlier, apparently elites were not involved in the anti-opium crusade among the provincial banner community nor were they systematically engaged in enforcing the prohibitions on poppy cultivation. The Opium Suppression Office in Fuzhou was established and staffed by the governor general on orders from the Opium Suppression Bureau-General in Beijing. Within the city of Fuzhou, it was often indistinguishable from the police force, and seemed to be in charge of preventing poppy cultivation, closing opium dens, regulating opium shops, counting, licensing, and treating common opium smokers, and setting up centers for the detection and treatment of opium smoking among provincial officials. The Fujian Anti-Opium Society acted as the government's foot soldiers, however, in carrying out many of these duties in the city. The society also appeared to play a prominent role in educating the public about the evils of opium. Well aware of the wide range of the society's activities, Song Shou was careful to report to Beijing that bureaucrats were sent to every meeting of the society, ostensibly to monitor these powerful elites.[45]

Fujian's provincial authorities and nonofficial elites were particularly efficient in dealing with opium dens (yanguan). In accordance with orders from Beijing, Song Shou ordered that all dens in the province be shut down as of 12 May 1907. The order was obeyed quickly, especially in areas close to Fuzhou, and most of the dens remained closed. He also stated that the number of stores selling prepared opium paste had been vastly reduced.[46] British sources confirmed that in Fuzhou alone, hundreds (and perhaps thousands) of dens were shut down, although these foreign observers attributed this accomplishment to the efforts of the elite-led Anti-Opium Society.[47]

In the early years, this blurring of the lines between bureaucratic and extrabureaucratic opium reform efforts often worked to the benefit of both parties. Close cooperation between officials and nonofficial elites allowed the state to exploit an eager and talented pool of volunteers. In a March 1908 memorial, Beijing explicitly lauded the efforts of Chinese gentry, and even praised foreign missionaries for condemning the opium trade and publicizing the evils of opium smoking.[48] In Fujian, Song Shou himself publicly encouraged gentry participation in the fight against opium smoking, singling out Lin Bingzhang and Chen Baochen for special praise, and he specifically encouraged nonofficial elites to act as watchdogs for the state:

> As for the local gentry, they are enthusiastically for the public good. They fix their eyes and ears on the petty officials, then eliminate those officials' use of public office to seek profit. By giving the local gentry authority, what is seen and heard in the community is particularly reliable. [The gentry] investigate and examine more closely than the officials.[49]

At the same time, elites used their ties to a patriotic nationwide movement to increase their own status and influence over local society.

Fuzhou became a showplace of public opposition to opium, and although mass demonstrations were largely orchestrated by the Anti-Opium Society, they were also supported by local officials and seemed to appeal to the general public. Among the most visible events were the public incineration of confiscated opium and opium-smoking implements, anti-opium demonstrations, and mass meetings, all conspicuously featuring likenesses of Lin Zexu or the prominent presence of his direct descendant. If these activities seemed more spectacle than substance, even pure spectacle had its role in a campaign such as this in illustrating the vigor of the society's efforts and attracting large and enthusiastic crowds.

THE BRITISH FACTOR

The Qing government could not have expected to succeed in eliminating China's opium problem unless it could count on the cooperation of the British in ending the importation of Indian opium into China. History had proven that domestic suppression simply spawned a thriving black market in the foreign drug if imports remained legal. By signing agreements with the British, the Chinese state not only guaranteed that its own efforts would be matched by the gradual elimination of foreign opium imports, but it also created a situation where local and provincial interests had to be subsumed under a broader national goal.

The first imperial edict of 1906 was issued only after British diplomats had hinted to Chinese officials that traditional British intransigence in this area was weakening because of a combination of developments in British domestic politics, growing public opinion against the opium trade, and the steady decline of Indian opium revenue. After a good deal of diplomatic wrangling, Great Britain and China signed an agreement in which the British pledged to reduce the amount of Indian opium imported into China by one-tenth each year. The agreement went into effect on 1 January 1908, and promised the end of Indian opium imports by 1917.

At the insistence of the British government, the Anglo-Chinese opium agreement of 1908 contained a provision for a three-year trial period after which the agreement could be abrogated if the British determined that significant progress in the suppression of opium had not been made by the Chinese. But when the agreement came up for renegotiation in the spring of 1911, even the most vocal of the Qing's foreign critics could not deny China's tremendous achievements. Duly empowered, the Chinese delegation brought enough moral leverage to the negotiating table to wrest important concessions from the British.

The signing of another agreement with the British on 8 May 1911 marked a new and important stage in China's anti-opium campaign. Most important for the purposes of this chapter, the new agreement clearly stated that a Chinese province could be closed to British opium imports if it could prove to a joint Sino-British inspection team that the province was free of the cultivation and importation of domestic Chinese opium. In other words, the possibility of ending Indian imports before 1917 now hinged entirely on eliminating domestic poppy cultivation.

The renegotiated agreement made explicit the need for all Chinese provinces to work toward a national goal. Indeed, it offered such an attractive incentive for unified action that the Chinese state reevaluated its own opium suppression strategy. One day after the agreement was signed, another imperial edict explicitly endorsed a change in course.[50] In practice, this meant less attention to the demand side of the opium equation in which nonbureaucratic urban elites had played such a crucial role. It was now assumed that as the domestic and foreign supply of the drug tapered off, consumption would evaporate of its own accord. But the new strategy would have to wait until after the 1911 Revolution.

REVOLUTION AND ITS AFTERMATH

Through their activism in the anti-opium campaign, Lin Bingzhang and the other members of the Fujian Anti-Opium Society found themselves able to regulate local society in ways that they had probably never imagined. But they also soon discovered that they had, in effect, become unofficial agents of state policy, and were bound by state-imposed constraints that increasingly came to be viewed as unacceptable by elite reformers. By late 1911, international pressures and domestic financial problems had restricted the ability of the Qing state to respond to the momentum for further and faster reform. The 1911 Revolution was welcomed by most urban reformist elites in Fuzhou, and many members of the Anti-Opium Society were involved in setting up the new state.

After the revolution, several developments worked to erode the influence of nonbureaucratic elites in Fuzhou's anti-opium campaign: the absorption of some of the society's most experienced and energetic leaders by the state bureaucracy; a shift in central government policy that signaled a new emphasis on curtailing the cultivation of opium in the countryside rather than its consumption in urban locales; the eventual elimination of legal foreign opium imports into China; and finally, the death of Yuan Shikai and the subsequent rise of warlord power. The public space occupied by the Fujian Anti-Opium Society merged with the state sometime after 1912, although the society itself did not formally disband until 1921.

The reins of government and control of the opium reform efforts in Fuzhou changed hands after the revolution as Song Shou and Pu Shou, the Manchus in charge of the official arm of the opium suppression campaign in Fuzhou and all of Fujian, both died in the political upheaval, the former by his own hand and the latter at the hands of the revolutionary forces.[51] The new Republic quickly endorsed the anti-opium campaign that had been initiated by its Qing predecessor, and pledged to honor the terms of the international agreements that had so strongly influenced the pace and conduct of opium suppression before the 1911 Revolution.[52] This meant that the Republican state had committed itself to the *second* Sino-British agreement on opium, which linked the end of Indian opium imports to the elimination of domestic poppy cultivation in every province in China. The new state's focus on the urgency of eradicating poppy cultivation seems to have acted to reduce the role of the nonofficial reform groups, such as the Anti-Opium Society, that had dominated attempts to reduce urban opium consumption in the late Qing. Although the society's attempts to curtail opium smoking continued, its efforts were accorded far less publicity and less vocal state approval.

In the city of Fuzhou and its environs, provincial authorities struggled to regain control after the Revolution but the restrictions on opium were hastily reimposed.[53] The new director of the Opium Suppression Office (*jinyan gongsuo*) reiterated the ban on prepared opium shops in the Fuzhou area in April 1912, and issued comprehensive new regulations that prohibited opium dens, opium smoking, the cultivation of opium poppies, and the sale and conveyance of English opium if the foreign opium cakes were not intact. This last restriction basically imposed a ban on foreign opium, since the cakes were notoriously brittle, and the restriction infuriated British opium merchants and diplomats.[54] In general, Republican opium reformers both within and outside the bureaucracy seemed far less solicitous of British sensibilities when unrelated to the prohibition of poppy cultivation.

The immediate aftermath of the 1911 Revolution was chaotic in Fuzhou, but the fall of 1912 marked a period in which the new state began in earnest to absorb the public space in which opium suppression was carried out. Initially, Peng Shousong, the head of Fujian's branch of the Tongmenghui, assumed control of both the police department and the Anti-Opium Society. The chief of police had, under the Qing dynasty, headed up the official Opium Suppression Office, but Peng seemed to have felt that the powers granted the nonofficial group were either more extensive or easier to manipulate. Peng was deeply enmeshed in Fujian's complex provincial politics, however, and by the fall of 1912 an armed confrontation in Fuzhou seemed inevitable. At this point Beijing stepped in, sending a high-ranking official with numerous soldiers to supervise Peng's departure.[55]

After Beijing compelled the resignation and departure of Peng, the state initiated the process of harnessing the public sphere within the confines of its bureaucratic framework. Several prominent nonbureaucratic reformers were given important positions in the state anti-opium bureaucracy. Chen Peikun, who had replaced Lin Bingzhang as head of the Fujian Anti-Opium Society in 1910, was now appointed director of the Fujian Provincial Opium Suppression Office *(Fujian jinyan ju zongban)* and head of Fujian's police department *(Fujian quansheng jingwuting tingzhang).*[56] In 1913 Chen Peikun was replaced by Chen Nengguang, a Chinese Christian who had served as an officer of the Fujian Anti-Opium Society before 1911 and was appointed director of the Provincial Board of Foreign Affairs after the 1911 Revolution. Chen Nengguang had first-hand knowledge of the power that nonofficial elites derived from the anti-opium campaign, and he was very careful to clarify the supervisory role of the official Opium Suppression Office over the unofficial Anti-Opium Society.

As Fujian's top anti-opium official, Chen was in charge when it came time in early 1914 to undergo the requisite inspection to determine if the province had eliminated poppy cultivation within its borders. His efforts paid off, and the official closing of the province to Indian opium in the spring of 1914 was greeted with great enthusiasm in Fuzhou. The festivities included a rowdy rally at the headquarters of the Anti-Opium Society, where a life-sized effigy of Lin Zexu was removed and conveyed in an exuberant procession throughout the city.[57] The figure of Lin Zexu was symbolic of many of the victories that the celebration represented. The exclusion of foreign opium was particularly poignant in Fuzhou because its venerated native son had himself failed to achieve it. Without foreign opium as its foil, however, Lin's image lost much of its symbolic power after this achievement.

The closing of Fujian and all of China to Indian opium did not mean the end of the opium problem. What it did mean was that without British pressure, the incentive for the state to continue to comply with opium suppression measures was considerably diminished, and the new Republican government was now able to turn more of its attention to other pressing internal problems. With foreign imports eliminated, the central Chinese state became far less concerned with the opium situation in the provinces, and the overarching policy framework through which it had guided and coordinated provincial campaigns began to fray. And after the death of

Yuan Shikai in 1916, power was appropriated by regional warlords. This weakening of central oversight was felt in Fuzhou almost immediately.

With foreign opium now officially prohibited in Fujian, the price of the drug soared and the Fujian Anti-Opium Society turned its energies to harassing opium smugglers, many of whom operated under the cloak of extraterritoriality with Japanese passports obtained in nearby Taiwan. As the situation in the countryside of Fujian began to deteriorate in 1915 and 1916, control of various regions of the province shifted hands repeatedly, and in many instances poppy planting was encouraged as a means to raise revenue for military expenses. The Fujian Anti-Opium Society held on for several years and finally disbanded in disgust and frustration in 1921.[58]

CONCLUSIONS

China's temporary but impressive progress in the nationwide campaign to halt the smoking, cultivation, and sale of opium from 1906 to 1915 generated pride among Chinese patriots and considerable surprise among many skeptical foreign observers. The results of the campaign were unexpected not only because of the addictive nature of the drug itself and the extent to which it pervaded the Chinese countryside, but also because the Qing state in its final years was often perceived as corrupt and decrepit, and thus incapable of launching such a comprehensive attack on an entrenched social evil. That the campaign was able to get back on track during the brief interlude after the upheaval following the 1911 Revolution and before the collapse of the early Republic made it all the more impressive. The course of the anti-opium campaign in Fuzhou indicated that the central Chinese state in the late Qing and early Republican eras was still capable of harnessing nationalistic sentiment both within and outside the bureaucracy.

Despite the prominent role of extrabureaucratic elites, China's central state was the guiding force behind the late-Qing / early-Republican antiopium movement in Fujian province. Paul Howard has emphasized the impressive extent of elite hostility toward opium, as expressed in a number of public literary forums.[59] But when it came time to eschew rhetoric for action in 1906, the Qing state established a legal and chronological framework for suppression that specifically encouraged nonbureaucratic elite involvement and left a great deal of room for provinces and localities to respond to peculiar situations. In 1908 and 1911 the Qing state signed agreements with the British to phase out the importation of Indian opium into China. This step made the success of the campaign attainable, but only if the Qing government adhered to the terms of the agreement. This was to prove problematic for both the Qing and Republican governments, but since fulfillment of the terms of the agreements was contingent upon a nationwide effort, the Chinese state had even more incentive to remain involved in provincial opium reform efforts.

For Fuzhou's elite reformers, Lin Zexu left a complex legacy, one that far exceeded the involvement of his descendant in the anti-opium movement. Commissioner Lin and his great-grandson exemplified the dilemma of many early-twentieth-century reformers. As Bin Wong explains in his chapter in this volume, the activities of Chinese elites in the context of opium reform were viewed by Beijing as "an extension of government capacity," much like traditional elite involvement in local social welfare and public works. But this chapter has demonstrated that the extraordinary powers granted the members of the Anti-Opium Society in Fuzhou went well beyond traditional public service roles. Narcotics control seems to have had a special appeal for China's elites, both as an outlet for budding nationalist sentiment *and* as an avenue for extending direct administrative control over local society. But in this case, that control could not have been established without the legitimizing presence of the state and the permeability of the public sphere. Permeability meant the ability of those in the public sphere to use the symbolic and actual resources of the state, but it also gave the state the ability to co-opt and control elites outside the official bureaucracy. In the end, it was the moral authority and regulatory presence of the Chinese state, shaped in large part by international pressures, that determined the course of the campaign and brought the absorption of the public sphere after the revolution and, with it, the downfall of the Fujian Anti-Opium Society.

NOTES

1. See Philip Huang, "'Public Sphere'/'Civil Society' in China?"; Rankin, "Some Observations on a Chinese Public Sphere"; Rowe, "Problem of 'Civil Society' in Late Imperial China"; and Wakeman, "Civil Society and Public Sphere Debate."

2. Rowe, *Hankow: Conflict and Community*, and *Hankow: Commerce and Society;* Rankin, *Elite Activism and Political Transformation in China;* Strand, *Rickshaw Beijing.*

3. Lin Man-houng, "Qingmo shehui liuxing xishi yapian yanjiu," and "Wan Qing de yapian shui."

4. For example, Wakeman, *Policing Shanghai;* Martin, *Shanghai Green Gang.*

5. The organizers of the Fujian Anti-Opium Society headquarters in Fuzhou were: Lin Bingzhang, Chen Baochen, Lin Shaonian, Shao Zhicheng, Liu Xuexun, Luo Jincheng, Zhang Zanting, Li Funan, Chen Maoding, and Lin Zhixuan. See Wu and Lin, "Fujian jinyan yundong 'qudu she.'" Many thanks to Ryan Dunch for sharing this source with me and providing such detailed notes that my research trip to Fuzhou was extremely productive.

6. Wu and Lin, "Fujian jinyan yundong 'qudu she,'" p. 15; *Mercy and Truth* (September 1907): 268–72; enclosure in Playfair to Jordan, 25 February 1907, in BFO 228/2415, doc. 66.

7. Wu Jiaqiong, "Lin Bingzhang shenping gaishu"; *Qingmo minchu Zhongguo guan shen renming lu*, pp. 240–41.

8. Li Guoqi, *Zhongguo xiandaihua de quyu yanjiu*, p. 559.

9. Faithfull-Davies, *Banyan City*, pp. 17–19.

10. Wu Jiaqiong, "Lin Bingzhang shenping gaishu."

11. Ibid.; Li Guoqi, *Zhongguo xiandaihua de quyu yanjiu*, pp. 558–59; *Friend of China* 27, no. 4 (January 1911): 71; *Qingmo minchu Zhongguo guan shen renming lu*, pp. 240–41; Archives de Ministère des Affaires Étrangères, Paris (MAE), Foutcheou to Paris, 3 July 1908, Nouvelle Serie (NS) 587, pp. 101–13; and MAE, Margerie to Pichon, 8 December 1910, NS 589, pp. 170–78.

12. The post was filled in 1907 by Song Shou, who belonged to the Manchu Plain White Banner and served the Qing dynasty for more than twenty years in a number of positions, both civilian and military. French diplomats also alleged that Song Shou was himself a habitual opium smoker, but I have yet to confirm that charge through other documentation. Zhao, *Qingshi gao*, 41:12787; MAE, Bourgeois to Bapst, 17 January 1908, NS 13, pp. 15–23.

13. Enclosure in Playfair to Jordan, 25 February 1907, in BFO 228/2415, doc. 66.

14. Yu Ende, *Zhongguo jinyan faling bianqian shi*, pp. 124–24; Great Britain Foreign Office, China no. 5, enclosure in *Correspondence Respecting the Opium Question in China*, China no. 1 (1908), pp. 4–8.

15. *India's Women and China's Daughters*, July 1908, p. 106.

16. Inspectorate General of Chinese Customs, *Decennial Reports*, Fuzhou, 1902–11, p. 91; Archives de Ministère des Affaires Étrangères, Nantes (MAE/Nantes), carton 71: translation from *Minbao*, 11 August 1908.

17. Werner to Jordan, 19 September 1911; September Quarter 1911, both in PRO, FO 228/1800. "Fujian qudu zongshe lishi," *Fujian qudu zongshe jibao*, pp. 3–4.

18. MAE/Nantes, "Enquête sur le nombre des fumeurs d'opium dans la cité," September 1908, cartons 71–72.

19. MAE, Foutcheou to Paris, 3 July 1908, NS 587, pp. 101–13: translation from *Fujian xinwen*.

20. Cheng, "Minchu jinyan yundong," p. 137.

21. Fletcher to Root, 8 April 1908, in the United States Department of State (USDS) Consular Despatches, Record Group 59, reel 105: 774/198–99; Brunnert and Hagelstrom, *Present Day Political Organization of China*, pp. 68–70; Quan, *Qingji xinshe shiguan nianbiao*, p. 66.

22. Des Forges, *Hsi-liang and the Chinese National Revolution*, pp. 95–101; Wyman, "Opium and the State in Sichuan Province during the Late Qing."

23. Brunnert and Hagelstrom, *Present Day Political Organization of China*, pp. 68–70.

24. Zhao, *Qingshi gao*, 41:12787; MAE, Bourgeois to Bapst, 17 January 1908, NS 14, pp. 15–23.

25. Pu Shou belonged to the Manchu Bordered Yellow Banner, and was awarded the *juren* degree in 1894. He was primarily a military man and served the Banner forces in several official capacities. Zhao Erxun's biography in the draft history of the Qing dynasty (*Qingshi gao*, 41:12805) emphasizes his bravery and integrity, and specifically praises his strict enforcement of opium restrictions. Pu Shou was ru-

mored to have once been plagued by the opium habit himself. His alleged addiction is discussed by American Board missionary George Newell in a letter that the board received on 7 April 1908 (Archives of the American Board Mission, Union Theological Seminary, New York, folder 2).

26. Crossley, *Orphan Warriors,* pp. 4, 92–93, 100–2, 117, 176, 195; Im, "Rise and Decline of the Eight Banner Garrisons in the Ch'ing Period."

27. This conception of opium addiction as a disease appears quite frequently in Chinese discussions of opium suppression at this time.

28. *Zhengzhi guanbao,* 11:410–12.

29. Ibid.

30. Letter from George Newell, received 7 April 1908, Archives of the American Board Mission, Union Theological Seminary, folder 2.

31. As for the Han officers and soldiers who staffed the naval garrison, Pu Shou stated that because they were stationed on an island, coming to the Fuzhou anti-opium office was very inconvenient for them; therefore he "immediately ordered the regulations sent to them [and] carefully selected and assigned officials and gentry to immediately establish an [anti-opium] office in that area [so as to] earnestly suppress [opium]"; *Zhengzhi guanbao,* 11:410–12.

32. Ibid., 20:108–10.

33. Ibid., 11:395–96.

34. Ibid., 20:108–10.

35. Ibid.

36. Ibid.

37. Ibid., 22:412–13, 30:173.

38. *North China Herald,* 6 February 1909, in MAE, NS 588, pp. 43–48.

39. Gracey to Bacon, 28 May 1907, USDS (1906–1910), reel 104.

40. *Zhengzhi guanbao,* 35:262–63, 37:27–29.

41. Ibid., 20:104–8, 32:159–60.

42. Ibid., 32:159–60, 36:473–77, 37:339–41.

43. Ibid., 37:27–29.

44. Ibid., 35:262–63.

45. Ibid., 20:104–8.

46. Ibid.

47. Enclosure no. 28 in *Correspondence Respecting the Opium Question in China,* China no. 1 (1908); Inspectorate General of Chinese Customs, *Decennial Reports,* Amoy, 1902–1911, p. 103.

48. Yu Ende, *Zhongguo jinyan faling bianqian shi,* p. 263.

49. *Zhengzhi guanbao,* 20:104–8.

50. BFO 233/134, Addendum to the "Opium Agreement, 1911."

51. *The Foochow Messenger,* January 1912, p. 13; USDS (1910–1929), reel 8: 893.00/720

52. Jordan to BFO, 18 March 1912, BFO 228/2446.

53. *The Republican Advocate,* 10 August 1912.

54. Multiple dispatches in BFO 1872.

55. Werner to Jordan, 30 September 1912 and 10 October 1912, BFO 228/1838.

56. Chen Peikun (b. 1874) had earned the *jinshi* degree but later went to a Japanese college. He served as head of several educational institutions in Fujian under the Qing. *Minguo renmin dacidian,* p. 1045.

57. *India's Women and China's Daughters,* July 1914, p. 130.

58. Wu and Lin, "Fujian jinyan yundong 'qudu she,'" p. 17.

59. Howard, "Opium Suppression in Late-Qing China."

ELEVEN

The National Anti-Opium Association and the Guomindang State, 1924–1937

Edward R. Slack Jr.

Following the death in 1916 of Yuan Shikai, the first head of the Chinese post-imperial state, the production, trafficking, and use of opium resurfaced in China. Two forces claimed the mandate for determining national opium policy. One was the Chinese state. Weakened and fractured by years of warlordism, it had become increasingly addicted to the lucrative revenues generated by a thriving narco-economy, yet it was also morally responsible for eliminating the most blatant symbol of Chinese humiliation and helplessness. As a result, the state found itself trapped in what Alan Baumler in the next chapter has depicted as the paradox of "suppression versus control." The other force was the Christian missionaries and their Chinese converts who resided in the treaty ports. They viewed this complex social, economic, and political problem through the stained-glass lens of good versus evil and embarked upon a holy crusade to destroy the Mephistopheles of morphine. The source of tension between these two forces lay in interpreting the double entendre of *jinyan* as it appeared in various government laws, institutions, and policy statements to the general public. Christians defined it as "complete, total, or absolute prohibition" (*juedui jinyan* or *jinjue*) and called for cultivation, trafficking, and use to be forbidden, a policy of zero tolerance on the part of national as well as local authorities. The state, more often than not, accepted the premise of "suppression through taxation" (*yujin yuzheng*), which meant something much less ambitious than zero tolerance. Its rationale was that the size and complexity of the opium problem were such that absolute prohibition was unrealizable. In the interim, therefore, it made sense to levy taxes on the trade while increasing control over it by means of a government monopoly, and only then to gradually reduce production and consumption of the drug.

Yujin yuzheng (suppression) was taken to be the means to achieve the goal of *juedui jinyan* (prohibition). This chapter explores the dynamic relationship that evolved between the state and urban elites, primarily Chinese Christians, over the contentious issue of opium policy by focusing on an important but now forgotten voluntary association called the National Anti-Opium Association *(Zhong-hua guomin judu hui)*. During its thirteen-year lifespan, the National Anti-Opium Association (NAOA) sought to control the *jinyan* discourse by assuming the role of the leading popular voice for prohibition in China. How the NAOA, its leadership, and public support were affected by Guomindang state-building in the realm of national opium policy highlights a previously unexplored region of state-society relations during the 1920s–1930s.

ORIGIN, STRUCTURE, AND ACTIVITIES OF THE NAOA

Early in 1918 the British physician Dr. W. H. Graham Aspland spearheaded an effort by Protestant missionaries against the Lazarus of narcotics by organizing the International Anti-Opium Association (IAOA). The espoused goals of the IAOA were "to secure restriction of the production and use of opium, morphia, heroin, cocaine and allied drugs to legitimate uses in all countries," and "to assist in procuring comprehensive legislation and its adequate enforcement, prohibiting the planting and cultivation of poppy throughout Chinese territory."[1] Within a year of its founding, the IAOA had established twenty branch associations in eleven provinces of China, primarily in treaty ports such as Shanghai, Tianjin, Hankou, and Shenyang.[2] The IAOA also began publishing an English-language quarterly titled *Opium Cultivation and Traffic in China,* which contained reports of the narcotics problem in the Republic gathered from its branch associations and foreign missionaries. Attempting to gain international support for its efforts, the IAOA unsuccessfully lobbied American, French, and British leaders at Versailles to include an anti-drug clause into the final draft of the 1919 treaty. IAOA was more successful, however, in convincing the League of Nations to create an Advisory Committee on Trafficking in Opium, which sought to halt the excess production of opium and its derivatives spurred by the Great War. Within China, the IAOA focused on pressuring the various warlord governments in Beijing to pass detailed laws against the sale and cultivation of opium, and even managed to attract important Beijing politicians such as Xu Shichang, Li Yuanhong, and Cao Rulin to serve as members.[3]

Despite such achievements, the IAOA failed to popularize its message among the Chinese masses because of the breakdown of central authority. From 1906 to 1916 the state had undertaken a serious effort to eliminate opium in China, widely circulating anti-opium literature and rigidly enforcing the laws. After the breakdown of central authority during the last year of Yuan Shikai's rule, however, warlords and local officials actively encouraged poppy cultivation and consumption. In virtually every province, Opium Suppression Bureaus (*Jinyan ju*) and similar-sounding agencies collected assorted taxes on the drug for local warlord administrations that were reluctant to support any anti-opium activities. Consequently, there were no Chinese-language posters, tracts, or publications distributed to the masses by any state or private interest, although volumes of information were being published by the IAOA in English.

Members of the National Christian Council of China (NCC) responded to this problem on 4 June 1923 by creating the Anti-Narcotics Commission (*Judu weiyuanhui*). Although several foreign missionaries, including Aspland, were commission members, the majority were Chinese Christians, most notably its general secretary Dr. R. Y. Lo (Luo Yunyan).[4] According to the NCC, the Anti-Narcotics Commission (ANC) was created to fill the void "where the International Anti-Opium Association has been compelled to leave off," in other words, to translate into Chinese the existing reports and literature on opium prepared by the IAOA.[5] To facilitate that all-important task, the ANC was originally located in the IAOA's Beijing headquarters, but later moved into the NCC's offices in Shanghai. Beyond the immediate goal of translating IAOA reports and literature into Chinese, the Anti-Narcotics Commission also collected data and information regarding the drug conditions in China and enlisted the support of other ecclesiastical organizations. More importantly, this movement was envisioned to transcend its Christian base and gain the support of all Chinese. According to its general secretary, the Anti-Narcotics Commission sought "to secure . . . the co-operation of Chambers of Commerce, Guilds, other religious bodies, educational associations, government schools, parliaments and provincial assemblies . . . and the press, to educate, mould and arouse public opinion."[6]

China's non-Christian urban elites were similarly concerned about the opium scourge that was ravaging the nation and desired to work with the ANC to create an all-Chinese public body to deal with the problem. On 5 August 1924 a group of more than five hundred Chinese, including representatives from thirty-eight leading public organizations, gathered at the General Chamber of Commerce in Shanghai to establish the National Anti-Opium Association. The original impetus for the creation of this organization was to prepare for the upcoming Geneva Opium Conferences sponsored by the League of Nations (November 1924 to February 1925). On 24 August the NAOA issued a manifesto to the entire nation, asking leading public bodies and patriotic individuals to join the crusade against opium and other drugs, and elected Cai Yuanpei, Wu Liande, and Gu Ziren (T. Z.

Koo) to act as "people's delegates" at the Geneva Opium Conferences.[7] The diversity of voluntary and professional associations constituting the thirty-eight founding organizations of the NAOA was not remarkable,[8] given the historical context within which such collaboration took place. The explosion of public associations, political parties, literary journals, and newspapers informing and mobilizing urban populations was at once both reaction and midwife to the growth of Chinese nationalism early in the 1920s. Owing to their distrust of the corrupt government in Beijing, student associations, chambers of commerce, and banking associations mobilized public opinion and put into practice "popular diplomacy." At the Washington Conference of 1921–1922, for example, the urban elite sent its own delegation abroad to represent "the will of the people" alongside the official Chinese delegation. The NAOA appeared to be a similar phenomenon.[9]

The genesis of the NAOA was linked to resolving contradictions between the forces of Chinese nationalism and Christianity. The aim of New Culture reformers was to modernize Chinese society, and traditional practices such as foot-binding and opium smoking were obvious targets of their efforts. As anti-imperialism also thrived in this emotionally charged atmosphere, Christianity was targeted as a most glaring example of foreign encroachment. Christian missionaries and often their converts were protected under the cloak of extraterritoriality, and the ubiquitous presence of Christian schools and colleges raised the specter of foreign domination over Chinese education. As a result, many Chinese Christians were caught between the Scylla of their foreign faith and the Charybdis of their "Chineseness," and desperately searched for a way to reconcile both forces without being crushed by one or the other.[10] The formation of the National Christian Council in 1922 was the first step away from the darkness of conservative missionary domination toward the light of Chinese nationalism. Although composed of both foreign and Chinese members, the sympathies of its constituency lay squarely with the goals of Chinese nationalists.[11] The fight against opium, containing both anti-imperialist and iconoclastic elements, was at once a moral and a nationalistic cause that all Chinese (excluding those who profited from it) could rally around. Because the National Anti-Opium Association was constructed around the nucleus of the ANC and headquartered within the offices of the National Christian Council, it provided Chinese Christians with an important tributary into the mainstream of Chinese nationalism. The National Anti-Opium Association was distinguished from its predecessors by its staying power. It did not dissolve immediately after the Geneva conferences, nor was its role solely limited to diplomacy. On the contrary, it grew in size and influence to assume leadership and responsibility in the populist movement to prohibit drugs when local and national governments failed to do so.

According to the association's constitution, the three principal aims of the NAOA were: (1) to enforce the laws prohibiting poppy cultivation and the illicit use, manufacture, and sale of opium and other narcotics; (2) to limit the importation of foreign narcotic drugs to the amount required for medicinal needs; and (3) to promote anti-narcotics education and the treatment of drug addicts.[12] The NAOA was composed of a national committee, executive committee, honorary directorate, secretariat, and numerous branch associations. The national committee, which met annually in Shanghai, consisted mainly of representatives appointed by its constituent organs, and the remaining one-third "co-opted from leaders in different walks of life who are strong supporters of the anti-narcotic movement."[13] Members of the executive committee and honorary directorate were notable figures in China's educational, political, business, and legal circles. Tang Shaoyi, Cai Yuanpei, and Shi Zhaoji (Dr. Alfred Sao-ke Sze) were among the honorary directors of the association.[14] Another well-known and respected member of the association's hierarchy was Dr. Wu Liande (Wu Lien-teh), a Cambridge University medical school graduate who headed the Manchurian Plague Prevention Service and served concurrently as an honorary director and chairman of the Harbin branch of the NAOA.[15] These men lent their names and prestige to the NAOA for public purposes, playing little or no role in the organization's day-to-day activities.

The real power within the association resided in the executive committee and secretariat, and both were dominated by members of the National Christian Council. The executive committee chair from 1924 to 1928, Li Denghui (T. H. Lee), had been very active in Chinese civil society. He was founder and chair of the World Students' Federation (1905–1915), and served as chair of both the League of Public Organizations, which protested against Chinese ratification of the Treaty of Versailles in 1919, and the People's National Federation, which represented 180 public bodies at the Washington Conference. Li also held directorships with numerous other associations.[16] His organizational skills and contacts with non-Christian groups benefited the NAOA immensely. Zhao Xi'en (Samuel U. Zau) likewise led a socially active life. He converted to Christianity in the early 1900s and later prospered as a government official, businessman, and philanthropist. Zhao's positions in the Beijing government included civil governorships of Zhejiang and Shandong, and his religious and philanthropic positions ranged from deacon of the Baptist Church to director of the Red Cross Society and Hospital. He also served as a director of numerous colleges, orphanages, modern banks, and industries.[17]

The very heart of the association was the secretariat. Headed by a general secretary, it had four departments: general administration, survey and sta-

tistics, local organization, and narcotics education. The secretariat was originally headed by Zhong Ketuo (Rev. K. T. Chung), a longtime member of
the National Christian Council. Zhong was a former Episcopal rector under
the American Church Mission, well known for his blunt talk and devotion
to the anti-opium cause.[18] He served as general secretary from the association's inception until he was succeeded by Garfield Huang (Huang Jiahui)
in late 1928. Huang had been very active in Christian organizations and
educational institutions since his youth in Xiamen (Amoy). His resume
shows that he taught at the Anglo-Chinese College in Shantou (Swatow) in
1921–1922, that he served as secretary for the National Committee of the
YMCA of China (1922–1923) and editorial secretary for the NCC (1923–
1924), and that he cofounded the NAOA.[19] In his roles as assistant secretary
and general secretary of the NAOA secretariat, Huang edited the association's Chinese and English-language journals and toured different parts of
China to establish branch NAOAs. After his appointment as general secretary in December 1928, Garfield Huang was the driving force of the
organization and became synonymous with both the NAOA and its work.
A crusader against the evils of opium, he never compromised his zealous
devotion to the cause.

The activities of the NAOA were legion. To educate the public on the
harmful effects of opium and other narcotics the association published a
welter of periodicals, tracts, books, pamphlets, and posters. Its most notable
publications included the monthly magazine *Judu yuekan* (Opium, A National Issue), the sporadically issued *Zhongguo yanhuo nianjian* (China
Opium Yearbook),[20] and the English-language quarterly *Opium, A World
Problem*. The NAOA also worked hard to get Chinese publishers to include
information on drugs in their publications, including school primers, and
sponsored essay and speech contests among Chinese students in Shanghai
and throughout the nation. The mobilization of public opinion that resulted from this work had a tangible impact. When Gu Ziren attended the
Geneva Opium Conferences and addressed its delegates as a representative
of the "Chinese people's anti-opium movement," he carried with him a
petition signed by 4,265 public bodies representing 4,663,979 Chinese
citizens.[21] In 1924 the association declared the last Sunday in September
"Anti-Opium Day." By 1926 the day had grown into an "Anti-Opium
Week" celebrated in the first week of October (see figs. 12 and 13). The
NAOA undertook aggressive organizational drives throughout China, especially in the cities along the Yangtze River and in Manchuria. As a result
of such efforts, the NAOA grew in size from 188 branch associations in
1924 to 450 in 1930.[22]

The National Anti-Opium Association also made a number of important studies of the drug situation in China and compiled records for domestic and international uses. In its capacity as the Chinese nongovern-

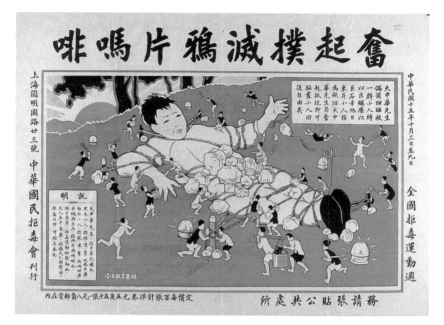

Figure 12. A poster produced by the Anti-Opium Association in Shanghai for the National Anti-Opium Week in October 1926. The black-shirted Lilliputians holding down "Master China" represent opium; the white-shirted, morphine. Reproduced with permission of the Hoover Institution, Stanford California.

mental equivalent of the U.S. Federal Drug Administration, the NAOA undertook chemical analysis of "remedies" advertised in Chinese periodicals as cures for opium addiction and found them generally to be morphine or heroin pills. As word of its work spread abroad, in January 1927 Zhu Zhaoxin (Chu Chao-hsin), China's representative to the League of Nations and honorary vice chair of the association, got the League's Opium Advisory Committee to recognize the NAOA for "its cooperation in the task of fighting the opium evil in the Far East."[23] In working against the opium trade and criticizing those who profited from it, the NAOA frequently found itself confronting Chinese governments at all levels, as well as national and international opium cartels and foreign governments. In February 1925 the Beijing government under President Duan Qirui proposed to legalize the opium trade because it was, in effect, quasi-legal throughout the country. The NAOA mobilized public opinion against the proposal, and the sponsors of the legislation, the Fengtian Clique, had to withdraw it.[24] A year later, the association revealed the names of thirty-six opium shops operating in the French concession in Shanghai, and its pro-

Figure 13. A poster produced by a women's association in Taiyuan, Shanxi, for the Third Anti-Opium Movement, sponsored by the provincial Anti-Opium Association in October 1926, and printed on the back page of *Judu tekan* (Anti-opium special issue). The title caption reads: "Hey, members of all social groups, do you really love your country and yourselves?" Students are shown approaching each of the four traditional occupational groups—gentry, peasantry, artisans, and merchants.

tests to the French administration resulted in police raids on several of the shops.[25] The NAOA was also a relentless critic of the opium monopolies operating in the Asian colonies of Britain, France, Holland, Portugal, and Japan, and of the "unequal treaties" that protected drug smugglers from Chinese law.

THE NAOA AND THE GUOMINDANG, 1926–1930:
FROM SUPPRESSION TO PROHIBITION

The revolutionary regime that Sun Yatsen founded in Guangzhou (Canton) in 1923 in the aftermath of the Guomindang-Communist alliance found itself facing financial problems it needed to solve quickly. In early January 1924, therefore, Sun announced the creation of an opium monopoly under an agency called the Opium Suppression Superintendency's Office *(Jinyan duban shu)*.[26] Eleven months later, Sun made the following statement to members of the branch NAOA in Tianjin:

> In my opinion, the problem of opium prohibition in China is synonymous with the problem of good government. For the traffic in opium cannot co-exist with a National[ist] Government deriving its power and authority from the people. Until political workers in China are in a position to implement civil authority in the administration of government, it will be nearly impossible to achieve absolute prohibition.[27]

Sun's ambiguous stance on opium at once justified Canton's policy of "suppression through taxation" while promising a policy of complete prohibition after the Guomindang had destroyed warlordism and established a national government. This statement was later canonized by the party as Sun's "Anti-Opium Will" *(Judu yixun)*.

Following Sun's death early in 1925, anti-Christian agitation carried out by Communist workers in the Guomindang became more pronounced as the Northern Expedition approached Shanghai. Christian churches and mission property were targeted for looting or occupation by the National Revolutionary Army, and Chinese Christians were frequently threatened or punished unless they joined in pro-Nationalist demonstrations. With the winds of Chinese nationalism blowing increasingly from Guangzhou, members of the NCC began taking a more patriotic stance on issues such as the May 30th Incident and Guomindang attacks against the "unequal treaties."[28] It is therefore not surprising that in 1926 the NAOA incorporated Sun Yatsen's "Anti-Opium Will" into its own anti-narcotics program.[29]

According to Joseph Fewsmith, when the "Thought of Sun Yat-sen" began to filter into the public mind during the Northern Expedition, the party's ability to control the interpretation of its professed ideology grew increasingly difficult. As a result, the Guomindang became vulnerable to criticism from critics quoting the words of its own founder.[30] As reports from both the IAOA and NAOA confirmed that the revolutionary army was encouraging poppy production and establishing opium suppression offices to collect opium taxes along its route, the National Anti-Opium Association stepped up its criticisms and damaged the public's perception of the Nationalist Party at a critical time during the drive for national unification.[31] When Guomindang troops entered Shanghai in late March 1927, the NAOA was a potent public force with which they had to reckon.

The first official contact between the NAOA and the Nationalists came in April 1927, when the association sent Zhong Ketuo and Garfield Huang to Wuhan to meet with party leaders and present to them a petition titled "Eight Demands to the Government." The petitioners asked the Wuhan government to prohibit the cultivation of poppies in areas under its control, to set a date for ending the opium traffic, to establish opium treatment clinics, to dismiss any of its own officials found smoking or trafficking in opium, to halt the importation of foreign drugs, to require publishers to include anti-opium materials in textbooks for primary and middle schools, to protest to those nations that permitted trafficking in their Asian colonies, and to appoint a national opium prohibition committee to implement the policies asked for in the petition.[32] This petition was the first of many attempts by the NAOA to stake its claim to leadership, or at least co-leadership, in the fight against drugs in China. The association's leadership envisioned an important role for itself in helping the party fulfill the second stage of Sun's "Anti-Opium Will."

In the aftermath of the Wuhan-Nanjing schism that brought about a separate Nationalist government under Jiang Jieshi (Chiang Kai-shek) in Nanjing, the Ministry of Finance had established an opium monopoly in Shanghai and other lower Yangtze cities to fund the Northern Expedition through to its completion.[33] Accordingly, in June 1927 the NAOA presented its "Eight Demands" to the Nanjing government, which responded by having the next (150th) meeting of the Central Political Council resolve that it would undertake a campaign to suppress opium use and trafficking within a three-year period.[34] In August 1927 the association convened a General Anti-Opium Conference to express its discontent over the government monopoly. Representatives of some sixty public organizations in Shanghai attended the conference to hear Li Jihong, director of the Ministry of Finance's Opium Suppression Office, explain Nanjing's policy, which essentially legalized the opium trade for three years. Outraged by the implications of the new policy, the NAOA launched an aggressive public campaign against the monopoly, insisting that it contravened Sun's "Anti-Opium Will."[35] As a result of the NAOA's pressure through publications and public rallies, Sun Fo (Sun Ke), head of the Ministry of Finance, telegrammed the association on 24 November asking that it dispatch a delegation to Nanjing to discuss opium policy. On 6 December Zhong Ketuo and Garfield Huang carried to Nanjing a five-point proposal urging the government to prohibit opium and other narcotics and to abolish opium taxes. Zheng Hongnian, vice minister of finance, admitted, "Presently,

our opium suppression plans are only a means to raise revenue. If you look
at the opium suppression policy, it does not prohibit opium, but actually
allows people to indulge in drugs."[36]

The main source of contention between the NAOA and Nanjing was the
former's insistence that *jinyan* could never be anything more than a scheme
to raise revenue as long as it remained under the jurisdiction of the Ministry
of Finance. Accordingly, the association began insisting that the government create an independent national Opium Suppression Committee (*Jinyan weiyuanhui*) to oversee state anti-narcotics activities. It called upon the
government to convene a National Opium Suppression Conference (*Quanguo jinyan huiyi*) to be attended by, among others, the government's leading
military and political figures.[37] Although Nanjing announced another "revision" of its opium laws in April 1928, the basic policy remained unchanged. On 1 May the NAOA condemned the revision with scathing criticism:

> As we look around at the conditions within China, opium is everywhere, how
> sickening! HOW SICKENING! We truly hope that the government authorities
> will comply with Sun Yat-sen's "Anti-Opium Will" and implement the
> Guomindang Party platform, address the suffering of the people, adopt the
> NAOA's proposals to completely prohibit opium and earnestly eradicate
> [opium], in order to save the tarnished reputation of our country, and forever
> consolidate the foundation of this nation![38]

In the summer of 1928, as the Nationalist government was attempting
to make the transition from the "Period of Military Rule" to the "Period
of Political Tutelage" in accordance with Sun's blueprint for national reconstruction, conditions were ripe for a change in policy. Garfield Huang
ventured to Nanjing and conferred with interior minister Xue Dubi and
Jiangsu governor Niu Yongjian, who told Huang that the government had
decided to prohibit opium and other drugs in accordance with the proposals made by the NAOA.[39] On 18 July Nanjing announced the new policy
of complete prohibition, and a week later made public the composition of
the newly created National Opium Prohibition Committee (NOPC), which
included as members Li Denghui and Zhong Ketuo, chair and general
secretary of the NAOA, respectively.[40] The NAOA's hard-fought victory
against a Guomindang opium monopoly was codified into law with the
Opium Suppression Act (*Jinyan fa*) and Opium Suppression Regulations
(*Jinyan fa shixing tiaoli*) on 10 September 1928. Nanjing subsequently convened the National Opium Suppression Conference, which met during the
first ten days of November (see fig. 14 for a poster produced at this time
to link opium suppression with Sun Yatsen). This conference was the climax
of the NAOA's crusade against the Nationalists' policy of *yujin yuzheng*.
Chairing the conference was Zhang Zhijiang, a Christian general concur-

Figure 14. "The people of the nation oppose the poison." In this National Anti-Opium Association poster of November 1928, the masses knock down the black figure of *yapian* (opium) and the white demon of *mafei* (morphine). The lead placard in the parade features Sun Yatsen's "Anti-Opium Will," tying the movement to the Guomindang Party. The poster follows a design that revolutionary propagandists used during the Northern Expedition to incite opposition to warlords and imperialists. From the association's magazine, *Opium, A World Problem* 2, no. 1 (November 1928): 27.

rently head of the NOPC, assisted by Li Denghui in the capacity of vice chair.[41] The conference was notable not because of any actions it took or proposals it made, but because of the revelations it made concerning the centrality of opium and the opium trade in Chinese life. The delegates learned, for example, that the Nationalist government derived at least forty million dollars annually from opium, which would presumably be lost if the prohibition policy succeeded. In addition, accusations of opium smoking and complicity in the trade were made against high-ranking military and government officials.[42] In light of such revelations, Jiang Jieshi boldly pledged, "Henceforth, the National government will absolutely not derive one copper from opium revenue. If anything of this sort is suspected and it is reported by this body, we could then regard this government as bankrupt, and place no confidence in it."[43]

Convening the opium conference, creating the NOPC, and passing prohibition laws marked the first phase of Guomindang state-building designed to reassert its leadership over national opium policy, leadership that the NAOA had exercised since 1924. The NOPC, an appendage of the Executive Yuan, contained two main departments (general administration, and inspection and medical analysis) and four subcommittees (international phases of opium suppression, examination of prohibition records, investigation of dangerous drugs, and examination of addicted officials).[44] One of its first acts was to establish 3 June as a national holiday, chosen in honor of Lin Zexu's burning of British opium on that day in 1839. Originally the brainchild of Wang Jingqi, an NAOA executive committee member who served concurrently as Chinese representative to the League of Nations, the celebration of Opium Prohibition Memorial Day was the state's answer to the association's Anti-Opium Week.[45] The NOPC was also instructed to oversee anti-narcotics education in China, and issued the monthly Chinese-language magazine *Opium Suppression Bulletin (Jinyan gongbao)*, as well as other posters and literature. Its most important tasks, however, were collecting statistics and formulating laws for the government. Each year the committee would compile data and publish an English-language annual report to the League of Nations titled *Traffic in Opium and Other Dangerous Drugs*. With members of the NAOA such as Li Denghui and Zhong Ketuo on the committee, it was not afraid to publicly criticize the government for flagrant violations of the prohibition laws.[46] This NAOA/ Guomindang alliance for prohibition provided tangible benefits for both sides: the NAOA received the stamp of state legitimacy and enhanced the political influence of the organization and its leaders, while Guomindang opium policy obtained the moral legitimacy and public support previous policies had lacked. Co-opting important leaders of the association, duplicating its function with a state bureaucracy, and muting public criticism were important first steps the Guomindang took along the road to controlling the *jinyan* discourse.

Despite such attempts to convince the public of Nanjing's sincerity in implementing Sun's "Anti-Opium Will," from the closing ceremonies of the National Opium Prohibition Conference, at which delegates signed an "Anti-Opium Oath," to the end of 1930, it became apparent that Nanjing's policy of complete prohibition was quixotic at best and hypocritical at worst. During that twenty-six month period, Guomindang opium policy evolved along a two-tiered path of de jure prohibition and de facto monopoly.[47] Although the government passed numerous anti-narcotics laws, and even created a national holiday in honor of Lin Zexu, the difficulties of enforcing prohibition were laid bare both by several domestic scandals and by the 1930 report of the League of Nations' Commission of Enquiry into the Control of Opium Smoking in the Far East.[48] More damaging to the policy of prohibition, however, was the Hubei-Hunan Special Tax Clearance Office *(Qingli Lianghu teshui chu)* that the Ministry of Finance established at Hankou in April 1929 to collect transit taxes on opium along the Yangtze River.[49] By mid 1930, numerous subbureaus of this central government agency were established in key market cities in Hubei and Hunan along important river and rail routes to provide revenues for both local and national governments. The heavy involvement of Jiang Jieshi and Song Ziwen (T. V. Soong) in the unofficial monopoly, moreover, was becoming increasingly difficult to hide from public scrutiny.[50] As the government became more and more reliant upon opium taxes to cover rising military expenditures associated with its campaigns against both warlords and Communists, on the eve of the twentieth year of the Republic, Nanjing's policy of complete prohibition appeared to suppressionist eyes to be a total failure.

THE DECLINE OF THE NAOA, 1931–1937: FROM PROHIBITION TO SUPPRESSION

The first indication of a shift away from the policy of complete prohibition of opium came with the appointment of Liu Ruiheng (J. Heng Liu), concurrently minister of public health, as chair of the NOPC in December 1930. Liu immediately asked F. W. Maze, inspector general of maritime customs, for advice on opium policy. Maze suggested that the best policy was "to place the opium trade and the cultivation of the poppy under strict Government control, with a view to eventually stopping smoking altogether. ... In other words, the existing irregular trade in opium ought to be regularized and come under the authority of the Government."[51] It appears that Maze's suggestion was taken to heart by Jiang and Song, for shortly thereafter the Nationalists attempted to make an opium monopoly official policy.

On 9 February 1931 the government announced a reorganization of the NOPC that included three high-ranking members of the NAOA, Zhong Ketuo, Wu Liande, and R. Y. Lo. Nanjing subsequently dispatched another member of the NOPC, Li Jihong, to Taiwan to study the Japanese opium monopoly there.[52] A day after the reorganization the *Shanghai Evening Post and Mercury* reprinted an article by Wu Liande titled "Opium Problem Reaches Acute Stage: Case for International Cooperation and Control." The piece had received little attention when it first appeared two weeks earlier in the *Chinese Nation*. According to Wu, China had produced almost 12,000 long tons of opium in 1930, and the Nationalist government had lost between C$50 and C$100 million annually for failing to tax it effectively because of the policy of prohibition. Wu then laid out a new policy that would abandon prohibition and, implicitly at least, give Nanjing a monopoly on the regulation and taxation of the drug.[53]

Wu's proposal ignited a firestorm of protest from the NAOA. Feeling betrayed by Wu Liande, the association proposed that henceforth it should not permit any of its executive members to serve concurrently on the NOPC. A few days later (19 February), Garfield Huang and Wang Jingqi brought together two hundred representatives from leading public bodies in Shanghai, who issued a "call to arms" to the people of China to oppose every effort to return to the monopoly system.[54] For weeks, arguments over that system raged in the press. It soon degenerated into a nasty personal battle between Wu Liande and Garfield Huang. Six months later, from May to July 1931, the Nationalist government made another attempt to establish an official monopoly under the guise of the Opium Smuggling Prevention Department (*Jinyan chaji chu*). In both instances, the NAOA forced Nanjing to back down on opium policy by rallying public opinion and using its organizational skills.[55]

To legitimize the monopoly system, the Nationalist government had to overcome public opposition to it. The leading force of public opposition was the NAOA and, more specifically, Garfield Huang. In the aftermath of the government's first failed attempt to establish an opium monopoly, Huang became the target of a concerted effort by Nanjing and Wu Liande to undermine public support for the NAOA as a means of undercutting public opposition to the monopoly policy. In mid March 1931, Huang and his wife, May Pai (Bai Zhiying), a Shanghai physician, went to Taiwan to conduct their own study of the Japanese monopoly.[56] While they were in Taiwan, reports in both Chinese and English-language newspapers in Shanghai alleged that maritime customs inspectors had once found opium in May Pai's luggage, while another version said that the drug was morphine and not opium and that Hong Kong customs had found it. On 29 March the *China Critic* ran a story headlined "Mrs. Garfield Huang and Mrs. Kao Ying," which unfavorably compared May Pai to the wife of the San Francisco consul involved in an embarrassing opium smuggling case in 1930. By late spring it had become evident that the charges against Huang and his wife were false and that the source of the allegations was someone at the NOPC. According to Huang, the source was "a high official connected with the Central Opium Suppression Commission at Nanking," the man who "was the chief sponsor of the legalization scheme . . . as a prelude of an extensive plot aiming at the total collapse of our labor."[57] The reference was obviously to Wu Liande.

The "monopolists" then attacked the finances of the NAOA. The main sources of income for the association were the American Boxer Indemnity Remissions Fund, advertisements in *Judu yuekan,* and private contributions. Back in 1927, the China Foundation, which oversaw allocations of the Boxer Fund, agreed to provide the NAOA C$30,000 a year for four years. In the summer of 1931, when the time came to renew this allocation in the aftermath of two failed attempts to legalize the opium trade, Nanjing used is influence to deny the renewal, thereby seriously crippling the organization since more than half of its budget came from these funds.[58] By late 1932 leading businesses in Shanghai that had previously advertised in *Judu yuekan,* such as the Bank of China and the Bank of Communications, quit doing so for fear of antagonizing Nanjing. Similar apprehensions probably explain why the NAOA moved its offices out of the Shanghai Banker's Association building in 1933.[59] Public contributions also declined as a result such efforts, especially those of Wu Liande, whose undermining of Garfield Huang and the NAOA proved highly effective.[60] This rather unflattering image of Wu Liande is worth noting, given the otherwise high regard most historians have for a man who probably contributed more to modernizing Chinese medicine than anyone else in the twentieth century. It is also interesting to note that in his autobiography Wu makes no mention at all of his work with either the NAOA or NOPC, and appears to have been wholly unimpressed with Nationalist anti-narcotics efforts.[61]

Another Guomindang tactic against the NAOA was intimidation. When Garfield Huang returned to Xiamen from Taiwan in 1931, men identified as "gangsters" boarded the Dutch steamer he was travelling on and attempted to kidnap him before he disembarked.[62] Also, when the association tried to publish information on the government's expanding unofficial monopoly in the fall of 1932, Nationalist censors prohibited the publication in various Chinese-language periodicals, including *Shenbao* and *Xinwenbao.* Soon afterward, on 25 November, someone planted a bomb in Garfield Huang's home with a letter warning him to discontinue his efforts against the monopoly. Similarly, unknown individuals frequented his home and his office threatening to kill Huang should they find him in residence.

Huang's subsequent movements and whereabouts were kept secret, and the activities of the NAOA were severely handicapped.[63]

Having effectively removed the main obstacle in his path for public acceptance of a monopoly in China, Jiang Jieshi continued to expand state control over the opium trade by absorbing the Hubei Special Tax Clearance Office under the control of his Military Affairs Commission in late 1932.[64] However, since Jiang had severed his ties with the NAOA, he had also undermined the moral foundation for his efforts to legalize the sale of opium. To remedy this situation, in early 1934 Jiang undertook two campaigns that would become inextricably linked and would provide the moral justification his policy of "suppression through taxation" heretofore lacked. They were the Six-Year Opium Suppression Plan *(Liunian jinyan jihua)* and the New Life Movement *(Xin shenghuo yundong).*

The six-year plan was presented to the public on 23 June 1934 as a military-supervised anti-narcotics campaign that would completely eradicate the cultivation, transportation, sale, and use of opium within six years, and later included a two-year plan to eliminate other drugs such as morphine, heroin, and cocaine (see Alan Baumler's chapter in this volume). The suppression of opium would be accomplished through the newly created Opium Suppression Inspectorate *(Jinyan ducha chu)* under Jiang's Military Affairs Commission, which had been operating in nine provinces since early April.[65] Although opium wholesalers and retailers were licensed and addicts were allowed to continue smoking opium for up to six years under a permit system, opium treatment clinics were opened to help smokers kick the habit. Those who dealt in harder drugs were judged in military tribunals and executed; addicts were sentenced to mandatory treatment and prison terms.[66]

Jiang's other effort was the New Life Movement (NLM), launched in February 1934 in a speech Jiang gave in Nanchang to Nationalist soldiers fighting the fifth and final "bandit suppression" campaign against the Communists in Jiangxi. The ideological tenets of the New Life Movement were centered around an eclectic mix of Confucianism, Christianity, and martial values.[67] For the average citizen, the movement was aimed at eradicating age-old Chinese social customs, such as spitting or urinating in public, that Jiang saw as hindrances to progress and modernization. Smoking opium was viewed through the same prism, in spite of its fiscal importance to the generalissimo's state-building objectives.

The impact of the resulting crusade was most evident in the city of Nanjing. In response to the mid-February announcement, Mayor Shi Ying promised to "thoroughly eliminate evil habits" and sponsored a Cleanliness Movement that culminated on 1 May with a Cleanliness Movement parade. It was at this parade that anti-opium propaganda first appeared in conjunction with NLM activities.[68] Three days later the mayor launched the

Movement to Exterminate the Three Evils (opium, gambling, and prostitution). According to Shi, the Japanese were flooding China with opium, heroin, and morphine as part of a diabolical plan to destroy the Chinese race, and it was his duty as mayor of the nation's capital to exterminate that threat.[69] During each night of the week-long Three Evils campaign, an important government figure gave a radio address or public speech against the use of narcotics. A fortnight later, another week-long Educational Conference to Exterminate the Three Evils took place, culminating on Opium Prohibition Memorial Day with speeches against opium and public bonfires of confiscated drugs and drug paraphernalia.[70] After six months of relative inactivity, in early December a Capital Committee to Exterminate Opium and Dangerous Drugs was created. It designated Nanjing as a drug-free zone. Unlike other parts of China where opium smoking was legal with a government permit, in Nanjing it was strictly forbidden. During 17–23 December this new organization cooperated with the New Life Movement Promotional Association and cosponsored "Exterminate Opium and Dangerous Drugs Education Week."[71] This event climaxed a year in which Nanjing became the national model for the espoused goals of the six-year plan, linking that campaign with the New Life Movement in the public's mind.

Following the announcement of the six-year plan, Garfield Huang stated that the "legalization of the opium trade and opium smoking by the Central government has proved a sad and retrogressive step in the morals of this modern government."[72] Even after his fellow Christian Jiang Jieshi in 1935 became director general for opium suppression, disbanded the NOPC, and assumed total control over Guomindang opium policy, the NAOA never wavered from regarding revenue derived by the state from opium sales as morally unacceptable. The NAOA continued its lonely crusade against the monopoly prior to the outbreak of war with Japan, but it was crippled by financial problems and lacked the public support it had had in the 1920s and early 1930s. In this phase of Guomindang state-building, Jiang endeavored, with the support of Chinese and foreign Christians, on whom he increasingly relied to revive the fading New Life Movement,[73] to force the association to adopt a new policy and program that were more sympathetic to the six-year plan. Early in May 1937, for example, Shanghai missionaries attempted to seize control of the organization, but Li Denghui and others on the executive committee rallied behind Garfield Huang, declaring that the association would rather suspend its work than compromise its long-held position against legalization of the drug, and would never hand over the NAOA to any party, including missionaries.[74]

Late in May, New Life figures close to Jiang met with NAOA executive committee members and some missionaries and offered to fund the NAOA indefinitely, with Garfield Huang as general secretary, so long as Huang and the association agreed not to criticize the six-year plan until after 1940.

The modified program of the NAOA would be limited to anti-narcotics education and exposés of Japanese drug trafficking in China for international and domestic purposes. The Nanjing group also offered to "clear up General Chiang's misunderstandings regarding Mr. Garfield Huang's strong anti-government and anti-monopoly activities in the past" if Huang consented to the proposal.[75]

While the NAOA was mulling over the government's offer, Jiang Jieshi as director general of opium suppression reviewed the initial results of his six-year plan at a public gathering to celebrate Opium Prohibition Memorial Day (3 June). Jiang claimed that opium cultivation had been eliminated in twelve provinces and reduced in several others, that more than 3.6 million smokers had registered with the government, and that facilities for treating opium addiction had been opened in 970 locations. The key to success, Jiang added, lay in the New Life Movement:

> *Jinyan* . . . is the most important foundation for implementing this New Life Movement. The movement places special emphasis on the virtues of orderliness, cleanliness, punctuality and diligence, which are directly opposed to the laziness and slovenliness of opium addicts. . . . While we ourselves must lead a new life, we must also use our utmost influence with a view to delivering the opium addicts from the Valley of Death. Only then can we fulfill the responsibilities imposed by the New Life Movement.[76]

By fusing biblical imagery, the New Life Movement, and his six-year plan, Jiang had seized the moral high ground in his military campaign against narcotics. Backed by legions of statistics to justify his policy of *yujin yuzheng*, the generalissimo's drug war impressed Chinese and foreigners alike. Several weeks after Jiang's sermon, Garfield Huang and the executive committee of the association decided to refuse Nanjing's proposal. On 28 June 1937 the association formally announced its dissolution, fulfilling its 1934 prophecy to American consular officials that it would "rather die as a martyr than to live an easy life."[77]

NOTES

1. *Annual Report of the International Anti-Opium Association* 4, no. 1 (May 1924): 18.
2. Ibid., pp. 4–5; Yu Ende, *Zhongguo jinyan faling bianqian shi*, pp. 193–94.
3. Yu Ende, *Zhongguo jinyan*, pp. 184–85.
4. The first general secretary of the Anti-Narcotics Commission was Dr. S. H. Chüan, who was soon replaced by R. Y. Lo; see *Chinese Recorder* 55 (March 1924): 176–80; Lo, *Opium Problem in the Far East*, p. 28.
5. *Chinese Recorder* 55 (March 1924): 176.
6. Ibid.; Yu Ende, *Zhongguo jinyan*, p. 185.

7. *North China Herald,* 9 August 1924, 24 August 1924; *Hankow Herald,* 26 July 1929.

8. According to *Opium, A World Problem (OWP)* 2, no. 4 (July 1929): ii, the constituent bodies were: National Christian Council, National Committee YMCA, National Medical Association, Shanghai General Chamber of Commerce, Jiangsu Educational Association, Shanghai Students Union, National Women's Federation of China, National Medical and Pharmaceutical Association, Shanghai Medical Practitioners Union, Women's Christian Temperance Union, World Chinese Students Federation, Red Cross Society of China, Council on Health Education of China, Overseas Chinese Union, Welfare Association for Chinese Abroad, Buddhist Association of Shanghai, Limen Anti-Opium League, Chinese Rate-Payers Union of the International Settlement, Newspaper's Union of Shanghai, Far East Association of Shanghai, Vocational Educational Association of China, China Christian Educational Association, Libraries Union of China, National Road Construction Association, Streets Union of Shanghai, Zhabei Chamber of Commerce, Fujian Association of Shanghai, Wenzhou Association of China, Shanghai YMCA, Shanghai YWCA, Young People's Lecture Bureau of Shanghai, Nandao Christian Institute of Shanghai, Shanghai Preachers Union, Shanghai Merchants Union, Shanghai Women's Union, Shanghai Farmers Union, and the All-Zhejiang Association.

9. Bergère, "Chinese Bourgeoisie," pp. 774–77.

10. Sovik, "Church and State in Republican China," pp. 128–248.

11. Lutz, *Chinese Politics and Christian Missions,* pp. 81–90; Latourette, *History of Christian Missions in China,* pp. 793–806; Sovik, "Church and State in Republican China," pp. 161–63.

12. *OWP* 1, no. 3 (March 1928): i.

13. *OWP* 3, no. 1 (October 1929): 16–19.

14. *OWP* 1, no. 2 (November 1927): i.

15. *OWP* 1, no. 3 (March 1928): 48; *Who's Who in China* (1931), pp. 445–46.

16. *Who's Who in China* (1931), pp. 240–41.

17. *Who's Who in China* (1933), p. 19.

18. USDS 893.114/2012; Latourette, *History of Christian Missions,* pp. 798.

19. *Who's Who in China* (1933), p. 110.

20. The English translations of *Judu yuekan* (Opium, A National Issue) and *Zhongguo yanhuo nianjian* (China Opium Yearbook) are by the NAOA, not the author.

21. *China Christian Yearbook 1926,* p. 329; *North China Herald,* 16 May 1925.

22. *Judu yuekan* 41 (February 1931): 50–52; *Chinese Recorder* 55 (November 1924): 751.

23. League of Nations, C.86.M.35.1927.XI, p. 130.

24. *Judu yuekan* 4 (September 1926): 24.

25. Ibid., p. 25; *China Weekly Review,* 3 April 1926.

26. *Luhaijun dayuanshuai dabenying gongbao* (Headquarters of the Commander in Chief of the Armed Services' Bulletin), no. 2 (February 1924), Zhiling; *Guangzhou shi shizheng gongbao* 115 (1924): 20–22, 117.

27. Sun Wen, *Guofu quanji,* 2:881–83; *Jinyan xuanchuan huikan,* pp. 6–8; *Dongfang zazhi* 21, no. 2 (1924): 154.

28. Sovik, "Church and State in Republican China," pp. 161–62, 198–200.

29. Ibid., pp. 214–20; Baumler, "Playing with Fire: The Nationalist Government and Popular Anti-Opium Agitation in 1927–28," p. 57.

30. Fewsmith, *Party, State, and Local Elites in Republican China*, pp. 89–166, 194.

31. *China Yearbook 1928*, pp. 524–39; *Judu yuekan* 23 (July 1928): 9–53.

32. *China Weekly Review*, 14 May 1927; *OWP* 1, no. 1 (1927): 7–8.

33. Slack, "Guomindang's Opium Policies," pp. 174–86.

34. *OWP* 1, no. 1 (1927): 8; Yu Ende, *Zhongguo jinyan*, p. 191.

35. *OWP* 1, no. 2 (November 1927): 5–6; Yu Ende, *Zhongguo jinyan*, p. 192.

36. *Judu yuekan* 22 (June 1928): 7; Yu Ende, *Zhongguo jinyan*, p. 202; *North China Herald*, 17 December 1927.

37. *OWP* 1, no. 3 (March 1928): 29–33, 36; *Judu yuekan* 18 (February 1928): 11.

38. *Judu yuekan* 22 (June 1928): 7.

39. *North China Herald*, 14 July 1928.

40. *OWP* 2, no. 1 (1928): 5–8.

41. Zhang Zhijiang, *Quanguo jinyan huiyi huibian*, pp. 1–32.

42. *China Critic*, 15 November 1928; *North China Herald*, 17 November 1928; *China Weekly Review*, 17 November 1928.

43. Zhang Zhijiang, *Quanguo jinyan*, pp. 39–40.

44. Yu Ende, *Zhongguo jinyan*, pp. 300–1; Tyau, *Two Years of Nationalist China*, pp. 305–9.

45. *Shibao*, 30 January 1929; *Guomin zhengfu gongbao* 177 (1929): 203.

46. *Dongfang zazhi* 27, no. 13 (1929): 127.

47. Slack, "Guomindang's Opium Policies," pp. 206–47.

48. Ibid., pp. 220–27.

49. *Shenbao*, 17 April 1929.

50. Slack, "Guomindang's Opium Policies," pp. 228–47.

51. BFO 6, F 1698/22/87, enc. 2.

52. Lai, *Guomin zhengfu liunian jinyan jihua jiqi chengxiao*, pp. 76–77; *China Weekly Review*, 14 February 1931.

53. *China Weekly Review*, 28 February 1931.

54. *Shenbao*, 14 and 20 February 1931; *North China Herald*, 17 and 24 February 1931.

55. *OWP* 4, no. 4 (1931): 2–4; *China Weekly Review*, 18 July 1931.

56. *OWP* 4, no. 4 (1931): 29; *China Critic*, 16 April 1931.

57. *OWP* 4, no. 4 (1931): 33.

58. USDS 893.114/625, 893.114/1992, enc. 1.

59. USDS 893.114/625. The NAOA was originally headquartered in the NCC from August 1924 to July 1927, then in the Shanghai Banker's Association until late 1932 or early 1933.

60. Ibid.

61. Lien-teh Wu, *Plague Fighter*, pp. 471–99.

62. *OWP* 4, no. 4 (1931): 32–33.

63. USDS 893.114/625; *China Weekly Review*, 3 December 1932.

64. Slack, "Guomindang's Opium Policies," pp. 273–91.

65. Neizhengbu, *Neizheng nianjian*, 2:574–77.

66. Ibid.

67. William Wei, *Counterrevolution in China*, pp. 76–81; T'ang, *Reconstruction in China*, pp. 33–46.

68. The titles of the two tracts issued in conjunction with the parade were "Qing guoren jichu yapiandu" (Appeal to citizens urgently to eradicate the opium poison), and "Yapian mafei baimian hongwan weifa qiangshen wangguo miezhong chedi saochu" (Thoroughly eradicate opium, morphine, heroin, and red pills, which are against the law, kill the body, subjugate the nation, and destroy the people); see *Zhongyang ribao*, 2 May 1934.

69. *Nanjing shi zhengfu gongbao* 141 (1934): 79–81.

70. *Zhongyang ribao*, 4 June 1934; *Shenbao*, 4 June 1934.

71. Xin shenghuo yundong cujin zonghui, *Minguo ershisannian xin shenghuo yundong zongbaogao*, p. 370.

72. *China Christian Year Book 1934–35*, p. 349.

73. Thompson, *While China Faced West*, pp. 151–95.

74. USDS 893.114/1992, enc. 1.

75. Ibid.

76. *Zhongyang ribao*, 4 June 1937.

77. *Chinese Recorder* 68 (August 1937): 533–34; USDS 893.114/625.

TWELVE

Opium Control versus Opium Suppression

The Origins of the 1935 Six-Year Plan to Eliminate Opium and Drugs

Alan Baumler

In the literature on Western societies, opium use has usually been presented as an issue of social deviance and its control. In Asia, however, opium is best seen as an issue of state and nation-building. The opium trade was a vital source of income and power for most of the colonial and national states of East and Southeast Asia. In China in particular dealing with opium was an important part of the project of defining China's nationhood. At the same time, growing public belief that opium was debilitating for both the individual user and society made it less and less acceptable for a government, especially a national government, to rely on opium profits.

A crucial point in the Chinese state's relationship to opium was the 1935 Six-Year Plan to eliminate opium and drugs. The plan was intended both to bring the opium trade and its profits under government control and to purify the nation by reducing the total amount of opium used in China. These two goals were seen as contradictory by many at the time and by most scholars today. Frederic Wakeman summarizes the goals of the plan and offers a typical dismissal:

> Well-meaning proponents of drug legalization like Dr. Wu Liande could argue quite cogently about the need for a government-controlled monopoly that would enable public health authorities to use the system of registration and detoxification clinics *(jieyan shi)* to cure addicts of their habit. Political "realists" like the Generalissimo's brother-in-law T. V. Soong could emphasize the importance to the state of appropriating vast private revenues that otherwise fell into gangsters' hands. And important military and police advisers such as Chief Cai Jingjun [head of the Shanghai Public Security Bureau] could underscore the urgency of depriving provincial warlords and Japanese "special organs" of such lucrative resources. But the fact remained that Chiang Kai-shek and his supporters fooled no one when they claimed that by

seeking to monopolize the sale of opium they were really "killing two birds with one stone" *(yi ju liang de)*: covering military costs on the one hand while curing drug addicts on the other.[1]

Although Wakeman seems to dismiss the campaign as mere window dressing, elsewhere he says that "there was no question about the government's sincere and serious intentions during the 1934–1936 opium suppression campaign."[2] Wakeman's ambivalence toward the plan is similar to that of contemporary Chinese and demonstrates two approaches to the opium problem, which I will label the moral or suppression approach and the control or state-building approach. The older one, the control approach, called for bringing the opium trade under government supervision so that it could be taxed. This would both provide revenue to the government and deny power to warlords and local elites. Since at least 1891 the Chinese government had attempted to control and tax the opium trade.[3] Like the many colonial governments that taxed opium the Qing court was not happy about its involvement with the drug, but opium was an excellent source of revenue and a mainstay of the government's finances. Policy therefore focused on controlling the trade and profiting from it more than eliminating it. In the late nineteenth century, however, new "moral" ideas about opium became common. These ideas portrayed the drug as a danger to the health of the individual and the nation. In China this led to the 1906–1917 antiopium campaigns, a classic case of moral suppression. Because the drug was now seen as a threat to the New China, the government could not possibly have anything to do with it, and a moral, modern, and nationalistic government should eliminate it, whatever the cost. The new ideas did not entirely replace the old, however, either at the popular level, where opium use remained common, or in the government, where the lure of opium revenue was still strong.

The ambivalence toward opium caused by these conflicting ideas created countless traps for twentieth-century Chinese governments. No government could afford to sacrifice its legitimacy by openly selling opium, yet none could resist the power and profits that came from control of the opium trade. The Qing had developed a system of opium suppression based on licensing that allowed the government to maintain some involvement in the trade while claiming to be morally pure. This could sometimes be effective, but the license model could not justify the large-scale opium system that Nanjing needed to finance its operations and bring its rivals to heel. Between 1932 and 1935 the Nationalists developed a new way of thinking about opium that would culminate in the 1935 Six-Year Plan to eliminate opium and drugs. The core of the new approach was to emphasize the importance of taking control of the trade before eliminating it, thus making opium control a necessary prerequisite for opium suppression. The new plan grew out of Nanjing's attempts to control opium for revenue purposes, but by 1935 the government's opium control system was efficient enough that it could be presented as a comprehensive solution to China's opium problem that transcended the dilemma of suppression versus control.

LICENSING SYSTEMS

During the late-Qing anti-opium campaigns the government developed an opium suppression system based on licensing opium growers and users to produce and consume gradually decreasing amounts of the drug. This model became the standard way for Chinese governments to deal with the opium problem. The license system grew out of the ambivalence toward opium caused by the conflict between the new ideas about opium and the old, and at the same time the license system encouraged this ambivalence. Gradual reduction was preferred because it was more lenient toward opium addicts and peasant poppy growers. In a strict moral approach the socioeconomic status of users and growers would not matter, since all those involved in opium were evil and deserved punishment. Many Chinese still had more old-fashioned ideas about opium, however. The users were likely to be one's family or acquaintances, and growers were poor peasants trying to make a living; shooting them, the ultimate "moral" policy, seemed cruel. The license system avoided excessive cruelty toward these people while still moving toward the moralist goal of opium suppression. At the same time the system solidified this ambivalence toward opium, first by certifying that poppy growing was not entirely criminal and by presenting users as victims rather than criminals, and second by bringing the government substantial revenue, revenue that implicated the government in the trade and that the state was reluctant to give up. Although the stated goal of these systems was always the moral goal of eliminating opium use, many of these systems were little more than covers for revenue-producing opium monopolies. The license system was ideally suited to a cover-up because there would be no difference in form between a revenue-oriented and a suppression-oriented license system. Only the government's honesty in its claims that it would eventually eliminate the trade could differentiate the two.

When the Chinese Nationalists united the country in 1927, they had been operating a standard warlord-style opium monopoly in Canton for some years. After their arrival in Shanghai they attempted to extend this system to the entire country, a move that met with strong resistance from the forces of modern public opinion in Shanghai and elsewhere. After the defeat of this first attempt to control the national opium trade, Nanjing contented itself with a profitable but circumspect involvement in the Yangzi opium trade. Nanjing's involvement in the Yangzi trade was protected by denying that the government was involved, that is, by lying. This was a time-honored tactic that the Communists used as well.[4] It could not, however, conceal a large-scale opium monopoly, and the government continued to look for a way to justify greater involvement with opium. In 1931 the government attempted to impose a national opium monopoly, justifying it on the grounds that the government was morally pure and could be trusted to eventually end the trade. This too was an old tactic, and it too failed. By 1932 Nationalist opium policy centered on the Hankou Special Tax Office, the center of Nanjing's involvement in the Yangzi river opium route, and from 1932 to 1935 the Hankou office's control over China's opium trade was gradually extended. The expansion of the Hankou office was originally aimed at control of the trade rather than suppression, but as the office's power expanded Hankou became an important part of Nanjing's campaign against its warlord rivals, and in 1935 the expansion of the Hankou model was reconceptualized and presented as a comprehensive and successful way to finally solve the opium problem.

THE HANKOU SPECIAL TAX OFFICE

The Hunan-Hubei Special Tax Office *(Lianghu teshui bu)*, the government's opium tax bureau in Hankou, was the center of the government's new policy. Hankou had long been a major station for taxing Sichuan opium on its way down the Yangzi River to Shanghai, and it also saw a good deal of Yunnan, Guizhou, and Hunan opium. Besides being the center of the national wholesale opium trade, Hankou was also the center of the lucrative Hubei retail market, and thus the city was always a bone of contention for the warlords. From 1927 to early 1929 the wholesale and retail trade were controlled by the Hankou Special Tax Office, technically in the name of the Ministry of Finance, but actually for the Guangxi clique. In May 1929 Jiang Jieshi (Chiang Kai-shek) took control of the city and gave control of the tax office to Huang Zhenxing, a central government loyalist. From this point on the revenues of Hankou would support Jiang, and he in turn would try to force as much of the trade as possible through Hankou.[5] He was helped in this by the economic logic of opium in China. The southwestern provinces of Sichuan, Yunnan, and Guizhou had always produced better and cheaper opium than other areas. During the disorder of the warlord period opium was particularly difficult to ship, and local producers all over China dominated the trade. With the reimposition of order after 1927, cheap, high-quality West China opium tended to drive other opium off the market. Hankou was a natural place for western opium to pass through on its way to the main markets, and thus the natural center of the opium trade. To realize the potential of this position Jiang would have to maintain and expand the Hankou office's control of the trade. Ultimately this would mean controlling every part of the trade from grower to smoker.

This was something of a departure from the existing pattern of opium control in China. Western warlords were already beginning to monopolize production in their areas, but they had no control over the marketing of their opium downstream. Distribution monopolies were also being set up downstream, but these relied on upstream suppliers. By taking the middle position the central government could put both the suppliers and the distributors at its mercy.

Although it would become the centerpiece of Jiang's opium control efforts, the Hankou office started out modestly, with limited control of the wholesale and retail trade in Hankou. The most important task of the office was controlling the wholesale trade. Although both Yangzi opium and Han River opium had to come past the city, opium shippers had no desire to pay taxes if they could avoid it, and many tried to do just that. Opium merchants had countless tricks that could be used to get a few chests of opium past Hankou, and the local police and the smugglers engaged in constant duels throughout the period.[6] Significant shipments, however, were more difficult to conceal, and the government tried to make tax avoidance still more difficult by extending its control up and down the river. By 1931 Hankou's Hunan suboffice had thirty men at its main office and more at the six other offices up and down the Han River.[7] The office was intended to prevent illegal opium shipments on the river, and there were similar offices on the other main opium routes, the goal being to keep the entire shipping route under surveillance and thus make smuggling much more difficult than just slipping past Hankou.

Besides preventing illegal opium shipments, the tax office began taking control of the legal trade. In 1929 the office's financial matters seem to have been run by the Central Bank, but in order to prevent T. V. Soong from getting involved, Jiang set up the Agricultural Bank of the Four Provinces, later the Farmer's Bank of China, to handle financial matters.[8] Given the scale of the trade, most merchants lacked the capital to buy opium outright, so they were reliant on loans. Now this capital would come from Jiang, providing him with both new profits and more control over the opium merchants.

Although it was not a major focus of the government's effort, the Special Tax Office was also expected to control retailers. Ideally the government would control the flow of opium from the producer to the consumer. In Hankou itself the government was willing to be fairly lenient with the merchants in order to get them under control. In 1930 the Hankou opium merchants were organized into the Hankou Special Enterprise Administrative Association *(Hankou teye qingli hui)*. The merchants were given six months to sell off their existing stocks of opium, and after that the association would be the marketing arm for official opium in Hankou.[9] Various levels of opium dens were set up to sell the opium directly to users, ensuring that all levels of the trade, from high-class dens for the rich to opium sheds (*yan penghu*) for poor laborers, were brought under government control. This system of retail control was fairly loose, which was to be expected. The government's chief goal at this point was to bring existing opium dealers into its system. Once this had been done control could be tightened.

The retail trade was open at both the top and the bottom, with few barriers to entry and little central control. In the mid 1930s the Yunnan warlords managed to set up a fourth opium *hang* in the city, and since they sold at a good price they did quite well.[10] Dens and sheds for opium smoking were licensed, but beyond that the government had little control. One family owned dens in several cities along the river, something that would be discouraged later because it made smuggling easy and made the den owner harder to control.[11] Besides the official opium sold by the *hang*, much illicit opium flowed through the city, and all the dens sold it. Theoretically opium users were also supposed to be licensed, although this seems to have been a dead letter. In the earlier anti-opium campaigns, which were based on eliminating opium use as a moral evil, this loose control would have been considered a disaster, but the primary purpose of this opium system was making money and denying money to potential rivals. Eliminating opium use was at best a secondary goal. Although this sort of policy was roundly condemned by moralistic critics like the Anti-Opium Association, it was a success in terms of controlling the opium trade.

The Hankou system was quite profitable, and during 1929 and 1930 the Hankou Special Tax Office brought in about one million yuan a month from the wholesale and retail trades. The Hankou office's success made it vital to the financing of the campaigns against the Communists, and in 1933 it was put under the authority of Jiang Jieshi's Anti-Bandit [that is, anticommunist] Headquarters. A statement made by the Anti-Bandit Headquarters on 1 November 1933 is explicit about the importance of opium revenue:

> Inasmuch as the income derivable from opium tax has long been the chief source of revenue from which the monthly expenses of Hupeh Provincial Government, and the Hupeh Dyke Construction and the emergency expenses of the anticommunist campaign within the three provinces are drawn, it has been designated as proper government revenue as distinguished from illegitimate extortion for selfish purposes so characteristic of the former militarist regime.[12]

Besides showing that the government was still relying on its supposed moral superiority to distinguish its opium policy from that of the warlords, this quotation also shows how dependent the Nationalists were on opium revenue. Rather than using their control to reduce the trade, as a moral model would require, the Nationalists began to expand and regularize the

Hankou office and expand its approach to the entire country. Control spread upriver, ultimately right up to the opium producer, and downriver to the end users. At the same time, the operations of the office came more and more under the direct control of Jiang Jieshi. As the office became an important source of power, it had to be kept under Jiang's control.

THE ANTI-OPIUM INSPECTORATE

Just as the Hankou office's control of the trade was fairly loose at first, so was Nanjing's control of the office, presenting many opportunities for corruption for Hankou opium officials. Huang Zhenxing, head of the original Special Tax Office, took advantage of most of these opportunities.[13] His dismissal for corruption was the initial impetus for the reform of the office, but the reforms went much further than a simple cleanup. The office was thoroughly revamped to put it more closely under Jiang Jieshi's control and its power began to expand.

In 1933 the Hankou Special Tax office was reorganized as the Opium Suppression Inspectorate (*Jinyan ducha chu*), with authority over ten provinces. The new inspectorate was deliberately divided into several sections, with control of each section given to members of different government cliques, thus preventing any one clique from dominating the office.[14] As the office became more and more powerful, keeping it directly under Jiang's control became more and more important, and even many of the day-to-day decisions that it made were referred directly to him.[15]

Part of the purpose of the inspectorate was to provide Jiang with at least one source of revenue that was not controlled by T. V. Soong, and both personnel and financial matters were handled accordingly.[16] The heads of the Shanghai and Hubei offices, the secretary of the inspectorate, and many of the other officials were Swatow men, connected to the old Swatow opium group that had controlled the opium trade in Shanghai before Du Yuesheng. They were experienced in the opium trade but had no connections to either Du or T. V. Soong.[17]

The first job of the new office was to perfect its control over the Hankou-Shanghai opium route. This involved eliminating opium smuggling and standardizing and regularizing the system for shipping legal opium. To control smugglers the government greatly increased the number of police detailed to stop smuggling on the Yangzi river. A new River Police was set up under Jiang Dingwen, in theory having 15,000 men and patrolling all parts of the river. In practice they may not have reached this number, and they dealt with smuggling of other goods besides opium, but the prime purpose of all of these new police was to control opium smuggling, and they were far more numerous than the earlier anti-smuggling teams.[18]

The inspectorate also regularized the shipping of legal opium. The route used by the inspectorate was essentially the same as that used by the old Special Tax Office, and the merchants seem to have been much the same as well, but the system was far more controlled. Most opium officials knew that the most successful opium smugglers were often legal opium traders. They had access to opium, they knew the market, and they had licenses to carry opium. It was not enough to simply license merchants; they had to be carefully supervised.

By 1934 the inspectorate was managing the Hankou to Shanghai opium route with a high degree of efficiency, although regularization had doubtless begun before this. Between June and October 1934 two ships, the *Chu Ying* and the *Wan Shou,* made the Hankou-Shanghai run nine times. Each stopped at several ports along the way to unload opium. The ships delivered opium to relatively large cities such as Anqing, Datong, and Wuhu, but also to tiny places such as Digang, Anhui. All of the Yangzi ports were apparently fully integrated into the retailing system. The opium was shipped in chests of about one thousand *liang* each. Smaller towns might get only three chests, whereas Shanghai would usually get about one hundred. Each chest was licensed, and the numbers of the licenses used were checked on arrival. Any discrepancies led to an investigation.[19] The departure and arrival of each shipment was reported directly to Jiang in his capacity as military affairs commissioner. In Shanghai at least some, and probably all, of the opium was delivered to Du Yuesheng's Three Prosperities Company.[20] In other places the opium was supposed to be marketed by opium shops run by the inspectorate, although in many cases low-level retailing was not fully under government control.

The financial end of the trade was also put under tighter control. By 1934 everything was under the control of Jiang's Farmer's Bank.[21] Before the opium arrived in Hankou, the merchant bought it in one of the southwestern provinces and shipped it to Hankou, paying various taxes along the way. Merchants seem to have purchased the opium on their own, or borrowed money from elsewhere, but to pay the transit taxes of 1,300 yuan per *dan* they needed help. Merchants who had a guarantor could mortgage their opium to the Farmer's Bank at 60–80 percent of the market price for up to three months and thus pay their taxes. Taxes owed to the central government could be paid directly to the Farmer's Bank. Once the opium arrived in Hankou, merchants could purchase opium with forty-five-day Farmer's Bank promissory notes. After selling the opium downriver they could pay off the note at any Farmer's Bank branch or, if there was no branch in the area, a representative would be sent to collect the money.[22] Although there seems to have been some involvement by other banks, the financial side of the trade was firmly in Jiang's hands.

At the same time that Nanjing was solidifying control over the center of the opium route, it was also guaranteeing supplies and markets by coming

to agreements with producers in Sichuan and distributors such as Du
Yuesheng in Shanghai. The Sichuan connection was Liu Xiang. Like most
of the warlords in this divided province Liu relied on selling opium downstream to finance his activities. From 1928 Liu Xiang was supplying opium
to the Hankou merchants, and by the mid 1930s he had some sort of
agreement the Jiang to do this on a regular basis; in 1936 he agreed to
"continue current arrangements" to send eight hundred *dan* of opium a
month to Hankou.[23] Opium from all over Sichuan was collected at Yichang,
paid Liu's taxes, and then moved downriver. Liu received weapons in return and gradually became the chief warlord of Sichuan because of this.[24]
He also became increasingly tied to the national government as he became
more and more dependent on marketing his opium through Hankou. He
attempted to wiggle out of this position by infiltrating Jiang's opium system
and by marketing refined drugs, but both efforts failed.[25] Besides making
money, Jiang's opium system was also helping him to control the warlords.

Jiang also entered into an agreement of some sort with Du Yuesheng,
China's Al Capone, to market opium in Shanghai.[26] Wakeman calls his
chapter on this matter "Criminalizing the Government" and contends that
in making this deal the Guomindang sold out its principles for opium
money.[27] In the context of Nanjing's larger control of the trade, however,
Du Yuesheng was not taking over the government but becoming the Shanghai opium farmer. Jiang needed Du to market his opium in Shanghai, but
Du was dependent on regular supplies of Jiang's opium. Brian Martin portrays Du's Green Gang as an example of an intermediate institution between the modernizing state society, providing the state with a degree of
control over local society that the state was unable or unwilling to exert for
itself and providing the gang with a bit of legitimacy.[28] In the case of opium
this is exactly how the Green Gang functioned.

This system was beneficial for Nanjing and for its clients at both ends of
the river, and they became willing to fight to defend it. In 1934 the Twenty-
first Army (Liu Xiang's army, stationed in Sichuan) heard rumors that a
group from French Indochina was trying to buy up a large amount of Yunnanese opium and ship it to Shanghai. The army passed this information
along to the inspectorate, which in turn passed it to Du Yuesheng. With
Du's help the inspectorate investigated the matter from the Shanghai end
and found nothing, but Du asked the inspectorate to keep looking into it.
Soon afterward the inspectorate reported that the whole affair was being
arranged by a Guizhou merchant, Ma Shi, who was arranging with important people in Yunnan to buy five hundred tons of opium. He planned to
pay half the value of the opium up front and then ship it to Shanghai via
French Indochina. The inspectorate had a complete list of taxes and bribes
that would have to be paid to get the opium to Shanghai and estimated
that it would cost about 1.2 yuan a *liang*. Given that the current price in

Shanghai was about 1.7 yuan a *liang*, this deal would easily undercut the government's monopoly. The inspectorate was, of course, worried about the impact that this would have on opium tax collection, but Du Yuesheng was all but frantic. He said that he agreed that tax revenues would fall, but more important, this plot would give foreigners the power to poison the nation with opium and would destroy all the progress that had been made so far in opium suppression. This statement was an example of Du's enormous chutzpah but also an example of how he assumed the government saw the problem of opium. The main point of opium suppression at this point was to put the trade under the government's control, and this Yunnan gambit threatened to destroy that control.[29] This case also reflects the considerable power of the inspectorate. It was capable of launching secret investigations even in places not under Nanjing's control, and gathered excellent data. One of the suggestions for foiling this plot was for the inspectorate to disrupt the opium harvest in Yunnan, which would suggest at least some capacity for covert action.[30]

In addition to regularizing the Hankou-Shanghai route and doing intelligence work, the inspectorate was constantly trying to extend its control geographically. These attempts often met with rebuffs, but inevitably the control of the inspectorate over the trade grew. The inspectorate tried to eliminate rivals in the wholesale business and force as much of the retail trade as possible into its system. In both of these endeavors it had success.

THE INSPECTORATE AND THE PROVINCES

By 1934 the Yangzi river opium route and the major western warlords were being integrated into Jiang's opium system. The semi-independent western warlords were only one of Jiang's problems. He also had to deepen his reach into local society in the areas in East China that Nanjing already controlled. The inspectorate was also involved in eliminating the problem of "residual warlordism."

Even in the areas controlled by Nanjing, local military commanders were involved in opium, and in most cases they were effectively beyond the law. Indeed, the two went hand in hand; opium was the source of revenue most likely to make a military commander financially independent and thus able to defy, ignore, or subvert government orders. Chi Hsi-sheng defines a warlord or regional militarist as someone who controlled armed force in a system where such force was the basis of political power,[31] but this definition is inadequate. In order to function as an independent militarist one also needed a regular source of income independent of one's theoretical superiors. Usually this came from exploiting a territory. Warlord armies could exist for a time without a territory to exploit, but if this condition lasted too long the army would disintegrate, with subcommanders either finding a new patron or finding a territory of their own to exploit and thus becoming warlords themselves. Opium was an excellent revenue source, and in many areas in China the return of poppy cultivation in the early Republic came because poppy cultivation was being encouraged, if not coerced, by the emerging warlords.

The Northern Expedition of 1927–1928 had ended open warlordism in much of China, but it left behind the problem of "residual warlordism." Many of those supposedly under Jiang's command were effectively independent, and his ability to demand and get compliance even in the areas he controlled was limited. Jiang's internal policies during the 1930s emphasized breaking the power of the remaining major warlords, but he also had to prevent his "own" commanders from getting control of their own financial resources and "reverting" to warlordism, that is, to independence. It was unlikely that any of the small commanders under Jiang would become independent warlords, but independence was relative. None of the regional militarists, not even those in the Southwest, were entirely independent of Jiang's government, the source of legitimacy and the acknowledged center of the Chinese nation. On the other hand, very few commanders could be considered completely loyal. Most of them oscillated along a continuum of greater or lesser loyalty as their power and Jiang's waxed and waned. One of the most important ways to keep these commanders under control was to deny them opium revenue. Opium was the most natural source of revenue for a local warlord, but it was also the easiest one for the central government to interfere with. Warlords could not publicly defend their control of the trade, nor could they compete economically with cheap government opium. Jiang began denying this revenue to local militarists and garrisons as one of the first steps of his opium control program. As the inspectorate was consolidating its control over the main Yangzi river opium route, it was also spreading its power into the provinces, taking over the smaller distribution routes all over East China and eventually reaching all the way down to the retail level with the goal of denying revenues to local militarists and local elites. The amount of effort Nanjing was willing to expend on this varied; Fujian, Hunan, and Henan are good examples of the different levels of penetration.

FUJIAN AND THE SUCCESS OF A COMPREHENSIVE DISTRIBUTION MONOPOLY

Fujian province had been taken over during the Northern Expedition, but even though it remained under Nanjing's de jure control after 1928, many of the garrisons became quite independent, often relying on opium revenue to make them so. Fujian elites had considerable success in suppressing opium in the early Republic, but during the warlord period most of these gains were lost.[32] Fujian was unlike other provinces in that it was close to both the center of the regime's power and to two of its greatest concerns, the Communists' Jiangxi Soviet and the semi-independent Canton group. The Fujian garrisons themselves were small and disunited and Fujian was thus important and relatively easy to bring under control. An attempt at what might be called heroic opium suppression, based on the moral model, was made early in the 1930s by the Nineteenth Route Army. The Nineteenth Route Army made no compromises on opium and exerted considerable effort to eradicate it. Poppy was uprooted and dealers were shot, but as usual with little effect.[33] Real success came only under Governor Chen Yi, who aimed first at control of the trade and only second at suppression. By 1934 Chen Yi had tamed the garrisons and brought the province solidly under control.[34] Once Chen was in control he brought opium under control as well. The inspectorate's control of wholesale opium shipments into the province made it easy for the central government to take over retail sales. Cheap official opium, along with steps taken to suppress poppy growing, reduced local production to a minor nuisance. Opium control in Fujian was not entirely aimed at revenue, however. As control was extended, private merchants were eased out of the system and smokers were registered and began to be put through programs intended to cure them. The province was thus a model of the new comprehensive opium policy and had success in achieving both control of the trade and eventually its suppression.

Poppy growers were prosecuted under Chen, but this was not the center of policy. Chen's actions against poppy growers were fairly typical. The province was divided into sections, and inspectors were sent out. If poppy was discovered, it was uprooted. This was not an ineffective policy, but it could not eliminate poppy cultivation entirely. Small-scale local poppy cultivation kept coming back. Given the fragmented nature of poppy cultivation in Fujian, this was not surprising. The plots that were being found were small, and the government could do little to entirely eliminate small peasant plots of poppy.[35] They could and did, however, reduce the problem of poppy growing in Fujian to a minor nuisance.

From the beginning of 1935 Fujian began putting opium sales under control with the help of the Opium Suppression Inspectorate. The inspectorate was to provide good-quality Sichuan opium at the price of one yuan per *liang*.[36] Licensed merchants brought opium into the province along approved routes and deposited it in official warehouses run by the Opium Suppression Inspectorate in Fuzhou and Xiamen.[37] The Yu Min (Enriching Fujian) Company bought the right to set up wholesale opium stores *(tugao hang)*, and they distributed the opium to licensed retail shops all over the province. The shops then sold the opium to licensed users. No doubt much opium was sold outside this system, but government opium was legal and of high quality and rapidly found a market. This system seems to have been quite successful in bringing opium retailing under control, and the inspectorate began plans to refine the system. The original goal seems to have been to bring everyone currently involved in the trade into the government system. Now the goal was to reduce the scope of the trade, both for the sake of reducing it and to make it easier to control. After June 1936 the number of opium shops started to be reduced with an eventual goal of having only one retail shop per county. During 1936 the number of wholesale shops was reduced from nineteen to six, and the next year it was reduced to four. The number of smaller shops remained steady at around seventy, but in 1937 they were split into four classes, with different license fees for different classes, presumably to ensure that even poor counties could afford a shop (keeping them from turning to smuggled opium) while assuring that merchants in richer counties paid high fees.[38] In April 1937 the wholesale monopoly was taken away from the Yu Min Company, and its manager was eventually arrested.[39] Wholesaling became the direct responsibility of the inspectorate.

Control of retailing was based on registration of users. Once the number of users in an area had been determined, only the amount of opium needed to maintain this number would be sent. The government pushed registration very hard, and it was the center of anti-opium propaganda. Dramatic performances and crosstalks were given all over the province, explaining to the common people that opium was not legal (this was stressed), but that users who were unable to quit at once would be allowed to register and continue use until they were called in to a detoxification center to be cured.[40] The process of registration began in 1935, but as in other provinces it was not as quick as had been hoped. By the middle of 1936 about half of the counties had completed registration, and a total of 111,482 users were registered. These counties were given quotas of opium based on the numbers of registered users. Quotas ranged from 0.5 to 1.6 *liang* per person per month, which may indicate that users were assigned to different categories based on their level of addiction.

The point of registering all these opium users was not just to determine the amount of opium needed, but also to begin the process of curing addicts. In 1935 Fujian had only one specialized anti-opium clinic, but in 1936 seventy-six more were opened, and by 1937 there were a total of eighty-four clinics or hospitals where addicts could go for cures. By 1937, 17,800 addicts had gone through the clinics.[41] Almost every county had a clinic of some sort. The smaller ones had as few as ten beds and budgets of as little as twenty yuan a month. Most of the clinics were probably supported largely by fees, although almost 90 percent of the users were on the special reduced-rate licenses for poor people. Each of the clinics was supposed to have at least one doctor, but it seems likely that many had minimal training. The clinics were supposed to make regular reports on numbers of addicts, ages, and numbers cured, and most seem to have done so fairly regularly.[42]

After the war started, the situation in Fujian changed. Wartime conditions called for even closer supervision of the opium trade. The opium *hang* were taken over by the government, and private merchants were removed from the process entirely. Each locality was to license a local person to set up a Smoker Cure Management Office *(Yanmin xian jie guanli suo)*, in effect an opium den, which would be the only place that male smokers were allowed to smoke. Women were to continue to be allowed to smoke at home, but this closer control over opium users was a major change.[43] All previous laws had forbidden opium dens entirely and required users to buy their opium and take it home to smoke it. This (if enforced) eliminated the opium den as a place for gathering and social interaction and presumably helped to reduce the number of casual users. Official opium dens had the advantage that they put the users under direct government supervision. Now all the legal opium in the province would be in government hands, which would make illegal opium easier to distinguish. Various fines were established for den owners who allowed nonregistered people to smoke or who allowed registered smokers to exceed their ration. The fines and the detailed reporting system show that these were not like the dens set up in Jiangsu, which, despite talk of registration, would sell to anyone.[44] In 1938 regulations were issued to allow the opium shops to go back to selling small containers of take-home opium, presumably because it had proved impossible to entirely restrict opium smoking to legal dens.[45] Fujian by this point had exactly what both the pro-revenue and the suppression forces in the government wanted, a small and fully controlled opium trade. There was no doubt still a good amount of private growing and smoking, and greater central control over the official system meant that this was now entirely outside the government system, but that was probably unavoidable.

The gradual suppression of opium use may be surprising if Nanjing's opium efforts are seen as aimed totally at revenue. Although Nanjing was eager to make profits from opium, the government also hoped to reduce the scope of the trade and eventually eliminate it. Besides the sincere convictions of at least some in the government that opium use was bad for China there was also a reluctance to encourage a trade that by its nature left considerable profits in the hands of local troops and local elites. One of the key goals of the entire effort was to take this money away from local power holders and thus reduce their independence. Nanjing thus had solid state-building reasons, as well as moral reasons, to reduce the scope of the trade.

Fujian would have to be called a success from all points of view. The power of the local garrisons had been broken, opium users were being cured, and only opium on which central government taxes had been paid could be sold in Fujian. This last point was the most important result of the system. It did not matter if Yunnanese warlords somehow managed to smuggle opium into Fujian. By 1938 the entire opium retailing system was controlled by the government. Even if outside opium did come, it would have to establish an entire new distribution network in order to compete with official opium. In 1929 the central government's opium control system consisted of Hankou. From the producer to Hankou and from Hankou to the consumer the trade was wide open, and avoiding the Special Tax Office in Hankou was not difficult. By 1938, at least in Fujian, the entire trade from one end to the other was under control. This control was not perfect, and attaining it took more resources than the government wanted to commit in most provinces, but Fujian was a model of what was wanted and an example of how effective the new system could be if run properly.

CO-OPTING THE EXISTING OPIUM SYSTEM IN HUNAN

In more remote areas and those where local resistance was stronger, the government pursued a more accommodationist policy than in Fujian. Hunan had an active opium trade with nearby Yunnan and Guizhou up until 1933 when the inspectorate began to close down the Hong river route, the main source of income for local garrisons.[46] In theory this should have put the entire trade under the control of the central government, but Nationalist troops began dealing in opium independently. In 1933 the Tenth Army of Xu Yuanquan was stationed in Changsha, the capital and main city of Hunan province, ostensibly to conduct anticommunist operations. Xu and his men actually proved to be more interested in buying up opium in the western part of the province and selling it in Changsha and Hankou. West Hunan had long been a producer of low-quality opium, and the government had usually ignored this, but when the opium began to move into more important markets, the government took action.[47] Jiang Jieshi's headquarters received news of Xu's actions and in August 1933 Jiang dispatched troops to help the Opium Suppression Inspectorate deal with the matter. They set up several inspection stations along the river, but Xu and his men had no trouble avoiding them. Sun Mingzhai, the head of the anti-smuggling detachment, knew that shipments were being received in Hankou by Yang Qingshan, the head of the Red Gang. Sun joined the Red Gang and became the brother of its leader in Changsha, Zheng Huatang. Zheng was unhappy with the cut he was getting, and was unable to do anything with Xu; he told Sun what routes Xu's boats and trucks used. Sun wired his superiors in Hankou and received permission to make a seizure, which he was supposed to do with the help of the local anti-smuggling office. They captured one truckload of opium and wired Nanchang for instructions. After first claiming that the truck belonged to the Tenth Army and should not be inspected, Xu and his men began trying to shift blame. It is not clear exactly what sort of a deal Jiang Jieshi made with Xu, but shortly orders came down that the Tenth Army, the garrison, and the local anti-smuggling office were to handle the case jointly. Xu returned to Changsha and had Zheng Huatang arrested and shot at dawn. The three sides then settled down to the business of buying up opium and shipping it.[48] This system was beneficial to all sides. In the long run it was easier for the local troops to take a cut from the distribution of Hankou opium, especially since prices of official and unofficial opium were about the same.[49] Cooperation was also easier for the central government. Peasants in West Hunan would have continued to grow opium regardless of what the government did; this way local opium became part of the system, not a rival to it. The central government had been forced to compromise somewhat with local forces but had still managed to take control of the wholesale opium trade without having to commit many resources to the effort.

HENAN AND LIMITED GOVERNMENT CONTROL

Both Fujian and Hunan were somewhat atypical. Fujian was close to both Shanghai and the Communists, so it received more attention than many other places. It also had an energetic and capable governor. Changsha was a major market and on a secondary opium route, so it too would receive a good deal of attention. Henan was more typical of the areas that did not matter as much. The province was poor, and since it was in the north it was not part of Jiang's power base. It was one of the ten provinces under the purview of the Opium Suppression Inspectorate, but before 1935 it received minimal attention.

Henan produced a certain amount of low-quality opium sold mainly inside the province. Better-quality opium came from Sichuan and Shaanxi. The main goals of the inspectorate in Henan were to make sure that the Sichuan opium smoked in the province came via Hankou and to try to lure as much of the Shaanxi opium as possible to Hankou for sale downriver. The central government was not much interested in the small local retail market. In some places the inspectorate could collect taxes itself; in others it used licensed merchants. Henan also had semi-independent garrisons that engaged in the trade. Even many of the officers of the inspectorate were collecting and pocketing extra taxes. Those officers who did try to carry out their duties often found that they had no support from the police or military, and a number of them were beaten or killed by opium smugglers. Although the inspectorate sold opium, most of the smoking happened in private opium dens that were not controlled by the government. Despite all this, much of the opium sold in the province was probably from the inspectorate. The inspectorate offered a better product at a better price, and even if its control of retailing was limited, it still dominated the market. In 1934 in a less important province like Henan this could be tolerated, but the government was already developing methods to put even these areas under fuller control.[50] By 1935 these new methods would start to be applied, and even in the less important parts of the province there would be efforts to put the trade under control.[51]

THE 1935 PLAN

In April 1935 the Nationalist government announced the Six-Year Plan to Eliminate Opium and Drugs. In most respects the plan was a continuation of policies that had already been started under the inspectorate, but whereas the old system was semi-secret, the new plan was publicly announced and heralded as the solution to China's opium problem. Almost nothing in the 1935 plan was new. Fundamentally, it was a grandiose licensing scheme: licensed growers in West China were to produce gradually decreasing amounts of opium for the Opium Suppression Inspectorate to distribute to registered users throughout China. What made the plan significant was its public honesty and the irresistible ideological force that this honesty and the government's previous successes in controlling opium gave it.

Jiang Jieshi had always been aware of the public relations problem that involvement with opium created. Accusations of opium dealing were dangerous to his standing both inside China and internationally. Before 1935 his reaction to this problem, like that of all his predecessors, was to run from it. Nanjing's involvement in the opium trade was kept as quiet as possible, working through intermediaries, shifting the focus to refined drugs, and emphasizing the do-nothing Opium Suppression Commission (*Jinyan weiyuanhui*) while keeping the inspectorate all but invisible. With the announcement of the 1935 plan, Jiang went on the offensive. The Opium Suppression Commission, which had been publicly waving the flag of opium suppression while the inspectorate took control of the trade, was abolished, and all opium affairs were put under a new Central Opium Suppression Commission (*Jinyan zonghui*) headed by Jiang himself. Jiang admitted that what the government would be selling was opium (*yandu*), not "anti-opium medicine" (*jieyan yao*) or any of the other euphemisms that had been used in the past. This honesty was possible because the plan was successfully presented as the only possible solution to China's opium problem. Jiang became China's savior rather than its betrayer, and those who resisted the plan became traitors.

In February 1936 Jiang Jieshi gave a speech outlining the benefits of the new plan. He refused to blame the problem on foreigners, which was a departure from previous discussions, locating the heart of the problem in the Chinese people themselves. The people lacked determination because they had lost faith in the government's ability to deal with the problem. Now that the government had found a method of controlling opium, the enthusiasm of the people could be reawakened and prove to the world that the Chinese were a strong race.[52] This speech neatly tied the moral approach to opium to the control approach: it was the government's ability to control opium, admittedly for revenue purposes, that would make possible the mass enthusiasm that would purify the nation. This purity was symbolized by the fact that students and government officials, as the leaders of society, would be forbidden to take out opium smoking licenses. Some places would also be designated opium-free, including Nanjing and Xiangshan, Sun Yatsen's home county in Guangdong.[53] The new plan thus did not entirely abandon the old moral view of opium, but combined it with a system that had originally aimed at controlling the trade rather than eliminating it. From a strictly moral viewpoint this was just another cynical gambit to allow the selling of opium, but few Chinese took the strictly moral viewpoint in 1935. This was a plan that offered real hope for success and might allow China to put the entire opium problem behind it. This was an intriguing possibility, and most of the government's potential critics allowed themselves to be seduced by it.

One of the critics who was won over was Ma Yinqu.[54] Ma had been an important critic of the Nationalists' opium suppression efforts, but the new plan won his approval despite the fact that it involved open opium sales. In a radio broadcast for the 3 June 1935 Anti-Opium Day, Ma explained why he supported the new plan. He mentioned the new spirit that had supposedly infused the government and made it serious about opium, but most of the speech discussed the success the government had achieved in taking control of the opium trade before 1935, and described how the new system would extend this success to the whole country. He stressed the orderliness of the new plan and the fact that it would be successful.[55] Ma at least was more interested in success than in purity.

Ma's attitude seems to have been typical of most other potential critics as well. The National Anti-Opium Association, once one of Jiang's most potent critics, closed its doors about the time the plan was announced, unable to muster any public enthusiasm to resist the plan or any donations from the groups that in the past had found the association's work worthwhile.[56] Reaction to the public announcement that the government would be selling opium, and in fact was already doing so, was very limited and not at all comparable to the reaction in 1927 or 1931. Cynicism probably played a part here. Many intellectuals had much lower expectations for Jiang's government than they had in 1928 and were probably willing to accept anything. The six-year plan was better than just anything, however. The government was showing real interest in curing users; it was bringing growing and shipping under control, and it had pledged to end the trade fairly quickly. None of these things was new, but together they added up to a comprehensive plan to deal with the opium problem. It was also a plan that would rise above the old moral interpretation of opium without abandoning it. Accepting the plan meant accepting the fundamental idea behind it: that opium control and opium suppression were compatible goals that Nanjing was already having success in reaching. Once this was accepted the impossible task of opium suppression became reasonable, and having faith in the government's motives no longer required absolute faith in its morality. When Nanjing said that this was a plan that the government would stick to, it did not require great faith in the government's morality to believe this. Nanjing was getting important financial and political benefits from this plan: simple self-interest would make the government stick with it.

Foreigners and foreign governments were also impressed with the new plan. Both the British and the Americans, who had been becoming more critical of Jiang and his opium and drug policies, were convinced that the new campaign was sincere. They were not as sanguine about its chances for success, but since their view of the problem was primarily moral, this was not as important.[57] The League of Nations also praised China's efforts. Public opinion in foreign countries was also changing. Jiang's government convinced Madame Toussaud's Wax Museum in London to remove a display of a Chinese opium den since China no longer had opium dens.[58]

The government won acquiescence to the new plan, but not enthusiastic support from either foreigners or Chinese. This was predictable, and Nanjing probably did not expect its opium policy to add to its legitimacy or international stature regardless of what it did. Opium was not like the New Life Movement. The entire purpose of the New Life Movement was to encourage a controllable public enthusiasm. This was the approach to opium that the National Anti-Opium Association had advocated in 1927–1928, but the new system neither needed nor wanted the help of the people. Nanjing wanted to use opium as a political and financial tool, and the Opium Suppression Inspectorate would allow the government to do just that without any help from the people. Opium was not an issue that was likely to help the government gain legitimacy, but it could make the government lose it. As long as public opinion left the government alone and allowed the opium control institutions to function, that would be enough. Grudging tolerance was thus an acceptable outcome.

Grudging acceptance would also be enough to allow the Nationalists to expand their plan to areas where they had little control. Yunnan province, led by Long Yun, was one of the most independent in China largely because of its opium revenues. Jiang had already begun to force Yunnan's opium into his distribution system, but the new plan gave him a position from which to criticize what Long was doing inside Yunnan, and eventually to force Long to accept Jiang's control over his opium policy. Prior to this Jiang had not criticized the opium policies of the warlords, since that would draw attention to his own involvement in the trade. Now that Jiang had a more successful opium control system in place, he could afford to criticize the policies of others. In a May 1935 speech, with Long Yun in attendance, Jiang attacked Yunnan's record on opium. Long pointed out that the province was reliant on opium revenues and asked for a subsidy from the central treasury to help defray the costs of suppression.[59] Long could not hope to defend his opium system in the face of a government that was simultaneously attacking his legitimacy and denying him markets. Long began encouraging tin exports as an alternative to opium, and eventually would be forced to reduce his opium exports and become a part of Jiang's opium system.[60] Long did not actually allow central government opium officials to work in Yunnan; the work was carried out by his own people. In the past this would have given Long an opportunity to pretend to suppress opium while profiting from it, but now he was caught in an ideological hammerlock. Even if he administered the plan himself, Long had no choice but to follow the course laid out by Jiang. Although Yunnan experimented with shipping opium through French Indochina and with flying it to the coast, the Yunnanese could not surmount Jiang's monopoly of their markets and the legitimacy that the six-year plan gave to his opium policy.

At the beginning of the war with Japan, Jiang Jieshi had more control over more of the country than he had ever had before and was as respected nationally and internationally as he had ever been. The money and power that opium control gave him helped him to accomplish the first of these, and his success in dealing with the opium problem and his ability to present his policy in a positive light helped with the others. Although it happened in a context of more general failure, Jiang's opium policies can only be considered a success, if a somewhat cynical one.

NOTES

1. Wakeman, *Policing Shanghai,* p. 274.
2. Ibid., p. 271.
3. Madancy "Ambitious Interlude," p. 122.
4. Chen Yung-fa, "Blooming Poppy under the Red Sun."
5. Guo, Xu, and Li, "Guomindang zhengfu 'yu jin yu zheng' zhi jinyan zhengce neimu," p. 221. Much of what follows is based on this article, whose three authors all served in opium-related offices continuously from about 1933 to 1942. The Guangxi Clique, of which Li Zongren was the most visible member, controlled Guangxi province and was one of Jiang's most important rivals throughout the period. The Guangxi Clique was financially dependent on opium shipping to maintain its independence; see Levitch, *Kuangxi Way in Kuomintang China.*
6. *Opium Trade, 1910–1941,* 28:89.

7. EDG 3.1013.

8. *Opium Trade, 1910–1941,* 28:91; EDG 3.1012.

9. EDG 3.934.

10. Tian, "Jiushehui yapian yanye zai Hankou," p. 186.

11. Wu Shuping, "Manhua yapian," p. 197.

12. Quoted in Marshall, "Opium and the Politics of Gangsterism in Nationalist China," p. 21.

13. USDS 893.114/729, 9 April 1934.

14. Guo, Xu, and Li, "Guomindang zhengfu," p. 226.

15. EDG 3.1012.

16. Chen Li, "Jinyan duchachu yu Zhongguo nongmin yinhang fanmai yapian," p. 54.

17. Zheng, "Chaoji yapianshang zai Shanghai de huodong ji qi yu Jiang Jieshi zhengquan de guanxi," p. 17.

18. USDS 893.144/738, 57.

19. EDG 33.25.

20. EDG 33.185.

21. Sun Xiufu, "Jiang Jieshi yu Zhongguo nongmin yinhang."

22. Xiao, "Jiang Jieshi de jinyan neimu," p. 169.

23. Hall, *Yunnan Provincial Faction,* p. 134.

24. *Opium Trade,* 28:90.

25. Baumler, "Playing with Fire: The Nationalist Government and Opium in china, 1927–1941," pp. 308–23.

26. Martin, *Shanghai Green Gang,* p. 139.

27. Wakeman, *Policing Shanghai,* p. 260.

28. Martin, *Shanghai Green Gang.*

29. EDG 33.67 It is not clear how this affair ended, but the opium apparently never arrived in Shanghai.

30. Xiao, "Jiang Jieshi de jinyan neimu," p. 161.

31. Chi Hsi-sheng, *Warlord Politics in China,* note 1.

32. See Madancy's chapter in this volume.

33. EDG 2.1466.

34. Gardella, *Harvesting Mountains,* p. 168.

35. *Fujian sheng jinyan gaikuang,* p. 22.

36. USDS 893.114/729, 4 April 1934.

37. EDG 41.251.

38. EDG 12.339.

39. *China Weekly Review,* 17 July 1937.

40. *Fujian jinyan likan,* n.p.

41. Jinyan weiyuanhui, *Ershiliu niandu jinyan nianbao,* table 12.

42. *Fujian sheng tongji nianjian,* pp. 617–26. Like many other sources this one divides users by sex, and like all the others it shows that the vast majority of registered users and clinic patients were men (107,240 registered men versus 4,242 registered women). This may have been because fewer women used opium, or because women were less likely to register, or most likely both.

43. *Fujian sheng jinyan gaikuang,* p. 26.

44. Ibid., p. 92.

45. Ibid., p. 95.
46. Fu, "He Jian zhu Xiang shiqi de teshui gaikuang," p. 202.
47. Ibid., p. 199.
48. Long, "Xu Yuanquan zai sha shifan yun yapian de zhixiang."
49. Fu, "He Jian zhu Xiang shiqi de teshui gaikuang," p. 199.
50. EDG 33.30.
51. Chen Huace, "Minguo nianjian de jindu qingkuang."
52. Li Zhonggong and Zheng Weijia, *Jinyan wenti*, pp. 30–34.
53. EDG 2.1375.
54. Ma was one of China's leading modern economists and would later become famous as a critic of Mao's population policies.
55. *Zhejiang sheng juduhui zongbaogao*, pp. 77–81.
56. See Slack's chapter in this volume; *China Weekly Review*, 14 August 1937.
57. Walker, *Opium and Foreign Policy*, p. 77.
58. *China Weekly Review*, 6 June 1936, p. 2.
59. Ibid., 25 May 1935, p. 421.
60. Hall, *Yunnan Provincial Faction*, p. 143.

THIRTEEN

The Responses of Opium Growers to Eradication Campaigns and the Poppy Tax, 1907–1949

Lucien Bianco

Any attempt at eradicating opium addiction "had to deal with a formidable array of vested interests."[1] One of those interests was the opium farmer, the subject of this chapter. In the face of state campaigns to eradicate poppy cultivation, peasants devised ways and means to resist the uprooting of their poppy in order to protect their livelihood. Opium farmers also resisted opium tax, a separate issue that I shall introduce briefly toward the end of the chapter. Patterns of resistance were shaped by patterns of suppression over the forty-three years from the first prohibition edict in October 1906 to the establishment of the People's Republic in October 1949. This period can be divided into two contrasting epochs. The first decade, which ends coincidentally with Yuan Shikai's death in 1916, was characterized by an uneven, but on the whole determined, implementation of the 1906 suppression policies.[2] The remaining three decades oscillated between half-hearted suppression measures and no suppression at all.

OPIUM SUPPRESSION

The late-Qing program against opium represented "the largest and most vigorous effort to stamp out an established evil."[3] It brought about quick, impressive results that proved wrong the initial skepticism of British and other Western diplomats. By early in 1911, opium production had, according to the foremost British investigator, almost stopped in Sichuan (the top producing province) and declined by three-fourths in Yunnan (which ranked second) and Guizhou.[4] The decline further north was less impressive, yet prohibition was effective in Shaanxi and Gansu and poppy cultivation practically disappeared from Shanxi.[5] In the country as a whole, no less than 80 percent of all poppy fields had by then been converted to food crops, at least according to the best British estimates. Even allowing for the unavoidable gaps in their surveys,[6] no one denies that in less than five years the late-Qing campaign against opium had achieved astonishing, unforeseen results.

After an initial interruption,[7] the new Republican regime tried to restore the momentum of the campaign. The program did not collapse suddenly in the wake of Yuan's death, but unraveled gradually. Failures and lapses in the implementation of the program, which were already noticed under Yuan,[8] became increasingly notorious from late 1916 to 1918, though much less so than from 1919 on, when what had been achieved during the 1907–1916 decade was thoroughly ruined. By 1926 poppy cultivation was as ubiquitous in China as it had ever been prior to 1906.[9]

The warlord decade brought back poppy cultivation, first because opium suppression was with few exceptions no longer implemented, and second because poppy planting was promoted and even imposed in order to tax the trade. Warlords desperately needed money to buy arms and soldiers, and in those areas where poppy had been extensively grown prior to 1907, opium profits quickly dominated the revenues of provincial governments and autonomous warlords. As early as 1915–1916, in the course of the war against Yuan Shikai, the National Protection Army *(Huguo jun)* brought from Yunnan into Sichuan no less than one million ounces of opium. At the time, opium could be bought in Yunnan for 4.2 yuan an ounce,[10] as compared to more than 15 yuan in Sichuan, where more effective suppression campaigns had raised the price of opium. The difference meant enormous benefits for Sichuanese opium merchants and an increase in the previously reduced number of smokers. It also meant the renewal of opium cultivation, first hidden, then (from about the spring of 1918) open in several eastern Sichuan counties, and an increase in taxes.[11]

The competition among warlords to get hold of opium and monopolize its sale was intense enough to bring about some wars of its own, christened "new opium wars." Although these occurred first of all in producing areas (e.g., the 1920 war among Sichuan, Yunnan, and Guizhou), armed conflict also happened in areas that grew little or no opium but benefited from its trade. For instance, the control over Shanghai traffic in both national and Indian opium (the latter providing enough revenues to finance three army divisions) was the most important factor triggering the 1924 war between Jiangsu and Zhejiang.[12] Guangxi's location made it a favorite exit route for Yunnan and Guizhou opium, especially once Sichuan's victory had closed the northern route through Sichuan. It was partly in order to open the Guangxi route for Yunnanese opium that Yunnan warlord Tang Jiyao attacked the New Guangxi clique late in 1924.[13] New Guangxi commanders seized huge amounts of Yunnanese opium, a feat they deemed as valuable as victory in battle and as a great contribution to their ultimate overall victory.[14]

Opium could also serve the cause of peace by inducing rival warlords to maintain peaceful relations in order to permit economic cooperation. After the ousting of Tang Jiyao's troops, revenues from opium traffic became so important to the New Guangxi leaders that they worked to prevent the recurrence of hostilities with either of their opium-producing neighbors, Yunnan and Guizhou, both of which were also concerned about business. The West River across Guangxi provided a major route for Guizhou opium to reach the Guangdong and foreign markets,[15] and it carried to Guangzhou and Hong Kong Yunnan opium, which also transited through northern Guangxi to Wuhan and Shanghai. Guangxi's much-publicized achievements in creating modern banks and promoting education, health, and economic development (the "Guangxi Way") owed much to the transit pass trade in opium.[16] Most of that trade was tightly controlled by Guangxi provincial armies.[17]

In southwest China, such practices outlived the establishment of the Nationalist regime. Although uprooting measures were sporadically enforced in the eastern provinces, which produced less opium, China as a whole remained the world's foremost opium producer. Officially Jiang Jieshi was in favor of eradicating opium, in conformity with Sun Yatsen's teachings, the wishes of the most vocal sector of Chinese public opinion, and international pressure. But whatever his public stand against the drug, Jiang could not single-mindedly pursue its eradication. The compelling reasons that had induced competing warlords to "raise the tax on opium in order to eliminate opium" led Jiang to turn the opium trade into a governmental monopoly to pay for his larger armies and more expensive arms.

Besides producing badly needed revenue, Jiang's opium policy provided him with both an excuse to increase his military strength[18] and powerful levers inducing recalcitrant provincial authorities to obey. His military blockade of Yunnan and Guizhou in 1936 prevented the delivery of opium to neighboring Guangxi, where the traffic fell from more than twenty million ounces in 1935 to a little over four million in 1936. New Guangxi leaders Li Zongren and Bai Chongxi had no choice but to accept Jiang's conditions.[19] Beginning in 1935, both Yunnan and Guizhou had to create anti-opium programs that fit into the national regulations prescribed by Nanjing.[20] The new provincial plans were not rigorously or continuously implemented, however.[21] Resistance fluctuated as campaigns went from vigorous to ineffective:[22] weak when policy was lax, and stronger or even violent in times of more determined offensives.

A QUANTITATIVE ASSESSMENT OF PEASANT RESISTANCE

Table 3 lists 131 cases of peasant resistance to opium prohibition. It is by no means exhaustive or representative of the time and space distribution of such incidents. The compilation that provided most cases (20 cases, and 16 more in conjunction with one or two other sources)[23] covers only the last decade of the Qing, resulting in an overrepresentation of the early years in my sample. My other materials have further amplified the predominance of the early period.[24]

Despite these and other deficiencies in my sample, it is not surprising to find that 63 percent (83 out of 131) of the incidents in table 3 are concentrated in the main opium-producing areas: 58 in the first producing area, the southwest (including 23 in Yunnan, 20 in Sichuan-Xikang, and 15 in Guizhou), and 25 in the northwest (including 14 in Shaanxi, 8 in Gansu, and 3 in Shanxi). Most of the remaining incidents (40 out of 48) occurred in eastern and southeastern China: 3 each in Jiangsu and Anhui, 7 in Jiangxi, 9 in Fujian, and 18 in Zhejiang alone! According to one source,[25] Zhejiang ranked third among China's opium-growing provinces during the early years of the Republic. If such was the case, which I doubt,[26] the high number of Zhejiang incidents, all of which happened between 1908 and 1914, would appear less abnormal.

More probably, my sample suffers from the classic bias favoring events that occurred in Zhejiang or, as evidenced by most other data, in Jiangsu province. It is not exceptional to learn about brief, almost benign incidents involving less than a hundred participants as soon as they took place in Jiangnan (southern Jiangsu and northern Zhejiang). By contrast, disturbances occurring in faraway, less developed western areas needed to reach a certain intensity (of deaths, damage, duration, and the like) to get reported in coastal newspapers and periodicals. The overwhelming majority of the bloodiest incidents listed in table 3 did indeed take place in the western "opium belt" from Gansu to Yunnan.

Temporal distribution is much more uneven than geographical distribution. Fifty-eight percent of all incidents (76 out of 131) took place during the first decade, from 1907 to 1916. Even more striking, 43.5 percent (57 cases) were concentrated during the brief Xuantong era (1909–1911), including 37 incidents in 1910 alone. By contrast, only 5 incidents occurred during the next decade (1917–1926), few (16 incidents) during the Nanjing decade, and not too many (34 incidents) during the last twelve years, from 1938 to 1949.

The bias in my sample does not alone account for this uneven distribution. Unsurprisingly, the unevenness is related to the relative determination with which successive prohibition campaigns were pursued, the strongest being during the first decade (1907–1916), the weakest during

TABLE 3   Cases of Peasant Resistance to
Opium Eradication Campaigns, 1907–1949

Year[a]	Date[a]	Province	County[b]	Source
1907	June	Sichuan	Kaixian, Wanxian	1
1908	Dec. 5	Zhejiang	Huangyan	2
	Dec 25	Fujian	Tong'an	2
1909	early	Yunnan	Chuxiong	3
	April 21*	Zhejiang	Sui'an	2
	July 21*	Shaanxi	Mizhi	2
		Jiangxi	Ji'an	4
1909–10		Sichuan	Fuzhou	1
1910	Feb. 3*	Zhejiang	Taiping, Xianju	2
	Feb. 6*	Zhejiang	Ninghai	2
	March 2	Zhejiang	Rui'an	2, 5
	March 8–9	Zhejiang	Wenzhou	5
	March 11/13	Shanxi	Jiaocheng, Wenshui	2, 5
	March 23–24	Shanxi	Jiaocheng, Wenshui	5
	March–April	Guizhou	Puding	6
	April 9	Zhejiang	Ninghai	2
	April 12	Zhejiang	Sui'an	2, 5
	April 13	Sichuan	Dianjiang, Liangshan	2
	April 21	Jiangxi	Yongxin	2, 4
	April ?	Zhejiang	Yueqing	5
	April/May	Gansu	Gaolan, Jinxian	2, 5
	May 5*	Henan	Shanxian, Ruxian	2, 5
	May 11 *	Jiangxi	Yushan	2, 5
	May 9/18	Zhejiang	Ninghai	2, 5
	May/June	Guangxi	Nandan	2
	June 2*	Shaanxi	Fufeng	2, 5
	June 19	Guizhou	Xingyi	2
	June–July	Gansu	Lanzhou prefecture	5
	June–July	Gansu	Gaolan	2, 5
	July 1	Jiangxi	Yushan	2, 5
	July 22	Sichuan	Meishan	2, 5
	August 9*	Sichuan	Deyang	2
	August 21*	Shaanxi	Fengxiang	7
	August 23	Zhejiang	Taiping	5
	August 29*	Heilongjiang	Dalaiting	2
	August	Liaoning	Yixian	8
	August	Zhejiang	(eastern part)	9
	Sept 16*	Zhejiang	Linhai	2
	Sept 30*	Gansu	Lanzhou prefecture	2, 5
	Sept 30	Zhejiang	Yuqian	5
	Sept	Zhejiang	Wenzhou prefecture	5
	Oct 3/12	Zhejiang	Zhuji, Lanxi, Jinhua	2, 5
	Oct	Sichuan	Changshou	1

TABLE 3   *(continued)*

Year[a]	Date[a]	Province	County[b]	Source
	Nov. 27	Yunnan	Dayao	2
		Shaanxi	Fufeng	10
1911	Jan. 25	Guizhou	Anshun	2
	Jan 26*	Guizhou	Zhenning	2
	Jan 26*	Guizhou	Shuicheng	2
	March 7*	Yunnan	Xuanwei	2
	April 10	Gansu	Zhangye	2
	May 16	Shaanxi	Xingping	2, 7, 10
	May 22	Gansu	Zhangye	2
	May 24–25	Shaanxi	Wugong	2, 7
	May or June	Shaanxi	Meixian	10
	July 2–3	Fujian	Putian	11
	Sept.	Gansu		12
	Sept	Shanxi		12
	fall	Shaanxi		10
1912	August	Fujian	Putian, Xianyou	13
		Shaanxi	Huxian	10
		Anhui		14
		Guizhou		15
1913	Jan. 30	Zhejiang	Wenzhou prefecture	16
	Febr. 8	Guangdong	Raoping	17
	Febr.	Fujian	Putian, Xianyou	13
	June–July	Shaanxi	Shenmu	5, 9
1914	March 15/19	Yunnan	Tongchuan	5
	April 10	Zhejiang	Xiangshan	5
1915	Jan. 12	Guizhou	Weining, Bijie	5
	June 24	Rehe	Chaoyang	5, 18
	summer	Gansu	Longdong	?
	Nov. 25	Yunnan	Shiping	5
	Dec. ?	Shaanxi	Huxian	7
1916	June 3	Rehe	Chaoyang	18
		Jiangxi	Wuning	19
		Yunnan		20
1917	Jan. 20	Yunnan	Qiaojia, Tengyue	5
	May 18	Shaanxi	Yijun	21
		Yunnan	Lancang, Huxian, Zhouzhi	22
1918	Oct.–June	Shaanxi	Xingping	7
1919		Yunnan	Lüchun	23
1927		Yunnan	Qiubei	24
1928	early	Jiangxi	northeast	25
		Jiangxi	Xingguo, Ningdu	25

TABLE 3 (continued)

Year[a]	Date[a]	Province	County[b]	Source
1929	March 1	Fujian	Yunxiao	26
		Anhui	Quanjiao	27
1930	Dec. 28	Fujian	Tongan	28
1931	Jan.	Fujian	Fuzhou	28
1932		Fujian	Tongan	29
1933		Fujian	Putian	30
		Jiangsu	Yangzhou	31
1934	April	Jiangsu	Siyang	28
		Anhui	Chaoxian	32
1935	Febr.	Jiangsu	Qingjiang, Suqian	28
1936–37		Yunnan	Jianshui, Mengzi, Shiping	22
1937	March	Yunnan	Yongsheng	33
	April	Yunnan	Lüchun	23
1938	Oct.	Shaanxi	Baoji	34
1939	Dec.	Yunnan	Yongsheng	33
		Yunnan	Huaping	33
		Yunnan	Zhenyuan, Jingdong	22
1940	Jan. 6	Yunnan	Yongsheng	33
	Jan.–May	Yunnan	Yongsheng	33
	March	Sichuan	Jinghua	35
		Yunnan	Zhenyuan	22
		Sichuan	Leibo, Maxian, Ebian, Pingshan	36
1941	summer	Sichuan	Jinghua	35
		Yunnan	Longwu	22
early 1940s		Xikang	Yingjing	37
1942	March	Guizhou	Songtao, Tongren, Jiangkou	38
	April 30	Yunnan	Qiubei	24
	spring	Guizhou	Dejiang	39
	summer	Sichuan	Maogong	35
	Oct. 28	Guizhou	Zhenyuan	39
	Nov.15	Guizhou	Taijiang	39
		Sichuan	Maoxian	35
1943	spring	Sichuan	Songpan	35
	Oct.11	Guizhou	Liping	40
		Yunnan	Luxi	22
1944	March 8	Sichuan	Puge	41
	March 19	Sichuan	Jiange	42
	April 16	Guizhou	Liping	40
	May	Sichuan	Jiangyou	42
	July	Sichuan	Songpan, Maoxian	35

TABLE 3 *(continued)*

Year[a]	Date[a]	Province	County[b]	Source
	summer	Sichuan	Lifan	35
	Nov.	Guizhou	Liping	40
1946	Feb. 21	Guizhou	Liping	40
	early	Sichuan	Ziyang	?
	April	Yunnan	Qiubei	43
1946/49		Sichuan	Jinghua	35
1947	April	Hunan	Longshan	44

SOURCES:

1. Adshead, *Province and Politics in Late Imperial China.*
2. Zhang Zhenhe and Ding Yuanying, "Qingmo minbian nianbao."
3. Roger Des Forges, *Hsi-liang and the Chinese National Revolution.*
4. Kamal Sheel, *Peasant Society and Marxist Intellectuals in China.*
5. *Dongfang zazhi.*
6. *Guizhou wenshi ziliao xuanji,* no. 15, pp. 169–75.
7. *Shuntian shibao,* 21 August 1910, 1 August 1910, 21 December 1915, 23 June 1918.
8. David Yun, "Mouvements populaires en Chine à la fin des Ch'ing."
9. *Shenbao,* 1910: lunar 8th month, 7th day; 1913: 7th month, 13th day.
10. *Minli bao,* 1911: lunar 4th month, first day; 6th month, 18th day; 1912: 5th month, 19th day; 10th month, 20th day.
11. *Putian wenshi ziliao* 2 (1981): 113.
12. John Lust, "Les sociétés secrètes, les mouvements populaires et la révolution de 1911."
13. Joyce Madancy, "Revolution, Religion, and the Poppy: Opium and the Rebellion of the 'Sixteenth Emperor' in Early Republican Fujian."
14. Yves Nalet, "Chen Duxiu 1879–1915, formation d'un intellectuel révolutionnaire."
15. David Owen, *British Opium Policy in China and India.*
16. Zhejiang sheng zhengxie wenshi ziliao weiyuanhui, ed., *Xinbian Zhejiang bainian dashiji, 1840–1940.*
17. *Raoping xianzhi* (1994), p. 30.
18. *Chaoyang wenshi ziliao* 1 (1986): 89–93, 130–37, 332–35.
19. *Wuning wenshi ziliao* 2 (n.d.): 34.
20. Alan Baumler, "Playing with Fire: The Nationalist Government and Opium in China, 1927–1941."
21. *Dagong bao.*
22. Li Zihui, "Yunnan jinyan gaikuang."
23. *Lüchun xianzhi* (1992), pp. 15–17.
24. *Wenshan zhou wenshi ziliao* 3 (1985): 99–110.
25. Stephen Averill, "Revolution in the Highlands: The Rise of the Communist Movement in Jiangxi Province."
26. Dong Yiming, "Étude sur le problème de l'opium dans la région du sud-ouest de la Chine pendant les années 1920 et 1930."
27. *Quanjiao xianzhi* (1988), pp. 706–8.
28. United States Department of State archives, National Archives and Records Administration, Washington.
29. *Tongan wenshi ziliao* 1 (1982): 50–52.
30. *Putian shi wenshi ziliao* 2 (1986): 102–12.
31. *Yangzhou wenshi ziliao* 3 (1983): 151–52.
32. *Anhui wenshi ziliao* 7 (1981): 107–13.
33. *Yongsheng xianzhi* (1989), pp. 508–10.
34. *Baoji wenshi ziliao* 2 (1985): 74–82.
35. Mi Qingyun, "Jiang zhengchuan zai Chuanxi bianju jinyan de zhenxiang."

36. Hsin-i Hsiao, "Économie et société rurale du Sichuan de 1927 à 1945," pp. 253–54.
37. Chen Yaolun, "Xikang yapian liudu zaocheng Yingjing shibian jingguo."
38. *Songtao wenshi ziliao*, no. 6, pp. 50–59.
39. *Guizhou jindaishi* (1987), pp. 367–71.
40. *Liping xianzhi* (1989), pp. 6, 20–22.
41. *Puge xianzhi* (1992), p. 7.
42. *Jiange wenshi ziliao xuanji* 7 (1986): 86–92, 103–4, 118–20.
43. *Qiubei wenshi ziliao* 3 (1989): 31–33.
44. *Xiangxi wenshi ziliao* 4 (1985): 132–35.

ᵃ Where two dates are given (e.g., 1909–10, 1936–37, 1946–49), either I have been unable to determine the exact year in which the incident occurred, or several incidents occurred during that period of time. Where neither month nor day is indicated, only the year in which the incident occurred is known; where the month is indicated but not the day, only the month is known. Slashed months (e.g., April/May) mean that I only know the lunar month and cannot determine whether the incident took place in April or May. A question mark by a month means that there is reason to believe, but no proof, that the incident took place that month. Where the day is indicated as 9/18, it means that I only know the decade of the lunar month during which the incident took place. By contrast, 24–25 means that the incident began on the 24th and continued on the 25th. Where an asterisk follows a date, the date refers to the day on which the incident was reported; the incident itself may have occurred on the previous day or the previous week, sometimes even during the previous month.

ᵇ Only counties, not localities, are indicated. When two or several counties are given, resistance to opium suppression took place in each county mentioned. When prefectures, not counties, are mentioned, it is either because incidents occurred in many or most counties in the said prefecture or because only the prefecture is known to me. When I include neither prefecture nor county, it is because I am aware only of the province or the area in the province in which the incident occurred.

the next (1917–1926). Following Yuan's death, the relapse into tolerance, not to mention active encouragement, of poppy cultivation happened rather quickly, yet could be neither sudden nor universal. This may account for the fact that four out of the five incidents registered during the warlord decade occurred or began during the first year (1917), although this may result from sheer coincidence, given the small numbers involved. It remains that table 3 does not list a single item from 1920 to 1926! The final increase in the number of cases following 1938, relative to the preceding twenty years, fits rather well with Baumler's description of Jiang's wartime turn to a more rigorous implementation of opium suppression.[27]

Table 4, which tabulates incidents of resistance to the poppy tax, does not bear detailed commentary. Neither the geographical nor the time distribution can be deemed representative of what happened in the real world, with 20 out of 46 incidents concentrated in eastern and southeastern China (including 10 in Fujian and 6 in Anhui, the latter all in 1932) and 12 out of 46 in a single year (1932)! In spite of that obvious bias—a single source[28] provided me with five of the twelve 1932 cases—that more than half of the incidents (26 out of 46) occurred during the Nanjing decade, as compared to so few at both ends of the time span (Qing and 1940s), may be more than a statistical artifact. The same can be said of the small number of anti-tax incidents in Yunnan (three cases, including one in 1903), where Long Yun made enough money from the opium trade "downstream" to be able to give up collecting poppy taxes.[29] I believe, however, that the main interest of table 4 consists in the small number of incidents: not much more than one-fourth of the whole sample (46 out of 177, or 26 percent).

OPIUM GROWERS' RESPONSES TO ERADICATION CAMPAIGNS

"Farmers have not been shot as in 1924."[30] This sentence refers to peasants being shot not for growing opium, but for refusing to grow it. From the early 1920s on, local powerholders resorted to every form of compulsion, from mild to military, to convince recalcitrant farmers to resume poppy planting. It was less easy for individual farmers to resist than for entire communities, as was the case in 1925 in Wanxian, Sichuan, where poppies had not been cultivated since 1909: the headman of every *jia* refused to comply when the military ordered the *jia* to return to planting poppies.[31] During the same year in neighboring Guizhou province, when the minor warlord Yuan Zhumin ordered Qijiang peasants to grow poppy, an "asso-ciation to ward off the poison" *(judu hui)* was established with the aim of inciting peasants to disobey Yuan's order.[32]

In some cases, the reluctance to comply may have come from the reali-zation that extremely high taxes made opium farming not worth the effort or the risk. More often, I believe, the crux of the matter was an analysis of the relative risks of compliance versus noncompliance. Deciding whether or not to obey the order to resume planting poppy amounted to deciding what one feared more: direct threats by local powerholders intimidating those who did not grow opium, or warnings by more distant authorities professing their determination to continue implementing harsh suppres-sion policies. Although the memory of the terrible repression suffered fif-teen years earlier was still very vivid, I would imagine that the local threat or sanction carried more weight, precisely because it was direct rather than distant, and that a majority of unwilling farmers complied and grew opium when ordered or urged to do so.

Nonetheless, although it is true that peasants from various parts of China were compelled to plant poppy, this has become a cliché. We need to put it in perspective: it is time to come to the heart of the matter, namely peasant resistance to poppy eradication, not to poppy growing. Even when initially ordered to grow opium, peasants were well aware of the profitability of poppy cultivation and were so eager to profit from it that after a year or two they were tempted into resisting uprooting rather than giving up their trade.[33] Most often peasants did not need to be coerced into planting poppy. A survey conducted in 1929 in thirty-one counties from twelve

TABLE 4 Cases of Peasant Resistance to Opium Tax, 1896–1949

Year	Date	Province	County	Source
1896		Zhejiang	Cixi	45
1898	June 8	Zhejiang	Yuyao	46
1903		Yunnan	Lianghe	47
1907	May 16–17	Zhejiang	Yuyao	46
1908	Sept. 2	Shanxi	Qinshui	2
1910	August	Liaoning	Yixian	8, 48
		Heilong-jiang		5, 8, 48
1915	spring	Gansu	Wudu	49
1916	July 2	Rehe	Chaoyang	18
1917	Oct.	Shaanxi	Zhouzhi, Xinping, Huxian	7
1920	summer	Gansu	Kangxian	50
1923	May 30	Shaanxi	Longxian	51
	fall	Fujian	south	52
1923–24		Sichuan	Shizhu	53
1924	Jan. 11–13	Fujian	Huian	52, 54
1925		Fujian		55
		Sichuan	east	55
1928	March	Fujian		28
	Oct. 16–17	Hubei	Zigui	56
1929		Hunan	Yuanling	44
		Liaoning	Lingyuan	18
1930	April	Hebei	Xingtai	57
	July	Rehe	Chaoyang	18
		Sichuan	Yongchuan	58
1931	Jan.	Fujian		28
	May 4	Fujian		20
1932	Jan.	Anhui	Fengyang	59, 60
	March	Anhui	Guoyang	59, 60
	spring	Fujian	Huian	28, 61
	spring	Henan	Luoning	62
	May–July	Anhui	Suxian	63
	August	Anhui	Lingbi	63
	August	Suiyuan	Bikeqi	59
	August	Anhui	Xiaoxian	59
	August	Jiangsu	Tongshan	60
	Aug.–Sept.	Anhui	Suxian	63
	Dec. 20	Fujian	Changle	64
		Fujian	south	59
1934	(or earlier)	Henan	north	65
	April	Fujian	Huian	28
	summer	Guizhou	Langdai	66

TABLE 4   *(continued)*

Year	Date	Province	County	Source
1935	April	Yunnan	Guangnan	67
	Oct.	Hebei	Xianghe	5, 68
1942		Guizhou	Mashan	
1943	Sept.	Sichuan	Danpa	7(
1947	April	Yunnan	Qiubei	43

SOURCES: For sources 1–44, see source note for table 3.

45. *Cixi xianzhi* (1992), p. 12.
46. *Yuyao wenshi ziliao* 4 (1987): 7–11.
47. *Lianghe wenshi ziliao* 1 (n.d.): 52–79.
48. *Lishi yanjiu*, 1956, no. 6.
49. *Wudu wenshi ziliao xuanji* 1 (1986): 8–9.
50. *Kangxian zhi* (1989), pp. 573–574.
51. *Longxian wenshi ziliao*, no. 1, pp. 32–34.
52. Zhang Youyi, *Zhongguo jindai nongyeshi ziliao*, vol. 2 (1912–1927).
53. *Sichuan wenshi ziliao*, no. 32, pp. 181–94.
54. *Huian wenshi ziliao* 5 (1986): 20–22.
55. *China Yearbook*.
56. *Zigui wenshi ziliao*, no. 6, pp. 149–51.
57. *Xingtai wenshi ziliao* 4 (1989): 159–64.
58. *Yongchuan wenshi ziliao* 2 (1986): 75–77.
59. Ma Chengfeng, "Zuijin Zhongguo nongcun jingji zhu shixiang zhi baolu."
60. Zhang Youyi, *Zhongguo jindai nongyeshi ziliao*, vol. 3 (1927–1937).
61. *Huian wenshi ziliao* 1 (1983): 45.
62. *Luoning wenshi ziliao* 2–3 (1988): 153–57.
63. Bianco, "Peasant Uprisings against Poppy Tax Collection in Su Xian and Lingbi (Anhui) in 1932."
64. *Zhongguo laodong nianjian* 4 (1933): 101.
65. *Henan nongcun diaocha*, p. 96.
66. *Liuzhi wenshi ziliao xuanji*, no. 4, pp. 122–41.
67. *Guangnan wenshi ziliao* 1 (n.d.): 145–49.
68. *China Weekly Review*.
69. *Qian xinan zhou wenshi ziliao* 1 (1982): 155–65.
70. *Ya'an wenshi ziliao*, no. 3, pp. 45–51.

provinces found out that eight out of nine opium farmers had voluntarily chosen to plant poppy.[34]

Of course, most farmers did not resist the uprooting of their poppy. Whether ordered to grow opium or not to grow opium, peasants felt that they had no choice but to comply. Rather than openly resist, they were more inclined to try less dangerous ways of getting round the interdiction. For an example in the mid 1920s in Anhui province, they planted poppy fields with alternate rows of other crops, such as wheat or beans, so that should the law against opium growing be enforced, they could pull up the opium and have another good crop remaining. If it was not, they weeded out everything but opium, which was left to mature.[35] Another popular trick

Figure 15. "The true patriot does not grow opium." This 1928 poster contrasts the healthy and prosperous peasant who does not grow opium, in the left panel, with the peasant who does, gets caught, and loses title to his land. From *Opium, A World Problem* 1, no. 4 (June 1928): 21.

was to uproot poppy plants alongside roads and main paths as soon as troops were reported on their way.[36] Still another was to plant poppy in remote areas, not likely to be inspected, or to hide it behind other crops.[37] As a late-Qing official commented, "they are greedy, not rebels; they disobey orders, but do not resist. The coming of the troops is enough to make them run away, forsaking their poppy fields."[38]

Beyond the kind of tricks and frauds labeled "weapons of the weak" by James Scott,[39] a further step, still short of open resistance, was bribing corrupt officials or military officers. In parts of Sichuan during World War II, poppy eradication amounted to a well-orchestrated farce, though not without its tragic moments, as troops made sure to kill two or three opium farmers during each raid as a warning to others. Everyone was, however, aware that lavish banquets and appropriate niceties restrained the soldiers' arms so that they gently struck at the poppy stalks in such a way that the plants would bend over intact, allowing the farmer to make them stand up again. When neither duly entertained nor bribed by villagers, troops would strike the poppy flowers hard, causing them to fall off and preventing the plant from bearing the precious product. In such cases, opium farmers would sometimes resist, a resistance made easier by the arms and ammunition provided to them beforehand by troops in exchange for their opium.[40]

Exchanging arms for opium can be considered a step beyond the ubiquitous bribes. As we shall see, bribes, when given to no avail, could trigger open, even violent resistance. The risks were, however, much bigger after troops had themselves armed those peasants they would have to repress later. That happened more than once in Sichuan, Xikang, and Guizhou during the war of resistance against Japan. Military officers first sold damaged or old rifles to Han, or more often non-Han, opium growers. Then, once the opium growers knew better, or in order to get more opium in exchange, these officers provided villagers with good, modern, sometimes imported arms and ammunition. To make up for the loss, which could be discovered during inspections, they bought cheaper, less effective arms. Not only the resistance, but the victory of Xikang opium farmers in Tianbao, Yingjing county, was thus facilitated during the early 1940s.[41]

The last step short of violent collective resistance amounted to another kind of deal having to do not with goods (such as arms exchanged for opium) but with the battle itself and the penalties for engaging in or abstaining from it. On 4 May 1944 three hundred troops suddenly appeared in Fuxing canton, Jiangyou county, Sichuan, ready to uproot poppy. Local opium growers were ready to defend themselves in two ways, by preparing for armed resistance (with the support of trained secret society members) and by offering bribes. Bribes had worked in the past, but this time the commander of the uprooting team, aware that he was under close surveillance by provincial authorities, could not let himself be bribed. He instead offered a compromise: "If your Paoge [the most widespread of the Sichuanese *Gelaohui*] do not fire, no one will be shot." This agreement was observed by both parties, even though the farmers had to allow their poppy stalks to be uprooted.[42] A little earlier in neighboring Beichuan county, the agreement, rather than preceding (and preventing) the battle, followed it. When an uprooting team consisting of two hundred troops and police arrived on 19 March 1944 at the villages of Xiaoyuan and Houyuan, it was met by some eight hundred opium farmers equipped with modern arms and entrenched in forts. Although victorious, the locals spent the next day getting ready to flee to avoid punishment. This proved unnecessary, however, because the "bandits" (the resisting opium farmers) were able to strike a bargain with the county magistrate, who had received from them the year before half a million yuan in "fines" (meaning bribes) for averting his eyes from their trade. According to a five-point agreement, the maturing poppies would not be uprooted, but in the following year no poppies would be allowed, at least along roads and lanes. Poppy fields hidden in forests or on mountain tops would be overlooked so long as no one denounced the county magistrate to provincial authorities, and should he be accused, local literati and the county consultative council would come to his defense.[43]

Deliberate violent resistance was rare and usually triggered by aggravating circumstances. One aggravating circumstance was timing. Farmers were especially prone to resist when their poppy was already "more than one foot high" (as was the case in Gansu in April 1910) or, worse, when it was almost ready to be harvested. In such cases, they complained that they should have been forewarned before planting[44] or given a year's delay.[45] Uprooting was also likely to arouse peasant anger and active resistance when officials had already been bribed. This could happen when a bribed official was transferred elsewhere. But sometimes officials were forced to reverse their stand because of pressure from above, as happened in 1910 when Shaanxi provincial authorities directly intervened in Fengxiang county because they were unhappy with the performance of the county magistrate.[46]

Policy reversal and inconsistent responses by eradication officials provoked violent action in a village north of Lanzhou in June 1910. During the previous year, Gansu authorities had acted as if they were oblivious to the imperial edicts forbidding opium cultivation. Lanzhou suburban farmers tested the waters by growing a few poppy plants at first, and once it was clear that there would be no official response, they grew more. Farmers from more distant villages were all the more eager to follow their example because prohibition had raised opium prices, and in the wake of the 1909 drought wheat seeds were in short supply and expensive. Abundant rains in the spring of 1910 meant that poppy plants were not only more numerous than during preceding years, but also more precocious and vigorous, making it difficult for provincial authorities to turn a blind eye. In mid April 1910 the Gansu government suddenly reversed its policy and ordered the immediate uprooting of poppy fields. Most officials deemed this implementation too stringent and uprooted just the fields bordering the main roads. By contrast, Lanzhou prefect Zhang Binghua had every poppy plant in the prefecture eradicated. He also sent subordinates to other areas where the uprooting had not been done properly. When they discovered that poppy growers would not allow their precious plants to be uprooted now that they were already more than a foot high, Zhang went personally to supervise the uprooting of poppy in Gaolan and Jin counties, north of Lanzhou. Newspapers reported that strong-willed farmers attempted to resist, while the more timid wept by their ruined fields. A few farmers hanged themselves, and some drowned themselves in a nearby river. In Jinyanyi village (Jin county), four or five elderly women in tears knelt in front of Prefect Zhang and asked him to spare a few poppy fields located in a remote valley, and when he refused, they begged for free wheat seeds. Either unwilling or unable to provide them with the seeds, he ordered them removed. When one of his escorts reportedly slapped one of the women in the face and dragged her away by the hair, several hundred peasants assembled. A tough called Yue Mazi hit Prefect Zhang and knocked him down. Some grabbed the staves of his sedan chair, and others beat his escort. The light wounds did not prevent Zhang's party from returning to Lanzhou. Zhang obtained Yue's head (he had asked for many more), but not the dismissal of the Jin and Gaolan county magistrates, whom he accused of having engineered the whole incident. Both officials retorted that they had been busy implementing the prefect's instructions by uprooting poppy in two localities six and nine miles away from the incident, and that when they heard of the attack, they hastened back, though too late to rescue the prefect.[47]

A policy reversal especially resented by opium farmers was the uprooting of poppies that they had been compelled to plant. In the fall of 1942 in Liping, Guizhou, Magistrate Xie Zhongliang had ordered peasants to grow poppy, reserving for himself 30 percent of the profit from the crop. The next year, poppy flowers in evidence throughout the county attracted the attention of the provincial government, which ordered Magistrate Xie to have them destroyed. Sensing that he must comply, Xie sent eradication teams to several villages. In two such villages, Tongguan and Shuangjiang xiang, opium growers violently resisted the incoming teams (11 October 1943). Escort troops went in with the teams the following spring, but when they plundered the villagers' goods and set fire to their homes, indignant peasants invaded the county yamen and seized the county magistrate and another official (16 April 1944). The next month, reinforcements were sent in to enable uprooters to carry out their task. When the latter planned to impose an opium tax at the same time, farmers concluded that the prohibition was over and planted poppy anew. But a new eradication campaign was launched in November 1944, which caused seven hundred armed peasants in the vicinity of Diping and Longhe to resist, eighty of whom were either killed or wounded in the encounter. Elsewhere in Liping county, troops uprooted 971 *mu* of poppy and shot thirty-seven opium growers who had not obeyed the interdiction.[48]

Peasants could also be driven to armed conflict when an official handled poppy control in a way they regarded as unfair. For example, even though an opium grower in Yi county, Liaoning, was persuaded by fellow villagers to uproot several hundred *mu* of poppy, he was nevertheless fined and taken to the police station (August 1910). When villagers set him free, the infuriated county magistrate sent police back to the village with military backup. The troops looted, raped, and set several houses on fire, and the villagers reacted by gathering to fight them off.[49]

Popular violence of this sort was usually a response to provocation, although occasionally peasants were moved to attack troops before they had begun to uproot poppy. A mob of hostile farmers might even succeed, though rarely, in intimidating soldiers into leaving and trying elsewhere.[50] The prospect of facing such opposition moved the magistrate of Shemnu county in northern Shaanxi in 1913 to lead troops from the county seat to suppress the seven or eight thousand followers ("bandits") of a leader who claimed that his talismans could protect their poppy plants from being eradicated. In the encounter, the magistrate and more than one hundred soldiers lost their lives. The road to Shenmu thus opened, the "bandits" plundered shops and grain warehouses in the county seat, where they also set churches ablaze and slaughtered priests. The agitation then spread to neighboring poppy-growing counties, compelling the governor to send reinforcements to the area.[51] Two years later, angry opium farmers in southern Shaanxi beheaded a county official in Huxian, southwest of Xi'an.[52] Sixteen months later in Yijun county, opium commissar Wang Jiechen and more than ten policemen escorting him were killed by bandits who had been commissioned by local opium growers to protect forbidden poppy plants in exchange for a share in the profits from opium sales. The bandits went on to occupy the county seat.[53] Such outright collusion between defiant opium farmers and bandits was exceptional, as were these bloody episodes. Farmers were far more likely to be killed than to kill, and their acts of violence rarely involved large-scale killing and destruction.[54]

CHANGING COMPOSITION OF RESISTANCE OVER TIME

So far I have been freely navigating or, more exactly, drifting from late-imperial to late-Republican episodes, on the implicit assumption that opium farmers' resistance basically retained the same features throughout all four decades. I am quite willing to make that assumption explicit, but distinctions can be made between the first decade and last three. One is sociological. As far as I know, most late-Qing and early-Republican efforts to resist poppy eradication were undertaken and managed by the farmers themselves. Later on, especially during World War II and when resistance became murderous, the murderers often originated from outside the ranks of opium farmers. Upon his arrival in the Jindong and Zhenyuan area in 1939, the Yunnan provincial prohibition commissioner was crushed under rice sacks at the instigation of local gentry. The county magistrate's report that the inspector had died from a violent illness did not convince the new inspector, who cautiously abstained from any inquiry when pretending to carry out his task in the same area.[55] The following year, another provincial inspector was killed in Zhenyuan county (he had, however, demanded five hundred ounces of opium for himself); his murderers were the county magistrate's agents.[56] In several bloodier incidents that erupted in Sichuan and Xikang provinces during the 1940s, peasants appear to have been manipulated by local powerholders or locally influential rich individuals. During one such incident (in Jinghua, Sichuan, in 1940), eight propagandists for the cause of opium prohibition were killed in an attack by men hired by the area's biggest landlord.[57]

While warlords, military and civil officials, and other opium traffickers (those rare ones who happened to be professional opium merchants) benefited most from the resumption of opium growing in southwest China, at the local level the most notorious profiteers belonged to a mixed elite consisting of large landlords, local powerholders, chieftains of national minority groups, and branch heads of Paoge and other secret societies. These influential people were better able to resist eradication campaigns by bribing, intimidating, or even fighting. Indeed, I have found many more cases than those I have related here of bloody encounters instigated by secret societies and/or local powerholders. Yet I cannot make very much of the difference between early and late resistance because I do not know much about the sociological lineup of early (1907–1917) resisters. Even cases of locally rich and powerful individuals manipulating a majority of poorer opium farmers in defense of their own interests do not contradict the traditional pattern of peasant resistance, which is fought by the entire community and on behalf of it. To be sure, large opium producers or traffickers belonging to the local elite stood to benefit much more than others from any victorious resistance, but that was also the case of those landlords and better-off farmers who led or instigated tax riots, which were perceived as being waged on behalf of each and every taxpayer.

A second, equally tentative, difference between early and late resistance is suggested by significant variations among the examples detailed above. Contrast the 1910 Gansu riot caused by Prefect Zhang's honest, if insensitive, conduct with the Liping disturbances of 1942–1944 brought about by Magistrate Xie's corrupt dealings and subsequent reversals. My impression is that during the 1930s and 1940s opium growers would proportionately more often resist extortion or abrupt policy changes, while a generation earlier their parents were more likely to resist eradication as such. Early resisters were more upset by the attack on opium as their livelihood than by abuses and exactions, which appear to have been less frequent under the declining Qing dynasty than they were later on under warlords or quasi-autonomous provincial and local officials in mostly remote or peripheral areas. Moreover, opium prohibition during the 1930s and 1940s came on the heels of laxity or even promotion of poppy cultivation during the 1920s, and the later prohibition was enforced in a less continuous and effective way than had been the case with the first prohibition campaign. Peasants were therefore inclined not to take it very seriously, or even to assume that it was over. They all the more resented the sudden, almost unexpected coming of new eradication campaigns following rather lengthy interruptions in the implementation of anti-opium policies, conducted within a political environment in which blatant disregard of the law looked more like the norm than the exception.

RESISTANCE TO POPPY TAX

Insofar as it was often directed against blatant abuses and extortion, resistance to opium interdiction during the 1930s and 1940s had more in common with contemporary resistance to opium tax than it did with previous resistance to opium suppression campaigns of 1907–1916. Resistance to poppy tax and resistance to poppy eradication not only were similar, but overlapped, if only because it was not always easy to distinguish imposition from interdiction. Should we consider the widespread heavy "fines" on opium cultivation as interdiction (which is how they appeared on paper) or as tax (which is what they amounted to in reality)? These were levied from the 1920s on by many warlords, first of all throughout the western "opium belt," but as far east as Fujian as well. That the purpose of such "fines" was to expand, not repress, opium cultivation in order to raise more taxes is corroborated by those instances when the continual increases of the fine eventually deterred peasants from planting poppies, as happened in various places during the season of 1925–1926. The authorities concerned then hurriedly reduced the amount of the fine in order to stimulate production.

The very name of the tax, *yanmu fajin* (abbreviated as *mufa*), conveys the fiscal nature of a "fine" assessed according to the size of opium fields, in the same way as the land tax. This was bluntly recognized by Sichuan warlord Liu Wenhui in a telegram sent in December 1931 to the Xuyong county magistrate in which he indicated in advance the amount of the fine (45,000 yuan) to be levied by the next opium crop throughout the county. He further instructed the magistrate to order each village head to make sure that every household planted poppies at the proper time, so that no area would fail to pay its quota of the "fine." The following year Liu sent a circular telegram on 5 October 1932 reminding every county magistrate within his jurisdiction to impose a fine on those cultivators who refused to plant poppies.[58] The latter fine, the equally infamous "lazy tax" *(lan yan-*

juan or, more commonly, *lanjuan)*, was supposed to equal the sum that poppy cultivators were required to pay. It was often doubled for a repeat offense, in other words, when the farmer refused to plant poppies for the second consecutive year. In Guizhou during the late 1920s, the lazy fine, when doubled in the second year, ran as high as fifty yuan per *mu*. No crop but opium could bring in enough for the farmer to be able to afford to pay such a sum.[59]

Before proceeding to tax resistance itself, let us give a few examples of transitional forms between resistance to opium interdiction and resistance to opium taxation. In 1943 the county magistrate of Luxi, Yunnan, first incited farmers to grow poppy, then pretended to uproot poppy plants in order to extract a bribe. Later on, he demanded a second bribe, allegedly for the benefit of provincial officials whose complicity was needed to safeguard the next crop. With the appearance of a civil inspector who insisted on getting his own share, farmers finally concluded that opium growing would no longer be profitable after a third extortion. When troops were sent in, peasants resisted and killed the magistrate as well as the commander and several soldiers.[60] Even in a nominally "anti-prohibition" affair such as this one, opium farmers were resisting not interdiction as such, but extortion by officials, a common feature of opium-tax resistance.

Such linkage applies even better in the case of resistance to heavy fines. In 1920 Kong Fanjin, a petty warlord in southern Gansu, imposed an extremely heavy "fine" on poppy cultivators. His agents arrested and tortured a local peasant leader from Baiyangtan, Kangxian, and made it known that they would not set him free until the fine due in Baiyangtan had been paid in full. After an agreement had replaced the captive by his son as hostage, the liberated leader obtained the help of the Red Lanterns, a local secret society. The Red Lanterns killed Kong's agent in charge of distributing and collecting fines, liberated the substitute hostage, and resisted two successive attacks by troops. Their successes eventually won exemption of the fine for those opium growers who had not yet paid it.[61] A similar overlap between opium suppression and opium taxation led to a riot in Wudu, Gansu, in the spring of 1915. The local warlord's emissaries to Wudu were directed both to represent opium prohibition committees and to collect tax on every field, whether planted in poppy or not (in the latter case, farmers owed the so-called lazy field fee). The bloody affair (fourteen people were killed or wounded) that ensued probably belongs more to the realm of tax resistance.[62]

As we have seen, and this is the first point to emphasize when comparing both kinds of resistance, opium tax resistance occurred much less frequently than resistance to opium suppression, at least according to my sample (46 incidents in table 4, compared to 131 in table 3). On the other hand, one of the largest revolts connected with opium during the half-century, and by far the best known, happens to have been caused by very high taxes. In fact, it amounted not so much to one as to three interrelated uprisings that troubled Suxian and Lingbi counties in northern Anhui throughout the summer of 1932. About twenty thousand opium farmers took part in some of these disturbances, and at least fifty-two were killed. In both cases, one of the most decisive factors triggering the revolt was official extortion and abuses. We have seen that the latter were often present, and notoriously so, in affairs related to opium prohibition. They were even more blatantly involved in the Suxian revolt. A few months before its outbreak, the Suxian county magistrate, going far beyond what was requested by the Northern Anhui "Special Tax" Bureau *(Wanbei teshui chu)*, abruptly raised the already exorbitant 900,000 yuan tax levied in 1931 to three million yuan by adding surcharges to the regular poppy tax, and established an elaborate system to control the size of poppy fields. That control proved more onerous to opium growers than the tax itself. Successive waves of opium commissioners exacted from poppy growers first a registration fee, then various fees for the rope used to measure poppy fields, for the stakes on which were written the name of the owners, the locality, and number of *mu* of the fields, for removing these stakes afterward, and for verifying the accuracy of the measurements, not to mention compensation for paper, ink, travel, and lodging expenses, and bribes to escape the larger penalties incurred in cases of inaccuracy or dissimulation in reporting the extent of the poppy fields. When these waves of commissioners reached the Suxian countryside in May to June 1932, their arrival coincided with a poor opium harvest, which left most opium growers unable to pay such high taxes and endless fees. A few committed suicide, but more fled and eventually rose in revolt when opium commissars and tax collectors began seizing buffaloes and torturing taxpayers to make them confess where their money was hidden.[63]

Suxian and Lingbi were far from the only rural places where local authorities deemed the profit from opium cultivation too juicy to be left to the producers. More than in the western poppy belt, such places appear to have been especially frequent—if the location of incidents of tax resistance can serve as an indicator—in the rest of Anhui province at the time of Chen Tiaoyuan's governorship and in Fujian province. Not only were such incidents much fewer in number in other eastern provinces, but one can detect in the unusually well documented Suxian and Lingbi affair a clear case of opposition between county and provincial authorities, on the one hand, and the central government and its representatives in northern Anhui, on the other. General Jiang Dingwen, then stationed in Bengbu, arrested and detained at his headquarters two corrupt powerholders from Suxian; he further requested and obtained the dismissal of the no less corrupt Suxian magistrate. Later on, the Central Executive Committee of the Guomindang expelled those Suxian and Lingbi party members who had exploited and oppressed local opium farmers, but when it ordered that some of them be punished severely, the Anhui provincial court pronounced them innocent of any crime. The GMD Central Executive Committee's Commission for the Guidance of Mass Movements *(Minzhong yundong zhidao weiyuanhui)* then asked for an investigation into the activities of the court, as well as for the arrest of all local GMD members guilty of exploiting or abusing peasant taxpayers—to no avail, as the offenders were consistently protected by county officials.

This is not to suggest that the sole flaw of the Nationalist government and the GMD headquarters in Nanjing was their inability to impose local obedience. Nonetheless, central government emissaries were on the whole more intent on reducing revenues from opium tax or opium traffic than were most local or provincial officials. A similar pattern could be observed during the late Qing, as we noted above in the case of Prefect Zhang, who pursued suppression more energetically than county-level officials. With few exceptions,[64] this pattern held during the last years of the Qing dynasty, but for reasons unlike those that account for divergences among Nanjing's representatives, quasi-autonomous provincial warlords, and local powerholders. To be sure, the laxity of many local Qing officials in suppressing the cultivation of poppy was often motivated by the sizable revenues they used to raise from opium tax, and sometimes also by the bribes they obtained for averting their eyes from conspicuously luxurious poppy fields, not to mention that they might have been opium smokers themselves. Nevertheless, caution appears to have been a fairly frequent motivation, too, as many on-the-spot officials were deeply concerned that disturbances were likely to ensue from a strict and swift implementation of the imperial edict of suppression. By contrast, conflicting interests and power relations between, say, Liu Xiang and then Jiang Jieshi, on the one hand, and local northern Sichuan strong men (whether "regular" officials or Paoge chieftains), on the other hand, explain much of their dealings with the opium question.

As far as peasant masses (as opposed to powerholders) are concerned, a significant difference between resistance to opium tax and opium suppression may be suggested by the admittedly rare instances of collusion between early-Republican Shaanxi opium farmers and bandits, who occasionally slaughtered officials, police, and troops. While they resented the loss of what had long been considered a legal revenue, opium farmers suddenly found their trade made them social outcasts. By contrast, most late-Republican opium farmers who resisted tax were no more than abused taxpayers.

CONCLUDING REMARKS

The distinction between open defiance of the law by opium farmers unwilling to give up their forbidden trade and the legitimate grievances of pressured taxpayers makes more sense to us than it did to involved peasants. From our point of view, it might seem strange that there were many more cases of resistance to opium prohibition than to opium tax, given the very high burden represented by the latter and the fact that poppy cultivation was less often repressed than tolerated during three of the four decades under review. After all, during the same period, tax resistance—including resistance not just to the land tax but also to the salt tax, the alcohol tax, the tax on pig slaughtering, and an infinite variety of miscellaneous taxes—predominated among rural disturbances not related to opium. Tax riots were in particular much more frequent than all cases of resistance to non-fiscal administrative measures or government policies, of which opium prohibition represents only one type.

A social movement contemporary with the peak of peasant resistance to opium prohibition that may help to point out the significance of opium resistance was the widespread, often violent opposition to the official campaign at the end of the Qing dynasty to register the population *(diaocha hukou)* and affix door plates *(menpai)* on residents' homes. Although the fees that were charged in connection with this program were occasionally perceived as a compensation for registration expenses, such measures were much less threatening to actual peasant revenues and lives than widespread, often extravagant rumors led many villagers and some urban dwellers to believe. Whatever the real threat or cost, which was in no way comparable to the loss of revenue suffered by opium growers, resistance to population surveys was linked to the ongoing opposition to the New Policies and "local autonomy" *(difang zizhi)*. Paying new taxes for establishing new schools, expanding local militia units, and the like no doubt contributed to this resentment, but so did the challenge to traditional ideas and beliefs and to conservative local elites.[65]

I mention this resistance in order to illustrate two final remarks concerning so-called "spontaneous" *(zifa)* peasant disturbances.[66] The first deals with both the reasons that incited peasants to rise and the timing of their reactions.[67] Far from questioning the status quo, however inimical it was to them, peasants usually reacted against new developments that represented a blow to the ways things had been done.[68] Notorious among such novelties were government campaigns or administrative measures that were either harmful to peasant interests, as opium prohibition was to opium growers, or deemed harmful, as in the case of population registration. Reaction against new developments triggered most tax riots as well: rather than question a long-established tax, peasant taxpayers resisted a newly established tax—or more often a fee surcharged on the land tax (*fujia shui*)—or the sudden increase of an old tax, or even the collection of the usual amount of tax in the wake of a poor harvest. This reaction applies to rent resistance as well. Very rarely did tenants resist rent in order to obtain new rights or improve their lot. Most rent resistance incidents followed bad harvests and the refusal of landlords to grant tenants a rent reduction (or one deemed sufficient), which was traditional in such circumstances.

In other words, peasant riots or revolts were defensive reactions to a local deterioration of their unenviable lot. The problem or the scourge of the moment, rather than any desire or hope for progress, was what led them to rebel. For poppy growers, the late-Qing imperial edicts prohibiting opium amounted to such a scourge. Although the sample of incidents listed in table 3 may not be truly representative of all cases of resistance, it is no coincidence that resistance was especially frequent during the beginning of the very first phase when poppy growers deemed poppy eradication an unheard of, unbearable calamity.

As a final observation, I would note that a privileged intellectual could be tempted to praise the rare collective actions or petitions aimed at re-fusing an official order to plant poppy and to condemn the much more common instances of resistance to poppy eradication. But we must be wary of classifying peasant revolts by projecting our values onto peasant con-cerns, instead of analyzing them on the basis of peasants' needs and per-ceived interests. Peasants reacted to notorious abuses or extortion by local powerholders, but they also opposed opium interdiction, or an overdue fiscal reform, or a land survey that might both alleviate the burden of most taxpayers and increase state revenues, or the official introduction of a type of silk-worm better able to resist Japanese competition, or a campaign against superstitions they believed to have offended the rain-dispensing dragon and therefore to be responsible for the drought.[69] Their responses to efforts at reform or modernization were reactive, not irrational. Like silk-worm cultivators who did not prefer their inferior, home-bred cocoons, but were simply unable to buy those that were officially promoted, many opium farmers could not but be struck with despair by an eradication campaign depriving them of their livelihood—the wonderful poppy that meddlesome authorities branded a poison.

NOTES

1. Spence, "Opium Smoking in Ch'ing China," p. 173.

2. The campaign from 1906 to 1916 was not abruptly terminated after Yuan's death, and performance in the first post-Yuan years was not as poor as it would be in the succeeding years. Alan Baumler extends the first phase of "concerted

nationwide campaign against opium selling, smoking, and growing" to 1919; "Playing with Fire: The Nationalist Government and Opium in China, 1927–1941," p. 57.

3. Wright, *China in Revolution*, p. 14.

4. Hosie, *On the Trail of the Opium Poppy*.

5. Butel, *L'opium*, pp. 248–52, 260.

6. They could not visit remote valleys and villages, where the suppression campaign was much more haphazardly implemented, and were at times forced to rely on the declarations of county magistrates and other officials. Compare the eastern Fujian situation described in Madancy, "Revolution, Religion, and the Poppy," p. 9. See also Baumler, "Playing with Fire: The Nationalist Government and Opium in China, 1927–1941," p. 180, for the superficial character of British inspections in Yunnan.

7. Compare again the situation in eastern and southeastern Fujian, where poppy cultivation resumed on a large scale; Madancy, "Revolution, Religion, and the Poppy," p. 12.

8. In Wudu, Gansu, a "lazy field fee" *(lantian kuan)* was collected as early as the spring of 1915 on fields not planted in poppy; *Wudu wenshi ziliao xuanji*, vol. 1, pp. 8–9.

9. Baumler, "Playing with Fire: The Nationalist Government and Popular Anti-Opium Agitation in 1927–28," p. 48; also Baumler, "Playing with Fire: The Nationalist Government and Opium in China, 1927–1941," p. 62.

10. Shortly thereafter prices would also rise in Yunnan as a result of the 1916 suppression campaign, though without approaching Sichuan levels; Baumler, "Playing with Fire: The Nationalist Government and Opium in China, 1927–1941," p. 180.

11. Dong, "Étude sur le problème de l'opium dans la région du sud-ouest de la Chine pendant les années 1920 et 1930," pp. 110–12.

12. Martin, *Shanghai Green Gang*, p. 55; Dong, "Étude," pp. 107–9.

13. Tang also had an eye on Guangdong. See Boorman and Howard, *Biographical Dictionary of Republican China*, 2:337, 3:225.

14. Dong, "Étude," pp. 120–23.

15. Levich, *Kwangsi Way in Kuomintang China*, p. 241.

16. Ibid., pp. 242–43.

17. Huang Shaohong, "Xin Guixi yu yapian yan," pp. 181–83.

18. After the participants in the 1929 Disbandment Conferences had committed themselves not to enlist new troops, it proved difficult for Jiang to increase his strength without inciting provincial warlords to do the same. The solution was to enlist troops in special units officially aimed at fighting opium traffickers (Xiao, "Jiang Jieshi jinyan de neimu," p. 161).

19. Huang Shaohong, "Xin Guixi," p. 193.

20. Baumler, "Playing with Fire: The Nationalist Government and Opium in China, 1927–1941," p. 290.

21. Baumler sees a shift in emphasis during the war in Jiang's opium policy: control and cure of smokers and elimination of poppy-growing took precedence over control of the opium trade (ibid., pp. 302–3).

22. Mi, "Jiang zhengchuan zai Chuanxi bianju jinyan de zhenxiang," details policy fluctuations in six north Sichuan counties.

23. Zhang and Ding, "Qingmo minbian nianbao," 49:108–81, and 50:77–121.

24. Two historians from the Institute of Modern History at Academia Sinica, Zhang Li (Chang Li) and Chen Yongfa (Ch'en Yung-fa), kindly gave me substantial materials relating to incidents in Shaanxi province, all of which occurred no later than June 1918. The last Shaanxi incident encompasses several disturbances triggered by opium suppression in central and western Shaanxi between October 1917 and June 1918 (*Shuntian shibao*, 23 June 1918). Likewise, I counted as one (or two, including the one on 6 January) the "more than ten incidents" that occurred from January to May 1940 in seven localities of Yongsheng county, Yunnan (*Yongsheng xianzhi*, p. 508). One can very well object to this way of tabulating events. I have followed it as a general rule when compiling rural disturbances of every kind, because I have deemed the obvious drawbacks resulting from this decision less important than those caused by, for instance, counting as scores of separate cases the almost uninterrupted rent resistance incidents that followed each other from November 1935 to June 1936 in Wuxian, Jiangsu. Although most of the latter were admittedly more important than many other rent resistance incidents listed separately, they nevertheless belong to a single rent resistance movement that needs to be treated as a whole, like the ones that previously mobilized Wuxian tenants in late 1929 and the fall of 1934.

25. *Dongfang zazhi* 10, no. 12 (June 1914): 43.

26. According to Baumler, "Playing with Fire: The Nationalist Government and Opium in China, 1927–1941," p. 166, Zhejiang "grew very little opium."

27. Ibid., pp. 12, 17, and chapter 8 passim.

28. Ma Chengfeng, "Zuijin Zhongguo nongcun jingji zhu shixiang zhi baolu."

29. Baumler, "Playing with Fire: The Nationalist Government and Opium in China, 1927–1941," p. 184.

30. *China Year Book* 1926, p. 620.

31. Ibid., p. 641. There were similar refusals in four other Sichuanese counties, in the southwest of the province (*China Year Book* 1926, p. 626; 1928, p. 524; 1931, p. 600).

32. *Qijiang xianzhi* (1991), p. 18.

33. For a 1944 example in Liping, Guizhou, see p. 307.

34. *Zhongguo yanhuo nianjian*, vol. 4, 1931, p. 12, quoted in Dong, "Étude," p. 203.

35. *China Year Book* 1926, p. 623. In Zhenyuan, Yunnan, in 1940, a similar ploy was tried, with rice taking the place of wheat and beans. Li Zihui, "Yunnan jinyan gaikuang," p. 122.

36. Examples in southern Yunnan during the 1936–1937 eradication campaign may be found in Li Zihui, "Yunnan jinyan gaikuang," p. 109.

37. Or under cover of earth: see Judith Wyman's chapter in this volume.

38. *Minli bao*, 18 June 1911.

39. See Scott, *Weapons of the Weak*.

40. Chen Yaolun, "Xikang yapian liudu zaocheng Yingjing shibian jingguo," pp. 176–77.

41. Ibid., p. 181.

42. *Jiange wenshi ziliao* 7 (1986): 118–19. On Paoge, or Gowned Brothers, see Ruf, *Cadres and Kin*, pp. 60–61 and 190.

43. *Jiange wenshi ziliao* 7 (1986): 103–4.

44. *Dongfang zazhi* 7, no. 5 (June 1910): 118. Compare an almost identical episode in the resistance by French tobacco growers in the late seventeenth century. On 4 August 1687, entire villages situated on the border of Artois and Picardie forcibly resisted eight police squads that had come uprooting tobacco a mere few days prior to harvesting time. The analogy extends to the illegal nature of the trade. As Artois was exempted from any tax on tobacco, villages close to Picardie had replaced wheat- with tobacco-growing in order to fraudulently and profitably sell tobacco to (not exempt) Picardie (Bercé, *Croquants et nu-pieds*, pp. 130–35).

45. The latter request did, in fact, coincide with a fairly common government policy. Because selling opium was considered worse than growing it, peasants were quite often allowed to harvest opium on condition that they plant no more (personal communication from Alan Baumler).

46. *Shuntian shibao*, 21 August 1910.

47. *Dongfang zazhi* 7, no. 6 (July 1910): 166–67; 7, no. 11 (December 1910): 347–48.

48. *Liping xianzhi*, pp. 20–22.

49. Yun, "Mouvements populaires en Chine à la fin des Ch'ing," p. 25.

50. For instance in Tong'an, Fujian, in December 1930 (USDS 893.00 PR Amoy/37, 1931.1.13).

51. *Shenbao*, 11 July 1913.

52. *Shuntian shibao*, 21 December 1915.

53. *Dagong bao*, 18 April 1917.

54. For instance, rioting opium farmers would invade the xian or prefectural city (e.g., in Nantan, Guangxi, in May 1910: Zhang and Ding, "Qingmo minbian nianbao," 50:98), where they might pull down or ransack the opium prohibition bureau (e.g., in Meishan, Sichuan, in July 1910, ibid., p. 102, and *Dongfang zazhi* 7, no. 7 [1910]: 199), as well as other official buildings such as tax bureaus or public salt stores, and private gentry residences, charitable halls, schools, and churches. Within six months, from October 1910 to April 1911, three such incidents occurred in Dongyang, Zhejiang (Zhang and Ding, "Qingmo minbian nianbao," 50:107; *Dongfang zazhi* 7, no. 9 [1910]: 251), Dayao, Yunnan (Zhang and Ding, "Qingmo minbian nianbao," 50:108), and Zhangye, Gansu (ibid., p. 115). More often, recalcitrant opium growers would not leave their farms or their fields, and simply clashed there with civil authorities (e.g., Fufeng, Shaanxi, 1910: Zhang and Ding, "Qingmo minbian nianbao," 50:98; *Dongfang zazhi* 7, no. 4 [1910]: 64; Anshun, Guizhou, January 1911: Zhang and Ding, "Qingmo minbian nianbao," 50:110; Dagongbao, Xuantong II.12.26 = 1911.1.26) or military officials (e.g., on the borders of Dianjiang and Liangshan counties, Sichuan, on 13 April 1910: Zhang and Ding, "Qingmo minbian nianbao," 50:92).

55. Li Zihui, "Yunnan jinyan gaikuang," p. 121.

56. Ibid., p. 122.

57. Mi Qingyun, "Jiang zhengchuan zai Chuanxi bianju jinyan de zhenxiang," p. 161.

58. *Sichuan wenshi ziliao,* vol. 10, 1963, p. 159.

59. Li Longzhang, "Lüetan Guizhou de yanhuo," p. 24.

60. Li Zihui, "Yunnan jinyan gaikuang," p. 124.

61. *Kangxian zhi,* pp. 573–74.

62. *Wudu wenshi ziliao xuanji,* vol. 1, pp. 8–9. For two similar cases that occurred in Xingtai, Hebei, in 1930, and Langdai, Guizhou, in 1934, see *Xingtai wenshi ziliao xuanji,* vol. 4, pp. 159–64, and *Liuzhi wenshi ziliao xuanji,* vol. 4, p. 124.

63. Bianco, "Peasant Uprisings against Poppy Tax Collection."

64. One such exception occurred in the spring of 1910 in Jiangxi. When Guang-xinfu poppy farmers assembled in Yushan, their county capital, in order to resist opium suppression, the Yushan magistrate requested that the provincial government send in troops. That request was, however, turned down by the governor of Jiangxi province, who advised the Yushan magistrate to try to persuade the crowd to disperse, rather than to use force (*Dongfang zazhi* 7, no. 5 [1910]: 118). In this case the subordinate (the county magistrate) was intent on suppressing the demonstration by opium farmers whereas the provincial governor was not.

65. Wang Shuhuai, *Zhongguo xiandaihua de quyu yanjiu: Jiangsu sheng, 1860–1916,* pp. 205–7; Esherick, *Reform and Revolution in China,* pp. 107–20.

66. No social movement is entirely spontaneous. That widely used term enables me to distinguish the minor rural disturbances in this chapter from communist agitation and the like.

67. According to Tilly's typology, most twentieth-century spontaneous Chinese peasant movements would be termed "reactive," as would most European peasant movements from the early seventeenth to the mid nineteenth centuries. See Tilly, *From Mobilization to Revolution,* and *The Contentious French.*

68. Bianco, "Peasants and Revolution," p. 322.

69. Details, including dates and localities, are given in Bianco, "Peasant Movements," pp. 280–89.

PART FOUR

Crisis and Resolution

FOURTEEN

Opium and Collaboration in Central China, 1938–1940

Timothy Brook

In September 1938, a year into the war with Japan, Song Meiling, the wife of Jiang Jieshi (Chiang Kai-shek), charged the Japanese invaders with using opium to defeat China. It was a piece of "diabolical cunning" intended, she insisted, "to drench a land with opium and narcotics with the primary object of so demoralizing the people that they would be physically unfit to defend their country, and mentally and morally so depraved that they could easily be bought and bribed with drugs to act as spies when the time came in order that their craving might be satisfied."[1] Was opium being pumped into China to promote the narcotization of the country? Was it part of an insidious Japanese plot to bring the Chinese people to their knees? Chinese active on the other side of the war, those who collaborated with the Japanese, insisted that they at least could not be tarred with this brush. At his war crimes trial, Liang Hongzhi (1882–1946), who as the former head of the Reformed Government (1938–1940) led the first Japanese-sponsored regime in Nanjing, agreed that opium had been a problem under his leadership. But he insisted that narcotization had not been his policy. His regime's Opium Suppression Bureau was not intended to promote the spread of opium for the financial benefit of his regime or Japan, he claimed; in fact, it had brought the trade under control by restricting the flow of drugs and registering addicts in order to rehabilitate them—just as Jiang's regime had done. He declared himself not guilty of narcotizing the Chinese people.[2] The Japanese, and not his government, were the traffickers.

Can we accept Liang's deflection of the charge of opium trafficking to the Japanese? His war crimes testimony implies more generally that his regime's involvement in opium was merely one element in a larger relationship that prevailed between his government and the Japanese occupation authorities: the Reformed Government could take no action independent of what Japan wanted, and those actions it did take were at Japanese direction. With respect to opium, however, he portrayed his regime in proactive terms. This chapter examines the opium trade in central China under Liang's regime from 1938 to 1940 in order to evaluate the extent of either his or Japanese responsibility for the trafficking that went on during those two years—and concludes that both played roles far more complicated than either Liang or Song suggests. The Reformed Government not only colluded in deriving substantial revenue from opium but competed, albeit unsuccessfully, with the Japanese to control that revenue. But this finding does not answer Song's charge of planned narcotization. For that, we will have to look at the issue of opium in relation to the logic of Japan's occupation—and in doing so, we will find the allegation hard to sustain. Whether Liang deserved to be found guilty as charged—and he was—may thus depend on perspective as much as on truth.

THE ORIENTAL HOTEL CASE

When the Japanese army launched its assault on Shanghai in 1937, it threw the center of the opium trade—the business of supplying it, the networks for selling it, and the regulations that asserted the government's monopoly over it—into chaos. Some of the effects of that chaos, and the first steps by figures in the occupation regime to take advantage of it, can be traced in the following typical story of a drug bust from the summer of 1938 in the Special Branch files of the Shanghai Municipal Police (SMP, the British-led force that policed the International Settlement).

In the early hours of 20 June 1938 the SMP raided the Oriental Hotel on Nanjing Road on a tip that "a number of Chinese traffickers in narcotics and arms were residing in either Room 707 or 708." The police entered room 707 and found Nozaka Takashi in his pajamas in bed. When he identified himself as a Japanese citizen, they "immediately withdrew without having attempted to search either the man or the room." On entering room 708, they found a brown leather traveling bag containing eleven packages of raw opium weighing eighteen pounds, with a street value of approximately two thousand dollars. The three occupants, two men and a female prostitute, were arrested. Jiang Yutian was a thirty-three-year-old rice merchant from Chuzhou, sixty kilometers northwest of Nanjing. Chang Bao Ping (Ch., Zhang Qifeng) identified himself as a Korean employed by the Chuzhou unit of the Special Service Department (SSD, *Tokumubu*), the Japanese agency charged with restoring civil administration in the wake of the military occupation. Faced with a subject of the Japanese empire, the arresting officers were obliged to call for the services of a Japanese detective on the staff of the SMP. When the Japanese officer arrived, Nozaka in room 707 came in to complain to him about the actions of the SMP detectives.

The officer was in turn obliged to call the Japanese consular police for assistance, as a Japanese national was now involved. While waiting for their arrival, Nozaka went back to his room and returned carrying a Browning automatic "and proceeded to demonstrate same to the Chinese detectives. He made no effort to coerce or intimidate them, but apparently only produced it to impress them with his own importance."[3] All four suspects were arrested and taken to the central police station.

Questioning at the station revealed that Jiang was a former university teacher who had taken up trading in rice and flour when wartime conditions made it impossible to survive on a teacher's salary. But Jiang was more than a merchant. He had served as the assistant manager of a refugee camp in Chuzhou (generating a happy conflict of interest with his grain business). He had also been a member of the Chuzhou Peace Maintenance Committee, a Chinese body that the Special Service unit there established to give a Chinese face to the occupation at the local level, though Jiang claimed to have resigned because he found the work "too strenuous." However he chose to represent himself, Jiang was clearly in active collaboration with the Japanese. This was not Jiang's first opium-buying expedition either, for he admitted that he had worked with other Koreans and Japanese to transport opium to Chuzhou several times before. On this occasion, Jiang testified, it was the Korean, Chang, who had initiated the run to Shanghai, though the capital for the venture was supplied by Jiang himself and two other Chinese merchants in Chuzhou.

Both Chang and Nozaka, it turns out, were civilian employees of the SSD. Jiang testified that they had traveled with him to ensure that he "was not molested," hence Nozaka's pistol. He also insisted that the Korean had been the one who made the actual purchase, from a Chinese man surnamed Xiao. Chang had claimed the same thing at the time of the arrest, insisting that the opium belonged to him and that the other two were not involved. Perhaps this was true. Chang's forthright admission may have been intended not just to spare Jiang (on whom, as a Chinese, penalties would fall more heavily) but to see that the opium was handed over to the Japanese consular police rather than remaining in SMP possession. In neither was he successful. The Shanghai Special District Court found Jiang guilty of trafficking and sentenced him to a prison term of nine and a half years and a fine of two thousand dollars. As for his accomplices, the Japanese Consular Court sentenced the Korean to two years for trafficking; the Japanese was released.[4]

Although this particular drug case occurred within the International Settlement and was not under the jurisdiction of the occupation authorities, it provides some initial impressions of the opium trade in the early phase of the Japanese occupation. First, it indicates that contraband drugs (including morphine) were available in Shanghai in the summer of 1938,[5] but that they were not available in the quantities that had circulated before the invasion. Opium was now moving in smaller packages, and under heavier guard. Both features may be noted in other SMP opium cases from this time, and indicate that supply had been badly disrupted: now opium in any amount was precious. The large-scale opium distribution networks that had operated under Green Gang supervision before 1938 were no longer functioning, and had been replaced by minor transactions through smaller operators.[6]

The second observation arising from this case is basic, but deserves to be stressed as we increase our awareness of Japanese involvement in drug operations during the occupation. Despite the disorder of the occupation, the suspension of judicial procedure, and the disappearance of the Guomindang system for drug control, opium remained a controlled substance. All regimes recognized the possession, consumption, and sale of private opium, as well as the ownership of unregistered opium-smoking equipment, as illegal and continued to police them as such. This illegality was recognized as much in occupied Shanghai in 1938 as in the concessions, to judge from the daily summaries of the first collaborationist police force in Shanghai, which are dominated by reports of arrests for possession of opium or morphine for the purposes of trafficking.[7] The illegality of opium was not yet written into law, however. The Reformed Government abrogated Guomindang laws and did not promulgate its own opium-control legislation until 20 March 1939, but in practice the earlier rules were still assumed to apply. When courts had to invoke laws to pass judgments, they used what the Jiangsu High Court in April 1939 referred to delicately as the "old laws,"[8] the regulations of the Guomindang regime. Chinese and Japanese officials and police of the occupation regime at all levels treated opium as a controlled substance and took action to reduce its consumption.[9] But this is not to assume that the goal of these efforts was necessarily to suppress consumption, because the revenue that an opium monopoly generated was too attractive to do without. What the occupation regime aimed for was not to get rid of opium entirely, but to ensure that consumers obtained their drug only through official channels. It was not consumption, but private dealing, that was illegal and the subject of police scrutiny and court discipline.

The Oriental Hotel case also exposes Japanese collusion in the opium trade. The ostensible dealer was Chinese but his bodyguards were imperial Japanese subjects: the drug run between Shanghai and Chuzhou was not the private transaction of a Chinese merchant working alone, but was organized under the protection, and probably at the direction, of the Chuzhou branch of the army's Special Service Department. Both a Japanese and a Korean were involved, though the latter found himself less well protected when judicial rules had to be applied, as was generally true of Koreans, who were ubiquitous in the China drug trade.[10]

These foregoing observations show that the opium trade in 1938 was operating across a disjuncture. On the one hand, both Japanese and Chinese authorities enforced the illegality of opium; on the other, at least some of them exploited it as a revenue producer. This disjuncture was a standard feature of many East Asian regimes in the first half of the twentieth century, which operated lucrative opium monopolies while also criminalizing the trade in which they participated. As we shall see, the Reformed Government found itself in this awkward but conventional position. It was an anomaly only to the extent that it may have slid back from the degree of control that its immediate predecessor, the National Government of Jiang Jieshi, had recently achieved. For this the Japanese bear more than a little responsibility.

THE OPIUM MARKET AFTER JAPAN'S INVASION

During the half-decade of Guomindang rule leading up to Japan's invasion of China, the opium trade in central China had attained an unprecedented degree of organization. The organization emanated from two sources: from the efforts of National Government officials who sought to suppress the trade in conformity with China's obligations under the Hague Convention of 1912, and from the energy of underworld operators such as Green Gang leader Du Yuesheng, who sought to expand it. On the one side, the Ministry of Revenue in 1932 set up an "opium suppression" system involving the public sale of opium by designated agents of the Opium Suppression Bureau (OSB, *Jieyan ju*). Through a program of registration and controlled access to opium, the system was designed to wean addicts from the drug, but also to provide the state with revenue during the weaning period. On the other, Du Yuesheng succeeded in gaining control of the importation and distribution of opium in Shanghai through competition within the underworld, but also with the cooperation of public officials. Du's cooperation was lucrative for both sides: once he had established his monopoly on the wholesale trade in Shanghai, he reportedly forwarded about two hundred thousand dollars a month to local authorities.[11] Eventually, however, Jiang Jieshi succeeded in imposing a monopoly over supply in 1935, as Alan Baumler describes in his chapter in this volume, giving the state the upper hand in the control of the trade.

When Japan attacked Shanghai in August 1937, the flow of opium into the region was disrupted and both the state's and the Green Gang's monopolies collapsed. (Du Yuesheng fled to Hong Kong and resisted Japanese attempts to lure him back, although some of his associates threw their lot in with the collaboration regime, possibly with his blessing.)[12] Scarcity drove up prices in the fall of 1937. A Shanghai newspaper reported that the price of opium and narcotics "rose by 300% to 400%. The markets dealing in noxious drugs in Nantao [Nandao] and Chapei [Zhabei] were destroyed, while the manufacturing plants in the Foreign Settlements ceased to function for lack of materials." But once the Chinese resistance around Shanghai was broken, the narcotics trade could resume. By December 1937 narcotics were flowing again into Shanghai, "imported here by a certain party," as the same newspaper euphemistically phrases Japan's involvement. As the old distribution network had collapsed, clandestine retailing went on inside the foreign settlements at certain vegetable stalls that became known to consumers. Narcotics prices fell almost to prewar levels by February 1938, but opium remained scarce, high prices apparently driving some opium addicts to switch to narcotics.[13] The same effect on prices was felt as the Japanese army pushed west. Following the occupation of Nanjing in December 1937, opium prices there rose and remained high through the spring and summer of 1938, inducing some to use refined narcotics to feed their opium addictions.[14] The price for official opium only stabilized in Nanjing in the autumn, when supply was resumed, at the rather high level of eleven yuan per tael.[15]

The disruption of prewar distribution and the attendant rise in prices made entry into the opium market attractive. The Japanese occupation force was lured. In November 1937, Lieutenant Colonel Chō Isamu of the Central China Area army asked a "journalist" named Fujita Isamu to approach Mitsui bussan to import two hundred thousand pounds of opium from Iran to Shanghai on the army's behalf. ("Journalist" was often the declared profession of fixers and clandestine Japanese agents.) Chō was acting on instructions from Colonel Kusumoto Sanetaka, head of what would become the General Affairs Bureau of the army's Special Service Department in Shanghai, and one of the Japanese instrumental in setting up Liang Hongzhi's Reformed Government the following spring. Fujita went to Mitsui headquarters in Tokyo to set up the deal. The company initially refused to get involved, but was soon persuaded to comply, allegedly under pressure from the Ministry of Foreign Affairs. Tokyo ordered its branch office in Iran to purchase 1,400 chests of opium (each chest weighed 160 pounds—72 kilograms or 2,656 taels) and to ship them to Shanghai. The first shipment of 428 cases arrived in April 1938, the remaining 972 chests the following January.[16]

While the opium was being acquired, Colonel Kusumoto approached another "journalist," Satomi Hajime, to handle wholesaling. As publisher of the Tianjin Chinese-language newspaper *Yongbao* under the pen name Li Ming, Satomi had in fact worked above ground as a journalist, but with the onset of war he used his intelligence-gathering skills for bigger projects.

He agreed to take on the job and approached Chinese merchants to distribute the drug. When the first shipment arrived in April, it was unloaded at a military wharf and placed in a guarded warehouse. A sign of the disorganization of the trade was that it took Satomi several months to distribute the stock even in a time of scarcity. He deposited the proceeds with the Bank of Taiwan, paid Mitsui from that account, and turned the remainder over to the SSD.[17] Although the source of the opium that the SMP confiscated in the Oriental Hotel bust was not disclosed, the timing suggests that it came from this first Mitsui shipment. Jiang Yutian in fact had started running opium out to Chuzhou earlier that spring, just at the time the Mitsui shipment landed in Shanghai: an agent of the SSD in Chuzhou acquiring what the SSD in Shanghai was making available to its local counterparts behind the screen of illegality.

DISTRIBUTION MONOPOLY:
THE OPIUM SUPPRESSION BUREAUS, 1938-1939

It is not difficult to understand why the Japanese revived the opium trade in Shanghai: both the Japanese army and the Reformed Government faced heavy financial burdens administering central China under wartime conditions. It is also easy to understand why they chose to run it as a government monopoly, since it earned revenue with a regularity that was preferable to the ad hoc distribution arrangement that Satomi set up for Kusumoto. Opium could be distributed in a more orderly and efficient fashion; consumers could be more readily identified and supplied; and the trade could be insulated from police interference, and might, in fact, avail itself of police protection to force rogue dealers out of the market.

Initially opium was handled at the local level by the Self-Government Committees that Special Service teams set up in every county immediately after it was occupied. Opium was not first on these committees' list of priorities, but it usually came to their attention within the first few months. In the absence of any sort of central direction, the committees appear to have followed pre-established practices of registering addicts and taxing the drug. The Self-Government Committee in Jiading county, just west of Shanghai, was directed by its Japanese handlers in mid March 1938 to ban heroin but to tax opium "at an appropriate rate." On 4 April the Japanese team ordered the committee's head of security to begin registering opium dens. In Taicang, the next county to the west, the Japanese Special Service agents directed the Self-Government Committee not just to register opium dens, but to arrange for them to reopen according to regulations subsequently published on 1 June. Controlling opium, it declared, was intimately related to restoring order and reviving the economy. Local regulations for the gradual elimination of opium use in Taicang over a three-year period were drawn up subsequently, and an Opium Suppression Bureau was set up to oversee this work in coordination with the police. Users were required to register, either for a twice-yearly fee of 0.4 yuan as a second-class addict, who could smoke opium in restricted amounts only at registered dens, or for a fee of two yuan as a first-class addict, who could smoke opium in his own home.[18]

Other counties and cities followed suit through the summer of 1938, according to articles published in the *New Nanjing Daily (Nanjing xinbao)*, the official newspaper in the capital. The Opium Suppression Bureaus (OSBs), as they were usually called, emerged in the absence of a national bureau or national regulations through the fall of 1938. By the spring of 1939 they were almost universal throughout the occupied lower Yangzi region. A state monopoly was beginning to take form through a process that was probably more centrally directed than surviving records indicate. The annual report of the Nanjing municipal police for 1938–1939 represents the founding of the OSB there as having occurred as a particular response to police pressure on the municipal government to do something about the growing number of addicts it was arresting and sentencing without recourse to the courts.[19] But other evidence indicates that the Special Service was the controlling agency. An article in the *New Nanjing Daily* on 23 June 1939 observes, for example, that the OSB in Wuhu, just upriver from Nanjing, reported neither to provincial authorities nor to the Reformed Government, but to the Special Service Department in Nanjing.

Those who agreed to register with their local OSB received the benefit of being allowed to purchase opium at a time when supplies of anything into the interior could not be guaranteed, and to do so legally. The opium they bought was supplied directly by the Japanese army. When the Nanjing OSB began to sell opium in October 1938, for example, it came from none other than Satomi, the journalist who operated the army's drug distribution operation in Shanghai. *New Nanjing Daily* articles about the OSB on 8 and 13 October do not actually name him or even say the suppliers were Japanese, but report only that Iranian opium being made available had been acquired through the assistance of "a friendly country." But in a postwar memoir, an employee of the Nanjing office of the South Manchurian Railway Company reveals that he was the one who arranged the initial supply for the Nanjing OSB. He purchased five chests from Satomi's warehouse in Shanghai and had them shipped to the capital in a sealed railway car.[20]

Opium retailing was more quickly and widely elaborated in Shanghai, where users were more numerous and supply more easily arranged. The Special Service Department in Shanghai did not set up an OSB there until December 1938, the delay apparently caused by tension between the Reformed Government and the Japanese army as to who should control revenues. The trade had already revived, however: as of November, twelve opium retailers had reopened in the Western District, the jurisdictional no-man's-land west of the International Settlement where the roads were po-liced by the SMP but local order was beyond settlement control. The alley-ways off Jessfield and Brenan Roads, just beyond the reach of the SMP, became Shanghai's wartime opium district. The director of the late-opening OSB was a Chinese named Yu Junqing, but the organization was controlled by three Japanese SSD appointees, among them none other than Satomi Hajime. According to a secret SMP analysis of 1941, "Osten-sibly the Bureau was a subordinate organ of the Reformed Government but in reality the Japanese Military Special Service Department was the real authority behind the scheme."[21]

The OSB in Shanghai was designed to serve not as a local organ, though, but as a regional coordinating body. Called the Jiangsu-Zhejiang-Anhui Opium Suppression Bureau, it was made responsible for distributing opium to local OSBs outside Shanghai. But the bureau was active within Shanghai as well. Among other undertakings, it sponsored a guild for opium distrib-utors under the name of the Special Enterprise Association *(Teye gonghui)*, "special enterprise" *(teye)* being the conventional euphemism for opium-dealing. The guild was in operation before February 1939, which is when the SMP first drew up a list of its thirteen members. It appears that the majority of opium dealers remained outside the guild at this time, for the SMP compiled a separate list of twenty-one opium retailers who were not members. By April, however, nine of these had joined the guild, presum-ably to improve their access to the OSB's supply of the drug.[22] By early summer, the Special Enterprise Association in Shanghai had twenty-nine members, all at addresses in the alleys off Jessfield and Brenan Roads, where dealers outside the guild continued to operate as well. A separate OSB office was finally established in the Western District in July 1939 to handle the booming trade there. I estimate that as of November 1939 eighty-two shops were selling opium in urban Shanghai, mostly in the West-ern District, and twelve in the outlying areas.[23] The opium trade may not have returned to prewar levels by 1939, but it was functioning reasonably well, at least in Shanghai, and was generating considerable revenue for those who controlled it.

SUPPLY MONOPOLY: THE HONGJI
BENEVOLENT SOCIETIES, 1939–1940

In setting up its OSB system, the Reformed Government had followed the practice of the collaborationist regime in North China, which placed its OSBs directly under the executive branch rather than under the judi-ciary in order to capture the flow of revenue for its own purposes. The monopoly became sufficiently lucrative by 1939 that the Reformed Government was not perceived to be making any real attempt to suppress opium consumption—the *New Nanjing Daily* on 1 May 1939 even carried an ad for the Mochou Opium Den in full view of readers and censors. But the revenue the regime controlled was limited to the extent that the monopoly was only partial. Its OSBs dominated distribution but could not touch supply, which remained in Japanese hands.

As proceeds rose, so did tension between the partners. Tokyo intervened on behalf of the Chinese in February 1939 against the Central China Liaison Office of the Kōain (or Asia Development Board, which replaced the SSD as Japan's development agency in Central China in December 1938, with Major General Kusumoto still in charge). It ordered the Kōain to hand the opium system over to Chinese management. With this support, the Reformed Government announced on 3 March that it would set up a national system of reorganized OSBs under its direct supervision. Provisional regulations were promulgated in March and April, and on 1 May the Opium Suppression Bureau General *(Jieyan zongju)* opened in Shanghai on North Sichuan Road in the Japanese concession. In his public pronouncement on the inaugural day, OSB director Zhu Yao went on the offensive. He did not hide behind vague platitudes about the need to control opium for the sake of improving public health. He declared rather that opium was a means by which powerful nations weakened the people of those they held in contempt.[24] The overt implication was that Great Britain was responsible for China's opium problem, though by not actually naming Britain, Zhu potentially reserved the charge for Japan. He may have been putting the Japanese on notice that they should keep their hands off the trade.

Zhu Yao's warning did not succeed. The Kōain did as Tokyo ordered, but compensated for its loss of control by engaging in two maneuvers that effectively nullified the concession.[25] First, it appointed more senior Japanese advisors to the local branches. Their control of the trade became less intrusive at the administrative center but tighter at the local operational level. The Kōain's second move became public at the end of May, when it reorganized the monopoly by separating distribution and supply from registration and taxation. The OSBs would continue to register addicts and collect the opium tax, but the opium itself was to be handled through a private business group called the Central China Hongji Benevolent Society *(Huazhong hongji shantang)*. The OSB was given the look of a state-centered bureaucratic entity, while the Hongji Society assumed the guise of a traditional philanthropic society. The declared purpose of this new arrangement was to forestall corruption by separating the functions of public servants and private merchants.[26] What the creation of the Hongji Society in fact achieved was the replacement of the General OSB as the dominant force in the opium monopoly. Despite Tokyo's directive, independence from Japanese military authorities was not achieved. The eight directors of the Hongji Society were all prominent Chinese opium wholesale merchants, but not one was appointed by the Reformed Government. The manager was Sheng Wenyi (Youan), president of the Jiangsu People's Bank and son of the eminent industrialist Sheng Xuanhuai (1849–1916), but the director general was none other than Satomi Hajime, once again. The organization had the appearance of being Chinese, but Sheng took his orders from the Japanese.[27] Henceforth, this society would be the principal organ for running the opium monopoly from the supply side.

The Reformed Government had no choice but to go along with the Kōain's scheme, for without the supply of opium, its distribution network would collapse. On 1 June 1939 the government announced new uniform regulations for the reorganization of the OSB and the installation of the Hongji Benevolent Society. The OSB reorganization took two months to complete, resulting in a two-tiered network of ten regional and thirty-one local (county-level) OSBs.[28] The head of the reorganized Suzhou OSB explained at a news conference on 10 July that the shuffle was designed to provide the Reformed Government with a unified opium administration.[29] This bureaucratic explanation is no match for the reality of unified control over opium distribution that the Hongji Society gave the Kōain. Given that the local OSBs in any case reported to local SSD units,[30] the retrocession of opium-control rights to the Reformed Government remained a fiction.

The Kōain was able to shadow and dominate the OSBs by setting up a Hongji Society branch in every city where a regional OSB existed. These local branches had at most five members, wealthy merchants who supplied local retailers from opium stocks they got from the main Hongji Society in Shanghai. The OSB was authorized to issue licenses, set prices, and inform the local Hongji merchants what these prices were,[31] but it lost control of most of the revenue collection. It was the Hongji Society, not the OSB, that affixed the OSB tax stamp when the tax ($1.80 on each twelve-ounce packet) was paid at the point of distribution to retailers, in addition to collecting its 10 percent processing fee. The local OSB simply received whatever portion of the receipts the Hongji Society chose to forward to it. The lion's share of opium revenues went directly into Japanese hands, and only then was a portion passed to the lambs.

The Hongji Society proved to be a successful vehicle for Japanese opium operations in Shanghai. In part this was because Japan could ensure its supply of opium: the official tally of the opium that Japan brought into Shanghai between April 1938 and March 1940 was 3,500 chests from Iran, of which Mitsui bussan was the importer, plus another fifty-seven chests from Xinjiang,[32] though this is only a portion of the total amount of opium reaching central China. The society obtained its opium from the Japanese warehouse at a fixed price of $195 per pound and sold it to smaller wholesalers for $374 (a profit of 80 percent). Its merchants, in turn, could sell it to retailers for $432 (a profit of only 15 percent). A confidential SMP report prepared in March 1940 states that the Hongji Society's distribution network was so well organized, well stocked, and carefully controlled that the police could make only small seizures of the drug. The SMP estimated that the Hongji Society distributed an average of four chests (288 kilograms) per day to at least fifty-eight large and small opium businesses in Japanese-controlled areas around the International Settlement, all of them registered with the Shanghai Opium Merchants Guild. This estimate is loosely corroborated by official statistics that the Kōain published on behalf of the Reformed Government in 1940 showing average monthly distributions of between 120 and 180 chests throughout 1939 (see table 5). The SMP report identifies the leading figures in the opium monopoly as Major General Kusumoto of the Kōain and Admiral Tsuda Shizue of the Bamboo (or Doihara) Agency, the unit instrumental in recruiting Wang Jingwei to replace Liang Hongzhi and form a new national government.[33]

A further step to enhance the effectiveness of the opium trade was to centralize its financial operations. The Farmer's Bank of China had served to finance the purchase and mortgaging of opium stocks before the war. Satomi chose to repeat this arrangement early in 1940 by setting up the Federated National Bank *(Lianmin yinhang)* to act as a clearinghouse for opium receipts. The regulations of the bank declared its purpose to be "to concentrate the floating capital in the local market for the purpose of developing the resources in the region of the Yangzi Valley, thus promoting the economic renaissance of the area."[34] But its purpose for those who organized it was to centralize the financial operations of the opium monopoly throughout the region. The new bank was an offshoot of the Bank of Taiwan, through which Satomi had financed his first opium operation. Its manager was Zhou Wenrui (Youchang), compradore of the Bank of Taiwan. Conveniently, Zhou was also commissioner of finance for the Shanghai municipal government.

SMUGGLING, 1939–1940

The greatest challenge to any state monopoly, which the monopoly itself produces, is smuggling. Smuggling flourishes to the extent that it can supply restricted goods at rates lower, or in volumes larger, than the state can, and to the extent that it can do so without incurring penalties that exceed its profits. The situation under which the Reformed Government operated its opium suppression system was just this. The system set higher prices than costs warranted, and in theory at least restricted the amount of the drug that a consumer could buy. As the OSB imposed restrictions on who could buy opium and in what quantities, private opium moved in to compete with official opium.[35]

TABLE 5   Amounts of Opium Distributed Monthly by the
Central China Hongji Benevolent Society According to
Official Reports, November 1938–March 1940

Year	Month	Number of Chests Distributed
1938	November	302.00
	December	103.50
1939	January	124.50
	February	137.50
	March	125.50
	April	121.00
	May	100.75
	June	161.25
	July	238.75
	August	143.00
	September	120.00
	October	179.00
	November	156.25
	December	121.50
1940	January	74.00
	February	43.00
	March	123.25
Total		2,375.25
Monthly Average		139.70

SOURCE: Kōain kachū renrakubu, *Chūka minkoku ishin seifu zaisei gaishi*,
p. 46.

The official monopoly was enforced by a variety of locally organized
paramilitary units that could not achieve any degree of coordination in
controlling the flow of opium in and out of regions. Retailers organized
and paid for a detective corps, but they were obliged to dissolve it on 15
May 1939 when the bureau general set up its own Narcotics Prevention
Service Corps. The undeclared intention was to prevent retailers from ac-
cessing, and guarding, sources of supply outside the OSB system. But the
competition did not stop there. In the spring of 1940, the Hongji Benevolent Society set about organizing its own armed unit. Its main task,
according to an unsympathetic observer, was "to cooperate with clandestine opium merchants in the foreign settlements of Shanghai and to dispatch officers to the various wharves along the waterfront for the purpose
of receiving and sending contraband goods" as well as to "prevent the
smuggling of contraband opium from the northern and southern ports
and control the activities of local merchants suspected to be so engaged."[36]

By keeping close watch over the movement of opium into and out of Shanghai, the corps helped to ensure the society's control over prices and revenue.

Despite the monopoly, smuggling went on throughout the region. A merchant from Wuxi filed a petition with the Reformed Government in the winter of 1938–1939 charging the Wuxi chief of police with smuggling private opium and narcotics into the city. The chief was able to get the drugs past the Japanese sentries at the city gates by having his policemen conceal them in their clothes. As evidence of smuggling, the merchant observed that official opium was not selling (private opium must have been coming into Wuxi in quantities and at a price that undercut the regulated market). This complaint suggests that this man was not so much against opium as against smuggling, possibly indicating that he himself was involved in the legal drug trade. His second observation was that morphine ("red poison pills") and heroin ("white happiness-beyond-all-happiness"), both contraband, were available at both the registered opium houses and private opium dens in Wuxi.[37]

We have no record of whether the police chief was prosecuted on opium charges, but other smugglers were. A county court in a Nanjing suburb noted in the spring of 1939 that the majority of the more than 120 convicts in its jail, plus roughly the same number of suspects awaiting trial, were there on theft or opium charges.[38] A report on the work of the Nanjing city police for 1939 reveals that opium offenses constituted the commonest charge filed, accounting for 42 percent of cases investigated. Fifteen percent of those charged were women. Opium cases tended to remain in the jurisdiction of local police administrations rather than rise to the "national" regime: of 4,881 cases referred up to the Ministry of Judicial Administration from mid 1938 to the end of 1939, only 830 (17 percent) were opium-related.[39] Despite the concern that opium was leaking through the state system, sentencing for private drug-dealing was relatively light. Someone caught dealing less than one hundred taels of opium had only to pay a fine. This sort of administrative sentencing, handled by the police, was designed to process smaller offenses quickly and economically.[40] Only the bigger dealers actually went through a trial or to prison. The report from the Ministry of Judicial Administration reveals that of more than nine hundred convicts held in provincial jails as of August 1939, only 8 percent had been convicted on opium-related charges (most were there for theft and violent crimes, which carried longer sentences). The ministry data also indicate that opium offenses were gender-influenced. In contrast to the low percentage of male opium offenders among male convicts, fully a quarter of female prisoners were there on opium convictions. After interference in marriage and family matters, opium was the second most common offense for which women were sentenced to prison.

REVENUE

Neither the Kōain nor the Reformed Government ever abandoned the conviction that opium use should be curtailed. And neither espoused opium trafficking as a worthy means of gaining revenue. Yet neither was able to do without opium revenue. The reliance on opium proceeds was not for want of trying other ways of raising revenue. While waiting for his first shipment of opium to arrive, Kusumoto set up the Jiangsu-Zhejiang-Anhui Consolidated Tax Bureau, which generated a monthly income of $300,000 for the Reformed Government and $1,000,000 for Japan.[41] Such sums were insufficient to administer occupied China and carry on a war. For Kusumoto, opium trafficking presented itself as one means among many for paying for the costs of occupation. But it proved sufficiently lucrative that neither Kusumoto nor Liang Hongzhi, nor any other Chinese or Japanese administrator in central China extracting revenue from the monopoly, could afford to do without it. And of course the trade proved profitable as well for the large Japanese corporations, notably Mitsui and Mitsubishi, that handled importation.

How important were opium revenues to Liang's regime? This question cannot yet be answered, as no full reporting of opium-related revenues was published, nor is there hard evidence as to the amount of revenue Japan extracted from the trade. But we do have official financial statistics that the Japanese published on behalf of the Reformed Government in 1940. These provide some sense of the support Liang's regime received from opium trafficking. According to this official source, revenue from opium between December 1938 and March 1940 totaled 33.3 million yuan (7.4 million in tax, the rest profit). The Reformed Government drew more than 28.4 million yuan of that amount for its administrative expenses; the rest went to local governments. By comparison, the two other principal revenue sources, the consolidated transit tax and customs, each contributed about sixty million yuan in 1939, again according to published figures. Opium was thus worth about half of these two items, amounting to about 20 percent of the reported total that the three revenue sources earned. Although not the leading source of state income, opium was nonetheless a critical component of the state budget. Consider the costs of running the regime: according to official reckoning, expenses for the period from December 1938 to March 1940 were 111,313,965 yuan. When stacked against these figures, opium revenues paid for 30 percent of the regime's costs. Opium was crucial in keeping the regime solvent.[42]

These statistics attest to little more than internal consistency. The total of 33.3 million yuan certainly undercounts the actual revenue derived from the opium imported into Shanghai. The revenues Japan extracted from the trade are not included in this budget, which shows only the Reformed

Government's finances. Nor are the earnings of local administrations, such as the Chuzhou Special Service unit. Nor, more significantly, are the unreported payoffs to powerful individuals in the regime. At his war crimes trial, the head of Liang's Legislative Yuan, Wen Zongyao, declared that the Reformed Government received about 200,000 yuan a month from opium operations, although he himself got none of it; more spectacularly, Hongji manager Sheng Wenyi claimed that every month he passed several million yuan of the society's take to Mei Siping, minister of industry under Wang Jingwei.[43] Sheng also claimed that his refusal to make payoffs to top collaborationist officials Chen Gongbo and Lin Bosheng was the reason that they sponsored the student demonstrations against opium in Nanjing in the winter of 1943–1944 (examined in chapter 16). We will never know exactly to whom and at what sums opium proceeds were paid out, but circumstantial evidence suggests that such payoffs were common.

Another way of tracking opium revenues is to look at the budgets of county administrations, which sometimes appear in the work reports of Japanese pacification teams. As these were internal documents not intended for circulation outside the SSD, they are reasonably accurate reflections of actual financial conditions. The handful of reports included in table 6 indicates that opium revenues accounted for about 25 percent of county income. In Dantu county, at least, the jump between November 1938 and January 1939 is explained as having occurred in relation to the Reformed Government's cancellation of the transit tax (which was subsequently reversed). In November, that tax had accounted for 76 percent of income. When it was no longer possible to raise funds this way, county administrations scrambled quickly to develop and augment other revenue sources, one of which was opium.

PUPPETS AND MASTERS

Opium may have earned revenue, but it did not earn it neutrally. It was under state monopoly and otherwise illegal; it was vulnerable to negative moral evaluation; and it generated large, easily collected sums that only fueled revenue hunger. By being imported and distributed on a large scale, opium fashioned a significant economic nexus between Japan and the Reformed Government. Opium helped Japan meet immediate financial needs as an occupying power. At the same time, it rendered puppets like Liang Hongzhi powerfully and helplessly dependent on the forces of occupation. It is difficult to imagine Liang's regime organizing and operating revenue-collection on the scale that Kusumoto was able to achieve through opium. But Japan also was trapped in this bargain and had to sustain the traffic to feed its hungry puppets. Tokyo strove halfheartedly to reduce its role in the opium trade in Shanghai in 1940, but it had to move slowly as it wound

TABLE 6   Monthly Opium Revenues in Two County Budgets, 1938–1939

County	Month	Total income (yuan)[a]	Opium revenue (yuan)	Percentage of total income from opium
Dantu	November 1938	34,081	3,760	11
	January 1939	72,353	21,040	29
	February 1939	29,554	9,520	32
	March 1939	135	1,000	24
Jiangdu	January 1939	38,494	9,640	25
Average				25

SOURCE: Inoue Hisashi, ed., *Kachū senbu kōsaku shiryō*, pp. 187–190, 250.

[a] Excludes surpluses transferred over from the previous month.

it down, since the revenue continued to contribute so much to Wang Jing-wei's budget.

Occupiers and collaborators alike understood that opium trafficking was not a strategy for the long term. It created easy revenue, but it also produced social and health effects, as well as a moral stain, that contradicted the renovationist posture of the occupation, which was to establish a stable and durable regime in place of a corrupt order that had to be swept away. The Japanese army could not continue to run opium in China and hope to establish international respectability for its clients. Nor could its collaborators be seen by the Chinese people as dealing in opium without a clear commitment to suppressing its use. Both in fact moved gradually away from opium after the Wang regime was installed in 1940. As Japan relinquished control over the trade, that regime was able to resurrect the full structure of the prewar opium suppression scheme.

What then of Liang Hongzhi's defense? Were the Japanese wholly responsible for expanding the opium trade in central China? Not wholly, perhaps, but principally. Contrary to doubts recently expressed concerning Japanese military involvement in the drug trade,[44] it is impossible to deny that Japan was not only engaged in, but directed and sustained, a substantial opium traffic in China during the years 1938–1940. As for Song Meiling's accusation of "diabolical cunning," my research has turned up no evidence on the Japanese side that there was a plot to narcotize the Chinese people, although many Japanese regarded the extent of addiction in China as grounds for treating Chinese with contempt. On the Chinese side, other collaborators besides Liang Hongzhi claimed that narcotization was not their goal. Mei Siping insisted at his war crimes trial, for instance, that the opium trade was purely a means for the Japanese army to provide funds for the SSD, as it was for other wartime regimes in China.[45] Rather than exposing a diabolical scheme to narcotize China, Japan's opium operations in central China point rather to its failure to anticipate the costs of occupation and to create an adequate and stable economic foundation for it.

What of Liang's second claim, that the Reformed Government's opium suppression program stemmed the opium trade? From one point of view, this claim should have earned some measure of acceptance. It did for Song Meiling and Jiang Jieshi in the 1930s, when the Guomindang profitably ran an almost identical opium monopoly that, despite domestic skepticism, was perceived internationally as an effective scheme for solving China's opium problem. But Liang Hongzhi's collaboration with the Japanese robbed him of the moral position of being able to make the sort of claim that Song or Jiang could make, even though his system was like theirs and both sides not only benefited from opium revenues but made little headway in reducing addiction. Regardless of these charges or his defense, opium was the rhetorical flourish to a sentence already passed. It was collaboration, not trafficking, for which Liang ultimately stood condemned.

NOTES

Research for this chapter was made possible by a grant from the Social Sciences and Humanities Research Council of Canada.

1. China Information Committee, *Japan's Narcotic Policy in China*, p. 1.

2. Masui, *Kankan saibanshi, 1946–48*, p. 108. The Reformed Government was dissolved in 1940 in favor of the Reorganized National Government of Wang Jingwei.

3. SMP file D-8717: "Arrest of Two Japanese Subjects and Two Chinese," 20 July 1938.

4. SMP file D-8717: "Records of Investigation," 1 and 10 August 1938.

5. SMP file D-8299: "Further to Assistance to Japanese Military Police," 18 June 1938.

6. Baumler, "Rhetoric of Independence," pp. 4–5.

7. Shanghai shi dang'anguan (Shanghai Municipal Archives), file R1–1–71: "Baogao gelu diaocha qingxing."

8. *Nanjing xinbao*, 13 April 1939.

9. Records from 1938 to 1939 repeatedly show the illegality of opium and the desirability of ending its use. For instance, the interior ministry imposed a ban on opium consumption among government officials; *Nanjing xinbao*, 24 January 1939. At the local level, collaborationist administrations regarded narcotics as illegal and used the *baojia* system to control their use; e.g., EDG file 2001(2), file no. 19: "Baojia zhidu zhi zhiwu," May 1938. Japanese pacification officers took the same approach, continuing Guomindang-style measures to suppress opium; e.g., Kumagai, *Shina kyōchin zatsuwa*, p. 33.

10. Jennings, "Forgotten Plague," pp. 810–12.

11. SMP file D-9319: "Memorandum on Mr. Tu Yueh-sung alias Tu Yuin," n.d., pp. 5–6.

12. SMP file D-9319: "Reported Change of Attitude of Tu Yueh Sung," 6 February 1940.

13. SMP file D-8215: "Narcotics in Shanghai," *Damei wanbao*, 1 March 1938.

14. *Nanjing xinbao*, 2 September 1938.

15. *Nanjing xinbao*, 13 October 1938. The price was lower where supply was better: it was six to seven yuan in Beijing and Tianjin (Eguchi, *Shiryō*, p. 198), and seven yuan in Shanghai (Kōain kachū renrakubu, *Chūka minkoku ishin seifu zaisei gaishi*, p. 47).

16. Eguchi, *Nit-Chū ahen sensō*, pp. 93–95. The doings of Chō Isamu and Kusumoto Sanetaka (misromanized as Kusamoto Sanetakc) are described in Meyer and Parssinen, *Webs of Smoke*, pp. 219–21.

17. Eguchi, *Nit-Chū ahen sensō*, pp. 95–98.

18. Katei senbuhan, "Katei senbuhan kōsaku shiryō," pp. 26, 48; Taisō senbuhan, "Taisō senbu kōsaku gaikyō," pp. 8–9; reprinted in Inoue Hisashi, *Kachū senbu kōsaku shiryō*, pp. 92, 97, 212–13.

19. Nanjing jingcha, *Nanjing jingcha gaishi, 1938–39*, p. 371.

20. Kojima, *Chōkō no nagare to tomo ni: Shanhai Mantetsu kaisōroku*, cited in Eguchi, *Nit-Chū ahen sensō*, p. 98.

21. SMP file D-9114(C): "Reports on the Situation in the Western District," 17 February, 28 February, 1 May 1939.

22. SMP file D-9114(C): "Reports on the Situation in the Western District during the Months of February, April, and June, 1939."

23. Shanghai Municipal Archives, file R1–3–127: "Shanghai teye gonghui huiyuan yilanbiao"; "Shanghai difang jieyan ju lingshou shang paihao xingming dengji didian yilanbiao"; "Shanghai difang jieyan ju gequ lingshou shang paihao xingming dengji didian yilanbiao."

24. Xingzhengyuan xuanchuanju, *Chūka minkoku ishin seifu gaishi*, pp. 82–83; Kōain kachū renrakubu, *Chūka minkoku ishin seifu saisei gaishi*, p. 44.

25. SMP file D-8292A(C): "Summary of the 'Central China Hong Chi Benevolent Society,'" 28 May 1941.

26. Xingzhengyuan xuanchuanju, *Chūka minkoku ishin seifu gaishi*, p. 84. The first Hongji Benevolent Society was formed by the Japanese authority in Dalian in 1915 to take over opium operations in Manchuria, and was similarly fashioned to appear as a philanthropic society of wealthy Chinese; Jennings, *Opium Empire*, p. 48.

27. Nanjing shi dang'anguan, *Shenxun Wangwei hanjian bilu*, p. 437.

28. Local OSBs were reorganized formally as of 1 June (*Nanjing xinbao*, 23 June 1939). According to the official newspaper in Nanjing, the new regional OSBs appeared in July; e.g., 2 July (Yangzhou), 3 July (Suzhou), 25 July (Wuhu), 28 July (Nantong), and 31 July (Bengbu). By the fall of 1940 thirty-four OSBs were in operation; EDG file 2001(2), no. 20: "Zhongyang zhengzhi weiyuanhui zhengzhi baogao: neizhengbu gongzuo," p. 16.

29. *Nanjing xinbao*, 13 July 1939.

30. *Nanjing xinbao*, 22 June 1939, concerning the Wuhu OSB.

31. Kōain kachū renrakubu, *Chūka minkoku ishin seifu zaisei gaishi*, p. 45. The

OSB's retention of nominal control over domestic shipping is suggested by a shipping contract issued in its name, preserved in Shanghai Municipal Archives, file R1–3–127.

32. Kōain kachū renrakubu, *Chūka minkoku ishin seifu saisei gaishi*, p. 45. The Xinjiang figures have been converted at a rate of 1,920 taels per chest, and March 1939 (as it appears in the source) changed to March 1940 as the terminal date. Mitsui brought in another five hundred chests in October 1940 and a further five hundred in November–December 1940; Eguchi, *Nit-Chū ahen sensō*, p. 104.

33. SMP file D-8292A(C): "Brief Review of Prevailing Opium Situation in Shanghai," 26 March 1940. This suggests that opium revenues were used to pay for the recruitment of Wang Jingwei. In the following chapter, pp. 346–347, Motohiro Kobayashi comes to the same hypothesis.

34. SMP file D-8292A(C): "Opium Merchants Organizing Big Bank in Shanghai," 29 January 1940. The chairman of the bank's board of directors was Sheng Wenyi.

35. The flow of private opium into Nanjing obliged the OSB to add a ten-day grace period to its registration deadline of 30 October 1938; *Nanjing xinbao*, 30 October 1938.

36. SMP file D-9114(C): "Report on the Situation in the Western District during the Month of May," 2 June 1939, p. 2; SMP file D-8292A(C): "Proposed Plan for Organization of a Narcotic Preventive Corps to Function in the Foreign Areas," 19 February 1940 (?).

37. EDG file 2001(2), no. 73: petition of Hou Weinan to Liang Hongzhi regarding Chief of Police Tao Heshu and Magistrate Qin Lianggong. The references to "official opium" *(guantu)* and registered opium houses suggest that the petition postdates the setting up of the Wuxi OSB in September 1938 (as reported in *Nanjing xinbao*, 6 October 1938).

38. EDG file 2001(2), no. 108: report from the Local Court of Jiangning to the Judicial Administrative Yuan, March 1939. The report predicted that the number of jailed people would increase, suggesting that opium trafficking was on the rise. A January 1940 report from the local court of review in Zhenjiang suggests that theft and opium trafficking were equally common offenses during this period, though the sample of cases (four) is too small to allow us to generalize; EDG file 2043, no. 9: "Weixin zhengfu Zhenjiang dijianchu xuangao wuzui ji huanxing yuebaobiao."

39. Nanjing jingcha, *Nanjing jingcha gaishi, 1938–39*, p. 369; Sifa xingzhengbu zongwusi, *Sifa zhuangkuang*, p. 137. The statistics of the former are of dubious quality, inasmuch as the number of cases resolved (4,581) is precisely the number resolved in the latter—in which, however, the breakdowns by crime are completely different!

40. Nanjing jingcha, *Nanjing jingcha gaishi, 1938–39*, p. 371.

41. SMP file D-8210/3: "Reported Compulsory Closure of Branch Offices of the Kiangsu-Chekiang-Anhwei Consolidated Tax Bureau," 15 November 1939.

42. Kōain kachū renrakubu, *Chūka minkoku ishin seifu zaisei gaishi*, pp. 2, 54–74. These figures do not include the Sichuan opium tax collected in Wuhan or the

"miscellaneous opium tax" levied on extra-monopoly opium sold in western Shanghai in the winter of 1939–1940 (pp. 48–49).

43. Nanjing shi dang'anguan, *Shenxun Wangwei hanjian bilu,* pp. 338, 438. Mei denied Sheng's charge, declaring himself a prohibitionist and committed to the ideals of the Guomindang's 1935 campaign (ibid., p. 432).

44. Walker, *Opium and Foreign Policy,* p. 124. Walker argues that Japan was unfairly faulted in the 1920s–1930s for its involvement in opium trafficking while the Guomindang regime was let off the hook for reasons of international diplomacy. Walker's rejection of the view that "Japan deliberately sought to use drugs as a weapon of war in China" (p. 91) withstands scrutiny only if one regards war financing as not being part of waging war.

45. Boyle, *China and Japan at War,* p. 100.

FIFTEEN

An Opium Tug-of-War

Japan versus the Wang Jingwei Regime

Motohiro Kobayashi

Translated by Bob Tadashi Wakabayashi and Aaron Skabelund

Involvement with opium and narcotics has been a very real and immediate issue for the modern Japanese state and people, but historians largely neglected it for decades until Eguchi Keiichi chanced to find a cache of primary sources related to the wartime collaborator regime, Mengjiang. Publishing these sources with a scholarly introduction in 1985, he exposed the imperial state's wartime involvement with opium in China. In 1986 Okada Yoshimasa and his associates came out with another volume of documents. These two volumes provide access to the basic sources on Japan's opium policy that Eguchi used to write *Nit-Chū ahen sensō* (The Japan-China Opium War) in 1988.[1] In this book he paints an overall picture of wartime Japan's opium operations and urges us to do more work, especially on opium under the Wang Jingwei, GMD, and CCP regimes. Some studies have appeared on the GMD and CCP,[2] but next to nothing has been done in Japanese on Wang's regime or the preceding Reformed Government.

Eguchi shows that the Mengjiang regime, set up in September 1939, relied heavily on opium exports for revenue. In 1939–1942, 55.4 percent of those exports went to Shanghai, whence they found their way to Hankou, Xiamen, and Guangdong as well.[3] After the war began in 1937, Japan occupied all of Shanghai except for its French Concession and International Settlement, which it took over in December 1941. Occupied Shanghai came under the jurisdiction of the Reformed Government in March 1938, and then of Wang Jingwei's Reorganized National Government in March 1940. Thus, these two Nanjing-based regimes controlled the area where 55.4 percent of Mengjiang opium went. In this chapter I briefly look at Japan's grip on opium under the Reformed Government, and then describe how the Wang regime tried to win a measure of autonomy by taking control of opium away from the Japanese. I seek to disclose one of the least-known dimensions of Japan's opium policy—how profits were used. All of that, I hope, will show how opium contributed to imperial Japan's goal of waging total war in conjunction with Chinese collaborator regimes.

BACKGROUND: THE HONGJI-KŌAIN SYSTEM

After the Konoe Fumimaro cabinet "refused to deal" with the GMD in January 1938, Japan had to create a collaborator regime in central China like the Provisional Government it sponsored in the north, so the army installed Liang Hongzhi at the head of the Reformed Government in Nanjing. Up to then, Colonel Kusumoto Sanetaka and Satomi Hajime, a civilian undercover agent for the army, had been smuggling Iranian opium to central China in league with Mitsui bussan. But U.S. delegate Fuller exposed those operations to the League of Nations in June 1938 and privately identified the perpetrators after Japan's delegate, Amō Eiji, denied the allegation.[4] Thereafter Japan had to make it look as if the Reformed Government itself were controlling the Iranian opium and using it to suppress addiction. Japan therefore pushed the Liang regime to create this feigned system based on plans drafted by the Foreign Ministry—although the regime had its own agenda in complying. The system took effect immediately in some areas but became grounded in law only the next year.[5] On 31 December 1938 the Liang regime abolished the 1936 GMD laws banning opium and narcotics, which formalized the GMD eradication campaign begun in April 1935.[6] Thus this regime repudiated and showed *dis*continuity with the old GMD policy of strict prohibition.

Japan created the Kōain, or Asia Development Board, in December 1938 and set up its Central China Liaison Office in March 1939. Vice Admiral Tsuda Shizue and Kusumoto directed this liaison office, which transferred opium operations from the Central China Expeditionary Army's Special Service Department (SSD) to the Kōain.[7] Harada Kumakichi, head of that division, was ordered by army authorities "to supply opium to the Chinese by creating a suppression bureau."[8] He raised this issue with the Reformed Government, which duly set up a new Opium Suppression Bureau General in Shanghai under its Interior Ministry and appointed Zhu Yao to head it on 4 March 1939. The bureau general eventually oversaw ten regional bureaus, each of which took charge of several county-level bureaus. On 30 April, the regime enacted detailed laws for registering addicts and dispensing drugs, and it set up a security force to thwart smugglers. On paper, the regime transferred the control of unsold opium from the Kōain to the suppression bureau general, but its general affairs chief, Major Hamada Tokukai, kept affairs on a tight rein for the Kōain.[9] Moreover, anyone could make, buy, or use opium with official permission, so this was a far cry from the old GMD policy of sentencing convicts to a maximum penalty of death.

Then in May 1939, the Kōain created and wrote the by-laws for the Central China Hongji Benevolent Society. The society was based in Shanghai, but local branches were soon set up in the same places as the regional Opium Suppression Bureaus.[10] The Hongji Society was an opium cartel comprising eight shareholders, each of whom entrusted ¥200,000 in security with the Kōain's representative, Hamada, whose seal was affixed to their receipts. Satomi Hajime became its de facto director and secured from the Reformed Government the right to determine the prices and amounts of the opium to be distributed.[11] Under his directorship, the Hongji Benevolent Society sold Iranian opium until the end of 1942, but poor harvests cut off this source of supply in 1939, so it was at this time that Mengjiang opium "imports" began.[12] The Kōain set the base price to be paid for the Mengjiang opium, then added transport and insurance charges plus a "Hongji handling fee" of up to 8 percent to arrive at its final cost.[13] Liang's regime thus not only could not set the price it paid for Mengjiang opium, but had to see a cut of that revenue go to the Hongji Society and the Kōain—all of which reduced the regime's income in proportion to the volume of opium it handled. This set of arrangements, established under the Reformed Government, is what I call "the Hongji-Kōain system" of exploitive Japanese intermediaries.

WANG'S NEED FOR OPIUM

On 30 March 1940 Wang Jingwei inaugurated a new regime to show the world that China's "real" Guomindang government had returned from Chongqing to its capital of Nanjing, and Hongji paid some of the expenses. According to Satomi's postwar recollections, "Hongji snared some $20 million in Iranian opium profits that went to the Special Service Department while it existed, and to the Kōain after that."[14] The SSD was already gone when Hongji was created, so Satomi's reference about Hongji payments to it is probably confused with those that he himself made. But we should note that profits did *not* flow from Hongji to the Liang regime even after it created the Suppression Bureau General; instead, opium profits went from Satomi to the SSD, or from Satomi to the Kōain, or from Hongji to the Kōain.[15] (Indeed, the consolidated transit tax from Anhui, Jiangsu, and Zhejiang also passed through sticky Japanese fingers on its way to Liang coffers.)[16] Thus Hongji profits did not go to the government; exploitive Japanese intermediaries were still skimming opium revenues apart from taxes. Where, then, did the $20 million in Iranian opium profits end up? In March 1946 Satomi testified that this money "went to create and sustain the [Wang] Nanjing regime." The Kōain, he said, amassed $20 million and paid one-third to Wang's Treasury Department, one-third to the Suppression Board-General, and one-third to Hongji (on credit).[17] Wang had to seek Japanese aid because he got almost none from business circles in China or overseas Chinese in Southeast Asia.[18] So in September 1939 he asked for forty million yuan in loans by which customs receipts deposited in the Yokohama Specie Bank would go to his "central government." But this loan could not have been used to establish Wang's regime because the contract was signed only on 29 March—one day before his inauguration.[19] It is possible that Hongji profits were used instead for that purpose.

On 21 September 1939, the Kōain's Economic Division adopted "Fiscal Policies to Deal with the New Central Authority," one of which was based on a secret pact that read: "besides consolidating finances [inherited from] the Reformed Government, the [Wang] central regime shall pay expenses with customs duties." In a highly imperialistic tone, this document demanded the hiring of Japanese fiscal advisors, more Japanese customs officers, and partial payment for Japanese "peacekeeping forces." It also called for "creating an opium system" whereby regional authorities would run and tax operations in their jurisdictions but the central government would "exercise management when needed"—thus hinting that opium revenues were a local prerogative over which Japan gave the Wang regime loose control.[20] In truth, the regime did not even control its own revenues. Zhou Fohai, who became head of Wang's Treasury Department, wrote on 17 March 1940: "Itō [Yoshio] invited Satomi to discuss the 'special tax' issue. This shows the Japanese won't give up control. Opium is one thing I don't want to fight them over, so I'll take that into account and tread lightly." Likewise, Jing Xiongbai, who joined the party Central Executive Committee, recalled that Satomi and Sheng Wenyi kept a tight grip on opium taxes and "Wang just had to accept that."[21] This tells us that the exploitive "Hongji-Kōain system" remained under the new Wang regime. Opium was crucial to Wang's finances, as seen from Zhou's diary entries of 8 February and 6 October 1940: "Inukai [Takeru] came to discuss finances, a ban on opium, and the issue of special service agencies." "We tried to draft monthly budgets for the new regime and come up short . . . by about 3 million each month. But when we figured in opium taxes we could somehow make ends meet." "We can't tell how much customs duties or the consolidated transit and salt taxes will come to; only the opium tax is a sure thing."[22]

The Hongji-Kōain system kept tight control over opium networks, so the "special tax" represents only part of the revenue from opium in central China, but it still came to between 3.0 and 5.9 percent of all revenue in the three fiscal years 1940 to 1942.[23] This came close to the 1938–1939 figure of 5.6 percent for Manchoukuo (Manzhouguo, J. Manshūkoku).[24] Opium taxes rates rose in 1942 because the *fabi (fapi)*, or GMD "legal tender," depreciated and many people used imperial army scrip to buy opium, causing its price to drop. Unlike the customs and consolidated transit tax receipts, which fell during the Asia-Pacific War, the "special tax" rose greatly, to a figure of 13.46 million yuan in the first half of 1942 alone.[25] Moreover, Hongji displayed staunch support for the new Wang regime by making monthly "donations" of 0.83 million yuan in the first half of 1943—quite apart from the "special tax."[26] Yet this also shows that Hongji's huge income could be disbursed only in that form, which in turn suggests a let-up in Japanese political pressure by 1943 that I discuss below. In any case, "special taxes" were one of Wang's biggest assets—after customs, consolidated transit, and salt receipts. That is why his regime felt a need to press Japan about revising the disadvantageous "Hongji-Kōain system."

For reasons that remain unclear, the head of the Suppression Bureau General was shifted from the Executive Yuan to the Interior Ministry just before the Liang regime expired.[27] But there was pressure to move the post back to its old jurisdiction when the Wang regime was born, and Japanese opinions were sought on this matter. On 21 August 1940 Hidaka Shinrokurō, a counselor in the Japanese embassy, cabled the following report to Suzuki Teiichi, head of the Kōain's political affairs department. Though admitting "this is a domestic Chinese matter," Hidaka said:

> In the present situation we are planning "internal guidance" to reorganize the opium control system in central China based on three guidelines:
>
> 1. End the GMD policy of putatively strict prohibition in favor of actual repentance [gradual prohibition].
> 2. Retain the current [Hongji-Kōain] sales mechanism for awhile in line with the East Asian Opium Policy and with market conditions for poppies in North China, Manchuria, and Mengjiang.
> 3. Place the head of the Suppression Bureau General under direct Executive Yuan control.[28]

Because Zhou Fohai saw the importance of opium revenues, he told Wang that "If we claim that acquiring these is vital while the Bureau General belongs to the Interior Ministry, we should raise the post's status."[29] That never took place, but Zhou's remarks disclose a subtle attempt to enhance both his own and the Wang regime's authority vis-à-vis the "Hongji-Kōain system" run by Japan. This was Zhou's attempt to raise his involvement with opium by getting the Suppression Bureau General upgraded from the Interior Ministry to the Executive Yuan at the very time when moves were afoot to make him its vice president. In response, the Japanese were willing to relocate the Bureau General, but insisted on keeping the current Hongji-Kōain system.[30]

In February and December 1938, the Provisional and Reformed Governments showed discontinuity with the old GMD by scrapping two 1936 ordinances that outlawed opium and narcotics in favor of their own systems of opium management. On 24 September 1940 Wang too abolished those GMD ordinances—which Liang's regime had already scrapped. This followed a decision by the Central Political Committee on 19 September that ordered courts to treat opium and narcotics offenses under ordinary criminal law.[31] The move clearly reflected Hidaka's "internal guidance" to "end the old GMD policy of putatively strict prohibition in favor of gradual prohibition," but it also had implications for opium revenues. Because Wang claimed to represent the "real" GMD government, he was obliged to uphold or revise old GMD laws or else create new ones in their place. Thus he kept old taxes on customs, stamps, salt, tobacco, alcohol, and some consolidated transit taxes; and he revised laws governing income and other consolidated transit taxes. But he abolished laws banning opium and narcotics without enacting new ones in their place, thus literally creating a condition of "lawlessness" and revealing discontinuity with the old GMD just as Liang had done.[32]

On 25 November 1940 the Kōain compiled "Guidelines on Opium and Narcotics Policy in China," which noted that "the [Wang] GMD government replaced the old regime's harsh criminal codes with centrally directed, rationally conceived laws based on a policy of gradual prohibition. We are preparing a similar system in Mengjiang." But on 27 December Kōain liaison heads approved a separate plan that called for "guidance if the [Wang] GMD regime seeks to enact centrally directed opium and narcotics laws" that seemingly aimed to check the Wang regime's urge to crack down. In any case, a situation of "no official laws enacted; current practices in effect" obtained until 1944, despite appearances to the contrary.[33] And it obtained in spite of opposition to Wang's position from within his own administration. On 9 December 1941, for example, Wang accepted a lower-level resolution to suppress opium and instructed the Executive Yuan to that effect, but this was a gesture designed to mollify malcontents. On 1 June 1942 Wang issued an ordinance to overturn or reduce sentences meted out under the old GMD anti-drug laws in areas that Jiang Jieshi still held after Wang had abolished those laws on 24 September 1940.[34] In other words, the ordinance took force in those court districts that the retreating GMD had abandoned. Moreover, Wang released from custody persons convicted under the old GMD laws. This mirrored what the Provisional Government had done in north China back in February 1938 amid criticism from the United States and Great Britain.[35] Wang made this move in tandem with a May 1942 imperial army offensive to expand areas under Japan's control. These areas now included Hong Kong and the Shanghai International Settlement, which Japan seized just after the outbreak of the Asia-Pacific War and would return to China (under Wang) in 1943. In

short, Wang overturned GMD policies of strict suppression in newly occupied areas, yet adopted a hands-off policy toward addicts in order to increase his opium revenues.

OPIUM FOR WAR MATÉRIEL

Wang's regime claimed to be *the* GMD government for *all* of China, when
in fact a North China Political Affairs Committee and a Mengjiang Federal
Regime for Mongol Autonomy continued to exist and to enjoy semi-
independent status. But Japan had to integrate the economies of Chinese
collaborator regimes because of problems arising from the long China war
and worsened relations with the United States. In March 1941 the Kōain
Central China Liaison Office held a conference devoted to "ending sec-
tionalism and creating economic integration" in Mengjiang and north and
central China.[36] Several topics were on the agenda: (1) trade pacts on specified matériel in fiscal 1941 and on general matériel between north and
central China, (2) leftover "pharmaceuticals" from barter with north
China in 1940, (3) the results of a "pact to equalize trade in specified
matériel between north and central China" as well as of "a trade pact with
Mengjiang for opium bought with north China currency" in 1940. According to the results of the barter in 1940, central China imported coal,
salt, and leaf tobacco from north China in return for flour, rice, and cig-
arettes. In general, though, north China supplied resources, and central
China supplied food. Opium charges to central China were: ¥36.9 million
to the Yokohama Specie Bank and ¥3.6 million to the Bank of Korea, plus
¥7.9 in unpaid funds to the Yokohama Specie Bank, for a total of ¥48.4
million. This broke down as: ¥15.5 million to Japan in cash; ¥22.9 million
to north China in the form of flour, ammonium sulfate, military-supply
cotton, hemp sacks, and rice worth ¥18.7 million; and ¥10 million to Mengjiang in the form of tea, cotton cloth, and flour worth ¥6.6 million. The
outstanding balances of ¥4.2 million and ¥3.4 million to north China and
Mengjiang respectively would be remitted in the form of other needed
commodities.

Similar conditions obtained with Manchoukuo in 1944, as graphically
described by Furumi Tadayuki, vice director of that collaborator state's
General Affairs Agency:

> My principle was to barter items like gold, opium, furs, and alcohol that
> weren't needed in the war effort, for Chinese goods that were. . . . I loaded a
> plane with one ton each of gold and opium and met my old acquaintance
> Zhou Fohai, vice premier and acting secretary of finance for the Nanjing
> Government, as well as president of its Central Bank. I placed those items in
> his bank vault and asked for help in buying war matériel. He replied, "When

making off with our goods, Japan comes empty-handed, but Manchoukuo has brought some precious commodities. I'm so grateful and will do my best to help you, Mr. Furumi." Of course, I always relied on my longtime friend Satomi Hajime while on these Shanghai shopping trips, and he never let me down.[37]

Thus payments for opium took place through barter, and Japan used opium profits to buy war matériel from central China.

As the danger of a Pacific War rose, so did Japanese economic dependence on China. The United States froze Japanese assets and embargoed all oil exports after Japan occupied southern French Indochina, so Japan had to adopt "measures to gain war matériel in China and Manchuria" that would "create a high-level defense state" able to pursue "total war." On 20 October 1941 the Kōain drafted plans to use GMD legal tender (fabi)—not the universally shunned "savings notes" that Zhou introduced in January 1941—to buy "raw cotton, flour, other regional crops, cotton cloth, and scrap textiles" in central China as well as other matériel from foreign sources via Shanghai between October 1941 and March 1942. The estimated 856 million yuan needed to do that would come from the Bank of Japan in China, the China Development Bank, the Savings Bank, textile firms in China, Japanese gold, and receipts from the sale of opium in central China. These opium receipts were to reach thirty million yuan from October to December 1941, and thirty million from January to March 1942, for a total of sixty million yuan used to procure the fabi.[38] This Kōain plan was revised on 12 November 1941, when this time frame was cut from six to two months, and the total estimated purchases were cut from 856 million to 453 million yuan. Procurement money to be secured through "receipts from the sale of special pharmaceuticals" also were cut from sixty million to fifty-two million yuan. But this opium money actually rose in terms of its ratio to overall expenditures. Passages such as "we will experience great difficulty in selling off the product due to the fabi's depreciation, but we'll do our best" show that things would not work out as desired.[39] Even so, the figures fifty-two million or sixty million yuan represent nearly three times the state revenues derived from Wang's opium tax in fiscal year 1941. Since the Kōain planned to procure these sums in either six or two months, we can imagine just how huge Japan's opium profits were.

The procurement of war matériel was not limited to occupied regions. Kumagai Hisao, acting director of Shōwa Trading, a company set up by the army in July 1939, noted that "the army used opium as a 'treasured pharmaceutical' to pacify conquered areas and acquire food and other goods from the populace." By the summer of 1942 "gold and opium were the only things left with which to conduct operations." "The army made liberal use of opium, forcing coolies to lug sixty-kilogram crates, because we couldn't buy provisions with imperial army scrip or the Wang regime's savings notes." "When I advanced with the army toward Wuzhou and Liuzhou on the Xijiang Campaign, thirty men up to the rank of sub-lieutenant were assigned to handle opium for their unit. They used it to procure war matériel or lay claim to tungsten mines when we came upon these."[40] Thus, opium itself served as tender to buy war matériel.

JAPAN BACKS DOWN

In August 1942 the Kōain Central China Liaison Office identified three causes of poor sales of Mengjiang opium in 1941. Continued depreciation of the *fabi* lifted the price of opium beyond the reach of poorer smokers; inflation in the cost of legal opium led to smuggling and encouraged people to give up opium for hard narcotics; and wartime conditions blocked the free circulation of goods. From 1942 on, the Kōain planned to: (1) use only the Wang regime's "savings notes," not *fabi*, to pay for opium in the three central provinces (Anhui, Jiangsu, and Zhejiang) as of April; (2) double tax rates on opium and related businesses as of June; and (3) lower the Hongji Benevolent Society's handling fees and use the savings to cut opium prices. Even more smuggled opium flowed in from border areas such as Henan and north Anhui, however, and the People's Enrichment Society of Guangdong, an opium monopoly set up in May 1939, folded in June 1942.[41]

When Japanese opium policy was already in a bind, the Pacific War forced revisions to it. Japan had to shift five divisions from China to the Pacific between fall 1942 and summer 1943, which could only weaken the army's grip on occupied China.[42] The imperial government decided to have Wang enter the war—an idea current since 1941. According to Greater East Asia Minister Aoki Kazuo, Tokyo wanted to exploit this opportunity "to bolster the [Wang] GMD government politically and allow it to win the Chinese people's hearts and minds." An imperial conference on 21 December 1942 resolved that Wang's declaration of war "would break a deadlock in Sino-Japanese affairs, so the Empire should take pains not to intervene in the [Wang] GMD regime, but rather urge it to act voluntarily" in "pursuing the Greater East Asian War to an end." When the Wang regime declared war on the United States and Great Britain on 9 January 1943, it also signed a treaty with Japan that returned treaty port concessions and ended extraterritoriality.[43]

Japan made these political concessions out of a need to prevent the alienation of Wang's regime and to ensure stability in occupied areas whence troops were being transferred to the Pacific front. But the backpedaling did not stop there. On 6 April 1943 Chen Gongbo, head of the

Legislative Yuan, asked Japan to revise the 1940 Sino-Japanese Basic Treaty and to annul its "special interests" in north China. A 31 May 1943 imperial conference accepted these requests and resolved to "conclude a Sino-Japanese Alliance" signed on 30 October by Wang as head of the Executive Yuan and Tani Masayuki as Japanese plenipotentiary. It ended the imperialistic Basic Treaty after only three years.[44] A Japanese retreat on opium policy took place from 1943 as well. On 18 June Takashima Kikujirō, head of the Central China Development Company, told Zhou Fohai that he had impressed Premier Tōjō Hideki with the need for tobacco and opium monopolies to strengthen the Wang regime. On 6 August Uyama Atsushi, an advisor to the regime, made the same argument to Zhou, saying that Hongji and its current opium merchants might be left intact for awhile but should gradually be phased out. Zhou agreed and ordered him to come up with a concrete plan. Uyama did so on 30 August, although its contents are unknown; in response to the plan, Zhou replied, "This is simple in plan and easy to implement, but there is still much opposition, so we can't be sure if it will really work." Zhou often broached reforms to the suppression bureau and opium tax with Sheng Wenyi.[45] Such attempts to create an opium monopoly designed to take distribution networks away from Hongji and remove exploitive Japanese intermediaries would enhance the Wang regime's revenue and authority. Zhou's diary shows that he and Japanese business and diplomatic personnel wanted such a monopoly, although they faced opposition.

On 17 December 1943 massive student rioting broke out in Nanjing, Shanghai, Suzhou, and Hangzhou, which destroyed opium retail shops and smoking dens.[46] One theory holds that Lin Bosheng, Wang's propaganda department head, incited the students to riot in order to show Japan just how much support the regime enjoyed and also to win over the people's hearts and minds. Lin, it is held, would seize this moment to trumpet the virtues of prohibition and deprive Hongji of its right to sell opium. This theory cannot be proven, and other theories are less flattering to Lin.[47] But given that Zhou Fohai was keen on establishing an opium monopoly, it is quite possible that the Wang regime was indeed behind these riots. And the riots did persuade Satomi to leave Hongji, although, he claimed, he had tried unsuccessfully three or four times before.[48] The imperial army refused to quash the rioting. Not only that, according to postwar testimonies by Mei Siping and Sheng Wenyi, Japan promised: "We will gladly send advisors to help the [Wang] Nanjing government revive prewar plans to prohibit opium if it so wishes—so long as it recognizes that opium profits are Mengjiang's prime source of revenue."

One reason for the offer was that "Japan now makes ten times more from commodity controls than from opium, so it has no worries about meeting political or military expenses."[49] Indeed, on 15 March 1943, a

General Association for Commercial Controls in China was convened, and subcommittees were formed later that year to implement controls on oil, rice, cotton, and other foodstuffs. Businessmen from Mitsui bussan, Mitsubishi shōji, and other Japanese concerns dominated these bodies and ignored attempts by the Wang regime to enhance its autonomy—with the result that Chen Gongbo was indicted after the war as a "Chinese traitor" partly for supplying strategic goods to Japan.[50] In short, most Japanese profits from opium in China went to procure strategic matériel for the war effort; so if this matériel could be obtained by other means, opium lost much of its allure for Japan. Thus the China opium market was dispensable—provided that the Mengjiang regime kept on receiving a modicum of opium revenues.

PROHIBITION / MONOPOLY: THE ANTI-CLIMAX

On 15 February 1944 the Executive Yuan approved a straightforward nine-point document titled "Principles Behind Prohibition" to be promulgated ten days later.[51] It stated that the war had cut short the five-year 1936–1940 prohibition plan, but the current regime would revive it from 1944 to 1946. In other words, Wang was reviving the very GMD prohibitions that he had abolished in 1940. The Executive Yuan excluded Mengjiang from this prohibition plan while in the drafting stages, but dropped that exclusion in the end. This shows how keenly the regime wished to pursue prohibition. Indeed, it adopted one measure after another in line with the "Principles."[52] By the end of February, the Hongji Benevolent Society dissolved and its six-year career came to an end although, as Satomi admitted, it had really stopped functioning after the student protests of December 1943. He claimed that Hongji had sixty million dollars when it expired, of which forty million went to the Wang regime, ten million went to pay off expenses, and ten million went to various Shanghai charitable institutions such as hospitals and orphanages.[53] The Wang regime set up a Suppression Bureau General to take over Hongji functions, thus bringing an opium monopoly to fruition. On 30 November the regime decided to transfer opium operations to a Military Affairs Committee headed by a superintendent, and this decision was ratified on 2 December at the Supreme National Defense conference, which named Chen Gongbo to the post on 8 February 1945, although the real powerholder was Yuan Yuquan. In addition to such reforms, the Wang regime set up suppression committees in Nanjing and Shanghai that began to register addicts.[54] But although it won the right to an opium monopoly from the Japanese, the Wang regime faced a dilemma. In order to win popular support, it had to laud the virtues of prohibition; yet in order to earn sorely needed revenue, it had to rely on opium.

For its part, the China Expeditionary Army high command drew up a directive that called for cooperation with the Wang regime in five areas. Japan should: (1) "create a Greater East Asian Committee on Narcotics" to upstage the League of Nations in achieving prohibition within the "Co-Prosperity Sphere"; (2) establish a permanent body tentatively named "The Task Force on Narcotics" to supplant the Wang regime's Suppression Bureau General, plagued as it was by "bureacratic evils"; (3) induce self-restraint among officials, suppress smuggling, and control addicts; (4) deny any request—such as from Wang Kemin's North China Political Affairs Committee—to create a permit system for large-scale poppy cultivation because "that would obstruct food production, be hard to implement, and contradict the [1944–1946] 'three-year' policy of prohibition"; and (5) repudiate as "evil" any policy that "makes opium revenue an end in itself; such revenue must be seen only as a means to achieve prohibition."[55] Thus Japan affirmed Wang's three-year prohibition plan, denounced opium policies designed to garner revenue, and strove to take the lead in stamping out addiction in "Greater East Asia." However, the reference to Wang Kemin's North China Political Affairs Committee shows that, beyond minimum needs for revenue under wartime conditions, the imperial army placed food above opium on its scale of priorities. In any case, Japan compromised greatly on opium policy in central China—and that policy reached its denouement at the end of 1943 with the Hongji Benevolent Society's demise.

Wang Jingwei died in November 1944, but the regime he had led issued a "Declaration of the GMD Government's Dissolution" one day after Japan's defeat.[56] Japan's surrender would have no bearing on a truly legitimate Chinese national government, but Wang's associates knew full well to whom they were beholden. Chen Gongbo went on trial as a "Chinese traitor" at the Jiangsu Higher Court in Nanjing on 5 April 1946. One of the indictments against him was that he had "poisoned the people through official opium sales."

> The enemy carried out a narcotics policy of selling poison indiscriminately. Your collaborator regime refused to ban that, but instead chose to profit by its revenues. You set up opium dens everywhere and gave official permission to smoke. In the spring of 1945, Yangzhou alone had fifty to sixty major dens. Sales amounted to 5.6 million yuan a day and the poison spread immeasurably. You called these dens "suppression bureaus" under the guise of controlling addiction, when in truth they exacerbated it. In one region alone, over 30 million people smoked this poison and the harm was incredible.[57]

In his defense, Chen protested that he closed one-third of existing opium retail outlets, forcibly shut dens, and set up treatment centers during the projected three-year prohibition plan begun in March 1944.[58] But as Mei Siping and Sheng Wenyi admitted in postwar testimonies, "even if Nanjing didn't mean to raise revenue through opium taxes, it gained $40 to $50 million from April to December 1944 which went to the Minister of Finance." So, vast sums of money did go to Wang's regime after the exploitive Japanese intermediaries were gone. Indeed, it even instituted an opium surtax of thirty yuan in April 1944 to cover the costs of provincial police and peace preservation units needed to uphold order.[59] In short, the Wang regime enacted policies to prohibit opium even while hoping to garner major fiscal benefits from it.

CONCLUSION

Japan established an exploitive, imperialistic "Hongji-Kōain system" of opium control under Liang Hongzhi's Reformed Government and carried it over into Wang Jingwei's GMD regime. But Wang sought a higher degree of "autonomy" from Japan than did Liang, especially regarding opium, and U.S. victories in the Pacific worked to his advantage, so the master-puppet relationship between Japan and Wang was less marked. The struggle over opium was a tug-of-war. Japan created the Wang regime, and bought matériel from other collaborator regimes, with profits from opium. Indeed, Japan depended on opium to wage "total war"—even after crushing defeats in the Pacific forced it to back down on the opium issue in China. Yet to the extent that Wang won limited autonomy from Japan, he compromised his position toward the Chinese masses, who would no longer endure conventional opium policies that raised revenue while spawning evils. In short, Wang was caught between the rock of awakening popular nationalism and the hard place of day-to-day fiscal necessity. Whereas the Liang regime, as described in chapter 14, was condemned more for its collaboration than for its opium policies, what damned Wang's regime was not so much having been a collaborator government as having relied on opium for its sustenance. This contrast discloses a historical development of some magnitude: the Chinese people's toleration of opium use had perhaps reached its breaking point.

NOTES

This chapter is an abridged translation of the author's "Ahen o meguru Nihon to Ō Chōmei seiken no 'sōkoku,'" first published in *Nenpō: Nihon gendaishi*, no. 3, ed. Akazawa Shirō et al., pp. 187–226. We thank the publisher, Gendai shiryō shuppan, for permission to translate the article.

The views expressed in this chapter are solely those of the author and do not reflect the opinions or position of the Foreign Ministry of Japan.

1. Eguchi, *Shiryō: Nit-Chū sensōki ahen seisaku;* Okada et al., *Zoku Gendai shi shiryō,* vol. 12, *Ahen mondai;* Eguchi, *Nit-Chū ahen sensō.*

2. On the GMD, see Sadatoki, "Nihon no ahen shinryaku to Chūgoku ahen no teikō ni tsuite"; on liberated areas, see Uchida Tomoyuki, "Chūgoku kō-Nichi konkyochi ni okeru ahen kanri seisaku," and "Sairon: Chūgoku kō-Nichi konkyochi ni okeru ahen kanri seisaku."

3. Eguchi, *Shiryō,* p. 169.

4. Okada et al., *Zoku Gendai shi shiryō,* 12:537–41.

5. Ibid., p. 550; also *Kyokutō saiban sokkiroku,* 1:727.

6. *Zhengfu gongbao* [Reformed Government] 36 (9 January 1939): 1, reprinted in Zhongguo di'er lishi dang'anguan, ed., *Wangwei guomin zhengfu gongbao,* vol. 14. The Provisional Government in North China had already abolished the GMD opium-control laws on 24 February 1938; see *Kyokutō saiban sokkiroku,* 1:817. On the GMD prohibition, see Lai Shuqing, ed., *Guomin zhengfu liunian jinyan jihua jiqi chengxiao,* especially pp. 440–47. See also the 1946 report of the Nanjing High Court on opium prohibition reprinted in Eguchi, *Shiryō,* pp. 627–28.

7. Ishikawa, *Kokka sōdōin shi,* 8:620; Awaya and Yoshida, *Kokusai kensatsu kyoku (IPS) jinmon chōsho,* 49:84; and *Tai-Shi chūō kikan setchi mondai ikken (Kō-A in) Kō-A in kōseki gaiyōsho,* vol. 1 (A.1.1.0.31–4), in Gaikō shiryōkan (Tokyo).

8. *Kyokutō saiban sokkiroku,* 1:807, 8:690.

9. *Zhengfu gongbao* 45 (13 March 1939): 2; 46 (20 March 1939): 3–4; 53 (8 May 1939): 2–7; 58 (12 June 1939): 4–5; 61 (3 July 1939): 1; Xingzhengyuan xuanchuanju, *Chūka minkoku ishin seifu gaishi,* pp. 82–84.

10. Testimony of H. F. Gill, in *Kyokutō saiban sokkiroku,* 1:727; Eguchi, *Shiryō,* p. 624.

11. *Kyokutō saiban sokkiroku,* 1:808.

12. "Satomi chōsho 5," in Awaya and Yoshida, *Kokusai kensatsu kyoku,* 49:91; see also Okada et al., *Zoku Gendai shi shiryō,* 12:305.

13. Eguchi, *Shiryō,* pp. 624–25.

14. Ibid., p. 625.

15. *Kyokutō saiban sokkiroku,* 1:809.

16. Imai Takeo, *Shina jihen no kaisō,* p. 320.

17. "Satomi chōsho 5 and 3," in Awaya and Yoshida, *Kokusai kensatsu kyoku,* 49: 61, 63, 90.

18. On Wang's relations with overseas Chinese, see Zeng Ruiyan, *Huaqiao yu kangri zhanzheng,* pp. 217–26.

19. Imai Takeo, *Shina jihen no kaisō,* p. 320; Cai, *Shū Futsukai nikki,* p. 179.

20. Tatai, *Zoku Gendai shi shiryō,* vol. 11, *Senryōchi tsūka kōsaku,* pp. 237–38.

21. Cai, *Shū Futsukai nikki,* p. 173; Jing, *Dōsei kyōshi no jittai,* p. 116.

22. On 9 February, however, Zhou Fohai wrote: "Income will increase to 18 million and outlays to 25 million, for a shortfall of 7 million" (Cai, *Shū Futsukai nikki,* pp. 157, 250).

23. "Kokumin seifu shūshi yosan oyobi jissekihyō (Shōwa 17-nen 10-gatsu)" and "Kokumin seifu kokkokin gaikyō (Shōwa 18-nen 4-gatsu Tsuitachi genzai)," manuscripts in the possession of Okabe Makio. The authors are unknown; the latter was probably compiled by economic advisors to the Wang regime.

24. Manshūkoku shi hensan kankō kai, *Manshūkoku shi (Kakuron),* p. 1224.

25. "Kokumin seifu kokkokin gaikyō," p. 4.

26. Manuscript in the possession of Okabe Makio, author unknown, "Minkoku 32-nendo kamiki Kokumin seifu yosan gaiyō (Shōwa 18-nen 1-gatsu)."

27. Eguchi, *Shiryō*, p. 630.

28. Cable from Yanagawa Heisuke of the Kōain dated 20 August 1940, in Okada et al., *Zoku Gendai shi shiryō*, 12:584.

29. Cai, *Shū Futsukai nikki*, p. 250.

30. Ibid., pp. 246, 400.

31. *Guomin zhengfu gongbao* 78 (27 September 1940): 3, 9, reprinted in Zhongguo di'er lishi dang'anguan, *Wangwei guomin zhengfu gongbao*, vol. 2.

32. Manuscript in the possession of Okabe Makio, Zai-Chūka minkoku Dai Nippon teikoku taishikan keizaibu, *Kokumin seifu kokuzei kankei hōrei to Kahoku sono ta chiiki ni okeru kokuzei kankei hōrei to no kankei (Shōwa 17-nen 7-gatsu genzai)*, pp. 5–8.

33. Okada et al., *Zoku Gendai shi shiryō*, 12:356, 360; Zai-Chūka minkoku Dai Nippon teikoku taishikan keizaibu, *Kokumin seifu kokuzei kankei hōrei*, p. 8; Eguchi, *Shiryō*, p. 630.

34. *Guomin zhengfu gongbao* 266 (15 December 1941): 4; 338 (5 June 1942): 1; reprinted in Zhongguo di'er lishi dang'anguan, *Wangwei guogmin zhengfu gongbao*, vols. 5, 6.

35. For Joseph Grew's testimony at the Tokyo trials, see *Kyokutō saiban sokkiroku*, 1:817; for a corroborating Japanese source, see Okada et al., *Zoku Gendai shi shiryō*, 12:536.

36. Information for this paragraph derives from Yokohama shōkin ginkō Tenshin shiten, *Tenshin jihō*, no. 134 (7 April 1941).

37. Furumi, *Wasureenu Manshūkoku*, pp. 125–26.

38. Tatai, *Zoku Gendai shi shiryō*, 11:558–59, 563–68.

39. Okada et al., *Zoku Gendai shi shiryō*, 12:xix–xxi.

40. Yamamoto, *Ahen to taihō*, pp. 164–65.

41. Okada et al., *Zoku Gendai shi shiryō*, 12:384–87, 592.

42. Bōeichō bōei kenshūjo senshi shitsu, *Senshi sōsho*, pp. 80–96.

43. Sanbō honbu, *Sugiyama memo ge*, p. 181; Gaimushō, *Nihon gaikō nenpyō narabini shuyō monjo ge*, pp. 580–81.

44. Cai, *Shū Futsukai nikki*, pp. 533, 547; Gaimushō, *Nihon gaikō nenpyō narabini shuyō monjo ge*, pp. 583, 591–93.

45. Cai, *Shū Futsukai nikki*, pp. 559, 572, 583, 590, 598, 602.

46. Nanjing shi dang'anguan, *Shenxun Wangwei hanjian bilu*, pp. 571–74; see the chapter by Mark Eykholt in this volume.

47. Eguchi, *Nit-Chū ahen sensō*, p. 197; for Sheng Wenyi's testimony, see the documents presented in Nanjing shi dang'anguan, *Shenxun Wangwei hanjian bilu*, pp. 484–85, 492–94.

48. "Satomi chōsho 2, 5" in Awaya and Yoshida, *Kokusai kensatsu kyoku*, 49:33–34, 93.

49. Eguchi, *Shiryō*, p. 630.

50. Cai and Li, *Wang Jingwei wei guomin zhengfu jishi*, pp. 199, 210, 223, 232. On Chen's trial, see Masui, *Kankan saiban shi*, p. 44. On the Wang regime's economic policies, see Furumaya, "Kankan no shosō."

51. Zhongguo di'er lishi dang'anguan, *Wangwei zhengfu xingzhengyuan huiyilu,* 24:267–68; *Guomin zhengfu gongbao* 606 (25 February 1944): 2, reprinted in Zhongguo di'er lishi dang'anguan, *Wangwei guomin zhengfu gongbao,* vol. 11.

52. The relevant laws on opium control in this period were published in *Guomin zhengfu gongbao,* nos. 610, 614, 615, 626, 631, 641, 643, 650, 656, 667, 689, and 705, reprinted in Zhongguo di'er lishi dang'anguan, *Wangwei guomin zhengfu gongbao,* vols. 11 and 12.

53. Nanjing shi dang'anguan, *Shenxun Wangwei hanjian bilu,* p. 484; "Satomi chōsho 2 and 6," in Awaya and Yoshida, *Kokusai kensatsu kyoku,* 49:34, 96, 99.

54. Cai, *Shū Futsukai nikki,* p. 728; Cai and Li, *Wang Jingwei jishi,* pp. 259, 265; Furumaya, "Ō Seiei seiken ni kakawatte," in *Geppō,* pp. 7–8, in *Iwanami kōza: Kindai Nihon to shokuminchi,* vol. 5; Eguchi, *Shiryō,* p. 631.

55. Okada et al., *Zoku Gendai shi shiryō,* 12:358–59. But it is unclear if this directive was actually issued to the army in China.

56. Cai and Li, *Wang Jingwei jishi,* p. 281.

57. Masui, *Kankan saiban shi,* p. 45.

58. Nanjing shi dang'anguan, *Shenxun Wangwei hanjian bilu,* pp. 50–51.

59. Zhongguo di'er lishi dang'anguan, *Wangwei zhengfu xingzhengyuan huiyilu,* 25:515, 525–26.

SIXTEEN

Resistance to Opium as a Social Evil in Wartime China

Mark S. Eykholt

At 9:00 P.M. on the night of Friday, 17 December 1943, a group of Chinese students marched through the streets of Nanjing. They came from National Zhongyang University, the leading government university in Japanese-occupied China, to protest against gambling parlors, dance halls, and opium dens as social evils that undermined Chinese morality and development. Undaunted by the specter of opposing the Japanese and the government of Wang Jingwei, both of which gained revenue from these businesses, the students paraded through the shopping area of Taiping Road and headed toward Fuzi Miao, the entertainment center of Nanjing. Along the route, students from middle schools joined the growing procession until the marchers numbered more than one hundred. Meanwhile, a second group of students gathered at the university to follow the first group. The first group continued its march as Taiping Road became Zhuque Road. Caught up in the energy of the demonstration, students broke down doors of street-side opium dens, smashed windows, and destroyed smoking tools. Around 10:00 P.M. they reached Fuzi Miao and spread out. Some students entered dance halls and tea houses to harass customers and destroy property. Others stayed outside and lectured people about the evils of opium, gambling, and dancing. Suddenly, Japanese gendarmes arrived and began to rough up the students. The students sent eight representatives forward to reason with the gendarmes. Then a second group of marchers arrived, numbering close to five hundred. The Japanese gendarmes ceased their aggressive tactics but would not allow the students to continue, even after the representatives claimed that Lin Bosheng, the minister of propaganda in Wang Jingwei's National Government, had sent them. The gendarme commander told the eight leaders to go to the police station the next day and discuss their activities with the proper authorities.[1]

By now it was well after midnight and the students had been on the streets for hours. The night's heady events had put the marchers in an ecstatic mood but left the student leaders in need of assurance that their actions would not be condemned. Shouting and unbowed, the students left Fuzi Miao, entered the western section of the city, and headed to the home of Lin Bosheng on Shanghai Road. Lin came out and told the students of his empathy for their deep emotions and strong patriotic spirit, but he also encouraged them to abide by the laws that ensured public safety and warned them he could not support reckless and rash acts. With that, the students dispersed, feeling that Minister Lin supported them.[2] Thus began five months of student demonstrations against dancing, gambling, and especially opium that spread beyond the confines of Nanjing. The actions of these students show that not all people in occupied China were overcome by passivity and despondency, and their public opposition to Japanese authority in Nanjing flies in the face of claims about stifling Japanese control.

CHINA'S OPIUM CULTURE AND NANJING

Just hours before the Marco Polo Bridge Incident of 7 July 1937 ignited the war between Japan and China, an article in the *Shanghai Evening Post and Mercury* claimed that seven hundred thousand people made a living from the billion-dollar opium industry in China.[3] The accuracy of the numbers is not as important as the implication that opium use was pervasive in China. Images of the dismal opium den, the ashen-faced opium addict, and the rich but seedy world of opium smoking and dance hall prostitution were really just partial aspects of opium's widespread use and acceptance. People smoked opium after meals just as people often enjoyed an after-dinner drink. When friends gathered in the evening to chat, opium—like tea or wine—might be part of the comfortable atmosphere, and opium was sure to be available for more convivial gatherings. People used opium to relieve stomach and intestinal pain, and some workers found that a quick smoke between shifts restored their energy. If such occasional use is taken into account, a large portion of the Chinese population had used opium at one time or another. The most frequent users were people of wealth and retired officials who had both the money and the leisure to enjoy themselves. Some families used opium to slow down an elderly relative, a disobedient child, or an intolerable spouse, thus making them easier to deal with. A wayward son who spent his money on opium was cheaper and easier to control than one who patronized prostitutes or spent his time gambling. A large percentage of the laboring classes also used opium as a cheap way to relieve the pain and drudgery of a laboring life. Only the middle classes did not use opium widely, and it is this class that voiced the loudest criticisms of opium use. Through middle-class criticism, momentum had increased for eradication of opium as part of a larger call for national development.

When the Japanese invaded China, they reversed this momentum. Restrictions against opium use melted away, government bodies officially promoted drug use, and narcotics poured into Chinese society. The Japanese established the Hongji Benevolent Society as the official opium supplier and thereby monopolized the trade.[4] Opium dens were gaily painted in red and white and advertised their product as "official paste" (guantu), playing up government approval of their business.[5] In Nanjing, the collaboration government distributed opium through the Opium Suppression Bureau to district sales agencies that in turn distributed the opium to individual dens, hotels, and entertainment halls.[6] Heroin use also spread rapidly, because heroin was easier to use and cheaper than opium. A moderate opium user might spend from one-half to one yuan per day whereas a heroin user could get by on one-third to one-half that. Though heroin was officially illegal, heroin dealers had close connections to opium networks, and Japanese agents kept up a steady supply to the many private distributors.

As to how much opium and heroin actually entered Nanjing, rough estimates have to be used.[7] The government reported monthly sales of about 2,150 kilograms of opium by mid 1939.[8] This is similar to unofficial reports of 2,550 kilograms (90,000 ounces) near the end of 1939, resulting in a wholesale trade of two million yuan per month.[9] This was enough opium for daily use by sixty thousand people out of a population of nearly five hundred thousand. We must remember, however, that of the five hundred thousand people in Nanjing, many were children who probably did not use narcotics, that the usage numbers did not account for the large illegal distribution of opium, that opium ash was reused two or three times by poorer users, and that not everyone who used opium was a daily user. Therefore, the above numbers were minimum estimates of actual use. There were no official numbers on heroin use, but an agent for the Japanese admitted that heroin revenue in and around Nanjing totaled three million yuan per month, leading to a minimum estimate of fifty thousand users.[10] In other words, a large proportion of Nanjing's adult population used drugs.

Japanese and Chinese representatives advertised and promoted opium use, but that does not mean that the nature of Chinese opium use suddenly became more sinister or evil than it had been before the war. Granted, the amount of opium in the market increased rapidly and opium use embedded itself more deeply into the society of occupied China; however, the atmosphere surrounding opium continued much as before. Local trade guilds and gangs handled much of the protection and daily opium operations amid an atmosphere of government involvement and merchant-official corruption. Fuzi Miao continued as the entertainment center, and beautiful hostesses amused high-rolling capitalists and government officials in an atmosphere of song, smoke, and pleasure. Farther out from the high-class halls were dens and shops that catered to a working-class clientele. This was a much rougher side of Fuzi Miao, a world of back alleys and violence as well as intoxicated song and camaraderie.

People also used opium on a personal and social basis. We know this because criticism of the trade mentions the large number of "domestic pipes" owned by families throughout the city.[11] The government sold week-long opium licenses so that people holding weddings, funerals, or other social get-togethers could properly entertain their guests. Opium was part of social intercourse and etiquette, and many families kept a pipe ready to offer guests when they visited.[12] Sellers touted their drug as a medicinal aid for stomach pains or as a quick pick-me-up.[13] This does not mean that addicts did not exist. No doubt addiction increased just as opium and heroin use increased, with a proportional amount of harm to society. Robbery was a common crime among addicts desperate for money to keep up their habit, and uncontrollable need led some even to exhume corpses to sell coffin wood for fuel.[14] The increased drug trade shocked few in the occupied areas, however, because they had been witnesses to the effects of opium and other narcotics all of their lives, and many had incorporated drug use into their daily lives.

The arrival of Wang Jingwei and his establishment of a new national government hardly affected the opium trade. As previous puppet leaders had done, Wang struggled to gain control of entertainment taxes that now totaled five million yuan per month, of which opium taxes made up the bulk. The Japanese resisted all of Wang's demands, making sure that opium supply remained in Japanese hands and allowing the Chinese government control of only the entertainment businesses.[15] Under Japanese occupation, the drug trade was lucrative, widespread, and continued to play a leading role in Chinese economics and society.

OPIUM AND THE NATIONAL RHETORIC OF STUDENTS

Opium was the focus of the popular song "Dingning" (Exhortations), about a young couple that must separate when the man goes to the South Pacific.[16] The wife warns her husband not to gamble, but the husband's worry about his wife is even more telling: "I hope my beloved will never smoke opium; opium is a waste of money; if you are unfortunate enough to become addicted, your health will suffer and your spirit will dissipate." Decades of living in a drug culture had made people aware of the hazards of opium use, especially use by people in lonely or desperate situations. China had been known as the "sick man of Asia" prior to the war in part because of its opium problem, and many people saw opium as a barrier to Chinese development and strength. Foremost among those worried about national development were students, and they connected opium use to Chinese failure.

After Japan's invasion, private and public schools had gradually reopened to create education opportunities for Chinese students. In Nanjing the government had overseen the establishment by fall 1939 of forty-two public schools with 17,233 students and 623 teachers. The price of education for the students was very cheap, averaging about one yuan (the price of two daily newspapers) per semester for elementary school students and ten yuan per semester for secondary school students. Furthermore, the government had registered thirty-six private schools and 160 family schools that taught an additional 12,673 students with 589 teachers. Overall, about 40 percent of school-age children were attending classes.[17] This was a very respectable percentage, especially considering the extreme amount of dislocation and destruction that citizens in Nanjing suffered during Japan's invasion and initial occupation. After seven years in Nanjing the Guomindang had achieved an attendance rate of about 55 percent of school-age children.[18]

In March 1940 Wang Jingwei and his advisors declared the return of the national government to Nanjing. One of their first acts was to reopen National Zhongyang (Central) University in Nanjing. Wang understood that the Republic of China had always been connected to students and higher education, and to help legitimize his government he needed to complement national schools at the elementary and secondary levels with a national university. Zhongyang had been the leading national university in Nanjing prior to the war, which made it a logical choice. Wang also wanted to get youth more involved in Nanjing society and China as a whole. He, more than some other leaders in the Guomindang leadership, had been cognizant of the progressive role played by education and youth in the growth of the Republic, and he was more prone to see the positive effects of student life on Chinese society. Finally, Wang understood the practical value of a national university as a source of talented government employees and a seedbed for government propaganda.

Wang's government propaganda called for Chinese development under Japanese tutelage, summed up in the motto "Peace, anticommunism, national development." Government-sponsored writers pointed out that every year China fought Japan was one more year that the people and the nation suffered. China needed peace in order to develop. Joining hands with Japan as a brother gave China the means to eradicate the evil influences that had plagued her throughout the twentieth century, namely Western imperialism and Communism. The Chinese people needed to unite under the banners of Greater East Asia and the Three People's Principles so that virtues of frugality, honesty, and cleanliness would surface and lead China to a better state.

Wang searched for an effective social tool to champion these ideas in the urban areas, and in early 1942 he launched the New Citizen Movement. Focused on youth as the disseminators, the movement meant to instill devotion and courage into the people of China. Propaganda was central, so the Minister of Propaganda, Lin Bosheng, played a leading role in the overall setup and development. Lin helped oversee the establishment of New Citizen Movement Youth Corps in all public schools. Students in these groups organized meetings, study sessions, parades, athletic meets, language contests, trips, music groups, and a host of other activities to attract citizens to their ideas. The Youth Corps proved popular with students for several reasons. For one, students were concerned with China's development, and development was a major theme of Youth Corps discussions and activities. The Youth Corps also received a lot of government attention and funding, so they were the center of many student activities. Finally, if we ignore the propaganda about a Greater East Asia, the "Peace, anticommunism, national development" ideas were very similar to Guomindang ideas before the war, and most students did ignore the Greater East Asia propaganda. They tolerated the pro-Japan rhetoric because they understood that this was part of Japanese occupation and Youth Corps participation. The same attitude applied to the hundreds of magazines that also had to pay lip service to pro-Japanese ideas. Old Wang remembers students getting together on weekends and holidays to study hygiene, practice military drills, do community service, and, in general, enjoy each other's company. On the surface there was nothing bad about it, and often students received free room and board over vacations. This was especially important to students who could not afford to go home over breaks.[19]

By using the Youth Corps to politicize student life, the government also attracted anti-government youth. Not only were they interested in discussions of China's future and the goals of student activities, but they also found the Youth Corps ideal for organizing students. As student life gained momentum under government guidance, students organized their own groups that brought more variety and possibilities for youth expression. For example, students formed the Student Mutual Aid Society under the sponsorship of Nanjing's mayor, Zhou Xuechang, and the society began publishing *Student* in 1943.[20] The opening issue of this magazine reflected the confidence and spirit that many students felt: "[We] need to assemble our comrades and dare to speak, dare to laugh, dare to cry, dare to curse, dare to fight; at this god-forsaken place, beat back this god-forsaken era."[21] No doubt, the militant tone of this opening issue was more imagined than real because Japanese censorship forced all publications to toe a careful line about what could and could not be printed. Furthermore, student-group sponsors, such as Mayor Zhou, made sure to leave their own close followers in charge. Still, students were able to talk at length about student life, development, Chinese identity, and the goals of students past and present. Articles about Sun Yat-sen's revolution, the power of China under great leaders of the past, and the evils of imperialism all stayed within censorship boundaries while also reflecting concerns about the relationship between Japan and China. Wang Jingwei allowed students more freedom than other social groups to express such ideas and to develop organizations. In Nanjing these activities centered around the students at National Zhongyang University, the center of the Student Mutual Aid Society and the site of its publication, *Student.*

Opium played a role in this rhetoric of national development. Just as in Jiang Jieshi's New Life Campaign, the government tried to get students more involved in opium suppression. For example, in May 1941 Lin Bosheng and the Ministry of Propaganda headed a week-long opium awareness campaign. Banners, parades, radio programs, and public speeches emphasized the evils of smoking opium. A special focus of the speeches and presentations were students, and speakers traveled to every elementary school in Nanjing.[22] Students themselves avoided the entertainment areas, and their periodicals often wrote about the social corruption surrounding drugs, gambling, and dance halls. Lin Bosheng encouraged these voices as part of the New Citizen Movement, and as leader of the Youth Corps he also sponsored his own student group at National Zhongyang University, the Struggle Committee.[23] This committee published the magazine *Struggle,* and the opening issue of this magazine again reflected the militant attitude felt by the students: "[A] generation of youth have not died, nor are they in a stupor. In response to these unreasonable times, they continue to look on angrily and only wait for the chance to explode."[24] The chance had already come when, at the end of 1943, Lin Bosheng headed up a campaign to cleanse society of opium, gambling, and dancing.

THE STUDENTS EXPLODE

In the fall of 1943 Wang's government moved to take direct control of the opium trade. Two contradictory reasons are given for this move. The first reason comes from testimony at the Tokyo War Crimes Trial, where witnesses claimed that by the fall of 1943 the government had sufficient finances to weather any disruption a battle for opium control might bring.[25] The other reason is offered in a book of recollections which claims that the government was desperate for revenues and had to act.[26] Either way, control over the lucrative opium trade, which had been an issue since the beginning of the war, was coming to a head, and Wang Jingwei began talking strategy with his advisors. Against a background of a convoluted chain of command and unclear factional battles, Lin Bosheng, either on his own or through the suggestions of others, laid plans for a youth cleanup campaign that would focus specifically on social evils such as opium. Because the Japanese and their underworld partners managed these aspects of life in Nanjing, Lin's campaign would add social pressure to any governmental pressure already being applied to the Japanese. At a time when Japan was promoting a more cooperative stance toward China for the sake of the war effort, such social pressure could make a difference. Furthermore, Lin's own prestige was sure to rise because he would guide the movement.

Lin contacted his followers among the Youth Corps and National Zhongyang University students. He wanted them to pass out fliers and make street speeches against opium, gambling, and dancing while the general student population of Nanjing would carry out a citywide youth purification campaign. On Friday 17 December, the government sponsored a meeting of student leaders from National Zhongyang University and outside areas to formally plan the purification campaign. The leaders set aside the week beginning 27 December for students to inspect classrooms, learn about sanitation, form committees, clean schools, and prepare a larger cleanup of Nanjing's streets.[27] On the evening of 17 December a handful of Lin Bosheng's student followers met to plan strategy for their own propaganda activities. Many wanted to do more than just pass out fliers and make speeches. The most aggressive claimed that Lin Bosheng's backing shielded them against police repression, so they had nothing to fear. The atmosphere heated up as students challenged one another's courage and devotion, pushing spirits to a feverish pitch. Agreeing the time had come for direct action, the students fanned out to organize their classmates.[28] The result was the demonstration with Japanese gendarmes at Fuzi Miao recounted at the opening of this chapter.

The afternoon following the night march to Fuzi Miao and Minister Lin's home, the atmosphere at Zhongyang University was electric. Information about the protest spread quickly, and Youth Corps groups held rallies and meetings to stir up student support for a parade against opium, gambling, and dancing. Unlike the previous day, the students had plenty of time to organize themselves. That evening they gathered at the National Auditorium on Guofu Road, which was also the national government center in Nanjing. Student leaders stirred people's emotions with fiery speeches and urged the crowd to take action. More than a few of those giving speeches and leading the shouts were also connected to underground student groups.[29] By 9:00 P.M., the crowd had grown to more than three thousand male and female students, and the marchers set off. They again headed through the main shopping district of Taiping Road and then turned on to Zhonghua Road, the central thoroughfare into southern Nanjing. Road names like Guofu (National Father) and Zhonghua (China's national name) gave great patriotic significance to the student's choice of parade routes, as did their use of a national site to begin their parade.[30] The front marchers carried a large white banner announcing to those lining the street that this was a demonstration of the Youth Purification Movement. The students all shouted "Three Evils" and punched their fists in the air each time. When they reached Jiankang (Healthy) Road, the marchers turned east and headed toward Fuzi Miao. As they passed opium dens, small groups of marchers smashed down doors, broke windows, destroyed furniture, and harangued customers. Some owners showed the students their government registration for selling opium and claimed they paid taxes on all of their accounts. The students responded by tearing up the registration certificates and removing any account books they could find, which in effect declared that the government could not recognize these dens and could not profit from them. Students were not just opposing the dens, they were also asserting their right to represent public interests against the government. Confiscated opium and paraphernalia were piled into empty rickshaws. Police and gendarmes intervened to protect as many shops as they could and to keep the marchers moving. Earlier, in another section of the city, about fifty students had attacked opium dens and police had arrested eight students; however, with three thousand students marching under the sponsorship of Lin Bosheng, security forces did not directly intervene.[31]

As the parade neared Fuzi Miao, the students split into groups and began their raids, attacking opium dens, destroying dance floors and mah-jongg tables, and confiscating more equipment to pile into the rickshaws. The students accosted those customers or owners who resisted and lectured the crowds who gathered to witness the spectacle. The demonstrators did not linger long in any one place and soon paraded out of Fuzi Miao. They headed down Zhuque Road and continued to destroy every opium den in sight. More than fifty establishments would issue reports to the police for the two days of demonstrations. Damages ranged from a few hundred yuan into the tens of thousands, with a total of almost five hundred thousand yuan. The biggest losses were from the hundreds of catties of opium now leaving in the student-pulled rickshaws.

The marchers returned to the National Auditorium. It was now after 11:00 P.M. The student pullers dumped the contents of each rickshaw into a pile and then set the pile ablaze. The bonfire was huge and re-energized the students. They entered the auditorium, and various student leaders made speeches. A 1991 article remembered the feisty rhetoric of one speaker: "The Chinese people must not live life in a stupor. As youth, we have to gather together and rise up. We must fight the dark forces of society."[32] The students formed a Capital Student Purification Committee and elected a president and vice president. When the police arrived to talk with the students, student leaders refused to vacate until Lin Bosheng himself arrived. Finally, Lin arrived and, as he had done the night before, offered a mixture of support for and criticism of the students' actions.[33] Regardless of what was said, Lin's presence showed the students that they still had government support.

On Sunday 19 December, the Purification Movement calmed down. The police had been told to allow peaceful gatherings but to arrest anyone trying to destroy property or upset public order. At 2:00 P.M. students began to rally, but the police arrived and put a stop to it. An hour later, about four thousand students gathered at the Chinese Youth Athletic Ground to hear Lin Bosheng speak. Once again his message was a mixed one. He offered his "unbounded sympathy" for the movement and expressed joy at the students' achievements. In his own words, the movement "roused a spirit of determination during wartime and set right the many evils in society." Lin also urged the students to strictly uphold the law and protect public safety.

Following the rally, students took to the streets to push their ideas. However, the police were on patrol to make sure that no disturbances occurred. When any of the scattered groups of students became aggressive or destroyed property, the police put a stop to it. Around 8:00 P.M. students began to gather at the police station where their eight comrades from the previous night were still being held. The students attempted a demonstration, but police reinforcements quickly calmed the students. Another group of three hundred students paraded from the city government area and arrived to meet the police reinforcements. A discussion ensued and the police invited a group of student representatives into the station to meet with their jailed comrades. At midnight the jailed students were set free.

On 20 December *Zhongbao* printed excerpts of Lin's speech from the day before as well as the results of meetings between Lin Bosheng and Mayor Zhou Xuechang. Mayor Zhou had ordered all dance halls to change their business immediately or face closure. The article noted that gambling had already been banned earlier in the year, and that the police desired the continuing help of the students in battling this menace. Finally, the article reported that Minister Lin and Mayor Zhou had taken to heart the students' and society's intolerance of opium and planned to urge the national government to act on this issue. By 20 December student actions and demands had achieved a tremendous amount. The government was acting.

THE GOVERNMENT TAKES CONTROL

On 17 December *Zhongbao* published a 15 December radio speech by Guo Xiufeng, Vice Minister of Propaganda, with a noticeable antiwar tone. The speech, titled "Youth and Production," lamented China's sorry state and admitted that China was a backward country which depended on foreign capital and technology. Never once did the vice minister mention Japan, and there was no anti-Japanese rhetoric in the speech. The concluding paragraph even spoke of World War Two as necessary to ensure safety and prosperity. The tone of this last paragraph, however, was quite different from that of the rest of the speech, more an addendum than a conclusion. The previous paragraphs had continually referred to China as a nation, saying that since 1937 and the beginning of World War Two, Chinese production had decreased each year and Chinese dependence on foreign aid had increased, thereby weakening China. Food was scarce and society had become unsafe. The number one priority, according to Guo's speech, was to protect the livelihood of the Chinese people, but the vice minister noted that war meant less food and the situation would only get worse. The war's negative effect on China's economic and social situation was repeated many times, and the constant connection between a weak China and foreign dependence could not be missed. Since China was dependent on Japan, "foreign" was masked only by the decision to avoid mentioning Japan directly. Finally, the strong emphasis on China as a nation throughout the speech overshadowed the passing references to Greater East Asia at the end.

In all these ways, this speech, coming a few days before the Purification Movement, expressed a mood in Lin Bosheng's Ministry of Propaganda of desire to draw away from dependence on Japan and toward more Chinese autonomy. Students expressed a similar mood through the patriotic symbolism of their demonstrations. Even the government's hope of wresting opium control from Japan carried a semblance of this mood. To connect all three aspects together in a direct way is not possible, since each group was acting out a different set of goals, but all three trends reveal dissatisfaction among students and government officials about the situation in China, and in all three cases this dissatisfaction expressed itself through the medium of opium suppression.

On Sunday 19 December, *Zhongbao* published a student manifesto with which the government began to assert its influence over the Purification Movement. Talking about not only the people of China but the people of East Asia, the message was to save China as well as to protect East Asia. The final paragraph stated, "For the nation, for East Asia, we hope the sincerity and passion of youth will call out to Chongqing to stop the war and unite in order to destroy Britain and America, help China flourish, and protect Asia." The manifesto's language about Greater East Asian unity and winning World War Two was very different than the patriotic and even anti-government actions of the students over the previous few days. The government was combining elements of cleansing society and creating national spirit with larger propaganda about Greater East Asia and the Pacific War.

The antiwar tone of Guo Xiufeng's previous speech had also been eliminated, suggesting a struggle within the ranks of government over its dealings with Japan. Wang's national government had tied itself to Japan and Greater East Asia, but this did not prevent struggles over issues of representation and propaganda.

The manifesto talked about a Nanjing Youth Resurgence Committee to uphold national policy, follow the nation's leaders, and destroy selfishness and hedonism. This student committee had been developed under government auspices in early December to oversee purification when it was still just a movement to clean schools. Now the government was pushing forward this committee as a leader of the Purification Movement in place of the student-formed Purification Committee. Lin's speech of 20 December had also made it clear that the government understood popular feelings and would now take charge. The students should help the government by raising citizen consciousness and coordinating with the police to enforce bans. Through media organs such as *Zhongbao,* the government planned to put its own spin on the meaning of purification.

The government proved adept at controlling the students, thanks to decades of experience that began with the 4 May and 30 May movements of the 1910s and 1920s. In the early 1930s the Guomindang had effectively begun to harness student energies to work toward government political goals by developing its own campus organs to control student political expression. Combining manipulation with an atmosphere of suppression, the government minimized spontaneous acts of mass participation, in sharp contrast to the 1920s. Furthermore, the patriotic outbursts that did occur came under the skillful manipulation of contending political groups.[34] These same tactics applied to the Purification Movement, and a few characteristics made government management easier. First, students framed their drive against opium, gambling, and dancing in terms of national development. This easily fit into Wang's national government propaganda of peace, anticommunism, and national development, thereby allowing the government to step in early and expand the meaning of this local demonstration to one of regional and national significance that in no way contradicted cooperation with Japan. Second, the government was already influential in the main student groups—the Youth Corps, the Student Mutual Aid Society, the Struggle Committee—and had contact with student leadership in the movement. Media control gave the government a means to spread its interpretation to a larger national audience, and Lin Bosheng's rallies with the students showed government sympathy for purification causes while also giving direction to student activities.

The events of 17 and 18 December had shown that students were willing to go beyond the boundaries imposed by their sponsors, and that this could lead students to resist government control and develop their own autonomy for action through student-controlled groups such as the Purification Committee. On 19 December this seemed to be the path that some leaders had taken as students from National Zhongyang University established committees for travel to Beijing, Shanghai, Guangzhou, and other cities in order to spread word of their movement. On 22 December, Hangzhou students formed their own Purification Committee in support of the Nanjing movement. Two days later, three thousand students in Hangzhou paraded through the streets. The Hangzhou committee also sent telegrams to students in other cities, wrote a petition to the city mayor and provincial governor, and helped form propaganda committees in each school to further spread the movement's ideas.[35] In Guangdong, students held meetings and demonstrations from 25 to 27 December. Shanghai students formed their Purification Committee on 23 December. On 27 December, ten thousand marched through the streets of Shanghai, attacking dens and collecting opium and gambling paraphernalia into ten rickshaws. The demonstration continued for more than seven hours and ended with shouts of "Long live the youth of China, long live China!"[36] Wuhu students held a demonstration with rickshaws on 30 December.

From the beginning, student autonomy had never been complete because student leaders had always looked to Lin Bosheng and the government for ultimate approval. Also, the government began to offer irresistible support. Lin Bosheng wrote letters of introduction for each student group that set out for other cities, and he funded various purification activities within Nanjing.[37] The government even agreed to let students broadcast purification ideas over the radio beginning in January.[38] Meanwhile, the government continued to play up the Resurgence Committee, organizing a series of national meetings headed by this committee from 29 to 31 December. The meetings discussed not only purification but also student spirit and the New Citizen Movement, thereby tying all demonstrations back into the government line on student activism. The overarching force for purification was the government.

The Purification Movement made the students feel that they were standing up for China, but the overwhelming majority of students were followers. The comments of Old Wang reflect what many students remember of the movement: "We only followed the group and caused some damage. The inside story was not clear. . . . Meetings were held among the leaders who planned what the next step would be. There were no meetings for all the people. Instead, prior to an action, the leaders would tell the students how to prepare."[39] Thus, student desires were defined by the role of the most active students, and the majority of demonstrators then followed these leaders. Yeh Wen-hsin has reported a similar situation with respect to student activism in the 1930s, when fewer than 10 percent of students were active and as few as 1 percent actually tried to be leaders. The majority of students kept to their studies and became aroused only for extraordinary crises.[40] The Purification Movement was an extraordinary crisis, as can be seen in the widespread student participation, and even though most students had no clear idea where the movement was headed, destroying property and marching in the street sent a strong message that something was wrong in society and that the students wanted to fix it. This movement showed that thousands of students had reached a point where public action outside of normal political channels had become necessary, even if there was no feeling of where such action might lead. In other words, student leaders may have been the instigators, but a larger student body was stating through parades, meetings, and demonstrations that the government was not doing enough to help China.

There were hints, such as the radio speech of the vice minister of propaganda, that some in the government may have been supportive of resisting Japan in indirect ways. More obvious was the government's involvement in the Purification Movement. But there were also those who wanted all demonstrations to cease. Lin Heng, head of the Nanjing Opium Suppression Bureau, wrote a letter of protest that was passed on to the Executive Yuan. In this letter Lin called the student demonstrations violent and illegal actions. On 17 December youth had destroyed government property, but the government had not acted. Therefore the destruction on 18 December had been even greater. Lin referred to the opium dens as opium suppression offices, emphasized that they paid taxes and abided by government regulations, and hailed them as central to government suppression of opium through ever-increasing prices. Lin recognized the need to gradually end opium use, but claimed that the Hongji Benevolent Society was overseeing gradual reduction. He strongly opposed the erratic actions of the students, which upset public order and created uncertainty in the business community. Lin closed his letter by asking for a strong order from the Executive Yuan to end the movement and restore the peace and order of society.[41]

Such a spectrum of opinion on the government's side hampered the government's control of the movement. On the students' side, a small but very active core leadership, the volatility of opium as an issue, and student savvy at using minimal opportunities to best advantage continued the Purification Movement well into 1944. Student groups spread propaganda and policed entertainment areas throughout Nanjing, making sure that opium, dancing, and gambling did not occur publicly. During winter vacation, the students organized winter camps under government sponsorship to continue their momentum. However, government media control continued to chip away at any separation between what the students were doing and government goals for China. In the midst of all of this an ominous article was published in early January 1944, which stated that entertainment taxes on opium, dancing, and other activities made up 40 percent of total government revenues, something the government was hardly willing to give up even for the moral improvement of society.[42]

Finally, the Ministry of Finance wrote directly to the Executive Yuan. The letter was a copy of a statement by the chairman of the Hongji Benevolent Society. He called the student demonstrators thugs *(baotu)* and criticized the Nanjing police for failing to protect property. The thugs attacked owners and customers, stole money out of the shops, and, worst of all, destroyed the account books so essential to the smooth operation of the tax system. The raided shops all had licenses, paid regular taxes, and supported the government. However, in December these shops had received no legal protection. Now businesses throughout China were nervous. This could severely upset revenue collection. At the end of December students in Shanghai had attacked stores, and in other areas students were causing similar disturbances. The chairman had notified opium suppliers to cease shipments to the Hongji Benevolent Society, but the society had already purchased a three-month supply of opium. Therefore, the opium monopoly still needed protection. Beginning 1 April the society would end its connection to opium distribution.[43] While the society prepared to cease its opium operations, Japan sent an economic advisor to China to negotiate the transfer of complete opium control to Wang's national government.[44]

The government had achieved its goal. In April, Wang's national government would be in charge of the opium monopoly and its revenues. Yet it seems strange that the Japanese government would give up control over such a lucrative monopoly. Unfortunately, there are only bits and pieces to help in understanding this changeover. Most important was that less and less opium revenue was going to the Japanese. During the tenure of the Reformed Government, the Chinese administration was small and ruled only three provinces. The Wang regime was much larger and more expensive. As Tim Brook notes in chapter 14, by 1941 the majority of opium revenues were being used to pay for the occupation government. We can assume that these costs continued to rise because of the growing size of Wang's national government, meaning that the Japanese government received less and less. On the other hand, Japan was making much greater profits through control of commodities in China, so there was no fear of losing substantial sources of income for Japanese political and military needs.[45] In Japan, there was concern about opium and other vices in China as early as 1941.[46] News of Japanese involvement in the China opium trade began to create a negative reaction among the Japanese people, and rumors suggest that even the emperor may have grown concerned.[47] Further, those Japanese directly involved in the buying and selling of opium were rogue businessmen *(ronin)* with shady connections. Finally, Japan had undertaken a more cooperative stance with respect to occupied China after Wang's government joined the fight against America in 1943. With student demonstrations making opium a public relations minefield, the Japanese turned their control of opium over to the Chinese.[48]

The government had proven effective at turning student energies against opponents of opium control. Students kept up their parades, discussed purification issues in their groups and committees, and raided uncooperative dance halls and underground opium dens, often with police support. At the end of January, students and police entered the home of "Heroin King" Cao Yucheng, a Chinese with close connections to Japanese security forces, and arrested him. Under increased vigilance against the heroin trade and illegal (meaning untaxed) opium sales, by April only government-approved centers could distribute opium. By then the government had taken over street propaganda and student activism was dwindling. When police began to investigate student leaders, student activists realized that purification had become a government program.

The Purification Movement remained a student affair: workers were never involved. Inflation was rampant, many necessary goods were being rationed, and standards of living were decreasing for the majority of Nanjing residents. Yet students never took advantage of this tension to connect with workers or other social groups in any major way. A few student societies opened night schools that supplied courses for a handful of shop workers, and students did go into the streets to spread their purification propaganda, but no larger cooperative organizations or networks had been established prior to the December demonstrations. Students only focused on organizing other students. Also, Nanjing was a political and education center full of service industries and did not have any large industries from which cohesive labor organizations might develop. Workers in the service industries organized themselves into government-sponsored labor groups, with membership numbering sometimes in the hundreds of workers. The diversified nature of labor in Nanjing would have made cohesion a time-consuming task even if students had wanted to undertake some kind of larger alliance. Furthermore, students led a pampered life. Their discussions focused on national issues of development rather than daily necessities for survival, government sponsorship gave them great leeway in their activities, and dormitory living made it easy for them to gather together. Laborers and others shared few if any of these advantages. Finally, the student spirit did not translate to the rest of society. The Japanese occupation forced people to repress many of their emotions, and inflation must have further dampened the spirits of those already struggling. Rather than fight back, many chose just to survive. Plus, opium was not a negative issue to all classes of people. As discussed before, among some groups, especially the rich and the working class, opium had been part of daily life for many decades. On top of that, what were the chances that the student demands for an end to opium, gambling, and dancing would really be met?

CONCLUSION

Like governments before it, Wang's national government set up a plan of registration and control that would gradually eradicate opium beginning April 1944. After the war, Mei Siping, at first minister of industry and commerce under Wang Jingwei and later minister of the interior, testified that drug use decreased and opium shipments from Mongolia and Xinjiang had been cut by approximately 60 percent.[49] According to comments by students at the end of 1944, opium and other vices seemed to be thriving as they always had.[50] We can conclude that opium use continued, differing as it always had only by the amount of opium being consumed. When students demonstrated against opium in 1943 and 1944, the government used its prewar experience with student protests to control and rechannel student energies. Even the students drew on prewar examples of protest and used familiar tactics such as street parades, banners, and propaganda. In many ways, the atmosphere surrounding opium in prewar and occupied China shows a continuity that no one has considered before.

A second element that needs closer examination is the pervasiveness of Japanese control. Students were by no means passive during the occupation of Nanjing. As the Purification Movement showed, students were able and willing to take to the streets in open protest. Furthermore, students themselves had built up this potential through public organizations, the open rhetoric of national development, and government-sponsored information networks such as magazines. Using these means, students achieved some voice in the affairs of Nanjing under occupation.

On the other hand, government officials took the lead in forming student organizations, maintained sponsorship over student activities, and monitored youth rhetoric to ensure that it did not violate government policy. Even when students lashed out, the government had enough tools at its disposal to channel youth enthusiasm in ways productive to the government. Furthermore, student activism played into the hands of government leaders who wanted to control the opium monopoly. By the time this control became a reality, government policies and activities had transformed the Purification Movement into a government-led movement that supported ideas of Chinese development under Japanese tutelage.

The final story seems to be the power of the state over the people. Although the state did have power over the people, these students also had power to manipulate the boundaries set by the state. Police and gendarme investigations as late as May 1944 showed that some students were not cowed by the inevitability of state power. Also, just because students cooperated with government plans did not mean that they completely agreed with the government or that they had sacrificed their ideals. Students were still opposing repression and attacking what they saw as social backwardness, and they remained committed to developing China. The students achieved much in five months, prompting official acknowledgment of social evils such as heroin use and illegal entertainment centers. The following summer the government-controlled *Zhongbao* carried a series of articles about the dark side of Nanjing life under the heading "The Social Atmosphere of Baixia." The articles describe a variety of negative social influences, such as the atmosphere of an opium den, women who sold tea and sex in movie theaters, swindlers' tricks, the lives of the homeless, and the slavelike existence of low-class prostitutes. These evil influences continued to be part of life in Nanjing and, with the help of the students, media attention became more focused on them as indicative of the problems in China. As for the students, they let go of the Purification Movement but continued to hold student camps, publish magazines, and organize activities until Japan's surrender. The end of the Purification Movement was not the end of a push to better China, just as occupation was not a silencing of voices for China's improvement.

NOTES

1. EDG file 2010-1950, "Shoudu jingjianshu cheng zhongda gexiao xuesheng ji qingshaoniantuan juxing jinyanduwu youxing shiwei ji sunshi qingxing, 1943–44"; file 2003(2), no. 35, "Nanjingshi xuesheng daohui jieyansuo an, 1943–44."

2. Pan Tian, "Wangwei tongzhi shiqi Nanjing xuesheng de 'qingdu' yundong," p. 75; "Quandao jinyan jinwu jindu."

3. Walker, *Opium and Foreign Policy*, p. 103.

4. Calling the monopoly supplier a "benevolent society" was intended to hide the nature of Japanese involvement from international scrutiny. Japanese involved in the monopoly used Chinese names for the same reason. See USNA (Washington), record group 59, LW63, roll 89, 893.114 Narcotics 2447: "Japanese Organizing Opium Merchants Union under Cover of Charity" (14 January 1939). The same logic applies to calling government distribution centers "Opium Suppression Bureaus."

5. Gould, "Nanking under Japanese Occupation," pp. 38–40; International Military Tribunal for the Far East, *Tokyo War Crimes Trial*, p. 2542.

6. Miner Searle Bates, papers, "Open Letter on the Narcotic Problem in Nanking," record group 10, box 4, file 52, 22 November 1938, Yale University, Divinity School Library, New Haven.

7. Government figures are given in *liang* (taels), the official unit of measurement, which is equivalent to 36 grams. One ounce of opium is equivalent to 28.4 grams.

8. Xingzhengyuan xuanchuanju, *Chūka minkoku isshin seifu gaishi*, p. 377.

9. Miner Searle Bates, "Narcotics in Nanking," *Shanghai Evening Post and Mercury*, 25–27 November 1939.

10. Bates, papers, "Open Letter" (see note 6).

11. Ibid.

12. Informant 40, male, interviewed June 1996; this was part of more than forty interviews conducted in China, Taiwan, and the United States with Chinese who had lived in Nanjing during the war.

13. Minnie Vautrin, diary, 18 November 1938, Yale University Divinity School Library; International Military Tribunal, *Tokyo Trial*, p. 2649.

14. Vautrin, diary, 26 December 1939.

15. International Military Tribunal, *Tokyo Trial*, pp. 4897–98.

16. Ibid.

17. Nanjing tebeishi zhengfu mishuchu, *Ershiba niandu Nanjing shizheng gaikuang*, pp. 112–39; Nankin Nihon shōkō kaigisho, *Nankin*, pp. 159, 163–71.

18. Nankin Nihon shōkō kaigisho, *Nankin*, p. 159. In the city the 1939 figures were more than 50 percent, whereas in areas outside the city they fell to 10 percent or less. The inner-city figures for the Guomindang in 1935 were 63 percent. Therefore, inner-city percentages were even closer for 1935 and 1939. From rough approximations it seems that by late 1937 as many as 80 percent of school-age children inside the city were enrolled in classes. See Nankin Nihon shōkō kaigisho, *Nankin*, pp. 152–53.

19. Informant 1, male, interviewed February 1995.

20. The society's formal name was Dongya lianmeng zonghui Nanjing fenhui xuesheng huzhuhui (Nanjing branch mutual aid society for the East Asia alliance Committee). Its magazine was called *Xuesheng*.

21. "Fakan ci," *Xuesheng*, no. 1 (April 1943).

22. Zhongguo guomindang zhongyang weiyuanhui dangshi weiyuanbu, *Zhonghua minguo zhongyao shiliao chubian*, part 6, *Kuilei zuzhi*, 3:777–78.

23. The committee's formal name was Ganzi yundong shixianhui (Committee to put the struggle movement into practice). Its magazine was called *Gan*.

24. Ping Wu, "Tietixia de huoyan," p. 17.

25. International Military Tribunal, *Tokyo Trial*, pp. 4914, 39324.

26. Dai, "Wang Jingwei xinguomin yundong neimu," p. 274.

27. "Xuexiao qingjie yundong zhou," *Zhongbao*, 18 December 1943, p. 3. *Zhongbao* was a newspaper run by the Wang Jingwei government.

28. Pan Tian, "Wangwei tongzhi shiqi Nanjing xuesheng de 'qingdu' yundong," p. 75.

29. Ibid., p. 76; *Zhongbao*, 19 December 1943, p. 3.

30. Whereas reminiscences claim that the students traveled south on Zhuque Road, just as they did the night before, police reports say that the students traveled south on Zhonghua Road. See EDG file 2010-1950.

31. Zhu Qiluan, *Nanjing renmin gemingshi*, p. 218; EDG file 2010-1950.

32. Ping Wu, "Tietixia de huoyan," p. 16.

33. The materials present a mixed message about Lin's speech. Police reports, such as EDG file 2010-1950, emphasize that Lin berated the students for their actions, whereas personal accounts, such as Pan Tian, "Wangwei tongzhi shiqi Nanjing xuesheng de 'qingdu' yundong," insist that Lin offered support. Another in-

dication that Lin and others supported the Purification Movement but not the student violence is that *Zhongbao* supportively reported the events of 17 and 18 December but left out all references to student destructiveness.

34. Israel, *Student Nationalism in China*, pp. 94–101; Yeh, *Alienated Academy*, p. 230; Li, *Student Nationalism in China*, p. 72.

35. "Hangxuesheng jihui xiangying," *Zhongbao*, 25 December 1943, p. 2.

36. "Juxing qingdu dayouxing," *Zhongbao*, 28 December 1943, p. 2.

37. Pan Tian, "Wangwei tongzhi shiqi Nanjing xuesheng de 'qingdu' yundong," p. 77; Zhu Qiluan, *Nanjing renmin*, p. 219.

38. "Taolun kuoda xuanchuan fangji," *Zhongbao*, 30 December 1943, p. 3.

39. Informant 1.

40. Yeh, *Alienated Academy*, p. 230.

41. EDG file 2003(2), no. 35.

42. "Jinyanduwu ying you zhi renshi," *Zhongbao*, 1 and 2 January 1944, pp. 3, 2.

43. EDG file 2003(2), no. 35.

44. Eguchi, *Nit-Chū ahen sensō*, p. 4913.

45. International Military Tribunal, *Tokyo Trial*, p. 4914.

46. Wakeman, "Shanghai Badlands," p. 367.

47. Chen Cunren, "Hongji shantang 'guangkai shanmen' Sheng Wenyi baoxiao xianqu yantu," p. 100; International Military Tribunal, *Tokyo Trial*, pp. 4914, 4789.

48. International Military Tribunal, *Tokyo Trial*, pp. 4912–14.

49. Ibid., p. 4918.

50. "Yier yiqi yundong yizhounian."

SEVENTEEN

Nationalism, Identity, and State-Building

The Antidrug Crusade in the People's Republic, 1949–1952

Zhou Yongming

In the period it calls "consolidation and reconstruction," from 1949 to 1952, the Chinese Communist Party took steps to consolidate its newly gained power. The most important undertakings were the campaigns to carry out land reform, to "resist America and aid Korea," to "suppress counterrevolutionaries," and to promote the "three antis" and "five antis." These mass movements, as well as the smaller-scale campaign to abolish prostitution, have drawn scholarly attention.[1] But the antidrug campaign from the same period remains untouched. This campaign involved most of China's urban population and successfully wiped out a two-centuries-long epidemic of opium abuse; it was also a political initiative involving a massive mobilization that had dramatic and penetrating effects on Chinese society. Yet it was kept invisible to the outside world. The lack of research on the antidrug campaign is mainly due to the fact that, in the campaign's decisive phase in late 1952, the Chinese government intentionally avoided creating any public records about the campaign. It has remained invisible until very recently.[2] In this chapter, which is based on newly available materials, I reconstruct a brief history of the campaign. By focusing on the ways the crusade was carried out in the context of the consolidation and reconstruction period, I demonstrate that the crusade served as a means for presenting the Communists' image of a "new China" and was an integral part of its state-building process in the early 1950s.

COMMUNISTS' DISCOURSE ON OPIUM BEFORE 1949

Antidrug crusades in modern China are based on a nationalistic discourse on the harmfulness of opium to the Chinese people, state, and society. Since the problem of opium is closely related to the Opium Wars (1840–

1842, 1856–1860) and always reminds Chinese of this history, the rampant opium epidemic was seen as a direct result of imperialist aggression in China. A general antidrug discourse achieved consensus among a wide array of social groups and became hegemonic in modern China, which meant that any regime or social group that conducted an opium-related business openly would risk its legitimacy. The Communists, like the Nationalists and previous regimes, had taken an antidrug stand in public well before they took full power in 1949.

The antidrug discourse of the Communists can be traced back to the late 1920s and early 1930s in those areas that were under their control, where the Soviet governments declared poppy cultivation illegal.[3] For example, in the Northern Sichuan Soviet established by Xu Xiangqian and Zhang Guotao in 1933, "opium cultivation was prohibited, and a graduated program to eliminate opium smoking was announced."[4] But it was during the Sino-Japanese War that the antidrug discourse focused on Japan as a tangible target to enhance the existing nationalist tone. In response to the opium monopoly policy in the territories occupied by the Japanese, the drug issue was tied even more tightly to the very existence of the nation.[5] On 29 February 1939 the Executive Council of the Communist-controlled Jin-Cha-Ji Border Region issued an order forbidding poppy cultivation. In addition to claiming that opium "sickens the country and harms the people," it warned that disobeying the order would undermine the anti-Japanese war effort and thus would further the Japanese plot to weaken China.[6] One article of the "Opium and Narcotics Suppression Regulations of the Shan-Gan-Ning Border Region" specified that Chinese using drugs endangered the vitality of the nation and would be subject to much more severe punishment according to the "Regulations for Punishment of Traitors."[7]

This antidrug rhetoric and regulation continued through the period of civil war. Various antidrug regulations were promulgated in the "liberated areas." With the countrywide victory over the Nationalists imminent, it was finally time for Mao Zedong and the Communists to put forward an identity for a "new China," which they had envisioned for years:

> For many years we Communists have struggled not only for China's political and economic revolution but also for her cultural revolution; all this aims at building up a new society and a new state for the Chinese nation. In that new society and new state there will be not only new politics and a new economy but also a new culture. That is to say, we want not only to change a politically oppressed and economically exploited China into a politically free and economically prosperous China, but also to change a China which has been ignorant and backward under the rule of the old culture into a China that will be enlightened and progressive under the rule of a new culture. In a word, we want to build up a new China.[8]

According to Mao, the new China would get rid of all "capitalist" and "feudal" cultural elements of the old China and have a "national, scientific and mass culture" instead.[9] It is in this broad context of discourse that opium, drugs, gambling, and prostitution were among the first targets of Communist state-building right after 1949.

THE FIRST PHASE OF THE CRUSADE, 1949 TO EARLY 1952

Signifying the start of a nationwide antidrug crusade, on 24 February 1950 the Government Administrative Council issued a "General Order for Opium Suppression." It presented several reasons to legitimize the initiative, with a clear demarcation line of before / after 1949 attached. Before 1949, the opium problem was associated with the regimes of compradors, warlords, and feudal bureaucrats, who had forced people to cultivate opium poppy, and with foreign imperialists, who had forced it upon the Chinese people. The "General Order" begins:

> It has been more than a century since opium was forcibly imported into China by the imperialists. Due to the reactionary rule and the decadent lifestyle of the feudal bureaucrats, compradors, and warlords, not only was opium not suppressed, but we were forced to cultivate it; especially due to the Japanese systematically carrying out a plot to poison China during their aggression, countless people's lives and property have been lost. Now that the people have been liberated, the following methods of opium and other narcotic suppression are specifically stipulated to protect people's health, to cure addiction, and to accelerate production.[10]

There is not much new in the antidrug rhetoric; however, the "General Order" did give specific instructions to local authorities for carrying out the crusade, which were generally followed during the whole process of the campaign. These steps include:

1. conducting propaganda to mobilize the masses;
2. having the People's Congress at various levels discuss the issue and set up methods to root out opium according to a limited timetable;
3. wiping out poppy cultivation in the areas where military operations have ended, followed by other areas immediately after the completion of military operations;
4. prohibiting production, trafficking, and selling of opium and other narcotics;
5. asking the general public to turn in their stores of opium;
6. registering addicts according to a timetable;
7. making medications and prescriptions available to drug addicts, but under the strict control of the Health Department in order to prevent them from being used as drug substitutes;
8. setting up rehabilitation centers in cities with severe opium problems; and

9. having each Major Administrative Region or Military Control Commission work out detailed methods and a specific timetable for opium suppression.[11]

The last item of the "General Order" was carried out within one year. And many provinces and big cities formulated their own regulations accordingly. For example, Yunnan Province, notorious for its high-potency *yuntu* ("Yunnan opium") and vast poppy cultivation, issued an "Opium Suppression Directive" on 27 June 1950, even before the issuance of the "Enforcement Regulation" by the Southwest Military Control Commission, its direct superior, on 31 July.[12] On 30 January, only thirty-five days after the establishment of Guizhou provincial government, the authorities issued an opium suppression notice and an open letter to its people, asking them to get rid of the opium evil inherited from the Nationalists and to strive to build a "new Guizhou." The notice was reiterated on 25 August in provincial enforcement regulations.[13]

From early 1950 on, the opium suppression campaign was carried out nationwide for the first time under the Communist rule. The actions taken ranged from registration and rehabilitation of addicts to curtailment of poppy cultivation and drug trafficking. Much progress was made. In Guizhou, opium dens were closed, addicts rehabilitated, poppy plants destroyed, and drug traffickers arrested. Many public trials were held and a number of large-scale traffickers were executed. In 1951, 49,646 *mu* (3,310 hectares) of poppies were wiped out and three thousand opium dens closed. A total of 11,700 opium addicts were rehabilitated and 6,333 drug offenders arrested. Among those arrested, two were sentenced to death, 4,163 were sent to prison, and 445 were remanded to labor camps.[14] But in a province estimated to have more than three million addicts out of a total population of fourteen million, curing twelve thousand addicts was not a particularly impressive achievement, even though the authorities seemed to pursue opium suppression quite aggressively compared to other areas.[15]

In fact, inconsistency and inefficiency were common during the first phase of the antidrug campaign. There was no systematic or well-constructed plan to coordinate the crusade with other initiatives taken by the central government. In that period, even though ideologically the government was determined to solve the problem, in reality the Communists were preoccupied with various other tasks they were facing, among which the most important were to revive the economy devastated by the civil war, to rebuild social order at home, and to fight the Americans in Korea. At this stage the Communists simply lacked the resources necessary to carry out this project completely. In Nanjing, the former capital of the Nationalists, the government gave up its efforts to set up rehabilitation centers because of lack of necessary medical resources.[16] In Guizhou, the government was preoccupied with the task of suppressing bandits in the first half of 1950, and opium suppression actually was not being pursued, as admitted by the provincial authority.[17]

A related problem is that in the case of drug offenses, the punishments were often too lenient or were substituted by fines. From May 1949 to December 1949, of the 472 drug offenders detained in Nanjing, only twenty-six were sentenced to prison terms of six months to two years. Of the 2,090 detained in 1950, 345 were sent to prison.[18] Compared with the percentage of those caught in 1952 (see table 7), these numbers are significantly low.

In an effort to intensify the antidrug crusade, in the fall of 1950, the Interior Ministry of the Government Administrative Council issued a directive asking for more severe punishment of drug offenders. More significantly, the directive abolished the practice of giving bonuses to law enforcement agencies or individuals according to the amount of opium seized. In November 1950 the Supreme People's Court also ordered that drug offenders not be allowed to avoid imprisonment by substituting fines. All offenders were to be sentenced to prison or labor camp for terms dependent on the degree of their guilt.[19]

In the early days of Communist rule, therefore, drug suppression simply could not be a high priority among the tasks of state-building. Meanwhile, local officials used their creativity to place the anti-opium crusade within the context of the initiatives that were deemed more important or more urgent at the time. In rural areas, reduction of poppy cultivation was achieved by linking it to land reform, which was conducted in the early 1950s. The redistribution of lands generally weakened the ability of big landowners to engage in mass cultivation of opium poppies and made it easier for the authorities to persuade peasants—the beneficiaries of land reform—to obey the government's opium suppression order. In the spring of 1951 more than 147,000 *mu* of opium poppies were pulled up in the course of rent reduction and land reform.[20] The discourse on opium suppression linked it with other concurrent government campaigns. Quitting opium was interpreted as an action to prove one's newly gained status, or as a response to the Communists' call to "increase production and practice economy," as well as to resist America and aid Korea when the Korean War broke out. And many antidrug public trials and gatherings were held in association with the Counterrevolutionaries Suppression campaign. Most drug traffickers executed during this period were identified as counterrevolutionaries. On 14 April 1951 about forty thousand people gathered at Dali, Yunnan, to hold a mass rally to "Resist America, Aid Korea; Oppose Reactionaries and Suppress Opium." In the session, six so-called counterrevolutionaries were executed and more than forty-three thousand taels

TABLE 7   Punishments Given to Arrested Drug Offenders
in Nanjing, 1952

Sentence	Number receiving sentence	Percentage of offenders receiving sentence
Death	19	1.6
>10 years' prison	13	11.7
5–10 years' prison	332	29
3–5 years' prison	285	24.7
Surveillance	138	11.9
Released	97	8.4
Not yet tried	146	12.7
Total number arrested	1,153	

SOURCE: Ning Gongshi, "Nanjing de jindu gongzuo," in *Jinchang jindu*, ed. Ma Weigang, p. 365.

(*liang*) of opium were burned in public.[21] I will come back to this issue of political spectacle later.

THE SECOND PHASE OF THE CAMPAIGN, 1952

After more than two years, it became clear that more efforts were needed to wipe out China's deeply rooted drug problem. These efforts were made by the Chinese authorities in the second half of 1952 in a campaign that has generally been seen as a very successful crusade against drugs. If the first phase of the campaign was sporadically and inconsistently carried out without much severity against the offenders, the second phase was the opposite. It was executed with well-formulated plans, intensive propaganda and mass mobilization, and harsher punishments on a nationwide scale. As a matter of fact, the decisive drug suppression action taken in the second half of the year was more or less a planned derivative of the Three Antis and Five Antis campaigns of 1951–1952. Leads and information obtained from these two campaigns prompted the highest authorities to initiate a drug suppression drive.

The Three Antis campaign (anticorruption, antiwaste, and antibureaucracy) was launched in November 1951, mainly against corrupt cadres. The Five Antis (antibribery, anti–tax evasion, anti–embezzlement of state assets, anti–shoddy work, and anti–pilferage of information about the state economy), launched in January 1952, targeted the national bourgeoisie. It soon appeared that many corruption cases involved drug trafficking. How to handle them became a concern to policy makers at various levels. The Jilin Provincial Council of the CCP reported the issue to the Northeast Bureau of the CCP in March 1952. The bureau responded by calling upon local authorities to cease antidrug action until a plan could be drawn up. This was in accordance with instructions from the Central Committee, which stressed that the focus should be on the ongoing Five Antis campaign; local authorities were told not to arrest drug traffickers in order to avoid disturbing the national capitalists, who were already under pressure from the Five Antis campaign. Therefore in the Three and Five Antis period the tasks of local authorities were to uncover and collect information on drug trafficking and to make lists of drug offenders until the Central Committee instructed the authorities to take action.[22]

The "Directive on Eradication of Drug Epidemic" came from the Central Committee on 15 April 1952, calling for a mass antidrug crusade to solve the problem once and for all, based on the information uncovered and leads developed in the Three and Five Antis campaigns. According to the directive's outline, drug trafficking was singled out as the main problem to be solved. Large and medium-sized cities, ports, and main areas of drug cultivation and distribution were targeted in the campaign. Punishments should be focused on drug kingpins and drug lords, especially those who refused to make confessions to the authorities.[23]

More than three months were spent on preparing for the upcoming campaign. The Central Ministry of Public Security was put in charge of coordinating the campaign nationwide. Peng Zhen, a member of the Politburo, was assigned to preside over the whole range of operations, which involved many relevant ministries and bureaus, including the ministries of railroads, communications, interior, and public health as well as the postal service, customs, courts, procuratorate, and so on. The need for thorough investigation and information gathering was once again emphasized, and local bureaus of public security were asked to delay any action against known traffickers until they got orders from the ministry.[24]

On 19 July 1952 the "Directive on Anti-Drug Propaganda" was issued jointly by the Central Propaganda Department of the CCP and the Central Ministry of Public Security. In it, the propaganda contents and forms to be adopted were clearly defined, and any form of propaganda in written format was prohibited. This issue will be explored later. In late July a working conference was held in Beijing to plan the coming campaign. Xu Zirong, vice minister of public security, gave a speech on the implementation of a concrete plan of operation. According to his speech, based on preliminary investigations nationwide, there were more than 165,000 drug offenders already uncovered, including drug producers, traffickers, and poppy cultivation promoters. The actual figure could reach 250,000. Of the total drug offenders, about 5 percent were drug makers and 95 percent were

TABLE 8   Drug Offenders Discovered in
Major Administrative Regions, 1952

Area	Number of offenders discovered	Percentage of total number of offenders discovered
South Central	38,000	22.8
North	28,000	16.8
Southwest	43,000	25.6
East	23,000	13.8
Northeast	23,000	13.8
Northwest	12,000	7.2
Total	167,000	

SOURCE: "Zhongyang gonganbu Xu Zirong fubuzhang zai jindu gongzuo huiyishang guanyu kaizhan quanguo guimo de jindu yundong de baogao" (Speech on Conducting National Antidrug Campaign by Vice Minister Xu Zirong in Work Conference on Drug Suppression), Ministry of Public Security Archives, file 1952-005.

drug traffickers; about 10 percent of the identified drug offenders were state employees.[25] The numbers of offenders in each Major Administrative Region were as listed in table 8.

The campaign started with a first wave of mass arrests around 10 August in different areas, followed by an intensive propaganda campaign and two or three more waves of mass arrests. Apparently the later arrests were based upon new leads and information gathered from the first. The second wave of arrests was carried out in late August or early September. By October, massive actions against drug offenders were suspended. The focus shifted to putting the arrested on trial and consolidating the results of the preceding work. In Tianjin the campaign started at 2:00 A.M. on 10 August, when 145 out of 150 targeted drug offenders were arrested during the eight-hour action, followed by intensive interrogation of detainees and intensive propaganda directed to the 800,000 people of the city. During that time the Bureau of Public Security planned the second phase of the campaign and the arrests to be made in the second and third waves—three hundred and more than one hundred, respectively, in addition to the 190 arrests made before September. On 3 September the second wave of arrests was made, with 301 detained. By the end of October the total number of arrests reached 677, which was in accordance with the original plan.[26]

Though the campaign targeted mainly drug makers and traffickers, drug addicts were forced to quit their habit, too. The Central Committee's policy on this issue was that addicts should be rehabilitated collectively or individually in programs administered by the government and under surveillance of the masses, with exceptions for the elderly and the sick, who could be granted extensions. This task was carried out mostly at the end of the campaign. With drug supply channels cut off and the masses mobilized, addicts had no choice but to give up. In Nanjing, there were still 1,120 addicts (711 male and 409 female) as of 1952. Two rehabilitation centers were set up, providing necessary medicine to those who required it. Most addicts were affected by the mass mobilization and undertook rehabilitation at home with the help of family members and "under surveillance of the masses"; only fifty addicts had to be put on compulsory rehabilitation under the supervision of the public security authority. By the end of the year it was claimed that all addicts were cured.[27]

Nationwide, the campaign was carried out in a coordinated manner and decisively. In his summary report on the national antidrug campaign dated 14 December 1952, Minister of Public Security Luo Ruiqing proclaimed that the campaign's concentrated crackdown had "triumphantly finished in the country's 1,202 targeted areas. The campaign had uncovered drug makers and traffickers totaling 369,705, more than the original estimation of 250,000. A total of 82,056, or 22 percent of the total, were arrested. Of those 51,627 who were prosecuted, 34,775 were sentenced to prison (including death penalty and life sentences), 2,138 were sent to labor camp and 6,843 were put under surveillance, 3,534 were released and 4,337 uncategorized."[28]

Among Luo's long list of campaign achievements, including confiscated instruments used to make and traffic drugs and weapons used to resist drug suppression, the amount of confiscated drug, the equivalent of 3,996,056 taels of opium, was well below the official estimate of drugs held by the public, which ranged from fifty million to one hundred million taels. Luo's explanation was that much had been confiscated prior to the campaign and there were a lot of drugs in rural areas that had not been touched by this campaign.[29] To resolve the latter problem the State Administrative Council issued a directive on 12 December 1952, which called on the people to quit opium smoking, forbade poppy cultivation, and authorized the confiscation of remaining drugs in rural areas.[30] The campaign of 1952 then basically ended nationwide.

AN INVISIBLE CAMPAIGN: ORAL PROPAGANDA AND MASS MOBILIZATION

To today's observers, the most puzzling question is why the Communists would not let the campaign leave any public records? Before 1952, newspapers had carried antidrug news regularly, but there were no reports about the 1952 campaign whatsoever in papers, books, pamphlets, or any other written format, except in government documentary archives. There was nothing on the radio, either. The crusade was deliberately kept invisible to foreigners by the highest authorities in China.

This was partly due to the Chinese government's reaction to an accusation made by the Americans that China was exporting drugs to Japan. It was reported on 19 February 1951 that Japanese narcotic agents seized twenty pounds of heroin in Kobe. Among the nineteen packages seized, four bore the labels "Duro-Well Pharmaceutic Laboratory, Luch Street, Tientsin (Tianjin), China." In the official *Report on the Traffic in Opium and Other Dangerous Drugs* of 1951, in which this was reported, the U.S. government expressed "considerable concern" about the "reported flow of heroin from Tianjin and points in Manchuria into Japan, via Hong Kong," and claimed that some of this heroin found its way into the United States and other countries. The report urged that "this traffic should be suppressed by the Communist authorities in China."[31] Yet the tone turned more acrimonious one year later. At the United Nations Commission on Narcotic Drugs, which held its seventh session in New York from 15 April to 9 May 1952, the U.S. representative alleged that the investigations, arrests, and seizures in Japan during 1951 were conclusive proof that the Chinese were smuggling heroin into Japan in order to finance Communist Party activities and to obtain strategic materials.

The accusation made by the United States, although not groundless, was based on evidence that was not as "conclusive" as was claimed. Historically Tianjin had been a major drug production and traffic center, especially during the period of Japanese occupation. It was known that prior to 1952, most of the drug selling in Tianjin originated from the Yuda Company. The company usually transported opium to Hong Kong to make heroin, then resold most of it to interior China via Guangzhou. In 1950, four hundred thousand taels of opium were transferred to Hong Kong by the company. It is not clear whether the Duro-Well Pharmaceutic Laboratory was related to Yuda, but the intensity and scale of drug trafficking in Tianjin decreased dramatically after the authorities ordered the Yuda Company to cease operation at the end of 1950.[32] In another case, a Chinese drug trafficking group in Wuhan bought Japanese-manufactured heroin in Hong Kong, then smuggled it into China.[33] Considering the active role Hong Kong had played in drug transit, it was highly possible that some heroin originating from Tianjin ended up in Japan through Hong Kong, as the U.S. representative reported to the United Nations. But there was little evidence that the Communist Party was running the operation or benefiting from it financially.[34] But Cold War rhetoric had been attached to the issue, and the United States continued to list Communist China as a principal source of heroin for many years.[35]

In a swift response to the American accusation, the Central Committee decided temporarily to suspend putting drug suppression news in newspapers. The Central Committee explained the issue in a directive to regional party bureaus on 10 June, saying that "since a systematic nationwide antidrug campaign is only at the stage of investigation and preparation, and the American imperialists are spreading rumors of us exporting drugs to Japan, the Central Committee has decided not to put drug suppression news in newspapers. You will be informed by the Central Committee on whether or not to issue drug suppression news, as well as the way of issuance in the future.''[36]

The ban was extended indefinitely in July. Jointly issued by the Central Propaganda Department of the CCP and the Central Ministry of Public Security on 19 July 1952, the "Directive on Antidrug Propaganda" ordered that the propaganda campaign be carried out orally among an inner circle of people, and all mention of this topic should be excluded from newspapers, magazines, radio broadcasts, and the New China News Agency. The reason was reiterated as "not to let the American imperialists use our drug suppression campaign to make up vicious rumors against us (not long ago the United States slandered us in the United Nations, saying that we exported drugs to Japan).''[37] To the Chinese, what was at stake was China's new image in the community of the nations in the world. The defensive stand they took looks a little bit awkward today. One may ask why the new regime did not turn the campaign into a successful image-making initiative by showing the world that only the Communists could deal with the problem at the root. This question has to be answered in historical context. At the initial stage of the Cold War, when the propaganda machines of both China and America were in full gear attacking each other and American media enjoyed some degree of hegemony in the Western world, the Chinese authorities operated on the assumption that America would use news of drug producing and trafficking in China to prove its accusation. The Chinese Communists would proudly claim credit for turning China into a "drug-free" country later in the 1960s and 1970s.

The directive on propaganda also focused on a counterattack against the Americans. It instructed local authorities that the first priority of propaganda should be to reveal the roles of imperialists and the previous Chinese rulers in using drugs to poison the Chinese people. It blamed the American imperialists and remnants of the Guomindang for the lingering drug activities in China, which posed severe threats to public order, production, reconstruction, and the people's health, customs, and morality. Thus, to the Chinese the antidrug campaign became a patriotic movement that would strike against the aggressive conspiracy of the American imperialists and protect people's interests. So any case related to producing, smuggling, or trafficking drugs by imperialist countries should be emphasized in propaganda, along with the history of their importation of drugs to China. The directive also sought to disclose those drug offenders who were also counterrevolutionaries or drug kingpins, and to publicize the policy that encouraged confession in exchange for lenient punishment.[38]

The Communists' concerns with image-making are also revealed by the directive's list of issues not (or less) subject to propaganda. This list included cases related to government organs, to prominent figures of the United Front, to minority peoples, and to drug smuggling to the outside world. The statistics of drug offenders arrested and drugs confiscated were also forbidden to be made public.[39] The directive also instructed local authorities to refrain from exposing drug cases related to industry and the commercial sector because by then the Five Antis campaign had caused a decline in production and an increase in unemployment in some big cities. Beijing did not want to distract national capitalists further from the main task of reviving the economy.[40]

Within the limits of keeping the campaign invisible to the outside world, local officials were set the task of mobilizing the masses. It turned out that these limits did not prevent them from carrying out a massive propaganda campaign that was pivotal to the success of the whole antidrug crusade. With few exceptions, the first wave of arrests did not have a strong enough impact to be felt by the drug offenders or by society as a whole. Many people saw this as a routine crackdown like many before it, and many doubted the government's resolution. In Xi'an, people thought that drug suppression was a good thing, but were not sure that the epidemic could be eradicated completely this time, given that neither the Qing dynasty nor the Nationalists had succeeded in doing this. The government sometimes had been lenient to drug criminals in the past couple of years. Though the city arrested 312 drug offenders in a single day on 11 August, the masses were not yet motivated to participate actively in the campaign. In the following week, only 917 drug traffickers came to be registered and the city received only 935 reports by the masses. Faced with this situation, the authorities decided to intensify the propaganda campaign. Within ten days, 5,843 propaganda meetings were held and 147,620 people were involved. The campaign turned the corner by combining propaganda efforts with a second wave of arrests on 22 August. During a mass antidrug rally the next day involving 150,000 participants, as many as 721 people asked to make confessions of their crimes and 19,464 reports were received on the spot.[41]

With newspaper and radio coverage excluded, the authorities took various other means, often very creative, to get their points seen and heard. The most common method was to use propaganda trucks circling the streets broadcasting the government's policy against drugs through loudspeakers mounted on top of the trucks. In Guilin, Guangxi province, arrested drug offenders were put on the circling trucks to demonstrate the government's resolution on drug suppression.[42] To make the message more accessible, the campaign's policy was elaborated through traditional opera, clapper talk, comic dialogue, yangge, dagu, cailianchuan, and other popular entertainment forms. Sometimes closed-circuit radio was set up to reach larger audiences. Yet the propaganda method that reached more people than any other were the thousands of group gatherings. The penetrating degree of this type of mass mobilization can be demonstrated by different types of antidrug gatherings held by almost all strata of the society. There were antidrug gatherings for people's representatives, party members and activists, members of the military, youth, senior citizens, women, students, and drug addicts and their relatives. In some places, it could be claimed without any exaggeration that the campaign was made known to every single resident. According to official statistics, the campaign held a total of 764,423 propaganda meetings nationwide, through which 74,595,181 people were educated. The numbers in Shenyang were 21,425 and 1,171,648, respectively. In Guangzhou, 11,046 gatherings were held and 1,239,283 people participated. In key targeted areas in the Southwest, it was said that the average number of antidrug education meetings attended per person was two to three.[43]

In retrospect, two characteristics of the propaganda campaign need to be emphasized. One is that the very reason for not making the campaign public was used to mobilize people's nationalist sentiment against the American imperialists, then China's number one enemy. The local authorities were instructed to portray the Americans as the main culprits in China's drug problem and, more recently, a vicious rumormonger against China's drug suppression campaign. They were also instructed to explain to the masses that the main purpose of conducting the campaign in this invisible way was to avoid providing the Americans with anything that they might use to attack China. They should explain that it was not true that the Chinese were afraid of letting the American imperialists know about our antidrug campaign.[44]

As a matter of fact, the Chinese were concerned about this issue sometimes obsessively. Not only was nothing allowed to appear in newspapers, in magazines, or on the radio, but nothing was allowed to appear in any other written form, such as posters, cartoons, billboards, or other exhibitions. Even putting titles like "Committee on Drug Suppression" on envelopes or letterhead was prohibited. And jumping the gun was viewed with deep suspicion. On 8 August, authorities in Lijiang county in Guangxi province held an antidrug mass rally. One hundred fifty copies of propaganda texts, one hundred seventy slogan posters, eighty pieces of propaganda instructions, and eight hundred forms were handed out to assist the propaganda drive. This incident, along with the fact that the county had carried out the first wave of arrests several days ahead of the plan, got a quick response from superiors all the way up to the Central Ministry, which ordered a thorough investigation of the incident.[45]

The second characteristic, related to the first, is that in the daily propaganda practice, it was not the nationalist antidrug arguments but those closely associated with people's real lives that played a more important and persuasive role. At the time of the Korean War, drug suppression was deliberately put in relation to "patriotism," the Communists' version of official nationalism.[46] In Xi'an, propaganda activists were asked to tell the masses that conducting antidrug crusades was a very concrete patriotic behavior that allowed them to participate in the campaign to "resist America and aid Korea."[47] But as some other local authorities acknowledged, talking generally about the history of the Opium Wars or the opium policy of the imperialists was not an effective way to reach the masses. Rather, the focus should be on how crimes committed by imperialists and local drug traffickers, such as seducing people to use drugs, forcing female addicts to become prostitutes, stealing others' property, and supporting bandits, had inflicted great misery on ordinary people.[48] In Beijing, the discovery of several heroin overdose victims in Tianqiao district every day during the Japanese occupation was used to condemn its opium monopoly policy.[49] Many relatives of drug addicts were encouraged to speak out about the misery drugs had brought to their family members and the addicts themselves. Angry sentiments were directed toward drug traffickers and makers so as to isolate them in society.

MASS RALLY AND PUBLIC TRIAL AS POLITICAL RITUALS

Professor Ma Mozhen, an acknowledged expert on the history of drug suppression in China, was motivated to study this subject in order to refute American scholars' misunderstanding that China had rid itself of its drug problem by simply killing drug offenders in the 1950s.[50] The number of executions in the campaign has been kept secret over the past several decades, which may have led Western scholars to make exaggerated estimates. The recorded number of executions turns out to be 880 nationwide in the second phase of the campaign in 1952.[51] Though this is not a small number, when we compare it with the number of executions in the campaign against counterrevolutionaries, estimates of which range from 500,000 to 800,000, it is relatively insignificant.[52] Most of the executions were proclaimed and carried out during mass rallies and public trials, which served as a main propaganda method to mobilize the masses and a psychological means to intimidate drug offenders.

The mass rally and public trial were the culmination of the propaganda drive during the campaign of 1952. In the early days after the first wave of arrests, most areas reported that the action did not seem to have much effect on society as a whole. The drive was intensified and various creative publicity forms were adopted. Yet in many cases it was mass rallies and public trials that gave momentum to the campaign. The situation in Wuhan was typical. After the first wave of arrests, most sectors of society remained untouched. Even a number of arrested offenders appeared not to take the matter seriously. Many of them did not acknowledge any wrongdoing. Some of them and their relatives even had direct confrontations with the authorities. Having experienced the Five Antis, which was very thorough in investigating offenders but quite lenient with punishment, those arrested thought the authorities could persuade only idiots to confess because few people were being executed for drug offenses. Of those who had not been arrested, some hid or escaped, some transferred drugs and properties to safe places, some threatened government informants, some circulated rumors that confiscated morphine would be resold in the department stores for fiscal gain by the authorities, and some even took advantage of the campaign to hike the price of drugs.[53] At this point the campaign for drug suppression was far from its basic goal.

To deal with the situation, mass rallies were used to launch an intensive propaganda drive by the authorities. On 16 August, three days after the first wave of arrests was complete, a conference attended by ten thousand people was held by the Propaganda Department of the Wuhan Municipal Party Committee. In the session, three hundred kilograms of narcotics were burned to show the government's resolution. It was not until 9 September, however, when a municipal public trial attended by more than twenty thousand people was held, that the whole campaign finally reached its climax. During the session, party and municipal leaders vowed to carry the campaign to a successful conclusion and representatives from democratic parties and people's organizations offered their support. Among the twenty drug offenders being tried, two were sentenced to death and immediately executed and eighteen were sent to prison—three for terms from seven to fifteen years, five for five to ten years, five for three to five years, and one for less than three years. One was put under the surveillance of the masses, and three were released after education. One of the released drug offenders expressed his appreciation for the leniency from the authorities, using himself as an example to call on others to follow. The public trial seemed to have an immediate effect on those drug offenders still holding out. Many rushed to confess in order to avoid a possible death penalty. Those who had not been arrested started to turn themselves in to receive lenient treatment. In the evening immediately after the public trial, it was said that 124 people voluntarily confessed, turning over 94 taels of morphine, 1,012 taels of opium, and 145 pounds of acetic acid. In conjunction with the mass arrests before and after this public trial, the campaign gained decisive results before the middle of October.[54]

Mass rallies and public trials had long been used by the Communists to mobilize the masses in other campaigns, and they were also used in the first phase of the antidrug campaigns, as they were in Dali, Yunnan. In Guizhou, numerous mass rallies and public trials were held before 1952.

In Guiyang on 16 June 1950 and 12 November 1950 mass rallies and public trials were held, with thirty-two thousand and twenty-three thousand taels of opium, respectively, burned in public, and two drug offenders were sentenced to death with immediate execution on the latter occasion. In Zunyi on 2 October and 17 November 1950, two and four drug offenders, respectively, were executed in the antidrug mass rallies attended by more than ten thousand people, and on both occasions great quantities of opium were burned. The same kind of antidrug mass rallies and public trials were held in Qianxi, Anshun, and Weining. Despite all these efforts, the drug problem was still pervasive in the province before the start of the second phase of the campaign.[55]

To explain the effectiveness of the mass rally and public trial in the 1952 campaign, it is necessary to consider the number of executions being carried out. As said before, the number is not excessive considering the vast scope of the campaign and in comparison to the numbers executed in the campaigns against counterrevolutionaries or for land reform. This time, however, the mass rally and public trial functioned mainly to generate psychological effects on society in general and on drug offenders in particular. If it was effective, it was because of several conditions that had not existed before. First, the period of consolidation and reconstruction had almost been completed: with the Land Reform and Counterrevolutionaries Suppression campaigns partially completed and the Three Antis and Five Antis finished, social order had been restored nationwide and Communist control had been enhanced. In fact, the antidrug campaign could be seen as a by-product of Three Antis and Five Antis because it was leads and information obtained from those two campaigns that prompted the highest authorities to initiate a drug suppression drive. Second, having completed various urgent tasks to consolidate their newly gained power, the Communists finally had the ability to put resources together and focus on drug issues. In the pre-1952 period, drug suppression was carried out around central tasks in different major campaigns at different times. This time, local authorities were asked to carry out campaigns that had suppression of drug trafficking and use as their main focus. Wuhan made these efforts the second priority of government work, right behind the campaign to "increase production and practice economy." It also asked that the campaign be directed by district leaders and that 80 percent of the resources of public security and the court system to be put into action to combat drugs.[56]

Third, the factor that made the biggest difference between the first and second phases of the antidrug campaign was that the latter was well planned and systematically and vigorously carried out. With the information accumulated during the Three Antis and Five Antis, and in light of the directive from the Central Committee, local public security organs spent almost four months preparing for the implementation of the campaign. The issue of how many executions ought to be carried out was specified in advance and modified during the operation. In the speech given on 28 July 1952 by Xu Zirong, vice minister of public security, about the operation of the national antidrug campaign, the percentage was temporarily set at 0.5 percent of the total number of drug offenders arrested. He instructed that only those who were guilty of the most heinous crimes should be executed in order to achieve the following three aims: to get rid of drug kingpins, to reform accomplices, and to educate the masses. He did mention that it was not appropriate to execute too many drug offenders and only those deserving capital punishment should be killed. In addition, only the provincial level authority could authorize the executions.[57] On 29 August, in response to a report by Luo Ruiqing, the minister of public security, the Central Committee agreed to hold public trials in specially targeted areas, and authorized each city to execute "several" to "more than a dozen" drug kingpins, but did not give a specific quota.[58] On 3 October the Central Committee instructed local authorities that "it is easier to get people's sympathy by killing drug offenders than by killing counterrevolutionaries. So at least two percent of those arrested should be killed."[59] The actual number of executions turned out to be 1 percent of the total number of arrests. The reason may be partly due to local differences in implementing the quota, and partly to *xianjin housong* ("strict in the beginning and flexible in the end") policies that were adopted in some places, so that real drug kingpins could be executed without exceeding the quota in the later part of the campaign.[60] The statistics given in table 9 are from mid December 1952, but considering that the national antidrug campaign ended at about this time, the number of executions carried out subsequently should not be much higher than those reported in the table.

It took all three conditions combined to give the authorities the leverage to generate such huge political effects through mass rallies and public trials. By accomplishing something no other regime had ever accomplished, the antidrug campaign in 1952 signified the unprecedented state hegemony the Communists had built in just a few years. Well-designed policy such as *yancha kuanban* ("strict in investigation and flexible in punishment"), in addition to public trials, enabled the Communists to achieve their aims at minimal cost in human lives and social upheaval.

THE ANTIDRUG CAMPAIGN AND THE ESTABLISHMENT OF URBAN CONTROL

As mentioned by Bin Wong in chapter 8, opium suppression was closely connected with the tasks of nation-building, especially with the state's attempts to establish rural and urban social control in China. In more than

TABLE 9   Numbers of Arrests and Executions in Major Areas, 1952

Area	Number of arrests	Number of executions	Percentage of arrested offenders executed
Yunnan	6,239	38	0.61
Guizhou	3,915	25	0.64
Fujian	1,659	27	1.62
Guangxi	4,476	24	0.54
Tianjin	677	10	1.48
Changchun	148	3	2.03
Nanjing	1,153	19	1.65
Xuchang	107	4	3.74

SOURCE: Ma Weigang, ed., *Jinchang jindu.*

two hundred years no regime had enjoyed substantial success in this area until the Communists did in the early 1950s. Why did the Communists succeed in wiping out opium where others failed? This complex question cannot be thoroughly addressed in this chapter. Based on the history of the campaign of 1952 described above, I want to emphasize that before the start of the campaign the Communists had already built a social control mechanism that was unprecedented in its power and effectiveness. The success of the antidrug campaign derived from the existing mechanism; at the same time the campaign strengthened the system.

At first the Communists connected the moral imperative of opium suppression with a nationalist interpretation concerning the nationhood of the new People's Republic. The concern with building and maintaining a "new" identity for Communist China had shaped the way the campaign was carried out. Unlike the rationales of other campaigns conducted during the same period, the rationale for conducting drug suppression was based not solely on the doctrine of class struggle, but on the concern for building a new national identity. In this process several contrasts were carefully elaborated: the Old China versus the New; the Nationalists versus the Communists; the imperialists versus the Chinese people. By proving that they could do what other regimes could not, the Communists enhanced the legitimacy of their rule. Not surprisingly, in the second phase of the campaign the Chinese took American accusations so seriously that they ordered that the campaign be invisible to the outside world. Thus the masses were mobilized through oral propaganda and public trials.

Through mass mobilization, the campaign became a well-orchestrated initiative to tighten social control over the urban public and an integral part of the state-building process. Derived directly from the Three Antis and Five Antis at the end of the consolidation and reconstruction period, the antidrug campaign contributed to the establishment of a social control system that eventually had "the means of totalitarian rule that preceding authoritarian regimes—the late Qing monarchy, Yuan Shikai's abortive republic, the Nationalists' Nanking regime—could hardly have imagined."[61] The ways that the antidrug campaign of 1952 was carried out have shown us that the state did not achieve social control merely by using state violence; rather, state hegemony was achieved through a combination of coercive force, surveillance, propaganda, and persuasion. This process was completed with the help of the social control institutions the Communists had built in China's urban society after 1949.

Franz Schurmann has pointed out that the Communists tried to control the urban population from two directions. One was through the expanded civil administration functions of the police, by staffing local police stations with so-called household register police whose main responsibility was to keep watch over almost everything in the community under his or her jurisdiction. The other was through mass organizations and their grassroot efforts.[62] These organizations included the Communist Youth League, the Women's Association, trade unions, and residents' committees. In the antidrug campaign, they were indispensable for conveying government policies to ordinary urban dwellers, especially to those unaffiliated with state-controlled institutions or enterprises. The growth of mass organizations in general and the residents' committees in particular enabled the campaign to be carried invisibly and yet to reach the vast majority of the urban population.

In fact, by the end of the Five Antis campaign, the Communists had set up a vast propaganda network in the big cities. In Shanghai, there were more than sixteen thousand propagandists, many of them from the Communist Youth League and other mass organizations. In August 1952 the Shanghai Party Committee announced that it would recruit fifty-four thousand new propagandists in the second half of the year.[63] Undoubtedly, these propagandists engaged in great mobilization efforts during the antidrug campaign. The decision to use only oral propaganda may have worked in favor of the authorities because the illiteracy rate was very high among city residents.[64]

Besides propagandists, the residents' committees played a big role in making the campaign touch each individual's everyday life. The neighborhood organization was first set up in big cities such as Shanghai and Tianjin in 1951, and gradually introduced to other cities in the first half of the 1950s. The main tasks of the residents' committees included making residents aware of government policies, providing community services, such as public sanitation and dispute arbitration, and collecting and reflecting the opinions and demands of the residents.[65] In Shanghai there were 2,083 residents' committees by December 1951.[66] If a residential unit consisted of between 150 and 500 households, and if we assume that the average size of a residents' committee was 300 households with four members each, the number of people belonging to residents' committees was around two and half million, about half of the total population of Shanghai at that time.

The residents' committees were prominent in the antidrug campaign. In the Jianghan district of Wuhan, more than 4,700 residential cadres and activists were mobilized to hold propaganda meetings with residents.[67] In Tianjin, cadres were dispatched to organize residents' meetings to publicize the antidrug campaign. Individual propagandists even held meetings at household complexes or conducted door-to-door propaganda campaigns. Police stations also used residential literacy classes to explain the government policy on drugs. More than eight hundred thousand were educated through various forms of propaganda.[68] In Qingdao, the propaganda was carried out by the public-security section of the residents' committees, newspaper reading groups, and women's groups, not only on the streets, but often within individual families. A total of 3,420 meetings were convened in the city.[69]

The unprecedented degree of mobilization achieved in the antidrug campaign was manifested not only in how broadly it touched China's urban society, but also in how deeply it was able to put individuals under direct government control. The police apparatus, the residents' committees, and other mass organizations, which had existed before the antidrug campaign commenced, all contributed to the formation of a social control network that could encompass every aspect of an individual's life. On the one hand, the antidrug campaign of 1952 took advantage of this existing network to accomplish its goal. On the other hand, the campaign also provided an opportunity for the authorities to consolidate this network further. Individuals were simply overwhelmed by this social control power. During the campaign, there were numerous cases of daughters being mobilized against their drug-trafficking fathers, sisters against opium-smoking brothers, wives against husbands.[70] These examples show that the social control was so effective that it could break connections even between family members.

By relying on a well-established antidrug discourse, the Communists realized that they could get public sympathy in executing drug kingpins. The authorities used the political rituals of mass rallies and public trials to generate psychological pressure and to force the people to acknowledge the party's power, consciously or unconsciously. This political ritual seemed so effective that it did not demand that the Communists kill many offenders to achieve their goal. The drug suppression campaign was both a part of a state-building process and a successful means of showing the social control and mobilization power the state had gained. By targeting drug traffickers and drug producers as the main culprits, the campaign of 1952 wiped out the backbone of this social epidemic in urban China, which had been rampant for more than a century. It is said that by the late 1950s the opium problem was virtually solved in most parts of China, except in several minority areas where the campaign was postponed.[71] From the late 1950s on, China claimed that it was a "drug-free" country, and it enjoyed this reputation for more than two decades before the problem of heroin re-emerged in the early 1980s.

After so many years of representing drugs as a problem belonging either to old regimes or to foreign imperialists, the re-emergence of drugs in the southwest border areas in the early 1980s put the Chinese government in an embarrassing position. Attempting to retain its "drug-free" status, the Chinese government was very reluctant to publicly acknowledge the drug problem. It was not until the end of the 1980s that a nationwide antidrug campaign was finally launched. From the very start of the current campaign, the highest authorities vowed to solve the drug problem by launching another "people's war," which required both broad participation by the general public and coordinated efforts by authorities at different levels. Insisting on the "people's war" strategy, which worked very well in the 1950s, the authorities failed to respond to the new situations that have made conducting a mass campaign against drugs very difficult in China in the 1990s. Given the weakening of the authorities' mobilization ability, the diminishing appeal of a nationalistic antidrug discourse, and the growing integration of China's economy into the world capitalist system, prospects for China's success in its war on drugs appear increasingly dim.

NOTES

1. For a general perspective on this period, see Teiwes, "Establishment and Consolidation of the New Regime"; Lin, Fan, and Zhang, *Kaige xingjin de shiqi*. For more recent works on the abolition of prostitution, see Hershatter, "Regulating Sex in Shanghai"; Henriot, "'La Fermeture.'"

2. I rely extensively on *Jinchang jindu*, edited by Ma Weigang, who heads the history office of the Ministry of Public Security. Most items in Ma's volume are archival materials from various local bureaus of public security.

3. "Zhongyang suweiai zhengfu jinyan tiaoli," in Ma Mozhen, *Zhongguo jindu shiliao xuan*, p. 4.

4. Kapp, *Szechwan and the Chinese Republic*, p. 89.

5. For a detailed review, see Zhu, Jiang, and Zhang, *Yapian yu jindai Zhongguo*, pp. 408–49.

6. "Jin-Cha-Ji bianqu xingzheng weiyuanhui guanyu yanjin bozhong yingsu de mingling," in Huang Shaozhi et al., *Jindu gongzuo shouce*, p. 79.

7. "Shaan-Gan-Ning bianqu jinyan jindu tiaoli," in ibid., p. 76. Ironically, in their struggle for survival during the years of Nationalist blockade of the Communist-controlled Shaan-Gan-Ning border region during the Sino-Japanese War, the Communists did cultivate and sell opium outside their base in exchange

for hard currency and strategic materials, although opium smoking and marketing were prohibited within the border region; see Chen Yung-fa, "Blooming Poppy under the Red Sun." This issue is still a forbidden topic in Chinese historiography.

8. Mao, "On New Democracy," p. 340.

9. Ibid., pp. 380–82.

10. "Zhengwuyuan guanyu yanjin yapian yandu de tongling," in Huang Shaozhi et al., *Jindu gongzuo shouce*, p. 97.

11. Ibid., p. 98.

12. *Yunnan dang'an shiliao* 4 (1991): 3–6.

13. Jin and Liao, "Guizhou sudu," p. 274.

14. Ibid., p. 280.

15. Ibid., p. 273.

16. Ning, "Nanjing de jindu gongzuo," p. 365.

17. Jin and Liao, "Guizhou sudu," p. 276.

18. Ning, "Nanjing de jindu," p. 364.

19. Ma Weigang, "Jianguo chuqi jinchang jindu shulu," p. 3.

20. Li and Fang, "Jinyan yu jinzheng," p. 193.

21. *Yunnan ribao*, 7 May 1951.

22. "Zhonggong zhongyang dongbeiju dui Jilin shengwei guanyu 'sanfan' 'wufan' zhong faxian daliang fanmai dupin de baogao de pishi," declassified government document.

23. MPS file 1952-016.

24. Ibid.

25. "Zhongyang gonganbu Xu Zirong fubuzhang zai jindu gongzuo huiyishang guanyu kaizhan quanguo guimo de jindu yundong de baogao," MPS file 1952-005.

26. Xiang, "Jiu Tianjin de yandu ji yijiuwuer nian de jindu yundong," pp. 352–62.

27. Ning, "Nanjing de jindu," p. 380.

28. Luo Ruiqing, "Quanguo jindu yundong zhongjie baogao" (14 December 1952), MPS file 1952-007.

29. Ibid.

30. In fact, anti-opium campaigns continued in rural areas in the middle and late 1950s, especially in non-Han areas, which were for the most part not covered in the campaigns of early 1950s. For example, whereas big cities such as Lanzhou and Tianshui were part of the campaign of 1952, in south Gansu, where Tibetans lived in compact communities, the anti-opium campaign did not start until 1954 and the problem was not solved until 1958. The people still kept a large quantity of opium on hand. In Sichuan, from July to December 1958, 55,000 taels of opium were confiscated in Xichang prefecture. The Ministry of Public Security issued a notice on 8 May 1959, ordering that the confiscation of opium continue. In Aba prefecture, Sichuan, the task of confiscating stock opium was finally completed as late as 1963. From Ma Weigang, *Jinchang jindu*, see Li and Fang, "Jinyan yu jinzheng," pp. 193–94; Sun, Shi, and Zhu, "Jinyan sudu zai Liangshan," p. 212; Yang Guangcheng, "Aba de jinyan sudu," p. 322.

31. United States Government, *Report of the Government of the United States on the Traffic in Opium and Other Dangerous Drugs, 1951*, pp. 2–3.

32. Xiang, "Jiu Tianjin de yandu," p. 345.

33. Ma Mozhen, *Dupin zai Zhongguo,* p. 130.

34. In November 1950 the Central Financial Committee forbade selling opium outside China; the directive was reiterated by the Central Committee in January 1951; "Zhonggong zhongyang guanyu jinzhi yantu waixiao de zhishi," declassified government document.

35. Except for 1960, China was listed as one of principal sources of heroin by the United States in its "Report on the Traffic in Opium and Other Dangerous Drugs" between 1953 and 1962.

36. "Zhuanfa xibeiju guanyu jindu yundong de zhishi zhongyang bing guiding quanguo jindu yundong zhuyao you zhongyang gonganbu zhangwo," MPS file 1952-005.

37. "Guanyu jindu xuanchuan de zhishi," MPS file 1952-016.

38. Ibid.

39. Ibid.

40. In his report to Mao Zedong and the Central Committee on 5 May 1952, acting secretary of the East China Bureau of the CCP Tan Zhenglin summarized that the side effects of the Three Antis and Five Antis in Shanghai were "unemployment, increased inventory, decreased prices, and irresponsible capitalists." Facing these unexpected consequences, the CCP decided to postpone conducting the Five Antis campaign in medium and small cities in May 1952. See "Zhonggong zhongyang guanyu 'wufan' dingan, butui gongzuo deng de zhishi" (5 May 1952) and "Zhonggong zhongyang guanyu tuichi xianquxiang de 'sanfan' he zhongxiao chengshi de 'wufan' de zhishi" (23 May 1952), in *Jianguo yilai zhongyao wenxian xuanbian,* 3:195–96.

41. Zhang Chengjun, "Xi'an de jinyan sudu," pp. 306–10.

42. Zhao Shikong, "Xiaomie Guilin de fandu huodong," p. 264.

43. Luo, *Quanguo jindu yundong zhongjie baogao.* (14 December 1952), MPS file 1952-007.

44. Central Department of Propaganda, "Guanyu jindu xuanchuan de yige tongbao," MPS file 1952-016.

45. "Guanyu Guangxi Lijiang xian jindu gongzuozhong shanzi xingdong jinxing wenzi xuanchuan de baogao," MPS file 1952-016.

46. In official discourse, *nationalism* often has the negative connotation of ethnic separatism. *Patriotism* is used in a broader sense, and requires citizens not only to identify themselves with the nation-state but also to be loyal to the Communist Party.

47. Zhang, "Xi'an de jinyan sudu," p. 307.

48. Propaganda Department of the Northeast Bureau of the CCP, "Jindu xuanchuan gongzuo zhishi," MPS file 1952-016.

49. "Beijing shi guanyu jindu xuanchuan de qingkuang he chubu jingyan," declassified government document.

50. Chen Jing, "Ma Mozhen jiaoshou fangtanlu,"p. 43.

51. Luo, *Quanguo jindu yundong zhongjie baogao.* (14 December 1952), MPS file 1952-007.

52. See Teiwes, "Establishment and Consolidation," p. 88n. 25. The number is consistent with newly revealed statistics from sources in the PRC, which say that by

May 1951 five hundred thousand had been executed; see Lin, Fan, and Zhang, *Kaige xingjin de shiqi,* p. 143.

53. Chen Shouqian, "Wuhan jindu yundong," pp. 236–37.

54. Ibid., pp. 239–43.

55. Jin and Liao, "Guizhou sudu," pp. 277–79.

56. Chen Shouqian, "Wuhan jindu yundong," p. 235.

57. "Zhongyang gonganbu Xu Zirong fubuzhang zai jindu gongzuo huiyishang guanyu kaizhan quanguo guimo de jindu yundong de baogao," MPS file 1952-005.

58. "Zhongyang pizhun Luo Ruiqing bayue ershiqiri guanyu zhaokai gongshen dufan panchu shixing de baogao," MPS file 1952-005.

59. "Zhuanfa xinanju guanyu shenru sudu yundong de jinji tongzhi,' " MPS file 1952-005.

60. Jin and Liao, "Guizhou sudu," p. 285.

61. Wakeman, "Models of Historical Change," p. 65.

62. Schurmann, *Ideology and Organization in Communist China,* p. 373.

63. Gardner, "Wu-fan Campaign in Shanghai," pp. 532–33.

64. Ibid., p. 499.

65. Schurmann, *Ideology and Organization,* pp. 374–76.

66. Gardner, "Wu-fan Campaign in Shanghai," p. 496.

67. Chen Shouqian, "Wuhan jindu yundong," p. 237.

68. Xiang, "Jiu Tianjin de yandu," p. 356.

69. Lan, "Qingdao qingchu yandu jishi," p. 395.

70. Chen Shouqian, "Wuhan jindu yundong," p. 238.

71. For a detailed description of antidrug campaigns in minority areas, see Zhou Yongming, *Anti-Drug Crusades in Twentieth-Century China,* pp. 149–67.

BIBLIOGRAPHY

A Ying [Qian Xingcun]. *Wan Qing wenyi baokan shulüe*. Shanghai: Gudian wenxue chubanshe, 1958.

Adshead, S. A. M. *The Modernization of the Chinese Salt Administration, 1900–1920*. Cambridge, Mass.: Harvard University Press, 1970.

———. "The Opium Trade in Szechwan, 1881 to 1911." *Journal of Southeast Asian History* 7, no. 2 (September 1966): 93–99.

———. *Province and Politics in Late Imperial China: Viceregal Government in Szechwan, 1898–1911*. London: Curzon Press, 1984.

Aisin-Gioro Pu Yi. *From Emperor to Citizen*. Trans. W. J. F. Jenner. 1964–1965; reprint, Oxford: Oxford University Press, 1987.

Alip, Eufronio. *The Chinese in Manila*. Manila: National Historical Commission, 1974.

Allom, Thomas. *China in a Series of Views*. London: Fisher, 1843.

Asahi shinbun, Yamagata shikyoku, ed. *Kikigaki: Aru kenpei no kiroku*. Tokyo: Asahi shinbunsha, 1991.

Assam Opium Enquiry Committee. *Assam Congress Opium Enquiry Report, September 1925*. Introduction by C. F. Andrews. Cinnamara (Assam): R.-K. Hatiburua.

Averill, Stephen. "Revolution in the Highlands: The Rise of the Communist Movement in Jiangxi Province." Ph.D. diss., Cornell University, 1982.

Awaya Kentarō. *Miketsu no sensō sekinin*. Tokyo: Kashiwa shobō, 1994.

———. *Tōkyō saiban ron*. Tokyo: Ōtsuki shoten, 1989.

Awaya Kentarō, Adachi Hiroaki, and Kobayashi Motohiro, eds. *Tōkyō saiban shiryō: Tanaka Ryūkichi jinmon chōsho*. Tokyo: Ōtsuki shoten, 1994.

Awaya Kentarō et al., eds. *Sensō sekinin, sengo sekinin*. Tokyo: Asahi shinbunsha, 1994.

Awaya Kentarō and Yoshida Yutaka, eds. *Kokusai kensatsu kyoku (IPS) jinmon chōsho*. 52 vols. Tokyo: Nihon tosho sentā, 1993.

Baumler, Alan. "Playing with Fire: The Nationalist Government and Opium in China, 1927–1941." Ph.D. diss., University of Illinois, Urbana-Champaign, 1997.

————. "Playing with Fire: The Nationalist Government and Popular Anti-Opium Agitation in 1927–28." *Republican China* 21, no. 1 (November 1995): 43–91.

————. "The Rhetoric of Independence: Collaborationist Anti-Opium Campaigns." Unpublished paper, 1997.

Bello, David. "Opium and the Limits of Empire: The Opium Problem in the Chinese Interior, 1729–1850." Ph.D. diss., University of Southern California, forthcoming.

Bercé, Yves-Marie. *Croquants et nu-pieds: Les soulèvements paysans en France du XVIe au XIXe siècle.* Paris: Gallimand, 1991.

Bergère, Marie-Claire. "The Chinese Bourgeoisie, 1911–1937." In *The Cambridge History of China,* vol. 12, ed. John K. Fairbank, pp. 722–825. Cambridge, Eng.: Cambridge University Press, 1983.

Berridge, Virginia, and Griffith Edwards. *Opium and the People: Opiate Use in Nineteenth-Century England.* New York: St. Martin's, 1981.

Beveridge, Henry. *A Comprehensive History of India, Civil, Military and Social.* 3 vols. London and Glasgow: Blackie and Son, 1862.

Bianco, Lucien. "Peasant Movements." In *Cambridge History of China,* vol. 13, ed. John K. Fairbank and Albert Feuerwerker, pp. 270–328. Cambridge, Eng.: Cambridge University Press, 1986.

————. "Peasant Uprisings against Poppy Tax Collection in Su Xian and Lingbi (Anhui) in 1932." *Republican China* 21, no. 1 (November 1995): 93–127.

————. "Peasants and Revolution: The Case of China." *Journal of Peasant Studies* 2, no. 3 (April 1975): 313–35.

Bird, Isabella. *The Yangtze Valley and Beyond.* 1899; reprint, London: Virago, 1985.

Bitō Masahide and Shimazaki Takao, eds. *Nihon shisō taikei,* vol.45, *Andō Shōeki, Satō Nobuhiro.* Tokyo: Iwanami shoten, 1977.

Bōeichō bōei kenshūjo senshi shitsu, ed. *Senshi sōsho: Shōwa 17–18-nen no Shina hakengun.* Tokyo: Asagumo shinbunsha, 1972.

Boorman, Howard L., and Richard C. Howard, eds. *Biographical Dictionary of Republican China.* 4 vols. New York: Columbia University Press, 1967–1971.

Boyle, John. *China and Japan at War, 1937–1945: The Politics of Collaboration.* Stanford, Calif.: Stanford University Press, 1972.

Braddell, T. T. "Gambling and Opium Smoking in the Straits of Malacca." *Journal of the Indian Archipelago and Eastern Asia* 1, new series (1857): 66–87.

Brenan, J. F. "The Cultivation and Consumption of Opium in Shansi." In *Despatches from His Majesty's Minister at Peking Forwarding Reports Respecting the Opium Question in China* (China no. 3), pp. 29–34. London: Harrison and Sons, 1909.

Brockway, Lucile. *Science and Colonial Expansion: The Role of the British Royal Botanic Gardens.* New York: Academic Press, 1979.

Brooks, Peter. *Reading for the Plot: Design and Intention in Narrative.* 1984; reprint, Cambridge, Mass.: Harvard University Press, 1992.

Brown, Ian G. "The End of the Opium Farm in Siam 1905–7." In *The Rise and Fall of Revenue Farming: Business Elites and the Emergence of the Modern State in Southeast Asia,* ed. John Butcher and Howard Dick, pp. 233–45. London: St. Martin's Press, 1993.

————. "Imperialism, Trade and Investment in the Late Nineteenth and Early Twentieth Centuries." In *The Rise and Fall of Revenue Farming: Business Elites and the Emergency of the Modern State in Southeast Asia*, ed. John Butcher and Howard Dick, pp. 80–88. London: St. Martin's Press, 1993.

———. "The Ministry of Finance and the Early Development of Modern Financial Administration in Siam, 1885–1910." Ph.D. diss, University of London, 1975.

Brunnert, H. S., and V. V. Hagelstrom. *Present Day Political Organization of China.* Trans. A. Beltchenko and E. C. Moran. 1910; reprint, Taipei: Ch'eng Wen Publishing Co., 1978.

Buell, R. L. *The International Opium Conferences.* Boston, Mass.: World Peace Foundation, n.d. [1926].

Burkman, Thomas. "Opium in China and the League of Nations." Paper presented at the conference on Opium in East Asian History, Toronto, 1997.

Butcher, John. "The Demise of the Revenue Farm System in the Federated Malay States." *Modern Asian Studies* 17 (1983): 387–412.

Butcher, John, and Howard Dick, eds. *The Rise and Fall of Revenue Farming: Business Elites and the Emergence of the Modern State in Southeast Asia.* London: St. Martin's Press, 1993.

Butel, Paul. *L'opium: Histoire d'une fascination.* Paris: Perrin, 1995.

Cai Dejin, ed. *Shū Futsukai nikki.* Murata Tadayoshi et al. Tokyo: Misuzu shobō, 1992. Originally published in Chinese in 1986 as *Zhou Fohai riji.* Trans.

Cai Dejin and Li Huixian, eds. *Wang Jingwei wei guomin zhengfu jishi.* Beijing: Zhongguo shehui kexue chubanshe, 1982.

Cameron, John. *Our Tropical Possessions in Malayan India: Being a Descriptive Account of Singapore, Penang, Province Wellesley, and Malacca; Their Peoples, Products, Commerce and Government.* London: Smith, Elder and Co., 1865.

Carstairs, Catherine. "'Deport the Drug Traffickers': The Racialization of Drug Use in 1920s Canada." Paper presented at the conference on Opium in East Asian History, Toronto, 1997.

Chan, Wellington K. K. "Government, Merchants and Industry to 1911." *Cambridge History of China,* vol. 10, ed. J. K. Fairbank and D. Twitchett, part 2, pp. 416–62. Cambridge, Eng.: Cambridge University Press, 1980.

Chang, Hsin-pao. *Commissioner Lin and the Opium War.* Cambridge, Mass.: Harvard University Press, 1964.

Chen Cunren. "Hongji shantang 'guangkai shanmen' Sheng Wenyi baoxiao xianqu yantu." *Zhuanji wenxue* 64, no. 4 (April 1994): 93–100.

Chen Huace. "Minguo nianjian de jindu qingkuang." *Gongxian wenshi ziliao* (Henan) 5 (1989): 100–4.

Chen Jing. "Ma Mozhen jiaoshou fangtanlu." *Beijing dangshi yanjiu* 1 (1995): 43–45.

Chen Li. "Jinyan duchachu yu Zhongguo nongmin yinhang fanmai yapian." *Lishi jiaoxue* 1994:7, 51–54.

Chen Shouqian. "Wuhan jindu yundong." In *Jinchang jindu,* ed. Ma Weigang, pp. 229–46. Beijing: Jingguan jiaoyu chubanshe, 1993.

Chen Yaolun. "Xikang yapian liudu zaocheng Yingjing shibian jingguo." *Wenshi ziliao* [national edition] 33 (1963): 174–86.

Chen, Yung-fa. "The Blooming Poppy under the Red Sun: The Yan'an Way and the Opium Trade." In *New Perspectives on the Chinese Communist Revolution,* ed.

Tony Saich and Hans van de Ven, pp. 263–98. Armonk, N.Y.: M. E. Sharpe, 1995.

Cheng Weikun. "Minchu jinyan yundong." *Jianghai xuekan* 1989:2 137–44.

Cheung, Lucy Tsui-ping. "The Opium Monopoly in Hong Kong, 1844–1887." M.A. thesis, University of Hong Kong, 1986.

Chi, Hsi-sheng. *Warlord Politics in China, 1916–1918.* Stanford, Calif.: Stanford University Press, 1976.

Chi Zhicheng. *Huyou mengying.* 1893? Reprinted in *Shanghai tan yu Shanghai ren congshu.* Shanghai: Shanghai guji chubanshe, 1989.

Chiang Kai-shek [Jiang Jieshi]. *China's Destiny.* Trans. Wang Chung-hui. 1947; reprint, Westport, Conn.: Greenwood, 1985.

The China Christian Yearbook, 1934–35. Shanghai: Christian Literature Society for China, 1935.

The China Year Book. Tianjin: Tientsin Press.

China Information Committee. *Japan's Narcotic Policy in China.* Hankow: China Information Committee, 1938.

Chung Shu-ming. "Nihon tōchi jidai ni okeru Taiwan no taigai hatten shi." Ph.D. diss., University of Tokyo, 1996.

Clunas, Craig. *Fruitful Sites: Garden Culture in Ming Dynasty China.* Durham, N.C.: Duke University Press, 1996.

Cohen, Paul. *Between Tradition and Modernity: Wang T'ao and Reform in Late Ch'ing China.* Cambridge, Mass.: Harvard University Press, 1974.

Collis, Maurice. *Foreign Mud, being an Account of the Opium Imbroglio at Canton in the 1830s.* New York: Alfred Knopf, 1947.

Connors, Rich. "British Justifications for the Opium Trade in East India Company Records, 1770–90." Paper presented at the conference on Opium in East Asian History, Toronto, 1997.

Correspondence Respecting the Opium Question in China (China no. 1, 1908). London: Harrison and Sons, 1908.

Costin, William Conrad. *Great Britain and China, 1833–1860.* Oxford: Clarendon Press, 1937.

Courtwright, David. *Dark Paradise: Opiate Addiction in America before 1940.* Cambridge, Mass.: Harvard University Press, 1982.

Cranmer-Byng, J. L., ed. *An Embassy to China: Being the Journal Kept by Lord Macartney.* London: Longman, 1972.

Crawfurd, John. *History of the Indian Archipelago: Containing an Account of the Manners, Arts, Languages, Religions, Institutions and Commerce of Its Inhabitants.* 3 vols. 1820; reprint, London: F. Cass, 1967.

———. Untitled note. *Journal of the Indian Archipelago and Eastern Asia* 10, new series (1854): 410.

Crossley, Pamela Kyle. *Orphan Warriors: Three Manchu Generations and the End of the Qing World.* Princeton, N.J.: Princeton University Press, 1990.

Cunynghame, Arthur. *The Opium War: Being Recollections of Service in China.* 1845; reprint, Wilmington, Del.: Scholarly Resources, 1972.

Cushman, Jennifer W. *Family and State: The Formation of a Sino-Thai Tin-Mining Dynasty, 1797–1932.* Singapore: Oxford University Press, 1991.

————. "The Khaw Group: Chinese Business in Early Twentieth-Century Penang." *Journal of Southeast Asian Studies* 17 (March 1986): 58–79.

Cushman, Jennifer W., and Michael Godley. "The Khaw Concern." In *The Rise and Fall of Revenue Farming: Business Elites and the Emergence of the Modern State in Southeast Asia*, ed. John Butcher and Howard Dick, pp. 267–71. London: St. Martin's Press, 1993.

Dai Yingfu. "Wang Jingwei xinguomin yundong neimu." In *Wangwei zhengquan neimu*, ed. Jiangsu sheng zhengxie wenshi ziliao weiyuanhui, pp. 264–75. Nanjing: Jiangsu wenshi ziliao bianjibu, 1989.

Davis, John Francis. *The Chinese: A General Description of the Empire of China and Its Inhabitants.* 3 vols. plus supplement. London: Cox, 1845.

Davidson, Robert, and Isaac Mason. *Life in West China, Described by Two Residents in the Province of Szechwan.* London: Headley Brothers, 1905.

Des Forges, Roger. *Hsi-liang and the Chinese National Revolution.* New Haven: Yale University Press, 1973.

Descours-Gatin, C. *Quand l'opium finançait la colonisation en Indochine: L'élaboration de la régie générale de l'opium (1860–1914).* Paris: Éditions l'Hartmann, 1992.

Despatch from His Majesty's Minister in China Forwarding a General Report by Mr. Leech Respecting the Opium Question in China (China no. 2, 1908). London: Harrison and Sons, 1908.

Diehl, F. W. "Revenue Farming and Colonial Finances in the Netherlands East Indies, 1816–1925." In *The Rise and Fall of Revenue Farming: Business Elites and the Emergence of the Modern State in Southeast Asia,* ed. John Butcher and Howard Dick, pp. 196–232. London: St. Martin's Press, 1993.

Dodwell, H. H., ed. *British India, 1497–1858.* Vol. 4 of *The Cambridge History of the British Empire.* Cambridge, Eng.: Cambridge University Press.

————. *The Indian Empire, 1858–1918.* Vol. 5 of *The Cambridge History of the British Empire.* Cambridge, Eng.: Cambridge University Press.

Dong Yiming. "Étude sur le problème de l'opium dans la région du sud-ouest de la Chine pendant les années 1920 et 1930." Ph.D. diss., École des Hautes Études en Sciences Sociales, Paris, 1997.

Duara, Prasenjit. "State Involution: A Study of Local Finances in North China, 1911–1935." *Comparative Studies in Society and History* 29, no. 1 (1987): 132–61.

Dumarest, J. 1938. "Les monopoles de l'opium et du sel en Indochine." Ph.D. diss., Faculté de Droit, Université de Lyon, 1938.

Dunch, Ryan. "Piety, Patriotism, Progress: Chinese Protestants in Fuzhou Society and the Making of a Modern China, 1850–1927." Ph.D. diss., Yale University, 1996.

Eames, James Bromley. *The English in China: Being an Account of the Intercourse and Relations between England and China from the Year 1600 to the Year 1843 and a Summary of Later Developments.* London: Curzon Press, 1909.

Eastman, Lloyd. "Facets of an Ambivalent Relationship: Smuggling, Puppets, and Atrocities during the War, 1937–1945." In *The Chinese and the Japanese: Essays in Political and Cultural Interactions,* ed. Akira Iriye, pp. 275–303. Princeton, N.J.: Princeton University Press, 1980.

Edkins, Joseph. *Opium: Historical Note; Or the Poppy in China.* Shanghai: Presbyterian Mission Press, 1889.

Eguchi Keiichi. *Jūgonen sensō shōshi: Shinpan.* Tokyo: Aoki shoten, 1991.

———. *Nit-Chū ahen sensō.* Tokyo: Iwanami shoten, 1988.

———. "Nit-Chū sensōki Kainantō no ahen seisan." *Aichi daigaku kokusai mondai kenkyūsho kiyō* 97 (September 1992): 117–35.

———. "Nit-Chū sensōki no ahen seisaku." In *Nankin jiken o kangaeru,* ed. Hora Tomio et al., pp. 226–36. Tokyo: Ōtsuki shoten, 1987.

———. *Shiryō: Nit-Chū sensōki ahen seisaku.* Tokyo: Iwanami shoten, 1985.

———. *Shōgen: Nit-Chū ahen sensō.* Tokyo: Iwanami shoten, 1991.

Esherick, Joseph W. *Reform and Revolution in China: The 1911 Revolution in Hunan and Hubei.* Berkeley and Los Angeles: University of California Press, 1976.

Etō Jun, ed. *Katsu Kaishū zenshū.* 22 vols. Tokyo: Kōdansha, 1972–1994.

Fairbank, John King. *Chinabound: A Fifty-Year Memoir.* New York: Harper & Row, 1982.

———. "The Creation of the Treaty System." In *Cambridge History of China,* vol. 10, ed. J. K. Fairbank and D. Twitchett, part 1, pp. 213–63. Cambridge, Eng.: Cambridge University Press, 1976.

———. *Trade and Diplomacy on the China Coast: The Opening of the Treaty Ports, 1842–1854.* Stanford, Calif.: Stanford University Press, 1969.

Fairbank, John K., Katherine F. Bruner, and Elizabeth M. Matheson, eds. *The I.G. in Peking: Letters of Robert Hart, Chinese Maritime Customs, 1868–1907.* 2 vols. Cambridge, Mass.: Harvard University Press, 1975.

Fairbank, John K., Edwin O. Reischauer, and Albert M. Craig. *East Asia: The Modern Transformation.* Boston: Houghton Mifflin, 1965.

Faithfull-Davies, Margaret E. *The Banyan City.* London: Church of England Zenana Missionary Society, 1910.

Fan Wenlan. *Zhongguo jindai shi.* Reprint of 9th (1955) edition. Beijing: Renmin chubanshe, 1962.

Fan Xian et al., eds. *Chongxiu Taiwan fuzhi.* 1747. Reprinted in *Taiwan fuzhi sanzhong,* ed. Chen Donglin. Beijing: Zhonghua shuju, 1985.

Fang Yingkai. *Xinjiang tunken shi.* 2 vols. Urumchi: Xinjiang qingnian chubanshe, 1989.

Fay, Peter Ward. *The Opium War, 1840–1842: Barbarians in the Celestial Empire in the Early Part of the Nineteenth Century and the War by which They Forced Her Gates Ajar.* New York: Norton, 1976.

Fei, Hsiao-t'ung. *Earthbound China.* Chicago: University of Chicago Press, 1945.

Feuerwerker, Albert. "Economic Trends in the Late Ch'ing Empire, 1870–1911." In *The Cambridge History of China,* vol. 10, ed. J. K. Fairbank and D. Twitchett, part 2, pp. 1–69. Cambridge, Eng.: Cambridge University Press, 1980.

Fewsmith, Joseph. *Party, State, and Local Elites in Republican China: Merchant Organizations and Politics in Shanghai, 1890–1930.* Honolulu: University of Hawai'i Press, 1985.

Finlayson, Geoffrey B. A. M. *The Seventh Earl of Shaftesbury, 1801–1885.* London: Eyre Methuen, 1981.

Fletcher, Joseph. "China and Central Asia, 1368–1884." In *The Chinese World Order,* ed. John K. Fairbank, pp. 206–24. Cambridge, Mass.: Harvard University Press, 1974.

———. "Ch'ing Inner Asia c. 1800." In *The Cambridge History of China,* vol. 10, ed. John K. Fairbank, pp. 35–106. Cambridge, Eng.: Cambridge University Press, 1978.

———. "The Heyday of the Ch'ing Order in Mongolia, Sinkiang and Tibet." In *The Cambridge History of China,* vol. 10, ed. John K. Fairbank, pp. 351–408. Cambridge, Eng.: Cambridge University Press, 1978.

———. "Sino-Russian Relations, 1800–62." In *The Cambridge History of China,* vol. 10, ed. John K. Fairbank, pp. 318–50. Cambridge, Eng.: Cambridge University Press, 1978.

Fogel, Joshua A. *The Literature of Travel in the Japanese Rediscovery of China, 1862–1945.* Stanford, Calif.: Stanford University Press, 1996.

———. "On Japanese Expressions for 'China.'" *Sino-Japanese Studies* 2, no. 1 (December 1989): 5–16.

Foster, John Watson. *American Diplomacy in the Orient.* Boston: Houghton Mifflin, 1903.

Friedman, Edward. "Revolution or Just Another Bloody Cycle? Swatow and the 1911 Revolution." *Journal of Asian Studies* 29, no. 2 (1969): 289–307.

Fu Yiguang. "He Jian zhu Xiang shiqi de teshui gaikuang." *Wenshi ziliao xuanji* 34 (1986): 196–209.

Fukumoto Yoshisuke. *Kusaka Genzui zenshū.* Tokuyama: Matsuno shoten, 1978.

Furumaya Tadao. "Kankan no shosō." In *Iwanami kōza Kindai Nihon to shokuminchi,* 6:149–71. Tokyo: Iwanami shoten, 1993.

Furumi Tadayuki. *Wasureenu Manshūkoku.* Tokyo: Keizai ōrai sha, 1978.

Gaimushō, ed. *Nihon gaikō nenpyō narabini shuyō monjo: 1840–1945.* 2 vols. Tokyo: Hara shobō, 1965.

Gaimushō tsūshōkyoku, ed. *Shina ni okeru ahen oyobi mayakuhin.* Tokyo: Gaimushō, 1925.

Gardella, Robert. *Harvesting Mountains: Fujian and the China Tea Trade, 1757–1937.* Berkeley and Los Angeles: University of California Press, 1994.

Gardner, John. "The Wu-fan Campaign in Shanghai: A Study in the Consolidation of Urban Control." In *Chinese Communist Politics in Action,* ed. A. Doak Barnett, pp. 477–539. Seattle: University of Washington Press, 1969.

Gavit, John Palmer. *Opium.* London: Routledge, 1925.

Ge Yuanxu. *Huyou zaji.* 1876. Reprinted in *Shanghai tan yu Shanghai ren congshu.* Shanghai: Shanghai guji chubanshe, 1989.

Gilbert, Marc Jason. "Lord Lansdowne in India: At the Climax of an Empire. A Study in Late-Nineteenth-Century British India Policy and Proconsular Power." Ph.D. diss., UCLA, 1978.

Godley, M. R. *Mandarin Capitalists from Nanyang: Overseas Chinese Enterprise in the Modernization of China, 1893–1911.* Cambridge, Eng.: Cambridge University Press, 1981.

———. "Thio Thiau Siat's Network." In *The Rise and Fall of Revenue Farming: Business Elites and the Emergence of the Modern State in Southeast Asia,* ed. John Butcher and Howard Dick, pp. 262–66. London: St. Martin's Press, 1993.

Goodman, Bryna. *Native Place, City, and Nation: Regional Networks and Identities in*

Shanghai, 1853–1937. Berkeley and Los Angeles: University of California Press, 1995.

Gould, Randall. "Nanking under Japanese Occupation." *The China Critic* 28, no. 3 (18 January 1940): 38–40.

Greenberg, Michael. *British Trade and the Opening of China, 1800–1842.* Cambridge, Eng.: Cambridge University Press, 1951.

Grousset, René. *The Empire of the Steppes: A History of Central Asia.* Trans. Naomi Walford. New Brunswick, N.J.: Rutgers University Press, 1970.

Guo Xu, Xu Yunju, and Li Peiqing. "Guomindang zhengfu 'yujin yuzheng' zhe jinyan zhengce neimu." *Hubei wenshi ziliao* 33 (1990): 221–30.

Haga Noboru. "Ahen sensō Taihei tengoku, Nihon." In *Chūgoku kingendaishi no shomondai,* ed. Tanaka Masayoshi sensei kinen ronbun kankōkai, pp. 87–123. Tokyo: Kokusho kankōkai, 1984.

Hall, J. C. S. *The Yunnan Provincial Faction, 1927–1937.* Canberra: Australian National University, 1976.

Han Bangqing. *Haishang hua liezhuan.* 1894; reprint, Beijing: Renmin wenxue chubanshe, 1985.

Hansard (British Parliamentary Debates), comprised of:

(a) *The Parliamentary Debates* (February 1803 to November 1820). 41 vols. London: T. C. Hansard et al., 1812–1820;

(b) *The Parliamentary Debates,* 2d series (April 1820 to July 1830). 25 vols. London: T. C. Hansard et al., 1821–1830;

(c) *Hansard's Parliamentary Debates,* 3d series (October 1830 to August 1891). 356 vols. London: T. C. Hansard et al., 1831–1891;

(d) *The Parliamentary Debates,* 4th series (February 1892 to December 1908). 199 vols. London: T. C. Hansard et al., 1892–1909;

(e) *The Parliamentary Debates,* 5th series (February 1909 to present). London: T. C. Hansard et al., 1909–present.

Hanshang mengren. *Fengyue meng.* 1848; reprint, Taibei: Hanyuan wenhua, 1993.

Hao, Yen-p'ing. *The Commercial Revolution in Nineteenth-Century China: The Rise of Sino-Western Mercantile Capitalism.* Berkeley and Los Angeles: University of California Press, 1986.

Harcourt, Freda. "Black Gold: P&O and the Opium Trade, 1847–1914." *International Journal of Maritime History* 6, no. 1 (June 1994): 1–83.

Hayes, James. "The Nam Pak Hong Commercial Association of Hong Kong." *Journal of the Hong Kong Branch of the Royal Asiatic Society* 19 (1979): 216–26.

He Simi. *Kangzhan shiqi zhuanmai shiliao.* Taibei: Guoshiguan, 1992.

Hedtke, Charles. "Reluctant Revolutionaries: Szechwan and the Ch'ing Collapse, 1898–1911." Ph.D. diss., University of California, Berkeley, 1968.

Henriot, Christian. "'La Fermeture': The Abolition of Prostitution in Shanghai, 1949–58." *China Quarterly* 20 (1995): 467–86.

Hershatter, Gail. *Dangerous Pleasures: Prostitution and Modernity in Twentieth-Century Shanghai.* Berkeley and Los Angeles: University of California Press, 1997.

———. "Regulating Sex in Shanghai: The Reform of Prostitution in 1920 and 1951." In *Shanghai Sojourners,* ed. Frederic Wakeman Jr. and Wen-hsin Yeh, pp. 145–85. Berkeley: Institute of East Asian Studies, University of California, 1992.

Hevia, James L. "Making China 'Perfectly Equal.'" *Journal of Historical Sociology* 3, no. 4 (1990): 380–401.

Hong Liangji. *Tianshan kehua.* 1800? Reprint. Beijing: Zhongyang minzu xueyuan, 1983.

———. *Yili jishi shi.* In *Zhou che suo zhi,* ed. Zheng Guangzu. 1843; reprint. Beijing: Zhongguo shudian, 1993.

Hosie, Alexander. *Despatch from His Majesty's Minister in China Forwarding a General Report by Alexander Hosie Respecting the Opium Question in China.* London: Harrison and Sons, 1909.

———. *Despatches from Sir A. Hosie Forwarding Reports Respecting the Opium Question in China.* London: Wyman and Sons, 1911.

———. *On the Trail of the Opium Poppy: A Narrative of Travel in the Chief Opium-Producing Provinces of China.* London: G. Philip & Son, 1914.

———. *Three Years in Western China.* 1897; reprint, Taipei: Ch'eng-wen, 1972.

Howard, Paul. "Opium Suppression in Late-Qing China: The Limits and Possibilities of Social Reform." Paper presented at the conference on Opium in East Asian History, Toronto, 1997.

Hsiao, Hsin-i. "Économie et société rurale du Sichuan de 1927 à 1945." Ph.D. diss., École des Hautes Études en Sciences Sociales, Paris, 1972.

Hsiao, Liang-lin. *Foreign Trade Statistics, 1864–1949.* Cambridge, Mass.: East Asian Research Center, Harvard University, 1974.

Hu Sheng. *Imperialism and Chinese Politics.* Beijing: Foreign Languages Press, 1955. Translated from the Chinese edition of 1954.

Huang Jianhua. "Qing zhi minguo shiqi Xinjiang Weiwuer zu zhasake zhi yanjiu." *Xibei minzu yanjiu* 1992:1, 149–57.

Huang, Philip C. C. "'Public Sphere' / 'Civil Society' in China? The Third Realm between State and Society." *Modern China* 19, no. 2 (1993): 216–40.

Huang Shaohong. "Xin Guixi yu yapian yan." *Wenshi ziliao xuanji* [national edition] 34 (1986): 175–95.

Huang Shaozhi et al. *Jindu gongzuo shouce.* Shanghai: Sanlian shudian, 1992.

Huang Shiquan. *Songnan mengying lu.* 1883. Reprinted in *Shanghai tan yu Shanghai ren congshu.* Shanghai: Shanghai guji chubanshe, 1989.

Hyde, Francis E. *Far Eastern Trade, 1860–1914.* London: A. & C. Black, 1973.

Ikeda Sumihisa. *Rikugun sōgi iinchō.* Tokyo: Nihon shuppan, 1953.

Im, Kaye Soon. "The Rise and Decline of the Eight Banner Garrisons in the Ch'ing Period (1644–1911): A Study of the Kuang-Chou, Hang-Chou, and Ching-Chou Garrisons." Ph.D. diss., University of Illinois, 1981.

Imai Shū. "Iwayuru 'Kitō mitsuyu' ni tsuite no ichikōsatsu." *Rekishigaku kenkyū* 438 (November 1976): 1–19.

Imai Takeo. *Shina jihen no kaisō.* Tokyo: Misuzu shobō, 1964.

Inglis, Brian. *Forbidden Game: A Social History of Drugs.* London: Hodder and Stoughton, 1975.

———. *The Opium War.* London: Hodder and Stoughton, 1976.

Inomata Masakazu. *Watashi no Tōtaku kaikoroku.* Tokyo: Ryūkei shosha, 1978.

Inoue Hisashi, ed. *Kachū senbu kōsaku shiryō.* Tokyo: Fuji shuppan, 1989.

Inoue Kiyoshi. *Nihon gendaishi I: Meiji ishin.* Tokyo: Tōkyō daigaku shuppankai, 1951.

Inspectorate General of Chinese Customs. *Decennial Reports for the Ports of Amoy, Foochow, and Santao.* Shanghai: Statistical Department of the Inspectorate General of Customs.

———. *Decennial Reports on Trade, Industries, etc. of the Ports Open to Foreign Commerce and on the Condition and Development of the Treaty Port Provinces,* 1882–1891; 1892–1901; 1902–1911; 1912–1921; 1922–1931. Shanghai: Statistical Department of the Inspectorate General of Customs.

International Military Tribunal for the Far East. *The Tokyo War Crimes Trial.* Annotated, compiled, and edited by R. John Pritchard and Sonia Magbanau Zaide. New York: Garland, 1981.

International Opium Commission. *Report of the International Opium Commission, Shanghai, China, February 1 to February 26, 1909.* 2 vols. London: P. S. King and Son, 1909.

Ishii Itarō. *Gaikōkan no isshō.* Tokyo: Chūō kōronsha, 1986.

Ishikawa Junkichi. *Kokka sōdōin shi.* 13 vols. Tokyo: Kokka sōdōin shi kankōkai, 1975–1987.

Israel, John. *Student Nationalism in China, 1927–1937.* Stanford, Calif.: Stanford University Press, 1966.

Iwao Seiichi. *Nihon no rekishi 14: Sakoku.* Tokyo: Chūōkōronsha, 1966.

Jennings, John M. "The Forgotten Plague: Opium and Narcotics under Japanese Rule, 1910–1945." *Modern Asian Studies* 29, no. 4 (1995): 795–815.

———. "The Opium Empire: Japan and the East Asian Drug Trade, 1895–1945." Ph.D. diss., University of Hawai'i, 1995.

———. *The Opium Empire: Japanese Imperialism and Drug Trafficking in Asia, 1895–1945.* Wesport: Praeger, 1997.

———. "The Rise and Fall of the Narcotics Industry in Japan, 1914–1945." Paper presented at the conference on Opium in East Asian History, Toronto, 1997.

Jin Shibao and Liao Yiwen. "Guizhou sudu." In *Jinchang jindu,* ed. Ma Weigang, pp. 267–92. Beijing: Jingguan jiaoyu chubanshe, 1993.

Jing Xiongbai. *Dōsei kyōshi no jittai: Ō Chōmei no higeki.* Trans. Ikeda Atsunori. Tokyo: Kyōdō tūshinsha, 1960.

Jinyan weiyuanhui, ed. *Ershiliu niandu jinyan nianbao.* Shanghai, 1938.

Johnson, Linda Cooke, ed. *Cities of Jiangnan in Late Imperial China.* Albany: State University of New York Press, 1993.

———. "Shanghai: An Emerging Jiangnan Port, 1683–1840." In *Cities of Jiangnan in Late Imperial China,* ed. Linda Cooke Johnson, pp. 151–81. Albany: State University of New York Press, 1993.

———. *Shanghai: From Market Town to Treaty Port, 1074–1858.* Stanford, Calif.: Stanford University Press, 1995.

Johnson, Paul. *The Birth of the Modern: World Society, 1815–1830.* New York: HarperCollins, 1991.

Kaempher, Engelbert. *Amoenitatum exoticarum politico-physico-medicarum: Quibus continentur variae relationes, observationes & descriptiones rerum Persicarum & Ulterior Asiae multa attentione in peregrinationibus per universum Orientem.* Lemgoviae: Henrici Wilhelmi Meyeri, 1712.

Kane, H. H. *Opium Smoking in America and China.* New York: G. P. Putnam, 1882.

Kapp, Robert A. *Szechwan and the Chinese Republic: Provincial Militarism and Central Power, 1911–1938*. New Haven: Yale University Press, 1973.

Kasahara Yōko. "Chūka kokumin kyodokukai ni tsuite no ichi kōsatsu." *Chikaki ni arite* 29 (May 1995): 2–16.

Katō Yūzō. *Kurofune zengo no sekai*. Tokyo: Iwanami shoten, 1985.

Keene, Donald. *Modern Japanese Diaries: The Japanese at Home and Abroad as Revealed through Their Diaries*. New York: Henry Holt, 1995.

Keiō gijuku, ed. *Fukuzawa Yukichi zenshū*. 22 vols. Tokyo: Iwanami shoten, 1960–1963.

Kesaba, Resat. "Treaties and Friendship: British Imperialism, the Ottoman Empire, and China in the Nineteenth Century." *Journal of World History* 4, no. 2 (fall 1993): 215–42.

Kikuchi Kazutaka. "Sensei-shō ni okeru gunbatsu shihai to ahen." *Kindai Chūgoku* 4 (1980): 127–53.

Kilborn, Omar. *Heal the Sick*. Toronto: Missionary Society of the Methodist Church, 1916.

King, Charles W. *Opium Crisis: A Letter Addressed to Charles Elliot, Esq*. London: Edward Suter, 1839.

Kōain kachū renrakubu. *Chūka minkoku ishin seifu zaisei gaishi*. Tokyo: Kōain, 1940.

Kobayashi Motohiro. "Ahen o meguru Nihon to Ō Chōmei seiken no 'sōkoku.'" In *Nenpō: Nihon gendaishi*, no. 3, ed. Akazawa Shirō et al., pp. 187–226. Tokyo: Gendai shiryō shuppan, 1997.

———. "Chūgoku ni okeru Nihon gendaishi kenkyū no dōkō." In *Nenpō: Nihon gendaishi*, no. 1, ed. Awaya Kentarō et al., pp. 249–63. Tokyo: Azuma shuppan, 1995.

———. "Tenshin jiken saikō: Tenshin sōryōjikan, Shina chūton gun, Nihonjin kyor-yūmin." *Nihon shokuminchi kenkyū* 8 (July 1996): 1–17.

———. "Tenshin no naka no Nihon shakai." In *Tenshin shi*, ed. Tenshin chiiki shi kenkyūkai, pp. 185–207. Tokyo: Tōhō shoten, 1999.

———. "Trends in Chinese Research on Modern Japanese History: The Fifteen-Year War." Trans. B. T. Wakabayashi and Bernard Luk. *Sino-Japanese Studies* 9, no. 1 (October 1996): 75–92.

Kojima, S. *View and Custom of North China*. Tokyo: Tokyo Publishing Co., 1910.

Kuhn, Philip A. *Soulstealers: The Chinese Sorcery Scare of 1768*. Cambridge, Mass.: Harvard University Press, 1990.

Kuma Rakuya. *Mayaku monogatari*. Tokyo: Inoue shobō, 1960.

Kumagai Yasushi. *Shina kyōchin zatsuwa: Chōkō senbu kiroku*. N.p.: n.p., 1943.

Kunaishō, ed. *Shōho junnanroku kō, kōhen*. Tokyo: Yoshikawa kōbunkan, 1933.

Kurahashi Masanao. *Nihon no ahen senryaku*. Tokyo: Kyōei shobō, 1996.

Kuroha Kiyotaka. "Mō hitotsu no ahen sensō." In *Jūgonen sensō shi josetsu: jō*, pp. 203–51. Tokyo: Sanseidō, 1984.

Kuroshima Denji. *Busō seru shigai*. Vol. 3 of *Kuroshima Denji zenshū*. Tokyo: Chikuma shobō, 1970.

Kyokutō saiban sokkiroku. 10 vols. Tokyo: Yūshōdō shoten, 1968.

Lai Shuqing, ed. *Guomin zhengfu liunian jinyan jihua jiqi chengxiao, 1935–40*. Taibei: Guoshiguan, 1986.

Lambert, Sheila, ed. *House of Commons Sessional Papers of the Eighteenth Century.* 173 vols. Wilmington, Del.: Scholarly Resources, 1975.

Lan Bo. "Qingdao qingchu yandu jishi." In *Jinchang jindu*, ed. Ma Weigang, pp. 390–97. Beijing: Jingguan jiaoyu chubanshe, 1993.

Latour, Bruno. *We Have Never Been Modern.* Trans. Catherine Porter. Cambridge, Mass.: Harvard University Press, 1993.

Latourette, Kenneth S. *A History of Christian Missions in China.* 1929; reprint, New York: Russell & Russell, 1967.

Le Failler, P. "Le mouvement international anti-opium et l'Indochine, 1906–1940." Ph.D. diss., Université de Provence, 1993.

League of Nations. *League of Nations Documents and Publications, 1919–1946.* Microfilm reprint. New Haven: Research Publications, 1970–1972.

———. *Report on the International Conferences on Opium and Dangerous Drugs.* London: His Majesty's Stationery Office, 1925.

Levich, Eugene William. *The Kwangsi Way in Kuomintang China, 1931–1939.* Armonk, N.Y.: M. E. Sharpe, 1993.

Li Guoqi. *Zhongguo xiandaihua de quyu yanjiu: Min-Zhe-Tai diqu, 1860–1916.* Taibei: Zhongyang yanjiuyuan, 1982.

Li, Lincoln. *Student Nationalism in China, 1924–1949.* Albany: State University of New York Press, 1994.

Li Longzhang. "Lüetan Guizhou de yanhuo." In *Guizhou wenshi congkan*, vol. 2, pp. 21–26. Guiyang: Renmin chubanshe, 1983.

Li Xiaomei and Fang Shijiao. "Jinyan yu jinzheng: Gansu lishi shang de jinyan sudu." In *Jinchang jindu*, ed. Ma Weigang, pp. 184–96. Beijing: Jingguan jiaoyu chubanshe, 1993.

Li Xingyuan. *Li Xingyuan riji.* 1849? Ed. Yuan Yingguang et al. 2 vols. Beijing: Zhonghua shuju, 1987.

Li Yongqing. "Youguan jinyan yundong de jidian xin renshi." *Lishi dangan* 1986: 3, 79–86.

Li Zhonggong and Zheng Weijia. *Jinyan wenti.* Zhengzhou: Zhengzhong shuju, 1941.

Li Zihui. "Yunnan jinyan gaikuang." *Yunnan wenshi ziliao xuanji* 3 (1963): 84–129.

Lin Enxian. *Qingchao zai Xinjiang de Han-Hui geli zhengce.* Taibei: Shangwu shudian, 1988.

———. "Qingdai Xinjiang huanfang bingzhi zhi yanjiu." *Bianzheng yanjiuso nianbao* 8 (1977): 159–213.

Lin Man-houng. "The National Opium Market within China, 1820–1906." Paper presented at the conference on Opium in East Asian History, Toronto, 1997.

———. "Qingmo shehui liuxing xishi yapian yanjiu: gongji mian zhi fenxi, 1773–1906." Ph.D. diss., National Taiwan Normal University, 1985.

———. "Wan Qing de yapian shui." *Si yu yan* 16, no. 5 (January 1979): 11–59.

Lin Yunhui, Fan Shouxin, and Zhang Gong. *Kaige xingjin de shiqi.* Zhengzhou: Henan renmin chubanshe, 1989.

Lin, Yutang. *Moment in Peking: A Novel of Contemporary Chinese Life.* Shanghai: Kelly & Walsh, 1939.

Little, Mrs. Archibald. *The Land of the Blue Gown.* London: T. Fisher Unwin, 1902.

Little, R. E. "On the Habitual Use of Opium in Singapore." *Journal of the Indian Archipelago and Eastern Asia* 2, no. 1 (1848): 1–79.

Liu Mingxiu [Itō Kiyoshi]. *Taiwan tōchi to ahen mondai.* Tokyo: Yamakawa shuppansha, 1983.

Liu Yingsheng. "Chahetai hanguo de fenlie." *Xinjiang shehui kexue* 1985:5, 99–105.

Lloyd, T. O. *The British Empire, 1558–1983.* Oxford: Oxford University Press, 1996.

Lo, R. Y. *The Opium Problem in the Far East.* Shanghai: Commercial Press, 1933.

Lodwick, Kathleen L. *Crusaders against Opium: Protestant Missionaries in China, 1874–1917.* Lexington: University Press of Kentucky, 1996.

Long Congqi. "Xu Yuanquan zai sha shifan yun yapian de zhixiang." *Jiangling wenshi ziliao* 4 (1988): 161–64.

Lowe, Kate, and Eugene McLaughlin. "Sir John Pope Hennessy and the 'Native Race Craze': Colonial Government in Hong Kong, 1877–1882." *Journal of Imperial and Commonwealth History* 20, no. 2 (May 1992): 223–47.

Luk, Bernard. "Recent Chinese Historiography on Opium on the Eve of the Retrocession of Hong Kong." Paper presented at the conference on Opium in East Asian History, Toronto, 1997.

Lust, John. "Les sociétés secrètes, les mouvements populaires et la révolution de 1911." In *Mouvements populaires et sociétés secrètes en China aux XIXe and XXe siècles,* ed. Jean Chesneaux, Feiling Davis, and Nguyen Nguyet Ho, pp. 360–92. Paris: Maspéro, 1970.

Lutz, Jessie G. *Chinese Politics and Christian Missions: The Anti-Christian Movements of 1920–28.* Notre Dame, Ind.: Cross Cultural Publications, 1988.

Ma Chengfeng. "Zuijin Zhongguo nongcun jingji zhu shixiang zhi baolu." *Zhongguo jingji* 1, no. 1 (April 1933): 1–43.

Ma Mozhen. *Dupin zai Zhongguo.* Beijing: Beijing chubanshe, 1993.

———, ed. *Zhongguo jindu shiliao xuan.* Tianjin: Tianjin renmin chubanshe, 1998.

Ma Weigang. "Jianguo chuqi jinchang jindu shulu." In *Jinchang jindu,* ed. Ma Weigang, pp. 1–13. Beijing: Jingguan jiaoyu chubanshe, 1993.

———, ed. *Jinchang jindu.* Beijing: Jingguan jiaoyu chubanshe, 1993.

Mackerras, Colin. *The Rise of the Peking Opera, 1770–1870: Social Aspects of the Theatre in Manchu China.* Oxford: Clarendon Press, 1972.

———. *The Chinese Theatre in Modern Times: From 1840 to the Present Day.* Amherst: University of Massachusetts Press, 1975.

Madancy, Joyce. "Ambitious Interlude: The Anti-Opium Campaign in China's Fujian Province, 1906–1917." Ph.D. diss., University of Michigan, 1996.

———. "The Fuzhou Anti-Opium Society (1906–1921) and China's Public Sphere." Paper presented at the annual meeting of the Association for Asian Studies, 1997.

———. "Poppies, Patriotism, and the Public Sphere: Nationalism and State Leadership in the Anti-Opium Crusade in Fujian, 1906–1916." Paper presented at the conference on Opium in East Asian History, Toronto, 1997.

———. "Revolution, Religion, and the Poppy: Opium and the Rebellion of the 'Sixteenth Emperor' in Early Republican Fujian." *Republican China* 21, no. 1 (November 1995): 1–41.

Malleck, Daniel. "Reformers, Medicine, and the Integrity of the Nation: Conceptions of Drug Addiction in Canada, 1869–1908." Paper presented at the conference on Opium in East Asian History, Toronto, 1997.

Mamdani, Mahmood. *Citizen and Subject: Contemporary Africa and the Legacy of Late Colonialism*. Princeton, N.J.: Princeton University Press, 1996.

Mander, Samuel S. *Our Opium Trade with China*. London: Simpkin, Marshall & Co., 1877.

Manderson, Lenore. *Sickness and the State: Health and Illness in Colonial Malaya, 1870–1940*. Cambridge, Eng.: Cambridge University Press, 1996.

Manshūkoku shi hensan kankō kai, ed. *Manshūkoku shi (kakuron)*. Tokyo: Manmō dōhō engokai, 1971.

Mao Zedong [Mao Tse-tung]. "On New Democracy." In *Selected Works of Mao Tsetung*, 2:339–84. Beijing: Foreign Languages Press, 1965.

Marshall, Jonathan. "Opium and the Politics of Gangsterism in Nationalist China, 1927–1945." *Bulletin of Concerned Asian Scholars* 8 (July–September 1997): 19–48.

Martin, Brian. *The Shanghai Green Gang: Politics and Organized Crime, 1919–1937*. Berkeley and Los Angeles: University of California Press, 1996.

Marx, Karl. *Marx on China*. London: Lawrence & Wishart, 1968.

Marx, Karl, and Friedrich Engels. *On Colonialism: Articles from the "New York Tribune" and Other Writings*. New York: International Publishers, 1972.

Masuda Wataru. *Seigaku tōzen to Chūgoku jijō*. Tokyo: Iwanami shoten, 1979.

Masui Kōichi. *Kankan saiban shi*. Tokyo: Misuzu shobō, 1977.

McMahon, Keith. *Misers, Shrews, and Polygamists: Sexuality and Male-Female Relationships in Eighteenth-Century Chinese Fiction*. Durham, N.C.: Duke University Press, 1995.

Medhurst, Walter Henry. *China: Its State and Prospects*. London: Snow, 1938.

Merrill, Frederick T. *Japan and the Opium Menace*. New York: Institute of Pacific Relations and Foreign Policy, 1942.

———. "The Opium Menace in the Far East." *Foreign Policy Reports* 7, no. 24 (1 March 1937).

Meyer, Kathryn. "Japan and the World Narcotics Traffic." In *Consuming Habits: Drugs in History and Anthropology*, ed. Jordan Goodman et al., pp. 186–205. New York: Routledge, 1995.

———. "The Sakata Group: Narcotics Trafficking as Military Strategy." Paper presented at the conference on Opium in East Asian History, Toronto, 1997.

Meyer, Kathryn, and Terry Parsinnen. *Webs of Smoke: Smugglers, Warlords, Spies, and the History of the International Drug Trade*. Lanham, Md.: Rowman & Littlefield, 1998.

Mi Qingyun. "Jiang zhengchuan zai Chuanxi bianju jinyan de zhenxiang." *Wenshi ziliao* [national edition] 33 (1963): 155–73.

Miao Pusheng. "Qingdai Weiwuer zu renkou kaoshu." *Xinjiang shehui kexue* 1985: 1, 70–80.

Miller, Stuart Creighton. *The Unwelcome Immigrant: The American Image of the Chinese, 1785–1882*. Berkeley and Los Angeles: University of California Press, 1969.

Millward, James. "Beyond the Pass: Commerce, Ethnicity and the Qing Empire in Xinjiang, 1759–1864." Ph.D. diss., Stanford University, 1993.

Miners, N. J., "The Hong Kong Government Opium Monopoly, 1914–1941." *Journal of Imperial and Commonwealth History* 11, no. 3 (May 1983): 275–99.

Mitohan shiryō bekki jō. Tokyo: Yoshikawa kōbunkan, 1970.

Miyajima Hiroshi. *Chōsen tochi chōsa jigyō shi no kenkyū.* Tokyo: Kyūko shoin, 1991.

Moorcroft, William, and George Trebeck. *Travels in the Himalayan Provinces of Hindustan and the Panjab; in Ladakh and Kashmir; in Peshawar, Kabul, Kunduz and Bokhara.* 2 vols. London: John Murray, 1841.

Mori Mutsuhiko. "Ahen sensō jōhō toshite no Tōfūsetsusho." *Hōsei shigaku* 20 (March 1968): 125–42.

Mōri Toshihiko. *Taiwan shuppei: Dai Nihon teikoku kaimakugeki.* Tokyo: Chūōkōronsha, 1996.

Morse, Hosea. B. *International Relations of the Chinese Empire.* 3 vols. Shanghai: Kelly & Walsh, 1910–1918.

———. *The Trade and Administration of the Chinese Empire.* Shanghai: Kelly & Walsh, 1908.

Moule, Arthur E. *New China and Old: Personal Recollections and Observations of Thirty Years.* London: Seeley, 1902.

Moulton, Edward C. *Lord Northbrook's Indian Administration: 1872–1876.* London: Asia Publishing House, 1968.

Muller, Max. "General Report by Max Muller Respecting the Opium Question in China." In *Despatches from His Majesty's Minister at Peking Forwarding Reports Respecting the Opium Question in China* (China no. 3), pp. 1–29. London: Harrison and Sons, 1909.

Munn, Christopher Charles. "Anglo-China: Chinese People and British Rule in Hong Kong, 1841–1870." Ph.D. diss., University of Toronto, 1997.

Nakajima Chūzaburō. *Aru ryōjikan no kaisōroku.* Tokyo: Kindai bungeisha, 1995.

Nalet, Yves. "Chen Duxiu, 1879–1915, formation d'un intellectuel révolutionnaire." Ph.D. diss., École des Hautes Études en Sciences Sociales, Paris, 1984.

Nanjing jingcha, ed. *Nanjing jingcha gaishi, 1938–39.* Nanjing: n.p., 1940.

Nanjing shi dang'anguan, ed. *Shenxun Wangwei hanjian bilu.* 2 vols. Nanjing: Jiangsu guji chubanshe, 1992.

Nanjing tebieshi zhengfu mishuchu, ed. *Ershiba niandu Nanjing shizheng gaikuang.* Nanjing: n.p., 1939.

Nankin Nihon shōkōkaigisho, ed. *Nankin.* Nanjing: n.p., 1941.

Nankoe, Hakiem, Jean-Claude Gerlus, and Martin J. Murray. "The Origins of the Opium Trade and the Opium Regimes in Colonial Indochina." In *The Rise and Fall of Revenue Farming: Business Elites and the Emergence of the Modern State in Southeast Asia,* ed. John Butcher and Howard Dick, pp. 182–95. London: St. Martin's Press, 1993.

Natsui Haruki. "Kanton kō-Ei tōsō." In *Kōza Chūgoku kingendaishi 1: Chūgoku kakumei no kigen,* ed. Nozawa Yutaka and Tanaka Masayoshi, pp. 181–203. Tokyo: Tōkyō daigaku shuppankai, 1971.

Neizhengbu. *Neizheng nianjian.* 2 vols. Shanghai: Shangwu yinshuguan, 1935.

Newman, R. K. "India and the Anglo-Chinese Opium Agreements, 1907–1914." *Modern Asian Studies* 23, no. 3 (1989): 525–60.

———. "The Opium Licensing System in India." Paper presented at the conference on Opium in East Asian History, Toronto, 1997.

———. "Opium Smoking in Late Imperial China: A Reconsideration." *Modern Asian Studies* 29, no. 4 (1995): 765–94.

Niimura Yōko. "Igirisujin no ahen bōekikan." *Rekishigaku kenkyū* 709 (April 1998): 18–34.

Ning Gongshi. "Nanjing de jindu gongzuo." In *Jinchang jindu*, ed. Ma Weigang, pp. 363–80. Beijing: Jingguan jiaoyu chubanshe, 1993.

Nohara Shirō. "Kyokutō o meguru kokusai kankei." *Iwanami kōza Nihon rekishi*, vol. 14, *Kindai I*. Tokyo: Iwanami shoten, 1962.

Norton-Kyshe, J. W. *History of the Laws and Courts of Hong Kong.* 2 vols., 1898; reprint, Hong Kong: Vetch & Lee, 1971.

Numata Jirō, Matsumura Akira, and Satō Shōsuke, eds. *Nihon shisō taikei*, vol. 64, *Yōgaku jō*. Tokyo: Iwanami shoten, 1976.

Ōba Osamu. *Edo jidai ni okeru Tōsen mochiwatarishi no kenkyū.* Osaka: Kansai daigaku shuppanbu, 1967.

———. *Edo jidai no Nit-Chū hiwa.* Tokyo: Tōhō shoten, 1980.

Okada Yoshimasa et al., eds. *Zoku Gendai shi shiryō*, vol. 12, *Ahen mondai.* Tokyo: Misuzu shobō, 1986.

Ōkōchi Kazuo. *Kokusaku gaisha Tōyō takushoku no shūen.* Tokyo: Sekibundō, 1991.

———. *Maboroshi no kokusaku gaisha Tōyō takushoku.* Tokyo: Nihon keizai shinbunsha, 1982.

Ono Mihoko. "Shanhai ni okeru gien no keisei to hatten." *Ochanomizu shigaku* 26–27 (1983): 50–70.

The Opium Trade, 1910–1941. Reprint of British Foreign Office (FO 415) documents in the Public Record Office. 6 vols. Wilmington, Del.: Scholarly Resources, 1974.

The Opium Trade and the United Nations Commission on Narcotic Drugs, 1945–1948. Microfilm of British Foreign Office documents, Public Records Office, Class FO 371. 4 reels. Marlborough: Adam Matthew Publications.

Owen, David Edward. *British Opium Policy in China and India.* New Haven: Yale University Press, 1934.

Pan Tian. "Wangwei tongzhi shiqi Nanjing xuesheng de 'qingdu' yundong." *Nanjing dangshi ziliao* 1983:4, 74–80.

Pan Zhiping. *Zhongya haohanguo yu Qingdai Xinjiang.* Beijing: Zhongguo shehui kexue chubanshe, 1991.

Ping Jinya. "Jiu Shanghai de yandu." In *Jiu Shanghai de yan, du, chang*, ed. Shanghai wenshi yanjiu guan, pp. 10–22. Reprint, Hong Kong: Zhongyuan chubanshe, 1990.

Ping Wu. "Tietixia de huoyan." *Xiaoyou tongxun* 4 (December 1991): 16–18.

Polachek, James M. *The Inner Opium War.* Cambridge, Mass.: Harvard University Press, 1992.

Pratt, John T. *Memorandum Respecting the Opium Problem in the Far East* (1929). In *The Opium Trade, 1910–1941* [a facsimile reproduction of the Foreign Office Collection (F.O.415) in the Public Record Office, London], vol. 6, part 26, pp. 11–43. Wilmington, Del.: Scholarly Resources, 1974.

Prinsep, George Alexander. "Remarks on the External Commerce and Exchanges of Bengal (1823)." In *The Economic Development of India under the East India Com-*

pany, 1814–1858: A Selection of Contemporary Writings, ed. K. N. Chaudhuri, pp. 51–163. Cambridge, Eng.: Cambridge University Press, 1971.

Qian Shifu. *Qingdai zhiguan nianbiao.* 4 vols. Beijing: Zhonghua shuju, 1980.

Qi Qingshun. "'Xinjiang nanlu jinyan zhangcheng' qiantan." *Xinjiang shehui kexue xuebao* 1 (1989): 94–100.

Qin Rongguang. *Shanghai xian zhuzhici.* 1903; reprinted in *Shanghai tan yu Shanghai ren congshu,* Shanghai: Shanghai guji chubanshe, 1989.

Qing huidian shili. 1899; reprint, Beijing: Zhonghua shuju, 1991.

Qingdai zhiguan nianbiao.

Qingmo minchu Zhongguo guan shen renming lu. Beijing: Zhongguo yanjiuhui kanhang, 1918.

Qingshi liezhuan. 20 vols. 1928; reprint, Beijing: Zhonghua shuju, 1987.

Quan Shifu, ed. *Qingji xinshe shiguan nianbiao.* Beijing: Zhonghua shuju, 1961.

Rankin, Mary Backus. *Elite Activism and Political Transformation in China: Zhejiang Province, 1865–1911.* Stanford, Calif.: Stanford University Press, 1986.

———. "Some Observations on a Chinese Public Sphere." *Modern China* 19, no. 2 (1993): 158–82.

Rawlinson, John L. *China's Struggle for Naval Development: 1839–1895.* Cambridge, Mass.: Harvard University Press, 1967.

Richards, John F. "The Indian Empire and Peasant Production of Opium." *Modern Asian Studies* 15 (1981): 59–82.

Rodzinski, Witold. *A History of China.* 2 vols. Oxford: Pergamon Press, 1979–1983.

Rothermund, Dietmar. *An Economic History of India: From Pre-Colonial Times to 1986.* London: Croom Helm, 1988.

Rowe, William T. *Hankow: Commerce and Society in a Chinese City, 1796–1889.* Stanford, Calif.: Stanford University Press, 1984.

———. *Hankow: Conflict and Community in a Chinese City, 1796–1895.* Stanford: Stanford University Press, 1989

———. "The Problem of 'Civil Society' in Late Imperial China." *Modern China* 19, no. 2 (1993): 139–57.

Royal Commission on Opium. *First Report of the Royal Commission on Opium: With Minutes of Evidence and Appendices.* London: H. M. Stationery Office, 1895.

Ruf, Gregory A. *Cadres and Kin: Making a Socialist Village in West China, 1921–1991.* Stanford, Calif.: Stanford University Press, 1998.

Rush, James R. *Opium to Java: Revenue Farming and Chinese Enterprise in Colonial Indonesia, 1800–1910.* Ithaca, N.Y.: Cornell University Press, 1990.

Sadatoki Hidekazu. "Nihon no ahen shinryaku to Chūgoku ahen no teikō ni tsuite." *Rekishi kenkyū* 30 (1993): 87–123.

Sadka, Emily. *The Protected Malay States, 1874–1895.* Kuala Lumpur: University of Malaya Press, 1968.

Said, Edward W. *Orientalism.* London: Routledge and Kegan Paul, 1978.

Saguchi, Toru. "The Eastern Trade of the Khoqand Khanate." *Memoirs of the Research Department of the Toyo Bunko* 24 (1965): 47–114.

Sanbō honbu, ed. *Sugiyama memo jō ge.* Tokyo: Hara shobō, 1967.

Satō Kenji, ed. *Satō Nobuhiro bugakushū jō.* Tokyo: Iwanami shoten, 1942.

Satō Saburō. *Kindai Nit-Chū kōshō shi no kenkyū.* Tokyo: Yoshikawa kōbunkan, 1984.

Satō Shōsuke. *Yōgakushi kenkyū josetsu.* Tokyo: Iwanami shoten, 1964.

Satō Shōsuke, Uete Michiari, and Yamaguchi Muneyuki, eds. *Nihon shisō taikei,* vol.55, *Watanabe Kazan, Takano Chōei, Sakuma Shōzan, Yokoi Shōnan, Hashimoto Sanai.* Tokyo: Iwanami shoten, 1971.

Satow, Ernest. *A Diplomat in Japan: An Inner History of the Critical Years in the Evolution of Japan.* Rutland, Vt.: Tuttle, 1983.

Schurmann, Franz. *Ideology and Organization in Communist China.* Berkeley and Los Angeles: University of California Press, 1966.

Scott, J. N. *The White Poppy: A History of Opium.* London: Heinemann, 1969.

Scott, James C. *Weapons of the Weak: Everyday Forms of Peasant Resistance.* New Haven: Yale University Press, 1985.

Sechter, Douglas A. "The Legal, Medical, and Social Status of Opium in Britain, c. 1867–1923." Paper presented at the conference on Opium in East Asian History, Toronto, 1997.

Seyf, Ahmad. "Commercialization of Agriculture: Production and Trade of Opium in Persia, 1850–1906." *International Journal of Middle East Studies* 16 (1984): 183–92.

Shanghai Mercury. *Opium Statistics in China, Foreign and Native.* Shanghai: Post-Mercury Co., 1889.

Shanghai wenshi yanjiuguan, ed. *Jiu Shanghai de yan, du, chang.* Reprint, Hong Kong: Zhongyuan chubanshe, 1990.

Sheel, Kamal. *Peasant Society and Marxist Intellectuals in China.* Princeton, N.J.: Princeton University Press, 1989.

Shenjiang mingsheng tushuo. Shanghai: Haishang rouyun guan, 1884.

Shenjiang shengjing tu. Shanghai: Dianshi zhai, 1884.

Shimada, Toshihiko. "Designs on North China." In *The China Quagmire: Japan's Expansion on the Asian Continent, 1933–1941,* ed. James William Morley, pp. 11–230. New York: Columbia University Press, 1983.

Shinano kyōikukai, ed. *Fukkoku Shōzan zenshū.* 5 vols. Tokyo: Meiji bunken, 1975.

Sifa xingzhengbu zongwusi. *Sifa zhuangkuang.* Nanjing: n.p., 1940.

Sima Qian. *Shiji.* Han dynasty; reprint, Beijing: Zhonghua shuju, 1959.

Singh, Narayan Prasad. *The East India Company's Monopoly Industries in Bihar, with Particular Reference to Opium and Saltpetre (1773–1833).* Muzaffarpur: Sarvodaya Bangmay, 1980.

Sinn, Elizabeth. *Power and Charity: The Early History of the Tung Wah Hospital, Hong Kong.* Hong Kong: Oxford University Press, 1989.

Sirr, Henry. *China and the Chinese . . . The Evils Arising from the Opium Trade.* 2 vols. London: Orr, 1849.

Skinner, G. W., ed. *The City in Late Imperial China.* Stanford, Calif.: Stanford University Press, 1977.

Slack, Edward R., Jr. "The Guomindang's Opium Policies, 1924–1937: Understanding 'Opium Suppression' in the Context of the Warlord System and the Republican Narco-economy." Ph.D. diss., University of Hawai'i, 1997.

Sly, H E. "Report on Opium Eradication by Acting Consul Sly." In *Despatches from His Majesty's Minister at Peking Forwarding Reports Respecting the Opium Question in China* (China no. 3), pp. 39–49. London: Harrison and Sons, 1909.

Smith, Carl T. *Chinese Christians, Élites, Middlemen, and the Church in Hong Kong.* Hong Kong: Oxford University Press, 1985.

Smith, George. *A Narrative of an Exploratory Visit to each of the Consular Cities of China, and to the Islands of Hong Kong and Chusan, in Behalf of the Church Missionary Society, in the Years 1844, 1845, 1846.* London: Seeley, Burnside and Seeley, 1847.

Smyth, H. Warington. *Five Years in Siam.* 1898; reprint, Bangkok: White Lotus Press, 1994.

Song, Ong Siang. *One Hundred Years' History of the Chinese in Singapore.* Singapore: University of Malaya Press, 1923.

Sovik, Arne. "Church and State in Republican China: A Survey History of the Relations between the Christian Churches and the Chinese Government, 1911–1945." Ph.D. diss., Yale University, 1952.

Spence, Jonathan. "Opium Smoking in Ch'ing China." In *Conflict and Control in Late Imperial China,* ed. Frederic Wakeman Jr. and Carolyn Grant, pp. 143–73. Berkeley and Los Angeles: University of California Press, 1975. Reprinted in Jonathan Spence, *Chinese Roundabout: Essays in History and Culture,* pp. 228–56. New York: Norton, 1992.

Stapleton, Kristin. "Police Reform in a Late-Imperial Chinese City: Chengdu, 1902–1911." Ph.D. diss., Harvard University, 1993.

Strand, David. *Rickshaw Beijing: City People and Politics in the 1920s.* Berkeley and Los Angeles: University of California Press, 1989.

Strauss, Julia C. *Strong Institutions in Weak Polities: Personnel Policies and State Building in China, 1927–1940.* Oxford: Clarendon Press, 1998.

Sun Wen. *Guofu quanji.* 6 vols. Rev. ed. Taibei: Zhongguo Guomindang zhongyang zhixing weiyuanhui, 1961.

Sun Xingsheng, Shi Tangxi, and Zhu Changhe. "Jinyan sudu zai Liangshan." In *Jinchang jindu,* ed. Ma Weigang, pp. 197–217. Beijing: Jingguan jiaoyu chubanshe, 1993.

Sun Xiufu. "Jiang Jieshi yu Zhongguo nongmin yinhang." *Minguo dangan* 1996:1, 91–98.

Sun Yusheng. *Haishang fanhua meng.* 1898–1906; reprint, Shanghai: Shanghai guji chubanshe, 1991.

Takeuchi Minoru. *Nihonjin ni totte no Chūgoku zō.* Tokyo: Shunjūsha, 1966.

Tan Chung. *China and the Brave New World: A Study of the Origins of the Opium War (1840–42).* Durham, N.C.: Carolina Academic Press, 1978.

T'ang, Leang-li. *Reconstruction in China: A Record of Progress and Achievement in Facts and Figures.* Shanghai: China United Press, 1935.

Tarrant, William. *Hongkong,* part 1, *1839 to 1844.* Canton: Friend of China, 1861.

Tashiro Kazui. *Kinsei Nit-Chū tsūkō bōeki shi kenkyū.* Tokyo: Sōbunsha, 1981.

Tatai Yoshio. "Hishi: Ahen ga sasaeta Nihon no tairiku shinkō." *Shinchō* 45 (May 1992): 195–202.

———, ed. *Zoku Gendai shi shiryō,* vol. 11, *Senryōchi tsūka kōsaku.* Tokyo: Misuzu shobō, 1983.

Taylor, Arnold H. *American Diplomacy and the Narcotics Traffic, 1900–1939.* Durham, N.C.: Duke University Press, 1969.

Taylor, J. Hudson. *China's Millions.* London: Morgan & Scott, 1886.

Teiwes, Frederick C. "Establishment and Consolidation of the New Regime." In

The Cambridge History of China, vol. 14, ed. Roderick MacFarquhar and John K. Fairbank, pp. 51–92. Cambridge, Eng.: Cambridge University Press, 1987.

Tenshin kōshinjo, ed. *Kita Shina zairyū hōjin kanshō roku.* Tianjin: Tenshin kōshinjo, 1932.

Tenshin kyoryūmindan, ed. *Tenshin kyoryūmindan sanjūshūnen shi.* Tianjin: Tenshin kyorūmindan, 1941.

Terry, Charles E., and Mildred Pellens. *The Opium Problem.* New York: Bureau of Social Health, 1928.

Thompson, James C., Jr. *While China Faced West: American Reformers in Nationalist China, 1928–1937.* Cambridge, Mass.: Harvard University Press, 1969.

Tian Meicun. "Jiushehui yapian yanye zai Hankou." *Wuhan wenshi ziliao* 7 (1989): 186–90.

Tilly, Charles. *The Contentious French.* Cambridge, Mass.: Belknap Press, 1986.

———. *From Mobilization to Revolution.* New York: Random House, 1978.

Ting, Joseph. "Native Chinese Peace Officers in British Hong Kong, 1841–1861." In *Between East and West: Aspects of Social and Political Development in Hong Kong,* ed. Elizabeth Sinn. Hong Kong: Centre of Asian Studies, University of Hong Kong, 1990.

Toby, Ronald P. *State and Diplomacy in Early Modern Japan.* Princeton, N.J.: Princeton University Press, 1981.

Traver, Harold. "Colonial Relations and Opium Control Policy in Hong Kong, 1841–1945." In *Drugs, Law and the State,* ed. Harold H. Traver and Mark S. Gaylord, pp. 135–49. Hong Kong: Hong Kong University Press, 1992.

Trocki, Carl A. "The Demise of Singapore's Great Opium Syndicate." In *The Rise and Fall of Revenue Farming: Business Elites and the Emergence of the Modern State in Southeast Asia.* ed. John Butcher and Howard Dick, pp. 166–81. London: St. Martin's Press, 1993.

———. *Opium and Empire: Chinese Society in Colonial Singapore, 1800–1910.* Ithaca, N.Y.: Cornell University Press, 1990.

———. *Prince of Pirates: The Temenggongs and the Development of Johor and Singapore, 1784–1885.* Singapore: Singapore University Press, 1979.

———. "The Rise of Singapore's Great Opium Syndicate, 1840–1886." *Journal of Southeast Asian Studies* 18 (March 1987): 58–80.

Tsai, Jung-fang. *Hong Kong in Chinese History: Community and Social Unrest in the British Colony, 1842–1913.* New York: Columbia University Press, 1993.

Turnbull, C. M. *A History of Singapore.* Kuala Lumpur: Oxford University Press, 1977.

Turner, F. S. *British Opium Policy and Its Results in India and China.* London: Sampson Low, 1876.

Tyau, Min Ch'ien T. Z. *Two Years of Nationalist China.* Shanghai: Kelly & Walsh, 1930.

Uchida Ginzō. *Kinsei Nihon, Nihon no kinseishi.* Tokyo: Heibonsha, 1975.

Uchida Tomoyuki. "Chūgoku kō-Nichi konkyochi ni okeru ahen kanri seisaku." *Ajia kenkyū* 41, no. 4 (August 1995): 25–65.

———. "Sairon: Chūgoku kō-Nichi konkyochi ni okeru ahen kanri seisaku." *Gekkan: Chūgoku tosho* 99 (June 1997): 2–6.

———. "Sanseishō no Nihongun senryō chiku ni okeru ahen kanri seisaku." *Tōyō kenkyū* 112 (September 1994): 29–54.

United States, Department of State. *Relations Relating to the Internal Affairs of China, 1930–1939*. Microfilm. Washington, D.C.: National Archives Publications, Series 893.

United States Government. *Report of the Government of the United States on the Traffic in Opium and Other Dangerous Drugs, 1951*. Washington, D.C.: Government Printing Office, 1952.

Usui Katsumi. *Chūgoku o meguru kindai Nihon no gaikō*. Tokyo: Chikuma shobō, 1983.

Vernon, Ken. *George Duddell, 1821–1857: A Hong Kong Pioneer and a Brighton Notability*. London: Privately published by the author, 1990.

Viraphol, Sarasin. *Tribute and Profit: Sino-Siamese Trade 1652–1853*. Cambridge, Mass.: Harvard University Press, 1977.

Wakabayashi, Bob Tadashi. *Anti-Foreignism and Western Learning in Early-Modern Japan*. Cambridge, Mass.: Harvard University Press, 1986.

———. "Japanese Wartime Opium Operations and Postward Political Correctness." Paper presented at the conference on Opium in East Asian History, Toronto, 1997.

———. "Opium, Expulsion, Sovereignty: China's Lessons for Bakumatsu Japan." *Monumenta Nipponica* 47, no. 1 (spring 1991): 1–25.

———. "Rival States on a Loose Rein: The Neglected Tradition of Appeasement in Late-Tokugawa Thought." In *The Ambivalence of Nationalism: Modern Japan Between East and West*, ed. James White, Michio Umegaki, and Thomas R. Havens, pp. 11–37. Lanham, Md.: University Press of America, 1985.

Wakeman, Frederic, Jr. "The Canton Trade and the Opium War." In *The Cambridge History of China*, vol. 10, ed. John K. Fairbank, pp. 163–212. Cambridge, Eng.: Cambridge University Press, 1978.

———. "The Civil Society and Public Sphere Debate: Western Reflections on Chinese Political Culture." *Modern China* 19, no. 2 (1993): 108–38.

———. "Models of Historical Change: The Chinese State and Society, 1839–1989." *Newsletter for Modern Chinese History* 11 (1991): 50–65.

———. *Policing Shanghai, 1927–1937*. Berkeley and Los Angeles: University of California Press, 1995.

———. "The Shanghai Badlands: Wartime Terrorism and Urban Crime." In *Guo Ting-yi xiansheng jiuzhi danchen jinian lunwenji*, pp. 345–69. Taibei: Institute of Modern History, Academia Sinica, 1995.

———. *Strangers at the Gate: Social Disorder in South China, 1839–1861*. Berkeley and Los Angeles: University of California Press, 1966.

Wakeman, Frederic, Jr., and Carolyn Grant, eds. *Conflict and Control in Late Imperial China*. Berkeley and Los Angeles: University of California Press, 1975.

Wakeman, Frederic, Jr., and Wen-hsin Yeh, eds. *Shanghai Sojourners*. Berkeley: Institute of East Asian Studies, University of California, 1992.

Waley, Arthur. *The Opium War through Chinese Eyes*. Stanford, Calif.: Stanford University Press, 1968.

Waley-Cohen, Joanna. *Exile in Mid-Qing China, 1758–1820*. New Haven: Yale University Press, 1991.

Walker, William O., III. *Opium and Foreign Policy: The Anglo-American Search for Order in Asia, 1912–1954*. Chapel Hill: University of North Carolina Press, 1991.

Wang Hongbin. *Jindu shijian*. Changsha: Yuelin shushe, 1997.

Wang Jinxiang. *Zhongguo jindu jianshi.* Beijing: Xuexi chubanshe, 1996.

Wang Licheng. "Yapian zhanzheng qianxi de jinyan juece pingxi." *Lanzhou daxue xuebao,* 18:4 (1990), pp. 9–15.

Wang Shuhuai. *Zhongguo xiandaihua de quyu yanjiu: Jiangsu sheng, 1860–1916.* Taipei: Zhongyang yanjiuyuan jindaishi yanjiusuo, 1984.

Wang Tao. *Yingruan zazhi.* 1875; reprinted in *Shanghai tan yu Shanghai ren congshu,* Shanghai: Shanghai guji chubanshe, 1989.

Watanabe Hiroshi. *Higashi Ajia no ōken to shisō.* Tokyo: Tōkyō daigaku shuppankai, 1997.

Ware, Vron. *Beyond the Pale: White Women, Racism, and History.* London: Verso, 1992.

Waung, W. S. K. "Introduction of Opium Cultivation to China." *Journal of the Chinese University of Hong Kong*5, no. 1 (1979).

Wei Guangqi. "Qingdai houqi zhongyang jiquan caizheng tizhi de wajie." *Jindaishi yanjiu* 1986:1, 207–30.

Wei, William. *Counterrevolution in China: The Nationalists in Jiangxi during the Soviet Period.* Ann Arbor: University of Michigan Press, 1985.

Wei Yuan. *Wei Yuan ji.* Beijing: Zhonghua shuju, 1976.

Wen Jingming. "Yapian yu jindai xi'nan shehui." M.A. thesis, Sichuan University, 1993.

Who's Who in China. 4th ed. Shanghai: China Weekly Review, 1931.

Who's Who in China. Supplement to the 4th ed. Shanghai: China Weekly Review, 1933.

Wickberg, Edgar. *The Chinese in Philippine Life, 1850–1898.* New Haven: Yale University Press, 1965.

Will, Pierre-Étienne, and R. Bin Wong. *Nourish the People: The State Civilian Granary System in China, 1650–1850.* Ann Arbor: University of Michigan Center for Chinese Studies, 1991.

Williams, Eric. *Capitalism and Slavery.* London: Deutsch, 1964.

Williams, Samuel Wells. *The Middle Kingdom: A Survey of the Geography, Government, Education, Social Life, Arts, Religion, &tc. of the Chinese Empire.* 2 vols. New York: Scribner's, 1883.

Willoughby, Westel W. *Foreign Rights and Interests in China.* 2 vols. Baltimore: Johns Hopkins University Press, 1920.

Wills, John E., Jr. "Maritime China from Wang Chih to Shih Lang: Themes in Peripheral History." In *From Ming to Ch'ing,* ed. Jonathan D. Spence and John E. Wills Jr., pp. 201–38. New Haven: Yale University Press, 1979.

Wilson, Constance M. "Revenue Farming, Economic Development and Government Policy during the Early Bangkok Period, 1830–1892." In *The Rise and Fall of Revenue Farming: Business Elites and the Emergence of the Modern State in Southeast Asia,* ed. John Butcher and Howard Dick, pp. 142–65. London: St. Martin's Press, 1993.

Wolpert, Stanley A. *Morley and India, 1906–1910.* Berkeley and Los Angeles: University of California Press, 1967.

Wong, J. Y. *Deadly Dreams: Opium, Imperialism and the Arrow War (1856–1860) in China.* New York: Cambridge University Press, 1998.

Wong, Lin Ken. "The Revenue Farms of Prince of Wales Island." *Journal of the South Seas Society* (1964–1965): 56–127.

Wong, R. Bin. *China Transformed: Historical Change and the Limits of European Experience.* Ithaca, N.Y.: Cornell University Press, 1997.

———. "Great Expectations: The 'Public Sphere' and the Search for Modern Times in Chinese History." *Chūgoku shigaku* 3 (1993): 7–50.

Wright, H. R. C. *East-Indian Economic Problems of the Age of Cornwallis and Raffles.* London: Luzac, 1961.

Wright, Mary C., ed. *China in Revolution: The First Phase, 1900–1913.* New Haven: Yale University Press, 1968.

Wu Chengming. *Zhongguo zibenzhuyi yu guonei shichang.* Beijing: Zhongguo shehui kexue chubanshe, 1985.

Wu Jianren. *Hen hai.* 1906; reprint, Tianjin: Tianjin guji chubanshe, 1987.

Wu Jiaqiong. "Lin Bingzhang shenping gaishu." *Fujian wenshi ziliao* 19 (1988): 98–104.

Wu Jiayu and Lin Jiazhen. "Fujian jinyan yundong 'qudu she.' " *Fuzhou wenshi ziliao xuanji* 2 (December 1983): 15–17.

Wu, Lien-teh. *Plague Fighter: The Autobiography of a Modern Chinese Physician.* Cambridge, Eng.: W. Heffer & Sons, Ltd., 1959.

Wu Shuping. "Manhua yapian." *Exi wenshi ziliao* 5 (1987): 193–98.

Wyman, Judith. "Opium and the State in Sichuan Province during the Late Qing." Paper presented at the annual meeting of the Association for Asian Studies, Boston, 1994.

———. "Social Change, Anti-Foreignism and Revolution in China: Chongqing Prefecture, 1870s to 1911." Ph.D. diss., University of Michigan, 1993.

Xiang Baosheng. "Jiu Tianjin de yandu ji yijiuwuer nian de jindu yundong." In *Jinchang jindu,* ed. Ma Weigang, pp. 336–62. Beijing: Jingguan jiaoyu chubanshe, 1993.

Xiao Juetian. "Jiang Jieshi de jinyan neimu." *Wenshi ziliao xuanji* [national edition] 34 (1986): 157–74.

Xie Guozhen, ed. *Mingdai shehui jingji shiliao xuanbian.* 3 vols. Fuzhou: Fujian renmin chubanshe, 1980.

Xin shenghuo yundong cujin zonghui, ed. *Minguo ershisannian xin shenghuo yundong zongbaogao.* Nanchang: n.p., 1935.

Xingzhengyuan xuanchuanju, ed. *Chūka minkoku ishin seifu gaishi.* Nanjing: Weixin zhengfu, 1940.

Xinhai geming qian shinianjian minbian dang'an shiliao. 2 vols. Beijing: Xinhua shudian, 1985.

Xu Jue. *Fuan xiansheng ji.* 1911; reprint, Taibei: Chengwen chubanshe, 1970.

Yamada Gōichi. *Ōrudo Shanhai ahen jijō.* Tokyo: Aki shobō, 1995.

Yamaguchi ken kyōikukai, ed. *Yoshida Shōin zenshū.* 12 vols. Tokyo: Iwanami shoten, 1939.

Yamamoto Tsuneo. *Ahen to taihō.* Tokyo: PMC shuppan, 1985.

Yang Guangcheng. "Aba de jinyan sudu." In *Jinchang jindu,* ed. Ma Weigang, pp. 316–22. Beijing: Jingguan jiaoyu chubanshe, 1993.

Yang Shenzhi and Huang Liyong, eds. *Wei Yuan sixiang yanjiu.* Changsha: Hunan renmin chubanshe, 1987.

Yapian zhanzheng wenxian huibian. Ed. Yang Chiu-lou. Taibei: Dingwen shuju, 1973.

Yawnghwe, Chao-Tzang. "The Political Economy of the Opium Trade: Implications for the Shan States." *Journal of Contemporary Asia* 23 (1993): 306–26.

Yeh, Wen-hsin. *The Alienated Academy: Culture and Politics in Republican China, 1919–1937*. Cambridge, Mass.: Harvard University Press, 1990.

"Yier yiqi yundong yizhounian." *Gan* 1, no. 11–12 (1944): 12–13.

Yongzheng chao hanwen zhupi zouzhe huibian. Ed. Zhongguo diyi lishi danganguan. 40 vols. Nanjing: Jiangsu guji chubanshe, 1989–1991.

Yu Ende. *Zhongguo jinyan faling bianqian shi*. 1934 reprint. Taipei: Wenhai chubanshe, 1973.

Yu Shengwu and Liu Cunkuan, eds. *Shijiu shiji de Xianggang*. Hong Kong: Unicorn Press, 1994.

Yun, David. "Mouvements populaires en Chine à la fin des Ch'ing." M.A. thesis, École des Hautes Études en Sciences Sociales, Paris, 1982.

Zeitlin, Judith T. *Historian of the Strange: Pu Songling and the Classical Chinese Tale*. Stanford, Calif.: Stanford University Press, 1993.

Zeng Wenwu. *Zhongguo jingguan xiyu shi*. 1936; reprint. Shanghai: Shanghai shudian, 1989.

Zeng Ruiyan. *Huaqiao yu kangri zhanzheng*. Chengdu: Sichuan daxue chubanshe, 1988.

Zhang Chang. *Yanhua*. Shanghai: Shenbao guan, 1878.

Zhang Chengjun. "Xi'an de jinyan sudu." in *Jinchang jindu*, ed. Ma Weigang, pp. 302–15. Beijing: Jingguan jiaoyu chubanshe, 1993.

Zhang Youyi. *Zhongguo jindai nongyeshi ziliao*, vol. 2 (1912–1927), vol. 3 (1927–1937). Beijing: Sanlian, 1957.

Zhang Zhecheng. "Hezhou, Haohan yu Chashegeer huibian." *Zhongguo bianzheng* 91 (1985): 32–35.

Zhang Zhenhe and Ding Yuanying. "Qingmo minbian nianbao." *Jindaishi ziliao* 49 (1982): 108–81; 50 (1983): 77–121.

Zhang Zhijiang, ed. *Quanguo jinyan huiyi huibian*. Nanjing: Xingzheng yuan, 1929.

Zhao Erxun. *Qingshi gao*. Reprint, Beijing: Zhonghua shuju, 1976.

Zhao Shikong. "Xiaomie Guilin de fandu huodong." In *Jinchang jindu*, ed. Ma Weigang, pp. 255–66. Beijing: Jingguan jiaoyu chubanshe, 1993.

Zhejiang sheng juduhui zongbaogao. 1935.

Zhejiang sheng zhengxie wenshi ziliao weiyuanhui, ed. *Xinbian Zhejiang bainian dashiji, 1840–1940*. Hangzhou: Zhejiang renmin chubanshe, 1990.

Zheng Yingshe. "Chaoji yapianshang zai Shanghai de huodong ji qi yu Jiang Jieshi zhengquan de guanxi." *Guangdong wenshi ziliao* 21 (1978): 1–30.

Zhongguo diyi lishi dang'anguan, ed. *Yapian zhanzheng dang'an shiliao*. 7 vols. Tianjin: Tianjin guji chubanshe, 1992.

Zhongguo di'er lishi dang'anguan, ed. *Wangwei guomin zhengfu gongbao*. Reprint, Nanjing: Jiangsu guji chubanshe, 1991.

———. *Wangwei zhengfu xingzhengyuan huiyilu*. Reprint, Shanghai: Dang'an chubanshe, 1992.

Zhongguo Guomindang zhongyang weiyuanhui dangshi weiyuanbu, ed. *Zhonghua minguo zhongyao shiliao chubian: dui Ri kangzhan shiqi*, part 6, *Kuilei zuzhi*. Taibei: Zhongguo Guomindang zhongyang weiyuanhui dangshi weiyuanbu, n.d.

Zhongguo Guomindang zhongyang zhixing weiyuanhui xuanchuanbu, ed. *Jinyan xuanchuan huikan*. Nanjing: Zhongguo Guomindang zhongyang zhixing weiyu-anhui xuanchuanbu, 1929.

Zhongyang wenxian yanjiushi, ed. *Jianguo yilai zhongyao wenxian xuanbian*. Beijing: Zhongyang wenxian chubanshe, 1992.

Zhou Jinfu, ed. *Qingdai zhuanji zongkan*. Reprint, Taipei: Mingwen shuzhu yinhang, 1986.

Zhou Yong and Liu Jingxiu. *Jindai Chongqing jingji yu shehui fazhan*. Chengdu: Si-chuan daxue chubanshe, 1987.

Zhou Yongming. *Anti-Drug Crusades in Twentieth-Century China: Nationalism, History and State Building*. Lanham, Md.: Rowman & Littlefield, 1999.

Zhu Jinpu. "Yapian zhanzheng qian Daoguang chao yanguan de jinyan lun." *Jindai shi yanjiu* 1991:2, 57–66.

Zhu Qiluan. *Nanjing renmin gemingshi*. Nanjing: Nanjing chubanshe, 1991.

Zhu Qingbao, Jiang Qiuming, and Zhang Shijie. *Yapian yu jindai Zhongguo*. Nanjing: Jiangsu renmin chubanshe, 1995.

CONTRIBUTORS

Alan Baumler is assistant professor of history at Indiana University of Pennsylvania.

David Bello is a graduate student in Chinese history at the University of Southern California.

Lucien Bianco is professor emeritus of modern Chinese history at the École des Hautes Études en Sciences Sociales in Paris. His best-known book in English is *The Origins of the Chinese Revolution*.

Gregory Blue teaches world and comparative history at the University of Victoria. He is most recently the coeditor (with Timothy Brook) of *China and Historical Capitalism: Genealogies of Sinological Knowledge*.

Timothy Brook is professor of Chinese history at the University of Toronto. His other coedited volumes include *China and Historical Capitalism: Genealogies of Sinological Knowledge* and *Nation Work: Asian Elites and National Identities*.

Alexander Des Forges is visiting assistant professor of Chinese literature at the University of Michigan.

Mark S. Eykholt holds a doctorate in history from the University of California at San Diego.

Motohiro Kobayashi works in the Japanese Consulate-General, Shengyang.

Joyce A. Madancy is assistant professor of history at Union College, Schenectady.

Christopher Munn holds a doctorate in history from the University of Toronto.

Edward R. Slack Jr. has a doctorate in Chinese history from the University of Hawai'i and is assistant professor of history at Indiana State University.

Carl A. Trocki is professor of Asian studies at Queensland University of Technology, and is most recently the author of *Opium, Empire, and the Global Political Economy: A Study of the Asian Opium Trade, 1750–1950.*

Bob Tadashi Wakabayashi is professor of history at York University. His books include *Anti-Foreignism and Western Learning in Early-Modern Japan* and *Japanese Loyalism Reconstrued.*

R. Bin Wong is professor of history at the University of California at Irvine. His most recent book is *China Transformed: Historical Change and the Limits of European Experience.*

Judith Wyman is senior program officer for the Hubert H. Humphrey Fellowship Program at the Institute of International Education. She received her doctorate in Chinese history from the University of Michigan.

Zhou Yongming is assistant professor of anthropology at the University of Wisconsin–Madison. He is the author of *Anti-Drug Crusades in Twentieth-Century China: Nationalism, History, and State-Building.*

INDEX

Text: 10/12 Baskerville
Display: Baskerville
Composition: Binghamton Valley Composition
Printing and binding: Thomson-Shore, Inc.